HITLER'S
LAST
GAMBLE

BOOKS BY R. E. DUPUY AND T. N. DUPUY

The Encyclopedia of Military History from 3500 B.C. to the Present

An Outline History of the American Revolution

Compact History of the Revolutionary War

Compact History of the Civil War

Brave Men and Great Captains

Military Heritage of America

To the Colors

BOOKS BY T. N. DUPUY

The Battle of Austerlitz

Revolutionary War Land Battles (with Gay M. Hammerman)

Revolutionary War Naval Battles (with Grace P. Hayes)

Modern Libraries for Modern Colleges

College Libraries in Ferment

Military History of the Chinese Civil War

Military History of World War I

Military History of World War II

Holidays

Civil War Naval Actions

Civil War Land Battles

Campaigns of the French Revolution and of Napoleon

Faithful and True

Military Lives—Alexander the Great to Winston Churchill

Almanac of World Military Power (ed., with John A. C. Andrews

and Grace P. Hayes)

A Documentary History of Arms Control and Disarmament

(ed., with Gay M. Hammerman)

People and Events of the American Revolution

(with Gay M. Hammerman)

Mongolia

A Genius for War: The German Army and General Staff, 1807–1945

Numbers, Predictions and War

Elusive Victory: The Arab-Israeli Wars, 1947–1974

The Evolution of Weapons and Warfare

Great Battles of the Eastern Front (with Paul Martell)

Options of Command

Flawed Victory: The Arab-Israeli Conflict and the 1982 War in Lebanon

(with Paul Martell)

Understanding War: History and Theory of Combat

Dictionary of Military Terms (with Curt Johnson and Grace P. Hayes)

Understanding Defeat

Attrition: Forecasting Battle Casualties and Equipment

Losses in Modern War

If War Comes: How to Defeat Saddam Hussein

(with Curt Johnson, David L. Bongard, and Arnold C. Dupuy)

Future Wars

The Harper Encyclopedia of Military Biography

(with Curt Johnson and David L. Bongard)

HITLER'S LAST GAMBLE

THE BATTLE OF THE BULGE, DECEMBER 1944–JANUARY 1945

TREVOR N. DUPUY,
DAVID L. BONGARD, AND
RICHARD C. ANDERSON JR.

HarperCollins*Publishers*

Photographs in the insert courtesy National Archives and Records Administration, Still Photographs Branch, College Park, Maryland.

Map 21 reprinted from R. E. Dupuy, *St. Vith: Lion in the Way* (Washington, D.C.: Infantry Journal Press, 1949), with permission.

HarperCollins books may be purchased for educational, business, or sales promotional use. For information, please write: Special Markets Department, HarperCollins Publishers, Inc., 10 East 53rd Street, New York, NY 10022.

FIRST EDITION

Designed by George J. McKeon

All maps and diagrams except Map 21 by Durf MacJoynt

Library of Congress Cataloging-in-Publication Data

Dupuy, Trevor Nevitt, 1916–
  Hitler's last gamble : the Battle of the Bulge, December 1944–January 1945 / by Trevor N. Dupuy, David L. Bongard, and Richard C. Anderson Jr.
    p. cm.
  Includes bibliographical references and index.
  ISBN 0-06-016627-4
  1. Ardennes, Battle of the, 1944–1945. 2. Hitler, Adolf, 1889–1945. I. Bongard, David L. II. Anderson, Richard C., Jr. III. Title.
D756.5.A7D86 1994
940.54'21431—dc20   94-19460

94 95 96 97 98 ❖/RRD 10 9 8 7 6 5 4 3 2 1

To the Allied and German soldiers who fought, bled, froze,
and died for their countries in the Ardennes

CONTENTS

Illustrations follow page 232.

MAPS

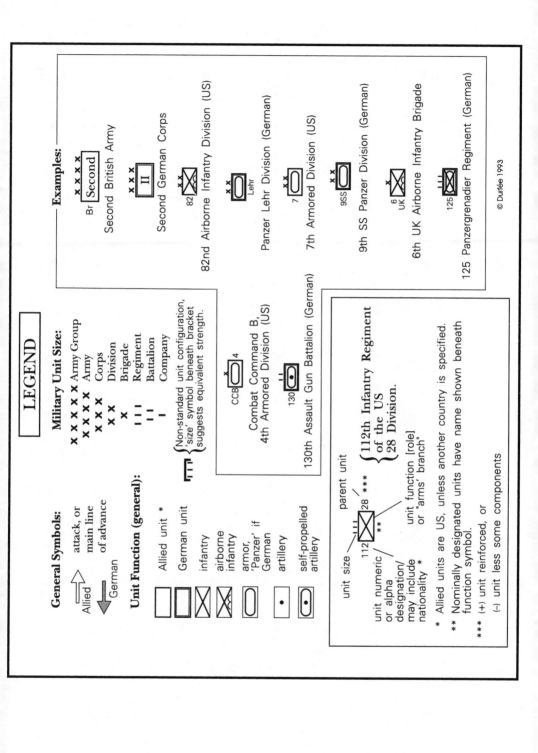

LEGEND

General Symbols:

Allied / German — attack, or main line of advance

Unit Function (general):

Allied unit *

German unit

infantry

airborne infantry

armor, 'Panzer', if German

artillery

self-propelled artillery

Military Unit Size:

x x x x x — Army Group
x x x x — Army
x x x — Corps
x x — Division
x — Brigade
||| — Regiment
|| — Battalion
| — Company

Non-standard unit configuration, 'size' symbol beneath bracket suggests equivalent strength.

Combat Command B, 4th Armored Division (US)
CCB | 4

130th Assault Gun Battalion (German)
130

{112th Infantry Regiment of the US 28 Division.}

unit size — parent unit
112 — unit numeric or alpha designation/ may include nationality *
28 *** — unit function [role] or "arms' branch"

* Allied units are US, unless another country is specified.
** Nominally designated units have name shown beneath function symbol.
*** (+) unit reinforced, or
(-) unit less some components

Examples:

Br | Second — Second British Army

II — Second German Corps

82 — 82nd Airborne Infantry Division (US)

Lehr — Panzer Lehr Division (German)

7 — 7th Armored Division (US)

9SS — 9th SS Panzer Division (German)

6 UK — 6th UK Airborne Infantry Brigade

125 — 125 Panzergrenadier Regiment (German)

© Durfée 1993

PREFACE

The genesis of this book is a conversation about seven or eight years ago between one of the coauthors and Edward B. Vandiver III, the Director of the U.S. Army's Concepts Analysis Agency, in Bethesda, Maryland. We were bemoaning the fact that none of the computer models of combat then in use by the Army for purposes of planning and budgeting had been validated. (A model is "validated" when it can reliably replicate real-world experience; without validation, no one can be sure that the forecasts or projections of the model are accurate.)

"The problem," said Ed Vandiver, "is that we do not have historical data for a modern combined-arms battle in sufficient detail to provide inputs to our models." He added that the battle would have to be one in which large numbers of tanks were engaged, since there would be large numbers of tanks in any future battle projected by today's models. We agreed that it would be nice if we could get data for the large tank battles in the 1973 October War in the Middle East. We also agreed that we could not get the data from the Israelis, Egyptians, or Syrians.

"What about the Battle of the Bulge?" the coauthor asked. Vandiver thought that would be a good idea. Then he probably forgot about the conversation. But our coauthor did not. He went back to his office and began to prepare a proposal. To make a truly long story short, many months later the proposal was submitted to Vandiver and was approved, and in due course our company went to work to produce what became officially known as "The Ardennes Campaign Simulation Data Base," or ACSDB. Two years later the ACSDB was officially submitted to Vandiver's Concepts Analysis Agency.

The ACSDB was a massive computer program containing some thirty-nine megabytes of data. It included detailed, daily information about more than 100 units over a period of thirty-two days: 16 December 1944 through 16 January 1945. The units were one German Army group, four German armies, eight German corps, thirty-five German divisions, three German brigades and a few smaller German units, two Allied army groups, two American armies, six American corps, forty-two American divisions, a few smaller American units, one British corps, two British divisions, two British brigades, elements of the German Luftwaffe, elements of the Royal Air Force, and elements of the U.S. Army Air Force.

The kind of information included was daily personnel strengths, daily inventory of major weapons, daily casualties, daily ammunition expenditures, daily fuel expenditures, daily unit locations, daily unit movements, names of commanders, and much more. The data were collected from archives in Washington, London, and Freiburg, Germany.

Aside from the coauthors of this book, the following people played major roles in the collection and organization of these data: Christopher Lawrence, Jay Karamales, Brian Bader, Vincent Hawkins, and Daniel Hammerman. The data were painstakingly reviewed, and praised, by two prestigious historians, authors of two of the most important books on the Ardennes campaign: Hugh M. Cole and Charles MacDonald.

We have been fortunate to have had the benefit of advice from three very knowledgeable reviewers of our manuscript: Lt. Gen. Dr. Franz Uhle-Wettler, German Army, retired; Col. George A. Daoust, Ph.D., U.S. Army, retired; and Lt. Col. Dr. Waldis Greiselis of the German Military History Research Institute in Freiburg, Germany. In addition to our debt to these three soldier-scholars, we owe one to M. S. Wyeth, the Editorial Vice President of HarperCollins, who painstakingly reviewed the manuscript and made many valuable suggestions to enable us to improve our presentation.

We are also grateful to our old colleague, Lt. Col. A. D. "Durf" MacJoynt, U.S. Air Force, retired, who prepared the maps for this book. Durf's efforts have given us, we believe, the best-mapped book of the Ardennes campaign ever to be published.

As is evident from the bibliography of this book, over the past fifty years there have been quite a few books written about the Battle of the

Bulge (the Ardennes campaign). Several of these are excellent, some are important, most range from mediocre to adequate, and a few are rather bad. But our book has something that not even the best of the earlier books have: the benefit of the Ardennes Campaign Simulation Data Base, the most comprehensive data research effort ever made with respect to the Battle of the Bulge. We hope that our attempts to be selective in retrieving data from that massive collection, to be painstaking in combining this data with those from other sources, to be meticulous in assembling the material, and to heed the comments of the reviewers of our manuscript will make our book at least as good and at least as important as the best of the earlier books on this subject.

The three coauthors have worked harmoniously together for well over a year in writing this book. Each has brought some special skill, talent, or experience to make a unique contribution to the project. But in the process of assembling, reviewing, and editing the results of our efforts, one of us has claimed the prerogatives of seniority in years, and has assumed final responsibility. So, while we should all share in whatever credit is due for the product of our endeavors, only one of us must shoulder whatever blame there may be.

All of us thank Ellen McCoy-Comstock and Yun Zhang, who were responsible for the organization and operation of our own miniarchive, our files, and our computer programs as we wrote and compiled this book.

GLOSSARY

AAA	Antiaircraft artillery
AAR	After-action report
Abn	Airborne
Abn D	Airborne division
AD	Armored division
AFV	Armored fighting vehicle
AGRA	Artillery Group, Royal Artillery (British)
Airborne division	A division-size unit organized and equipped for airborne operations, designed to enter into battle by parachute or glider
APC	Armored personnel carrier, a lightly armored vehicle used to transport armored infantry into battle
Arm	Armored
Armored division	A division-size unit organized to conduct combat mostly from tanks and other armored vehicles
AT	Antitank
AW	Automatic weapons, as in AAA-AW
Battalion	A medium-size unit, usually 500 to 1,000 men in strength, usually commanded by a lieutenant colonel or a major
Battery	An artillery unit of company size
Bazooka	American handheld antitank rocket
Bde	Brigade

Bn	Battalion
Brigade	A large unit composed of either three battalions (comparable to an infantry regiment) and commanded by a colonel, or two regiments and commanded by a brigadier general
CCA	Combat Command A in a U.S. armored division
CCB	Combat Command B in a U.S. armored division
CCR	Reserve combat command in a U.S. armored division
CCS	Combined Chiefs of Staff
Chief of staff	Senior staff officer of a division or higher formation; coordinates all staff activity of the formation
Chiefs of Staff Committee	The three senior British military leaders: Chief of the Imperial General Staff (Army), The First Sea Lord (Navy), and Chief of the Air Staff (RAF)
CO	Commanding officer
Co	Company
Combat command	A combined-force component (in flexible task force organization) within a U.S. armored division, usually about one-third of the division strength, usually commanded by a brigadier general or colonel
Combined Chiefs of Staff	The senior Allied military decision makers, consisting of the British Chiefs of Staff Committee and the U.S. Joint Chiefs of Staff
Company	A basic military unit usually composed of two or three platoons. An infantry company usually consists of 100 to 200 men; it is usually commanded by a captain
COM-Z	Communications Zone; that portion of a theater of operations behind the Combat Zone
CP	Command post or headquarters
Div	Division
Division	The smallest standard combined-arms formation, usually 10,000–18,000 men in strength, usually commanded by a major general
Eng	Engineer

Exec	Executive officer
Executive officer	Second in command and (usually) chief of staff of a brigade or smaller unit
FA	Field artillery
FLAK	Antiaircraft artillery fire or gun
G-1	Personnel staff officer of a division or higher formation
G-2	Intelligence staff officer of a division or higher formation
G-3	Operations staff officer of a division or higher formation
G-4	Logistics or supply staff officer of a division or higher formation
H-hour	The specific time for a particular operation to begin
ID	Infantry division
Inf	Infantry
Jabo	German slang for jagdbomber (fighter-bomber)
JCS	Joint Chiefs of Staff (U.S.)
JgPz	Jagdpanzer, or "hunting tank," a self-propelled tank destroyer
Joint Chiefs of Staff	Committee of four senior military decision makers of the United States: Chief of Staff to the President, Chief of Staff of the Army, Chief of Staff of the U.S. Army Air Forces, and the Chief of Naval Operations
Kampfgruppe	German equivalent of task force; combat team
Luftwaffe	German Air Force
M1 (Garand)	U.S. semiautomatic infantry rifle
M4 (Sherman)	U.S. medium tank
M5 (Stuart)	U.S. light tank
M10	U.S. tank destroyer with 3-inch gun
(–) (Minus)	Understrength, or with components detached
Nebelwerfer	German multiple rocket projector
OB West	Oberbefehlshaber West (Commander in Chief, West, or his headquarters)
OKH	Oberkommando des Heeres (Army High Command)
OKW	Oberkommando der Wehrmacht (Armed Forces High Command)
Panzer	Armor (German)

Panzer division	German armored division
Panzerfaust	German handheld antitank rocket
Panzergrenadier	Mechanized or semiarmored organization, or infantry soldiers within such an organization
(+) (Plus)	Overstrength, or with attached units
POL	Petrol (gasoline), oil, and lubricants
POW	Prisoner of war
POZIT	U.S. proximity fuse for artillery and antiaircraft (see also VT fuse)
PzD	Panzer division
PzGrenD	Panzergrenadier division
PzJg	Panzerjäger, an antitank gun or unit
PzKw-IV	Panzerkampfwagen (armored fighting vehicle or tank); an upgunned and improved version of a prewar German design
PzKw-V	Model designation for the Panther medium-heavy tank
PzKw-VI	Tiger heavy tank
RAF	Royal Air Force
RCT	Regimental combat team (American), usually part of a division, consisting of an infantry regiment, its normal supporting artillery battalion, and other small supporting units
Regiment	A large single-arm unit, usually consisting of three battalions; a typical infantry regiment is 2,000–3,000 men in strength, usually commanded by a colonel
Rgt	Regiment
S-1	Personnel and administrative staff officer, or adjutant, of a brigade or smaller unit
S-2	Intelligence staff officer of a brigade or smaller unit
S-3	Operations staff officer of a brigade or smaller unit
S-4	Supply staff officer of a brigade or smaller unit
SHAEF	Supreme Headquarters, Allied Expeditionary Forces
SP	Self-propelled
Squadron	A cavalry unit of battalion size

SS	Schutzstaffel (elite guard), designation of military or paramilitary organizations of the Nazi Party
StuG	Sturmgeschütz, or "assault gun," in several models (-IIIG, -IV, etc.)
T	Towed
TAC	Tactical Air Command
TD	Tank destroyer; antitank personnel or organization, or an armored, self-propelled antitank gun
T/O&E	Tables of organization and equipment; list of equipment and personnel for a regular or standard unit or formation
TOT	Time on target; a method of timing the firing of different artillery units so that their fire falls simultaneously on a target
Troop	A cavalry unit of company size
VGD	Volksgrenadier division
Volksgrenadier	Designation of an infantry unit or formation organized late in World War II
VT fuse	U.S. proximity (variable-time) fuse with a tiny radar that automatically provides air bursts
Wacht am Rhein	Watch on the Rhine; German code name for Ardennes offensive
Waffen-SS	Regular military, army-type formation of the Nazi Party
Wehrmacht	German armed forces—land, sea, air—not including the Waffen-SS

See also the list of abbreviations in appendix D.

1

BEFORE THE STORM

HITLER'S DECISION: 16 SEPTEMBER 1944

August 1944 was "the Black Month of the German Army."[1] In the east the German Central Army Group was shattered by a massive Soviet offensive that overran all of eastern Poland. In the west two German armies were virtually destroyed by the breakout of the Anglo-American armies from Normandy and their subsequent pursuit of the defeated Germans across northern France. In Italy the remnants of two German armies streamed north of the Arno River, hotly pursued by the American Fifth Army and the British Eighth Army. To many Germans, and to most Allies, total German collapse seemed inevitable and imminent.

Then, in early September, all three Allied drives came to surprising, shuddering halts. The Allied supply systems could not keep pace with their racing armies, and without fuel and ammunition those armies could not move or fight. The Germans, skillful and resourceful soldiers, took immediate advantage of the unexpected respite. They regrouped, reorganized, and began—incredibly—to counterattack.

Thus, the daily briefing for German Führer Adolf Hitler on 16 September at Hitler's field headquarters, the so-called Wolf's Lair in East Prussia, took place in an ebullient atmosphere. Successful German counterattacks, launched by scratch battle groups from the 2d Panzer and 2d SS Panzer "Das Reich" divisions, had erased most of the small American lodgments on German soil in the Ardennes region, a rugged area of forest on the German-Belgian frontier. One of these counterattacks had pushed back elements of the 4th Infantry Division in the woods of the Schnee Eifel. Another had repulsed the 28th Infantry Division at Pronsfeld just east of the Our River.

Hitler had been sitting quietly as the briefing officer, pointer in hand, stood before a large map summarizing the previous day's major events along the front in the Netherlands and northern Belgium. But as the briefer began to describe the Ardennes counterattacks, the German dictator suddenly came to life.

"Stop!" he exclaimed. "I have come to a momentous decision. I shall go over to the counterattack!" He strode to the map, seized the pointer from the astonished briefing officer, and touched the map at the Ardennes. "That is to say, here!" He turned to face the assembled commanders and staff officers.

"Out of the Ardennes, with the objective: Antwerp!"

The stunned audience was silent. Not only was the proposal bold, perhaps past the point of foolhardiness, but Hitler was exhibiting an energy and enthusiasm that he had not shown for many months.

IN AND AROUND REIMS: 29 NOVEMBER–15 DECEMBER 1944

On 17 September 1944, the U.S. 82d Airborne Division, as part of Operation Market Garden, carried out a brilliantly successful airborne landing at Nijmegen, in Holland, fifty miles behind the German lines. For three bloody days the "All-Americans" (derived partly from the stylized *AA* on their shoulder patch and partly from the division's "national" recruitment in World War I) of the 82d Airborne fought through desperate German defenders before they were able to seize the Nijmegen Bridge over the Waal River. There they were joined by British tanks, which had advanced overland from the south through Eindhoven (with the help of the U.S. 101st Airborne Division). As the tanks continued their dash toward Arnhem, the All-American airborne soldiers established defensive positions and repulsed vicious German counterattacks attempting to cut off the British armored spearhead. For nearly seven more weeks of grueling battle, the 82d Airborne held off repeated German efforts to break through. Finally, on 11 November, after the arrival of British reinforcements, the division was pulled out of the line and sent by train to Reims, France, to rest and refit in old French caserns (barracks) on the outskirts of the Cathedral City.

The 101st Airborne Division, after a similarly successful airborne drop at Eindhoven, had had only a slightly less difficult time in securing crossings over the Wilhelmina Canal on 18–19 September. Then, after British tanks had dashed north across the canal toward Nijmegen and Arnhem, the "Screaming Eagles" (the nickname drawn from their shoulder patch, which showed a bald eagle's head with open beak) had followed them to hold the line there against an insistent German counteroffensive. The 101st paratroopers were not pulled out of the line until 25–27 November. Then they, too, were sent to France for rest and refit in caserns on the other side of Reims from the 82d Airborne.

There was considerable rivalry between the two airborne divisions, both made up of soldiers proud that they had been specially selected, trained, and indoctrinated to be elite fighters. The 82d had been activated five months before the 101st in 1942. Because the 82d's paratroopers had had combat experience landing by parachute and glider in Sicily in July 1943 and at Salerno in September 1943, they considered the Screaming Eagles to be Johnny-come-lately recruits. And they knew that, as seasoned veterans, they had been given the tougher job in Operation Market Garden. The troopers of the 101st, aware that they had done just as well as the 82d in the D-Day landings in Normandy and in seizing the bridges in Holland and in the subsequent tough defensive battles there, would no longer tolerate the condescension of the All-Americans.

Every evening, small groups of soldiers from the two divisions would encounter one another as they wandered through the streets and gathered in the bars of Reims. It did not take many drinks or muttered insults to start a brawl, which was usually quickly broken up by alert military police (MPs) working with local French police. But on some occasions the fights were big enough, and lasted long enough, to damage private property and injure French citizens. At least twice between 29 November and 6 December Gen. Maxwell Taylor (the only senior officer of the XVIII Airborne Corps who was fluent in French) visited the mayor of Reims at the Hôtel de Ville, near the cathedral, to apologize.

The night of 16–17 December was a particularly busy one for the MPs in Reims. There were a number of broken noses, black eyes, and cut cheeks and lips treated by unit doctors at sick call on the morning of the seventeenth. That night most unit commanders in both divisions kept all or most of their men in barracks, which was just as well because, not long after dinner, all units were alerted for a motor movement to the front the following morning. The belligerent airborne soldiers were about to go back to the primary business of fighting Germans instead of each other.

"LET THEM COME!": 7–15 DECEMBER 1944

As early as 1 October, intelligence intercepts had revealed that many German armored formations, especially elite SS Panzers, had been withdrawn from the front lines for rebuilding. Most did not reappear in the line, but remained in reserve throughout October and November. Furthermore, intelligence also revealed the creation of the Sixth Panzer Army on 20 October, although the information was not released in intelligence summaries until the first week of November. (This was standard procedure for protecting the intelligence source; the source was noted to be a German deserter.)

There were marked differences of opinion among Allied intelligence officers. By 12 December Col. Benjamin Dickson, G-2 (intelligence officer) of the American First Army, seemed convinced that a German offensive was imminent. He repeated his warning to his staff on the fourteenth, pinpointing the Ardennes as the Germans' likely objective. However, his concerns did not prevent him from leaving for Paris that evening for a long-delayed four-day leave of absence.

Similar concerns were voiced by Col. Oscar Koch, G-2 of the neighboring American Third Army. On 9 December he presented a special intelligence briefing to his commander, Lt. Gen. George S. Patton Jr., suggesting that the First Army's VIII Corps, in the Ardennes, was particularly vulnerable to German attack. He pointed out that a successful German attack in the Ardennes would pose a threat to the left flank of the Third Army. Patton was sufficiently impressed to order his Third Army staff to prepare contingency plans to deal with any threat to the army's flank as a result of such a German attack.

Even earlier, on 7 December, British Maj. Gen. Kenneth Strong, intelligence officer at SHAEF (Supreme Headquarters, Allied Expeditionary Force), submitted a new intelligence estimate. He suggested that the increasingly strong German reserve could be used by the German High Command to rupture the Allied lines. He suggested that a possible German objective might be to disrupt the overstretched U.S. VIII Corps in the Ardennes.

General Dwight D. Eisenhower, the Supreme Allied Commander of American and British forces in Western Europe, was impressed by this estimate. His Chief of Staff, Lt. Gen. W. Bedell Smith, directed Major General Strong to visit Lt. Gen. Omar N. Bradley, commander of the American forces of the 12th Army Group, at his headquarters in Luxembourg City to give him a briefing. Strong went to Luxembourg and presented his estimate to Bradley and selected officers of the 12th Army Group staff. To Strong's surprise, Bradley and his officers seemed unimpressed with his estimate. Particularly outspoken in disagreement was Brig. Gen. Edwin Sibert, G-2 of the 12th Army Group.

Sibert's views were expressed in his weekly summary of 12 December: "It is now certain that attrition is steadily sapping the strength of German forces on the Western Front and that the crust of defenses is thinner, more brittle, and more vulnerable than it appears on our G-2 maps, or to the troops in the line."[2] For Strong's benefit, Sibert now repeated the conclusion of the analysis he had recently presented to General Bradley: "The enemy divisions . . . have been cut by at least fifty percent. . . . The [German] breaking point may develop suddenly and without warning."

Bradley backed up Sibert. He told Strong that he was "aware of the danger," and that he had "earmarked certain divisions to move into the Ardennes should the enemy attack there."[3] But he made it clear that he did not take the German threat too seriously. He dismissed Strong with the flippant remark: "Let them come!"

A PROMOTION AND A WAGER: 15 DECEMBER 1994

General Eisenhower was in good humor on 15 December 1944, as he went about his duties at his headquarters in the Grand Trianon Palace at Versailles. That morning he received official notification from Washington of his promotion to the rank of General of the Army, the equivalent of field marshal in other armies. He had been aware, of course, that this promotion was imminent, and depended only upon the formality of the signing of an act of Congress by President Franklin D. Roosevelt. U.S. Army Chief of Staff General George C. Marshall had already sent Ike a set of his new insignia—five stars arranged in a circle. When he recieved the radio message from Washington, Eisenhower removed his four-star general's insignia from his uniform shoulder straps, and Lt. Gen. "Beetle" Smith then pinned on the new insignia.

A few hours later Ike received a radio message from Field Marshal Sir Bernard Law Montgomery, commander of the Allied 21st Army Group, holding the northern part of the Allied line in the Netherlands and Belgium. Monty, a widower, asked Ike's permission "to hop over to England" to celebrate the Christmas holiday with his son. In his message Monty also reminded Ike that at Carthage, near Tunis, on 11 October 1943, he and Ike had made a wager of five pounds. Eisenhower had bet that the war would be over before Christmas 1944. Montgomery now asked him to "pay up."[4]

In his jovial response Ike told Monty that he had no objection to the field marshal's proposed holiday in England. However, he refused to pay the bet. It was still nine days to Christmas, he wrote, "and while it seems almost certain that you will have an extra five pounds for Christmas, you will not get it until that day."

After discussing with Beetle Smith an expected visit the next day from General Bradley, Ike left his office and was driven back to the hotel suite that was his home in Versailles. He looked forward to Bradley's visit. It should be another good day.

THE LETTER: 16 DECEMBER 1944

Early in the course of the Ardennes battle, soldiers of the U.S. 99th Infantry Division, fighting on the northern shoulder of the "Bulge," retrieved a letter that had been written by a young SS panzergrenadier a few days earlier. The letter, written in the predawn hours of 16 December, was to the German soldier's sister, Ruth. He had been unable to post it before the battle began, and he was still carrying it when he was killed east of Elsenborn.

I write during one of the great hours before we attack, full of expectation for what the next days will bring. Everyone who has been here for the last two days and nights, who has witnessed hour after hour the assembly of our crack divisions, who has heard the constant rattling of our panzers, knows that something is up. We attack to throw the enemy from our homeland. That is a holy task!

On the back of the envelope the young soldier had scrawled a hasty postscript, demonstrating his enthusiasm for the task ahead: "Ruth! Ruth! Ruth! WE MARCH!"

2

GERMAN DISPOSITIONS AND PLANS

By December 1944, the German forces deployed facing the western Allies along the western German frontier were organized into four army groups (Heeresgruppen). Three of these—Army Groups H, B, and G— were under the direction of Commander in Chief West (OB West), a post held by Generalfeldmarschall (Field Marshal) Gerd von Rundstedt. OB West controlled all ground operations in western Germany, Belgium, the Netherlands, and France.[1] OB West reported in turn to the Armed Forces High Command (Oberkommando der Wehrmacht, or OKW), but Luftwaffe operations on the western front were handled by the Luftwaffe High Command (OKL).[2] The exception was the fourth army group in the west—Oberkommando Oberrhein (High Command Upper Rhine), which had since November been commanded by Reichsführer-SS Heinrich Himmler, who did not report to Rundstedt but directly to OKW. OB West only had responsibility for logistic support of the 19th Army, the major element of Army Group Upper Rhine, which extended from the vicinity of Karlsruhe to the Swiss border.

The northernmost army group in the west was Army Group H. The Germans habitually gave their army groups either letter designations or geographical names like North, South, and Vistula. Army Group H, commanded by Luftwaffe Col. Gen. Kurt Student, contained two armies, and was deployed in the Netherlands and as far south as Roermond on the Meuse River. South of Army Group H lay Field Marshal Walter Model's Army Group B, which contained four armies and held the front from Roermond south to the vicinity of Echternach. As army group commander, Model was the senior officer with command authority for the Ardennes offensive.

Model had been born outside Magdeburg on 24 January 1891, the son of a Lutheran schoolmaster.[3] Soundly and widely educated as a youth, he eschewed the family profession and gained a commission in the 52d Infantry Regiment in August 1910. As a lieutenant, he served in combat on the west-

NETHERLANDS

The Hague
Rotterdam

xxxx
Twenty-Fifth
Arnhem

Neder Rijn

Waal
Nijmegen
Grave

xxxx
First Para

Wesel

Maas

Cdn
xxxx
First
Eindhoven

Krefeld
Duisburg

The Ruhr

GERMANY

Br
xxxx
Second

H
x xxxx x
B
Düsseldorf

Antwerp
Albert Can.

Geilenkirchen
Cologne

21
x xxx x
12
Maastricht
Heerlen

xxxx
Fifteenth

BRUSSELS

US
xxxx
Ninth

Rur

Aachen
Hürtgen
Bonn

BELGUIM

Liege
Verviers
Eupen

Remagen

Namur
Meuse
Huy
Stavelot
Malmédy
Monschau

Koblenz

Sambre

Ardennes
St. Vith

xxxx
Sixth Pz

Frankfurt

Houffalize
Bastogne
LUX

xxxx
Fifth Pz

Moselle

Rhine

Givet

US
xxxx
First

xxxx
Seventh

Mainz

Sedan
LUXEMBOURG

Trier

B
x x
G

Mannheim

Saar

xxxx
First

Meuse

x xxx x

Metz
Saarbrücken

Karlsruhe

G
x xxx x
Oberrhein

Verdun

FRANCE

US
xxxx
Third

Saar

US
xxxx
Seventh

12
x xxx x
6

Nancy

Strasbourg

Fr
xxxx
First

xxxx

Moselle

Colmar

xxxx
Nineteenth

Mulhouse

Belfort

Strategic Map: West Front
15 December 1944

————— Westwall
– – – – FEBA, 15/16 Dec 44

0   60 miles
0   80 km

ern front during the first fifteen months of World War I, but after passing an abbreviated wartime General Staff Officer course (April 1916), he spent the remainder of the war as a staff officer, mostly on the Russian front. After the Treaty of Versailles, he was retained in the 100,000-man Reichswehr, serving in staff and troop assignment and gaining a reputation as a capable staff officer. At the start of World War II, Model was a Generalmajor and Chief of Staff of the IV Corps and was involved in considerable action in the Polish campaign. After promotion to generalleutnant (April 1940), he was Chief of Staff of the Sixteenth Army during the 1940 campaign in the Low Countries and France.

Model was appointed to command the 3d Panzer Division in late 1940, and led it in the first months of the Russian campaign. Promoted to General der Panzertruppen on 1 October 1941, he took command of the XLI Panzer Corps on the same day, and was assigned to command the Ninth Army the following January. Promoted yet again, to generaloberst in late February, Model spent the next two years leading the Ninth Army, part of Army Group Center on the Russian front. By mid-1943, Model's energy, determination, and sangfroid had made him one of Hitler's favorite generals, and had earned him the nickname "the Führer's Fireman." He weathered his part in Operation Zitadelle, the unsuccessful offensive against the Soviet Kursk salient in July 1943, with his reputation intact. He commanded Army Group North (January–March 1944) and then, newly promoted to field marshal, led Army Group North Ukraine (March–June 1944). He replaced Field Marshal Ernst Busch as commander of Army Group Center (June–August 1944) during the devastating Soviet summer offensive. He was unable to prevent the near-destruction of Army Group Center, but prevented a complete catastrophe. On 17 August 1944, Model was sent west to take over as OB West in the wake of the dismissals of von Rundstedt (3 July) and Field Marshal Hans Günther von Kluge, who had replaced him. (Both were scapegoats for Allied successes in Normandy.) He was simultaneously made commander of Army Group D and Army Group B (17 August 1944). This unusual catalog of responsibilities was reduced a few days later, on 5 September, to command of Army Group B when Hitler brought von Rundstedt back as OB West. Short, pugnacious, and energetic, Model expected maximum effort from his subordinates, and was ruthless with those who did not measure up.

Colonel General Gustav Adolf von Zangen's Fifteenth Army, the northern-most of the four in Model's army group, was not slated to play a major role in the Ardennes offensive. The other three armies in Model's army group were preparing for the Ardennes offensive: Oberstgruppenführer der Waffen-SS (Generaloberst) Josef Dietrich's Sixth Panzer Army,[4] General der Panzertruppen Hasso von Manteuffel's Fifth Panzer Army, and General der Panzertruppen Erich Brandenberger's Seventh Panzer Army.

South of Model's Army Group B, General der Panzertruppen Hermann Balck's Army Group G held the front from just south of the Moselle River to the vicinity of Karlsruhe, and its major component was General der Infanterie Hans von Obstfelder's First Army. Farther south was General der Infanterie Friedrich Wiese's Nineteenth Army, holding the Colmar pocket west of the Rhine in Alsace. In addition, there were several smaller formations directly under Army Group G's command, holding the line of the Rhine between the Colmar pocket and the left flank of the First Army, north of Strasbourg. This was the principal component of Oberkommando Oberrhein, commanded by Reichsführer-SS Himmler.

HITLER'S STRATEGIC CONSIDERATION

By the early autumn of 1944, even Adolf Hitler knew that the Germans were in serious danger of losing the war after suffering heavy and costly defeats on the eastern, western, and Italian fronts. In the east, the Soviet summer offensive had nearly destroyed Army Group Center, and operations in the southern Ukraine in the spring had led to a triumphant Soviet advance through Romania and Bulgaria into Yugoslavia and onto the Hungarian Plain. The German Army was essentially being rebuilt, especially in the west, and this reconstructed army with its new supplies of tanks, aircraft, and munitions would have to be employed skillfully if it were to do anything more than briefly postpone Germany's defeat.

By this time, after five years of war, Hitler's mind was no longer reliably clear, and many of his actions were quixotic and illogical, if not the outright products of a disturbed mind. Considering the emotional shock of the assassination attempt of 20 July 1944, and the injuries he suffered in that bomb blast, this was perhaps not surprising. However, he did retain some strategic vision, which on 16 September he began to apply to the formulation of a plan that might avoid defeat by compelling the Allies to agree to a negotiated peace. Hitler recognized that against the enormously powerful and massive Soviet Army, an offensive on the eastern front would accomplish little. The Soviets had no strategic weak spots, no points where they were really vulnerable. The western Allies, on the other hand, were demonstrably not the Soviet monolith. Their logistical support depended not on railroads, but on the shipping capacity of several ports, of which Antwerp was undoubtedly the most important.

Hitler's plan, in essence, was to concentrate forces in the west in order to break through a weak, American-held sector of the Allied front line and retake Antwerp, simultaneously isolating most of the British-Canadian 21st Army Group while seizing the major Allied logistical nexus. Hitler wanted to attack the Americans because he believed that they were less capable soldiers than the British and unlikely to put up much of a fight. While this assessment might have been true for the U.S. Army in Tunisia in the winter of 1942–1943, it was certainly *not* true for the U.S. Army two years later.

At the least, Hitler planned that even if the British and Canadians escaped encirclement, the Allies would be back where they were in late August, and

Germany would have three or four months' grace to deal with the Soviets. In the best case, the rout of a major element of the 12th Army Group and the loss of Antwerp might create such a rift between the British and the Americans that the western Alliance would fracture, and Germany would face only a one-front war by early spring 1945.

As the target area for the offensive, Hitler chose the Ardennes region. This was an area of winding river valleys and steep hills, covered by dense conifer forests. The Ardennes was thinly settled with many small villages but few significant towns. It was the region where, following General Erich von Manstein's plan for Operation Yellow (German prewar plans were named for colors—"Green" was Czechslovakia, and "White" was Poland) in May 1940, the Germans had ruptured the French defenses and effectively won the Battle of Flanders en route to winning the Battle of France. Hitler intended to repeat that victory. He also knew, from reports of battlefield reconnaissance and from communications intercepts, that the area was only thinly held by the Americans, and he believed that an immediate breakthrough there would be relatively easy.

These considerations and their accompanying analysis were what had led Hitler to astound his officers with his declaration of his offensive plan in the command conference at the Wolf's Lair on 16 September 1944 (see chapter 1). Several of the attendees at that conference noted that, despite the recent experience of the assassination attempt, Hitler showed much of his former energy, spirit, and determination when telling the assembled generals of his plan. The listlessness that had characterized his behavior since 20 July had evaporated.

The chief of operations at OKW, Generaloberst Alfred Jodl, was uneasy about Hitler's plan, which he believed to be beyond the capabilities of the German Army. Born on 10 May 1890 in Würzburg, Bavaria, Jodl was the son of a retired artillery officer in the Bavarian Army. Following in his father's footsteps, he joined the 4th Bavarian Field Artillery Regiment in 1910, and saw considerable combat during World War I. Selected as one of 4,000 officers in the 100,000-man Reichswehr, he served in a series of staff posts in the early 1930s.

Jodl was a Generalmajor by autumn 1938. He served as Artillerieführer 44 (Artillery Leader 44) in Vienna from October 1938 to 23 August 1939, the eve of the German invasion of Poland, when he was called to Berlin to become chief of the Operations Staff at OKW, and was subsequently promoted to general der artillerie in 1940 and to generaloberst on 30 January 1944. Tall, intelligent, and hardworking, Jodl was a thoroughly professional staff officer. By autumn 1944 he found it increasingly difficult to work with Hitler, but, as a loyal German officer, he steadfastly remained at his post for the duration of the war. Curiously, Hitler liked Jodl's open (and un-Prussian) manner, and had developed substantial respect for the general's considerable military abilities.

Before he fine-tuned Hitler's basic concept into an operational plan, Jodl also developed an offensive option of his own, later dubbed the "Small Solution," which envisaged an offensive by the Fifth and Sixth Panzer armies aimed at seizing Liège. This main arm of the assault would meet a smaller offensive mounted by the Fifteenth Army coming from the northeast. Together, these two attacks would isolate the bulk of the First and Ninth American armies, and seize the Allied supply dumps and forward airfields around Liège. Although Jodl was one of the few General Staff officers whom Hitler either listened to or trusted, he refused to consider Jodl's less ambitious plan, and remained steadfastly committed to his own concept.

The matter did not end there, however. Although Jodl had been rebuffed, he could be nearly as stubborn as the Führer. Moreover, Hitler's field generals, including Model and Manteuffel, had experienced the might of the western Allies' tactical airpower, and were skeptical of the required movement rates for units to reach their assigned immediate and final objectives. "This plan hasn't a damned leg to stand on," Model snarled when informed of the Führer's intentions.[5] Also critical was Hitler's old street-fighting crony "Sepp" Dietrich, commander of the Sixth Panzer Army, who held little expectation for the offensive's success.[6]

Most other senior German generals were likewise distressed by the operation's optimistic goals. They persuaded Jodl to bring up the Small Solution once more. By this time Hitler had been compelled to accept a postponement of the offensive from 25 November to 10 December. It was postponed twice more, first to 15 December and then, on the twelfth, to 16 December.

In a major staff meeting at the Reichskanzlerei (Reich's Chancellery) in Berlin on 2 December, the assembled generals tried one last time to limit the goals of the offensive. Hitler, typically, was no more amenable to this suggestion than he had been before, although Manteuffel was able to gain a few minor tactical modifications. Dietrich said nothing to further the generals' goals during the meeting. Hitler believed that he alone, and not the generals who had collectively betrayed him in the 20 July assassination plot, could save Germany. He also recognized, more clearly than the generals, the political significance of the offensive. The destruction of six or twelve or even twenty Allied divisions would not end the war with Britain and the United States. The Germans must inflict on the western Allies a reverse of such great political magnitude that it would split the coalition and shift public opinion in one or both countries against the war. As risky, overly ambitious, and full of hubris as the plan for the Ardennes offensive might be, the underlying analysis was sound in concept if unrealistic in practical terms: It was literally the Third Reich's last chance for survival.

What the generals knew from their statistics, situation maps, and status reports, and what Hitler must have known, at least subconsciously, was that the Third Reich was close to the end of its resources. Combat casualties had been so high during 1944 that, coupled with the standing need for factory workers and farmers, the armed forces had few if any untapped reserves of manpower available. (Germany, true to Nazi ideology, did not employ women in large numbers in war industries until late summer 1944.)[7] The ongoing relentless Allied strategic bombing campaign, coupled with the loss of raw materials sources in the Balkans (especially the Romanian oil fields), finally reduced factory outputs, despite Production Minister Albert Speer's effective leadership and inventive problem solving. Morever, the enemy was at the frontiers of the Reich itself, and there was no more conquered territory to give up to buy time. Something clearly had to be done, and soon. Hitler had already discarded the rational course of making peace. The alternative was a desperate gamble for victory by staking all the resources carefully hoarded for months. It was an all-or-nothing throw of the dice.

In the end, Hitler's plan, elaborated by Jodl with Hitler's personal approval, specified an offensive by three armies along a ninety-six-kilometer (sixty-mile) front in the Ardennes, beginning on 16 December 1944. To support this effort, and to distract the Americans, the Fifteenth Army was to open a secondary offensive north of Aachen on 18 December, and early in January the First Army of Army Group G was to undertake Operation Nordwind in Alsace.

Hitler dubbed the proposed Ardennes offensive Wacht am Rhein ("Watch on the Rhine"), a deceptively defensive-sounding designation for what was to be the last all-out German offensive of World War II. Jodl's detailed operational plan for the offensive was christened Herbstnebel, or "Autumn Fog," appropriately reflecting the expected and necessary weather conditions for the attack.

DECEPTION, SURPRISE, AND OPERATION GREIF

The deceptive name for the offensive was a small indication of the importance Hitler attached to keeping the preparations secret and maintaining the advantage of surprise. In addition to the usual steps of concealing and camouflaging supply dumps and other static facilities for supporting the offensive, several other measures were undertaken.

The foremost of these was code-named Operation Greif (Condor) and placed under the direction of the experienced commando officer Obersturmbannführer der Waffen-SS (lieutenant colonel) Otto Skorzeny, who had gained Hitler's attention by his spectacular glider-borne rescue of Mussolini from Gran Sasso in the Abruzzi Mountains on 12 September 1943. Skorzeny was a tall, burly man with a notable facial scar from his university days in Vienna, when he was a member of a dueling society.[8] Born in Vienna on 12 June 1908, the son of an engineer, he earned an engineering degree from the University of Vienna and was running his own engineering firm when Germany annexed Austria on 11–12 March 1938. When he tried to volunteer for the Luftwaffe, he was rejected because of his age. He then entered the SS and served in the Leibstandarte Division during the 1940 campaign. He was commissioned a lieutenant and transferred to the Das Reich Division with which he served in the opening months of the Russian campaign. Seriously wounded that winter, he was invalided back to Germany and on recovery was assigned to the Leibstandarte Division's depot. Promoted to captain on 18 April 1943, he became commander of the new Friedenthal Hunting Groups, designed as a commando and special operations force. Personally supervising recruitment and training, he molded these units, staffed by volunteers from all services, into efficient special operations forces, animated by his own enterprising approach and inventive, often inspired, leadership.

Skorzeny had recently carried out an operation in Hungary (15–16 October 1944) that had deposed the Regent, Admiral Miklós Horthy, who had been secretly seeking an armistice with the Allies. Skorzeny met with Hitler shortly after his return from Hungary, and was briefed on the particulars of Wacht am Rhein and on the role planned for him in the operation. He was to establish infiltration teams, made up of English-speaking soldiers, who were to slip through the American front line and seize and hold the crucial bridges over the Meuse River for the panzer spearheads. The soldiers in the infiltration teams would wear American uniforms and use American equipment to support their deception, and also were to spread confusion and disorder in the rear areas, thereby hampering communications and disrupting the defense. Skorzeny immediately began to recruit English-speaking soldiers for his teams.

Those early recruitment efforts nearly compromised the entire program when a senior staff officer at OKW issued an order to units throughout the army requesting that they forward the names of English-speaking personnel who were prepared to serve under Skorzeny for a special operation. The commanders were also directed to turn in any captured American vehicles, uniforms, weapons, and other equipment. Clearly such a widely disseminated document would eventually reach the hands of Allied intelligence agents. Skorzeny, understandably furious at such a gross breach of security, at first tried to cancel Greif. His superiors forbade that move, and he eventually made the best of the matter by deliberately letting rumors about his unit and its purpose circulate freely. This unorthodox but clever approach permitted the true goals of Operation Greif and Skorzeny's unit, the 150th Panzer Brigade, to remain hidden from Allied intelligence until after the offensive began.

WACHT AM RHEIN

The main effort for the Ardennes offensive, as we have seen, was to be provided by Sepp Dietrich's Sixth Panzer Army. Dietrich had been born in Memmingen in the Allgäu on 28 May 1892.[9] After finishing primary school, he served a successful apprenticeship in the hotel business in Zürich. Returning

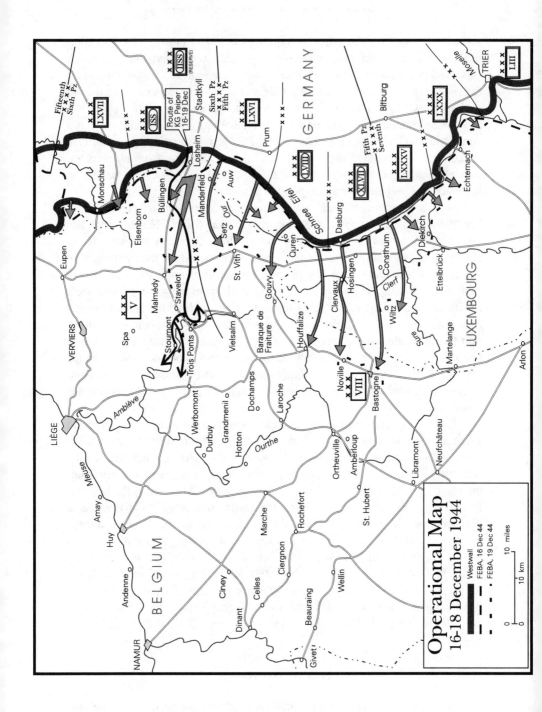

**Operational Map
16-18 December 1944**

Westwall
FEBA, 16 Dec 44
FEBA, 19 Dec 44

10 miles
10 km

Fifteenth
Sixth Pz
LXVII
ISS
Route of
KG Peiper
16-19 Dec
ISS (RESERVE)
Stadtkyll
Sixth Pz
Fifth Pz
LXVI
GERMANY
Prum
XLVIII
LXVII
Fifth Pz
Seventh
LXXXV
LXXX
TRIER
LIII
Moselle
Bitburg
Echternach
Dasburg
Diekirch
Schnee Eifel
Ouren
Consthum
Ettelbrück
Clerf
Sure
Martelange
LUXEMBOURG
Arlon
Neufchâteau

Monschau
Elsenborn
Büllingen
Losheim
Manderfeld
Setz
Auw
Out
St. Vith
Gouvy
Hosingen
Clervaux
Wiltz
Eupen
Malmédy
Stavelot
Stoumont
Trois Ponts
Vielsalm
Baraque de
Fraiture
Houffalize
Noville
Bastogne
VIII
Werbomont
Durbuy
Grandmenil
Dochamps
Laroche
Ortheuville
Amberloup
Libramont
Spa
Amblève
Hotton
Ourthe
St. Hubert
VERVIERS
V
LIÈGE
Meuse
Amay
Huy
Andenne
BELGIUM
Cliney
Marche
Ciergnon
Celles
Rochefort
Wellin
Beauraing
Givet
Dinant
NAMUR

to Germany, he joined the 4th Bavarian Field Artillery Regiment in 1911, and at the outbreak of World War I was a corporal training mounted troops. During that war, he served first with the 6th Reserve Field Artillery Regiment and then with the 7th Bavarian Field Artillery. Transferred in 1917 to the infantry-gun unit of the 10th Infantry, and armed with a high-powered rifle, he gained a reputation as a tank-killer. The next year Dietrich joined the infant German armor force, and was assigned to the 13th Assault Tank Detachment. As a sergeant, he commanded a tank at St. Quentin in March 1918, the debut of the German tank arm. By the end of the war he had won several medals, including the First and Second classes of the Iron Cross.

Dietrich was discharged from the Bavarian Army in March 1919, and joined the Freikorps 1st Defense Regiment in Munich. There he played a role in deposing the short-lived Communist government in Bavaria. The next year he joined the Bavarian National Police as a sergeant-major, and was at the same time a member of the "Oberland" Freikorps. He saw action with the latter unit in Upper Silesia, against Polish volunteers, in 1921. He left the police in 1927 and managed a gas station while also working as a forwarding agent for a large publishing firm. In May 1928, he joined the Nazi SS, and he was appointed Sturmbannführer (Major) of the SS on 1 August. Winning Hitler's favor, he rose very rapidly through the ranks of the SS: Standartenführer (Colonel) and commander of the SS Bavarian Brigade (18 September 1929), then Oberführer (Brigadier) and commander of SS Group South (11 July 1930), then Gruppenführer (Major General) in January 1932. After Hitler became Chancellor on 30 January 1933, Dietrich became one of his close advisers and also supervised the formation of the SS-Wacht-Abteilung Berlin, which became the Leibstandarte SS Adolf Hitler that September.

Dietrich's actual involvement in the humbling of the SA (Sturmabteilung or "Brownshirts") in the brutal "blood purge" of 30 June–1 July 1934 was minor. However, the SS provided many of the "hit squads" that struck at the SA, and SS men manned the firing squad that summarily executed SA leader Ernst Röhm and five others at Stadelheim Prison in Munich. The next day, Dietrich was promoted to Obergruppenführer (Lieutenant General). Dietrich spent much of the next four years training the Leibstandarte and supervising its expansion from a battalion to a large brigade, at the same time gaining some formal military education, much of this by way of personal attention from Army Chief of Staff General Werner Freiherr (Baron) von Fritsch and Defense Minister Werner Blomberg. Dietrich led the Leibstandarte with some skill and considerable zeal and enterprise in Poland in 1939 and in Belgium in 1940.

Dietrich again led the Leibstandarte in the Balkan campaign (April 1941), winning particular distinction in Greece. His unit, hastily expanded to a motorized infantry division, did not enter action in Russia until July, as part of Army Group South's First Panzer Group. After heavy combat in the late autumn and winter in southern Russia near the Sea of Azov, Dietrich and the

Leibstandarte were withdrawn to refit in March 1942. Sent to Paris in June, Dietrich and his division spent several months there reorganizing and reequipping as the 1st SS Panzer Division Leibstandarte Adolf Hitler. By year's end, the division contained more than 20,000 personnel of all ranks, and in January 1943 returned to combat duty in Russia.

Arriving in southern Russia in the aftermath of the debacle at Stalingrad, Dietrich led the Leibstandarte as part of Obergruppenführer Paul Hausser's I SS Panzer Corps in Manstein's famous "back-hand-blow" counteroffensive around Kharkov. This effort badly mauled the triumphant but weary Soviet mechanized and cavalry forces that had driven the Germans hundreds of miles westward and led to the recapture of Kharkov itself by Dietrich's troops on 11–13 March.

Following this success, Dietrich led his division alongside the other formations of Hausser's (now redesignated) II SS Panzer Corps (2d Das Reich and 3d Totenkopf divisions) in the unsuccessful Kursk offensive (4–19 July 1943). Most of Hausser's units, Dietrich's included, were hastily withdrawn from the waning offensive effort at Kursk and hurried to northern Italy to provide some backbone to the Italian war effort after British and U.S. forces landed in Sicily. This move also was intended to indicate to the Italians the fate awaiting them should they try to surrender. While resting and reorganizing in the Po valley (as part of Rommel's Army Group B), Dietrich was ordered to form the I SS Panzer Corps on 27 July 1943. Within six months Dietrich reported that this task was complete and that the brand-new I SS Panzer Corps was ready for action. Dietrich himself was promoted to Oberstgruppenführer on 20 April 1944.

Two days after the Allied landings in Normandy on 6 June 1944, the I SS Panzer Corps, comprising the 1st and 12th SS Panzer divisions, was committed to the Normandy front, and was soon heavily engaged with British and Canadian troops before Caen. Dietrich himself was hastily appointed commander of Panzer Group West on 12 June. He retained command of that unit through the disaster of the Falaise pocket and on into the autumn, when it was redesignated the Fifth Panzer Army. After Dietrich turned its command over to Manteuffel, Hitler appointed his old associate to command the still-forming Sixth Panzer Army.

Hitler planned to use the Sixth Panzer Army to deliver the decisive blow in his planned offensive into the Ardennes. Consequently Dietrich was able to have most of his requests for personnel and equipment filled promptly. He had, however, few illusions about the chances for success. Something of a grumbler, and with an old front-line soldier's distrust of the promises from higher headquarters, he was too much of a realist (or a pessimist) to expect much chance of success, but too good a soldier to raise more than a token protest. He was particularly unhappy with the lack of training among the new replacements in his divisions, and considered the Ardennes highly unsuitable country for mass armored operations, especially in early winter.

Frequently and unjustly portrayed as an uneducated, boorish, dim-witted thug, Dietrich was in fact a skillfull and aggressive tactician. He probably had more experience with tanks than almost anyone else in the Wehrmacht (he was the only senior officer who had served in armored units during World War I). Moreover, as a former enlisted man, he showed more consideration and concern for his men than did many other officers.

The Sixth Panzer Army contained four SS Panzer divisions (1st Leibstandarte, 2d Das Reich, 9th Hohenstaufen, and 12th Hitlerjugend), the 3d Parachute Division, and the 12th, 272d, 277th, and 326th Volksgrenadier divisions (VGDs). The infantry formations, under the I SS Panzer and LXVII Corps, were to tear holes in the American lines between the Losheim Gap and Monschau for the 1st and 12th SS Panzer divisions of I SS Panzer Corps.

Once the gap was made, the two panzer divisions were to advance over five preselected routes called *Rollbahnen*[10] to seize a series of bridges over the Meuse River from Huy northeast to Liège. The Hitlerjugend had the three northern routes leading from Hollerath and Losheim across the Elsenborn Ridge, then through Stavelot, Malmédy, and Spa to the four northern bridges. The Leibstandarte was assigned the two southern routes, which passed through Amblève, Vielsam, and Trois Ponts to reach the Meuse bridges around Huy. To lead the exploitation, Leibstandarte created a powerful kampfgruppe (battle group) or task force under veteran tank commander Obersturmbannführer der Waffen-SS (Lieutenant Colonel) Jochen Peiper to lead the armored breakthrough. Kampfgruppe Peiper contained more than half of the 1st SS Panzer Division's armor, along with supporting panzergrenadier, engineer, and artillery troops. As a second echelon, the 2d and 9th SS Panzer divisions in II SS Panzer Corps were to support and exploit whatever successes I SS Panzer Corps might produce.

The plan called for the infantry attacks to breach the American front line within twenty-four hours, and for the lead panzer elements to reach the Meuse that same day.[11] Most of the field commanders thought this was highly optimistic, considering the terrain and weather conditions. Regardless of when they actually reached and crossed the Meuse, the panzers were to push on rapidly toward Brussels and then Antwerp, leaving the volksgrenadier and parachute divisions to protect their northern flank. Those screening infantry formations would later be supplemented by infantry divisions from the Fifteenth Army to the north, and by additional divisions committed to the offensive but not assigned to the assault echelon. As a final objective, the Sixth Panzer Army would hold a line from Antwerp east to the Meuse, roughly along the Albert Canal.

To the south of the Sixth Panzer Army's sector lay General der Panzertruppen Hasso von Manteuffel's Fifth Panzer Army. Manteuffel, the scion of an aristocratic Prussian family that had bred generals since the seventeenth century, was also an experienced armor commander. He had risen to prominence as commander of the Grossdeutschland unit in Russia. Manteuffel had supervised its expansion from a motorized infantry brigade to an oversized panzer division.

The Fifth Panzer Army's northernmost unit, the 18th VGD of the LXVI Corps, was assigned the task of isolating and destroying the U.S. 106th Infantry Division in the Schnee Eifel massif and seizing the important crossroads of St. Vith immediately west of the Eifel. Two of the 18th Division's regiments, reinforced by assault guns and self-propelled antitank guns, were to drive west, north of the Eifel itself, while the third regiment would advance northwestward, around the southern end of the Eifel massif. The LXVI Corps's other division, the 62d VGD, was directed to capture the Our River bridges at and south of Steinebrück to facilitate the advance of the 116th Panzer Division's right wing.

Farther south, the 116th Panzer Division and 560th VGD of the LVIII Panzer Corps were supposed to break through the American 28th Infantry Division's lines and advance through Houffalize toward the Meuse crossings around Namur. Farther south, the XLVII Panzer Corps's 2d Panzer and Panzer Lehr divisions were supposed to advance to the Meuse and seize the bridges north of Namur, and the 26th VGD was assigned the immediate task of capturing Bastogne, another crucial crossroads, before pushing on to the Meuse. Once the initial breakthrough had been achieved and the immediate geographic objectives seized, the Fifth Panzer Army was supposed to shield the southern and eastern flanks of the Sixth Panzer Army, which was to advance across the Meuse, eventually gaining a line running roughly west-northwest from Givet to Antwerp.

The southernmost of the three armies committed to Wacht am Rhein was General Erich Brandenberger's Seventh Army. It contained the 5th Parachute Division and 352d VGD in the LXXXV Corps, and the 212th and 276th VGDs in the LXXX Corps. These units were to protect the southern flank of the Fifth Panzer Army as it crossed the Meuse, and to hold the front between Echternach and the vicinity of Givet on the Meuse, as the panzers headed for Brussels and Antwerp. The Seventh Army was initially allotted only four divisions, but contained a third corps headquarters (the LIII Corps) to handle several volksgrenadier divisions expected as reinforcements. Even Hitler realized that four divisions could not adequately defend a 100-kilometer front.

In all, the initial German forces committed to the Ardennes offensive totaled almost 410,000 men, as well as about 1,400 tanks and assault guns, 2,600 artillery pieces and rocket launchers, and just over 1,000 combat aircraft in support.[12] While this constituted a considerable matériel and personnel advantage over the American forces then deployed in the Ardennes, even this impressive array was dwarfed by the potential forces the Americans could bring to bear.

PROBLEMS

The initial operational plan for Wacht am Rhein called for twelve panzer and panzergrenadier divisions and eighteen infantry-type (parachute and volksgrenadier) divisions to be committed to the attack. In fact, there were only five panzer and thirteen infantry-type divisions in the initial assault with two more panzer divisions and a panzer brigade in immediate support, or only 70 percent of the forces Hitler had originally slated for the offensive.[13] These planned forces were not all in position by 15–16 December due to difficulties in disengaging them from other sectors and, more significantly, because the German logistical transportation system was not up to the task. Using the rail lines available, it was simply impossible to move combat units forward and at the same time to assemble the stocks of fuel, ammunition, and other supplies required for the offensive. For instance, although the Germans had, through considerable effort, stockpiled the 500 million gallons of gasoline their planners estimated was required for the initial phase of the operation, half of it remained east of the Rhine because the transport system could not move it forward. The transport routes, especially the marshalling yards, were under steady Allied air attack. Although each train was protected by Luftwaffe-manned flak cars, and the trains ran principally at night and during bad weather to avoid Allied aircraft, the movement plans were sometimes interrupted. For this reason, several units that had initially been slated to take part in the offensive never reached the battle area, including most of the 15th Panzergrenadier Division. The 10th Frundsberg SS Panzer Division and 11th Panzer Division both reached the battle area later than originally planned, and were diverted south to take part in the Nordwind offensive in Alsace in early January. Several of the units committed to the offensive went into action without their full complement, and parts of other divisions (including both the 2d SS and 9th SS Panzer) had only been in position for a matter of hours when the offensive began.

ASSESSMENT

Put bluntly, Hitler's plan for the Ardennes offensive was overambitious and ridden with unrealistic assumptions. Even with their best efforts, the Germans were unable to commit to the offensive the force levels called for in the original plan—which many of the generals considered inadequate. Even if those forces had been available, adding perhaps another 400 tanks and assault guns, 500 combat aircraft, several hundred artillery pieces, and at least two more panzer or panzergrenadier divisions to the initial lineup, the objective determined by Hitler when he first outlined his plan in mid-September was not achievable.

This is not to say that his overall strategic assessment was incorrect. The Germans had assembled enough resources for a final counterstroke capable of inflicting considerable damage on the Anglo-American allies. But while there was logic in the concept, Hitler's assessment was fundamentally flawed. The American Army in Europe was by and large an experienced and combat-capable force. It was blessed with abundant matériel resources, and steady, reliable supply arrangements. Its artillery was particularly powerful and effective, and by late 1944 its commanders at corps level and above were experienced, able, and comfortable with command. Hitler also failed to understand the crucial differences between the Franco-British armies of 1940, which had lacked combat experience, unified command, sound doctrine, and effective tactical airpower, and the Anglo-American armies of 1944, which had all four in abundance. Considering the actual conditions that prevailed on the western front in the late autumn and early winter of 1944, rather than Hitler's fantasy-fogged appreciation, the best the Germans could hope for in the Ardennes was a modestly successful spoiling attack.

3

ALLIED PLANS
AND DEPLOYMENTS

GATHERING AT MAASTRICHT

The principal Allied leaders in the west had no inkling of the planned
German offensive when they met at Maastricht, in the southern Nether-
lands, on 7 December. Attending the meeting were General Eisenhower, the
Supreme Allied Commander (SAC); Air Chief Marshal Sir Arthur W. Tedder,
Deputy SAC; Field Marshal Sir Bernard Law Montgomery, commander of
the British 21st Army Group; Lt. Gen. Omar N. Bradley, commander of the
American 12th Army Group; and senior members of their staffs.

Born in Denison, Texas, on 14 October 1890, Eisenhower had spent most
of his youth in Abilene, Kansas. Of the 164 graduates of the West Point Class
of 1915, he ranked 61st in academics and 125th in discipline; he was one of
59 members of that class who became general officers. To his great regret, he
did not get overseas in World War I. Despite his undistinguished record at
West Point, he graduated first in his class from the Command and General
Staff School at Fort Leavenworth, Kansas, in 1926. He graduated from the
Army War College in 1928.

In 1933 Eisenhower became an aide to Gen. Douglas MacArthur, then
Chief of Staff of the U.S. Army. When MacArthur retired, Eisenhower
accompanied him to the Philippines in 1935. Later, as a colonel and Chief of
Staff of the Third Army in the Louisiana Maneuvers of 1941, he attracted the
attention of Army Chief of Staff Gen. George C. Marshall, who appointed
Eisenhower chief of the Army War Plans Division with the rank of brigadier
general. In March 1942 he was promoted to major general and made chief of
the newly created Operations Division of the General Staff. In June Marshall
sent him to England to command all U.S. troops in Europe, and the next

month he was promoted to lieutenant general. He was then appointed Commander in Chief of Allied Expeditionary Forces for Operation Torch, the landings of American and British troops in North Africa in November 1942.

Eisenhower's rapid promotions in 1941 and early 1942 were due to both his exceptional military competence and the effect of his outgoing, genial manner on General Marshall. Now, however, he had an opportunity to display a facet of his personality that until this time had been only fleetingly discernible. Ike was a natural-born diplomat. He charmed his British subordinates—as well as most Americans—by his tact and wit, while his solid military virtues won their respect.

Eisenhower was promoted to general in February 1943 while commanding Allied operations in Tunisia. As Commander in Chief Allied Force Headquarters, he directed the invasion of Sicily in July 1943, and then the invasion of Italy at Salerno in September. In December 1943 he was appointed Supreme Commander of Allied Expeditionary Forces and went to England to prepare for Operation Overlord, the invasion of France by way of Normandy.

There had been at least two other candidates for Supreme Allied Commander. One of them was U.S. Army Chief of Staff Gen. George C. Marshall. The other was Marshall's British countrpart: Chief of the Imperial General Staff of the British Army, Gen. Sir Alan Brooke (later Field Marshal Lord Alanbrooke). The fact that Brooke was British, however, precluded him from ever achieving what was undoubtedly his dream. Both Allied leaders—President Franklin D. Roosevelt and Prime Minister Winston S. Churchill—and their senior political and military advisers recognized that the greater manpower and resources of the United States would demand that the Supreme Commander be an American. At the same time, President Roosevelt insisted that Marshall remain in Washington as the military man upon whom the president most relied. Reluctantly accepting this fact of life, Marshall then made certain that his protégé, Eisenhower, would get the job.

D-Day for Overlord was 6 June 1944. Ike's Allied troops broke out of the Normandy Beachhead in late July 1944. Soon after the liberation of Paris on 25 August Eisenhower moved his Supreme Headquarters, Allied Expeditionary Forces (SHAEF) to Versailles. From there he exercised control over Allied ground forces, by then comprising more than 2 million men, consisting of, in addition to a massive logistic support force, seven armies in three army groups: The 21st Army Group (British Second Army and Canadian First Army), commanded by Field Marshal Montgomery; the 12th Army Group (U.S. First, Third, and Ninth armies) under General Bradley; and the 6th Army Group (U.S. Seventh Army and French First Army) under Lt. Gen. Jacob L. Devers. Another 500,000 American troops were on their way to Europe, most staged through Britain, about to join Eisenhower's field armies.

Ike's deputy, Air Chief Marshal Tedder, was born on 11 July 1890, in Glenguin, Stirling, Scotland. He entered the British Army in 1913 as a subaltern and was transferred to the Royal Flying Corps in 1916 during World War I. He remained in the Royal Air Force (RAF) after the war, and rose steadily to high rank and command. In 1941, early in World War II, he was appointed Commander in Chief of the RAF Middle East Command. In concert with the ground commanders in that theater he developed the concepts of close air support of ground forces that became the doctrine for the British, and later the Americans, to the end of the war. After commanding the successful RAF support of operations in North Africa, Sicily, and southern Italy, he returned to England early in 1944 to become deputy to Eisenhower.

In his wartime memoirs *Crusade in Europe*, Eisenhower described his pleasure at the appointment of Tedder as his deputy. They had worked closely together in the Mediterranean Theater and, as Ike wrote, "[There Tedder] had won the respect and admiration of all his associates, not only as a brilliant airman, but as a staunch supporter of the 'allied' principle as practiced in that command."[1] In the months following his appointment as Ike's deputy, Tedder was responsible for policy and control of all Allied air operations in northwest Europe, both before and after Operation Overlord. He developed a close and cordial relationship with Eisenhower during that time. Unquestionably there was personal chemistry at work; their respective national origins did not in the slightest influence the viewpoints of these two men, which were amazingly consistent.

Bernard Law Montgomery's family came from Northern Ireland, but he was born on 17 November 1887, near Alton, in Hampshire, England. A graduate of St. Paul's School and the Royal Military Academy at Sandhurst, he distinguished himself as a junior officer in World War I. At the beginning of World War II he commanded a division in the British Expeditionary Force in France. After being evacuated from the Continent at Dunkirk in May 1940, he was placed in command of British forces in southeastern England, where a German attack was anticipated momentarily. The attack never came, and in August 1942, Montgomery was placed in command of the British Eighth Army in Egypt, which had recently been defeated in Libya by German Field Marshal Erwin Rommel and pushed back into Egypt. He defeated Rommel in the decisive Battle of El Alamein in November 1942, and slowly pursued the Germans across Libya and into southern Tunisia. Halted by the German Mareth Line, the Eighth Army, in eastern Tunisia, drove northward, converging with the Allied First Army from the west, until the German surrender in Tunisia in May 1943.

Montgomery continued to command the Eighth Army during the invasion of Sicily in July 1943 and the invasion of southern Italy in September. Monty commanded Allied land forces in the invasion of Normandy in Operation Overlord in June 1944. He was then appointed to command the 21st Army Group in the subsequent breakout from the Normandy Beachhead and in the pursuit of German forces across northern France in August and September.

Over the years Montgomery had alienated many of his fellow British officers by his arrogance and egotism. Not least among them was Air Chief Marshal Tedder, who had found it difficult to cooperate with Montgomery in the Mediterranean Theater. The same traits almost automatically antagonized most Americans with whom he came in contact in the campaigns in North Africa, Sicily, and Italy.

The fourth senior Allied commander at the Maastricht conference was American Lt. Gen. Omar N. Bradley. Born in Clark, Missouri, on 12 February 1893, he was a West Point classmate of Eisenhower's. In the early 1920s he was a mathematics instructor at West Point. After graduation from the Infantry School at Fort Benning, Georgia, in 1925, he spent three years in Hawaii, and then attended the Command and General Staff School at Fort Leavenworth. From 1929 to 1934 he served as an instructor at the Infantry School, under then Lt. Col. George C. Marshall. He was later the Assistant Commandant at West Point. In 1941 he was promoted from the rank of lieutenant colonel to brigadier general (and thus was the first in his West Point class on whom stars fell) when the Chief of Staff, General Marshall, appointed him Commandant of the Infantry School. In early 1942, as a major general, he became the commander of the reactivated 82d Division. His success in training the 82d led to his appointment in June as commander of the 28th Division, Pennsylvania National Guard, which had gained a reputation for laxness in discipline and training.

Early in 1943, after American troops were defeated by Field Marshal Erwin Rommel at the Battle of Kasserine Pass, Bradley was sent to Tunisia to be General Eisenhower's personal representative in the field. On 15 April he took command of the II Corps, which concluded the Tunisian campaign in May with a stunning victory in the capture of Bizerte from the Germans. He then led his corps in the successful invasion of Sicily in July 1943. Soon after this he was selected to command the U.S. First Army in the coming invasion of Normandy. On 20 October 1943 he opened his headquarters in Bristol, England. He landed in Normandy on 6 June 1944 a few hours after the assault landings of his troops. Shortly after the breakout from Normandy, on 1 August 1944, he assumed command of the newly established 12th Army Group, which included the First Army, now commanded by Lt. Gen. Courtney Hodges, and Gen. George Patton's Third Army. A few months later the Ninth Army, commanded by Lt. Gen. William H. Simpson, was added to his army group, which now included nearly 1 million men. The Fifteenth Army would be added to his group in December.

Bradley's quiet, homespun, almost gawky personal appearance and mannerisms appealed to almost everyone with whom he came in contact. Also appealing to colleagues and associates were his innate courtesy and unfailing consideration of others—qualities that did not, however, inhibit him from making quick, usually sound, military decisions.[2]

DISAGREEMENT AT MAASTRICHT

Montgomery had suggested the 7 December meeting, which took place at the headquarters of General Simpson's Ninth U.S. Army. Although the others had apparently not realized it, Monty was hopeful that at this meeting he could persuade Eisenhower to modify the existing command arrangements before the initiation of Allied offensives planned to begin in mid-December.

Eisenhower and Montgomery had met earlier at Monty's headquarters at Zonhoven on 28 November, when Montgomery had tried to persuade Ike to place him in overall direction and command of land operations with Bradley under Montgomery's operational control. Monty passes over this meeting very briefly in his memoirs. Ike does not mention it in *Crusade in Europe*, but it is evident from both Montgomery's and Bradley's memoirs that Eisenhower discussed the meeting at considerable length with Bradley, who obviously was very annoyed by Monty's suggestions.[3] After the Zonhoven meeting, Ike agreed to Monty's suggestion for a meeting at Simpson's headquarters at Maastricht on 7 December.

Bradley, who was not well, thought the meeting was "a long and tedious affair."[4] Eisenhower began the meeting with a survey of the anticipated Allied offensives: In the north, the British Second and Canadian First armies of the 21st Army Group would drive toward Germany's strategic industrial region of the Ruhr. In the center, just south of the Ruhr, the U.S. Ninth and First armies of the 12th Army Group would thrust through the Roer River region toward Cologne and Coblenz. Further to the south, the U.S. Third Army, also part of the 12th Army Group, was to begin an offensive toward Frankfurt.

When asked to present his views, Montgomery strongly disagreed with this plan. He argued that Eisenhower had in reality decided upon what was essentially a two-pronged thrust into Germany. He suggested that the northern thrust, involving the Ruhr and Cologne, should be under one command—that of his 21st Army Group—while Bradley's 12th Army Group should be responsible for the southern offensive toward Frankfurt. As it stood, Montgomery said, Eisenhower's plan had the American First and Ninth armies, under Bradley's 12th Army Group, conducting one offensive north of the Ardennes toward Cologne (which he said was really a part of the Ruhr), while south of the Ardennes, Patton's Third Army—also under Bradley—would be carrying out a divergent offensive toward Frankfurt. Monty argued that Bradley should concentrate either on the offensive toward Cologne or on the drive to Frankfurt. In either case, one overall commander (obviously Monty) should have command responsibility for the offensive toward the Ruhr-Cologne industrial region.

Eisenhower disagreed, although (to Bradley's annoyance) he agreed that Monty should make the main effort and accepted Monty's idea of putting the Ninth Army under the 21st Army Group.[5] So the Allied offensive, the preliminaries of which would begin on 9 December, would be three-pronged, as

Eisenhower had stated, instead of the two-pronged thrust that Monty recommended. Monty wrote in his memoirs

So we really achieved nothing at the Maastricht conference on the 7th December. I had hoped to get agreement that we would shift our main weight toward the north. I then wanted the activities of 12 and 21 Army Groups [under Montgomery's command, although left unsaid] to be directed against the Ruhr, and to the task of imposing mobile war on the enemy in the north German plain in the early spring. But no decision was given.

Meanwhile Bradley's 12 Army Group was disposed in two main concentrations, each deployed for attack. In between was a gap of some 100 miles, held by [VIII] American Corps of four divisions—under Middleton.[6]

As subsequent events were to demonstrate, the abrasive Montgomery, thoroughly disliked by many American colleagues—not least by Bradley and Patton—was to show that his strategic vision and tactical competence were considerably greater than the Americans were willing to acknowledge—even though considerably less than Montgomery himself obviously believed.

VII CORPS ROER OFFENSIVE: 9–13 DECEMBER

On 9 December the U.S. First Army began an offensive that was to have consequences that would be crucial to the outcome of the Battle of the Bulge. The VII Corps, under the command of Maj. Gen. Joseph Lawton "Lightning Joe" Collins, began operations to eliminate the German bridgehead on the west bank of the Roer River, west of Düren.

Joseph Lawton Collins was born in New Orleans on 1 May 1896. He graduated from West Point on 20 April 1917, just after the United States entered World War I, as a second lieutenant of infantry. He was assigned to the 22d Infantry Regiment at Fort Hamilton, New York, and remained with the regiment throughout the war. He never left the vicinity of New York City, although he rose to the rank of major and was commanding a battalion at the end of the war. Early in 1919 he reverted to the rank of captain and sailed to Europe to join the Army of Occupation in Germany. After two years in Germany he returned to the United States to begin twelve solid years of school duty, either as an instructor or student. From August 1921 to June 1925 he taught in the chemistry department at West Point. He then attended the Company Officers' course at the Infantry School in Fort Benning, graduating in July 1926. Then, in an unusual instance of cross-training for an infantryman, he attended the Advanced Course at the Field Artillery School in Fort Sill, Oklahoma, graduating in June 1927. He returned to Fort Benning as an instructor at the Infantry School until August 1931, when he became a student at the Command and General Staff School at Fort Leavenworth, Kansas, graduating in June 1933. He was promoted to major while at Fort Leavenworth.

After serving for three years in a troop assignment in the Philippines,

Collins attended the Army Industrial College and then the Army War College in Washington from August 1936 to June 1938. He stayed on for two more years as an instructor at the War College. After seven months as Assistant Secretary of the Army General Staff in Washington, he served as Chief of Staff of the VII Corps in Birmingham, Alabama, from January to December 1941. Immediately after the Japanese attack on Pearl Harbor brought the United States into World War II, he became Chief of Staff of the Hawaiian Department. Promoted to brigadier general in February 1942, he was assigned on 8 May to command the 25th Infantry Division and was soon promoted to major general. From 26 November 1942 to 15 December 1943 he led his division in combat on Guadalcanal and New Georgia in the Solomon Islands.

Collins was then ordered to England, arriving in February 1944 to take command of the VII Corps. (He was one of very few American officers who served in high command positions in both the war against Japan and the war against Germany.) The 9th and 90th divisions of his corps landed in Normandy at Utah Beach on D-Day. His corps was selected to make the breakout from the Normandy Beachhead at St. Lô in Operation Cobra, beginning on 25 July 1944. Through the month of August the VII Corps was in constant aggressive pursuit of the defeated Germans, and Collins confirmed the nickname he had first received on Guadalcanal: "Lightning Joe." His corps was the first to penetrate the German frontier, and it captured Aachen, the first major German city to fall to the Allies, on 16 October. Generals Bradley and Hodges selected the VII Corps as the spearhead for the Roer River offensive, which began on 9 December 1944.

The major units of Collins's VII Corps—the 104th Infantry Division, the 9th Infantry Division, elements of the 3d Armored Division, the 83d Infantry Division, and elements of the 5th Armored Division—executed a concentric attack on a defensive line held by the German LXXXI Corps. After an initial repulse, the 104th made good progress, closing up to the river by the evening of 12 December. This unhinged the German right flank and allowed the veteran 9th Division—supported by tanks of the 3d Armored—to roll up the German position in its sector from north to south. Large numbers of prisoners were taken, but the Americans in turn also suffered heavy casualties. Farther south the 83d Division—making its combat debut—had many of the problems of units new to combat and became embroiled in a close-quarters fight in the eastern edge of the Hürtgen Forest. However, despite severe losses, the division profited from the success of the 9th Division to its north and on 13 December was attacking the remaining German positions west of the Roer, which were eliminated by late on 15 December.

ENTER THE V CORPS: 13–15 DECEMBER

Farther to the south on 13 December, the V Corps, commanded by Maj. Gen. Leonard T. Gerow, also entered the offensive. Its thrust aimed at eliminating the threat presented by the Roer River dams to an Allied crossing of the Roer. In the north of the corps sector the 8th Infantry Division advanced to seize the villages of Hürtgen, Brandenburg, and Bergstein, with objectives secured, or about to be secured, by late 15 December. The 78th Infantry Division in the center drove east to seize Kesternich and was still engaged in a seesaw battle for the village on 16 December. To the south, the 2d Infantry Division, supported by the 99th Infantry Division, drove north toward the crossroads of Wahlerscheid. These assaults by the V Corps threatened the flanks and rear of both the German LXXIV Corps—in its positions southeast of Bergstein and east of Kesternich—and of the LXXVII Corps—southeast of Kesternich and north of Wahlerscheid.

The significance of these actions, just north of the German concentration east of the Ardennes, to what happened later in the Bulge has been largely ignored by most histories of the campaign. In attempting to stem the U.S. advance on Düren (Hitler had decreed that the Düren bridgehead was crucial to the success of the Ardennes offensive), the Germans were forced to commit several major combat units scheduled to participate in the Sixth Panzer Army's offensive on 16 December.[7]

The 3d Parachute Division was intended to deploy as the leftmost of the three divisions forming the assault echelon of the Sixth Panzer Army. By the morning of 16 December—when the German attack was to begin—the division was still straggling into its assembly area, and most of its 8th Regiment (one-third of its infantry strength) had not even left Düren. The parts of the division that were in position were badly disorganized, had suffered significant casualties, and were unable to orient themselves prior to the order to jump off.

A heavy antitank battalion, which included the deadly self-propelled (SP) 88-mm Jagdpanthers as well as SP 75-mm guns, intended to reinforce the Sixth Panzer Army's initial attack, did not arrive until three days later. Two assault gun brigades and an artillery corps supposed to support the LXVII Corps also were delayed, leaving the German infantry in that sector without armored support and lacking a major part of their artillery support. Perhaps even more important, the American attacks forced the LXVII Corps to retain in line three battalions of one of the divisions assigned to lead the assault of the Sixth Panzer Army, and those three battalions constituted one-half of that division's infantry strength.[8] This meant that the two divisions of the corps could muster only five and a half battalions of the twelve that had been counted on for thrusts on Monschau and Höfen.

Just as important, by 13 December the advance of the U.S. VII Corps on Düren had pinched out of the Allied line the 3d Armored Division and the bulk of the 9th Infantry Division, both of which immediately went into corps reserve. Furthermore, the successful conclusion of the Düren battle meant that the veteran 1st Infantry Division, which had suffered heavy casualties in the first week of December in an earlier, unsuccessful attack on Düren, did not need to be committed, and remained in reserve. Thus three divisions, two of which (the 1st and 9th) were considered by many to be the among the best American divisions in Europe, were in reserve behind the First Army front—ready at hand to counter the initial threats presented by the planned German attack on 16 December.[9]

Meanwhile, the divisions of the V Corps were executing a concentric attack to seize the Roer dams. On the corps left flank, the 8th and 78th Infantry divisions were driving east and southeast into the LXXIV Corps sector of the Fifteenth Army. On the right flank, the 2d Infantry Division, supported by the 99th Infantry Division, attacked north into the sector of the LXVII Corps of the Sixth Panzer Army. Linking the two flanks of the corps was a security screen composed of the 102d Mechanized Cavalry Group, and elements of the 2d and 99th divisions (the division reconnaissance troops and the 3d Battalion of the 395th Infantry).

THE 2D INFANTRY DIVISION ATTACK

As part of the general offensive by the U.S. V Corps, the 2d Infantry Division was to drive northeast from the vicinity of the twin villages of Krinkelt-Rocherath, through a corridor formed by the 99th Division, to take the German defenses protecting the Roer River dams in flank and rear. As we have seen, the U.S. 8th Division was already attacking from the north, while the 78th Division was attacking from the west. The operation was intended to pinch off the German salient west of the Roer, ending once and for all the threat the dams presented to forces attempting an assault across the lower reaches of the Roer.[10]

On the evening of 12 December the 2d Division moved into position to the left of the 395th Infantry Regiment of the 99th Division.[11] Artillery support for the attack was amply provided by four organic and two and one-third attached battalions plus the reinforcing fires of three and one-third V Corps battalions.[12] However, the bulk of the V Corps artillery was out of supporting range of the 99th Division and the right flank of the corps. This was not perceived as a problem, however, inasmuch as the role of the 99th Division (supported by its four organic and two and two-thirds attached artillery battalions) was to be primarily passive in the support of the 2d Division attack.

The 2d Division was further reinforced by the attachments usual for an infantry division, including a tank battalion, a tank destroyer battalion, an antiaircraft battalion, a 4.2-inch heavy mortar battalion, and miscellaneous minor units.[13] There were other important reinforcements. One was Combat Command B of the 9th Armored Division, which was intended to exploit any breakthrough. The other was a second tank destroyer battalion.

Unfortunately for the attackers, the German defenses, although thinly held, were well sited and camouflaged. Furthermore, the densely wooded terrain offered significant advantages to the defenders. At the same time, there was little undergrowth, which allowed good fields of fire for the defending Germans along most of the possible avenues of approach. Also, the densely packed trees significantly limited long-distance visibility, obscuring the German positions and making it almost impossible for the American artillery observers to make accurate visual sensings. Perhaps worse for the exposed American attackers, incoming German mortar and artillery fire usually resulted in deadly tree bursts with splinters and falling tree limbs magnifying the normal explosive effect of the actual round. (Of course, tree bursts were also damaging for the defenders, although to a lesser degree because of dug-in positions.)

The 2d Division's main effort was to be executed initially by the 9th Infantry Regiment, attacking through positions held by the 2d Division Reconnaissance Troop and the 99th Infantry Division, striking to the northeast astride a road (actually more of an improved trail than a road) that led through the German positions. The 1st Battalion was deployed on the left (west), the 2d Battalion was on the right (east), and the 3d Battalion was held in reserve. The 9th's mission was to penetrate the German lines and then swing left to capture the town of Rohren and trap the German forces holding the line farther north. The 38th Infantry was held in immediate reserve, behind the 9th, and was to be prepared to come on line to the right of the 9th and expand the breach to the north and east. The 23d Infantry Regiment was held in divisional reserve at Camp Elsenborn.

Initial attacks by the 9th Infantry (Col. Chester J. Hirschfelder) made little progress and incurred heavy casualties. For nearly three weary days (13–15 December) the 9th Infantry battered at the defenses of the German Westwall in an attempt to seize the road junction near Jägerhaus Wahlerscheid. (Jägerhaus means "hunter's house" or "forester's house," but it was actually a customs post on the German-Belgian border.) The only significant result was the cutting of a four-yard-wide gap in the German wire entanglements by a squad from G Company on the evening of 13 December. Unfortunately, since the company commander had been wounded and communications had broken down, no immediate effort was made to exploit the gap.

On the night of 15 December Lt. Col. Walter M. Higgins Jr., commanding the 2d Battalion of the 9th Infantry, decided to gamble and utilize this needlelike opening in the German lines. Higgins, a West Point graduate of the Class of 1939, had joined the 2d Division as a brand-new second lieutenant, and was now a hard-bitten, much-decorated veteran. First one company, then the rest of the battalion (except one company detailed to hold the gap and the right flank), slipped single-file through the German lines and fanned out to surround the first German pillbox. The 3d Battalion soon followed and deployed to the left. Shortly thereafter, the assault began; within minutes the German defenses collapsed as the bewildered defenders were swiftly routed from their positions. Fifteen pillboxes and the customs house were seized, and more than 130 prisoners were taken in this quick success. Higgins had reinforced his reputation as one of the best battalion commanders in one of the best divisions of the U.S. Army.

By the morning of 16 December, the outlook seemed to be bright for the 2d Infantry Division. The German defenses had been ripped open on a 1,000-meter-wide front and nearly 300 German casualties had been inflicted. Losses in the 9th Infantry had also been heavy: the three battalions of the 9th Infantry had suffered 338 casualties.[14] However, the 38th Infantry had been moved up from reserve and was now prepared to exploit the breach.

During the engagement the 2d Division G-2 had reported the enemy as being an Alarm Company of the 277th Volksgrenadier Division, composed of personnel from the division's Transport and Supply Regiment and Veterinary Company. However, on 15 December a confused German (a messenger who had walked unawares through both the German and American lines in the dark) was taken prisoner by the 38th Cavalry Squadron near Kesternich. He proved to be a member of the I Battalion, 751st Grenadier Regiment, 326th Volksgrenadier Division, which was moving into position to the north, opposite Monschau (garrisoned by the 38th Cavalry Squadron) and Höfen (held by the 3d Battalion of the 395th Infantry of the 99th Division). More ominously, prisoners had begun to report that the defenses at Wahlerscheid were now backed up by SS troopers.

VIII CORPS: QUIET SECTOR

Throughout this period of intense activity along the Roer River, the Ardennes front just to the south remained quiet. On the left of the VIII Corps, the 18th Cavalry Squadron of the 14th Cavalry Group remained in its billets in the Losheim Gap, leisurely observing the German positions to the east and occasionally sending contact patrols to the 99th Infantry Division to its north. Two troops of the 18th and a reinforced company of the 820th Tank Destroyer Battalion (towed) were deployed in the gap—mostly in platoon-size strongpoints. The squadron Headquarters Troop, Assault Gun Troop, and the Tank Company were in immediate support at Manderfeld, while one troop was deployed to the south covering the juncture of the 423d and 424th Infantry regiments (of the 106th Division) at Grosslangenfeld. The 32d Cavalry Squadron was in the 14th Group reserve at St. Vith, where it was performing scheduled maintenance on its vehicles.

To the south of the 14th Cavalry Group, the 106th Infantry Division (to which the 14th was attached) settled into the former positions of the 2d Infantry Division while the division commander, Maj. Gen. Alan Jones, attempted to adapt the 2d's contingency plans to the capabilities of his green division.

A major problem soon cropped up: The 2d Division's plan to meet a possible German counterattack called for a commitment of the divisional reserve—a tank battalion, an infantry battalion, and a self-propelled tank destroyer battalion. The 106th simply did not have such a reserve. (The division's attachments, aside from the 14th Cavalry, consisted of a single towed tank destroyer battalion.) Jones made do with a single infantry battalion in reserve; he counted on the availability of the VIII Corps armored reserve (CCR, 9th Armored Division) in the event of an emergency. Furthermore, his division was supported by six of the ten corps artillery battalions. He was not unduly worried—the 106th was in a "quiet sector" of the front.

Jones's 422d Infantry Regiment, the division's left wing, was in positions along the Schnee Eifel, a heavily wooded ridge that ran roughly northeast to southwest along the east bank of the Our River. The line was extended to Bleialf by the 423d Infantry with two battalions (its 2d battalion was in division reserve near Born). The distance from Bleialf to the left flank of the division's remaining regiment—the 424th—was nearly six kilometers. This gap was covered by the aforementioned squadron of the 18th Cavalry, the 106th Division's Cavalry Reconnaissance Troop, and the 424th Regiment's Cannon Company, which was fighting as infantry—barely 400 men. The 424th was in well dug-in positions to the south, but if the screening force in the gap was overwhelmed, the regiment's left flank would be badly exposed, and the division's front line would be ruptured.

In theory, the 14th Cavalry Group and the 106th Division were amply supported by artillery. In addition to the four organic artillery battalions of the 106th, there was a self-propelled battalion with the 14th Cavalry (the 275th), plus six additional corps artillery battalions scattered along this four-regimental sector of the front.[15] Unfortunately, coordination between the 106th Division and the supporting artillery was not firmly established. Jones's inexperienced artillerymen had little knowledge of the artillery plan that had been established by the 2d Division. Worse perhaps, the extensive communications net established by the 2d Division had to be—at least partially—reestablished by the 106th, because the frugal signalmen of the 2d Division had taken their field telephones with them. Veteran divisions had found that field telephones were an indispensable asset and assiduously collected large numbers of unauthorized telephones and switchboards, including captured German equipment. The signalers of the 106th encountered a bewildering array of telephone lines, and had little idea with whom they communicated.

Next in line to the south on the VIII Corps front was the 28th Division. This veteran division was recovering from a violent drubbing suffered in the Hürtgen Forest during the first two weeks of November. The 28th's regiments were now back at nearly full strength, but had been filled by green replacements. The division had gained the nickname "Bloody Bucket" from its red Pennsylvania Keystone shoulder patch and its heavy casualties in earlier battles. The 28th had begun to earn the unenviable distinction of being the unluckiest division of the American Army, a distinction confirmed in the Ardennes.

On the left of the 28th Division was its 112th Infantry Regiment, deployed to the right of the 424th Infantry on the east bank of the Our River. Like the 424th, the 112th was well dug in, but its tenuous connection to its right-hand neighbor (the 110th Infantry Regiment) posed a major threat to its right flank.

The 110th Infantry was deployed with two battalions (the 2d Battalion was in division reserve) in company-size strongpoints along the west bank of the Our River from Heinerscheid to Weiler—a distance of nearly sixteen kilometers. South of the 110th was the 109th Infantry, which had only a slightly less extensive front. Behind the 110th Infantry, at Trois Vierges, was the sole armored reserve of the VIII Corps, CCR of the 9th Armored Division. These two regiments of the 28th Division were supported by three artillery battalions (two light and one medium)[16] organic to the division, but there was only a single corps artillery battalion (the 687th) in this sector.

South of the 109th Infantry was the rump of the 9th Armored Division: the Division Headquarters and Combat Command A (CCA). (CCB was in V Corps reserve far to the north.) CCA held a narrow sector along the Our River, covering the gorge of the Schwarz Ernz with a single infantry battalion. The combat command's tank battalion and artillery battalion were in support.

The right flank of the VIII Corps was formed by the 4th Infantry Division, arguably one of the best U.S. divisions in Europe. However, like the 28th Division, the 4th had been badly battered in recent fighting in the Hürtgen Forest and was still seriously understrength. Furthermore, it was so dispersed along a wide front that its commander, Maj. Gen. Raymond O. Barton, was unable to assemble an effective infantry reserve. The division's reserve consisted of the 4th Engineer Combat Battalion, the 4th Division Reconnaissance Troop, and the badly depleted and broken-down 70th Tank Battalion. (This description is quite literally correct; the battalion was depleted in the sense that it had only thirty-three of its authorized fifty-four medium tanks available, and only eleven of these were operational.) Artillery was also limited: The 12th Infantry in its positions around Echternach was supported by the 42d Field Artillery Battalion,[17] elements of the 802d Tank Destroyer Battalion (towed)—utilized as artillery—and, at the limits of their range, the 20th, 81st, and 174th Field Artillery battalions. There was no corps artillery support available along this portion of the VIII Corps front.

FORCES IN RESERVE

Most histories of the Ardennes Offensive make much of the fact that Eisenhower's sole strategic reserve consisted of the two divisions (U.S. 82d and 101st Airborne divisions) of the U.S. XVIII Airborne Corps. In a very strict sense this was true. However, it is more accurate to say that the XVIII Airborne Corps was Eisenhower's *immediately available* strategic reserve. Additional divisions were moving onto the Continent from England or the United

States. Only one of these, the U.S. 11th Armored Division, participated directly in the response to the offensive. However, many others moved forward to take over defensive positions elsewhere on the front, thereby relieving veteran units that responded to the threat. In addition, both the veteran British 6th Airborne Division and the new U.S. 17th Airborne Division were in England, ready for deployment to Europe. They were assigned to the First Allied Airborne Army and could also be considered part of the SHAEF strategic reserve. The 17th Airborne Division, which was originally part of the XVIII Airborne Corps, would play a major role in the final phase of the campaign, as part of a reorganized VIII Corps.

Furthermore, the operational reserves available (that is, those reserves available to the armies and corps in Europe) were substantial. In the 12th Army Group zone the Ninth Army had two divisions (30th Infantry and 7th Armored) in reserve; the First Army had all or parts of four divisions (1st and 9th Infantry, 3d and 5th Armored) in reserve; and the Third Army also had all or parts of four divisions (26th and 80th Infantry, 4th and 10th Armored) in reserve. Finally, two new U.S. divisions (75th and 94th Infantry) were fully deployed on the Continent and were preparing for their baptism in combat.

4

"THE ARDENNES OFFENSIVE . . . COULD HAVE BEEN FORESEEN"[1]

THE INTELLIGENCE FAILURE

At daybreak of 16 December the German Army had concentrated a total of twenty divisions—with nearly 410,000 men, more than 2,600 artillery pieces and multiple-rocket launchers, and about 1,400 tanks and assault guns—on a 110-kilometer front facing the U.S. First Army.[2] That this concentration was completed almost without the Allies noticing is one of the most troubling aspects of the Ardennes campaign. The Allies had near-complete air superiority, their signals intelligence was of the highest order, and they had built up an accurate accounting of the disturbing resurgence of strength in the German armed forces since their crushing defeats of the previous summer. How then were the signs missed? How did the preparations for this massive counteroffensive go almost unnoticed? Legions of historians have pondered these questions, and reams of paper have been consumed in addressing them.

Answers range from the fantastic to the mundane. One of the most fantastic is a supposed plot by Bradley, Eisenhower, Churchill, and/or others to make the American forces fight harder. Typically mundane is the argument that nobody listened to the warnings of Col. Benjamin "Monk" Dickson (First Army G-2, or chief of intelligence) about the German buildup because he was a known pessimist and thought to be overstressed. The true answers are neither as simple as the convoluted theories of conspiracy buffs nor as simplistic as the belief that Allied arrogant overoptimism provides the explanation.

The true answer (if it can be called that) is neither immediately obvious nor easily understood. As in many historical events, the Allied intelligence failure was the result of a congruence of many events, the interplay of complex and forceful personalities, the misappreciation of a large number of subtle clues, and the pernicious inertia inherent in any massive human organization. However, an understanding of how the Allied intelligence failure occurred is essential to an understanding of how and why events transpired as they did in those gloomy days of December 1944.[3]

MILITARY INTELLIGENCE

Frequently derided as an oxymoron by ignorant buffoons, military intelligence is the term applied to the collection, assimilation, analysis, and distribution of information or knowledge regarding enemy strengths, dispositions, capabilities, and intentions in war. Military intelligence has played a role in wars since the dawn of recorded history. (The biblical tale of the fall of Jericho was probably a feat better attributed to Hebrew spies than to the hand of God.) In recent military history, the functions of military intelligence have become more sophisticated, formalized, and complex.

In the U.S. Army of World War II, military intelligence was (as it still is today) the responsibility of the G-2 section of the General Staff. There is an intelligence section at all command levels, from the U.S. and UK Combined Chiefs of Staff of World War II, or the current Joint Chiefs of Staff organization in the Pentagon, to the battalion in the field.[4] Intelligence in war is gathered from all possible field sources, including front-line information gained from observation of enemy movements and positions by combat reconnaissance patrols and by the capture and interrogation of enemy prisoners of war; interception and decryption of enemy radio traffic;[5] aerial reconnaissance and photography; and spying, the oldest form of intelligence gathering. Despite the exploits of fictional characters, spies have little impact on the gathering of military intelligence at the tactical and operational level in combat.

GERMAN COUNTERINTELLIGENCE MEASURES

Adolf Hitler insisted on complete secrecy from the beginning of planning for the Ardennes offensive. All officers associated with planning were required to sign a special declaration of secrecy regarding the offensive—in effect making their own lives and the lives of their families hostage to their honor. Even the code name of the operation—Wacht am Rhein (defense or guard of the Rhine River)—was chosen by Hitler for its ambiguity.

Perhaps more important, Hitler had come to believe (and he was right) that German radio traffic was no longer completely secure, so he ordered that all preparations for Wacht am Rhein were to be conducted by telephone and telegraph land lines rather than by radio. This merely confirmed as a direct order what was already an established fact. Radio had been necessary to deliver messages to the far-flung elements of the German armed forces in the heyday of the greatest expansion of the German Reich. However, as the German fighting frontier contracted in 1944 to the old prewar boundaries, there was less need for radio transmissions.

As the German forces assembled for the attack, all units and their commanders were given fictitious designations; thus, the Fifth Panzer Army became Feldkommando z. b. V. (Corps Headquarters for Special Purposes), implying a purely administrative command; Fifteenth Army became Gruppe von Manteuffel, implying the ad hoc formation of a corps-size task force; and Sixth Panzer Army became Auffrischungsstab 16 (Replenishment Staff 16). As the Germans should have expected, these designations only partly deceived Allied intelligence. Nevertheless, they contributed to a degree of confusion within Allied intelligence circles.

Furthermore, the assembly of German forces was deliberately carried out in a fashion intended to be ambiguous to Allied intelligence. It began in the area northeast and east of Düren, on the Roer River, a placement that would have enabled the gathering forces to intervene effectively in the battles then taking place at Düren, in the Hürtgen Forest, or at Geilenkirchen. These were logical moves—at least from the point of view of Allied intelligence. The final movement to the start line for the offensive did not begin until 13 December for the panzer formations, and then the movement was made at night to hide from possible aerial observation and under the cover of the noise of overflights by the German Air Force to drown out the noise of the motor vehicles.

ALLIED INTELLIGENCE

Information gained by the Allies from their standard intelligence sources was limited. The terrain of the Ardennes (wooded and hilly) allowed the Germans to make good use of masking ground to hide the deployment of their assault units, negating much of the effectiveness of ground-based observation.

One major clue, however, the sounds generated by the massive movement of German motor vehicles into the area, was well confirmed by reports made on the night of 14–15 December by the 106th and 28th Infantry divisions. Nevertheless, these reports were quickly discounted by the VIII Corps G-2. In the case of the 106th Division, little credence was given to the reports due to the division's combat inexperience; it had not yet been engaged in combat, and had only begun relieving the 2d Division in place on 11–12 December. The failure of the corps intelligence section to heed the reports of the 28th is less understandable. A veteran (if unlucky) division, the 28th had been badly battered by the 116th Panzer Division in the Hürtgen Forest in early November and had been brought up to strength by a massive infusion of green replacements. Although it was never explicitly stated in the records of the First Army or VIII Corps G-2, it is likely that the importance of the 28th Division's reports was overlooked as being the nervous overreaction of a demoralized outfit to normal enemy road traffic.[6]

More damning and more serious than the failure of higher headquarters to investigate these front-line reports of large-scale enemy vehicular movement was the failure by these same divisions to patrol their own front lines properly. Defensive combat patrolling was never a strong suit of the U.S. Army in World War II, a fact frequently cited by German officers after the war as a common failing in American infantry tactics. Due to the defensive posture and overextended fronts of the 28th and 106th divisions, their commanders should have realized that aggressive patrolling was vital for the security of their front lines. It was also the only means to capture prisoners (perhaps the primary source for tactical intelligence). The only POWs interrogated on the front prior to the start of the offensive were two men the 106th Division "captured" on 15 December. (Army Group B's war diary noted—with some anxiety—that the 18th Volksgrenadier Division had lost three men to desertion that night.) These men revealed that rumors of a major counteroffensive were circulating in the German Army. But such rumors had been common over the past months. Again, the VIII Corps and First Army G-2s failed to follow up on the information.

SIGNAL INTELLIGENCE (SIGINT)

The release in the 1970s of hitherto secret details regarding the astounding signal intelligence capabilities of the Allies in World War II (the "ULTRA" secret) forced military historians to make wide-ranging reevaluations of many Allied actions taken during the war. Unfortunately the role of ULTRA has been misunderstood in many cases.

ULTRA decryptions were of high-level German Army, Navy, and Air Force radio messages that frequently gave great detail on German dispositions, strengths, and intentions. Because ULTRA was limited to radio traffic only, the Germans' reversion to land-line telephone and teletype transmissions in late 1944 eliminated a major source of ULTRA information. As a result, ULTRA decryptions that had value for the Allied intelligence staffs dwindled to a trickle in early December.

The Allies' reliance on ULTRA had infected the high-command intelligence staffs (direct ULTRA information was not disseminated below the level of field army) with a pervading sense of complacency. The older means of intelligence gathering were not only less depended on but considered to be less dependable. Unfortunately, to a great extent the lack (or apparent lack) of data on German capabilities and intentions was interpreted as a loss of strength on the part of the Germans rather than a loss of information on the part of the Allies.

Nevertheless, tactical signal intelligence (as opposed to the strategic intelligence of ULTRA) did provide some clues to the buildup of the German forces.[7] It is interesting to note that many postwar historians have accepted without question the frequent German criticism of faulty American signal security. The Germans were often able to track the whereabouts of American formations simply by listening in on the many transmissions that were made "in the clear" (without encryption). Many of these historians have failed to realize that this was neither always true (the Germans completely missed the presence of the 2d Infantry Division in the sector of the Sixth Panzer Army) nor one-sided.

U.S. documents declassified in 1988 reveal that American operational and tactical signal intelligence services operated on a par with ULTRA, and were far beyond German capabilities. During the war, American signal interception units utilized superior cryptoanalysis systems to decipher large numbers of German tactical messages and relay them to Allied commanders, often within hours of the initial transmission. (An analysis of German signal security found in these Allied documents is almost disdainful.) Unfortunately, although tactical signal intelligence did allow Allied planners to build up an accurate German order of battle (revealing to the Allies the true nature of the Twenty-fifth Army, Gruppe von Manteuffel, and Feldkommando z. b. V. 16, for instance), it could not reveal the intentions of those units until operations began due to Hitler's orders prohibiting any radio signals dealing with planning for the attack. On the other hand, the evidence of the large number of formations, and of their unusual strengths, should have prompted far more serious attention than they received.

AERIAL RECONNAISSANCE

To a great extent the almost complacent and somewhat lackadaisical American attitude with respect to the value of ground reconnaissance was offset by the excellent Allied aerial reconnaissance capabilities. The nearly complete Allied control of the air allowed photo and visual reconnaissance aircraft full freedom to rove deep behind the German lines. Allied photo-analysis services were highly efficient and provided many insights into the whereabouts and capabilities of the German ground forces. However, weather and darkness (due to the time of the year) greatly reduced the effectiveness of Allied aerial reconnaissance in December 1944.

The atrocious fall weather severely restricted Allied flying time. Many combat and reconnaissance missions were scrubbed due to either the obscuration of potential targets or the inability to get off the ground. This was crucial because the Germans had learned from bitter experience to execute all major ground movements either at night or during poor weather, and had become highly proficient at it.

The 422d and 425th Night Fighter Squadrons of the Ninth Tactical Air Force had the only night and all-weather-capable aircraft available to U.S. forces. These two squadrons were badly overtaxed; each had fewer than twenty aircraft operational at any one time. They also had many other responsibilities, including interception of harassing raids by German night bombers, night intruder missions against German communications lines, and night armed reconnaissance. The limited number of aircraft coupled with the multiplicity of missions reduced the overall capability of the force.

Nevertheless, missions flown by the night fighters revealed some clues (concentrations of vehicles and crowded rail lines east of Gemünd), but little that was conclusive, although the fact that there was a German buildup in the area east of Düren was confirmed. However, this finding still did not stimulate questions that should have been asked as to the Germans' probable intentions.

ALLIED EXPECTATIONS

The final flaw in Allied intelligence prior to the Battle of the Bulge was perhaps the most damning of all, for it violated the basic tenet of sound military intelligence operations. That tenet holds that the best intelligence analysis is based on knowledge of an enemy's capabilities rather than assumptions as to his intentions.[8]

In the context of the Ardennes offensive, careful analysis by Allied intelligence showed a steady growth in German strength during late November. Unfortunately, in the euphoric aftermath of the successful drive across France and the stunning Soviet victories in the east, Allied intelligence predicated all their estimates on the expected early collapse of the German war effort. Thus all courses of action expected of the Germans were assumed to be reactions to the ongoing Allied assaults on the Reich frontiers. What the Allies expected were small-scale counterattacks, some of which might be relatively powerful, to delay the U.S. advance to the Roer River, north of the Ardennes, rather than an all-out counteroffensive. Almost without exception, the Allied intelligence circle refused to consider the possibility that Hitler might gamble everything to wrest the initiative from the western Allies.

There were a few who saw that all was not rosy in the Allied intelligence picture, but they did not begin to speak out until it was too late. By late November and early December it was well known that a massive strategic reserve built around the reconstituted panzer divisions of the Sixth Panzer Army (1st, 2d, 9th, and 12th SS Panzer) and Fifth Panzer Army (Lehr, 2d, and 116th Panzer) existed and were available for commitment anywhere along the front of the U.S. 12th Army Group. Additional panzer formations were known to be rebuilding while in reserve or were moving to augment the force already assembled (10th SS, 9th, 11th, and 21st Panzer divisions; 3d and 15th Panzergrenadier divisions; and Führer Begleit and Führer Grenadier brigades).

Major General Kenneth Strong, SHAEF G-2 (a Britisher who was General Eisenhower's intelligence officer), began in early December to sense the growth of a threat. As we have seen, this led to a confrontation between Strong and American Brig. Gen. Edwin Sibert, the 12th Army Group G-2, in

General Bradley's office. Bradley, possibly influenced by the fact that Strong was British, backed Sibert. He said he refused to be cowed by the German threat, and dismissed Strong with the flippant remark, "Let them come!"

A similar fate befell another voice in the wilderness, Col. Monk Dickson, First Army G-2. Until late November Dickson, despite his reputation as a pessimist, had firmly believed that the Germans had been reduced to a completely defensive posture by their heavy losses in the summer and fall. However, the identification of the Sixth and Fifth Panzer armies on the Cologne Plain began to change his perspective. The growing German strength seemed to point to either a preemptive strike to forestall the American advance to the Roer River or, just possibly, a counteroffensive. On 10 December Dickson distributed an intelligence estimate (his no. 37) that addressed the German threat. His concern, however, was with a potential counterattack *north* of the Ardennes and although the possibility of a major counteroffensive or an attack in the Ardennes were apparently on Dickson's mind his estimate did not suggest either one. But by 12 December, Dickson had become convinced not only that a blow was about to fall but that it would be in the Ardennes. In a conference with his staff on the evening of 14 December Dickson exclaimed, almost to himself, "It's the Ardennes!" Even so, the supposed threat was not enough to prevent Dickson from leaving later that night for a long-delayed four-day leave in Paris.

One other voice preaching caution was that of Col. Oscar W. Koch, Third Army G-2. He believed that the Germans, although badly hurt in the summer and fall battles, were still full of fight. The mounting evidence regarding the steady growth of the German reserves had Koch worried. What worried him most was the threat that would be posed by a German attack at the seam of the boundary between the First and Third armies in the southern Ardennes. The overextended front held by the VIII Corps, combined with the difficulties in coordinating the actions of two armies in that area, appeared ripe for potential disaster in the eyes of the Third Army G-2. On 9 December Koch invited the army commander, Lt. Gen. George S. Patton Jr., to a special intelligence briefing.

George Smith Patton Jr. was born on 11 November 1885, near San Gabriel, California. He spent a year at the Virginia Military Institute (VMI), from which his father and grandfather had graduated, before entering West Point in 1904. Because of failure in mathematics at the end of his first year, he was "turned back," and graduated with the West Point Class of 1909 as a second lieutenant of Cavalry. (He was later fond of saying, "West Point is a five-year course, sometimes completed in four years.") In 1912, at the Olympics at Stockholm, he was the first American to compete in "Modern Pentathlon," placing fourth out of forty-three contestants. During the Mexican Punitive Expedition in 1916, Patton pursued, fought, and personally killed Gen. Julio Cárdenas, one of the principal bandit leaders under Pancho Villa. Early in World War I he went to France with General Pershing, commanding the American Expeditionary Forces Headquarters Troop. As a lieutenant colonel he commanded a tank brigade and was seriously wounded in the Battle of the Meuse-Argonne. When, after the war, the army decided not to establish a separate tank corps, instead putting tanks under the Infantry, Patton decided to remain in the exclusively horse-mounted Cavalry.

Patton's service between the wars was a mixture of schools, staff, and command. In 1940 he went to Fort Benning, Georgia, as a colonel to train the nucleus of an armored force. Promoted to brigadier general, then to major general, he was assigned in 1941 to command the recently activated 2d Armored Division. After distinguishing itself in maneuvers, the division was selected to take part in Operation Torch, the invasion of North Africa in November 1942. Patton was no longer the division commander, though: He had been selected to command the Western Task Force that would land on the Atlantic coast of French Morocco. Because of his successful conduct of that operation, after the defeat of the U.S. II Corps by Rommel at Kasserine Pass, Tunisia, in February 1943, Patton was placed in command of the corps as it prepared for the final Allied offensive in Tunisia. However, before the offensive began, he turned the corps over to Gen. Omar Bradley, since he had been selected to command the new U.S. Seventh Army for the invasion of Sicily in July 1943. Patton's performance in that brief campaign was exemplary, but at its conclusion, during a visit to a field hospital, he almost ended his career. Infuriated by what he believed to be the cowardice and malingering of a soldier who suffered from "shell shock," or "combat fatigue," he slapped the soldier, and the incident was reported in the national press. General Eisenhower relieved him of command of the Seventh Army, although both he and Army Chief of Staff General Marshall recognized Patton's exceptional combat leadership.

During the planning for the invasion of Normandy, Patton was sent to England to establish the staff of the Third Army. That army became active on 1 August 1944 as part of the 12th Army Group, and Patton was again in action as a battlefield leader, though now serving under his former subordinate, General Bradley. In the next few months Patton's brilliant leadership of the Third Army overcame the bad publicity he had received for the slapping incident, and by December he was being lauded in the press as the bold, flamboyant combat leader that he was.

When Colonel Koch presented his special briefing to General Patton on 9 December, he expressed his concerns for the Third Army's left flank. Patton was impressed by Koch's reasoning. In one of the most important decisions made prior to the start of the German offensive, Patton ordered that contingency plans be prepared to meet any threat to the Third Army's left flank resulting from a possible German attack on the VIII Corps. The Third Army staff immediately went to work drafting plans to employ the newly operational III Corps, in reserve near Luxembourg City, as the primary counterattack force. Three possible axes of advance were contemplated: from the vicinity of Diekirch due north, from the vicinity of Arlon north to Bastogne, and from the vicinity of Neufchâteau due north.

Despite these scattered last-minute flurries of activity, the Allied forces in Europe continued to exhibit a remarkable degree of complacency regarding the continued German buildup. The VIII Corps positions in December remained virtually unchanged from what they had been at the end of September, when the front had stabilized. This deployment of the VIII Corps in the Ardennes was explicable only if the Allies had no knowledge of the German buildup. Originally a calculated risk by Eisenhower that freed forces for an assault on the German positions along the Roer River, the VIII Corps deployment had become an invitation to disaster by December 1944.

That some intelligence officers were beginning to reassess their formerly rosy picture of the situation is aptly illustrated in the memoirs of Col. David Niven, the late actor, who was a liaison officer at SHAEF.

In the middle of December I was at Spa, American First Army Headquarters in the Ardennes. I spent the day with Bob Low [a former *Time* reporter and friend of Niven's, who was now a member of the First Army G-2 staff] and he showed me the map room of the Intelligence Section.

"What happens here?" I asked.

"You mean here in Spa?"

"Yes."

After all these years I can quote what he said, word for word—it was impossible to forget. He pointed out of the window. "You see those trees on top of those hills?"

"Yes."

"Well, on the other side of those hills, there is a forest, and in that forest they are now forming the Sixth Panzer Army and any day the Sixth Panzer Army is going to come right through this room and out the other side, cross the Meuse, then swing right and go north to Antwerp."[9]

This incident was probably partly apocryphal. (For instance, according to Niven, Low supposedly went on to tell him that this was the first of three estimates presented daily to the First Army commander, which it most emphatically was not.) Nevertheless, Niven's story does serve to illustrate the increasing tension within the Allied intelligence community. The conviction was growing that something was about to happen. The remaining intangible was where it would occur.

Thus intelligence on the German threat was being built up piecemeal along the front of 12th Army Group. But it was not being integrated, partly because of a major failure in the U.S. intelligence organization: the insularity of the various G-2 staffs. There was little intercommunication among the intelligence officers of the army group and those of the armies, due in part to a clash of personalities. For instance, Colonel Dickson, the First Army G-2, was engaged in a long-running feud with General Sibert over Dickson's accusation that intelligence data flowed up to army group, but never down from army group to army. The situation was not helped by Sibert's opinion (shared by others) that Dickson was an alarmist and Dickson's belief (also not unfounded) that Sibert did not fully credit his reports.

If responsibility were to be assigned to one or two men, it is difficult to avoid the conclusion that Sibert failed to exercise leadership, or to provide integrating guidance to the fractured intelligence community of the army group. He was disdainful in dismissing any opinion contrary to his own assessments. Had he acted to integrate the army group intelligence process, the German capability—dimly perceived by the two army G-2s—would have been much clearer to all. General Bradley must also share some of the blame since he so unquestioningly backed Sibert.

The Allied intelligence failure was not due to a lack of information, although information was scarce and the overreliance on ULTRA intercepts meant that other significant intelligence was being overlooked. In fact, the Allies had reasonably good information on the strength and whereabouts of most of the German strategic reserve. The failure was in the Allies' interpretation of how the Germans would make use of the reserve. Allied expectations were based on the supposition that the Germans could no longer win the war—which was correct—and that enemy actions could only delay the inevitable. Unfortunately, the Allies failed to allow for Hitler's penchant for opportunism, and neglected to see that Hitler could envisage the possibility, no matter how remote, for a substantial, though not decisive, German victory—a possibility achievable in the Ardennes.

5

ORDEAL IN THE KRINKELTER WALD

THE DIMENSIONS OF THE BATTLE

The vast series of month-long World War II combat actions that were initiated by the great German counterattack early on 16 December 1944 is known to history as either "The Battle of the Ardennes" or, more popularly in the United States, "The Battle of the Bulge." However, in the strict sense of both normal English-language usage and standard military terminology, this conglomeration of fighting operations is more properly designated as a campaign rather than a battle. A campaign is defined in an authoritative military dictionary as "A phase or stage of a war, involving a series of related operations [and] may involve a single battle but more often comprises a number of battles conducted over a protracted period of time or considerable distance but within a single specific theater or delimited area."[1] A battle is defined as "A major combat encounter between the military forces of two belligerents, each seeking to impose its will on the opponent by achieving its objective, while preventing the enemy from achieving his."[2]

Thus within the Battle of the Bulge or Ardennes campaign, which continued for a little more than a month, there were a number of distinct battles, some lasting a day, some lasting a week or longer. One of the earliest clearcut battles of this campaign was fought from early 16 December until late 18 December in the sectors of the 99th and 2d Infantry divisions of the U.S. V Corps, and centered around the villages of Krinkelt and Rocherath in the Krinkelter Wald (Forest). This hard-fought engagement is therefore generally known as either Krinkelter Wald or Krinkelt-Rocherath.

GERMAN PLANS AND DISPOSITIONS

The main attack of Hitler's grandiose counterstroke in the Ardennes was to be executed by the powerful Sixth Panzer Army, commanded by SS Gen. Sepp Dietrich, the northernmost of the three attacking armies of Army Group B. Dietrich's two SS Panzer and one infantry corps commanded a total of four SS Panzer and five infantry-type divisions, and was heavily reinforced with gun and rocket artillery units.

One major question for the planning staffs of the Sixth Panzer Army was how best to utilize this concentration of forces to break through the American lines and reach their assigned objective—the Meuse River crossings—in the shortest possible time. German assault doctrine was in flux; proponents of the old-style blitzkrieg-type attack of massed armored units were opposed by those who believed that it was necessary for infantry to first open a breach before armor was committed, or else the armor would be massively attrited in breaking through the enemies' defenses, as had happened at Kursk in July 1943. As a result of this controversy, the Sixth Panzer Army adopted tactics somewhat different from those employed by its southern neighbor, the Fifth Panzer Army.[3]

On the army's right, the LXVII Corps, commanded by Generalleutnant Otto Hitzfeld, with two divisions, the 272d (commanded by Oberst Georg Kosmalla) and 326th Volksgrenadier (VGD) (commanded by Oberst Erwin Kaschner), was to seize the towns of Monschau and Höfen and advance to take control of the Hautes Fagnes (the high moorland west and northwest of the German-Belgian frontier). This area controlled the major American communications routes running north to south behind the V and VII Corps—the route that all American reinforcements from the north would of necessity follow to reach the beleaguered VIII Corps. To aid in this blocking mission, the last jump-trained parachutists available to the Luftwaffe—Oberstleutnant Baron Friedrich August von der Heydte's 1,200-man battalion—were to be dropped onto the Hautes Fagnes on the night of 15–16 December. The attacking German forces were forbidden to fire artillery into the town of Monschau itself.[4]

Farther south, on the panzer army's left, three infantry divisions (in order from north to south: 277th VGD under Oberst Wilhelm Viebig; 12th VGD, under Generalmajor Gerhard Engel; and 3d Parachute, under Generalmajor Walther Wadehn), nominally part of the LXVII Corps, were attached to the I SS Panzer Corps, commanded by SS Gruppenführer Hermann Priess, for the breakthrough. No armored units were assigned from the SS panzer divisions, however, to participate in the initial attack. Instead, the infantry divisions were expected to depend on their organic panzerjäger company and attached assault gun battalions to provide the armored support necessary. Furthermore, the powerful preassault artillery barrage (intended by Hitler to be of the weight and intensity of those of World War I) was expected to blast gaping holes in the American defenses.

Two SS panzer divisions, 12th "Hitlerjugend" (under SS-Standarten-führer Herbert Kuhlmann)—on the right—and 1st "Leibstandarte Adolf Hitler" (commanded by SS-Oberführer Wilhelm Mohnke)—on the left—were deployed behind the infantry divisions. These two divisions were the panzer spearheads aimed at the Meuse. They were assigned five specially designated *Rollbahnen*, or routes of advance, lettered A, B, C, D, E, from north to south. These routes were to be used only by the two panzer divisions—D and E by the 1st SS; A, B, and C by the 12th SS. Each of the routes was in turn assigned by the divisions to a single kampfgruppe or combat team.[5]

In army reserve was the II SS Panzer Corps (commanded by SS-Ober-gruppenführer Wilhelm Bittrich) with two divisions, the 2d "Das Reich" (under SS-Brigadeführer Heinz Lammerding) and 9th "Hohenstaufen" (under SS-Oberführer Sylvester Stadler) SS Panzer divisions—a total of 231 tanks, assault guns, and tank destroyers. They were to follow in the wake of the I SS Panzer Corps, prepared to continue the push toward Antwerp.

The German divisions varied greatly in the quality of their officers, enlisted personnel, and equipment. None of them approached the superb qual-ity of the German forces at their zenith in 1942–1943, but neither had they reached their nadir. Competence levels of officers and men were generally high.[6]

The volksgrenadier divisions were in the worst shape. Most of their offi-cers were experienced, as were some of their noncommissioned officers. Most of their enlisted personnel, however, were retrained Luftwaffe or navy men who had little experience in infantry combat. Few of these divisions had even the limited number of motor vehicles allotted to them by their tables of organization. The 3d Parachute Division was in little better condition. It had been badly battered in the fighting at Düren in the previous week and was missing a regiment that was still in transit. The quality of its personnel was about the same as that of the volksgrenadiers, except that most of its regimen-tal commanders had little or no combat experience.

Even the SS divisions were in relatively poor shape. Technically they were overstrength in personnel, but their tactical units were slightly under-strength. This seeming contradiction was due to the fact that their recently inducted, poor-quality personnel (more Luftwaffe and navy men, as well as a fair number of ethnic Germans from conquered countries) were held in the division's training battalion and were intended to be used as individual replacements. Combat equipment was generally good, although a shortage of motor vehicles remained a problem.

THE GERMAN ATTACK BEGINS

The attack of the German Sixth Panzer Army began at 0530 hours on 16 December with a massive artillery barrage. At least 657 light, medium, and heavy guns and howitzers and 340 multiple-rocket launchers opened fire on

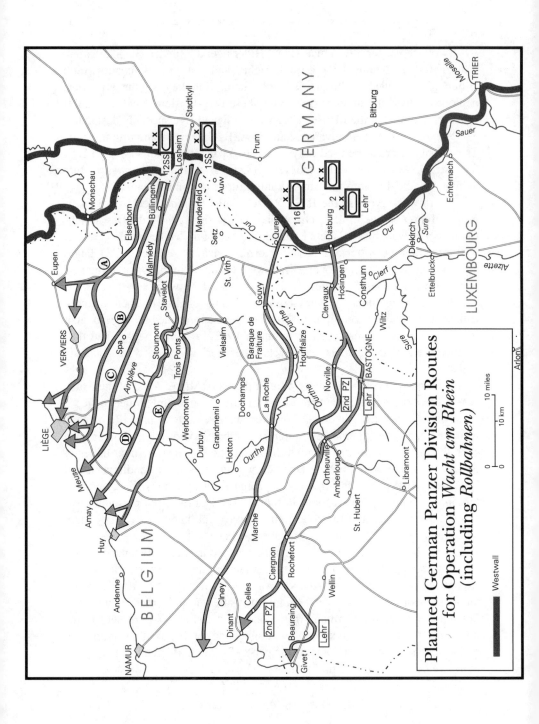

Planned German Panzer Division Routes
for Operation *Wacht am Rhein*
(including *Rollbahnen*)

American positions between Höfen and the Losheim Gap. Although much of this fire was ineffective (due in part to Hitler's orders against preregistration of fire, the lack of trained fire-control personnel and equipment, and the dug-in posture of the defenders), the sheer volume of fire was an unpleasant surprise to the Americans. The Germans had pressed every available piece into service, from 75-mm antitank guns firing as artillery to massive 280-mm railway guns.[7]

16 DECEMBER: THE MONSCHAU-HÖFEN SECTOR

Unfortunately for the Germans, a number of the elements of the 326th VGD, which had been scheduled to be shifted south from the Düren area for attack missions at Monschau and Höfen, had been tied down by the earlier offensive of the U.S. VII Corps toward Düren. Fully embroiled in defending against the 78th Infantry Division at Kesternich and Simmerath, the 272d VGD, on the LXVII Corps's right flank, was also unable to participate in the attack as planned. As a result, the Germans were only able to deploy two and a half battalions of the 326th for the Höfen-Monschau attack.

At Monschau the 38th Cavalry Squadron held well-organized positions that had been steadily improved over the previous weeks. The commander of this squadron, Lt. Col. Robert E. O'Brien Jr., was a Regular Army officer. A native of Illinois, O'Brien had graduated from West Point in 1936.

The town of Monschau lay in the bottom of a deep, canyonlike valley, surrounded to the north, east, and south by high ground. The high ground to the east (Monschau Hill), northwest (Mutzenich Hill), and southeast (Höfen Hill) of town was key to control Monschau. Between the three hills were two deep draws that were the natural routes to approach the town, one to the north of Monschau Hill (known to the Americans as Stillbusch, from the name of a nearby farmhouse) and one to the south, the Roer River gorge. From these hills the ground fell away gradually to the east and to the German-held pillboxes of the Westwall, which were in the western fringes of Monschau Forest.

Two cavalry troops (B and C) were available for the defense, as well as the squadron's light tank company (F), and the assault gun troop (E). The squadron's third cavalry troop (A) was detached to the north at Kesternich in the zone of the 78th Division. A platoon of combat engineers was attached to the squadron as well as a company of tank destroyers. The 62d Armored Field Artillery Battalion was in direct support, and the corps artillery guns of the 406th Field Artillery Group and the 955th Field Artillery Battalion were on call.

The squadron was deployed with B Troop to the left on a north-south line running from Mutzenich Hill along a railroad that ran from Mutzenich to Konzen Station, a front of 3,400 yards. F Company occupied Monschau itself with its three tank platoons deployed to cover the main routes into the town.

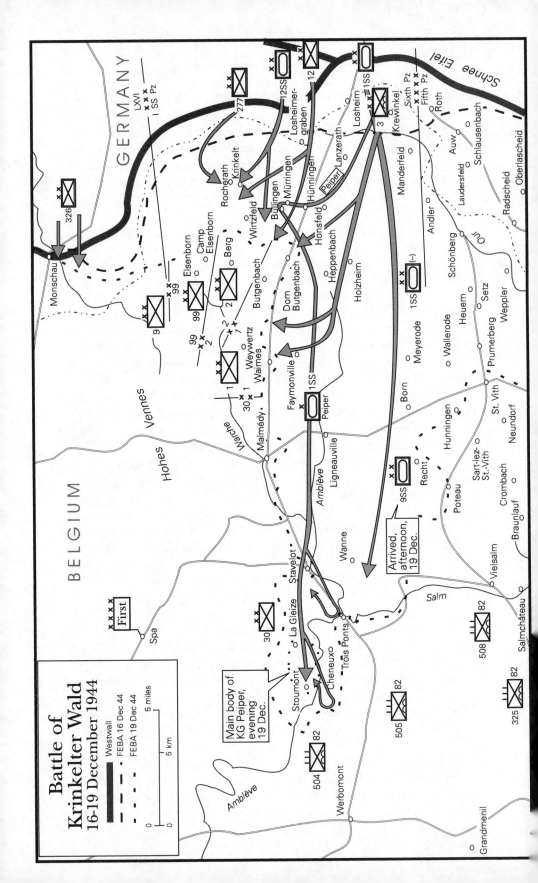

C Troop held the center and right with two platoons in a 600-yard-long natural trench on Monschau Hill and one platoon farther south, extending a line of outposts south to Höfen. The total length of the line was nearly 8,000 yards with about 750 men available to man it. The firepower of the cavalry troops had been augmented by dismounting the .50-caliber antiaircraft machine guns from their armored cars. The platoon strongpoints were organized for all-around defense and were liberally protected by barbed wire entanglements, minefields, and trip-flares.

Farther south at Höfen the 3d Battalion of the 395th Infantry (under Lt. Col. McClernand Butler) held similar positions. The battalion, from the 99th division, had moved into position in the middle of November and had spent the intervening month improving the field fortifications by "digging in deep." A company of towed tank destroyers was attached to the battalion, and the 196th Field Artillery Battalion was in direct support.

At 0530 hours on 16 December the German preassault barrage began. It continued without letup for the next thirty-five minutes, destroying wire communications throughout the 38th Cavalry Squadron sector. Wire crews went to work before the barrage had ceased and rapidly reestablished the vital telephone links. The initial German attack was directly into the center of the squadron's defenses at Monschau. The 3d Company of the 751st Regiment, 326th VGD moved forward, only to be met by a hail of fire from the F Company tanks (using the deadly 37-mm "canister" antipersonnel round), the 75-mm howitzers of E Troop, the 62d Field Artillery, and enfilading fire from the 81-mm mortars of C Troop. The assault collapsed in minutes as the panic-stricken Germans fled.

During the rest of the day scattered German patrols were repulsed as they attempted to find weak spots in the line. By nightfall it had become apparent to the defenders of Monschau that a major German attack was being prepared as more elements of the 326th Division became available. Reinforcements were brought up, including six machine guns and crews furnished by the 186th Field Artillery Battalion that were used to augment the security of the F Company tanks in Monschau. At 1700 hours an even more welcome reinforcement was received: Company A of the 146th Engineer Battalion, which was immediately deployed to strengthen the lines of B and C troops. Astoundingly, the squadron had suffered a total of only seven casualties and inflicted at least fifty on the Germans.

At Höfen, the 3d Battalion, 395th Infantry (3/395th), suffered through a twenty-minute-long barrage with an estimated 250 to 300 rounds falling in the battalion sector. At 0550 hours the Germans (evidently from the 2d Battalion of the 751st Regiment) attacked at five points along the battalion's front. The main effort was made at the battalion center, at the boundary between I and K companies. All wire communications were out and communication with the 196th Field Artillery was not reestablished until 0650. Thus the brunt of the attack was met by the rifles, machine guns, and mortars of the infantry. "There were a number of cases where BAR [Browning automatic rifle] men and rifle-men withheld their fire until the entire platoon which was advancing towards them was in view and without cover, and in three known cases, bodies of Germans fell into the foxholes from which the men were firing."[8]

By 0745 the surviving Germans had withdrawn except one penetration in the center of the battalion position. After an hour-long fight this small group was annihilated by personnel pulled back from the front line. German losses in front of Monschau were horrifying: 204 German bodies were counted in front of and behind the lines of the 3/395th; 19 prisoners were captured. Casualties sustained by the 3d Battalion were 4 killed, 7 wounded, and 4 missing.

The night of 16–17 December was far from quiet, although the Germans made no effort to execute an attack. Large numbers of heavy German aircraft were reported to be flying over the front line between Monschau and Höfen. Reports of paratrooper drops behind American lines began to filter in. Sporadic heavy artillery fire continued to fall on the positions of the 38th Cavalry and the 3/395th during the night.

THE WAHLERSCHEID-KRINKELT-ROCHERATH SECTOR

At Wahlerscheid, in the early hours of 16 December, the 2d Division prepared to consolidate its gains of the previous day and to exploit its advantage to the utmost. Its commander, Maj. Gen. Walter M. Robertson, a Regular Army officer, was born on 15 June 1888 in Nelson County, Virginia. A 1912 West Point graduate, he served with infantry regiments in Hawaii, at the Presidio of San Francisco, and at Fort Missoula, Montana, before World War I. To his regret he did not get overseas during the war, but was assigned to training units in the United States. Between the wars he held the usual school, staff, and command assignments, including duty on the General Staff in Washington.

Just before World War II, Robertson, then a colonel, commanded the 9th Infantry Regiment of the 2d Infantry Division and then the 23rd Infantry in the same division. Promoted to brigadier general, he was briefly the Assistant Division Commander before assuming command of the division as a major general in 1942. On 7 June 1944 Robertson and his division landed into combat on Omaha Beach. The 2d distinguished itself in fighting its way through the hedgerows of Normandy, and was one of the spearhead divisions in the breakout. Briefly part of the Third Army, and then assigned to the newly activated Ninth Army, the 2d Division swept through Brittany to Brest, and Robertson participated in accepting the surrender of the German garrison of that city. Transferred east to the VIII Corps, the 2d took over a portion of the Westwall in the Schnee Eifel from the 4th Division, then shifted north to join the V Corps to spearhead the drive through the Westwall near Monschau in the Roer offensive.[9]

* * *

Pleased with the results of the previous day's attacks, Robertson ordered two battalions of the 38th Infantry from his reserve to move forward to reinforce the 9th Infantry's penetration at Wahlerscheid. The early-morning quiet was disrupted by the noise of the German barrages falling on Höfen and Monschau to the north and on the 99th Division to the south. However, within the 2d Division corridor there was little activity as the division edged forward, deeper into the salient.

It soon became obvious to Robertson that the activity developing to the south had ominous portent for his division. In the late morning of 16 December his concerns were brought to a head by a conversation with his Division Artillery Commander, Brig. Gen. John H. Hinds.

Hinds, a native of Virginia, was a Regular Army officer. He graduated from West Point in November 1918, just before the Armistice that ended World War I. He had spent the next year as a student officer at West Point, and became an artilleryman after his second graduation late in 1919. Between the world wars he rose in rank to colonel, and was promoted to brigadier general in 1943, when he was appointed commander of the 71st Infantry Division's artillery. In subsequent months he commanded the artillery of the XIII and XXI corps. He had joined the 2d Infantry Division as artillery commander in early 1944.

The reason for Hinds's visit to Robertson in the late morning of 16 December was a telephone call Hinds had received from a captain on the 99th Division's staff. The unknown caller asked that the towed tank destroyers attached to the 2d Division be sent to support the 99th. Hinds considered the nature and the source of the request to be sufficiently unusual as to warrant discussion with the division commander. Robertson decided to visit the headquarters of Maj. Gen. Walter E. Lauer, commander of the 99th Division in Butgenbach.

Walter Ernst Lauer was born in Brooklyn, New York, on 29 June 1893. He was in his junior year at Cornell University when the United States entered World War I in April 1917. A student in the Reserve Officers' Training Corps, he was appointed a second lieutenant in the Officers' Reserve Corps on 15 August 1917 and was then commissioned in the Regular Army on 26 October. He arrived in France in late 1918 in time to join the Army of Occupation in Germany. He returned to the United States in 1923, and his career between the wars was the usual mixture of school assignments, troop duty, and staff appointments. He was sent to North Africa in 1943 to become the Chief of Staff of the 3d Infantry Division. He returned to the United States later that year to take command of the newly activated 99th Infantry Division. Now he and his division were undergoing their baptism of fire.

Robertson was shocked at the conditions he found in the 99th Division command post (CP). Staff officers and enlisted men were milling aimlessly about the large villa that housed General Lauer's CP, all seeming to talk at once; the din was deafening. General Lauer himself was in a corner, playing a piano. Robertson's request for information was met by Lauer's calm insistence that all was well in hand: The 99th Division had been attacked at a number of points but had not lost any ground. Robertson returned to his own CP sure that the situation in the 99th Division's sector was not quite "well in hand."

That afternoon CCB/9th Armored Division was detached from the 2d Division and sent south to reinforce the VIII Corps, which was also reported to be under heavy but localized attacks. The detachment significantly weakened the division's right flank. General Robertson, realizing that the 99th Division was very thin in the south, had planned to use CCB/9th to cover that flank and protect the main supply route through Krinkelt-Rocherath until a route from Wahlerscheid to Höfen could be opened. The 23d Infantry became the division's sole reserve, and it was ordered forward from the vicinity of Camp Elsenborn to Wahlerscheid.

A short while later Robertson received orders from V Corps Headquarters not to commit the 23d without further orders from the corps. Shortly thereafter the 3d Battalion of the 23d Infantry was detached by the corps from the division. The battalion was attached to the 99th Division and was ordered to move eastward into the Krinkelter Forest to support the 393d Infantry of the 99th Division, which was under heavy German pressure. Soon thereafter, the 1st Battalion of the 23d Infantry was also detached from the division, attached to the 99th Division, and sent south to Büllingen. Thus by 2300 hours the reserve available to the 2d Division had been reduced to the 2d Battalion of the 23d Infantry.

The reason for this sudden and unexpected dispersal of the 2d Division's reserve became apparent that evening when Robertson met with Maj. Gen. Clarence R. Huebner, deputy commander of the V Corps. Huebner told him that the 99th Division was being heavily pressed along its entire front, and contact had been lost with the 14th Cavalry Group in the Losheim Gap. Huebner advised Robertson to keep his division well in hand. Although he was to continue the attack, he should anticipate an early change in his orders.

Robertson immediately directed his Chief of Staff to prepare a contingency plan for withdrawal from the salient to an intermediate position at Krinkelt-Rocherath. The twin villages dominated two road networks: one that ran north to Wahlerscheid and south to Murringen, Hunningen, and Losheimergraben in the Losheim Gap, and one that ran west to Wirtzfeld and Elsenborn. The only troops available for the defense of Krinkelt-Rocherath on 16 December were the 38th Infantry's Service Company and the 38th's Antitank Company.

THE OPENING GERMAN ATTACKS ON THE 99TH INFANTRY DIVISION

The 99th Infantry Division was an untried and inexperienced unit: It had arrived on the Continent in early November 1944. On 9 November, it began taking over positions of the 9th Infantry Division in the southern part of the V

Corps sector. Until 13 December, when the division's 395th Infantry Regiment had attacked in support of the 2d Division, the front had been quiet.

On the morning of 16 December the positions of the 99th Division were as follows: To the north, the 3d Battalion of the 395th Infantry held Höfen. On its right (south), the 99th Reconnaissance Troop held a thin line centered on the town of Kalterherberg. The 2d Division Reconnaissance Troop held equally dispersed positions to the north boundary of the 2d Division corridor, which ran through the 99th Division front.

The main line of the 99th Division in effect began south of the 2d Division corridor. First came the 2d and 1st battalions (in order from north to south) of the 395th Infantry, and then the 2d Battalion of the 393d Infantry, which had been attached to the 395th. These three battalions had been attacking to support the right of the 2d Division's 9th Infantry Regiment. They had suffered moderate casualties and were consolidating hasty defensive positions on their objectives.

Farther south the 99th Division's positions remained as they had been in November. The 393d Infantry, with its 3d Battalion on the left and 1st Battalion on the right, held positions within the Krinkelter Forest. Commanding the 393d was Col. Jean D. Scott, a native of Texas and a Regular Army officer. He was one of a group of 405 officers known in the U.S. Army as "the thundering herd," the graduates of the West Point Class of 1924, the largest class to graduate from the U.S. Military Academy before 1939.

The 394th Infantry, commanded by Col. Don Riley, held positions just within the edge of the forest, paralleling the so-called "International Highway" (a hard-surfaced road that ran along the prewar Belgian-German border), with its 2d Battalion on the left and 1st Battalion on the right.

General Lauer, concerned with both the extensive front his division was responsible for and the weakly held Losheim Gap to his south, had elected to refuse his right flank. The 3d Battalion of the 394th Infantry, in division reserve, was at Buchholz Station on the southern flank, but several thousand yards west of the main line. This battalion was to be prepared to move to any needed sector on one hour's notice.

The southernmost of the division's units was the Intelligence and Reconnaissance (I&R) Platoon of the 394th Infantry, commanded by Lt. Lyle J. Bouck, Jr. This platoon occupied a position on a hill overlooking the road running from Lanzerath in the south (held by elements of the 14th Cavalry Group, see chapter 6) to Losheimergraben to the north (held by the 1/394th).

The German initial barrage was followed by probing attacks along the entire division front. Telephone communications had been badly disrupted by the German artillery fire (as they were along the entire Ardennes sector), and radio communications remained only sporadically functional in the face of German jamming, poor terrain,[10] and abysmal weather. The situation remained unclear at division headquarters—a major reason for General Lauer's sanguine attitude during General Robertson's visit in the afternoon.

Division headquarters knew that a deep penetration had been made into the 393d Infantry sector and that it had only been beaten back in part. In fact, the 393d was fighting for its very existence by the end of the day.

At about 0600, as the artillery barrage was lifting, the initial German probes by the 989th and 991st Grenadier regiments of the 277th VGD struck the regiment. The German attack hit between the two battalions: Company K on the right of the 3d Battalion was surrounded, and Company C on the left of the 1st Battalion was driven back. I Company of the 394th Infantry (in reserve at Buchholz) was committed to reinforce the 3d Battalion, while A Company of the 393d counterattacked to seal the penetration. Some ground was regained, but by nightfall the 3d Battalion was almost completely surrounded.

The situation in the 394th Infantry sector was somewhat better. Most of the 394th had, unlike the 393d, clear fields of fire and made the most of them. Machine-gun, small-arms, and mortar fire caused heavy casualties to the attacking battalions of the 27th Fusilier Regiment of the 12th VGD. The left and center flanks of the 394th were able to hold their ground, but the right flank was more seriously threatened. B Company was under heavy attack; German elements pushed up to 1,000 yards toward the right rear of the battalion.

Near Lanzerath, Lieutenant Bouck's I&R Platoon reported that the tank destroyer men in the village had pulled out. Shortly thereafter a battalion of the 3d Parachute Division marched calmly by on the road to Losheimer-graben, unaware of the presence of Bouck's men. A near-perfect ambush was thwarted when a young girl from the village warned the Germans at the last moment. The Germans quickly deployed and confidently advanced to assault the tiny twenty-man American unit. However, Lieutenant Bouck had carefully chosen his position: His men were well dug in and well equipped with automatic weapons. A barbed wire fence, hidden in the deep snow, broke up the initial German assault: Scores of the inexperienced German paratroopers were cut down by American fire. Renewed attacks were also beaten back, until the hillside was carpeted with German bodies. However, the outcome was never really in doubt: Almost continuous German machine-gun and mortar fire whittled down the American defenders. A German sergeant finally rebelled against the continued frontal attacks across open fields aimed directly at the Americans. He collected fifty men and after dark hit the flank of the position. Bouck and his handful of men surrendered to the Germans, who were astounded to discover how few men they had faced. Lieutenant Bouck's gallant stand had delayed the advance of the 3d Parachute Division from early morning until nearly midnight of 16 December. This in turn stalled the movement of the 1st SS Panzer Division, which was impatient to begin its race to the Meuse.

As Bouck and his survivors trudged into captivity, the situation on the V Corps front remained unclear for both the Germans and the Americans. Generals Robertson and Lauer were both becoming increasingly concerned about their exposed southern flank. Robertson concluded that events were moving too rapidly, and he was prepared to exercise what discretion he was allowed. He decided that the 2d Division would not renew its attack unless he received a direct order from Maj. Gen. Leonard T. Gerow, commander of the V Corps. He quietly told his regimental commanders to hold off attacking in the morning. Meanwhile, Lauer had dispatched his reinforcements—two battalions from the 2d Division—to shore up the shaken 393d Infantry and his open right flank. However, the massive extent of the German attack had not yet become clear. News of events on the VIII Corps front, farther south, was scanty to nonexistent.

For SS-General Priess the situation was also unclear. He knew that the infantry attacks of his I SS Panzer Corps had not gained a clean breakthrough of the American position, although advances had been made and it was obvious that resistance was slackening in front of the 277th VGD and the 3d Parachute Division. Priess decided to commit the armored strength of his panzers and ordered both divisions to move forward during the night to prepare for an attack at first light.

17 December: The Monschau-Höfen Sector

The Germans renewed the attack on Monschau early on the morning of 17 December. The remnants of the II Battalion of the 751st Grenadier Regiment were concentrated with the I Battalion opposite the positions of the 38th Cavalry. Frontal assaults in reinforced company strength were again made on the F Company positions around the town. The Germans were met by a rain of rifle, machine-gun, mortar, tank-gun, and artillery fire from front and flank and were quickly repulsed. However, farther north on Mutzenich Hill, in the B Troop sector, the situation was becoming critical. A second German battalion was putting heavy pressure on the thinly spread cavalrymen. At one point a group estimated at 50 to 100 strong simply "walked" through the American lines and overran a mortar position in the rear. By late morning B Troop was seriously threatened with encirclement.

The situation was restored by using the engineer company as a reserve to backstop the B Troop positions. Elements of B Troop then counterattacked to seal the gap. Around noon, A Company of the 47th Armored Infantry Battalion, 5th Armored Division, arrived in the rear of B Troop. (This element of the division's CCR had recently passed into the VII Corps reserve after a week of fighting south of Düren. It had then been sent to V Corps as part of the response to an urgent call for reinforcements on the night of 16 December.) The armored infantrymen were immediately sent forward to sweep the squadron rear area, where they met scattered resistance and captured some prisoners.

Further reinforcements for the beleaguered squadron were obtained by

Captain Meyer, who commanded A Company of the 146th Engineer Combat Battalion. While directing traffic on the Eupen road, Meyer commandeered A Company of the 10th Tank Battalion, 5th Armored Division, which was moving south to Monschau, and sent them to support B Troop.

Shortly before noon the situation had stabilized. The infiltrating Germans had all been killed, captured, dispersed, or driven back to their own lines. The remainder of the day was spent routing out the few Germans remaining behind American lines.[11] As the Germans endeavored to mass troops for a renewed assault in their frontline pillboxes, American artillery observers brought fire down to break up these concentrations. German casualties were again heavy: More than 200 dead were counted in front of the squadron lines; 26 were captured. One of the prisoners captured behind the lines of B Troop confirmed one earlier disturbing report—he was a paratrooper, a member of a battalion-size unit dropped behind American lines the previous night.[12] Casualties to the 38th Cavalry were only 2 wounded, one of whom later died.

At Höfen the 3/395th Infantry had a quiet day on 17 December, although reports of enemy penetrations farther south and the increasingly heavy fire heard from that direction seemed to bode ill for the isolated battalion. Renewed reports of German paratroopers in their rear and the news of the penetrations on the left flank of the 38th Cavalry further worried the battalion. Visual observations and noise from the German movements suggested that additional troops were being massed opposite the battalion. Later it became clear that the greater part of the 752d and 753d Grenadier regiments (probably equivalent to three battalions) had been concentrated opposite Höfen.

WITHDRAWAL OF THE 2D INFANTRY DIVISION

At 0630 hours on 17 December reports of German armor penetrations to the south began to filter in to the 2d Division CP. Honsfeld was overrun and German tanks were advancing on Büllingen. General Robertson took steps to bolster his division's open southern flank. Colonel Paul D. Ginder, commander of the depleted 23d Infantry, was directed to take command of forces assembling in the Wirtzfeld area. Colonel John H. Stokes, the Assistant Division Commander, was to take command in the area of Krinkelt-Rocherath. Stokes, a native of New Jersey, was another graduate of the West Point Class of November 1918. The division CP in Wirtzfeld was organized for all-around defense.

Colonel Ginder immediately ordered his remaining battalion, the 2d, a tank destroyer company, and a tank company to move to cover Rocherath, Krinkelt, and Wirtzfeld. Four tanks and three tank destroyers arrived in the battalion area shortly thereafter, and E Company and the antitank platoon moved out to their positions mounted on the armor and their own organic vehicles. The remainder of the battalion followed on foot. When E Company reached Krinkelt-Rocherath, it was directed south to Büllingen by Colonel

Stokes, who had received reports of the presence of enemy armor in that area. The remainder of the battalion continued on to Wirtzfeld.

Near Büllingen, E Company encountered elements of Kampfgruppe Peiper and knocked out a number of German vehicles. Peiper's force had bypassed the 3/394th Infantry at Buchholz, raced through Honsfeld, and was now turning west toward Moderscheid. The company and its accompanying armor then took up positions overlooking Büllingen. At Wirtzfeld, German armored vehicles were engaged and knocked out by tank destroyers that had arrived to bolster the CP defenses. By 0845 the remainder of the 2d Battalion had arrived in Wirtzfeld and drove away the few German infantry that had been harassing the CP area with small-arms fire.

At 0730 hours Robertson received a call from General Gerow, commander of the V Corps. Gerow said that the Germans were attacking all along the front of the V and VIII Corps, and that the situation was generally chaotic. He confirmed what Robertson already surmised: the Germans had broken through the 99th Division to the right and rear of the 2d Division and had penetrated the seam between the V and VIII Corps in the Losheim Gap. Gerow ordered Robertson to stop his attack and to undertake an immediate withdrawal. His division was to occupy a position along the Elsenborn Ridge covering the roads leading to Eupen and Verviers. Gerow left to Robertson's judgment the manner and execution of this new mission—a perilous daytime withdrawal.

The events of the next two days would show that Gerow's confidence in Robertson and his division was justified. Walter Robertson was about to prove himself one of the outstanding combat leaders in the U.S. Army.

Immediately after this momentous phone conversation, Robertson's headquarters received a more chilling call. General Lauer told Robertson that the 99th Division had in effect been overrun by German armored and infantry units; the division CP was at that moment being evacuated. Robertson directed his Chief of Staff to implement the withdrawal plan at once.

Meanwhile, to reinforce the threatened right flank of the division, the 3d Battalion of the 38th Infantry, which was in regimental reserve at Wahlerscheid, was ordered south at 0835 hours. Lieutenant Colonel Olinto Barsanti, the battalion commander, drove ahead with a reconnaissance party through Krinkelt toward Büllingen and observed the engagement nearby. His battalion closed in around Rocherath at 1130 hours and took up positions defending the southern and eastern edges of town.

By about 1000 the confused situation at Wirtzfeld had stabilized somewhat. It was fortunate that the engagements at Büllingen and Wirtzfeld were with minor elements covering the right flank of Peiper's main column. At a time when the major striking power of the 1st SS Panzer Division was driving westward little more than a mile to the south, the southern flank of the entire V Corps was protected by little more than the 2/23d Infantry and the Headquarters Company of the 2d Infantry Division. Oblivious to the situation to the north, Peiper continued westward, his attention focused totally on his assigned route to the Meuse (as it should have been).

At 1015 Robertson issued orders to the 9th and 38th Infantry regiments to execute an immediate withdrawal from the salient. They were directed to break contact and to move south as fast as possible. Colonel Hirschfelder of the 9th Infantry was placed in charge of the disengagement and withdrawal from the Wahlerscheid area. This was one of the most hazardous of combat operations: withdrawing units in close contact with an enemy in broad daylight. To complicate matters, the line of march of the withdrawing troops would be across the front of an advancing enemy of unknown but clearly formidable strength.

Shortly after 1015 General Robertson ordered his CP to displace to Elsenborn. He then got into his jeep and drove north to supervise the withdrawal. He stopped first at Rocherath, where he spoke to Colonel Stokes about the defense plan for the twin villages. He then drove to the CPs of the 9th and 38th Infantry regiments to discuss the withdrawal plans with the two regimental commanders. His next stop was the CP of the 395th Infantry, one and a half miles northeast of Rocherath, where he found that the two battalions of the 395th and the attached battalion of the 393d were still effective.

On his own authority, Robertson assumed command of the 395th and its attached battalion. He explained to Col. Alexander J. Mackenzie, commander of the 395th, that the withdrawal would be conducted by "skinning the cat"— the foremost units would be withdrawn first, followed by the rearmost. The mission of the 395th was to face to the north and east, covering the north flank of the 2d Division defensive position at Krinkelt-Rocherath.

By 1045 the leading units of the 2d Division had begun the movement south over the narrow snowbound road. The 9th Infantry moved out first, in column, in the order 2d, 3d, and 1st battalions. The 38th Infantry (minus the 3d Battalion) moved out shortly thereafter, the 1st Battalion at 1530 hours and the 2d Battalion half an hour later.

For several hours, General Robertson moved up and down the road supervising and expediting in every possible way the rearward movement of his units. He exhorted laggards to move faster, sorted out traffic jams, and literally drove the exhausted GIs rearward to safety. Fortunately, wire communications functioned well during the day and Robertson was able to maintain close contact with his division and regimental CPs.

The 2/9th Infantry arrived at Wirtzfeld at 1330 and took up positions to the west of town. At 1730 the battalion was ordered to shift to new positions on a ridge northwest of the town. It quickly dug in and held these positions without major incident for the next thirty-six hours.

At 1530 the 3/9th Infantry moved into position southwest of Krinkelt, overlooking Büllingen. Elements of the battalion were diverted en route and were attached to the 1/9th, which took up positions north of Rocherath. Like the 2d Battalion, the 3d Battalion would hold this ground until 19 December.

At about 1600 hours Robertson received word that the Germans had broken through the positions of the 393d Infantry and the attached 3/23d Infantry in the forests northeast of Rocherath (see below). This breakthrough posed an immediate threat to the safety of his entire division and that of the 99th Division. At once Robertson gathered and rushed to the area whatever blocking forces could be assembled northeast of Rocherath: elements of the 3/9th Infantry (Company K, 1st Platoon Company M, and the Battalion Ammunition and Pioneer [A & P] Platoon), a platoon from the 644th Tank Destroyer Battalion with three self-propelled guns, and the 1/9th Infantry, all under Lt. Col. William D. McKinley, commander of the 1st Battalion. (A native of Georgia and a 1937 graduate of West Point, McKinley was a great-nephew of the twenty-fifth president.) Antitank mines obtained from the 644th Tank Destroyer Battalion were placed at the crossroads. Soon after, survivors from the 3/23d Infantry arrived from the east and attempts were made to reorganize the shattered battalion.[13]

The two battalions of the 38th Infantry had a more hazardous journey to join Colonel Barsanti's 3d Battalion at the twin villages. The 1st Battalion was slated to go into position to the east of Krinkelt-Rocherath, and the 2d Battalion was supposed to extend the line from the left of the 1st Battalion, north to the 1/9th and 395th Infantry (and the ad hoc groupings from the 3/23d and 393d).

The march of the 1st Battalion was marked by a series of mishaps. The initial reconnaissance by the battalion advance party revealed one major problem with the position east of the twin villages that had been selected for the battalion—it was already occupied by the Germans! Hurried consultations between Col. Francis H. Boos, the regimental commander, and Major Coopersmith, the commander of the advance party, resulted in a shift of the battalion position to the ridge southeast of Krinkelt. Boos, a native of Wisconsin, was a 1928 graduate of West Point.

The battalion began its march well after dark, in column, in order A, B, C, and Headquarters companies. (Company D, the battalion heavy weapons company, was dispersed throughout the column; the machine gun platoons were attached to the rifle companies. The mortar platoon and Company Headquarters marched with the Battalion Headquarters and Headquarters Company.) The battalion S-3, Capt. Fred L. Rumsey, led the column with orders to go straight down the road to meet guides posted at the crossroads in Rocherath. As he neared the town, Rumsey realized that the area of the crossroads was under extremely heavy artillery fire. Rumsey at first thought that the fire was friendly, but as he got closer he realized that it was coming from the Germans. Suddenly the route of march of the entire battalion was inundated with artillery, mortar, and Nebelwerfer fire. A Company, at the head of the column, escaped with few casualties. B Company was badly hit, and C Company suffered heavy casualties and became disorganized.

To cap this disaster, only the guide for the battalion CP group could be found in Rocherath—the guides for the rifle companies were nowhere in sight. Rumsey elected to act on the principle that it is better to do the wrong thing than to do nothing at all, and pushed onward, hoping that the guides would be somewhere on the road ahead. The battalion moved on, still under relentless shell fire, until the head of the column began to receive small-arms fire from the front. Rumsey quickly turned about the head of the column, then doubled back the line of march and turned southeast, still hoping to find guides in the pitch-dark night. He finally found the battalion Executive Officer, who had located the missing guides. Doubling back again, the battalion began to move into position at about 1930 hours.

The battalion, which had been nearly fresh a few hours earlier, was now only in fair condition. B, C, and D companies had all suffered heavy casualties, and C Company was also disorganized and demoralized. To add to the woes of C Company, its guide was wounded before the company could get into position. B Company's guide volunteered to lead them in, but they were destined never to occupy their position—they were attacked by the Germans.

Sergeant Joseph Jan Kiss Jr., a squad leader in C Company, 38th Infantry, moved forward on the morning of 16 December to put his squad in positions near Wahlerscheid. On the afternoon of 17 December Kiss and the rest of the 38th Infantry's 1st Battalion were pulled back toward Krinkelt and Rocherath. When Kiss's squad trudged into Krinkelt, they came across an American major general, whom Kiss recognized as Robertson. The general asked Kiss, "What outfit, son?" After hearing his reply, Robertson told Kiss, "Down this road two blocks to a brown brick house on the end." Kiss replied "Yes, sir," collected his squad, and hurried off. He later heard that Robertson had been all over the area, on the night of 16–17 December, strengthening the main line of resistance and gathering up stragglers. When Kiss and his squad reached the brown brick house, they found it was under direct fire from a German tank. The tank was driven off by a helpful M-10 tank destroyer, and Kiss's squad and the rest of C Company settled into their positions.[14]

The 2d Battalion of the 38th also suffered the gantlet of fire at the crossroads but was able to get into position with relatively few casualties. Company F was placed in positions protecting the crossroads; Company E was next in line to the south, extending from the crossroads to the positions of the 38th Infantry's Service Company. G Company was sent to defend the regimental command post in Rocherath. Sporadic small-arms fire was received from the front, but there was no major attack.

As these defensive preparations were being completed, a series of German attacks struck the 2d Division. The first probes were received by the 1/9th Infantry in its exposed position northeast of the villages, shortly after 1830 hours. McKinley's men had been warned that stragglers from the 3/23d and 3/393d Infantry would be retreating through their positions; it was impressed upon them that they should not mistakenly fire on their own men. Thus, when three tanks approached the defense perimeter from the east, no shots were fired at them. The big vehicles roared into the positions of B Company. By the time anyone realized that they were German it was too late. Firing would only have revealed the defenders' positions to close-range retaliation from the tanks' big guns. Discretion prevailed, and the Germans were allowed to pass unmolested, down a road behind the positions of Company A, where they pulled off the road and halted.[15] D Company's 81-mm mortars soon opened fire, followed by several volleys from the 15th Field Artillery. It was extremely fortunate for the men of McKinley's battalion that his artillery liaison officer, 1st Lt. John C. Granville, had been able to regain radio contact with the 2d Division's artillery fire direction center shortly before the attacks began. One tank was knocked out; the others, and the infantrymen who had ridden them, opened fire into the rear of A Company.

Shortly thereafter four more tanks approached B Company. Two were disabled by mines, and two were knocked out by bazooka teams. The German infantry accompanying this group sought what cover they could find and opened a desultory fire on the company.

About half an hour later, the main body of Kampfgruppe Müller was spotted approaching the 1st Battalion. Heavy artillery and mortar fire dispersed the armored vehicles and caused severe casualties to the exposed German infantry. However, individual tanks and small groups of German infantry were infiltrating through the battalion lines in the dark. SS-Sturmbannführer Helmut Zeiner, commander of the 12th SS Panzerjäger Battalion, took three of his tank destroyers and a platoon of panzergrenadiers and slipped past the defenders, heading for Krinkelt. Roving patrols were organized by Colonel McKinley and his commanders to deal with the infiltrators. They knocked out four more tanks.

The final attack of the night on McKinley's battalion erupted less than an hour later. Three columns of tanks and infantry struck the battalion. In response to Lieutenant Granville's desperate pleas for support, the massed fires of all four of the 2d Division's artillery battalions and three corps 155-mm howitzer battalions were brought down on the attackers. The Germans were unable to stand the pounding and fell back into the forest.

Farther south, in front of the twin villages, the 1/38th Infantry was hit at about 2130 by German tanks and infantry that had slipped past McKinley's battalion. C Company collapsed immediately and fell back in confusion to the regimental command post in Krinkelt. B Company was overrun and lost its commander and most of two platoons. A Company managed to hold its positions and finally drove off the Germans, probably only Zeiner's small party of three assault guns and a few infantry.

At 2100 hours Lt. Col. Barsanti's 3/38th Infantry was also hit, probably by more German units that had infiltrated past McKinley's battalion. Five tanks and about eighty infantrymen struck K Company's left flank and forced it back some 150 yards. However, its reserve platoon was committed and, in turn, pushed the Germans back, destroying one tank in the process. The remainder of the night was marked by recurring minor clashes between Americans and Germans.

Shortly after midnight, a relative calm fell over the battlefield. The initial German probes had been thrown back, but had created some havoc, particularly with Lt. Col. Frank T. Mildren's 1/38th Infantry. (Mildren, destined to achieve four-star rank, was a native of Arizona and a 1939 graduate of West Point.) Assembling in the woods east of the twin villages were the 12th SS Panzer Regiment and the 26th SS Panzergrenadier Regiment, as well as elements of the 277th VGD.

THE RIGHT FLANK

The Germans continued sporadic attacks on the 393d Infantry Regiment during the night of 16–17 December. By dawn the 3/23d Infantry had arrived to back up the two battered battalions, but at the same time German pressure increased. By noon the situation had reached the breaking point: German armor was hitting the 3d Battalion of the 393d in strength, contributing to the battalion's disorganization; the 1st Battalion on the right was also under great pressure, and its right flank was becoming exposed as the 394th Infantry Regiment to the south gave ground. The 3d Battalion of the 393d was ordered to withdraw behind the 3/23d. The 1st Battalion was ordered to withdraw and tie in with the right of the 3/23d.

The withdrawal of the 1st Battalion of the 393d was a success, but that of the 3d Battalion was an escape from disaster. The 3d Battalion was surrounded and had to fight its way out. The 3/23d barely had time to prepare before the Germans were upon them. Attack after attack was beaten back by the fresh troops of the 2d Division. However, in the late afternoon the Germans again committed the tank destroyers of the 12th SS Panzerjäger Battalion. The unprotected left flank of the 3/23d quickly collapsed under the pressure. By 1500 hours all three battalions were streaming back toward the twin villages.

Events were also rapidly deteriorating on the front of the 394th Infantry. The 2d Battalion began to lose ground as the 393d Infantry folded on its left. The 1st Battalion began to shift to the right rear as it tied in with the 3d Battalion (minus I Company) at Buchholz Station. The 1/23d Infantry then came up on the right (west) to hold east of Hunningen and prevent total collapse of the 394th.

WITH KAMPFGRUPPE PEIPER

SS-Lieutenant Colonel Peiper was not a man to suffer fools gladly. By the predawn hours of 17 December his task force had advanced only a few kilometers to the west. Peiper stormed forward to determine the cause of the delay. He discovered a colonel of the 3d Parachute Division near Lanzerath (quite possibly the same officer who had so badly botched the effort to dislodge Lyle Bouck's men the day before). The colonel warned Peiper of mined roads and strong resistance in front of his regiment. Peiper then went forward to investigate—and returned shortly in disgust. There were no Americans to be seen. He commandeered one of the hapless colonel's battalions (presumably as cannon fodder to husband his own panzergrenadiers) and began to push forward. Also at about this time, Kampfgruppe Hansen began to move forward, surprising men of the 14th Cavalry Group at Andler (see chapter 6). Kampfgruppe Hansen then pushed forward into the Losheim Gap, further threatening the southern flank of the V Corps.

At 0600 Peiper's men overran Honsfeld; twenty minutes later they moved toward Hunningen. The Germans then advanced on Büllingen at 0830, having penetrated nearly ten kilometers into the American lines. The defenders of Büllingen, a company of the 254th Engineer Combat Battalion, had just arrived and were forced to retreat after a short firefight. Peiper sent other elements toward Wirtzfeld while the main column turned west.

From Büllingen, Peiper's column continued west to Moderscheid, then on to Schoppen, Ondneval, and Thirimont. At Thirimont his column was forced to backtrack when the country road it was following turned into an impassable quagmire. The column moved to the northwest, toward Malmédy and a tiny crossroads known as Baugnez. By this time Peiper's Kampfgruppe had penetrated more than twenty-five kilometers.

At about 1300 hours Peiper's men encountered an American convoy moving south from the crossroads. The Germans shot up the vehicles and rounded up the survivors, the men of Battery B of the 285th Field Artillery Observation Battalion. They were guarded in an open field next to the road as Peiper's men continued south to Ligneauville. What followed some time later has always been referred to as the "Malmédy massacre," although Malmédy was several kilometers to the north. According to trial testimony after the war, the German guards opened fire unprovoked on the helpless American prisoners. At least 72 of some 130 men held in the field were killed in the firing. Forty-three men escaped, although most of them were wounded. Fourteen more bodies were found in the area, although some had probably been killed when the convoy was attacked.

That the massacre occurred is indisputable as is the fact that it was not done "in the heat of action." The prisoners had been disarmed and held for some time before the firing began. Whether or not Peiper was directly responsible is not known, but it is unlikely since he was far to the south when the firing began. However, his troops committed other atrocities in the fighting in the Ardennes (against both soldiers and civilians); therefore he must bear some of the blame. (However, see appendix G for an assessment of the massacre and its aftermath.)

Peiper's column advanced about eight kilometers to Ligneauville, where it surprised the headquarters of the 49th Antiaircraft Brigade. Following a short firefight (and apparently some additional atrocities), the Germans continued on ten kilometers to Stavelot and a bridge leading to the north bank of the Amblève River. At 1830, elements of Company C of the 291st Engineer Combat Battalion engaged and damaged the lead tank of Peiper's column on the steep and winding road south of Stavelot. Peiper decided to halt for the night and to seize the bridge in the morning.

On the evening of 17 December the atmosphere remainded tense in Robertson's CP. No one was sure when Peiper's command would turn north to rend the flank of the V Corps again. A fairly complete, albeit at points insubstantial, line had been formed by the 2d and 99th divisions to cover the corps front. Welcome news from V Corps was that both the 1st and 9th Infantry divisions were being dispatched from the VII Corps to reinforce both flanks. The 9th Division would fill the gap near Monschau held by the 38th Cavalry Squadron and the 3/395th Infantry, and the 1st Division would secure the southern and western flanks of the corps. And more reinforcements were reportedly on the way. From the Ninth Army the 7th Armored Division was en route to VIII Corps; the 30th Infantry Division was moving to guard the road junctions at Malmédy and Spa.

18 DECEMBER: THE MONSCHAU-HÖFEN SECTOR

At 0435 on 18 December the storm broke over the 3/395th Infantry as the Germans made their strongest attack to date in the sector. The heaviest concentrations of artillery and rocket fire yet encountered blanketed the battalion's positions. Infiltrators surrounded the battalion observation post in the center of the position and were not driven back until after daylight.

At 0900 the Germans, reinforced by twelve "tanks" and seven armored cars (probably the assault guns and self-propelled antiaircraft guns of the 326th Panzerjäger Battalion), made their main thrust at three points along the battalion lines. The principal effort was made against the left front (Company I), a secondary effort against the right front (Company K), and a minor attack against the juncture of the two companies in the center of the battalion.

The attack on the right was made by tanks and infantry that advanced through heavy American small-arms, mortar, and artillery fire right up to the battalion front. The battalion commander, Lt. Col. McClernand Butler, called for a five-minute artillery concentration to be delivered directly on Company K's position. When it lifted, the men came up out of their foxholes and fired point-blank into the assaulting troops. The artillery fire and close-range small-arms fire devastated the exposed German infantry, leaving the assault guns unsupported. Without infantry support the German armor was unwilling to press on into the American position, where they would be vulnerable to attack by bazookas. The assault guns therefore quickly withdrew to the woods to the east.

The attack against the battalion's center followed the same pattern: Two five-minute American artillery concentrations forced the Germans to withdraw. By 0930 hours the attacks on the right and center were over, and the Germans had been "liquidated," according to Butler.

The attack on the left front continued unabated. At 1010 the Germans reinforced the assault and penetrated the battalion's line on a 400-meter front. The positions were restored only after Butler ordered three more five-minute artillery concentrations on I Company's lines and committed his remaining reserve, one platoon of I Company. By 1230 the main line had been restored, and the situation became stabilized, although heavy artillery and rocket concentrations fell throughout the day.

As at Monschau, German casualties were severe. The 3/395th Infantry reported counting more than 550 bodies in front of the battalion (many of these were almost certainly casualties of 16 December, double-counted) and 42 prisoners were taken. Losses to the 3/395th were 5 killed and 7 wounded. Minor actions later in the evening resulted in 2 killed, 2 wounded, and 6 missing, for a total of 22 casualties for the day.

Also on 18 December the Germans made their last attempt to capture the vital road centers at Monschau-Höfen. The 326th VGD had been gutted. By actual count the number of bodies found in front of C Troop of the 38th Cavalry at Monschau was 156. The count in front of B Troop was not precisely given but was probably similar. As noted above, casualties to the units facing the 3/395th were even more severe. From these American counts and from the scanty German reports available, it may be estimated that the total casualties to the 326th VGD on 16–18 December were more than 1,000 killed and wounded.

There were several reasons why the German attacks at Monschau-Höfen were debacles. The first mistake made by the Germans was to even attempt an assault on 16 December, when little more than a reinforced regiment was available to attack at two separate points. A second mistake was the unimaginative execution of the attacks, although that was due in part to the constraints of the terrain. Most were directed into the center of the American positions; little effort was made to infiltrate the widespread cavalry positions at Monschau or to envelop the weakly held flanks of the infantry at Höfen.

The failure of the final, strong, armor-supported attack at Höfen was primarily due to the magnificent support provided to the front-line defenders by the American artillery. In a nine-and-a-half-hour period, the supporting 196th Field Artillery fired more than 3,600 rounds from its twelve 105-mm howitzers.[16] This expenditure was nearly matched at Monschau, where the eighteen 105-mm SP howitzers of the 62d Armored Field Artillery Battalion expended 1,828 rounds, and E Troop's 75-mm SP guns fired a total of 941 rounds on 18 December.[17] The Germans were unable to suppress the massive firepower of the defenders, and ultimately failed to gain their objective. Major Charles E. Rousek, Assistant Executive Officer of the 38th Cavalry, later summed up the German failure: "On the 16th the Germans tried to drive directly into Monschau. On the 17th they tried to cut our line in half. On the 18th they tried the other side of the line. On the 19th they gave up."[18]

FIGHT FOR THE TWIN VILLAGES

On the morning of 18 December the 2d and 99th divisions had achieved a measure of stability. General Lauer's division was now fighting under the effective command of General Robertson, who was integrating the defenders into a cohesive force. (This command relationship was confirmed by V Corps at 1800 hours on the 18 December.) In effect Robertson was now command- ing a near-corps-size task force.[19] General Gerow, commander of the V Corps, had wisely decided to leave tactical control of the battle to Robertson for the time being. Gerow was fully occupied with coordinating the move- ment of reinforcements to the battle and their integration into the new defense line that was taking shape to Robertson's rear. Gerow was also greatly con- cerned by the yawning gap to his right rear. Except for the defenders of St. Vith (see chapters 6 and 10), there was little more than a variety of engineer units, antiaircraft units, and service support troops to hold the area west of Butgenbach. Peiper was still driving to the west, and the First Army Head- quarters at Spa was seriously threatened.

Rear-area personnel were working on a new V Corps position on Elsen- born Ridge to the west. The 395th Infantry and its attached battalion from the 393d anchored the left flank and were under little pressure. The situation to the south was more serious.

Sergeant Kiss and his squad of C/38th Infantry were in a barn across the street from a church. They received a few shots from a German sniper in the church steeple (one of which came within inches of Sergeant Kiss's left ear), but they were soon too busy with other concerns to make much of an effort to dislodge him. The sniper took an ill-advised shot at Colonel Mildren, the commander of the 38th Infantry. In response, according to Sergeant Kiss, Colonel Mildren ordered a tank to blow the steeple off the church.[20]

The fighting erupted again on Lieutenant Colonel McKinley's front at first light. Twelve tanks and an estimated battalion of German infantry advanced. These were elements of the 12th SS Panzer Division. The infantry were halted by intense American artillery fire. However, the tanks continued to advance and by 0800 hours had overrun the entire front line. A Company was com- pletely overrun by tanks and infantry by 0900 hours. The company comman- der, Lt. Stephen E. Truppner, said: "My men all have holes and I want the artillery poured in on my own position because the situation is hopeless any- way." An artillery battalion fired the concentration requested by Truppner for thirty minutes. Nothing else was heard from A Company or its commander: Only twelve men escaped—the rest were killed, wounded, or missing.

At 1000 hours McKinley received word that the 2/38th Infantry had secured the position to his rear and had linked with the 395th Infantry to the northwest. Ordered to withdraw at 1300, McKinley thought he would be unable to get any of his troops out from their very close contact with the enemy. Then fate intervened. Four Shermans of the 741st Tank Battalion were spotted by Lt. Eugene Hinski, the antitank platoon leader, on the road behind the battalion. Hinski intercepted them and asked if they would like to do some fighting. The tank platoon leader responded "Hell yes" and was directed to the battalion CP.

The four tanks were a godsend. McKinley quickly organized a counterattack led by the armor to clear his front. The battalion would then withdraw under cover of the tanks. The plan worked perfectly. Two of the Shermans decoyed the four most troublesome German tanks into the open, and the other two American tanks then shot them up from the rear. Three of the German tanks were knocked out, and the fourth withdrew. The four American tanks then looped onto both flanks of the German infantry and began to spray them with machine-gun and 75-mm-gun fire at point-blank range. The German attack collapsed completely.

Under cover of this vicious counterattack, the 1st Battalion was able to withdraw in twenty minutes. The entire battalion with attachments had gone into action the night before with about 600 men, and by the evening of the eighteenth there were only 197 men left who were combat effective. The others were killed, wounded, or missing. Of the four rifle companies, A Company had twelve men, B had twenty-seven, C had forty-six, and K had twelve. The battalion weapons company, D, had sixty men, and Headquarters Company had forty. The survivors were reorganized as a composite rifle company in Krinkelt and were held there as a reserve until they were withdrawn to Elsenborn on 19 December.[21]

The 2d and 3d battalions of the 38th Infantry suffered a number of sporadic attacks by the Germans throughout the day. However, the stand by McKinley's battalion had erased the threat from the northeast and had severely battered the 25th SS Panzergrenadier Regiment. Nevertheless, the situation to the east and southeast of the villages remained grave as the battered remnant of the 1/38th tried to prevent a breakthrough on its front.

At about 0800 on 18 December five German tanks (probably Panthers), accompanied by a company of infantry, broke through A/38th and drove into the center of the twin villages. The defenders of the battalion CP met them with a hail of machine-gun fire and managed to disperse the infantry. The tanks continued to range through the villages for some time until they were all hunted down and destroyed. Later attacks, in battalion strength, were repulsed by artillery fire, although small groups of German tanks and infantry continued to probe at the defenses throughout the day.

18 DECEMBER: KAMPFGRUPPE PEIPER

Early in the morning of 18 December, far to the west at Stavelot, Peiper's men prepared to seize the bridge leading north. The accompanying paratroopers were sent forward to test the defenses as the armored column prepared to race down the road and across the river.

By coincidence a small American force was advancing from the north toward Stavelot to secure the same bridge over the Amblève River. This was a company of the 526th Armored Infantry Battalion (part of the Headquarters Guard of the First Army) with two engineer platoons and a platoon of A Company, the 825th Tank Destroyer Battalion (towed), attached. At about 0400 the American advance guard reached the bridge and began to deploy to defend it. Lieutenant Jack Doherty, commanding the tank destroyer platoon, heard the sound of tanks revving up over the hill beyond the river. These were Peiper's tanks, preparing to assault the bridge.

In accordance with aggressive tank destroyer doctrine, Lieutenant Doherty sent two of his units across the bridge to investigate. As the tank destroyers cautiously approached the top of the hill, the lead one hit a trip wire, which triggered a flare beside the road. Waiting German tanks in an overlooking position on the outskirts of Stavelot opened fire, setting the prime mover of the second tank destroyer on fire. At the same time, behind them, the American troops holding the bridge began to fire in response, catching the lead tank destroyer in a crossfire. Unable to retreat because of the burning tank destroyer behind them, the crew bailed out. Sergeant James A. "Bob" Hammons from Lewisville, North Carolina, grabbed the .30-caliber machine gun from its pedestal mount as he jumped out of the vehicle. He and the three other crew members took shelter in a shed beside the road.

By this time the German infantry began to advance to seize the bridge in accordance with Peiper's plan. The four Americans ran into a nearby farmhouse. As the Germans rushed past them, toward the bridge, the American soldiers took shelter in the basement.[22]

At the bridge, the Germans had the advantages of surprise, more troops, and superior firepower. The structure was rushed in minutes, before it could be blown up. The defenders withdrew to the north, protecting a secret: Lining the road to Spa were a series of huge fuel dumps with enough fuel available to get II SS Panzer Corps (temporarily stalled by the shortage of gas) forward, indeed, with enough fuel to supply the needs of all of Army Group B for some time. Peiper, however, had no hint of this, and was intent on regaining his assigned route and reaching the Meuse River. The Germans, having penetrated more than forty kilometers into the American lines, continued west toward Trois Ponts.

At Trois Ponts elements of the 51st and 291st Engineer Combat battalions blew up all three bridges in the face of the approaching Germans. Peiper had insufficient bridging material with his columns to span the Salm River, so he was forced to turn north in search of another crossing point.

Near Cheneux was an intact bridge that led west toward Werbomont and the more open country sloping down to the Meuse. However, the Germans had one more bridge to cross—at Habiemont. Like so many others, it was blown up in Peiper's face by men of the 291st Engineer Combat Battalion. Peiper had been thwarted again, and for good this time, by the "damned engineers."[23] This was the deepest penetration by Peiper and his men, about sixty kilometers west of the original German positions.

Meanwhile, back at Stavelot, Sergeant Hammons and his three companions found that their shelter was a trap. They were soon captured and held prisoner in the basement where the Germans had found them. That night, however, they escaped when left briefly unattended. The four men worked their way back to the river, but it was too deep and swift for them to attempt to cross, so they walked and crawled westward along the bank of the Amblève for several miles until they found a dam. They were able to get across the river without getting completely drenched, but as they approached the far bank they were shot at by Americans of the 119th Infantry Regiment, part of the 30th Infantry Division that had been rushed south from the Ninth Army. Hammons and his companions were not hit, and their shouts caused the fire to stop. After spending the night with the infantrymen, the four tank destroyer artillerymen were walking to the rear the next morning, when they saw their commander, Lieutenant Doherty, driving along the road in a jeep looking for them. They were soon back at the A Company CP in Malmédy, which was bombed several times over the next three days by American planes. Apparently the airmen had been told that the Germans held Malmédy.[24]

Had Hammons and his companions stayed where they were (prisoners in the basement of a house on the outskirts of Stavelot) they would have found themselves in an even more exciting situation. During the night the 117th Infantry Regiment of the 30th Division attacked and seized the bridge and then occupied the northeastern half of Stavelot. Peiper was unpleasantly surprised when informed of this development.

19 DECEMBER: WITHDRAWAL

By late evening of 18 December, the situation on the V Corps front had improved tremendously. Elements of the 9th Infantry Division were approaching Monschau, preparing to shore up the left flank of the corps. The 1st Infantry Division, moving behind the 2d and 99th divisions, was taking positions at Butgenbach and Elsenborn. This gave Major General Robertson the vital backup—and protection for his right flank—that he needed to complete his withdrawal.

Aiding the American withdrawal was the slow realization at I SS Panzer Corps that the Germans were now butting heads against a brick wall. SS-General Priess tardily decided to attempt to flank the position from the gap to the south by moving the 12th SS Panzer Division farther west and then turning it north to hit Butgenbach. Meanwhile, all elements in contact with the Americans in the twin villages were ordered to withdraw.

Helped by slackening pressure from the front, the 2d and 99th divisions were able to execute the withdrawal after nightfall with relative ease. The 395th Infantry withdrew west over logging trails. The 38th Infantry peeled off one battalion at a time from north to south. Elements of the 741st Tank Battalion, the 644th Tank Destroyer Battalion, the 2d Engineer Battalion, and the 38th I&R Platoon formed the rear guard. After the 38th's withdrawal through Wirtzfeld, the 9th Infantry, the 2/23d Infantry, and the 394th Infantry followed. The remnants of the 393d Infantry had already withdrawn for reorganization at Elsenborn.

Private John B. Savard, a nineteen-year-old rifleman from Minnesota then assigned to G/38th Infantry, spent most of 19 December dodging and hunting German tanks in the twin villages. At one point, he emerged from a cellar to find himself facing down the barrel of a PzKw-IV, and quickly dived back into the cellar as the tank fired its main gun. Savard escaped injury, and a bazooka team took out the tank. That evening G Company and the remainder of the 38th Infantry withdrew from the twin villages to the new positions to the west.[25]

By 0200 hours on 20 December the withdrawal was complete. Krinkelt-Rocherath had been reduced to a burning shambles. Sixty-nine German tanks and assault guns and countless other German vehicles littered the area. Hundreds of dead Germans lay in heaps at the approaches to the villages. The stand taken by the 2d Division had gutted the vaunted 12th SS Panzer Division: The steam had gone out of the Sixth Panzer Army attack.

19 December: Kampfgruppe Peiper

Far to the west, Peiper again began to move. He had decided to attempt to follow the Amblève valley northwest through Stoumont and Remouchamps in a new bid to reach the Meuse. However, two new opponents had just entered the fight.

During the night of 18–19 December the engineers at Trois Ponts had been relieved by the arrival of elements of the 82d Airborne Division. Farther north, the 119th Infantry of the 30th Division moved toward Stoumont and La Gleize. To the northeast, at Stavelot, the 117th Infantry prepared to close Peiper's supply route to the east. A ring was beginning to close around the spearhead of the 1st SS Panzer Division.

At Stoumont, the Germans advanced confidently, expertly brushing aside the 3d Battalion of the 119th Infantry. However, hastily scraped together armored forces counterattacked and crushed Peiper's advance guard. Peiper hesitated, unwilling to lose too many tanks in an unclear situation, and fell back to La Gleize.

At Stavelot, the American attackers seized most of the rest of the town in house-to-house fighting. A counterattack across the river by the 2d SS Panzergrenadier Regiment collapsed under heavy artillery fire. When the Germans sent some tanks forward in an attempt to cross the bridge, carefully sited American tank destroyers quickly disabled them. An attempt by the 1st SS Reconnaissance Battalion (which had joined Peiper by slipping its light vehicles across a rickety bridge over the Amblève River near Trois Ponts) to attack eastward from La Gleize also failed. After dark men of the 105th Engineer Combat Battalion of the 30th Division moved carefully forward and blew up the bridge over the Amblève. Peiper was now trapped on the wrong side of the river.

6

DISASTER IN THE SCHNEE EIFEL

O f the many battles that are now known collectively as "the Battle of the Bulge," none was more dramatic, or more fateful, than that of the Schnee Eifel, fought from early 16 December to late 19 December. The name is derived from the dominating terrain feature of the battle, the Schnee Eifel (*Schneifel*, or Snow Eifel) ridge.

The hilly, forested region of western Germany known as the Eifel is a continuation of the Ardennes region of contiguous France, Belgium, and Luxembourg. The Eifel lies west of the Rhine River, north of the Moselle River, and south of the Aachen-Cologne line. Most of the subregion in the rugged area between the Prüm and Our Rivers, just north of Luxembourg, is known as the Schnee Eifel, but the term is usually applied to a forested ridgeline just east of the German-Belgian border. Shortly before World War II German engineers had enhanced the natural defensive qualities of this ridgeline by a series of fortifications, part of the so-called Siegfried Line, or Westwall, protecting Germany from attack from the west. The Westwall, just inside Germany's western frontiers, extended from the Rhine River near Nijmegen, south to Switzerland. A segment of the Schnee Eifel portion of the Westwall had been seized by the American 4th Infantry Division in September 1944. This was one of two short stretches of the Westwall that fell into Allied hands before the stiffening of German resistance later that month.

OPPOSING FORCES: GERMAN ATTACKERS

As we have seen in chapter 5, the main effort of the planned German offensive was to be made by the left-flank corps of the Sixth Panzer Army, spearheaded by two panzer divisions driving toward the Meuse River. Just to the south of the Sixth Panzer Army was the Fifth Panzer Army. Its main effort was also to be a two-division panzer drive to the west.

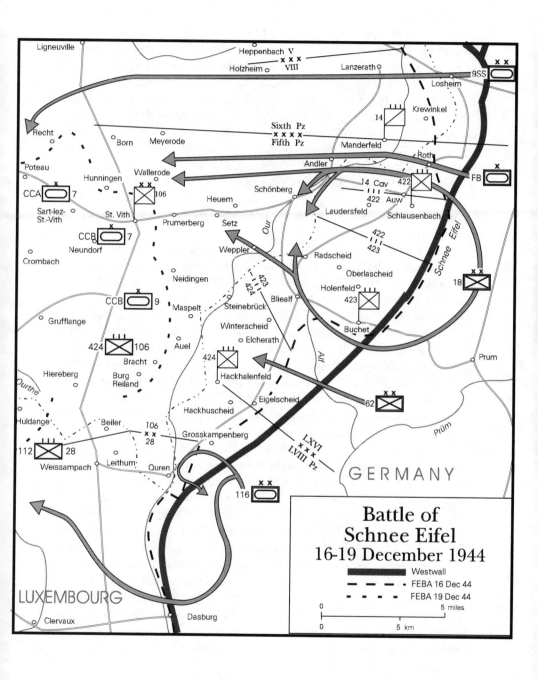

Battle of
Schnee Eifel
16-19 December 1944

Ligneuville

Heppenbach V
Holzheim   xxx   VIII
Lanzerath

9SS   xx

Losheim

Recht

Born   Meyerode

Krewinkel

14

Sixth Pz
xxxx
Fifth Pz

Manderfeld   Roth

FB   x

Poteau

Wallerode

Andler

14 Cav   422   xxx

CCA   x   7

Hunningen

Schönberg

422   Auw

Sart-lez-
St.-Vith

St. Vith

Heuem

Laudersfeld

Schlausenbach

CCB   x   7

Prumerberg

Setz

Radscheid

Oberlascheid

18   xx

Neundorf

Weppler

Holenfeld

Crombach

Neidingen

423
424

Bliealf

423

Buchet

Schnee Eifel

CCB   x   9

Maspelt

Steinebrück

Grufflange

Winterscheid

Auel

424

Elcherath

Prum

424   xxx   106

Bracht

Hackhalenfeld

Hiereberg

Burg
Reiland

Eigelscheid

62   xx

Huldange

Beiler

Hackhuscheid

Ourthe

112   xxx   28

106
xx
28

Grosskampenberg

Weissampach

Leithum

Quren

LXVI
xxx
LVIII Pz

GERMANY

116   xx

Prüm

LUXEMBOURG

Clervaux

Dasburg

Westwall
FEBA 16 Dec 44
FEBA 19 Dec 44

0   5 miles
0   5 km

The Fifth Panzer Army's secondary effort (midway between the main efforts of the two panzer armies) was to seize the road hub of St. Vith, just west of the Schnee Eifel ridge. This attack was hardly less significant than the two main efforts since its purpose was to open up the roadnet of the central Ardennes to assure adequate road communications to support and sustain the main efforts in their parallel drives toward the Meuse River. This secondary effort was to be made by the right wing of the Fifth Army, the LXVI Corps, commanded by General der Artillerie Walter Lucht.

Born in Berlin on 26 February 1882, Lucht served in World War I as an artillery captain. After the Treaty of Versailles he was retained in the Reichswehr, and in 1937 became commander of the 215th Artillery Regiment. In February 1942, as a major general, he was placed in command of the 87th Infantry Division. In November 1943, he was promoted to command the LXVI Corps.

The mission of Lucht's corps was to drive through or around the defensive positions of the American 106th Infantry Division in the Schnee Eiffel. It was to attack on a two-division front, its boundaries almost exactly matching those of the defending 106th Division.

On the right was the 18th Volksgrenadier Division (VGD), commanded by Generalmajor Günther Hoffmann-Schönborn. The principal combat components of the 18th VGD were the 293d, 294th, and 295th Grenadier regiments. The division was formed in Denmark during the late summer of 1944 by grafting the 2,500-odd survivors of the 18th Luftwaffe Field Division into the newly established and still-forming 571st Reserve Division. It contained many former Luftwaffe and Reichsmarine (navy) personnel like a number of other divisions rebuilt during the summer and autumn of 1944. By late November 1944 it had a strength of nearly 10,000 officers and men, and had benefited from a month of training in the eastern Ardennes, or Eifel, region. The division had about thirty armored vehicles: its self-propelled antitank company contained eleven JgPz-38(t) Hetzer (a self-propelled 75-mm antitank gun) and attached were about twenty StuG-IIIGs in the 244th Sturmgeschütz (Assault Gun) Brigade, loaned from LXVI Corps. (The Hetzer and the StuG-IIIGs were both fearsome-looking, tanklike armored vehicles, which any American infantry soldier would almost automatically assume was a Tiger Tank—the most fearsome, and most feared German armored vehicle.)

Hoffmann-Schönborn was born on 1 May 1905 in Posen, West Prussia. He joined the army as an artillery officer in 1924, and was a battery commander by 1936. In October 1940 he became commander of the 1st Assault Gun Battalion. Promoted to major general in September 1944, he took command of the division in Denmark.

Hoffmann-Schönborn's mission was to encircle the Schnee Eifel positions of the American 106th Infantry Division by a daring double-envelopment (simultaneous attacks against or around both flanks of an enemy). For an experienced commander with a veteran division this might have been considered a reasonable risk since the Germans knew that the Americans were overextended. For the newly promoted commander of a scantily trained division, however, it was a daunting task. Nevertheless, when the chips were down, Hoffmann-Schönborn and his men did it with distinction.

Exploiting a gap between the left-hand regiment of the 106th Division and the attenuated line of the attached 14th Cavalry Group to the north, Hoffmann-Schönborn put two regiments in the northern arm of his pincer, and one in the southern arm. He held out from the enveloping forces only one battalion to hold the six-mile front opposite the American positions on the ridge. Then, having encircled and neutralized the Schnee Eifel positions, the division would advance westward to St. Vith.

South of the 18th VGD, opposite the left wing of the 424th Infantry and the right wing of the 423d Infantry, was the 62d Volksgrenadier Division, commanded by Oberst Friedrich Kittel. (He was promoted to generalmajor on 1 January 1945.) This division was to drive northwestward for St. Vith between the Our and Alf river valleys. The two divisions were expected to converge at St. Vith by the evening of 17 December or early on 18 December.

Opposite the right wing of the 424th Infantry was part of the 116th Panzer Division and elements of the 560th Volksgrenadier Division. This was the right wing of the LVIII Panzer Corps, whose commander was Generaloberst Walter Krüger. This corps was to play only a minor role in the Schnee Eifel battle, since its main weight was to be thrown against the 112th Infantry Regiment of the 28th Infantry Division farther south.

OPPOSING FORCES: AMERICAN DEFENDERS

When the German blow fell before dawn on 16 December, the U.S. VIII Corps held its eighty-eight-mile-long Ardennes front with four overextended divisions: from north to south, the 106th Infantry Division, 28th Infantry Division, 9th Armored Division (–), and 4th Infantry Division. Considered generally unsuitable for armored operations, and with no major objective to the east in Germany, this quiet, defensive sector was suitable for giving battle-weary divisions like the 28th and the 4th an opportunity to rest and recuperate, and for giving inexperienced divisions like the 106th and the 99th an opportunity to become gradually acclimated to battle.

The commander of the VIII Corps was Maj. Gen. Troy H. Middleton. Born near Georgetown, Mississippi, on 12 October 1889, he graduated from Mississippi A&M College, a military school, in 1909. Unable to get an appointment to West Point, he enlisted in the Army in 1910 with the intention of gaining a commission as a second lieutenant through a competitive examination. He was successful in 1912, and found himself two years ahead of his prospective West Point classmates. He took part in the expedition to Vera Cruz in 1914. In World War I he served with the 4th Division and was promoted rapidly through the ranks to major and then lieutenant colonel, winning

the Distinguished Service Cross for gallantry in command of an infantry battalion in the Meuse-Argonne. He was promoted again, becoming the youngest
colonel in the AEF by the time of the Armistice. After the war he was
appointed to the first faculty of the Infantry School at Fort Benning, where he
reverted to his peacetime rank of captain.

In the years between the wars Middleton was an outstanding student at
the Infantry School's Advanced Course, at the Command and General Staff
School at Fort Leavenworth, and at the Army War College in Washington. He
retired from the army in 1937, still a major after twenty-seven years of military service. He became a dean and then assistant vice president of Louisiana
State University. After the outbreak of World War II Middleton was recalled
to active duty as a lieutenant colonel early in 1942. By June he had risen to
the rank of brigadier general as the assistant commander of the 45th Infantry
Division. A few months later he became the commander of the division and a
major general. The 45th Division distinguished itself in combat in Sicily in
July 1943 and later—in September—in the amphibious invasion of Italy at
Salerno. Illness forced him to return to the United States later that year. His
career should have been over, but Generals Marshall and Eisenhower agreed
that Middleton's unique talents as a combat commander were too valuable to
lose. In March 1944 he was sent to Britain to take command of the VIII
Corps, which was activated on 12 June 1944. After the breakout from Normandy, the VIII Corps was responsible for the siege of Brest and the clearing
of Brittany. Transferred east in late fall, it was assigned to the First Army and
took over the Ardennes sector.

The northernmost of the VIII Corps divisions in the Ardennes was the
106th Infantry Division, commanded by Maj. Gen. Alan W. Jones. Born in
Goldendale, Washington, in 1896, he was a junior at the University of Washington when the United States entered World War I in 1917. He left college to
join the Army. He served with the 43d Division in France in World War I.
During the years between wars he served in the Philippines and in Hawaii,
and had the usual mixture of school assignments, troop duty, and staff
appointments. After the outbreak of World War II Jones became the Assistant
Division Commander of the 90th Infantry Division. On 20 January 1943 he
was assigned to command the new 106th Infantry Division, which was activated on 15 March. Three days later Jones was promoted to major general.

Although the 106th Division had been activated in Tennessee, it did most
of its training at Camp Atterbury, Indiana. In October and November 1944 the
division was transported overseas on three British steamers: the *Queen Mary*,
the *Aquitania*, and the *Wakefield*, landing in Greenock, Scotland, and Liver-
pool, England. Assembled briefly in the English Midlands, the 106th moved
from England to France on 1–2 December, and then by train and motor to
eastern Belgium to a quiet sector held by the 2d Infantry Division, which was
about to move north. The 106th Division now held the northernmost division
sector of the VIII Corps. (The veteran 2d, having had an opportunity to rest,

was already playing a major part in the planned offensive of the U.S. V Corps, just to the north, which had begun on 13 December; see chapter 5.) The 106th Division's sector, stretching about twenty-two miles from north to south, was in turn divided into four subsectors.

The northernmost of these subsectors, northwest of the Schnee Eifel ridge, and just west of the Belgian-German border, was in a low-lying depression from which the headwaters of the Our River rise. The depression was called the Losheim Gap, named after the principal town in the vicinity. (Losheim was a border town just inside Germany; most of the Gap itself was in Belgium.) This sector, with a front of about six miles had been held since mid-October by the 14th Cavalry Group, which consisted of two reconnaissance squadrons (18th and 32d), and to which were attached the 275th Armored Field Artillery Battalion and Company A of the 820th Tank Destroyer Battalion. Commanding the 14th Cavalry Group was Col. Mark Devine, whose command post was at Manderfeld, just west of the headwaters of the Our River. One of Devine's two squadrons (the 32d) was in reserve, west of St. Vith. (By coincidence, most of the 32d Squadron's vehicles were temporarily "deadlined"—not available for duty—on the morning of 16 December, because the unit was going through a scheduled maintenance overhaul.) The other squadron of the 14th Cavalry Group (the 18th) held the front with eight platoon- or troop-strength strongpoints (most reinforced with two towed 3" tank destroyer guns) with intervals averaging nearly a mile between strongpoints. Most of the strongpoints had been set up in small villages that were in depressions (described by one participant as being "in the bottom of sugar bowls") with poor observation and limited fields of fire. B Troop of the 18th was detached to cover a gap between the 423d and 424th Infantry regiments, about ten miles to the south.

The 14th Cavalry Group was on the extreme left (north) of the VIII Corps line. To its left was the 99th Infantry Division, which held the right flank of the V Corps. There was a two-mile gap between the northernmost strongpoint of the 14th Cavalry Group and the southernmost positions of the 99th Division. This gap was covered by periodic patrols from the cavalry group and the 99th Division. The rightmost strongpoint of the cavalry group was about a mile and a half north of the positions of the 422d Infantry of the 106th Division; the infantry had the responsibility for patrolling this area. In the four days since the 106th Division had taken over the sector there had not been time for more than preliminary discussions of coordination between the staffs of the division and the attached 14th Cavalry Group.

Unknown to the Americans, and totally unsuspected, was the fact that the left flank of the thinly held 14th Cavalry Group sector had been selected by the Germans as the locale for launching the main effort of their planned major offensive. The power of this attack would be totally unimaginable to the Americans, who believed Germany was on the verge of collapse. (By coincidence, the boundary between the German Sixth and Fifth Panzer armies was almost identical to that between the American 14th Cavalry Group and the 422d Infantry.)[1] Furthermore, as a result of patrolling, the Germans were aware of the gap between the 14th and the 422d, and the 18th VGD planned to exploit that gap in its daring double-envelopment of the Schnee Eifel position.

The positions of the 422d Infantry were completely inside Germany, just east of the Our River. (From Losheim south the eastern border of Belgium more or less follows the Our River until it runs into the Sauer River.) The 422d was ensconced in a four-mile strip of pillboxes of the old German Westwall defenses running along the northwest slopes of the hogback Schnee Eifel ridge, just beneath the crest on the western side. The three battalions of the 422d were in line in the pillboxes: the 2d, 1st, and 3d, from left to right. The command post of Col. George L. Descheneaux Jr., commanding the 422d, was in the village of Schlausenbach, where the ridge rises from the Our valley.

To the right of the 422d lay the 423d Infantry Regiment, also holding about two miles of old German Westwall pillboxes, plus another two miles of field fortifications just west of the old line, but still inside the German frontier. Colonel Charles C. Cavender, commanding the 423d, had two battalions in line: the 3d on the left in the Westwall positions, the 1st on the right. (The regiment's 2d Battalion was in division reserve, back at Born, near St. Vith.) Cavender's command post was in Buchet, a village just east of the source of the Alf River, which flows south to join the Prüm River at Pronsfeld.

There was a gap of about three miles between the right flank of the 423d Infantry and the left flank of the 424th. This was covered on the north side of the boundary between the two regiments by B Troop of the 18th Reconnaissance Squadron, and on the south side of that line by the 106th Reconnaissance Troop. Continuing west and southwest of the Alf River was the six-mile line of the 424th Infantry, commanded by Col. Alexander D. Reid. The 424th, also completely inside Germany, had two battalions in line, the 3d on the left, the 2d on the right; the 1st Battalion was in regimental reserve. Reid's command post was at Heckhalenfeld, just east of the frontier, and about a mile east of the Our River.

Supporting the three infantry regiments were the four battalions of the 106th Division Artillery. The 589th Field Artillery Battalion was located west of Auw and east of Laudesfeld, positioned to provide direct support to the 422d Infantry; the 590th Field Artillery Battalion was similarly located with respect to the 423d Infantry (northeast of Radscheid), as was the 591st Field Artillery Battalion with respect to the 424th Infantry (near Heckhalenfeld). These three light artillery battalions were each equipped with twelve 105-mm howitzers, allocated four to a battery. The division's medium battalion—the 592d Field Artillery Battalion—with twelve 155-mm howitzers, was centrally located, just west of the 589th Field Artillery Battalion, near Laudesfeld. The width of the division front was such that most of the front could be covered by no more than two of these artillery battalions. However, more than making up for this deficiency were eight corps artillery battalions, most deployed generally behind the 423d Infantry, available to support the division.

Just behind the front line, and running generally parallel to the front, was a ridgeline road that the Americans called the "Skyline Drive." Perhaps less aptly named than a similar but nonconnected Skyline Drive in the 28th Division sector, it performed a comparable function. It ran from the right flank of the 424th Infantry at Grosskampenberg, generally north through Bleialf, Radscheid, Auw, and Roth, close behind the forward positions of the 424th, further behind the Schnee Eifel positions of the 423d and 422d, into the right-hand strongpoints of the 14th Cavalry Group. This was the principal means of lateral road communications in the 106th Division sector.

General Jones had taken over the old command post (CP) of the 2d Division in St. Vith, the principal road center of the northeastern Ardennes. The 106th Division Artillery commander, Brig. Gen. Leo T. McMahon, had his CP adjacent to that of General Jones. McMahon had joined the division a year earlier at Camp Atterbury. Also located with Jones's CP were the CPs of the 331st Medical Battalion (part of the division) and of the attached 634th Antiaircraft Artillery Battalion, the 820th Tank Destroyer Battalion, and the 168th Engineer Battalion.

THE BREAKING STORM

At 0530 on 16 December a massive German artillery barrage of all calibers swept over the 106th Division sector. St. Vith was hit by fourteen-inch shells from German railroad guns. Since most of the Americans were in dug-in positions, casualties were light, but the sudden impact of the shelling and its ferocious intensity filled many hearts with terror. The intensity lessened after 0600, however, but by 0615 the front-line Americans detected movement to the east.

The first serious ground movement came in the 14th Cavalry Group sector, north of the Schnee Eifel, as paratroopers of the 3d Parachute Division (many clad in white snowsuits) began to move into the Our valley south and north of Losheim. (These were spearheads of the I SS Panzer Corps, making the main effort on the left flank of the Sixth Panzer Army; see chapter 5.) By dawn (about 0730) the cavalrymen were being driven from their positions near Lanzerath, Krewinkel, and Roth by overwhelming mortar and small-arms fire. The 18th Squadron's tank company counterattacked east of Manderfeld early in the morning, but was soon halted by German antitank units. Without infantry support, and threatened with encirclement by the German paratroopers, the American tanks had to fall back.

Colonel Devine asked for and obtained the permission of division headquarters to call up his 32d Squadron from reserve near Vielsalm, twenty miles to the rear. The advance party from the 32d arrived at the group CP at Manderfeld at about 1100 hours, around the same time that Devine realized that German armor (apparently assault guns attached to the 12th VGD) had penetrated into the northern part of his sector, while on his right flank other armor (the assault group of the 18th VGD) was pouring through Roth toward Auw, threatening to cut off the cavalrymen from the 106th Division.

The German pressure mounted against both flanks of the cavalry group. Massed artillery barrages were followed by infantry assaults. As the garrisons of his strongpoints were either overwhelmed or driven back, Devine asked division headquarters for permission to fall back to a new position along the Holzheim-Andler road. Early in the afternoon he received permission to withdraw to the new line. Also about this time Lieutenant Colonel Ridge, the commander of the 32d Squadron, strangely disappeared, telling his executive officer that he was "going back to get ammunition."

By dark there was a semblance of a cavalry line along the Holzheim-Andler road. But both Honsfeld and Holzheim were in enemy hands, and farther south Schönberg was threatened by German tanks and infantry in Auw.

At division headquarters the situation was seen as both grim and confused. There were reports (apparently greatly exaggerated) that German armored spearheads were streaming west through the Losheim Gap north of the 14th Cavalry Group line, threatening the division with envelopment from the left. Division was also aware that strong German infantry groups were moving north through the center of the division line toward Schönberg through Bleialf. This meant that both the 422d and 423d regiments were in danger of being surrounded. All that prevented the incipient encirclement was intense fire from the 589th, 590th, and 592d Field Artillery battalions against the enemy troop concentrations in and around Auw and Bleialf, and along the roads farther south and east. (These fires were directed by forward observers in the infantry positions.) In midafternoon German armored vehicles from Auw (reported to be "tanks" by the Americans) attempted to overrun the battery positions of the 589th. Using direct fire, the cannoneers knocked out several of these "tanks," and the survivors withdrew toward Auw.

Meanwhile, in light of the danger of encirclement, General Jones had ordered the division reserve to Schönberg. The 2d Battalion of the 423d, under Lt. Col. Joseph F. Puett, arrived near Schönberg from Born and St. Vith shortly after noon. It soon became evident to Brigadier General McMahon, the division artillery commander, that Puett's battalion could help extract three of the division's four artillery battalions from imminent overrun. The 589th Field Artillery Battalion, west of Auw and east of Laudesfeld, was in the most immediate danger, but the 592d and 590th were also threatened. By late afternoon General McMahon had instructed both the 589th and 592d to displace as soon as possible. At about 2030 General Jones personally called Puett, ordering him to take his battalion east from Schönberg to relieve the left flank of the 422d, and at the same time to facilitate the displacement of the 589th and 592d Field Artillery battalions. Puett moved at once, but apparently he took a road different from the one directed by General Jones.[2] Nevertheless, moving by truck on a snowy, blustery night, by about midnight the battalion reached the vicinity of the 589th, which was ready to move out. Under heavy German artillery and small-arms fire, the American artillery began to move soon after midnight. However, all four guns of C Battery of the 589th had to be abandoned. The only exit from C Battery's position onto the Auw-Radscheid road was through a German armored concentration.

Throughout the day and into the night the two arms of the pincers of the 18th VGD had been hammering at the northern flank of the 422d Infantry and the southern flank of the 423d. This meant that the left flank battalion of the 422d Infantry (2d Battalion) and the right flank battalion of the 423d (1st Battalion) had been heavily engaged. The 2d Battalion of the 422d had been pulled back into the Westwall fortifications at an angle of more than 100 degrees from the original front, facing an enemy that had taken over the former positions of the 14th Cavalry Group in Kobscheid and Auw. To the right of the fortifications, the 1st Battalion of the 423d had been severely shaken by the left hook of the 18th VGD, and had fallen slowly back to Bleialf. In between, however, all was quiet in the Westwall positions held by the 1st and 3d battalions of the 422d and the 3d Battalion of the 423d.

On the division's extreme right, the 424th Infantry had also been badly pounded during the day by assaults from the 62d VGD. In this sector the German main effort was northwest along the Eigelscheid-Winterspelt road, driving through the left flank of the 3d Battalion toward the Our River bridge at Steinebrück, and heading toward St. Vith just beyond.

In midmorning, near Eigelscheid, a German captain, a staff officer of the 116th Panzer Division, was apparently reconnoitering the route his division was planning to take in exploiting this main effort of the 62d VGD. He was unlucky enough to meet the commander of the Weapons Platoon of I Company of the 424th Infantry, who was also on reconnaissance, 1st Lt. William V. Shakespeare, a former All-American football star at Notre Dame University. I Company had been in 3d Battalion reserve and had just been ordered to bolster the threatened lines of K and L companies. Shakespeare, who had been reconnoitering positions for his platoon, tackled and quickly subdued the German, then marched him to the rear as a prisoner. The German was carrying a map case crammed with papers, including the plan for Operation Greif and the attack plans of the 116th Panzer Division.[3]

The captured papers were immediately sent to Division Headquarters at St. Vith. This was the first hard information the American intelligence community had received on the plans of Skorzeny's 150th Panzer Brigade to cause disruption behind the American lines.[4] The plans of the 116th Panzer revealed that that division expected to be committed that day, and that its objective by nightfall was Crombach, nine miles northwest of where the German officer had been captured, and two miles southwest of St. Vith. As it turned out, thanks largely to the determined defense of the 424th Infantry, the

116th Panzer Division was not committed that day, and it would be five more days before other Germans reached Crombach.

Another big former football player accompanied I Company as it moved forward to reestablish the threatened line of the 3d Battalion: Capt. Lee Berwick, a burly 220-pounder who was the S-3 (operations officer) of the 3d Battalion. He was prisoner-hunting because he wanted to know the identification of the unexpected German attackers. I Company received fire as it emerged from the forest near the village of Heckhuscheid. Berwick organized a skirmish line just inside the edge of the woods. He got support from the nearby Weapons Platoon of L Company, and sent one of I Company's platoons, under Lt. Joseph E. Dresselhaus, to outflank the village from the north. He then led his skirmish line out of the woods toward the outskirts of the village. The Germans in Heckhuscheid opened fire on Berwick and his men. Then they were taken under fire from the flank by Dresselhaus's platoon. Berwick, who spoke some German, shouted to the Germans to surrender. Suddenly German soldiers came streaming from the houses, waving handkerchiefs, napkins, tablecloths, anything white they could find in the houses. To his amazement, Berwick found that he had captured 107 prisoners, including two officers.[5]

Despite this setback, the 62d VGD continued its violent assault into the 3d Battalion of the 424th Infantry. By noon the battalion was again close to collapse. Colonel Reid committed his reserve, the 1st Battalion, which counterattacked, threw back the German spearheads, and then reestablished the defensive line just to the left of the 3d Battalion. Farther south the remainder of the 3d Battalion and the 2d Battalion had held their positions against less intensive attacks. Unexpectedly, the 2d Battalion of the 424th was augmented late in the day by B Company of the 112th Infantry of the 28th Division. This company had been cut off from its place on the left flank of the 28th and driven northwest by the fury of the Fifth Panzer Army's main effort. Nearly out of ammunition, the battered B Company men soon had their ammunition replenished by the 2d Battalion of the 424th, and took up a position on the right flank of the 106th Division.

At midnight General Jones saw the situation of his division as follows:

To the north, the collapse of the cavalry group laid his left flank completely open to enemy armor reportedly moving toward Amblève. In the center, two of his infantry regiments and three of his artillery battalions were threatened with encirclement. But the converging enemy columns advancing through Auw and Bleialf had at least been slowed, and most of his artillery seemed to be displacing from immediate danger. He could also take some comfort from the fact that his right flank was holding firm, although loss of communication with the 28th Division to the south was worrisome.

Furthermore, Jones had been promised substantial reinforcement.

During the afternoon Maj. Gen. Troy Middleton, commanding the VIII Corps, had promised Jones that Combat Command B of the 9th Armored

Division, commanded by Brig. Gen. William M. Hoge, was being placed under his command. Hoge's tanks and armored infantry were at Faymonville, north of St. Vith, and would be available to him before dawn on 17 December. Jones decided to move that combat command to St. Vith to help defend that vital road junction from the attack he expected momentarily from enemy armor to the east and north.

Then, later in the evening, Jones had been informed that Combat Command B of the 7th Armored Division, commanded by Brig. Gen. Bruce Clarke, was on its way from the Ninth Army area to the north, and would be available to him by 0700 on 17 December. Jones then decided that with arrival of this additional armor he would sideslip CCB of the 9th farther south in the morning. It would counterattack east in the Bleialf area to break up the left arm of the threatened encirclement of his two regiments in the Schnee Eifel. Then, when CCB of the 7th arrived, he would use it to defend St. Vith and, if possible, counterattack to drive the Germans north and east of the town back toward Losheim. (Jones still had no idea of the weight and power of the German drive.)

THE SECOND DAY, 17 DECEMBER: THE GERMANS TAKE STOCK

The commanders of the two German divisions attacking the 106th Division— Generals Hoffmann-Schönborn and Kittel—had mixed feelings about the results of the first day's fighting. Their attacks had been successful, yet the success had not been as overwhelming as they had hoped. The two pincers of the 18th VGD had clearly broken through the crust of the American defenses, but unexpectedly strong resistance from American reserves had prevented these thrusts from completing the planned encirclement of the troops on the Schnee Eifel. The 62d VGD had met with even greater frustration. The drive toward St. Vith had come close to seizing the Our River bridge at Steinebrück. Then the apparently crumbling defenses of the 424th had stiffened when its reserve battalion had been committed. Both division commanders had given up their earlier hope of taking St. Vith before dawn on 17 December.

Behind the two infantry divisions, the German tankers were growing impatient. The Führer Begleit Brigade was ready to move on St. Vith, but the Americans had to be cleared from Schönberg first.

South of the 62d VGD the 116th Panzer Division had also been frustrated, in this case by the unexpectedly firm defense of the 424th and 112th Infantry regiments. The commander, Generalmajor Siegfried von Waldenburg, had anticipated being in Crombach, southwest of St. Vith, by this time. Now, with the direct line of advance seemingly blocked, the 116th began to sideslip to the south, through Dasburg, taking advantage of a gap that had been opened between the 110th and 112th Infantry regiments in the 28th Division sector.

THE BATTLE FOR SCHÖNBERG

Despite the combination of snow in the air and a mixture of mud and ice on the ground, the 592d Field Artillery Battalion had successfully evacuated its position east of Schönberg before midnight and was rolling west toward St. Vith. Two 155-mm howitzers got so badly stuck that they had to be abandoned, but before dawn on 17 December the remaining ten howitzers were in position just north of St. Vith, near the Division Artillery airstrip.

The 589th Artillery was less fortunate. The displacement from the battalion's original position began with the abandonment of the four guns of C Battery, which were destroyed by their crews. The other two batteries had to cope not only with the abominable weather but with the harassment of infiltrating German infantrymen. Both batteries got out successfully (except for one B Battery gun, which had to be abandoned) and pulled back to new positions east of the Schönberg-Bleialf road and about a mile and a quarter south of Schönberg. Just before dawn, about 0700 hours, they were ready to resume their mission of supporting the 422d Infantry.

The howitzers of the 589th were hardly in their new positions before German infantry overran the battalion CP and began to approach the firing batteries. With communications cut between the battalion commander, Lieutenant Colonel Kelley, and the gun positions, and with German infantry closing in, the Battalion Executive Officer, Major Arthur C. Parker III, took command of the seven remaining howitzers (three of B Battery and four of A Battery). Deciding to evacuate the new positions, he ordered the two battery executives to get their guns out individually and to reassemble west of St. Vith.

The battery executive of Battery A, 1st Lt. Eric Fisher Wood, was able to get three of his guns out of position and on the road, but the fourth was stuck, and German infantry and tanks were approaching. He sent the three waiting guns on ahead, telling them he would join them west of Schönberg, and then went to help the crew of the stuck gun. When they finally got the gun out, Wood, the last man out of the position, which was under heavy small-arms fire, swung himself onto the back of the truck and told the driver to head for Schönberg. They found the town full of Germans. Nevertheless, the truck and howitzer careened through the town, throttle to the floorboard, while the crew crouched behind the truck's sidewalls returning the poorly aimed fire of the surprised Germans. Near the west end of the town a tank blocked the road. The truck screeched to a halt, and the men jumped out and into a ditch. As one of them later said, they "were alone in a world of Krauts." As German infantrymen swept toward them, Wood suddenly jumped out of the ditch and dashed under heavy fire to a nearby forest, where he disappeared from the view of both the Germans and his own men, who promptly surrendered.

Battery B of the 589th was cut off by German infantry and a tank. Captain Arthur C. Brown, the battery commander, ordered his men to abandon and destroy their howitzers. He then got his men and his remaining trucks on the road and followed Lieutenant Wood and A Battery's last gun into Schön-berg. Like Wood's truck and gun, the B Battery trucks were forced to stop near the center of the town. Surrounded by Germans, the men of B Battery had no choice but to surrender.

Perhaps two hours earlier, about dawn, just southeast of Auw, Lt. Col. Puett's 2d Battalion of the 423d Infantry—the former division reserve—attempted to carry out the orders he had received from General Jones to join the 422d Infantry. However, the advance of masses of German tanks and infantry from Auw made that impossible. Puett then tried to fall back to Schönberg, only to discover that Germans from the north and south now held that town. Fighting Germans all the way, Puett fell back to the southeast, accompanied by the 590th Artillery Battalion, to join the 423d Infantry in the Schnee Eifel.

The battle for Schönberg was over.

ON THE SCHNEE EIFEL

Aside from some harassing German artillery fire, the morning of 17 Decem-ber was relatively quiet for the men of the 422d Infantry, who were only dimly aware of the bitter battle going on to their west. They were even less aware of how important that battle was to their own fate. The 2d Battalion, having pulled back and now facing north, was no longer under pressure, although Germans were streaming past the battalion's new front. Nor was there any pressure from the east—the regiment's original front. Colonel Descheneaux passively awaited orders.

By early afternoon Descheneaux realized that his regiment and the 423d had been encircled by the enemy. Late in the afternoon or early in the evening he received a radio message from Division Headquarters telling him to expect a drop of food and ammunition supplies during the night. (It never arrived.)

It is easy in retrospect to see that had the 422d been committed early on 17 December, either to the north or to the west (preferably to the west), the battle for the Schnee Eifel might have had a very different outcome, and the entire campaign would have been changed dramatically. Descheneaux's regi-ment was probably the only large American unit along the entire VIII Corps front that was not fighting desperately that day. Had it been committed deci-sively, not only could it have saved or recovered Schönberg, it could have saved itself. Someone somewhere in the chain of command from regiment through division to corps had made a terrible blunder. Colonel Descheneaux, General Jones, and General Middleton must share the blame. But Desche-neaux, a West Point graduate of the Class of 1933, was most culpable. His regiment was being encircled. The main body of the encircling force was passing just in front of his 2d Battalion. He could have committed two battal-ions—indeed, his entire regiment—into the struggle for Schönberg. In that case, the 18th VGD could have been destroyed. As it was, Gen. Hoffmann-Schönborn had taken a great risk, and by the evening of 17 December he had won his battle. But we are ahead of our story.

The 423d Infantry had had a much different day than the 422d. Before dawn the southern pincers of the 18th VGD had renewed its pressure up the Alf River valley, along the boundary between the 1st Battalion of the 423d and the left wing of the 424th. Before midnight the attackers had reached the vicinity of Winterscheid, and were now attacking northeast, toward Bleialf, into the right rear of the 1st Battalion of the 423d. By 0400 all contact had been lost with the 424th.

By 0600 on 17 December the 293d Volksgrenadier Regiment, the left arm of the 18th VGD pincer, had fought its way into Bleialf, and the 423d Infantry had lost communications with the supporting 590th Field Artillery Battalion. The Germans continued their drive to the northeast, toward Buchet and Schönberg. By 0830 they were at Schönberg, where they linked up with the other pincer arm to complete the encirclement of the 422d and 423d Infantry regiments. This was at the very moment that the 589th Artillery was trying to escape through Schönberg.

With his right wing driven back and his regimental CP at Buchet threatened, Colonel Cavender was now very much in the middle of the battle. He shifted elements of the 3d Battalion from their Westwall dugouts to bolster the crumbling 1st Battalion. By 1000 hours his situation was much improved by the unexpected arrival of the 2d Battalion and the 590th Field Artillery Battalion. This development confirmed the fact that his regiment and the 422d were now isolated from the rest of the American Army.

The enemy pressure on the 423d suddenly subsided. The Germans, having achieved, even if somewhat belatedly, their primary objective of encircling the Schnee Eifel, were now focusing their attention to the west, primarily toward St. Vith. Later in the day there was an encouraging message from 106th Division Headquarters to both beleaguered regiments promising a counterattack "to clear the area west of you this afternoon with reinforcements." The message continued: "Withdraw from present positions if they become untenable." Cavender, who had moved his CP to a Westwall emplacement, next to the 3d Battalion CP, must have wondered how his encircled regiment would carry out such a withdrawal. In any event, he established a three-sided regimental perimeter defense with the 2d Battalion facing generally north, the 1st Battalion covering the west, and the 3d Battalion continuing to face south.

Another radio message from division promised the 423d a supply airdrop during the night. Cavender's staff sent back a message listing the most urgently needed items of food, equipment, and ammunition. Although the airdrops never happened, both of the isolated regiments spent a relatively quiet night.

THE 424TH INFANTRY ON THE SOUTHERN APPROACHES TO ST. VITH

The 62d VGD resumed its attacks in the sector of the 424th Infantry before dawn on 17 December. Winterspelt was captured by 0600, and the Germans pressed north toward Steinebrück, inflicting heavy casualties on the 1st Battalion. At about 1300 hours the German advance was brought to a sudden halt when the first tanks of CCB of the 9th Armored Division rolled over the Steinbrück bridge to join the hard-pressed 424th. Colonel Reid felt greatly relieved.

By this time, however, it became obvious to Division Headquarters that German advances to the northwest from Winterspelt, Bleialf, and Schönberg, combined with the drive of the 116th Panzer Division through the 112th Infantry sector farther south, could result in encirclement of both the 424th and CCB/9. At about 1515 hours Reid was ordered to withdraw across the Our River to establish a new defensive line. The move began shortly after dusk and was carried out efficiently. When the displacement was complete, the 424th held a line from Maspelt in the north to a point midway between Burg Reuland and Beiler in the south.

Meanwhile, about noon, CCB of the 9th Armored Division received its baptism of fire just south of Steinebrück as it came to the relief of 1/424. The Germans were thrown back to Elcherath, which was taken by CCB at 1530. General Hoge was preparing to attack Winterspelt when he received orders from the 106th Division to fall back behind the Our River. Shortly after dark this withdrawal was completed, and CCB held about three miles of riverbank from Weppeler in the north to Auel in the south.

TRAVAILS OF THE 14TH CAVALRY GROUP

As dawn broke on 17 December, the depleted 14th Cavalry Group still held the northern wing of the 106th Division's sector. About half of the group had disappeared—casualties, prisoners, or refugees. Nevertheless, Colonel Devine had been able to hold substantial elements of his remaining cavalrymen together. The battered remnants of the 18th Squadron were on the left, near Heppenbach; the 32d was stretched southeastward to Andler and Schönberg. But early on the morning of 17 December the troopers of the 18th Squadron were pushed back toward Born by elements of the 1st SS Panzer Division. At the same time, German armor from the 18th VGD mobile group was hitting the 32d Squadron, deployed near Andler, from both north and east.

Colonel Devine pulled his shattered units back to a new line from Born to Wallerode. The Amblève valley was now completely open to the 1st SS Panzer Division, while only a handful of artillerymen, engineers, and division signalmen in Schönberg were between St. Vith and the Führer Begleit Brigade on the main road from Auw and Schönberg.

Shortly after noon the 14th Cavalry Group got the following order from Division Headquarters: "Stay on line where you are."

Despite this order, Devine did not change the withdrawal orders he had previously issued. The 32d Squadron fell back from Wallerode through the northern outskirts of St. Vith to reach the road that led through Poteau to Vielsalm. The cavalrymen suddenly found themselves part of a mammoth traffic jam. Most of the congestion was created by the eight corps artillery battalions that had been ordered to withdraw from the danger posed by the German pincers closing on Schönberg from Auw and Bleialf. Mixed with them, however, were a few panic-stricken stragglers from units that were supposedly fighting farther east.[6] This concentration of vehicles (most in organized formations, but a few in individual trucks and jeeps) created a massive obstacle that prevented the 32d and 18th Cavalry squadrons from carrying out Colonel Devine's order to fall back to Vielsalm and Poteau. Nevertheless, by following a circuitous route on smaller roads, Devine and much of his staff reached Poteau. After establishing his CP, Devine and several of his staff officers went on reconnaissance to the northeast.

The traffic jam between St. Vith and Vielsalm was having a far more serious effect than hindering the movements of the squadrons of the 14th Cavalry Group. The leading elements of the 7th Armored Division had arrived in the vicinity of Vielsalm late in the morning, and were now attempting to follow orders to move eastward to bolster the defense of St. Vith. The situation approached chaos after some vehicles attempted to get around the stalled columns by pulling into half-frozen farm fields and wound up getting stuck in the icy mud.

Meanwhile, Colonel Devine and his reconnaissance party had just passed Recht when they ran into Germans who opened fire. Their vehicle was wrecked, but all of the occupants dove into nearby ditches and miraculously none of them was injured. Traveling singly on foot, all got back to the CP at Poteau after dark.

First to arrive was Devine, badly shaken by the experience. He abandoned his responsibility and turned command of the 14th Group over to Lt. Col. William F. Damon Jr., commander of the 18th Squadron. Soon after, a message was received from corps ordering the cavalry commander to report immediately to VIII Corps headquarters at Bastogne. Before leaving, Damon turned over command to Lieutenant Colonel Ridge of the 32d Squadron, who had returned to the Group CP after his mysterious search for ammunition. Not long after that the Group Executive Officer, Lt. Col. Augustine D. Dugan, who had been on the reconnaissance that ended so abruptly near Recht, arrived back at the CP. By virtue of seniority he assumed command of the group. Thus in a period of about three hours the 14th Cavalry Group had had four commanders.

More important than this game of command musical chairs, however, was that by its unauthorized withdrawal the 14th Cavalry Group had left the northern approach to St. Vith completely open. Fortunately for the Americans, the only German unit in a position to take advantage of the opportunity was Kampfgruppe Peiper of the 1st SS Panzer Division. Intent upon his dash to the Meuse at Huy the German commander, Lieutenant Colonel Peiper, would have ignored the opportunity even if he had been aware of it. Other German units were charged with seizure of the roadnet hub, and they were intent upon carrying out their missions, even though they were being thwarted in their efforts.

Two Lieutenant Colonels Hold the St. Vith Road

Contributing to this German failure were the actions of two American lieutenant colonel staff officers and a small group of valiant soldiers on the road east of St. Vith. Their courage and initiative reflected enough credit on their army to offset the shameful scene of panic on the road west of the town.

Early on 17 December, the division signal officer, Lt. Col. Earle Williams, and his wire chief, M.Sgt. Clyde F. Foster, were at Schönberg, the location of the division's forward switching central. About 0830, as German tanks approached from Andler to the north and Auw to the east, Williams called Division to report the situation. He then ordered the switchboard destroyed and sent the signalmen back to St. Vith. He and Foster climbed into their jeep and under small-arms and mortar fire drove slowly westward toward Heuem. They stopped from time to time to tap into the phone line and report to Division. At Heuem they found a self-propelled M8 TD gun and collected a few artillerymen, engineers, and signalmen to establish a delaying position beside the gun.[7]

A German tank poked its nose cautiously over a rise in the road and was promptly knocked out by the TD gun. Williams then pulled his detachment west of Heuem, put the gun in another good position, and ordered his men to start felling trees for a roadblock. Again he tapped into the phone line and called for artillery fire. Within minutes 155-mm shells from the 592d Field Artillery Battalion put interdiction fire on the road between Heuem and Schönberg.

Later in the morning—probably after 1030—Williams was joined by Lt. Col. W. M. Slayden, Assistant G-2 of VIII Corps, who had been with the 106th Division G-2 section for the past two days. Slayden, apparently on his own initiative, was reconnoitering to find out where the Germans were, and soon came under small-arms fire from Germans in Heuem. He then tapped into the line and called the Division G-2, reporting that he was "the last man between St. Vith and Schönberg." Gathering together an artillery forward observer team and a few stray cavalrymen, Slayden fell back to join Williams.

As German armored vehicles and infantrymen poked cautiously westward along the road from Heuem, they were continually slowed by small-arms fire and TD fire from the polyglot Williams-Slayden task force, and particularly by air-OP-directed fire from the 592d Field Artillery Battalion.[8] Every time the Germans built up enough strength to threaten them, Williams and Slayden pulled back to the next ridgeline or the next clump of trees and resumed their delaying tactics. By 1430 they had fallen back to within a mile of St. Vith, but with the invaluable help of the 592d Artillery, and its observers in their light planes, they had delayed the spearhead of the 18th VGD by at least three hours.

THE DEFENSE OF ST. VITH

At 0935 on 17 December General Jones had designated Lt. Col. Thomas J. Riggs, commanding the 81st Engineer Combat Battalion, as the defense commander of St. Vith. From his battalion Riggs had available the Headquarters and Supply Company and part of A Company, which had been in the Schönberg-Heuem area. (The other companies were with the infantry regiments.) He also had about half of the attached 168th Engineer Combat Battalion, commanded by Lt. Col. W. L. Nungesser. Also available were the Division Defense Platoon and a platoon of B Company of the 820th Tank Destroyer Battalion with three towed guns. Finally, there was the 592d Field Artillery Battalion in position just northeast of St. Vith with ten of its original twelve 155-mm howitzers and a replenished supply of ammunition.

Riggs had planned to establish his defensive line near Heuem, but he and Nungesser soon discovered what Williams and Slayden already knew: The Germans held Heuem and were advancing westward as rapidly as they could push the two staff officers and their informal task force. As the German advance continued, Riggs finally picked the high ground one mile east of St. Vith as his defensive position, and at 1300 hours his men began to dig in north and south of the Schönberg road.

The three precious hours gained by the Williams-Slayden task force were enough for the 81st Engineer Battalion to establish a viable defensive position just east of St. Vith. At 1400 hours the 81st Engineers and the 592d Field Artillery brought the German advance to a halt. Two hours would pass before the Germans accumulated sufficient strength to mount a coordinated attack on the front and flanks of this last-ditch position in front of St. Vith.

Darkness was falling when German artillery fire began to fall on the 81st and 168th Engineers. At that time they were joined by Brig. Gen. Bruce Clarke, commander of CCB of the 7th Armored Division, who had been in St. Vith conferring with General Jones since late morning. Now he was joined by a handful of the leading tanks of his command, which had finally worked their way through the clogged road west of St. Vith. He made a quick reconnaissance and began feeding his tanks into the fight. At 1745 hours Clarke, with the approval of General Jones, assumed command of the defense of St. Vith. We shall return to St. Vith in chapter 10.

THE THIRD DAY IN THE SCHNEE EIFEL

Division Headquarters had fairly good radio communications with the 423d Infantry. Contact with the 422d was not so good, due in part to the forested and rugged terrain and to German jamming. But when direct communications from Division to the 422d became impossible, messages could be passed through the 423d. Under these circumstances, it is surprising that Division Headquarters did not simplify the communications situation by forming the two encircled regiments into a task force, particularly since communication was best with Colonel Cavender, and he was the senior of the two regimental commanders. Even without the communications situation that would have been the logical thing to do militarily. But, stubbornly, General Jones decided that he would deal individually and directly (to the extent the radio permitted) with all three of his regimental commanders.

At 0215 on 18 December Jones sent an order to the commanders of the 422d and 423d to shift northwest to "dug-in positions south of Schönberg-St. Vith Road" to "destroy by fire" the Germans on that road. "Ammunition, food and water will be dropped," the message continued. "When mission accomplished, move to area St. Vith-Wallerode-Weppler, organize, and move to west."[9]

The message was received by the two regimental commanders about 0400 hours. Descheneaux is reported to have said, when he read the message, "My poor men—they'll be cut to pieces."[10] We have no information on Cavender's reaction. However, regardless of their feelings, both colonels began to issue orders to carry out this directive.

Wire communication, which had been cut by German artillery fire, had been restored between the two regiments, and the two regimental commanders conferred briefly by phone. They agreed that they would each move at dawn, but that the 423d would move first. This seeming contradiction probably means that they agreed that they would move simultaneously, which automatically put the 423d in the lead. And evidently they agreed upon adjacent assembly areas. There appears to have been no further synchronization of effort.

In fact, the 422d began to move first. Leading elements seem to have been on the trails by dawn, shortly after 0730, and the main bodies of the regiment began to move at about 0900 with the 2d Battalion in the lead, followed by the 1st and then the 3d. There was a thick fog and steady rain; the trails and few roads were incredibly muddy. It was terribly slow going. The selected assembly areas, southeast of Schönberg, were only three to four miles from the starting positions, but the units didn't reach the bivouac area until dark. There was almost no enemy opposition, although the 1st Battalion had a few skirmishes on its right flank, south of Auw. This contact was enough to alert the Germans that the 422d seemed to be on the move.

For all the promises of Division, there had not yet been an airdrop, and food was short. Yet, despite the dreadful conditions, the men were generally cheerful. They had been told that when they attacked the next morning, there would be armored reinforcements hitting the Germans simultaneously from the west.

After dark Colonel Descheneaux held an officers' call, at which he issued orders for the attack on Schönberg the next morning. The 1st Battalion would be on the right, 2d Battalion on the left, 3d Battalion to the left (south) rear in reserve. He did not mention the 423d, because he did not know what the 423d would be doing. He had not spoken to Cavender since long before dawn, and the two regiments were now completely out of communication with each other, even though there was probably less than 500 yards between the left (south) of the 422d and the right of the 423d.

At dawn on 18 December the major elements of the 423d Combat Team were disposed in a rough perimeter defense as follows: The 3d Battalion was still in its Westwall fortifications just east of Halenfeld. The 590th Field Artillery Battalion was in positions in the 3d Battalion's area, also east of Halenfeld, the guns laid in the general direction of Schönberg to the northwest. The 1st Battalion was in and around Halenfeld, facing generally west. The 2d Battalion was south of Radscheid, facing north. The Regimental CP was with the 3d Battalion in the Westwall.

Colonel Cavender laid out the following route of march: Halenfeld-Oberlascheid-Radscheid-Schönberg. The order of march, largely dictated by locations, was the 2d Battalion, the 1st Battalion, Regimental Headquarters, the 3d Battalion, and the 590th Field Artillery. The 2d Battalion moved out at 1000 hours.

About noon the 2d Battalion received fire from Germans in and to the south of Radscheid. Lieutenant Colonel Puett characteristically attacked immediately to the southwest and drove the Germans from Radscheid. By 1400 the 2d Battalion had advanced as far as the Bleialf-Schönberg road. The attack was supported by A Battery of the 590th; the other batteries were on the road. But ammunition was short, and only a few artillery concentrations were fired. Then radio communications failed, and the 2d Battalion was without artillery support. Puett radioed regimental headquarters, recommending that a counterattack be made against the enemy right flank to the west, toward Bleialf, by one of the battalions behind him.

Cavender did not follow that recommendation, however, because he had just received a radio message from Division changing the previous order, which had been to take up preattack positions south of Schönberg for an attack the next day. Instead he was now directed to seize the town that day.[11]

Accordingly, he ordered the 3d Battalion, now at Oberlascheid, to push on directly for Schönberg, passing to the east of the 2d Battalion. The 1st Battalion sat on the trails for several hours without orders.

As German resistance to the 2d Battalion attack to the southwest increased, Cavender committed the 1st Battalion on Puett's left. By dusk a fierce battle was raging along the two-battalion front, but German reinforcements soon brought the American advance to a halt along a line that had stabilized about a mile southwest of Radscheid. In fact, the 2d Battalion had actually cut the Schönberg-Bleialf road, but was halted and thrown back by fire from German 20-mm self-propelled AAA guns.

Meanwhile, as ordered, Lt. Col. Klinck's 3d Battalion had pushed on to the north across the Skyline Drive toward Schönberg. Soon after that German resistance was encountered. Klinck pressed on, however, and by evening, against ever-increasing opposition, was within half a mile of Schönberg. He tried to report his situation to Cavender, but could not reach the regimental commander by radio. He sent runners, but these men never reached the regimental CP. However, shortly after dark a patrol from regimental headquarters found Klink's CP.

During the day Cavender had moved his CP to Oberlascheid. After dark he moved again, to a position just north of Radscheid. His quick estimate of the situation was as follows: Two battalions were engaged, facing southwest, in the opposite direction of his objective. One battalion was very close to the objective. His artillery was well in hand, in position near his CP, but almost out of ammunition. (By this time, all ammunition was in short supply.) Despite efforts to call by radio and patrols sent to the east, there was no contact with the neighboring 422d Infantry Regiment. At 2200 hours a message was received from Division: "Attack Schönberg, do maximum damage to enemy there, then attack toward St. Vith. This mission is of gravest importance to the nation. Good luck. Brock."[12] (Lieutenant Colonel Brock was the Division G-3.) Soon afterward another message came in, promising an early airdrop of food and ammunition in a spot just south of the 3d Battalion.

Before doing anything about these messages, Cavender decided to visit the 3d Battalion. After getting a report from Klinck, he issued his orders in response to the bombastic attack message he had received from Division. The 2d and 1st battalions were to disengage and to concentrate north of Radscheid, just behind the 3d Battalion. While the exhausted and battle-worn men of those battalions wearily trudged north in the dark through heavy mud, the 590th Field Artillery also displaced to new positions just northwest of the regimental CP. Except for the artillery, the regiment had no transportation. Any vehicles that had not run out of fuel were hopelessly bogged down in the mud. Thus Cavender had to abandon the hundreds of wounded men in the aid stations of the 1st and 2d battalions, along with their overworked surgeons and medics. Nevertheless, before dawn, the 423d Infantry was concentrated just south of Schönberg, ready to attack as ordered.

Colonel Cavender has been criticized, and with some reason, for his failure to make use of the 1st Battalion during the middle of the day on 18 December. On balance, however, given the circumstances and the orders he had received from Division, his performance warrants high marks. And so does the performance of his green, inexperienced, exhausted soldiers, who became veterans that long, cold, wet, hard-fighting day.

THE THIRD DAY ON THE RIGHT FLANK

At dawn on 18 December the 424th Infantry found itself with both flanks open. Colonel Reid knew that CCB/9 was somewhere to his north, and he assumed that the 112th Infantry of the 28th Division was somewhere to his south. In light of what had happened to the 112th on the two previous days, and the way that CCB/9 had performed on 17 December, he was less concerned about his left flank than he was about his right. In fact, he considered that his principal mission was to hold the right flank of the 106th Division sufficiently secure to provide a base for the counterattack he still expected the 9th Armored Division to make toward the Schnee Eifel.

There were no major German attacks on the 424th on 18 December. Enemy activity was focused either to the north or to the south. The three battalions licked their wounds, dug in on their new positions, and patrolled actively to the front and to the flanks. Around noon patrols from the 1st Battalion established contact with the 27th Armored Infantry of CCB/9 south of Maspelt. Shortly after dark, about 1800 hours, Reid reestablished contact with his liaison officer with the 112th Infantry, which was near Weiswampach. At about the same time patrols from his 2d Battalion finally made contact with the 1st Battalion of the 112th Infantry near Beiler, a village in the northern tip of Luxembourg.

Farther north, General Hoge had been worried by the fact that his left flank at Weppler was completely open. There was a gap of about three miles between the left rear of his 14th Tank Battalion and the right flank of the defenders of St. Vith. He had no contact with the 424th Infantry on his right.

After repelling a thrust of the 62d VGD across the Our at Steinebrück, Hoge decided in the early afternoon to pull back to a less exposed defensive position along the Neidingen Ridge. He put the right flank of the 27th Armored Infantry Battalion at Maspelt with orders to patrol aggressively south to regain contact with the 424th. His left flank linked up by patrols with the defenders of St. Vith in the north.

Late in the afternoon patrols from the 424th and the 27th Armored Infantry reestablished contact south of Maspelt. The 424th and CCB/9 were now an integral part of the defense of St. Vith. We shall return to them later. (See chapter 10.)

THE FOURTH DAY ON THE SCHNEE EIFEL

At 0610 on 19 December the 106th Division headquarters sent the following message to the 423d Infantry Regiment:

"Display 50-foot panel orange at (P962867) [these were the map coordinates of the point previously set for the airdrop]. Make every attempt to establish contact with the 422d Inf in regard to dropped supplies."

There was no response. The message was repeated every fifteen minutes throughout the day and the following night.

Having received no word from the regiments, and without information about the airdrops from Corps, at 1430 Division sent a message to VIII Corps: "Please advise at once if supplies were dropped to units this division in vicinity Schönberg." At 2200 the following reply was received: "Supplies have not been dropped. Will be dropped tomorrow, weather permitting."[13]

At daybreak on 19 December, the 423d Infantry Regiment, which had been expecting the airdrop that never came, was concentrated just to the south and east of Schönberg. The regiment was at about half strength. The 3d Battalion, on the left, had not suffered severe casualties in the previous days of fighting, and so was near full strength. To its right was the 1st Battalion, which also had not suffered severe casualties, but had misplaced two companies. Still farther to the right and slightly to the rear was the 2d Battalion, which had been in near-continuous combat for three days, and was at about half strength. Both the 1st and 2d battalions were exhausted by their march through the mud after a full day of fighting. All three battalions were practically out of mortar and machine-gun ammunition, but were in pretty good shape with .30-caliber rifle ammunition. Just behind them was the 590th Field Artillery Battalion, which had only 300 rounds left.

At 0830 Cavender called his battalion commanders together and issued his orders. He told them the situation as he knew it, and then ordered an attack in line of battalions, in echelon, beginning with the 3d Battalion on the left. The 2d Battalion, while moving on line with the others, was to be in reserve and was not to attack without orders. The 3d Battalion attack was to begin at 1000 hours. Cavender coordinated their watches at 0900. At that moment a volley from a German artillery battery dropped on the regimental CP, killing and wounding several officers and men, including Lieutenant Colonel Craig, the 1st Battalion commander. The others dashed for cover.

This was the beginning of a thirty-minute barrage. When the fire lifted, a German infantry attack of at least battalion strength from the direction of Bleialf followed. Cavender's reaction was praiseworthy. He ordered the battalion commanders to deploy covering forces to their left rear, but to continue the attack as ordered. The 590th Artillery positions were overrun before the guns could be destroyed, but the German attack was halted all along the line.

Lieutenant Colonel Klinck's 3d Battalion then began its attack at 1000, as scheduled. It quickly ran into opposition from the front, and then its left flank was again attacked by the Bleialf-based Germans. That attack was driven off, and two of Klinck's companies actually reached the outskirts of Schönberg. They were stopped there by heavy German artillery fire and an infantry counterattack. Klinck pulled his men back to a hill overlooking the southern edge of the town and dug in.

After Lieutenant Colonel Craig was mortally wounded, his executive, Maj. Carl H. Cosby, took command of the 1st Battalion. Despite casualties from the German barrage, Cosby moved his two companies to the start line, then received orders from Regiment to leave one company in regimental reserve, leaving only B Company for the attack. These men reached the Schönberg-Auw road, only to be halted by heavy infantry fire, followed by a tank attack. By noon B Company had ceased to exist. Cosby and a few survivors joined K Company of the 3d Battalion to their west.

The 2d Battalion moved out on schedule to reach its assigned position. From a hill overlooking the road, Lieutenant Colonel Puett could see Schönberg to the west. With no opposition in front of him, Puett felt he could mount a successful attack on the village. He sent a message to this effect by runner to Regiment, but received no response. By 1400 the aggressive Puett decided that he should attack. Shortly after he moved out, only 1,000 yards east of the town, the battalion was hit by heavy fire from the east. Puett responded to this unexpected attack commendably. But just as he was about to counterattack, he realized the fire was from the 422d Infantry. In a few minutes the situation was clarified, but both American units had been badly disorganized.

At 1600 hours Colonel Cavender, who was with Klinck's 3d Battalion, assessed his situation as follows: One battalion (the 1st) was wiped out. Another (the 2d) was out of communication, location unknown. He had lost his artillery. The 3d Battalion, under increasingly heavy attack by German artillery and small arms, was almost out of all ammunition. There was no water. The men had not eaten for more than twenty-four hours. The advancing Germans would probably overrun his position within half an hour. Reluctantly, he raised a white flag, and ordered his men to destroy their weapons.

Meanwhile, the 422d Infantry, undoubtedly being observed by German patrols, began to move from its bivouac area at 0730. It advanced generally to the northwest, intending to hit Schönberg from the east, with the 2d Battalion on the left, the 1st on the right, and the 3d following to left rear, in reserve. The leading battalions passed across the Skyline Drive around 0900 and began to run into opposition. Suddenly, from the direction of Auw, German tanks drove into the right flank of the 1st Battalion. (These were elements of the Führer Begleit Brigade moving toward St. Vith.) Within minutes, struck from front and flank simultaneously, the battalion was overwhelmed. Some survivors were able to join the 2d Battalion to their left. The others scattered or surrendered.

The 2d Battalion, meanwhile, had advanced quickly against light opposition, and came out into the open from the woods near the Andler-Schönberg road, about 1,000 yards northeast of Schönberg. The road in front of them was full of vehicles. Lt. Col. William D. Scales and his staff tried to determine if these were friendly or enemy vehicles but soon learned the hard way. They were raked by fire from several German FLAK half-tracks. Badly disorganized, the Americans fell back into the woods. Pursued by German infantrymen, the surviving Americans fell back to establish two small defensive perimeters, completely isolated from the rest of the regiment and from each other. For all practical purposes the 2d Battalion had ceased to exist.

The 3d Battalion, under Lt. Col. Donald F. Thompson, had moved across the Skyline Drive to the left of the 2d Battalion. They observed and opened fire on a body of armed men to the west, across the Linne Creek ravine. This was Puett's 2d Battalion of the 423d. By about 1400 hours the immediate damage from this tragic encounter had been ameliorated. Puett, who had long ago lost communication with Cavender, now learned that Colonel Descheneaux was with the 3d Battalion of the 422d. Puett reported to him and joined his battalion to the 422d.

Although under desultory German artillery fire, this combined two-battalion force of the 422d and 423d was for the moment not engaged directly with any enemy. That soon changed, as Germans closed in from all directions. Descheneaux now established a perimeter defense with his two battalions. It was about 1530 hours.

While Puett was out on a personal reconnaissance, Descheneaux pondered the situation. He was out of ammunition. His men had not eaten for more than twenty-four hours. There was no water. He sent out a white flag, ordered a cease fire, and told his men to destroy their weapons. Puett came back and was shocked to find that Descheneaux was in the process of surrendering. He asked permission to try to fight his way out with his battalion, but the colonel refused. He said it would only make matters worse. Puett, considering that he had received a direct order to surrender, nonetheless spread word through his battalion that any men who wanted to could try to escape. (Nearly 100 of them slipped away; a few of these got back to the American lines at St. Vith.) And so, at 1600 Lieutenant Colonel Nagle, the Regimental Executive, went out under a white flag to surrender the regiment to a German major. At almost exactly the same time Cavender was also surrendering.

Near Oberlascheid was Company A of the 423d Infantry, commanded by Captain Nauman, which had become lost early in the day. There were other rags and tags of units there, including part of F Company of the 422d. Major Sanda B. Helms, the S-4 (supply officer) of the 423d, took command of the group. Shortly after noon Helms and Nauman decided to try to work their way out, planning to move to the northeast between Auw and Schönberg. However, they soon ran into Germans and were broken up. One platoon of A Company, commanded by Lt. Harold A. McKinley, and the regimental I&R

Platoon, under Lt. Ivan H. Long, escaped from the debacle and joined forces. Moving only at night, and traveling generally west by compass, this small group of about forty men dribbled into St. Vith on 21 December.

A number of other American soldiers, some individually and some in small groups, also tried to work their way back to the American lines. A few made it; most did not. Of those that didn't, some were captured, others were killed.

One group, despairing of fighting their way out, seems to have decided to stay behind the German lines until the inevitable American counteroffensive rolled back to the German frontier. The leader of this group of probably no more than four or five men was apparently Lt. Eric Wood, Executive Officer of A Battery of the 589th Field Artillery, whom we last saw escaping capture at Schönberg on 17 December. How they subsisted is not known, but they seem to have killed a number of unsuspecting Germans in the wooded area around Meyerode and lived off captured German supplies and occasional handouts from Belgian farmers.[14] The Germans searched for them and killed them off one by one. The last to survive seems to have been Wood. The Germans never caught him, but they mortally wounded him, and his body was found after the Americans reoccupied the area in mid-January. Apparently he died shortly after the New Year.

7

FIGHTING FOR TIME ON THE "SKYLINE DRIVE"

THE 28TH DIVISION AND ITS OPPONENTS

Nearly half of the American front in the Ardennes on 16 December was held by one division, the veteran but battle-worn 28th Infantry Division (Pennsylvania National Guard), informally and somewhat lugubriously nicknamed the "Bloody Bucket" by relating the division's red keystone insignia to the heavy casualties it had suffered in Normandy and in fighting during the autumn on the German frontier (notably at Schmidt in early November). The 28th, commanded by Maj. Gen. Norman D. "Dutch" Cota, held a long sector, totaling thirty-seven kilometers (twenty-three miles).

The 28th Infantry Division, officially nicknamed the "Keystone Division," was first activated in August 1917 from Pennsylvania National Guard units. It was sent to France in May 1918 and entered combat in July. Deactivated in early 1919, it remained in existence as a National Guard division. The 28th was reactivated in February 1941 and after thirty months of training and organization was sent to Britain in autumn 1943.[1] The division arrived in Normandy on 22 July 1944, six weeks into the campaign. It was immediately committed to combat as part of the XIX Corps, but its initial attacks were unsuccessful and there were heavy casualties. The division commander was relieved and replaced by Major General Cota on 13 August.

Norman Daniel Cota was born on 30 May 1893 in Chelsea, Massachussetts. He and his classmates graduated from West Point two months early, on 20 April 1917, due to U.S. entry into World War I earlier that month. Assigned to the 22d Infantry Regiment, Cota spent the war training recruits and so, to his regret, did not see action. His career between the wars was the usual mix of staff, troop, and school assignments. In November 1940, as a colonel, he became Chief of Staff of the 1st Infantry Division, and landed at

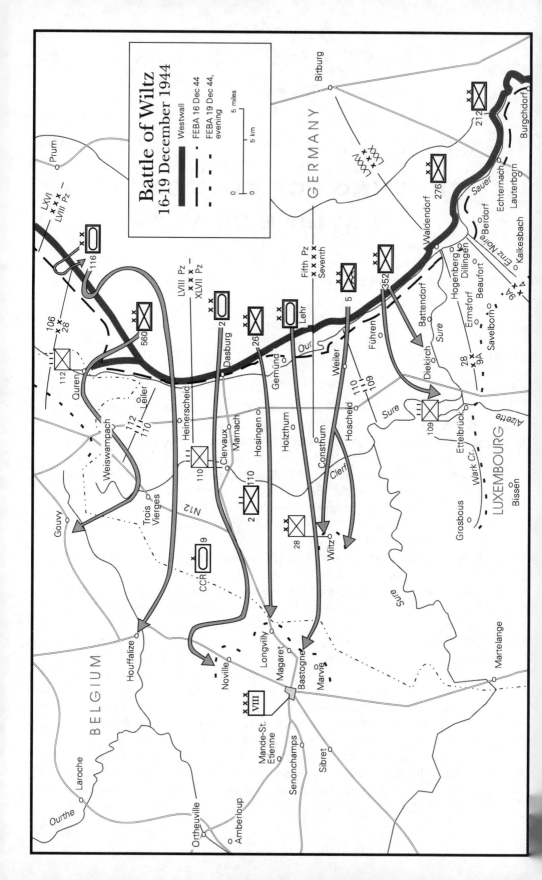

Oran in Algeria on 9 November 1942 as part of Operation Torch. Cota served with the 1st Division until February 1943, when his amphibious experience led to his appointment as U.S. adviser to Admiral Lord Louis Mountbatten, commander of British Combined Operations. Later that year, Cota was promoted to brigadier general and became Assistant Division Commander of the 29th Infantry Division. As commander of the division's assault elements, he was the first U.S. general officer to land on Omaha Beach on 6 June. On 13 August, Cota became commander of the 28th Division.[2]

Under Cota's leadership, the 28th Division took part in the pursuit of the beaten German forces across France in August and September, and paraded through Paris on 29 August. By the beginning of autumn Cota's division was pushing through Luxembourg as part of the V Corps. The division took part in fighting along the Westwall, or "Siegfried Line," in September and October as part of the V Corps offensive. In late October, the 28th Division was shifted northward and committed to an offensive against German forces in the Hürtgen Forest. Beginning on 2 November, the division spent two weeks unsuccessfully battering its way toward Schmidt. Despite Cota's valiant and determined efforts, the 28th made little progress and suffered very heavy casualties. Finally, on 19 November, the division was transferred south to the quiet VIII Corps sector in Luxembourg. There Cota devoted himself to rebuilding the 28th, absorbing the extensive replacements made necessary by the losses suffered at Schmidt, and trying to revive the division's shaken morale.

The 28th Division's putative main line of resistance stretched along the highway leading south from St. Vith through the villages of Heinerscheid, Fischbach, Hosingen, and Hoscheid, then through Diekirch and into the 9th Armored Division's sector near Medernach. Since the road ran along a ridgeline three to six kilometers west of the Our River in a manner reminiscent of the scenic Skyline Drive above the Shenandoah valley in Virginia, the troops nicknamed it the "Skyline Drive."

Although the 28th held the high ground above the west side of the narrow, steep-sided Our valley, it was in an unenviable tactical position to withstand a major German attack. The best route of lateral communication in the division's sector was Skyline Drive itself, and because of the length of front he was supposed to cover, General Cota had committed all three of the division's infantry regiments (the 112th, 110th, and 109th) in line, north to south, holding out only one battalion (from the 110th) in reserve. With all three regiments deployed along the front, and with limited lateral communications, Cota's division could not possibly concentrate against a major enemy threat. Moreover, if the Germans broke through anywhere along this thin cordon front, the 28th would have little capability to plug the hole or restore a continuous front line.

The 112th Infantry, under Col. Gustin M. Nelson, held the northernmost sector, just south of the 106th Infantry Division's positions in the Schnee

Eifel.[3] Nelson was a member of the West Point Class of 1921, which had only seventeen graduates—the smallest West Point class of the twentieth century—due to readjustments of the Military Academy as it returned to normal after World War I. The 112th's sector ran roughly southwest from Lützkampen to the vicinity of Kalborn, a distance of about six kilometers (3.75 miles). Half of this front lay on the east bank of the Our, held by the 1st Battalion (around Lützkampen) and the 3d Battalion (around Sevenig). The 2d Battalion, serving as regimental reserve, had its main position around and to the south of Leiler, along the Skyline Drive. The 2d Battalion's outpost line on the Our, like that of the other two regiments to the south, was manned only during daylight, and German patrols roamed relatively freely through the Our valley in front of Leiler during the hours of darkness.

The 110th Infantry, commanded by Col. Hurley E. Fuller, holding the line just to the south, covered a much larger sector than did the 112th.[4] Its front ran for more than fifteen kilometers (9.4 miles) from Kalborn south to Stolzembourg. There was a thin screen of outposts along the west bank of the Our, but the regiment's main positions were in a line of village strongpoints, each held by about a company.[5] The gaps between these village strongpoints were covered by patrols, but no troops held those areas permanently. Worse, there was no regimental reserve to backstop this long, intermittent line: The 110th's 2d Battalion had been detached by General Cota to form the division reserve, and was located just west of the 110th's command post (CP) at Clervaux.[6]

The 109th Infantry, next in line, led by Lt. Col. James E. Rudder, held the southern portion of the division's sector, occupying positions along 16.5 kilometers (10.3 miles) of wooded heights above the west bank of the Our as it bent south-southeastward toward Echternach. Before he was given command of the 109th, Rudder had led the 2d Ranger Battalion in its epic battle during the assault landing at Pointe du Hoc, on the western flank of Omaha Beach at the start of D-Day. Twice wounded in that desperate battle, he had also won the Distinguished Service Cross.

Although the 109th covered a slightly longer front than did the 110th, it at least had all three of its battalions available, with the 1st Battalion in regimental reserve.[7] The 2/109th held the northern part of the regiment's sector, from Stolzembourg south to Longsdorf and Bettel, while the 3/109th held the line from Bettel to positions opposite Wallendorf on the German side of the Our, where the Clerf River flows into the Our. Still, like the neighboring 110th Infantry, Colonel Rudder's men could cover neither the Our River line nor the gaps between their company strongpoints twenty-four hours a day.

Facing the 28th Division were large German forces, comprising the bulk of General von Manteuffel's Fifth Panzer Army. By mid-December, the two divisions (one panzer, one volksgrenadier) of General Walter Krüger's LVIII Panzer Corps were deployed opposite the 28th's 112th Infantry and the 106th Division's 424th Infantry. Born at Zeitz in Saxony on 23 March 1892, Krüger had served in combat as a junior cavalry officer during World War I. At the start of World War II he was a colonel, commanding Infanterie Regiment 171, part of the 56th Infantry Division, during the Polish campaign. After further service in the French campaign and the opening stages of the invasion of the Soviet Union, he was made commander of the 1st Panzer Division in July 1941 and promoted to generalleutnant in October 1942. Krüger had been made commander of the LVIII Panzer Corps on 1 January 1944 and was promoted to general der panzertruppen the following month.[8]

South of Krüger's LVIII Panzer Corps sector lay General der Panzertruppen Heinrich Freiherr von Lüttwitz's XLVII Panzer Corps with three divisions, two panzer and one volksgrenadier. Born in Krumpach in Silesia on 6 December 1896, Lüttwitz had, like Krüger, been a cavalry officer during World War I, and as a lieutenant colonel he commanded the 1st Panzer Division's 1st Reconnaissance Battalion during the Polish and French campaigns. In late summer 1940 he was promoted to colonel and took command of the 59th Rifle Regiment in the newly formed 20th Panzer Division. Shortly after the invasion of the Soviet Union, Lüttwitz became commander of the 20th Panzer and led it on the eastern front for the next thirty months. In February 1944 he took command of the veteran 2d Panzer Division, which he led through the Normandy campaign. Promoted to general der panzertruppen, he took command of the XLVII Panzer Corps the following September.[9] Tall and stocky, Lüttwitz wore a monocle and affected the image of an old-fashioned Prussian cavalryman. Remarkably for a man of his belligerent mannerisms, he had a reputation within the army of being especially kind to his troops. He was also a combat commander of considerable experience, but his performance in the Ardennes could lead an objective observer to conclude that he was past his prime.

The southern boundary of the XLVII Corps also marked the southern boundary of Fifth Panzer Army's sector. To its south was General Erich Brandenberger's Seventh Army, which contained four divisions in two corps. The Seventh Army's northern wing comprised General der Infanterie Baptist Kniess's LXXXV Corps. Kniess was born on 17 April 1885 in Grünstadt in the Rhenish Palatinate. He joined the 5th (Bavarian) Infantry Regiment as an officer-candidate in 1906 and saw considerable active service as a junior officer in World War I. Selected as an officer for the Reichswehr, he served in infantry units between the wars, rising to generalmajor on 1 June 1938. He commanded the 215th Infantry Division in the 1940 campaign in the Low Countries and France and in the opening stages of the invasion of Russia, and was promoted to generalleutnant in July 1940. Named commander of the LXVI Corps in November 1942, he was promoted to general der infanterie the following month. Kniess held a series of corps command and senior staff appointments over the next two years before his appointment to command the LXXXV Corps on 10 August 1944.[10]

The LXXXV Corps's two divisions, the 5th Fallschirmjäger (literally

"Parachute Light Infantry," but often simply translated as "Parachute") and 352d Volksgrenadier, faced most of the 109th Infantry's sector. The extreme right, or northern, wing of the LXXX Corps to the south would brush the southern flank of the 109th, in the Bettendorf-Eppeldorf area.

All of this meant that the 17,000-odd personnel of the 28th Division and its attached units faced three panzer divisions, three volksgrenadier divisions, and the 5th Parachute Division, plus supporting artillery and engineer units, totaling something over 110,000 men. Unfortunately for the 28th Division, but perhaps fortunately for the short-term peace of mind of its officers and men, the onset of the German offensive came as a great surprise to the Americans.

THE ONSLAUGHT BEGINS

The assault by the Fifth Panzer Army and the Seventh Army against the thinly held 28th Division sector began at 0530, two hours before dawn on 16 December, with a furious thirty-minute artillery bombardment. Although the artillery onslaught marked the formal beginning of the offensive, elements of the Fifth Panzer Army had begun their tasks shortly after midnight, moving into assault positions and infiltrating the American front line. Most of the infiltration effort and nearly all of the artillery preparation was directed against the positions of the 112th and 110th Infantry. The 560th Volksgrenadier Division (VGD), slated to attack the 112th Infantry in the north, was supposed to infiltrate the U.S. positions and seize two bridges across the Our River near Ouren by surprise. Consequently, the 112th's outpost line reported seeing gun flashes and hearing fire to the south, which gave them some warning that trouble was on the way.

Some sections of the 28th Division's front line had more detailed indication that something was up. Private Clarence Blakeslee, a native of Rockford, Michigan, assigned to M Company (heavy weapons) of the 112th Infantry, was given the mission of spotting German gun positions from their muzzle flashes and the sound of their fire. His reports, including some that indicated increased truck traffic, were well received at 3d Battalion headquarters, and earned him a citation. Unable to sleep on the night of 15–16 December, he had left his dugout to go forward and see what was happening. He noticed the Germans were creating "artifical moonlight" by shining antiaircraft searchlights off the low-hanging clouds. Blakeslee returned to his dugout and told his fellow soldiers there to keep their shoes on because something was up. One buddy told him to "quit scaring the men." (There were many new men in his unit, replacements who had arrived since the division withdrew from the Hürtgen Forest.) Blakeslee replied that the Germans weren't doing this just to be nice, and hurried outside to the perimeter to listen.

He soon heard several German voices and frequent mention of someone named Carl, whom Blakeslee surmised was their leader. He found a sentry post and borrowed their field telephone to call the M Company CP. The lieutenant he talked to was initially reluctant to alert the company, but Blakeslee's previously established reliability, and the details he was able to provide evidently persuaded him, and he told Blakeslee to "stick with them and I will alert the company." Blakeslee followed the Germans as they infiltrated the U.S. lines and made their way between the mortar positions and the cook tent. By this time the sky was growing light and Blakeslee was crawling to avoid being seen. Someone from neighboring K Company fired his carbine at the Germans; they turned and bolted for their lines, barely avoiding Blakeslee as they hurried past. As he recalled later, this experience gave him "a front center seat" for the start of the Battle of the Bulge.[11]

Krüger's LVIII Panzer Corps had two divisions: the 116th Panzer and the 560th VGD. The 560th had been activated from garrison and occupation troops in Norway in October, and contained the 1128th, 1129th, and 1130th Grenadier regiments. The division was nearly up to strength in manpower (9,150 of 10,500) and most equipment, but transportation difficulties meant that by mid-December the 1129th Grenadier Regiment, the self-propelled antitank gun and FLAK companies, and one of the four artillery battalions were still not present in the LVIII Panzer Corps area, and did not join the division until 20 December.[12]

When the infantry of the 560th VGD attacked the 112th's positions, they managed to overrun two company kitchens. One platoon reached a small stone bridge south of Ouren, where it was repulsed and dispersed. The Americans commented afterward that the attackers seemed "awfully green," and indeed many of the German infantrymen were poorly trained and inexperienced.[13]

At Ouren, where the main body of the 112th Infantry's Cannon Company occupied the town itself (along with the regimental headquarters), the German infantry attack across the Our bridge was shredded by heavy machine-gun fire.[14] Again, the tactics of the German assault troops were clumsy. "The Germans were so bunched up, almost marching in a column of twos, that some of the men thought for a moment they might be prisoners coming to the rear," recalled Lt. Richard V. Purcell, the Cannon Company's executive officer and reconnaissance officer, in a combat interview soon after the battle. The Cannon Company quickly realized the Germans were not POWs, Purcell went on, and ". . . everybody, including the three .50 caliber machine guns, opened up all at once on the enemy on the bridge, and they were literally 'mown down.'" That effectively ended the German efforts against Ouren, at least for the time being. Elsewhere in the 112th's sector, the situation was similar. The German attacks were heavy, but generally had not seriously threatened U.S. positions.

Farther south in the 110th Infantry's sector, the artillery bombardment was intense but brief; most of the German guns and Nebelwerfer (rocket launchers) had only enough ammunition to fire for half an hour. By 0600 or a little later, the bombardment had tapered off to sporadic salvos and single shots. The German preparatory fire had been less effective than the Germans hoped. Their artillerymen (especially their forward observers) were inexperienced and indifferently trained; the artillery units had been prohibited from registering on likely targets by the desire for surprise; and the assault companies, especially those of the 560th VGD, were slow in following the preparation. Consequently, the startled American defenders were given a valuable opportunity to recover before the infantry battle began.

In contrast to the situation with the 560th VGD, the attack of Col. Heinz Kokott's 26th VGD was more polished and considerably more effective. As the 26th Infantry Division, containing the 39th, 77th, and 78th Grenadier regiments, it had been a prewar Regular Army division.[15] Its home depot was at Cologne, and its personnel were drawn originally from Prussia and the nearby Rhineland. After limited participation in the 1940 campaign, it saw extensive action in Russia, and took part in the Kursk offensive in early July 1943, where it suffered heavy casualties. Between June 1941 and early 1944 the division was destroyed and rebuilt no less than six times, an indication of its involvement in continuing heavy combat.

The 26th was destroyed a seventh time in late August 1944 on the eastern front, and was rebuilt later that month in Holland, employing a large cadre of survivors from the "old" division and the still-forming 582d Division. In addition to its core of veterans, the 26th was blessed with an unusually able and talented commander, Col. Heinz Kokott.[16]

Kokott was born on 14 November 1890 in Gross Strelitz. After service in World War I, he was selected as an officer for the Reichswehr. By training an infantryman, he commanded the 2d Battalion of the 196th Infantry Regiment (part of the 68th Infantry Division) in the 1940 campaign in France and during the first months of the invasion of Russia the next July, and was promoted to lieutenant colonel in October 1941. He commanded the 176th Infantry in the 61st Infantry Division from December 1941 to May 1942 and then, following his promotion to colonel (April 1942), commanded the 337th Infantry in the 208th Infantry Division until June 1943. Kokott next served as commandant of Infantry Officer-Candidate School No. 6, and commanded the 1135th Grenadier Brigade for a few weeks during July and August 1944. He then took command of the 26th VGD just after its seventh "destruction" in late August 1944. With a slight build and scholarly visage, Kokott was physically unimpressive. He had an even temperament and was able to coordinate the activities of several different military units engaged in battle.

By mid-December the 26th VGD contained nearly 10,600 men in the standard seven infantry battalions of a volksgrenadier division. (It has often been inaccurately reported that the 26th VGD contained 17,000 men and nine infantry battalions.) The division's antitank battalion had fourteen JgPz-38(t) tank destroyers.

Colonel Kokott had taken advantage of the American habit of occupying the outpost line only during daylight. (To be fair to General Cota and to Colonel Fuller, the 110th Infantry had fewer than sixty infantrymen to cover each kilometer of front, and simply lacked the manpower to hold both the outpost line and its main positions twenty-four hours a day.) After dark on the evening of 15 December Kokott's patrols, heavily reinforced, pushed into the two-to three-kilometer zone between the Our River and Skyline Drive just to the west. About 0300 on 16 December, the 26th VGD's engineers began ferrying the division's assault companies across the Our in inflatable boats, and these units moved rapidly inland. By the time the bombardment began at 0530, Kokott had most of the 77th Grenadier Regiment (GR) formed in front of Hosingen and K Company's positions, and the 39th Fusilier Regiment (FusR) slightly to the south and rear in the woods just north of Wahlhausen. Colonel Kokott's operational timetable required his division to be across the Clerf River, eight to ten kilometers west of the Our, by the end of the first day. Accordingly, he directed the 77th GR to seize the bridge across the Clerf at Drauffelt, while the 39th FusR slipped past the American-held villages to its front and seized the Clerf crossings at Wilwerwiltz and Lellingen.

The 26th VGD's advance was frustrated by unexpectedly stubborn American resistance and hampered by other unforeseen problems. The narrow, winding, and muddy roads leading west from the Our River to the Skyline Drive were clogged by mines and other manmade obstacles emplaced by the Americans. German engineers were unable to complete the bridge over the Our at Gemünd until after nightfall, when at last the 26th Aufklärungs Abteilung (armored reconnaissance battalion) and a reinforced company from the 2d Panzer Division's 2d Panzer Aufklärungs Abteilung moved west across the bridge. Although troops of the 26th VGD captured Buchholz and Holzthum, the fortified American position at Hosingen held out. The Germans' failure to open the road through Hosingen created severe traffic jams to the east, delaying the movement of the 26th VGD's artillery as well as elements of the 2d Panzer Division.

The 2d Panzer Division was the second-oldest panzer division in the Wehrmacht, having been established under the command of then-Colonel Heinz Guderian in the fall of 1935.[17] After the Anschluss in 1938 the division was moved into Wehrkreis (Mobilization District) XVII in Austria and began recruiting Austrians. The 2d Panzer served with distinction in Poland in 1939 and then in France in 1940. The division also took part in the invasion of the Balkans in early 1941 and then was shifted to Russia in September. Subsequently it served primarily in Army Group Center, and in July 1943 took part in the Kursk offensive (Operation Zitadelle) as part of Gen. Walter Model's Ninth Army. The 2d Panzer was transferred from the middle Dnieper to France in midspring 1944, shortly before the Allied landings in Normandy. It was badly mauled in Normandy and during the retreat across northern France that summer, but was refitted and reorganized in September. Although its pool of experienced officers and enlisted personnel was greatly reduced, most of the replacements were of better than average quality. Because the division was short more than 300 trucks the II Battalion of the 304th Panzergrenadier Regiment was mounted largely on bicycles (the I Battalion was in half-tracked carriers). By mid-December the division's strength stood at 12,700 officers and men with another 1,800 in attached units. Its armored strength totaled seventy-two tanks and thirty-odd assault guns, and the artillery regiment had several batteries of 170-mm guns and 210-mm howitzers attached. General George S. Patton called it "one of the best god-damned panzer divisions in the German army."

Unlike Lieutenant General von Lüttwitz, Col. Meinrad von Lauchert (born at Potsdam, outside Berlin, on 29 August 1905, and thus one of the youngest division commanders on either side during the Ardennes campaign) had been too young to see action in World War I.[18] He had joined the 5th Cavalry Regiment in 1924, and then transferred to the infant panzer force in the mid-1930s. He led the I Battalion of the 4th Panzer Division's 35th Panzer Regiment in Poland and France, and by May 1943 commanded the 35th. While leading the 35th, and later the 15th Panzer Regiment of the 11th Panzer Division, von Lauchert gained an impressive reputation as a hard-driving, cunning, and talented panzer commander. He had been appointed to command the 2d Panzer only one day before the Ardennes attack was due to begin. His extensive eastern front experience as an armor leader would serve him well in coming days.

As the traffic jams near the Our River delayed the mass of the 2d Panzer, leading elements of that division's Kampfgruppe Cochenhausen crossed the river in inflatable boats and pushed forward swiftly, reaching Marnach about 0800.[19] Without their heavy weapons and self-propelled guns, however, the German battalions made little progress against the resolute and well-entrenched American defenders. Uncoordinated but moderately successful counterattacks by tanks of the 707th Tank Battalion threw the panzer-grenadiers into disorder, and temporarily left them scattered across the countryside in front of Marnach. In the meantime, German engineers had thrown a tank bridge across the Our at Dasburg (about 4.5 kilometers east of Marnach). This, coupled with the late-opening bridge at Gemünd six kilometers to the south (where the Panzer Lehr Division was waiting to cross), at last allowed large numbers of German vehicles and heavy equipment across the Our. Shortly before dusk German tanks of the 3d Panzer Regiment and other armored vehicles began moving forward against the American positions. With this added support, other units of the 2d Panzer overwhelmed the defenders of Marnach soon after dusk, and pushed toward the headquarters of the 110th Infantry at Clervaux, barely 2,000 meters west of Marnach.

The Panzer Lehr Division, which would play an important role in the Ardennes campaign, had been activated in early winter 1944 from several Lehr (demonstration and training) units.[20] Only a few of these units had been in combat, and as a result the division's personnel were exceptionally well trained but untested. Although the new division was numbered as the 130th Panzer Division, it was usually known (both informally and officially) as Panzer Division Lehr.

After it was formed, Panzer Lehr was dispatched to France, and fought in Normandy in June 1944. Unique among Wehrmacht or SS panzer divisions, all four of Panzer Lehr's panzergrenadier battalions were mounted in half-tracked carriers (most other divisions had only one half-tracked battalion). Unfortunately for Panzer Lehr, however, its divisional boundaries conformed almost exactly to the zone selected by the Americans for "carpet bombing" near St. Lô on 25 July 1944, and the proud division was almost destroyed in that cataclysm and the ensuing U.S. ground attack.

Although only partially rebuilt by early autumn, Panzer Lehr was committed to combat in early November near the Saar, and once more suffered heavy losses. Again hurriedly rebuilt by mid-December, the division's overall strength had reached nearly 12,700 officers and men with another 2,200 in attached units. Its infantry units were short of riflemen, and many of its newer replacement officers and men were of indifferent quality. With a weak panzer regiment of only fifty-four tanks, the division was reinforced with close to forty assault guns and tank destroyers, which did much to alleviate the shortage of tanks.

Panzer Lehr's commander, Lt. Gen. Fritz Bayerlein, was born in Würzburg in Lower Franconia on 14 January 1899.[21] Like most men of his generation, he fought in the later stages of World War I, serving as an officer-candidate (fahnenjunker) in the 2d Jäger Battalion on the western front. After a brief sojourn in civilian life, he joined the new Reichswehr in 1921 and was commissioned a lieutenant in the 21st Infantry Regiment on 21 January 1922. During the next sixteen years, Bayerlein rose slowly through the ranks of Germany's small peacetime army. Promoted to major, he was posted to the new 3d Panzer Division as a staff officer in 1938, beginning a long-term association with that division and with Germany's new mechanized forces.

Bayerlein served with the 3d Panzer in the Polish campaign and then joined the staff of Gen. Heinz Guderian's Panzer Corps for the campaign in the Low Countries and France. Promoted to lieutenant colonel in September 1940, he became a staff officer with Guderian's Second Panzergruppe (panzer army) in early 1941, as it was preparing for the invasion of the Soviet Union. Bayerlein saw action during the opening stages of Operation Barbarossa, but was sent to Libya as a staff officer with the Afrika Corps in September. His service in North Africa won him the Knight's Cross (Ritterkreuz) on 26 December 1941 and appointment as Chief of Staff of the Afrika Corps a few weeks later. He was promoted to colonel on 1 April 1942. Following the devastating British offensive at El Alamein, Bayerlein, now a generalmajor, briefly commanded the Afrika Corps when its commander, General Nehring, was wounded and evacuated to Europe. Bayerlein himself was wounded and evacuated to Italy shortly before the Axis forces in Tunisia surrendered in early May 1943.

After his recovery, Bayerlein took command of the 3d Panzer Division in Russia in early August 1943, and saw considerable combat under Army Group South in operations around Kharkov and in the Ukraine. On 4 February 1944 he took command of the newly formed Panzer Lehr Division. While preparing it for combat in France, he was promoted to generalleutnant on 1 May. Bayerlein led his well-equipped division in hard fighting in Normandy, largely in the western sector of the front, facing the Americans, until it was virtually destroyed near St. Lô.

A genial and relatively easygoing man, Bayerlein was a field commander with considerable concern for his troops. His experiences in Normandy, especially dealing with the overwhelming effect of Allied airpower, followed by the bitter defeats of the Lorraine campaign, forced him to conclude that the war was lost. This assessment may have contributed to his somewhat lackluster leadership during the Ardennes offensive, in sharp contrast to his distinguished earlier record.

On the American side, the experience at Hosingen of Company K of the 3d Battalion, 110th Infantry, was typical of what happened to American company posts near and along Skyline Drive during the first days of the German offensive. Company K had suffered heavy casualties in the fighting around Schmidt during the Hürtgen Forest battles in November, but with replacements had been rebuilt to a strength of 160 officers and men.[22] Like several other companies in the 109th and 110th Infantry regiments, the company was covering a sector far too wide for its resources, in this case, nearly two miles of front. Situated on a ridge about 6.5 kilometers west of the Our River, Hosingen was little damaged when K Company arrived with the rest of the 28th Division in mid-November. Skyline Drive ran through the center of town. Without sufficient manpower to cover his assigned sector, K Company's commander, Capt. Frederick Feiker, elected to concentrate his defenses in Hosingen proper. The company's slender resources were supported by a thirty-man platoon from the 110th's Antitank Company with three 57-mm antitank guns and three .50-caliber machine guns. Despite considerable contact with German patrols on the west side of the Our, one of the last reports Company K received from Division before the attack rated the 26th VGD as capable of little more than vigorous patrol work.

The officers and men of Company K heard some vehicle sounds on the evening of 15 December and also saw German searchlights shining on the low cloud cover to provide reflected light. Beginning at 0530 on 16 December they were subjected to a forty-five-minute artillery barrage. In the first hour after the German artillery fire ended, the U.S. troops heard German infantry moving up the draws and ravines toward Hosingen, but there was no visual contact with the enemy since dawn wasn't until 0730.

As dawn broke the Americans could see some of the German activity and began firing mortars and machine guns. They had considerable success on the north side of Hosingen in pinning down the advancing infantry and halting the German advance. To the south of town, the first German infantry rush carried the attackers around and over the platoon from the regimental antitank company and K Company's own 3d Platoon, which were cut off from the troops holding Hosingen. Since the southern outskirts of the village lay astride an east-west road now identified by the Americans as one of the 26th VGD's main supply routes, this area received unusually vigorous German attention. Captain Feiker called for artillery fire in that area, where he could see heavy German traffic heading west from the Our. Surprisingly, however, there was no fire from U.S. guns.

A little after 0800 the defenders of Hosingen realized that they were surrounded. Feiker established a perimeter defense, aided by a handful of engineers from B Company of the 103d Engineer Combat Battalion, who had been busy doing road maintenance on Skyline Drive. The Germans did not attack, however; they simply bypassed Hosingen to the north and the south. About 1600 a platoon of five American M-4 Sherman tanks of the 707th Tank Battalion entered Hosingen from the north along Skyline Drive. The tankers, under 1st Lt. Robert A. Payne, were pleasantly surprised to find U.S. troops in town. Three tanks of this platoon went south of Hosingen to harass the Germans' supply route while the other two remained in town. The three tanks south of the village were driven back into Hosingen when two German tanks got into position on the high ground southeast of town. These German tanks were identified as "Tigers" by the Americans, but were probably Panthers or PzKw-IVHs. Although K Company and Lieutenant Payne's tanks received sporadic small-arms and automatic-weapons fire, no serious attack was made against the town during the night.

Meanwhile, in the 109th Infantry's sector between Stolzembourg and Wallendorf, just south of the 110th's shattered lines, the 5th Parachute Division and the 352d VGD of the LXXXV Corps pushed across the Our, the paratroopers advancing some seven kilometers. The 5th Parachute Division had been formed as part of a general large-scale expansion of Luftwaffe ground combat forces in late 1943.[23] Assembled and organized near Reims, the division was built around a cadre of experienced personnel, especially the 3d battalions of the 3d and 4th Parachute regiments of the 1st Parachute Division. In early 1944, the division was transferred to Brittany for training, and was committed to combat in Normandy alongside the 3d Parachute Division in early June. After fighting through most of the Normandy campaign, the division was essentially destroyed in the Falaise Pocket in mid-August.

The 5th Parachute Division was rebuilt in Germany and Holland that autumn, employing large numbers of Luftwaffe ground personnel and a woefully small cadre of veterans. By early December the 5th was considered ready for action with a total of 13,500 officers and men in the division and another 2,800 in attached units. However, it lacked sufficient motor transport assets. Less than a week before the start of the Ardennes offensive the division commander was relieved and replaced by Colonel Ludwig Heilmann, who although a veteran officer with considerable combat experience, was unknown to, and soon became unpopular with, the officers of the division.

Heilmann was born near Würzburg in Franconia in August 1903, and volunteered for duty in the Reichswehr shortly after his eighteenth birthday. He served twelve years as an enlisted man, and in 1934 was commissioned an officer as part of the early stages of the army's expansion following Hitler's accession to power. By 1939 Heilmann was a captain and company commander in the 21st Infantry Regiment, and saw considerable action in Poland and France. Attracted by the exploits of the new parachute troops in Belgium in 1940, he volunteered for parachute duty and was accepted. After completing parachute training, Heilmann, now a major, joined the 3d Parachute Regiment (FJR) as commander of its 3d Battalion. His first combat action came in the air assault on Crete (20–31 May 1941), where he was involved in particularly bitter fighting around Galatas and Daratso.

In Russia, Heilmann's battalion was committed to battle near Leningrad, and performed with exceptional skill and bravery at the Vysborgskaya bridgehead in October 1941. After rest and refit in France, Heilmann and his regiment returned to Russia and fought at Velikiye Luki and Orel in the summer and autumn of 1942. In December 1942 Heilmann and the regiment returned to France and took part in a reorganization that abolished the old 7th Flieger (Flying) Division and created the 1st and 2d Parachute divisions. In the ensuing command shuffle, Heilmann was appointed commander of 3d FJR of the 1st Parachute Division. Designated a strategic reserve for the Mediterranean theater of war, elements of the division were committed to Sicily in response to the Allied invasion of 10 July 1943.

On 12 July, Heilmann led his regiment in a parachute assault on the Catania Plain in southeastern Sicily, landing at the same time as, and within a few miles of, British airborne troops. The ensuing fighting, especially the struggles for the crossings of the Simeto, Marcelliono, and Malati Rivers, considerably enhanced his reputation as a tactician and battlefield leader. Heilmann's regiment was one of the last German units to leave Sicily during the night of 16–17 August. Subsequently it was committed to the defense of Italy against the northward Allied advance, fighting mostly on the Adriatic coast. Transferred to the Monte Cassino region in the west in December, Heilmann and his regiment held that formidable mountain stronghold for almost six months, repelling three major Allied assaults, before evacuating their positions there on 17 May 1944.

After the fall of Rome and the German retreat to the Gustav Line in northern Italy, Heilmann was sent north to command the re-forming 5th Parachute Division. Since the 5th FJD was missing its divisional reconnaissance company, Heilmann improvised a replacement by contriving to motorize one of his infantry battalions.

After crossing the Our River on 16 December, the 5th Parachute's 15th Parachute Regiment, reinforced by the division's engineer battalion, captured Vianden, four kilometers south-southeast of Stolzembourg, and Walsdorf, 2,000 meters west of Vianden. At the same time, the 14th FJR, on the division's northern or right flank, captured the hamlet of Putscheid about three kilometers southeast of Weiler, but there was little contact between the two advancing columns of German paratroopers.

To the south of Heilmann's paratroopers, the 352d VGD, the left wing of the LXXXV Corps, advanced about six kilometers.[24] This division, comprising the 914th, 915th, and 916th Grenadier (infantry) regiments, had been activated in France as a static coast-defense unit in late 1943. Holding a section of shoreline in Normandy that closely corresponded to Omaha Beach, the division had stoutly contested the American landing, but was destroyed in the early stages of the Normandy campaign. The handful of survivors were withdrawn to the Flensburg-Schleswig area for refit in September 1944.

Strengthened by drafts of naval personnel in October, which brought the total strength to more than 10,000, the 352d VGD was moved into the Eifel region in November, occupying a section of front east of the Our River between Vianden and Echternach. Although its rank and file were poorly trained, and the division suffered from a lack of experienced officers and noncommissioned officers, it had at least had time to become familiar with the terrain in which it would operate during the offensive. By mid-December its self-propelled antitank company contained six JgPz-38(t)s, and the 352d's strength, including attached units, totaled 11,900 officers and men.

Leading the way, the 915th Grenadier Regiment captured Tandel, three kilometers northeast of Diekirch, on its right (northern) flank. This effectively isolated E Company, 2d Battalion, 110th Infantry, at Führen, barely 1,000 meters northeast of Tandel, since the 15th FJR was advancing north of Führen. The Germans, however, were advancing without most of their heavy equipment, which was still on the east bank of the Our, waiting for the necessary bridges to be completed.

THE SECOND DAY, 17 DECEMBER: THE PANZERS ENTER THE FRAY

By midnight on 16–17 December, General Cota knew that his division in general, and the 110th in particular, were in serious trouble. Particularly alarming was the presence of the 2d Panzer Division, identified in front of Marnach that afternoon. While the Americans still held most of Skyline Drive, they had lost Marnach, and German infantrymen were known to be moving cross-country through the 110th's entire sector. In an effort to restore the situation,

Cota organized a counterattack on the morning of 17 December. He committed his divisional reserve, the 2d Battalion, 110th Infantry, to this effort. The infantrymen, with little artillery and no tank support, were only able to advance about 1,000 yards from their start line, barely reaching the ridgeline between Urspelt and Reuler. The riflemen of the 2/110th were stopped cold by German mortar and machine-gun fire, and efforts to advance further were halted by German tanks and assault guns (part of the 2d Panzer Division, which had crossed the Our). By noon the attack had stalled completely and casualties were mounting.

Meanwhile, D Company of the 707th Tank Battalion, comprising seventeen M-5 Stuart tanks, pushed south along Skyline Drive from the 112th Infantry's sector. The tanks encountered German antitank guns near Heinerscheid (four kilometers north of Marnach and halfway to Weiswampach), and with their thin armor only five of them survived a ten-minute engagement with the Germans' deadly high-velocity guns. The survivors eventually withdrew to Urspelt, leaving a dozen burning or disabled tanks behind. They took position near the headquarters of the 2d Battalion, 110th Infantry, about two kilometers north-northeast of Clervaux.

Although General Cota's counterattack was repulsed, the situation was not much clearer to the German commanders. In the LVIII Panzer Corps sector, Col. Rudolf Bader's 560th VGD, continuing its attacks to gain the Our bridge at Ouren, made scant headway, while to the south the division's left wing closed on Heinerscheid. Colonel Kokott brought some order from the confusion on the 26th VGD's front in the XLVII Panzer Corps sector, and the American bottleneck at Hosingen was eliminated during the morning of 17 December. By afternoon, the 26th held bridgeheads across the Clerf River at Alscheid, Wilwerwiltz, Enscherange, and Drauffelt, and the leading elements of Gen. Fritz Bayerlein's Panzer Lehr Division, with the 26th Reconnaissance Battalion attached, were moving west of the Clerf toward the important crossroads at Bastogne. Colonel von Lauchert's 2d Panzer Division, advancing just to the north of Bayerlein's troops, spent the day battering its way into Clervaux. There, the dogged if disorganized defense of the town by elements of the 2/110th and fragments of other units continued until early morning on 18 December, when the survivors finally decamped westward toward Wiltz. The American defense of Clervaux prevented unarmored vehicles and unprotected infantry from moving through the town on the main road.

The situation of the 28th Division deteriorated steadily on 17 December. Elements of the 560th VGD finally captured the bridge at Ouren but were repulsed at Sevenig. Other units of the 560th, assisted by the 116th Panzer Division's reconnaissance battalion, took Heinerscheid in the afternoon from its defenders, A Company, 110th Infantry. Ironically, the bridge at Ouren was found too light to support tanks, and during the evening the 116th Panzer was diverted southward to utilize the bridge at Dasburg, on the road to Marnach, about eight kilometers south of Ouren.

The 116th Panzer Division, nicknamed the "Windhund (Greyhound) Division" and commanded by Generalmajor Siegfried von Waldenburg, was positioned around Leidenborn in mid-December. It had begun its existence as the 16th Motorized Infantry Division, formed in early 1940 from cadres of the 16th Infantry Division, a Prussian-Westphalian regular unit. The 16th Motorized took part in the fighting around Sedan in the Ardennes in May 1940 as part of Heinz Guderian's XIX Panzer Corps (and so was the only major unit to serve in both Ardennes campaigns!). The division also served in the Balkan campaign (April 1941) and in the invasion of Russia as part of Army Group South (June 1941). Redesignated a panzergrenadier division in late 1942, it fought with particular distinction throughout 1943.

Transferred to the west to refit, the division was reorganized as the 116th Panzer Division by expanding its panzer battalion to a regiment in early 1944. Thus restructured, the division fought in the Normandy campaign, where it suffered heavy losses of men and matériel. Hastily rebuilt around Düsseldorf, the 116th was bloodied again in the Hürtgen Forest in November, fighting against the U.S. 28th Infantry Division. Withdrawn to refit a second time, the division was still underequipped in mid-December 1944, although it had nearly 15,500 officers and men. Furthermore, the panzer regiment had only forty-nine tanks (less than half the authorized total), and the division was missing close to 30 percent of its motor transport. However, the 116th had twenty JgPz-IVs in its antitank battalion, and was generally a high-quality formation.

General von Waldenburg had commanded the 116th since September. Despite his wide military experience, especially as a staff officer, he had relatively little familiarity with large-scale troop command or with mechanized units. He was born in Gross Leipe on 30 December 1898, and had been commissioned a lieutenant in the elite 1st Guard Grenadier Regiment in August 1917. He was selected for service in the Reichswehr at the end of World War I. By the start of World War II he was a major, assigned to the Operations Section (Ia) of the 6th Infantry Division, and was promoted to lieutenant colonel in March 1940. He saw action with the 6th Division during the campaigns in Poland and France, and was then assigned to the staff of the XII Corps in October 1940. Waldenburg served in that assigned through November 1941, when he was posted to Rome as an assistant military attaché and German representative to the Italian Armed Forces High Command. He remained in Rome for almost two and a half years, and was promoted to colonel in February 1942. Posted to the 26th Panzergrenadier Regiment in April 1944 (part of the 24th Panzer Division), he saw action on the eastern front. Transferred west to take command of the 116th Panzer on 14 September, he was promoted to generalmajor in early December.[25]

At Ouren, the 112th Infantry's Cannon Company continued to hold the town proper with only four howitzers (the other two were being repaired).[26] About 0900 at least twelve German tanks advanced down the road toward

Ouren, unwittingly providing excellent flank shots for the Americans. Although the 105-mm howitzers were not intended as antitank guns, on this occasion they served that role quite well. In the opening shots, the Cannon Company destroyed one German tank. This was again listed as a Tiger. (The combat interviews suggest that the Americans believed the Germans had only Tiger tanks.) The ensuing firefight, which lasted more than an hour, ended when the surviving German tanks withdrew, although not before the Cannon Company had virtually exhausted its 105-mm ammunition. The cannoneers claimed four tanks destroyed and two more badly damaged with one howitzer destroyed, several crewmen dead, and at least ten more wounded. At one point Cpl. Howard Minier manned the #3 gun alone, loading, aiming, and firing the piece by himself for "eight or ten rounds."

During the afternoon, several barrages of "screaming meemies" (Nebelwerfer) landed near Ouren, but the situation was otherwise quiet.[27] At 1700, shortly after dark, the company received orders to withdraw to Weiswampach beginning at 1800. It withdrew in good order, and had assumed new firing positions along Skyline Drive at Weiswampach by 2030. German infantry entered Ouren as the company headquarters and support elements left town. Technician 4th Grade (T/4) John Wheeland, a mechanic, escaped capture only by slugging a would-be captor in the jaw and hurriedly making his getaway into the darkness. At Weiswampach the company recovered its other two howitzers from division ordnance workshops, and thus disposed of five guns by the early hours of 18 December.

The infantry battalions of the 112th had also had a busy day. An early-morning attack by German PzKw-IV medium tanks and panzergrenadiers in half-tracks near Lützkampen had broken through the lines of the 1st Battalion. Although the Germans were unable to exploit this success fully in the face of determined American resistance and several local counterattacks, the rest of the 112th was unable to reestablish contact with the 1st Battalion. With the permission of both General Cota and Maj. Gen. Troy H. Middleton, commander of VIII Corps, Colonel Nelson began to withdraw his men to preselected positions on the west bank of the Our River. Fortunately, radio communications had been reestablished, so he was able to order the 1st Battalion to withdraw as well; that unit's A, C, and D companies arrived in their new positions well before dawn on 18 December.

The 112th Infantry's B Company, holding the northern flank of both the 1st Battalion and of the entire 112th Infantry, was unable to withdraw westward. It fell back to the northwest during the night of 17–18 December into the sector of the 424th Infantry of the 106th Infantry Division, and came under command of that regiment's 1st Battalion. The company was finally able to return to its proper regiment on the afternoon of 19 December, after nearly two days with the 424th and the 106th Division. By that time, both regiments were falling back toward the important crossroads of St. Vith.

To the south, the 26th VGD had moved its artillery forward to the vicinity of Buchholz, between Hosingen and Drauffelt. During the day, the division's infantry units crossed the Clerf River and established a bridgehead, arcing in a rough semicircle from Drauffelt in the north to Wilwerwiltz in the south. The 2d Panzer Division spent most of the day battering its way into Clervaux against stubborn resistance from the headquarters elements of the 110th Infantry and assorted units, fragments of units, and individual stragglers who had drifted into the town. Although organized resistance in Clervaux ended by late evening, scattered groups of American troops continued to resist; there were a few impromptu skirmishes as they withdrew to the west. These efforts and the attendant confusion hampered German efforts to move forward. Meanwhile, the 901st Panzergrenadier Regiment of Panzer Lehr captured Holzthum and advanced southeast to Consthum. The division's reconnaissance battalion, with the 26th Fusilier Regiment attached, bypassed Hosingen and headed west toward the Clerf. The division headquarters and the 902d Panzergrenadier Regiment moved forward to Marnach. These successes left the 110th Infantry's line so full of holes and breaches that by evening it essentially ceased to exist as a coherent unit, although its scattered elements continued to resist.

Farther south in the LXXXV Corps sector, the 5th Parachute Division also continued to advance. However, its progress was slowed by more coherent American resistance, as well as by the division's lack of motor transport. The 15th FJR reached the outskirts of Landscheid and captured Bourscheid, about four kilometers south of Hoscheid, overlooking the Wiltz River valley. The bulk of the 15th FJR attacked Hoscheid itself, while advance elements bypassed the town. Fighting for Hoscheid continued throughout the night; the town was finally secured before dawn on 18 December. To the south of the 5th Parachute Division, troops of the 352d VGD worked steadily to complete bridges across the Our near Gentingen and Bettel (barely 1,000 meters apart, and about two kilometers east of Führen) by evening, while the division headquarters moved forward. Meanwhile, the 2d Battalion of the 352d's 915th Grenadier Regiment captured Bastendorf, nearly five kilometers west of the Our. Bastendorf fell to the Germans only after a hard fight against the A batteries of the 107th and 108th Field Artillery battalions, which, fighting as infantry, had fended off the attackers for most of the day.

Company K of the 110th Infantry continued to hold Hosingen. The defenders of the village were little disturbed during the hours of darkness, but heard traffic on the main road just south of town, which the 26th VGD was employing as a main supply route. They also heard tank and motor vehicle activity to the north of the town, but were unable to find or identify the vehicles. There was little enemy activity in the vicinity through the morning of 18 December, but about 1300 two German tanks (again misidentified as Tigers) opened fire on the village water tower, which was Company K's observation post. The water tower had thick concrete walls with a steel-walled staircase in the center that sheltered its occupants, so the fire caused no casualties. Soon after the two German tanks north of town were joined by six more tanks and a body of infantry, and an attack began in earnest. By 1430 German infantry were moving forward cautiously from both the north and west, and Hosingen's defenders also observed continuous movement past the town to the south.

About dusk, a force of German tanks and infantry reached the north edge of town and soon after drove the observation team out of the water tower. The Germans then began to work their way into town, taking buildings one at a time with the aid of antitank rocket teams and direct tank support.[28] As the night went on, the organized U.S. defenses contracted to the area around the company CP in the southern end of Hosingen. Lieutenant Payne's tanks were limited to movement on the main street. Two were knocked out, but the three survivors were worked into the CP's defenses. Some of the engineers, along with men from the 1st Platoon on the north side of town, were isolated from the main body of defenders.

Until 0400 on 18 December, Battalion Headquarters (3d Bn/110th Infantry) had insisted that Hosingen be held and that reinforcements were on the way. At 0400 or a little later, Battalion Headquarters ordered Company K to separate into small groups and break out to the west. By that time, however, such an effort was impossible, and Captain Feiker met with the company's other officers to decide what to do. With ammunition running low (rifle ammo was down to twenty-five rounds per man or less, and there were only two smoke rounds for the 81-mm mortars) and Germans on all sides, Captain Feiker decided to surrender after final contact with Battalion Headquarters. The surviving U.S. soldiers destroyed their remaining equipment, burning their vehicles and supplies, wrecking their weapons, and shooting out or slashing tires. The surrender was completed between 0900 and 1000 on 18 December.

The defenders of Hosingen totaled 8 officers and about 300 men, including the engineer company and Lieutenant Payne's tank platoon from the 707th Tank Battalion. This force suffered seven killed, ten wounded (two seriously), and none missing during the action. According to Lieutenant Flynn (Company K's executive officer), the ranking German officer (a colonel) expressed surprise that so small a force had put up such a stiff fight and had suffered so few losses while inflicting heavy casualties on the attacking German troops.

Elsewhere in the hard-pressed 110th Infantry's sector, the situation was grim and unraveling rapidly. As resistance at Hosingen ended, other village strongpoints (Kauthenbach, Holzthum) surrendered or were overrun, and most personnel at the hard-pressed headquarters defense at Clervaux left shortly after dark, making for Wiltz and other points west. Colonel Fuller, who accompanied one of the parties escaping, was captured later that evening while attempting to break out to the west. The 2/110th, surrounded on a ridge east of Clervaux, attempted to break out during the night, but only about sixty officers and men reached safety. Most of the 3/110, except K Company at

Hosingen, managed to concentrate at Consthum and hold off several German attacks, but withdrew during the hours of darkness. The 1/110 to the north had essentially ceased to exist, although refugees from that unit trickled westward toward Bastogne for several days.

On the southern flank of the 28th Division, the 109th Infantry continued to hold its positions. Although subject to heavy German infantry attacks, it faced little armor, and many of the infantrymen in the 5th Parachute Division and the 352d VGD were former Luftwaffe or navy personnel, poorly trained and indifferently led. E Company was isolated at Führen, and Lieutenant Colonel Rudder organized a two-company counterattack to reestablish contact with the beleaguered troops in Führen. Neither A nor B company made much progress, and as the day wore on small forces of German infantry began to slip through the 109th's front lines and threaten its rear areas. With his position becoming rather porous, Rudder ordered the regiment to fall back to Bastendorf and Diekirch during the evening.

18 DECEMBER: THE PANZERS ADVANCE

The general situation remained grim for the 28th Division. The weather was still cloudy with scattered light and misty rain and occasional dense but patchy ground fog. The battered 110th Regiment was effectively out of action. The divisional headquarters at Wiltz, defended by a hodgepodge of units and located behind the southern flank of the 110th's former position, came under assault during the day. Isolated positions at Clervaux, Buchholz, Munshausen, Hoscheid, Hosingen, and Holzthum surrendered during the day, although the troops at Consthum continued to hold. On the division's north flank, the 112th Infantry abandoned Ouren and took up new positions along Skyline Drive, and the 109th Infantry finished its withdrawal to Diekirch and positions just west of Bastendorf.

The Germans continued their forward progress, now with a clearer idea of what was actually happening. The 560th VGD pushed ahead about three kilometers, maintaining contact with the 112th Infantry. The 116th Panzer, continuing its roundabout approach, also pushed forward, although the main body was slowed by lack of fuel. By early evening the division's reconnaissance battalion, no longer helping the 560th VGD, had reached the vicinity of Houffalize, fourteen kilometers north of Bastogne and more than eighteen kilometers due west of Weiswampach. The 116th Panzer's main body was able to resume its movements under cover of darkness, when it received new fuel supplies. The 560th's opponent, the 112th Infantry, was still being pressed hard by the Germans, and its redoubtable Cannon Company spent the day firing on targets of opportunity in its sector, including columns of armored vehicles and horse-drawn transport. Much of the German traffic was moving north from the vicinity of Heinerscheid, along Skyline Drive.

South of the LVIII Panzer Corps, the three divisions of von Lüttwitz's

XLVII Panzer Corps also advanced. The 2d Panzer pushed forward nine kilometers against waning American resistance with advance elements reaching Hamiville. Although the 26th VGD advanced more than ten kilometers, its progress was hampered by traffic jams on the narrow and muddy roads. Moreover, the slowness of the 5th Parachute Division's advance compelled Colonel Kokott to detail the 39th Fusilier Regiment to form a security screen on the 26th VGD's southern flank between Alscheid and Nortrange.

However, several elements of Bayerlein's Panzer Lehr Division began to "break into the clear" and headed for Bastogne. The division's reconnaissance battalion and the 902d Panzergrenadier Regiment advanced from Drauffelt through Erpeldange and Oberwampach to Magaret (barely four kilometers from Bastogne). There the advance units were joined by the division's headquarters that evening. Meanwhile, the 901st Panzergrenadier Regiment pushed through Rellingen and Wilwerwiltz to Benonchamps, just southeast of Magaret.

In the Seventh Army's LXXXV Corps the 15th FJR, comprising 5th Parachute Division's southern wing, had halted just west of Bourscheid (partly to cover the Sure River crossings nearby), while the 14th FJR pushed on toward Wiltz. The division was able to utilize a Fifth Panzer Army bridge to move its artillery and other heavy equipment across the Our. The 915th Grenadier Regiment was thrown back more than two kilometers to Bastendorf by a strong counterattack made by A and C companies of the 1/109th, supported by a few Sherman tanks. In light of that reverse, the division worked to bring up its heavy weapons and artillery for the renewed assault.

19 DECEMBER: U.S. FORCES REGROUP AND THE GERMANS EXPLOIT

The situation of the sorely pressed 28th Division remained extremely difficult. To reduce the difficulties of communication and coordination between the division's scattered elements, the 112th Infantry was transferred to the tactical control of the 106th Infantry Division Headquarters at St. Vith. The 28th's own headquarters was withdrawn from Wiltz and moved to Sibret, twenty kilometers to the west and about five kilometers southwest of Bastogne. Wiltz came under increasing German pressure. The town's U.S. defenders were commanded by Lt. Col. Daniel Strickler, the Executive Officer of the 110th Infantry. Strickler assumed command at Wiltz about noon on 19 December, arriving with the 200 remaining officers and men of the 3d/110th. Aside from these new arrivals, the defenders comprised the 44th Engineer Combat Battalion with elements of the 707th Tank Battalion, 630th Tank Destroyer Battalion (towed), and 687th Field Artillery (FA) Battalion (105-mm howitzers).[29]

Fighting grew more intense as the afternoon wore on, and the American defenders (many of whom had been in continuous combat for four days) were increasingly hard-pressed to repel the German attacks. By nightfall, the perimeter had been pierced in several places, and the defense had contracted to a small area within Wiltz itself. The 687th FA, struck by the advance guard of the 15th FJR in midafternoon, had withdrawn southeast of Harlange. The defenders of Wiltz were tired, very low on ammunition, and virtually without tank support. Their radio communications were essentially gone, and contact between units was maintained, tenuously, with runners. Unknown to Strickler, a supply column from Sibret had been unable to pass through the German troops on the road.

With no prospect of immediate relief, at about 2100 Strickler decided to evacuate the town and withdraw through the German lines by infiltration. Understandably beset by confusion, the withdrawal was hampered by German roadblocks west of Wiltz. The main road column of the 28th's "Provisional Battalion" (assembled from stragglers, medical and support troops, and personnel at the 28th Division's rest facilities in Wiltz) broke up after encountering its third German roadblock sometime after midnight, about eight kilometers west of Wiltz on the highway to Bastogne. Some of its personnel reached Bastogne, and other refugees from Wiltz, including Lieutenant Colonel Strickler himself, reached Vaux-les-Rosières during the course of the following day, 20 December. The 687th FA, surrounded and attacked again at its positions southeast of Harlange, managed to escape after two hours of close combat, but with only three of its twelve howitzers.[30]

On the division's southern flank, the 109th Infantry drew back about a kilometer and began to take up defensive positions on the high ground south and west of Ettelbruck with Combat Command A and some supporting elements of the 9th Armored Division on its southern flank. With the collapse of the 110th Infantry's sector, the 109th was virtually on its own, and tactical control of the regiment was transferred from the 28th Division to the 9th Armored Division (which was, like most U.S. armored divisions, happy to get more infantry, however temporarily).

Facing the 112th Infantry, the 560th VGD of the LVIII Panzer Corps pressed forward some seven kilometers, capturing the villages of Tavigny and Cetturu. Gruppe Schumann remained attached to the 62d VGD, attacking northward toward St. Vith. The 116th Panzer Division captured Houffalize and its leading elements advanced westward another fourteen kilometers to the southwest to reach the village of Ortheuville, where they encountered elements of the U.S. 158th Engineer Combat Battalion. The division headquarters moved up to Wandebourcy. Late in the day, the division was directed by LVIII Panzer Corps to withdraw from Ortheuville and shift its axis of advance through Houffalize, to prepare for an advance along the north bank of the Ourthe River.

To the south, the hard-driving divisions of the XLVII Panzer Corps continued westward toward Bastogne. The 2d Panzer Division advanced about 4.5 kilometers and met very heavy resistance around Bourcy. A counterattack by American armor from CCB, 10th Armored Division, was repulsed several kilometers southeast of Bourcy, and elements of the 2d Panzer Recon Battalion neared the eastern outskirts of Bastogne by evening. The Panzer Lehr's rate of advance was not as rapid. Around the village of Longvilly, about nine kilometers northeast of Bastogne, Bayerlein's troops and the 77th GR of the 26th VGD ran into elements of CCR, 9th Armored Division. In several hours of heavy fighting, the Germans drove the Americans back with heavy losses, opening the road to Bastogne, but the 9th Armored Division tankers had bought several precious hours for the gathering defenders of Bastogne.

Meanwhile, Lehr's 901st Panzergrenadier Regiment advanced westward around the southeast side of Bastogne, but was halted by heavy fire at Marvie that came from troops of the 101st Airborne Division, who had been rushed in by truck from SHAEF reserve to secure the vital crossroads of Bastogne. Although the Germans did not yet know it, Bastogne was no longer defended by odds and ends of combat engineers and the remnants of armored task forces, but by a reinforced division of battle-hardened paratroopers. They would have a serious fight on their hands to take Bastogne and its crucial crossroads.

The headquarters of the 26th VGD was able to move forward into Magaret by late afternoon, and most of the division took up positions around the hamlet of Bizory and in the Bois de St. Jacques. Unfortunately for the Germans, the 39th Fusilier Regiment was still occupied providing a security screen on the southern flank of the XLVII Panzer Corps penetration.

Despite the check administered to the 915th Grenadier Regiment on 18 December, Seventh Army troops also continued their advance. The 5th Parachute Division advanced seven to eight kilometers during the day. The 14th FJR captured Nocher, and advance elements of the regiment reached Roullingen, less than 600 meters south of Wiltz. The 15th FJR, supported by the assault guns of the 11th Fallschirm Sturmgeschütz Brigade, pushed ahead to capture Dahl and Guesdorf. The other division of LXXXV Corps, the 352d VGD, managed a four-kilometer advance. The 915th Grenadier Regiment reached Erpeldange (a scant 1,000 meters northeast of Wiltz) with the rest of the division's front line stretching south for about five kilometers.

The original American forces holding the Our River line from Ouren and Lützkampen south to Wallendorf had either been driven back or, in the case of the unfortunate 110th Infantry, virtually destroyed. However, the German success was at best a highly qualified one. It had taken them not a mere twenty-four to thirty-six hours to create their breakthrough—as they had planned—but the better part of four days, and the delay was to prove crucial. With the 101st Airborne Division now holding Bastogne, the Germans would be hard-pressed to seize the town and make use of its vital transportation routes. This meant that, at least for the time being, they would be compelled to use the inadequate roadnet north and south of the town, thereby further slowing their advance. Their already precarious logistical situation would deteriorate further. Unless they could take Bastogne there could be no German success in the Fifth Panzer Army's zone, and no advance past the Meuse.

8

THE BATTLE OF THE SAUER RIVER

GERMAN PLANS AND DISPOSITIONS

The German Seventh Army, commanded by General der Panzertruppen Erich Brandenberger, was the weakest of the three armies assembled for the great counteroffensive in the west. It was composed of only two corps with four infantry-type divisions; although it was heavily reinforced by artillery it had little armored support. The army had another corps headquarters under its command (the LIII), but initially this corps included only a few fortress troops on the extreme left of the army.

Born in 1894, Erich Brandenberger entered the German Army in 1913 and fought in World War I as a junior infantry officer. He was retained in the 100,000-man Reichswehr, the tiny professional army the Weimar Republic was allowed under the terms of the Treaty of Versailles. By 1942 he had risen to command the 8th Panzer Division, and took part in extensive hard fighting in Russia as part of Army Group North. He was promoted to general der panzertruppen on 1 August 1943 and given command of the XIV Corps in Italy, but soon after he was reassigned to command of the XXIX Corps on the eastern front. He gained a reputation as a skilled, careful, and resourceful defensive tactician and commander.

Brandenberger was a slightly pudgy man of average height. Field Marshal Model, who did not like him, charged that he "had the features of a scientist." While Brandenberger may not have been the most aggressive corps or army commander in the Wehrmacht, his attention to details made him well suited to the strains of directing defensive operations. He was called away from the eastern front in September 1944 to assume command of the Seventh Army, which was holding a section of the Westwall in the Ardennes-Eifel region. It is doubtful if anyone could have excelled his performance in the

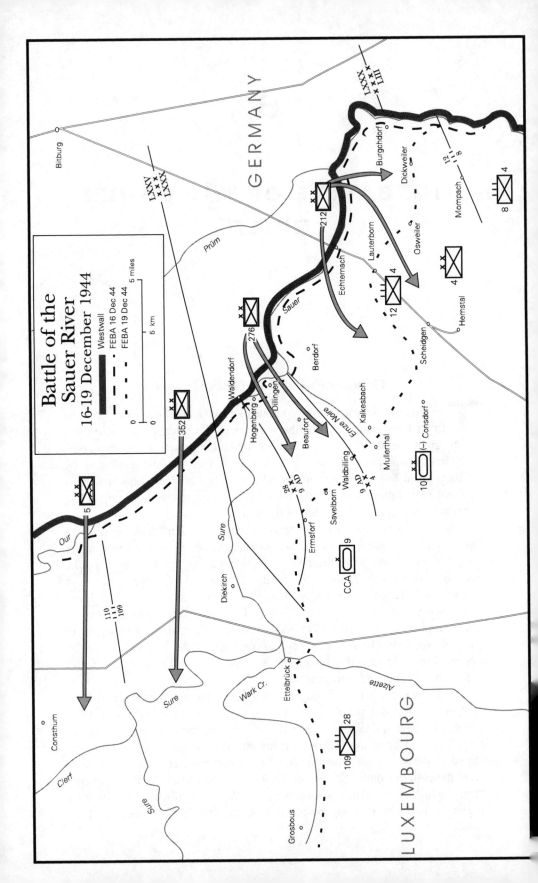

Battle of the
Sauer River
16-19 December 1944

Westwall
FEBA 16 Dec 44
FEBA 19 Dec 44

0   5 km

0   5 miles

GERMANY

LUXEMBOURG

Bitburg

Prüm

Sauer

Echternach

Burgchdorf

Dickweiler

Lauterborn

Osweiler

Mompach

Hemstal

Scheidgen

Consdorf

Mullerthal

Kalkesbach

Waldbilling

Berdorf

Beaufort

Ernze Noire

Hogenberg

Dillingen

Waldendorf

Our

Sure

Diekirch

Sure

Wark Cr.

Ettelbrück

Grosbous

Clerf

Sure

Consthum

Alzette

Savelborn

Ermsdorf

CCA

Our

212

276

352

5

28

109

4

4

12

8

4

8

28 AD
9 AD

9 AD
4

9

10 (-)

LXXX
LIII

LXXV
LXXX

LXXXV
LXXX

110
109

next few weeks of the offensive in terms of good progress with meager resources.

On the Seventh Army's right, opposite the U.S. 109th Infantry Regiment, was General der Infanterie Baptist Kniess's LXXXV Corps. Kniess controlled two divisions: on the right, Luftwaffe-Oberst Ludwig Heilmann's 5th Parachute Division, and, on the left, Oberst Erich Schmidt's 352d Volks-grenadier Division (VGD). (See chapter 7 for additional details of the organization and the initial attacks by the LXXXV Corps.)

On the left of the Seventh Army was General der Infanterie Franz Beyer's LXXX Corps. Beyer's mission was not well defined. His corps was to cross the Sauer River,[1] advance to destroy U.S. forces on the high plateau southwest of the river, and establish blocking positions to protect the left flank of the Fifth Panzer Army from the threat of a U.S. counterattack from the vicinity of Luxembourg City. It was expected that the corps, due to its limited mobility, would be able to advance no more than twenty kilometers before it would be forced to assume a defensive posture. As a result—contrary to later American G-2 estimates—neither Luxembourg City nor the powerful transmitters of Radio Luxembourg, outside the city at Junglinster, were ever included in the corps's objective. Like the LXXXV, the LXXX Corps had only two divisions: the 276th VGD on the right, and the 212th VGD on the left.

The 276th VGD, commanded by Generalleutnant Kurt Möhring, was probably the least effective in the Seventh Army. It was formed from the shell of a division that had been destroyed in Normandy and was almost entirely composed of poorly trained recruits and inexperienced officers and noncommissioned officers. General Möhring was a skillful and dedicated officer, but his abilities could not compensate for the inexperience of his men. The division had a fully organized artillery regiment (eighteen 75-mm guns, twenty-four 105-mm howitzers, and twelve 150-mm howitzers) but no organic panzerjäger company.[2]

The sector assigned to the 276th VGD ran from the confluence of the Sure and Our Rivers (to become the Sauer River) near Wallendorf on the right (the boundary with the LXXXV Corps) to the juncture of the Sauer with the gorge of the Ernz Noire River north of Berdorf. The division would attack with two regiments abreast and a third in reserve. The initial objective was a line running roughly northwest to southeast through the villages of Ermsdorf-Savelborn-Waldbillig-Müllerthal. Further objectives would be determined by the degree of success achieved by the division and by the divisions on its right and left.

In contrast to the 276th, the 212th VGD, commanded by Generalleutnant Franz Sensfuss, was considered to be the best division in the Seventh Army. It had suffered heavy losses on the eastern front, but had retained a strong cadre of experienced officers and noncommissioned officers. Furthermore, the replacements assigned to the division were considered to be better than average and had been well trained. The division's artillery regiment was organized and equipped like that of the 276th. One advantage the 212th had over the 276th was that its panzerjäger company was present at the start of the offensive even though its complement was only at half-strength (five Stug-III assault guns).

The division was to attack south across the Sauer with two regiments (the 316th Grenadier Regiment was in corps reserve). The 320th Grenadier Regiment was to cross the river west and east of Echternach. The 423d Grenadier Regiment was to cross farther east. Supporting the attack were two battalions of fortress troops south of the bend of the Sauer River that were to attack west across the river toward Dickweiler to divert attention from the main assault.[3] The division was to seize the high plateau south and west of the Sauer, denying to the powerful American artillery the use of the excellent positions to be found there.

Corps and army artillery support was ample: about 190 guns and howitzers ranging in caliber from 75 mm to 210 mm, plus thirty-six 280/320-mm Nebelwerfer.[4] The quality of the artillery, however, was mixed.[5]

Engineer support for the river crossing was inadequate, to say the least. Each of the volksgrenadier divisions had a two-company engineer battalion, but they were only capable of emplacing infantry footbridges. Although infantry heavy weapons could be transported on rafts, bridges were needed for heavier weapons like artillery and armored vehicles. The LXXX Corps was forced to share with the LXXXV Corps the services of a single engineer bridge battalion and a few poorly equipped and almost immobile bridging columns. Furthermore, all available bridge construction sites were under observation from the American-held side of the river. The German engineers' problems were to have a major impact on the success of the LXXX Corps's attack.

AMERICAN DISPOSITIONS

Opposing the LXXX Corps was the U.S. 9th Armored Division (CCA and Division Headquarters and Service Troops only) and elements of the 4th Infantry Division (the 12th Infantry and attachments).[6] Commanding the 9th Armored Division was Maj. Gen. John W. Leonard. Born in Toledo, Ohio, on 25 January 1890, he was a West Point classmate of future generals Eisenhower and Bradley, graduating from West Point in June 1915. He joined the 6th Infantry Regiment as a second lieutenant and served with the regiment in Mexico with General Pershing's Punitive Expedition in 1916. In France in 1918, he commanded its 3d Battalion in the Battles of St. Mihiel and the Meuse-Argonne. He won the Distinguished Service Cross for (according to the citation) "extraordinary heroism in action near Romagne, France, 14 October 1918." At the conclusion of the war he was selected as the executive officer of the Third Army's Composite Regiment, which served as General

Pershing's honorary bodyguard at victory parades in Paris, London, New York, and Washington.

At the beginning of World War II Leonard was commanding the 6th Armored Infantry Regiment at Fort Knox, Kentucky. In September 1942 he was appointed commanding general of the newly activated 9th Armored Division. After staging through Great Britain, the three combat commands of the division were committed to the front in November 1944 in widely separated locations. Combat Command A (CCA) and the Division Headquarters were assigned to the VIII Corps, and held a position in line along the Sauer River between the 28th Infantry Division and the 4th Infantry Division; Combat Command B (CCB) was assigned to the V Corps, and was in reserve behind the right-flank divisions of that corps; Combat Command R (CCR) was assigned to the VIII Corps reserve between Bastogne and Neufchâteau.

The 9th Armored Division's CCA was commanded by Col. Thomas L. Harrold, a Regular Army cavalryman who had graduated from West Point near the top of the Class of 1925. He placed one battalion—the 60th Armored Infantry Battalion—on the high bluffs overlooking the Sauer River in his sector. The battalion was commanded by Lt. Col. Kenneth W. Collins, a 1939 graduate of West Point. The battalion's sector ran from the juncture of the Sure and Our Rivers opposite Wallendorf on the left to the juncture of the Sauer and Ernz Noire (Schwarz Ernz) River on the right—a frontage of almost four miles. Complicating the defensive problem was the fact that neither the Sure nor the Ernz Noire gorge was included within the battalion's sector. Lieutenant Colonel Collins refused to overextend his unit, and kept A and B companies in a tight perimeter running east, north, and northwest of the village of Dillingen. C Company was in reserve with Battalion Headquarters at Beaufort. A single squad held an outpost on the far left at Hogenberg, overlooking German-held Wallendorf across the Sauer to the east and positions of the 109th Infantry Regiment across the Sure to the north.

The 3d Armored Field Artillery Battalion, in firing positions between Savelborn and Waldbillig, was in direct support of the infantry. Also supporting the 60th Armored Infantry Battalion was the bulk of CCA, deployed between Ermsdorf and Waldbillig.[7]

On the right of CCA/9 was the 12th Infantry Regiment of Maj. Gen. Raymond O. Barton's 4th Infantry Division. Both the division and its commander were a cut above the average.

Raymond Oscar Barton was born in Colorado on 22 August 1899. To the bafflement of those who served with and under this lithe, athletic soldier in later years, he was known to his West Point classmates as "Tubby." He graduated on 12 June 1912 as a second lieutenant of Infantry. Like many of his classmates, he failed to get overseas in World War I because he was needed as a trainer in the United States. Between the wars he held the usual school, command, and staff assignments. When World War II broke out he was a brigadier general and chief of staff of the IV Corps. In 1942 he was promoted to major general and assigned to command the 4th Infantry Division.[8] In January 1944 he brought the "Ivy Division" (so called because its shoulder patch was a four-leafed sprig of ivy) to the United Kingdom. Because the division had demonstrated a high state of training in tests and exercises, it was selected as the principal assault division for Utah Beach on D-Day. Ernest Hemingway, who was a war correspondent, was with Barton much of the time as his division fought its way through and out of Normandy. After the war he told Barton, "You had one of the greatest divisions in American military history." The 4th's performance led General Patton to remark later that he "knew of no American division in France which excelled the magnificent record of the 4th Infantry Division." After the breakout from Normandy, the 4th Division advanced on Paris, but halted briefly outside the city to allow a French division to claim the honor of liberating the city. In the subsequent dash across France, Barton's 4th Division was the first American unit to cross the border into Germany, on 14 September, and seized a portion of the Westwall on the Schnee Eifel. (This was the sector held by the 106th Division on 15 December.) Following that, Barton and his division were ordered north to take part in the bitter and inconclusive struggle for the Hürtgen Forest. Early in December, after suffering more than 5,000 casualties, the division was pulled out of the line to rest in a "quiet sector" of the VIII Corps zone in the southeastern Ardennes of Luxembourg. Between 4 and 11 December the division took over a thirty-five-mile-long front along the Sauer and Moselle Rivers from the 83d Division.

There in the wild and rugged country south and west of the Sauer, Barton and one of his regimental commanders invited Hemingway to join them for relaxation. The famous author divided his time between Barton's command post and that of his old friend, Colonel "Buck" Lanham, colorful commander of the 22d Infantry. From either of these command posts, seated in the early evening with predinner drinks in hand, Hemingway and his hosts could see the occasional glimmer of moving lights in the dark void beyond the Sauer River that was Germany.

The 4th Division, like the 28th Division, had suffered very heavy casualties in the Hürtgen Forest. However, unlike the 28th Division, which had received many replacements, the 4th Division was still badly understrength. All three infantry regiments were 20 to 30 percent below the manning tables; some rifle companies were short as much as 50 percent.[9] In addition, the attached 70th Tank Battalion was not only badly understrength, most of the tanks on hand were undergoing long-delayed maintenance.[10]

Holding the left flank of the 4th Division's long line was the 12th Infantry Regiment, commanded by Col. Robert H. Chance. The left flank of the regiment was held by the 2d Battalion with Company E in Echternach, Company F in Berdorf, and Company G in Lauterborn. The battalion Weapons Company, H, was split with a heavy machine-gun platoon and an 81-mm mortar section assigned to each of the rifle companies. The right flank of the regiment was held by the 3d Battalion with Company I in Dickweiler and Burschdorf, Company K in Herborn and Dickweiler, and Company L in Osweiler. The battalion Weapons Company, M, like that of the 2d Battalion, was split among the rifle company positions. The 1st Battalion was in reserve at Hemstal. The 12th Regiment Cannon Company was in firing positions near Berdorf. The Regimental Antitank Company was split with the 2d Platoon at Berdorf, the 3d Platoon at Dickweiler and Osweiler, and the balance of the company at Hemstal. The regimental front was nearly ten miles long.

The widely separated company positions of the 12th Infantry were loosely connected by a number of squad- and platoon-size outposts. The outposts maintained observation of the ground between the main positions and ran contact patrols between the companies. Most of the positions were set up in the strongly built farmhouses that dotted the area.

In support of the 12th Infantry Regiment were the twelve 105-mm howitzers of the 42d Field Artillery Battalion (which had been reequipped in the fall with M7 self-propelled howitzers) and the twelve 155-mm howitzers of the 20th Field Artillery Battalion, both assigned to the 4th Division's artillery. Also in support (although at extreme range) were the twelve 155-mm self-propelled guns of the 174th Field Artillery Battalion, a nondivisional unit attached to the 4th Division. Other support was provided by the guns of the 802d Tank Destroyer Battalion (towed) and the 803d Tank Destroyer Battalion (self-propelled), which were dispersed along the length of the 4th Division's line.

To the right of the 12th Infantry Regiment were the 8th and then the 22d Infantry regiments, which extended the 4th Division line to the boundary between the VIII Corps of the First Army and the XX Corps of the Third Army. Both regiments had a single battalion in reserve. The only other reserves available to General Barton were the division's 4th Reconnaissance Troop, the 4th Engineer Combat Battalion, and the attached (and badly depleted) 70th Tank Battalion.

16 DECEMBER

At 0530 hours the German preassault bombardment began. In this sector, unlike those of the Sixth and Fifth Panzer armies, the Germans benefited from relatively good observation of the American positions. Heavy fires were directed with extreme accuracy against company and battalion command posts and artillery observation posts. Wire communications within the 12th Infantry broke down almost immediately when the wires were cut by shell fragments.

Closely following the barrage, the first German assault teams crossed the Sauer River by boat and prepared to attack the forward American outposts. On the far left of the 60th Armored Infantry Battalion, the isolated squad at Hogenberg was quickly overwhelmed; all men were either killed or captured.

However, the main battalion positions at Dillingen held firm. Excellent observation and fields of fire from the river bluffs allowed the armored infantrymen to cut down the inexperienced men of the 276th VGD in droves. By the end of the day only minor German pockets had been established on the American-held side of the river in this sector.

Farther to the east, the 212th VGD enjoyed greater success. Company F of the 12th Infantry Regiment, in platoon-size positions outside of Berdorf, was overwhelmed by a well-coordinated attack of the 320th Grenadier Regiment. Only nine men escaped from the three forward rifle platoons to the Company Headquarters at the Parc Hotel outside of Berdorf. First Lieutenant John L. Leake, commander of F Company, and fifty-eight other officers and men of F Company, and elements of the 2d Platoon of the 12th Regimental Antitank Company, held out there for the rest of the day against repeated German assaults. After dark the survivors infiltrated out to the south.

Outside of town, men of the 12th Regimental Cannon Company fired their 105-mm howitzers over open sights at the advancing Germans until they were forced to displace to the rear for the lack of infantry support. Despite this valiant resistance, by nightfall elements of at least one German battalion were advancing past Berdorf up the Ernz Noire gorge. This posed a grave threat to the flanks and rears of both the 60th Armored Infantry Battalion and the 2d Battalion of the 12th Infantry.

The second battalion of the 320th Grenadier Regiment was also successful. By nightfall it had crossed the river and bypassed Company E in Echternach and was threatening the right flank and rear of Company G at Lauterborn. Three squad-size outposts of Company E were surrounded but were able to make their way back to the main company positions in Echternach during the night.

The 423d Grenadier Regiment, crossing farther to the east, had greater difficulty, but despite heavy losses was also able to advance far into the American position. By 1100 hours it had nearly surrounded Dickweiler and Osweiler, and had forced the 42d Field Artillery to displace from its forward positions.

The commander of the 2d/12th, Maj. Herman R. Rice, boldly counterattacked with eleven men of K Company and the three medium tanks of Company B of the 70th Tank Battalion. The tiny force struck and surprised the Germans outside of Dickweiler with devastating effect. One German company was nearly annihilated; more than fifty men, including its commander, were killed or wounded. A second company commander and thirty-five men surrendered.

Meanwhile, Colonel Chance reacted quickly to restore the situation. General Barton released to him his 1st Battalion, which had been in division reserve, along with elements of the 70th Tank Battalion. Colonel Chance ordered the 1st Battalion to send Company B, with light tanks from D Company, 70th Tank Battalion, to Berdorf. (They were joined by three newly repaired mediums from A Company of the 70th Tank Battalion shortly before moving out.) Chance sent Company A with light tanks from D Company, 70th Tank Battalion, to Lauterborn, and Company C to Osweiler and Dickweiler. In addition, he sent forward B Company of the 70th Tank Battalion to join Major Rice of the 2d Battalion in striking the Germans outside of Dickweiler. Company A made contact with G Company a mile southwest of Echternach, but the combined force was unable to reach E Company in the town. B and C companies also made little progress but were at least able to slow the advancing German columns.

By late evening the situation had stabilized somewhat. General Barton, in addition to sending elements of the 70th Tank Battalion to the 12th Infantry Regiment during the day, had also formed a new reserve by motorizing the 2d Battalion, 22d Infantry, which had been in reserve, and dispatching it to the 12th Infantry Regiment sector. The 2d Battalion of the 8th Infantry Regiment, also in regimental reserve, was also alerted for a possible redeployment to the threatened sector. General Barton was writing to risk stripping the remaining reserves from the rest of his division's front because of the almost complete lack of activity in the sectors of the 8th and 22d Infantry regiments.

On the German side the situation was also chaotic. The 276th VGD had taken a severe pounding, as had elements of the 212th. More worrisome for the Germans was the lack of progress in bridge construction. It was difficult to move equipment forward, and all the major bridging sites were frequently harassed by American artillery. Without the bridges in place, the forward troops could not be reinforced by heavy weapons and could be supplied only with great difficulty.

On the positive side for the Germans, the American lines, if not broken, had been severely dislocated. The road following the course of the Ernz Noire was a clear avenue into the flank and rear of the American defenders. The thinly spread defensive lines were still highly vulnerable to infiltration. General Beyer thus decided to continue the attack in an effort to break through the American defensive crust before further reinforcements could make an appearance. The corps reserve, the 987th Grenadier Regiment of the 276th VGD, was committed to the drive up the Ernz Noire.

17 DECEMBER

In the sector of the 60th Armored Infantry Battalion, sunrise of 17 December was met with some apprehension. Both flanks of the battalion were vulnerable to envelopment. The steadily deteriorating situation of the 109th Infantry to the north (see chapter 7) meant that the Sauer-Sure river line was no longer a defensible barrier. The German advance up the Ernz Noire gorge was even more dangerous. Colonel Harrold of CCA/9 made some attempt in the early-morning hours to block the threats to his flanks. D Company, 19th Tank Battalion's light tanks, were sent to screen the northern flank. Two troops of the

89th Cavalry Reconnaissance Squadron and Company B of the 811th Tank Destroyer Battalion were dispatched to cover the exits from the gorge to the south.

During the morning the threats developed as had been feared. Elements of the 276th VGD worked south from Hogenberg into positions behind the forward armored infantry companies. At the same time, a full regiment from the 276th, as well as elements of the 212th VGD, pushed into the Ernz Noire. Some drove to Müllerthal at the head of the gorge, others debouched at the foot of the gorge and drove on Beaufort, headquarters of the 60th Armored Infantry Battalion.

In the early afternoon Colonel Harrold attempted to drive the Germans out of Müllerthal. A cavalry troop and a platoon of tank destroyers advanced on the twisting roads leading to the gorge—and were stopped cold by German antitank guns and panzerfausts. Lacking sufficient infantry, the small American force withdrew to the top of the gorge before dark.

By evening the situation for CCA was critical. The defending armored infantrymen were effectively surrounded, and Colonel Collins had abandoned Beaufort in a fighting withdrawal. Hope for the trapped infantry rested with a counterattack planned by Colonel Harrold for dawn on 18 December. For the attack he assembled two medium tank companies (B and C companies) of the 19th Tank Battalion, A Company of the 9th Armored Engineers, a troop of cavalry, and the Intelligence & Reconnaissance (I&R) Platoon of the 60th Armored Infantry Battalion.

On the German side the problems were equally severe. General Brandenberger was very displeased with the performance of the 276th and had decided to replace General Möhring. Word of the impending relief reached Möhring at his forward command post near Müllerthal. Ignoring warnings from his staff regarding the danger to vehicles on the roads, the despondent general climbed into his commandeered American staff car and headed down the Ernz Noire to the rear. Near Beaufort a machine gun from Colonel Collins's rearguard riddled the car, killing Möhring instantly. The death of this well-liked and respected commander severely affected the already low morale of the grenadiers of his division. (He was posthumously promoted to Generalleutnant.)

South of the beleaguered 9th Armored Division, the 12th Infantry also faced a hectic day. The great distance between the company positions and lack of communications made it impossible for Colonel Chance to keep up with the German movements. However, all German advances were eventually checked during the day, and by night a fairly solid defensive line had been established. Two factors in the American defense made this possible: All the surrounded American troops doggedly held on in their positions until relieved, and additional reinforcements were pushed into the sector by General Barton as rapidly as they became available.[11]

Early in the morning, the 2d Battalion, 22d Infantry Regiment (with A

Company, 19th Tank Battalion attached), was attached to the 12th Infantry Regiment and went into action in the sector of the 3d Battalion. At the same time a pickup group of various units was formed into a makeshift task force under Col. James S. Luckett.[12] (He was a former commander of the 12th Infantry Regiment, and then carried as an excess officer at Division Headquarters.) Task Force Luckett was sent to guard the exit from the Ernz Noire just east of Müllerthal.

In the 2d Battalion sector, Company E in Echternach remained isolated in relative quiet during the day. Companies A and G, sent to relieve E, were still stalled about halfway between Lauterborn and Echternach. At Scheidgen, the Antitank Company of the 12th Infantry Regiment (fighting as infantry), Headquarters Company of the 2d Battalion, one platoon of A Company, and several tanks halted a German attack during the day. At Berdorf, Company B counterattacked and broke through to join the remnants of Company F still holding the village.

Farther to the east, the Germans continued to attack Osweiler and Dickweiler in battalion strength. Additional German units (probably the fortress battalions attached from LIII Corps) were pushing on Dickweiler from the southeast. With the small party from Company K and two tanks (the third had broken down again) that had counterattacked the day before, Company I continued to hold in Dickweiler. Company L held Osweiler. Company C, with thirty men, advanced north between the two villages. Counterattacks by the 2d Battalion greatly improved the situation. Company F reached Osweiler and restored contact with Company L. The remainder of the 2d Battalion beat off a number of battalion-size attacks west of Osweiler during the day.

By the end of the second day, the situation had improved remarkably for the 4th Division. With the exception of Company E at Echternach, contact had been restored with all of the companies that had been isolated the day before. In addition, General Barton had redeployed two more infantry battalions, as well as an engineer battalion to the area—substantially improving the original imbalance in infantry forces. Further reinforcements were also on the way: the 10th Armored Division—dispatched to the VIII Corps front from the XX Corps of the Third Army on the direct orders of General Bradley over General Patton's vehement protest—and the 159th Engineer Combat Battalion.

When CCA of the 10th Armored Division arrived, it was not attached to the 4th Division. Major General William H. H. Morris Jr., commanding the 10th, set up his command post in Consdorf, then went to General Barton's nearby command post. The two division commanders agreed that the 10th Division's armor would attack the next morning toward Müllerthal and Berdorf, through the positions of the 12th Infantry. The objective was to drive the Germans back across the Sauer River.

The original German superiority in infantry strength had nearly disappeared. They had started the battle with the equivalent of about fourteen infantry battalions facing four American battalions. Two days later, the same fourteen German battalions—considerably depleted—were facing the equivalent of nine American battalions. The armor ratio was far worse. Having so far failed to get a bridge into place, none of the relatively few German armored vehicles had been able to get across the Sauer. On the American side, the 19th Tank Battalion and the broken-down 70th Tank Battalion were about to be joined by a third battalion, pitting about 180 American medium and light tanks against a German force without armor.

18 DECEMBER

Colonel Harrold's counterattack to relieve the surrounded armored infantrymen west of Beaufort jumped off at dawn. The main element of the attacking force advanced east from Savelborn. Unfortunately for the Americans, General Möhring's last act before leaving for his fatal car ride the night before had been to organize an attack of his own: An infantry battalion and a light antitank company, with about fifty-four handheld panzerfaust antitank rocket launchers, was to be sent west toward Savelborn.

The two attacks collided east of the village. To the still green tankers of the 19th Tank Battalion it appeared as if the German antitank teams were everywhere. Six medium tanks were quickly knocked out, and the I&R Platoon of the 60th Armored Infantry Battalion was nearly wiped out in an ambush. The American attackers were badly shaken and quickly withdrew to Savelborn. The Germans, equally shaken, fell back to Beaufort.

The isolated men of the 60th Armored Infantry Battalion were thus left in a hopeless situation and were ordered to break out by infiltration. The result was messy. About 400 men of the battalion made it to safety, but 350 were killed or captured, mostly during the withdrawal.

Following the collapse of the forward position of CCA/9, Colonel Harrold formed a new line to the rear that ran from a tenuous connection with the 109th Infantry Regiment south of Ettelbruck, through Ermsdorf, Savelborn, and Waldbillig. Although the men of battered CCA/9 had no way of forecasting this, the new line marked the limit of the German advance.

The new commander of the equally battered 276th VGD, Oberst Hugo Dempwolff, attempted to reorganize his somewhat demoralized division. General Brandenberger abandoned his attempt to build a bridge in the sector of the 276th and directed that supplies and heavy weapons be moved across bridges in the area of the 352d VGD to the north. During the day the divisional panzerjäger company finally appeared with a total of three assault guns. By the evening of 18 December it was clear that the German attack in this sector had been stalled—permanently as it turned out.

Farther south, the counterattack by CCA of the 10th Armored Division fared no better than that by CCA of the 9th Armored. Two task forces pushed toward Müllerthal in the Ernz Noire and at Berdorf, farther north and east. The task force on the left was stopped cold by German panzerfausts. Initially the attack on Berdorf was more successful. Task Force Lang (named for the commander of C Company of the 11th Tank Battalion), with a company of the 61st Armored Infantry Battalion attached, drove into the village under heavy fire by Germans in the Parc Hotel and nearby houses. Corporal Sam Silverman, gunner of the leading tank of C Company, fired his machine gun into windows and doors of the hotel, and then into other houses, as the tank lumbered down the street. A panzerfaust hit the tank, stopping it, and wounding Silverman in the face and shoulder. He later remembered "the feeling of being in a whirlpool with all kinds of flashing colors and being pulled down. . . ." [13]

The other tanks of C Company moved past Silverman's stricken tank, but they too were soon stopped by the Germans' effective use of panzerfausts. With his tanks stalled and his infantry unable to move further without tank support, Captain Lang withdrew from Berdorf in frustration.

The terrain and the heavy stone construction of the village houses greatly facilitated infantry defense against armor; however, the inexperience of the tankers of the 11th Armored Battalion of CCA/10 made the job much easier for the Germans. After suffering minor casualties for little gain, CCA withdrew.

A third task force (composed of a company of armored infantry, a tank company, and two companies from the 159th Engineer Combat Battalion) had more success in an attack to relieve E Company at Echternach. Meeting little resistance the task force reached Lauterborn, where it halted for the night. Two tanks and two infantry squads were sent forward and reached the command post of E Company in the center of town.

A tragicomedy of errors then ensued. Lieutenant Colonel John R. Riley, commanding the task force, was unwilling to push additional tanks into the town without more infantry support. The commander of E Company, 1st Lt. Morton A. Macdiarmid, was completely out of contact with the 4th Division, and assumed that General Barton's order of 16 December (to hold in place) was still in effect. Macdiarmid wanted the tankers to assist him in restoring contact with his 1st Platoon, which had been isolated from the company on the first day of the attack. General Barton had directed Colonel Riley to order the isolated company to withdraw once contact had been reestablished. Unfortunately, no such order was issued. The two tanks withdrew that night from town to the positions of Task Force Riley after promising that they would return in the morning.

Meanwhile, the Germans had attempted to push forward again between Osweiler and Scheidgen. This nearly resulted in a clean breakthrough, as there were virtually no troops available to meet the threat. However, the two German battalions were exhausted from two days of heavy fighting and severe casualties. Scattered elements of American rear-area personnel managed to pin the Germans until reinforcements arrived.

On the German side, General Sensfuss had decided to eliminate the pocket at Echternach on the next day. He then planned to resume the attack on Osweiler and Dickweiler.

19 DECEMBER

On the morning of 19 December, the commander of CCA, 10th Armored Division, Brigadier General Edwin W. Piburn, decided to halt the attacks into the Ernz Noire. Instead, forces were deployed to keep the Germans from exiting the gorge. The main power of CCA was then directed at Berdorf to cut off the German salient in the gorge at its base. In bitter fighting the tankers succeeded in clearing the village by late in the day.

At Echternach, the two American tanks returned as they had promised and helped free the isolated 1st Platoon of E Company. The tanks then withdrew again from Echternach to join the main body of Task Force Riley at Lauterborn. Again, no effort was made to inform Lieutenant Macdiarmid of General Barton's order for him to withdraw.

Soon thereafter General Sensfuss's assault to clear Echternach began. Despite American artillery harassment, the Germans had finally completed a bridge over the Sauer that morning, and assault guns were available to join the attack on the company positions. Under cover of assault-gun fire, troops of the 212th Fusilier Company closed in on the positions of E Company. An urgent request for support from Task Force Riley was denied. Riley apparently assumed that E Company was about to withdraw, so he saw no reason to risk his tanks in the streets of the town again.

In fact, before dawn E Company had finally received a direct order to withdraw. Unfortunately, Lieutenant Macdiarmid replied that he could not withdraw in the dark: There was too great a risk that some of the troops would be left behind by mistake. He said that E Company would withdraw later in the morning. (It was probably already too late.)

20 DECEMBER

Little occurred in the southern sector. The badly shaken opponents faced each other and sporadically shelled opposing positions. The exception to this relative quiet was at Echternach, where the tragic conclusion to the story of E Company was about to take place.

During the night, the Germans had closed every possible exit route from the E Company positions. Task Force Riley was withdrawing to form a new reserve, leaving a platoon each of tanks and infantry behind to cover E Company's anticipated withdrawal. Unfortunately, withdrawal was now impossible. By 1400 hours four assault guns were pounding the Americans at close range. The company soon surrendered.

9

COMMAND DECISIONS

BRADLEY'S DECISION

Lieutenant General Omar N. Bradley, commanding the 12th Army Group, was meeting with General Eisenhower and senior members of the SHAEF staff on the afternoon of 16 December, when the conferees were informed of the German attacks in the Ardennes. The subject of the conference quickly changed from replacement policy to the ongoing battlefield operations. Through the evening and into the next morning Eisenhower and Bradley discussed the situation as a flood of messages began to suggest the scope of the German offensive.

Early that evening Bradley called Lt. Gen. George S. Patton, commander of the Third Army, and told him to send the 10th Armored Division, in Third Army reserve near Thionville, to report to the VIII Corps commander, Maj. Gen. Troy Middleton. Patton protested, because he intended to use the division in a planned offensive in the Saar region. Nevertheless, Bradley insisted.[1] He then called Maj. Gen. Leven C. Allen, his Chief of Staff at the 12th Army Group advanced headquarters at Luxembourg, and told him of the order he had just issued to Patton. Bradley then directed Allen to order the 7th Armored Division, which he knew was in Ninth Army reserve, to move south at once to help stop the German drive. The 7th Armored was to report to the VIII Corps as quickly as possible.[2] Bradley's prompt decision to commit those divisions to move to the threatened area was perhaps the most important command action of the entire campaign. (General Allen, knowing that the 30th Infantry Division was also in reserve in the Ninth Army area, also ordered it to move south at once to the support of the V Corps.)

Early the next morning, before Bradley left to drive back to his headquarters in Luxembourg, Lt. Gen. "Beetle" Smith, the SHAEF Chief of Staff, said to him, "Well, Brad, you've been wishing for a counterattack. Now it looks as

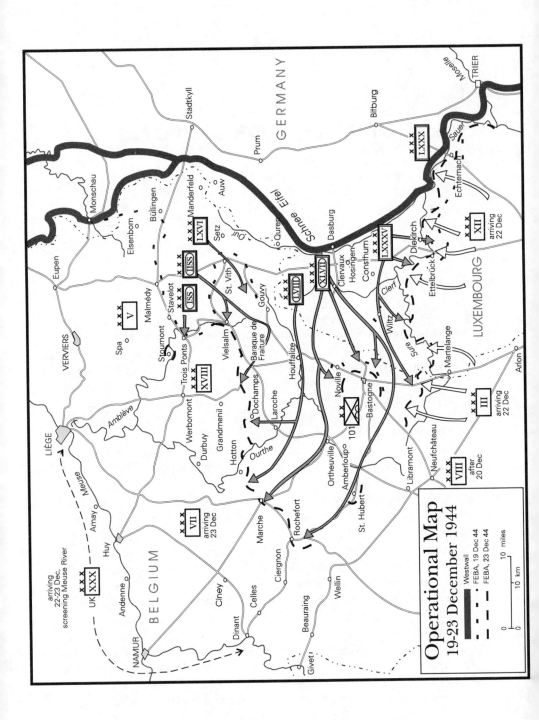

Operational Map
19-23 December 1944

Westwall

FEBA, 19 Dec 44

FEBA, 23 Dec 44

0   10 km

0   10 miles

TRIER

Moselle

Bitburg

Stadtkyll

GERMANY

Prüm

Schnee Eifel

Monschau

Büllingen

Manderfeld

Auw

Setz

Our

Queren

Dasburg

Eupen

Eisenborn

Malmédy

Stavelot

St. Vith

Gouvy

Clervaux

Hosingen

Consthum

Diekirch

Ettelbrück

Echternach

Sauer

LXXX

XII
arriving
22 Dec

LXXXV

LXVI

ISS

ISS

V

Spa

Stoumont

Trois Ponts

Vielsalm

Baraque de
Fraiture

Houffalize

Clerf

Wiltz

Sure

Martelange

Arlon

LUXEMBOURG

XVIII

LVIII

XLVII

Noville

Bastogne

III
arriving
22 Dec

VERVIERS

Werbomont

Grandmenil

Durbuy

Hotton

Dochamps

Laroche

Ourthe

Amblève

101

Ortheuville

Amberloup

St. Hubert

Libramont

Neufchâteau

VIII
after
20 Dec

LIÈGE

Amay

Huy

Meuse

VII
arriving
23 Dec

Marche

Rochefort

Ciergnon

Wellin

Beauraing

BELGIUM

UK XXX
arriving
22-23 Dec,
screening Meuse River

Andenne

Clney

Celles

Dinant

Givet

NAMUR

though you've got it." Bradley responded wryly: "A counterattack, yes, but I'll be damned if I wanted one this big."[3]

EISENHOWER'S CONFERENCE AT VERDUN

For the next two days Eisenhower kept a close watch on the situation, conferred with his staff, and issued orders. First, he directed that all ongoing Allied offensive operations be halted. Then he ordered the deployment of the SHAEF Reserve—the XVIII Airborne Corps and its two divisions, the 82d and 101st Airborne divisions—to move in the general direction of Bastogne, where the VIII Corps command post was located. He directed his staff to identify other divisions in reserve elsewhere along the front that could be shifted to help stop the German drive, should such moves become necessary. By the evening of 18 December he had formulated a general defensive plan and a concept for a counter-counteroffensive. Since this would involve major shifts in units and in boundaries, he decided to meet with several of his senior subordinates to discuss the situation. He directed Bradley, Patton, and Lt. Gen. Jacob Devers (commanding the 6th Army Group) to meet with him the next morning at Verdun, the main, or rear, headquarters of the 12th Army Group. He asked Air Chief Marshal Sir Arthur W. Tedder, Deputy Supreme Allied Commander, to accompany him. He did not send for Lt. Gen. Courtney Hodges, commander of the First Army, because he knew that Hodges, with his headquarters at Spa threatened by a German armored column, was literally in the center of the battle.

Late on the morning of 19 December the four generals and air chief marshal, and senior members of their staffs, met in a chilly barracks room of the old French casern in Verdun where the 12th Army Group main headquarters was located. In opening the meeting Eisenhower said that the situation was not one of disaster but of opportunity. Patton quickly agreed with him, adding with a grin, "Hell, let's have the guts to let the sons of bitches go all the way to Paris. Then we'll really cut them off and chew them up."[4]

Ike then outlined his idea of a counteroffensive to the north, toward Bastogne, by the Third Army, and discovered that both Patton and Bradley were already preparing for this eventuality. Eisenhower asked Patton when he could mount such an attack. He was dubious when Patton responded that he could attack with three divisions in forty-eight hours—in other words, by 21 December. Ike told Patton to make certain that he took enough time to mount a powerful, coordinated attack. "You'll start on the 22nd," he said. "I'd even settle for the 23rd if it takes that long to get three full divisions."

Actually Patton had already issued orders for the Third Army reserve (the III Corps and three divisions) to get ready to shift westward in order to carry out the attack. After the meeting he called his Chief of Staff, Maj. Gen. Hobart Gay, at Third Army headquarters in Nancy, and found out that the 4th Armored Division of the III Corps had actually begun to move on the previous evening.

It was also agreed at the Verdun meeting that the Third Army's XII Corps, commanded by Maj. Gen. Manton Eddy, would also shift its location to the west and shift its axis from facing northeast to facing northwest. It would counterattack against the left flank of the German Seventh Army.

These changes of front for two of the Third Army's three corps meant that Maj. Gen. Walton Walker's XX Corps, continuing to face northeast, would have to extend its front to the east. At the same time the 6th Army Group, farther to the east, would also have to extend its front westward to take over part of the former Third Army sector. General Devers agreed to that.

Late that evening Eisenhower returned from the meeting in Verdun to his headquarters in the Trianon Palace at Versailles.

Monty to Stage Center

Earlier that same day, 19 December, Field Marshal Sir Bernard Law Montgomery had called British Maj. Gen. J. F. M. Whiteley, deputy G-3 or operations officer of the SHAEF staff at Versailles. Monty suggested to Whiteley that the German penetration would make it very difficult for Bradley to exercise command over the Ninth Army and that part of the First Army (all except the VIII Corps) that was north of the penetration. Monty was prepared to assume "operational command" (apparently implying that it would be a temporary measure) of these American armies as part of his 21st Army Group, and seems also to have suggested that such an arrangement would facilitate the commitment of British reserves to help stop the German advance.[5]

Like many other senior British officers, Jock Whiteley was not a strong adherent of Montgomery. He naturally saw the relevance of this suggestion to the debate that had taken place—and that Monty had lost—twelve days earlier at Maastricht. There were obviously both political and personality problems inherent in any such change in command relationships and command geography. Many Americans might well interpret such a move as an effort by Monty to lord it over the Americans, as he posed as their savior, while at the same time justifying his previous strategic suggestions. But Whiteley also saw the military logic of the field marshal's suggestion.

Early that evening, after his conversation with Montgomery, Whiteley decided to discuss it with his British colleague, Maj. Gen. Kenneth W. D. Strong, SHAEF G-2, or intelligence officer. Whiteley and Strong shared an apartment, as well as some antipathy for Montgomery. The two British generals agreed, nevertheless, that Monty's suggestion was logical from a military standpoint. They also agreed that it was a sensitive matter because of American attitudes toward Montgomery. They decided to go together to discuss the idea with General Smith, the SHAEF Chief of Staff

The initial reaction of Smith, who was known for his short temper and abrasive manner, was just what the Britishers had expected. He rejected the idea out of hand. Apparently he accused Whiteley of acting like "a damned British staff officer" instead of maintaining "a completely Allied outlook." But Whiteley and Strong persisted. They soon convinced Smith that their arguments were sound, and that they were not trying to foist a British plot on him. He agreed to discuss the matter with Eisenhower when the general returned to the Trianon Palace from Verdun.[6] They spoke sometime after 2300. Although Eisenhower said he would hold off making a decision until the next morning, apparently he pondered the matter before going to bed and seems to have made up his mind in favor of the change of command.

Possibly sensing that Eisenhower had decided to make the change, Smith called Bradley around midnight and discussed the matter with him. Bradley, not surprisingly, was completely opposed to the change, but when pressed by Smith, he agreed that it made military sense and that his opposition was due more to Montgomery's personality than anything else.[7]

The next morning Eisenhower met with Tedder, Smith, Strong, and Whiteley, and discussed the question of command geography. Despite some concern that placing the American armies north of the Bulge under Montgomery's command would hurt American pride, Eisenhower was obviously convinced that military realities were more important.

Shortly after 1000 Eisenhower called Bradley and told him about the decision to shift to Monty's command all American forces north of the Bulge created by the German penetration. He assured Bradley that the shift was only temporary, until the German penetration was eliminated. Bradley, forewarned by Smith's phone call a few hours earlier, did not argue.

About 1030 Eisenhower called Montgomery at his headquarters in Zonhoven and told the field marshal that he was to assume temporary command over the American forces north of the Bulge. (The boundary between the two army groups was later designated as a line from Prüm in western Germany to Givet in eastern France.)

After a brief conference with his two army commanders, Generals Dempsey and Crerar, Montgomery decided to visit General Hodges, the First Army commander at his new headquarters at Chaudefontaine. (The First Army command post had been moved from Spa on 19 December to get it out of the immediate battle area.) By this time Monty probably knew more about the general situation in the U.S. VIII and V Corps than did any senior American commander, including General Hodges. On 18 and 19 December he had sent two liaison officers to visit the headquarters of all front-line units in the embattled region except St. Vith. Just before he left for Chaudefontaine, the officers reported to him what they had found. Hodges had one advantage over Montgomery, however. Thanks to a letter just received by his Chief of Staff, Maj. Gen. William B. Kean, from Brig. Gen. Robert W. Hasbrouck, who commanded the 7th Armored Division, Hodges now had a clear picture of the situation in the crucial St. Vith region.[8]

When Monty arrived at the First Army headquarters shortly after noon, one of his accompanying British staff officers later said that "the Field-Marshal strode into Hodge's H.Q. like Christ come to cleanse the temple."[9] He then insulted the Americans (probably inadvertently) by refusing an invitation to join them for lunch. Instead, as was his standard custom when away from his headquarters, he sat down to eat a bagged sandwich and to drink some coffee from a thermos.

Monty discussed the situation at some length with General Hodges. He instructed Hodges to use the VII Corps, under Maj. Gen. Joseph Lawton Collins, for a counterattack against the leading German divisions before they reached the Meuse. Montogmery refused to consider any alternative commander; he had formed a high opinion of Collins, and considered him the most aggressive and competent of all the American corps commanders. (It appears, in fact, that Hodges had already selected Collins for exactly the role that Monty had in mind for him.) Montgomery then left to pay a visit to Lt. Gen. William Simpson at Ninth Army headquarters.

During his visit to the First Army headquarters Monty got the impression that General Hodges looked tired. He also came to the conclusion that the headquarters was disorganized. The next day he made a private phone call to "Beetle" Smith, suggesting that Hodges should be replaced. Smith passed this on to Eisenhower, who refused in a handwritten note to Monty. The initially tense relationship between Montgomery and Hodges seems to have improved as a result of subsequent daily meetings. The general and the field marshal met on 21 December at General Simpson's headquarters to arrange, among other things, the transfer of the 2d Armored Division to the First Army. On 22 December Monty again visited Chaudefontaine, and informed Hodges that the British 29th Armoured Brigade would protect the Meuse River bridges at Namur, Dinant, and Givet, and would cover the west (right) flank of the newly assembling VII Corps. At the same time, the veteran British XXX Corps, under the experienced General Sir Brian Horrocks, was moving into position just north and west of the Meuse, west of Liège and east of Namur, ready to counterattack should any German spearheads cross the river.

As a result of the Montgomery-Hodges meeting on 20 December, Collins was directed to report to the First Army command post early the following day. Collins was then instructed by Hodges to leave in place the divisions that had been in his corps in the Roer sector. He would now have the 84th Infantry Division, moved south from the Ninth Army; the inexperienced 75th Infantry Division, recently arrived in Europe; and the veteran 2d Armored Division, also from the Ninth Army. He was told that he might also receive the experienced 3d Armored and 30th Infantry divisions, if they could be pulled out of their defensive commitments with the XVIII Airborne Corps farther east along the northern shoulder of the German penetration.

10

THE BATTLE OF ST. VITH

THE BATTLE BEGINS

The Battle of St. Vith began on 17 December 1944. The exact hour it began is debatable. It could have been 0935, when Maj. Gen. Alan W. Jones, commanding the 106th Infantry Division, appointed Lt. Col. Thomas J. Riggs Jr., the commander of the 81st Combat Engineer Battalion (and also division engineer officer), as the defense commander of the town. Or it could have been any time later that morning as spearheads from the German 18th Volksgrenadier Division (VGD) pushed westward from Schönberg and Heuem along the Schönberg–St. Vith Highway against a pickup task force of engineers, artillerymen, cavalrymen, and signalmen commanded by two staff officers: Lt. Col. Earle Williams, signal officer of the 106th Division, and Lt. Col. W. M. Slayden, Assistant G-2 (intelligence officer) of the VIII Corps, temporarily assigned to the 106th Division. Another possible starting time might be shortly after noon, when General Jones directed Brig. Gen. Bruce C. Clarke, commander of Combat Command B (CCB) of the 7th Armored Division attached to the 106th, to take over responsibility for the defense of St. Vith. Or it could have been about 1300, as Riggs's troops of the 81st and 168th Combat Engineer battalions began to dig in along a line athwart the Schönberg highway, near the village of Prümersberg, about one mile east of St. Vith. Or it could have been about 1530 as German spearheads began to probe at the line of Riggs's Engineers. Certainly the battle was well under way at dusk, at 1720, when Clarke began to commit the leading elements of his CCB into the defensive line beside the Engineers.

The story really begins at 1730 the previous day in the Netherlands, in the vicinity of Heerlen, and in Scherpenseel, Germany, northwest of Aachen, more than sixty miles north of St. Vith. This was where the 7th Armored Division was in XIII Corps reserve as part of the Ninth Army. Brigadier General Robert W. Hasbrouck, commanding the 7th Armored, was ordered to get

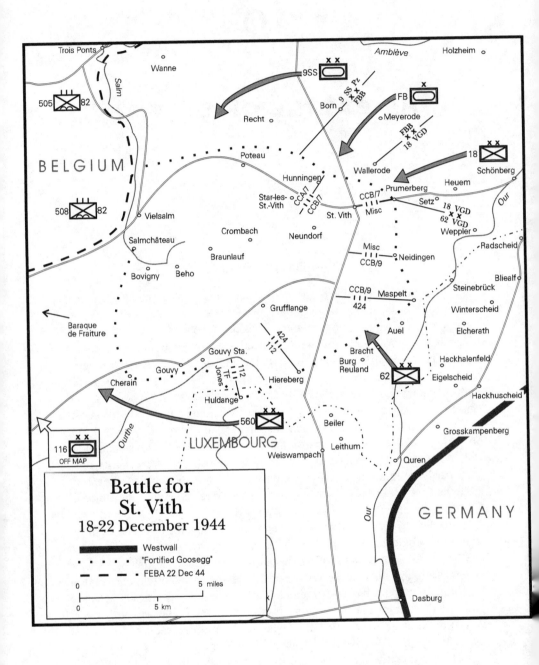

Trois Ponts
Wanne
Amblève Holzheim
9SS
505 82
Salm
Recht
Born 9 SS Pz
FBB
FB
Meyerode
FBB
18 VGD
18
Schönberg
BELGIUM
Poteau
Hunningen
Wallerode
Heuem
Prumerberg
Our
508 82
Vielsalm
Star-les-
St.-Vith
CCA/7
CCB/7
St. Vith
CCB/7
Misc
Setz
18 VGD
62 VGD
Weppler
Radscheid
Crombach
Neundorf
Salmchâteau
Braunlauf
Misc
CCB/9
Neidingen
Bliealf
Steinebrück
Bovigny
Beho
CCB/9
Maspelt
Winterscheid
424
Baraque
de Fraiture
Grufflange
Auel
Elcherath
424
112
Bracht
Hackhalenfeld
Gouvy Sta.
112
Burg
Reuland
62
Eigelscheid
Gouvy
Jones
TF
Hiereberg
Hackhuscheid
Cherain
Outhe
Huldange
560
Beiler
Grosskampenberg
116
OFF MAP
LUXEMBOURG
Leithum
Weiswampach
Quren
Our

Battle for
St. Vith
18-22 December 1944

Westwall
•••••• "Fortified Goosegg"
– – – FEBA 22 Dec 44

0   5 miles
0   5 km

GERMANY

Dasburg

ready to move south to an assembly area near Vielsalm, where he would come under the VIII Corps. He was supposed to be ready to move as soon as he received information about his route of march. At 2000 he called Brig. Gen. Bruce Clarke and ordered him to go to Bastogne as soon as possible to report to Maj. Gen. Troy Middleton, commander of the VIII Corps, for instructions and information.[1]

Shortly before midnight Hasbrouck was told he was to take two parallel roads behind the VII and V Corps of the First Army. The western road went through Heer, Verviers, Stavelot, and Trois Ponts to Vielsalm; the eastern road went through Aachen, Eupen, Malmédy, Recht, and Poteau to Vielsalm. He immediately directed the following units to start out at midnight, taking the western road: the 87th Cavalry Reconnaissance Squadron, CCB, CCA, the 814th Tank Destroyer Battalion, Main Division Headquarters, the 33rd Armored Engineer Battalion, and the division trains. On the eastern road, starting at 0800 on 17 December, would be CCR (Combat Command Reserve), Division Tactical Headquarters (TAC), Division Artillery, the 203d Antiaircraft Battalion, and smaller units.[2] No one told Hasbrouck that VIII Corps had already informed General Jones that the leading elements of the 7th Armored Division would reach St. Vith and the 106th Division by 0700 on 17 December.

As it was, after three false starts because the Ninth Army MPs were having trouble clearing the roads, the 7th Division's western column started moving about 0430, three hours before dawn. Once on the move, CCB covered the sixty-five-mile route quickly, reaching the Vielsalm assembly area without trouble at 1100. Orders were waiting there for CCB from its commander, General Clarke.

Clarke had gone ahead, pursuant to the orders he had received earlier from General Hasbrouck, and had reached Bastogne at 0400. He reported to Major General Middleton, who told him that his CCB would be attached to the 106th Division with headquarters at St. Vith. After getting as much information about the situation as he could from the Corps staff, Clarke proceeded to St. Vith, where he reported to General Jones at 1030. He then radioed orders to CCB to join him at St. Vith.

At about this time the 7th Armored Division column on the eastern road was encountering trouble.[3] The spearhead of Kampfgruppe Peiper of the 1st SS Panzer Division hit the 7th Division column just south of Malmédy. The Germans captured B Battery of the 285th Field Artillery Observation Battalion, which had inserted itself into the column between the TAC Headquarters and Division Artillery, unbeknownst to 7th Armored Division Headquarters. (The tragic fate of B Battery is recounted elsewhere.) The last few vehicles of TAC Headquarters were also hit by the Germans, and in the ensuing firefight the Division Chief of Staff, Col. Church M. Matthews, was killed. (When Hasbrouck learned of Matthews's death a few hours later, he appointed Col.

John L. Ryan Jr., commander of CCR, as the new Division Chief of Staff; Lt. Col. Fred M. Warren was appointed acting commander of CCR.)[4]

CCR and TAC Headquarters, largely unaware of what was going on behind them, continued south. The Division Artillery and the rear elements of the column turned back, shifted to the western road, and followed the division's western column into Vielsalm, arriving late that night without further incident. Meanwhile, near Stavelot, CCR ran into more of Peiper's Germans—who were as surprised as the Americans by the encounter. CCR brushed them aside, and arrived at Vielsalm with no serious damage late in the afternoon.

CCB, following Clarke's instructions, was trying to march eastward to St. Vith. The 7th Division tankers found themselves in a maelstrom of confused traffic, most of it headed west. (This was the disgraceful traffic jam described in chapter 6.)[5] It took the leading vehicles of CCB six hours to make the twelve-mile march from Vielsalm to St. Vith. When the leading tanks arrived shortly before 1730, they were immediately thrown into the line piecemeal by Clarke.

During the night Clarke supervised the extension and thickening of the original thin Engineer line that ran roughly from Hunningen, north of St. Vith, through Prümersberg to Weisenbach, where it somewhat loosely joined the left flank of CCB of the 9th Armored Division.[6] In reserve were the 31st Tank Battalion, the 23d Armored Infantry Battalion, and Company B of the 33d Armored Engineer Battalion.

Because of the delay in the arrival of the 7th Armored Division's artillery in Vielsalm, Clarke had no organic artillery. But he found a substitute that was at least as good. Lieutenant Colonel Roy U. Clay was the commander of the 275th Armored Field Artillery Battalion, which had been attached to the 14th Cavalry Group. His battalion had performed magnificently in support of the cavalrymen on 16 and 17 December with little guidance or direction from the 14th's commander, Colonel Devine. As the 14th Cavalry fell back in front of the German onslaught, Devine and his command post (CP) often forgot to inform Clay of their movements, on several occasions leaving the artillery battalion in front of the cavalrymen, engaging the advancing Germans with direct fire. Learning of Clarke's arrival at St. Vith, Clay reported to him, saying, "I want to shoot." Clarke welcomed Clay and assured him he would have plenty of opportunity to fire his weapons.

THE BATTLE ON 18 DECEMBER

By early morning on 18 December, St. Vith had become important to SS-General Sepp Dietrich and his Sixth Panzer Army. Unexpectedly blocked by determined American opposition from Elsenborn Ridge to the north, he believed it essential to widen the gap in the south so that his impatient panzer divisions could join the 1st SS Panzer Division in the drive to the Meuse

River near Huy. The 1st SS Panzer Division corridor between Büllingen-Stoumont on the north, and Vielsalm–St. Vith on the south, was only seven miles wide. Obviously the road hub at St. Vith was the key to this bottleneck.

Dietrich communicated his frustration to Field Marshal Walter Model, who passed it on to General Hasso-Eccard von Manteuffel, commander of the Fifth Panzer Army. Manteuffel reluctantly diverted his attention from the successful breakthroughs achieved by his LVIII and XLVII Panzer corps in the 28th Division sector (see chapter 7). He was much more concerned with, and interested in, the early seizure of Houffalize and Bastogne, the next objectives of his onrushing panzers. Nevertheless, he took time to order General der Artillerie Walter Lucht to expedite the seizure of St. Vith by his LXVI Corps. At the same time Dietrich moved his reserve, the II SS Panzer Corps, into the corridor behind the I SS Panzer Corps. Leading this move was the 9th SS Panzer Division, which began at once to probe for weak spots on both sides of the corridor.

General Lucht must have wondered if his superiors fully understood why he had not yet taken St. Vith. On his right, his 18th VGD had been completely successful in its daring encirclement of two American infantry regiments and an artillery battalion. And General Günther Hoffmann-Schönborn's men had also smashed open the roads to St. Vith from the east. But they could not ignore the powerful force that was encircled and already showing signs of attempting a breakout to the west. On his left, the 62d VGD, after initial success, had been halted by the combined efforts of an American infantry regiment (the 424th) and a powerful armored brigade (CCB/9). The Führer Begleit Brigade—really a small armored division—was uncommitted. Early on 18 December General Lucht ordered Col. Otto Remer, its commander, to move north and west toward St. Vith.

South of the German corridor in the Amblève valley, the relationship between the 7th Armored and 106th Infantry divisions had seemingly been established by VIII Corps. The 7th Division (without CCB) was responsible for the zone north and west of the Gouvy–St. Vith line. The 106th Division was responsible for St. Vith and everything to the south.

By this time, of course, the 106th Division consisted of only a division headquarters, one infantry regiment (the 424th), two artillery battalions (the 591st, the 592d, plus three guns of the 589th), and the engineers in the line east of St. Vith. However, attached were CCB of the 7th Armored Division and CCB of the 9th Armored Division. (The substantial remnants of the 112th Infantry Regiment would become attached the next day.) General Jones, realizing that his CP in St. Vith was now virtually on the front lines, shifted his headquarters back to Vielsalm. That afternoon General Clarke also moved the CP of CCB/7 out of St. Vith, back to Crombach.

General Hasbrouck had already established the 7th Armored Division CP in Vielsalm. It was immediately obvious to him that the enemy was in force in the area north of his zone of responsibility. He therefore had to prevent the

Germans from exploiting the open northern flank. Occupation of Poteau by elements of the 1st SS Panzer Division was the most immediate threat to holding the Vielsalm–St. Vith line. He ordered Col. Dwight A. Rosebaum, commander of CCA, to seize Poteau. The mission was accomplished, but only after a hard, three-hour fight that lasted until dusk. While this fight was going on, Lieutenant Colonel Warren put CCR into a backup defensive line behind CCA, covering Vielsalm and the St. Vith highway.

The 18th VGD by this time was launching a series of halfhearted attacks against St. Vith. Some of the fighting was bitter, but the Germans were never able to attack in sufficient strength to make a breakthrough. General Hoffmann-Schönborn was at least as concerned with the situation in his rear, where he had encircled the 422d and 423d Infantry regiments, as he was with the situation in St. Vith.

It was during this day that CCB of the 9th Armored Division and the 424th Infantry Regiment began to consolidate their positions west of the Our River into a southern extension of the St. Vith defensive line (see chapter 6). They were not seriously threatened during this day by the repeated but uncoordinated attacks of the 62d VGD.

THE BATTLE ON 19 DECEMBER

As German panzers approached, VIII Corps closed its CP at Bastogne and reopened it at Neufchâteau, about twenty-five miles to the southwest. The panzers approaching Bastogne were now deep in the rear of the American defenders at St. Vith. On both German and American situation maps the plotted positions of these defenders began to look more and more like a peninsula jutting from Vielsalm and Salmchâteau about ten miles east of the Salm River, and extending about ten miles north and south from Poteau to Huldange. But both above and below the peninsula, German spearheads extended almost another ten miles west of the Salm. Should those spearheads suddenly decide to close upon each other, the St. Vith peninsula might quickly become an island.

This possibility was obvious to the two American generals whose separate commands made up the peninsula: Brigadier General Hasbrouck of the 7th Armored Division and Major General Jones of the 106th Infantry Division. For the moment, however, their attentions were primarily fixed to the situations to their immediate front and flanks. Jones was concerned with the front; Hasbrouck, initially assigned the left flank, also assumed responsibility for the right flank and rear. Jones was also still nominally responsible for the Schnee Eifel islet to the east of the St. Vith peninsula.

Through most of that day, the attention of General Hoffmann Schönborn and that of his 18th VGD was also fixed primarily on the Schnee Eifel islet and on the determined but totally uncoordinated efforts of the 422d and 423d Infantry regiments to link the islet to the peninsula. Hoffmann-Schönborn could not direct his attention for more than a few minutes at a time to St. Vith until the two American regiments surrendered late in the afternoon.

Nonetheless, German artillery was being displaced in the direction of St. Vith, and the defenders were subjected to near-incessant artillery and mortar harassment. Elements of the Führer Begleit Brigade began to arrive near Wallerode, to the northeast of St. Vith. This foreshadowed great activity near St. Vith on the following day. During the day General Clarke received more artillery support. The 434th Armored Field Artillery Battalion of the 7th Armored Division and two batteries of the 965th Field Artillery battalion (VIII Corps artillery) were attached to CCB.

Also during the day General Clarke appointed Lt. Col. William H. G. Fuller, commander of the 38th Armored Infantry Battalion, as the defense force commander in front of St. Vith. Lieutenant Colonel Riggs, who had commanded the defense force since 17 December, became the defense force executive officer.

In the south the 62d VGD took advantage of the attenuated deployment of CCB/9 to cross the Our River and press westward in the Steinebrück, Hemmeres, and Auel area. After conferring with General Clarke at Crombach, General Hoge of CCB/9 planned to withdraw to higher ground, where he could coordinate his defense more closely with that of CCB/7 to the north. That withdrawal was carried out after dark as planned, permitting elements of the 62d VGD to occupy Niedingen and Maspelt during the night. Efforts by the Germans to infiltrate up the railroad from Steinebrück were blocked.

The 424th Infantry also received considerable attention from the 62d VGD. But its commander, Col. Alexander Reid, had by now established a substantial defensive line on the high ground between Bracht and Burg Reuland, and the Germans were unable to break through. During the day patrols of the 424th were unable to reach either CCB/9 to the north or the 112th Infantry to the south.

At 1500 Colonel Reid reported by radio to 106th Division Headquarters from his CP at Grufflange that the positions of the 424th were holding firm against moderate pressure, but that both of his flanks were open. His regiment was down to about 50 percent effectiveness. He was determined to hold his positions, but reported that he had prepared plans for withdrawal if necessary.

During the night a strong combat patrol of the 424th's 2d Battalion made contact with outposts of the 1st Battalion of the 112th Infantry near Beiler. The 424th had been unable to make earlier contact with the 112th Infantry because that regiment had been trying to comply with orders from the 28th Division to withdraw from its positions northeast of Weiswampach to Trois Vierges, and then to fall back on Bastogne. Aware of considerable German activity in the vicinity of Trois Vierges, the 112th's commander, Col. Gustin Nelson, had elected to fall back to the vicinity of Huldange, and then to try to comply with the division order. The move to Huldange was completed early in the afternoon of 19 December. Soon after that Colonel Nelson was visited in Huldange by the ubiquitous Lieutenant Colonel Slayden. After Slayden returned to Vielsalm to inform General Jones of the situation of the 112th, Jones issued an order assuming control of the 112th Infantry, which was received by Nelson shortly after dark, at 1745. Soon afterward Brig. Gen. Herbert T. Perrin, assistant division commander of the 106th, arrived at the 112th CP, having been directed by General Jones "to organize the southern flank." Perrin told Nelson to seize Beiler Berg, a ridge commanding the Our valley, and to establish a firm link with the 424th. During the night, as we have seen, contact was reestablished between the 112th and the 424th, and B Company of the 112th, which had been fighting with the 424th for three days, returned to regimental control.

General Hasbrouck, out of communication with VIII Corps headquarters, was worried about the south flank and rear of the St. Vith salient. He sent Lt. Col. Robert B. Jones, commander of the 814th Tank Destroyer Battalion, and some elements of CCR, to the south, and attached to this task force various odds and ends of units, including the remnants of the 14th Cavalry Group. Task Force Jones established screening positions at Bovigny, Cherain, Gouvy, and Gouvy Station.

20 December: The Battle Intensifies

By early on 20 December it had become obvious to the German high command that their great offensive had no possibility of success unless the St. Vith salient was promptly eliminated. With no possibility of a breakthrough north of Elsenborn Ridge, the II SS Panzer Corps could not operate unless it could be unleashed in the rear of the American front lines. Increasing pressure was placed on General Lucht to not only energize his LXVI Corps to drive through St. Vith from the west. Also the LVIII Panzer Corps, which had sideslipped south, was to turn north through Houffalize, threaten the salient from the south, and, if possible, encircle it.

On the Allied side organization was beginning to replace chaos at higher levels of command. As we have seen, General Eisenhower placed American forces north of the Givet-Prüm line, that is, north of the German penetration, under the command of Field Marshal Bernard Law Montgomery's British 21st Army Group. This included all of the American First Army except VIII Corps, as well as the Ninth Army farther north. General Omar Bradley's 12th Army Group would retain under its command only General Patton's Third Army and that part of the First Army south of the German penetration—the VIII Corps, which would become part of the Third Army.

North of the penetration, the XVIII Airborne Corps would be responsible for holding the north flank from Malmédy (where it would link up with the VII Corps' 1st Infantry Division), to Houffalize, where it was planned to link up with the VIII Corps and the Third Army. As a result the 106th and the 7th Armored divisions would come under XVIII Airborne Corps. Also in the corps would be the 82d Airborne, 3d Armored, and 30th Infantry divisions, all of which were rushing to the Werbomont-Stavelot area from the west and from the north.

Neither General Hasbrouck nor General Jones could reach VIII Corps Headquarters by radio. Thus neither of them had any official information about these high-level developments, although they had heard rumors. Hasbrouck decided to do something about this frustrating situation. He sent an officer courier to First Army Headquarters at Spa with a personal letter to the First Army Chief of Staff, Maj. Gen. William B. Kean, which was delivered before noon.

Dear Bill:

I am out of touch with VIII Corps and understand XVIII Airborne Corps is coming in.

My division is defending the line St. Vith-Poteau both inclusive. CCB, 9th AD, the 424th Inf Regt of the 106th Div and the 112th Inf Regt of the 28th Div are on my right and hold from St. Vith (excl) to Holdinger [Huldange]. Both infantry regiments are in bad shape. My right flank is wide open except for some reconnaissance elements, TDs and stragglers we have collected and organized into defense teams at road centers as far back as Cheram [Cherain] inclusive. Two German Divisions, 116 Pz and 560 VG, are just starting to attack NW with their right on Gouvy. I can delay them the rest of today maybe but will be cut off by tomorrow.

VIII Corps has ordered me to hold and I will do so but need help. An attack from Bastogne to the NE will relieve the situation and in turn cut the bastards off in rear. I also need plenty of air support. Am out of contact with VIII Corps so am sending this to you. Understand 82AB is coming up on my north and the north flank is not critical.

Bob Hasbrouck[7]

This was the first hard information that First Army Headquarters had received about the situation in the area already becoming known as "the Bulge." At 1230 an answer to Hasbrouck's letter from Gen. Courtney Hodges, the First Army commander, was dispatched to Hasbrouck via his officer courier.

Ridgway [XVIII Airborne Corps] with armor and infantry is moving from west to gain contact with you. When communication is established you come under command of Ridgway. You retain under your command following units: 106th Div, RCT 112, and CCB 9th Armed Div. All above units presently attached. Ridgway has CP in vic of Werbomont. He holds Malmedy, Stavelot and Trois Ponts.[8]

An interesting aspect of Hasbrouck's remarkably clear and comprehensive letter was his obvious personal assumption of responsibility for the defense of the St. Vith salient. While VIII Corps had not placed either division subordinate to the other, it was obvious to Hasbrouck that decisions were needed, and he made them. Apparently he worked through the 106th head-quarters with respect to all matters nominally the responsibility of General Jones, and he kept Jones fully informed. By this time General Jones seems to have been little more than a spectator. General Hodges's letter to Hasbrouck simply confirmed the already tacit relationship of Jones and Hasbrouck. (This arrangement would also put Brigadier General Hoge, also senior to Has-brouck, under the latter's command.) In fact, the relationship between Gener-als Jones and Hasbrouck does not appear to have been changed by this letter.

Actually both generals had learned more about the evolving Allied plan before the messenger got back to Hasbrouck with the letter from General Hodges. Early on 20 December, Lieutenant Colonel Slayden—there he is again!—visited VIII Corps Headquarters at Neufchâteau, where he learned everything that the VIII Corps G-2 section knew. He returned to Vielsalm in the early afternoon and reported the information, including the new command relationship, to both Jones and Hasbrouck.

Slayden then volunteered to go to Werbomont, where the XVIII Corps was setting up its CP, to find out its plans for the two divisions. With Jones's approval, the colonel went off to investigate. He learned little new informa-tion, other than that General Ridgway had not realized that the 106th Division would be part of his command. Slayden returned to Vielsalm after dark.

Intensive fighting flared intermittently along the southern perimeter of the St. Vith salient, but—with a few exceptions—things were generally quiet in the north. Although the 62d VGD continued to try to exploit the gap between CCB/9 and the 424th Infantry, by evening the situation was gener-ally unchanged all along the perimeter. The only significant development was that the 112th Infantry had firmly established the southern section of the St. Vith defensive line between Beiler and Leithum. Patrols covered the ground as far west as Huldange. The regiment's left was now firmly linked with the 424th.

21 December: All-out Assault on St. Vith

The following American forces held the perimeter of the St. Vith salient, clockwise from the north on the Salm River: CCA, 7th Armored Division, Salm River to Hunange, about one-third of an armored division; CCB, 7th Armored Division, Hunange to Prümersberg, about one-third of an armored division on the line, about one-sixth of an armored division in local reserve; miscellaneous engineers and other detachments, Prümersberg to near Niedin-gen, about the equivalent of an infantry battalion; CCB, 9th Armored Divi-sion, near Niedingen to Maspelt, about one-fourth of an armored division; 424th Infantry, Maspelt to Hierberg, about one-half of an infantry regiment; 112th Infantry, Hierberg to Huldange, about one-half of an infantry regiment; and Task Force Jones (CCR/7+), Gouvy-Cherain-Salmchâteau, about one-sixth of an armored division. The total strength approximated one armored division plus two-thirds of an infantry division—about 22,000 men holding a perimeter approximately thirty-three miles (or fifty-three kilometers) in length. It was about this time that someone, somewhere, began to refer to this dug-in perimeter, now prominent on German and American situation maps, as "the fortified goose-egg."

The following German forces half-encircled the salient, clockwise from the Salm River on the north: elements of the II SS Panzer Corps (9th SS Panzer Division and part of the 2d SS Panzer Division), Salm River to Nieder Emmels, about one and a half panzer divisions; Führer Begleit Brigade, Nieder Emmels to Wallerode, about one-half of a panzer division; 18th VGD, Wallerode to south of Prümersberg; about three-fourths of an infantry division; 62d VGD, south of Prümersberg to Maspelt, about three-fourths of an infantry division. This was a total of about two armored divisions and one and a half infantry divisions (perhaps 54,000 men) prepared to move directly against about half of the defending American perimeter. In addition, to the south and west, within striking distance were most of two panzer divisions (the 116th and the 2d, although the 2d was soon shifted toward Bastogne), most of two infantry divisions (the 340th and 560th VGDs, although the 340th also soon moved toward Bastogne), and about half of another panzer division (part of the 2d SS Panzer, which had been shifted south from II SS Panzer Corps to take advantage of the fifteen-mile gap in the old 28th Division sector). Thus, on the morning of 21 December, a total of about four and a half panzer divisions and three and a half infantry divisions (well over 100,000 men) were available to assault and/or encircle the St. Vith salient. The potential odds were probably more than five to one. In fact, the Germans elected to attack with the forces deployed against the northern and eastern faces of the salient with the main effort from the east, odds of about three to one. But (and this is a big but) the three panzer divisions to the south and west of the salient were racing north and northwestward, through and past La Roche and Houffalize, to cut off any possibility of withdrawal from the salient to the west. That morning there was serious fighting at the Baraque de Fraiture crossroads, seven miles due west of the command posts of the 7th Armored and 106th Infantry divisions at Vielsalm.

The potentially touchy command relationships involving three general officers (two of them division commanders) again emerged that morning. General Ridgway sent a radio message to General Hasbrouck, telling him that the 106th Division was relieved from attachment to the 7th Armored; henceforth the two divisions were to cooperate in carrying out corps orders.[9] At the same time General Hoge received a radio message telling him that his CCB/9 was no longer attached to the 7th Armored Division. What had appeared to be a clear if unorthodox relationship was now again in potential chaos. Who commanded whom? Who was responsible for the St. Vith salient?

Beginning at dawn there was increasing activity all along the eastern face of the salient. German artillery fire was severe, particularly against CCB/7 and CCB/9. There was also activity by the 9th SS Panzer Division against CCA/7 in the north, and by the 116th Panzer Division against the 424th and 112th Infantry regiments in the south, although this activity was more in the nature of probes that were easily repulsed.

At 1500 hours the Germans initiated an intense barrage against CCB/7 in the Prümersberg area. The fire lifted shortly after dark, and there was a lull during which the defenders could hear German tanks moving behind the line of engagement. Shortly before 2200 there was a powerful, carefully prepared assault by infantry and armor.

The line of the 38th Armored Infantry Battalion began to crumble about 2200. Corporal Kenneth M. Neher, of Tacoma, Washington, the radio operator in the darkened battalion command post, in a stone house, was alone on the second floor waiting for the battalion commander's jeep to pick him up to take him and his radios to a new CP further to the rear. Suddenly a message came over the radio: "German tanks are operating behind our lines." Looking out the window, he could see the dim outline of a tank approaching the command post, firing its big gun into every house that it passed. Just then he heard someone come into the command post on the ground floor. Thinking it was the jeep driver, he called out: "Jimmy, is that you?"

There was no response, which caused Neher to realize that he was alone in the dark with one or more German soldiers. Hearing steps on the stair, he waited silently until the intruder had almost reached the top, at which point he shoved all of his radio equipment down the steps, and jumped out of a rear window. He braced himself for a hard fall, but unexpectedly found his drop cushioned by a soft, yielding substance—the omnipresent pile of manure collected outside of almost every Ardennes village house for use as fertilizer in the spring. Pulling himself gingerly from the pile, Neher realized that he was now completely cut off from his battalion. He worked his way westward, hoping to soon rejoin his unit.[10]

The German assault into St. Vith continued. By midnight they held much of the town. General Clarke ordered a withdrawal of his command from the town to new positions along a line running southeasterly from just east of Sart-lez-St. Vith to Bauvenn. There seems to have been an attempt at a counterattack shortly before dawn, but it was never undertaken.

Sometime earlier that afternoon or evening an incident occurred that was never officially recorded. General Clarke seems either to have called personally on the radio, or sent a message back, to Hasbrouck informing him of his plan to withdraw to the new line if the intensity of the attack warranted this. Word of this message somehow got back to Ridgway, who peremptorily forbade any withdrawal. Whether or not this order was given *directly* to Clarke by Ridgway is not known; Clarke received the order but ignored it, and pulled back when he deemed that withdrawal was wise. It seems likely that soon thereafter Ridgway and Clarke had words about this apparent insubordination, but Ridgway took no official action.[11]

22 DECEMBER: THE SALIENT CONTRACTS

Soon after Clarke withdrew CCB/7 from St. Vith, General Jones sent warning orders to General Hoge (CCB/9) and Colonels Reid (424th Infantry) and Nelson (112th Infantry) that they must be prepared to withdraw. This was consistent with plans that had already been drawn up for a possible contraction of the salient. The 7th Armored Division sector, including CCB, would extend eastward from the Salm River (just north of Vielsalm) past Poteau to Sart-lez-St. Vith, then southeast to Neubrück. CCB/9 would hold a line extending southwesterly to Auf dem Gericht. From there the 424th would hold a southwesterly line to Beho. The 112th Infantry would continue this line due west to Bovigny, and would also be responsible for patrolling a western perimeter from Bovigny to contact with the 82d Airborne, which was expected to move in at Vielsalm. This would be a reduced perimeter for the "fortified goose-egg," about twenty-two miles in circumference.[12] At 0900 the withdrawal orders were issued to CCB/9 and the 424th and 112th Infantry regiments.

Shortly after dawn, the 9th SS Panzer Division began the first of several efforts to push CCA/7 out of both Poteau and Sart-lez-St. Vith. Driving snow cut down visibility and made the attacker's job more difficult. The visibility was usually adequate for the waiting Americans to seek and hit their targets. German panzers managed to penetrate between CCB and CCA, threatening the left rear of CCB as well as its withdrawal route to the Salm River. The north flank held, but barely.

General Hoge began the withdrawal of CCB/9 at about 1000. At his request, Colonel Reid of the 424th assigned his 3d Battalion to CCB/9 to act as armored infantry and to facilitate Hoge's withdrawal. By nightfall CCB/9 had reached its new positions, generally in front of Braunlauf, with little trouble. Firm contact was established on the north with CCB/7, and to the southwest with the 424th Infantry.

There was surprisingly little German interference with the snowy march of the 424th. By midafternoon the regiment was in a perimeter defense around Commanster; links were secure with CCB/9 to the left and the 112th Infantry to the right.

It was a similar story for the 112th Infantry. Well before nightfall the regiment was on its long defense line from Beho to Bovigny and northward. At the same time, Task Force Jones, in coordination with the 112th Infantry, was organizing a defensive screen around the mouth of the Bovigny-Salmchâteau corridor.

Sometime on 22 December Field Marshal Montgomery was briefed on the situation in the salient, and was told of the plan to hold a diminished perimeter. Monty quickly concluded that nothing more was to be gained by delay in the St. Vith salient, and that the troops there were in grave danger of complete encirclement. He directed that all the troops in the salient should be withdrawn behind the 82d Airborne Division.

American historians are often reluctant to give Monty the credit that he deserves. It is clear in retrospect that in this instance the British field marshal was absolutely right, and his decision saved the equivalent of two American divisions from disaster.

Shortly after midnight on 22 December General Ridgway passed on Monty's decision to Generals Jones and Hasbrouck, telling them that they would have to decide on how to conduct the withdrawal. Apparently recognizing that failing to assign single responsibility or authority in the salient was a command cop-out, Ridgway sent a letter to Hasbrouck by courier early the next morning with a copy (also by courier) to Jones. In fact, his letter made the situation potentially worse.

1. The following msg. sent you at 0100 is repeated for your information: "Confirming phone message to you, decision is yours. Will approve whatever you decide. Inform Jones he is to conform."
2. In addition to his force, Major General A.W. Jones will command 7th AD effective receipt of this message.

As one commentator has observed: "Hasbrouck would make the decision, Jones would conform, but—Jones would command Hasbrouck. As puzzling double-talk, it would be hard to beat this fifty-odd-word message."[13]

Hasbrouck apparently decided to act on the first part of Ridgway's letter and to ignore the second part. He sent a message to corps headquarters saying that if a withdrawal were to take place, it should either be through the Vielsalm bridgehead or across the front of the 82d Division. Corps responded, approving either of these alternatives, but adding, "Plans should contemplate maximum use of corridor including two bridges rather than west across the front of 82d but both are available. Inform me of plans. Expedite movement of trains. Destroy all gasoline where necessary to prevent capture."[14]

By this time Ridgway seems to have been having third thoughts about the command mess to which he had contributed so much confusion. Late that evening, he visited Hasbrouck's command post at Vielsalm. He summoned General Jones and his second-in-command, General Perrin. Ridgway then told Hasbrouck, Jones, Perrin, and a few staff officers that the withdrawal would be expedited. It was to be completed by noon on 23 December, fourteen hours hence.

Ridgway then told Jones that he would become deputy commander of the XVIII Airborne Corps. This left Hasbrouck as the single commander in the salient. Hoge was to become deputy commander of the 7th Armored Division. (Ridgway was obviously confused; this did not modify the fact that

Hoge's date of rank preceded Hasbrouck's; it did, however, confirm unequivocally that Hasbrouck would be in command.) At Ridgway's request, Jones designated Perrin as commander of the 106th.

As the meeting was ending, Jones suddenly collapsed. He had had a heart attack. As he was rushed by ambulance to the nearest field hospital, Ridgway unambiguously repeated that the 106th and all of its attached units were now attached to the 7th Armored Division. He also confirmed Perrin as commander of the 106th. He then left, leaving Hasbrouck and Perrin to complete plans for the withdrawal.

PARKER'S CROSSROADS

Inextricably linked to the fighting that was taking place in the St. Vith salient on 20–23 December was a small but bitter struggle that was going on eight miles west of the Salm River at an obscure crossroad hamlet called Baraque de Fraiture. The story of the epic fight there begins on 19 December.

At 1500 the remnants of the 589th Field Artillery Battalion arrived at Baraque de Fraiture. There were three 105-mm howitzers (the three guns from A Battery that Lt. Eric Wood had sent west from Schönberg early on 17 December), about twenty trucks and jeeps, a few machine guns, and nearly 100 officers and men. In command was Maj. Arthur C. Parker III, formerly the Executive Officer of the 589th, and now commanding this remnant of the battalion.

Parker's rump battalion had been commandeered near Bovigny on 18 December by Col. Herbert W. Kruger, commander of the 174th Field Artillery Group. Totally out of communication with the 106th Division, Parker saw no reason not to obey the orders of a senior artillery colonel who seemed to know what he was doing, and who apparently was going to fight. So, when ordered by Colonel Kruger to establish a roadblock at Baraque de Fraiture to keep supply lines open, Parker obeyed.

Parker soon learned that Division Headquarters was a few miles away at Vielsalm. He reported to General McMahon, the Division Artillery commander, who told him he should continue to hold the roadblock, to keep open the division's supply route, should there be an attack from the west or south. McMahon also saw that this could be a useful position with respect to the new line that the 82d Airborne Division and 3d Armored Division were establishing south of Manhay. (Actually, as Parker later discovered, there were outposts of the 82d Airborne and 3d Armored a bare mile north of the crossroad.)

Parker went back and began to organize the area for defense. He incorporated on his perimeter a platoon from the 87th Reconnaissance Squadron and a detachment of three quadruple .50-caliber machine guns and a self-propelled 37-mm gun. The arrival of some stragglers from Service Battery now gave him 110 officers and men.

When the 87th Recon Squadron reported that there were Germans in Samree, about four miles to the southwest, Parker was asked if he could fire on the village. He could and did: Adjusted by radio reports from the front, two of his howitzers dispersed the enemy patrol.

That night German cyclists probed the crossroads. They were driven off by machine-gun fire. There were further probes the next two days. On 21 December Parker was wounded. He refused to be evacuated until he lost consciousness. Major Elliot Goldstein then took over the command of the area now known as "Parker's Crossroads."

Baraque de Fraiture was at the extreme northern flank of the German Fifth Panzer Army drive toward the Meuse River and Dinant. It was not until 23 December that the local German commanders thought the position important enough to warrant serious action. Late in the day the 2d SS Panzer Division mounted a major attack. At 1600 the defenders were overwhelmed, and the three howitzers captured. The survivors fell back to the north to join the 3d Armored Division. The 589th Field Artillery Battalion had been in battle almost continuously for eight days. It no longer existed.

23 December: End of the Fortified Goose egg

The most dangerous operation in modern war is a daylight withdrawal. In General Hasbrouck's command post, late on 22 December, General Ridgway had ordered a daylight withdrawal from the St. Vith salient.

One analytic historian has compared a daylight withdrawal with one done at night as follows:

A retirement under the cover of darkness is a ticklish affair. It must be planned; the elements getting out must move on a specific timetable; those remaining must be steady, calm, unruffled. Above all, the enemy must, if possible, be deceived. Daylight retirement by troops already engaged is another affair. In the first place, one does not retire unless by force of circumstances; *ergo*, the enemy has superiority. He is pressing, harassing, perhaps definitely assaulting. To put it bluntly, in a retirement, one gets out the heavy stuff first, "to let a man run who can run," as one famous instructor at Leavenworth used to remark. Then the remaining troops divide themselves into two categories, those who can march out more or less unhampered, and those who form the last crust—the men on the actual fighting line, now reduced in number to a minimum, who must at a given moment, get out and stand not on the order of their going. Any dislocation of the timetable, any interruption in the movement can, and frequently does, produce panic. The retirement changes to a rout. That's just too bad.[15]

Amazingly, General Hasbrouck and his staff prepared and issued the orders in time for the withdrawal to begin at an H-hour of 0600 on 23 December. In only one case were orders late in arriving (see below). In accordance with standard doctrine, the orders saw to it that they got "out the heavy stuff first." Medium artillery units and heavy engineer organizations were on the roads before 0600. Those able to march out "more or less unhampered" began to move at H-hour, although not always quite in accordance with the plan. And those units in "the last crust" made their preparations to start their final dash for the rear at 1600. This was not quite the fourteen hours that General Ridgway had directed, but it was an amazing eighteen hours, nonetheless.

While CCA/7 held the northern flank against mounting German pressure, CCB/7 began its withdrawal to the Salm River according to plan. There was some trouble initially, since enemy units had infiltrated down the railway from St. Vith. Nevertheless, the step-by-step withdrawal began as ordered before dawn. The withdrawal was facilitated by a hard freeze during the night, permitting the Americans to use forest tracks that would otherwise have been impassable to vehicles.

CCA/7 had to repulse repeated German attacks on Poteau that began before dawn, but leapfrog movements were initiated on schedule and carried out smoothly according to plan. At dark, CCA closed on the Salm River behind CCB, which was already across the river in the sector of the 82d Airborne Division.

The only major unit that did not receive its orders on time was CCB/9. At 0605 General Hoge got his orders to move at 0600. He simply opened up his radio net and issued orders in the clear simultaneously to all of his units. CCB/9 was only about fifteen minutes late in getting started, but it was not an easy start since the Germans were just beginning an attack on Grufflange, with the Beho-Bovigny road apparently their objective. Hoge mounted a counterattack, halted the enemy attack, and then resumed his phased, leapfrog withdrawal.

The 424th had little enemy interference with its withdrawal. Many of the infantrymen were able to take advantage of the proximity of the 9th Armored Division's tanks, and by the time the armored vehicles reached Beho infantrymen were clustered on them like flies.

Facilitating the withdrawal were clearing skies, which enabled American fighter aircraft to appear over the battlefield. But the aircraft dared not hit any activity on the ground in or near the "goose egg" because they could not possibly tell friend from foe. Their mere presence, however, forced the Germans to be more cautious and gave the Americans more confidence than they probably should have had.

The 112th Infantry and Task Force Jones were the most seriously engaged units that day. The only grave mistake made by the 7th Armored Division staff affected the 112th. Colonel Nelson had been ordered to hold his last battalion in position as a covering force until he received positive radio orders from Hasbrouck personally to withdraw. At 1530 Nelson reported that everything had cleared out behind his covering force and that enemy tanks were closing in. He asked permission to withdraw his 2d Battalion. There was no response. Communications had been lost. At 1630, with German tanks within 200 yards of his command post and still no word from Hasbrouck, Colonel Nelson ordered the 2d Battalion to withdraw at once.

As dusk turned to darkness, the roads leading to the two bridges were all clogged, and the enemy—now well aware of what was going on—was pressing in behind. However, the covering forces all kept their heads and held the Germans off as the columns slowly moved northward and westward. Most seriously damaged was Task Force Jones, which was the last unit to get back to the bridges. It was hard-pressed by the 2d SS Panzer Division's Reconnaissance Battalion, which had been on the right flank in the attack on Parker's Crossroads and which struck the withdrawing Americans from the west.

In the now-stripped 7th Armored Dvision's command post in Vielsalm, Hasbrouck and Perrin were checking off reports from the covering forces to be certain that all of their units were getting out. Finally, with most tallies complete, they were told that enemy tanks were in Vielsalm. They decided it was time to go. As they were leaving the headquarters building, a German tank came around the corner. It destroyed one American half-track, but the remaining jeeps and half-tracks dashed away down side streets, heading for the bridge. Hasbrouck halted his jeep on the far side of the bridge and jumped out. There were no more American vehicles coming. He nodded his head to the waiting engineer captain. A detonator was pushed; there was a great explosion; the bridge collapsed. The St. Vith salient was no more.

11

HOLDING THE NORTHERN SHOULDER

On the morning of 20 December, events on the northern flank of the Ardennes battle, originally centered upon the swirling battle at Krinkelt-Rocherath, were shifting to the west. The 2d and 99th divisions were about to receive an unexpected but well-earned rest, while the 1st Infantry Division was about to become the unwelcome center of attention for the 12th SS Panzer Division. And even farther to the west, Kampfgruppe Peiper was fighting for survival in the middle of a steadily constricting ring of enemies.

By this time the 26th Infantry Regiment of the 1st Division had established a firm position in and around Dom Butgenbach, which had become the key point of the German penetration of the northern shoulder. The 2d Battalion of the 26th, reinforced by four tank destroyers from the 2d Platoon, Company A, 634th Tank Destroyer Battalion, and four Sherman tanks of Company C, 745th Tank Battalion, formed the main line of resistance at Dom Butgenbach itself. The battalion was commanded by Lt. Col. Derrill M. Daniel, who had a Ph.D. from Clemson University. Daniel and his men had engaged in a few minor skirmishes with German reconnaissance units on 18 and 19 December, but had not been seriously challenged by the enemy. The 1st Battalion was at Elsenborn, protecting the right and rear of the 2d Division, while the 3d Battalion occupied the high ground north of Dom Butgenbach with its left flank in contact with the 2d Division.

The 16th Infantry Regiment extended the line west from Butgenbach, to the vicinity of Waimes, east of Malmédy. The 1st Battalion of the 16th was on the left, the 3d Battalion was on the right, and the 2d Battalion was in reserve. The third regiment of the 1st Division, the 18th Infantry, was east of Eupen and prepared to defend the roadnet running through the Hohes Vennes from the 500 to 700 paratroopers that had been reported to have been dropped in that vicinity on 17 December.

The area farther west was now the responsibility of the newly arrived

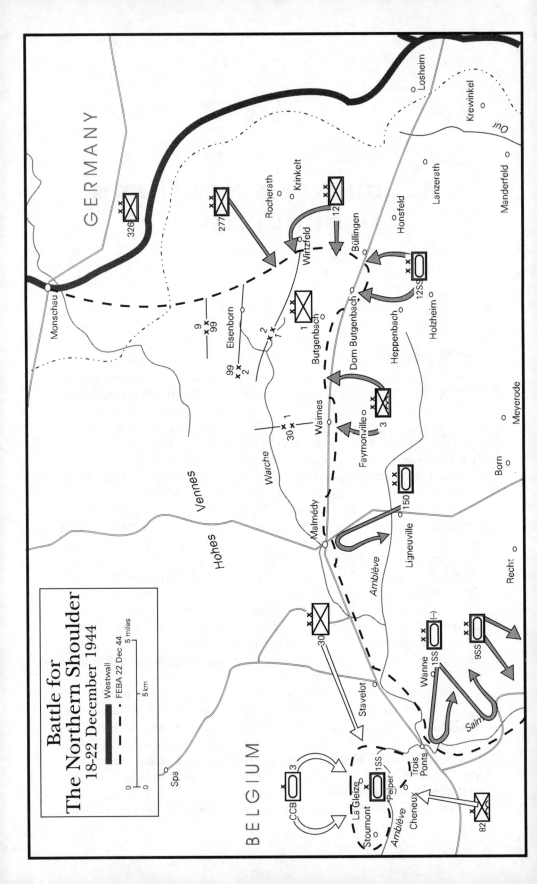

Battle for
The Northern Shoulder
18-22 December 1944

Westwall
FEBA 22 Dec 44

0   5 km
0   5 miles

GERMANY

BELGIUM

Monschau

Rocherath
Krinkelt
Wirtzfeld
Büllingen
Losheim
Krewinkel
Manderfeld
Lanzerath
Honsfeld
Holzheim
Heppenbach
Dom Burgenbach
Butgenbach
Elsenborn
Waimes
Faymonville
Born
Meyerode
Malmédy
Ligneuville
Recht
Stavelot
Trois Ponts
Wanne
Spa
La Gleize
Stoumont
Cheneux
Peiper

Hohes   Vennes

Warche

Amblève

Amblève

Salm

Our

326
277
12
12SS
99
99
2
1
1
99
2
30   1
3
150
30
30
3
CCB
1SS
1SS(-)
9SS
82

XVIII Airborne Corps. From Waimes, the line continued west to Malmédy, which was held by the 120th Infantry of the 30th Division.[1] Stavelot was now firmly held by the 117th Infantry of the 30th Division, which was pushing west against the rear of Peiper's position at La Gleize. North and west of La Gleize the remaining regiment of the 30th Division, the 119th Infantry, was attempting to push through the bottleneck of the Salm River defile against a desperate defense by Peiper's men. The 30th Division was about to receive a powerful reinforcement in the form of CCB of the 3d Armored Division, which had been attached to the XVIII Airborne Corps. From Stoumont the American line curled sharply south to Trois Ponts, which was held by the 505th Parachute Infantry Regiment of the 82d Airborne Division. The line of the Salm River to Vielsalm was held by the 506th and 508th Parachute Infantry regiments of the 82d Airborne.

From the German point of view, the situation on the front of the Sixth Panzer Army must have appeared bleak but not hopeless. The infantry and armored units of the I SS Panzer Corps had failed in repeated efforts to batter a hole in the V Corps defense. However, they had inflicted significant casualties on the 2d and 99th divisions and had forced them to withdraw from Krinkelt-Rocherath. As a result, General Hermann Priess ordered the 12th SS Panzer Division to sideslip south and west in an attempt to follow Peiper's route through Butgenbach. The 560th Panzerjäger Battalion was to be committed along with the remnants of the 12th SS Panzer Regiment and the 25th SS Panzergrenadier Regiment in a last ditch effort to break through.

20 DECEMBER

Near dawn the first German attacks were made on the new positions that had been taken up by the 2d and 99th divisions on Elsenborn Ridge. Situated on a forward slope looking toward Krinkelt and Wirtzfeld, these positions had excellent visibility and fields of fire. The first attack was repulsed easily, as were two others later in the day.

Farther south and west, in the sector of the 1st Infantry Division, at about 0330 hours, a force estimated to consist of twenty tanks and a battalion of infantry had earlier attacked from Büllingen west toward the 26th Infantry's 2d Battalion position at Dom Butgenbach. The German tanks hit a roadblock of mines and turned off the road to the south. They moved cross-country to the north-south road running into Dom Butgenbach and continued their attack. The Germans struck F Company, knocked out three bazooka teams and a machine-gun section, but were then repulsed by the massed fires of three artillery battalions and a 90-mm antiaircraft gun battery firing from positions at Elsenborn. By 0415 the attack had been repelled.

Another attack against the 2d Battalion of the 26th Infantry began at about 0600 hours, again striking the front of E and F companies west of the road. Some German tanks were able to penetrate the position, but the American infantrymen stayed in their fighting holes and called for artillery fire. Three 1st Division artillery battalions responded, and were soon reinforced by the fire of some of the artillery of the 2d Division. At about 0800 elements of G and C companies were dispatched from reserve to plug the gap; however, they were not needed. The artillery had done the job. The Germans withdrew, leaving the wreckage of eight tanks burning in the fields. These unsuccessful assaults at Dom Butgenbach and Elsenborn Ridge cost the 12th SS Panzer Division about 30 dead and more than 100 wounded, the majority of a total of 180 killed and wounded suffered by the division that day. More serious, the Germans lost nearly two dozen tanks, cutting its effective armor strength by nearly half.

A little later, at 0900, farther west at Waimes, the 3d Battalion of the 16th Infantry was struck by elements of the III Battalion, 8th Parachute Regiment, 3d Parachute Division. The Germans were repulsed by American artillery fire. This attack was renewed at 1625 hours, and the Germans were once more turned back in little less than an hour. These attacks cost the 8th Parachute Regiment dearly; losses amounted to twenty killed, sixty wounded, and close to eighty missing.

American losses had been heavy as well, particularly in the 2d Platoon of the 26th Infantry's Antitank Company, attached to the 2d Battalion. The platoon lost two of its four 57-mm guns. Since the 3d Battalion near Schwarzen-büchel had not been so hard-pressed, at about 1300 the regiment sent the Antitank Company's 3d Platoon to join the 2d Platoon in the sector of the 2d Battalion at Dom Butgenbach. By direction of Colonel Daniel, the battalion commander, the four new guns were quickly dug in to the west of E Company's sector. The 3d Platoon's guns were soon heavily engaged. A German force of ten tanks and eight jagdpanzers smashed into the lines of E and F companies of the 2d Battalion.

One of the 57-mm gun commanders was Sgt. Stanley Oldenski. He had sent most of his crew out to get some tanks with their bazookas, leaving only him and his gunner, Cpl. Henry "Red" Warner, to man the gun. Oldenski loaded, and Warner slammed four rounds into a jagdpanzer, which was quickly consumed by flames. Warner then shifted his fire to another German tank destroyer, knocking it out with two rounds. As he fired another shot, to make sure the enemy armored vehicle was destroyed, his gun jammed. A third jagdpanzer appeared out of the mist, heading straight for Warner and his gun. The German tank destroyer commander apparently decided to run over the gun, and stuck his head out of the turret, to guide the monster. By this time the jagdpanzer was no more than ten yards away. Warner pulled out his .45-caliber pistol, fired a quick shot at the tank commander, then dove into a slit trench near the trail of the gun, fully expecting to be crushed to death. Suddenly the tank stopped, went into reverse, and raced backward. Warner raised his head and saw the tank commander slumped half out of the turret— he had been killed by the single pistol shot.

At Malmédy and Stavelot the day was quiet. American reinforcements from many different commands continued to trickle into Malmédy until a respectable, if somewhat thinly spread, line had been formed south of the town. At Stavelot the situation was even better. With the bridge destroyed the icy river now provided a strong deterrent to a German attack. Nevertheless, the American defenders remained wary.

Farther to the west, the net around Kampfgruppe Peiper was tightened as the newly arrived CCB of the 3d Armored Division began to drive south from Spa to Trois Ponts. Brigadier General Truman E. Boudinot divided his command into three task forces that were to drive south along separate, roughly parallel roads leading into the valley of the Amblève River.

The easternmost task force, under Lt. Col. William B. Lovelady, was the strongest, and it enjoyed the greatest success. Task Force Lovelady drove all the way to the river and en route surprised and destroyed a small German fuel supply column guarded by infantry and a few assault guns, which had been moving up from Petit-Spa and Trois Ponts to replenish Peiper's force. This advance hammered the final nail into the coffin of Kampfgruppe Peiper, which was now completely isolated at La Gleize.

The other two task forces, under Maj. Kenneth T. McGeorge in the center and Capt. John W. Jordan to the west, were less successful. Striking Peiper's main body, they made little progress, but were able to reinforce the 119th Infantry. The concentrated firepower of Peiper's tanks, half-tracks, assault guns, and automatic weapons stalled the American advance. The lively exchange of fire produced significant losses on both sides.

West of La Gleize the 119th Infantry Regiment began operations to retake Stoumont. The 1st Battalion of the 119th Infantry, under Lt. Col. Robert Herlong, supported by the 740th Tank Battalion, attempted to drive down the defile of the Amblève. However, the Germans had strongly garrisoned the St. Edouard Sanatorium, which overlooked the only route of advance.[2] Difficulties with the steep terrain, which impeded or prevented off-road movement, as well as the fortresslike nature of the sanatorium, stymied Herlong's efforts during the day. Two of his companies succeeded in driving the Germans from the sanatorium, which they then occupied. They were immediately subjected to a vicious counterattack. It now became evident that it was impossible for supporting American tanks to negotiate the embankment leading from the road to the strongpoint. The Germans, with an easy slope running from Stoumont to the sanatorium, were able to provide effective tank support to the counterattacking infantry. As a result, the two American companies in the sanatorium were nearly destroyed, and the survivors were driven back to their start line.

Saint Edouard sheltered 250 Belgian civilians, mostly children and elderly people who had been patients there, as well as the sanatorium's staff. Fortunately, they were able to escape most of the battle by taking refuge in the basement, which was deep enough to provide a safe haven from the fighting. There, along with a few wounded Germans and Americans, shaken by artillery and mortar fire, they waited for the battle above them to end.

Farther south and west, the newly arrived 82d Airborne Division began to add its weight to the American defense. The 504th Parachute Infantry Regiment probed toward Cheneux, finding it strongly occupied by the greater part of the 74th FLAK Battalion. The commander of the 504th, Col. Reuben H. Tucker, ordered an immediate attack on the village. Although heavy German fire halted the attack, the survivors managed to get a toehold in the village. However, they found themselves isolated. Reinforcements were unable to get through the terrific volume of German fire over the open fields. Fortunately for the Americans, the Germans were short of infantry and were thus unable to do more than keep the paratroopers pinned down.

Farther south, the 505th and 508th Parachute Infantry regiments were moving into position between Trois Ponts and Vielsalm. The last regiment in the division, the 325th Glider Infantry, remained in reserve. Late in the day patrols from the 506th Parachute Infantry established contact with patrols of the 7th Armored Division west of St. Vith. With that contact, all the forces in the vicinity of St. Vith passed to the command of General Ridgway and the XVIII Airborne Corps.

21 DECEMBER: HOLDING THE SHOULDER

The position of the 2d and 99th divisions on Elsenborn Ridge remained firm despite a determined German attack at midday. Artillery fire again disorganized the attackers, who were forced to withdraw to their starting point. A lull ensued on the Elsenborn front. Until 28 December this sector remained relatively inactive as the Germans sought to reorganize and bring up sufficient artillery to counter the large number of pieces V Corps massed behind the ridge. Eventually, Brig. Gen. John H. Hinds, the 2d Division Artillery commander, who was acting as de facto corps artillery commander, was controlling a total of 348 pieces, including 16 divisional and 7 corps artillery battalions plus several tank destroyer and antiaircraft artillery battalions.[3]

Much earlier, at 0130, the Germans had struck again at Dom Butgenbach. The attackers were the 12th SS Panzer Division and elements of the 3d Parachute Division. SS-Colonel Hugo Kraas, commander of the 12th SS Panzer Division, was determined to smash through the positions of the 26th Infantry. He organized an attack by three grenadier battalions supported by all of his available tanks and assault guns. Machine-gun and tank-gun fire opened up on the positions of the 2d Battalion of the 26th Infantry southeast of the town. American artillery quieted the Germans for a time, but at 0300 they answered with a heavy barrage from artillery, mortars, and Nebelwerfer, which succeeded in knocking out telephone communications in the battalion. However, the American infantrymen retained radio contact with the artillery, and once more heavy American shell fire was able to throw back a German attempt to advance at 0500.

Under Kraas's driving leadership, the strongest German effort against Butgenbach began at 0715—an effort that nearly overran the battalion's position. Twelve tanks and a reinforced battalion of infantry advanced and broke through despite heavy American shell fire. Two of the German tanks drove up and down the hedgerow that formed the basis for the defensive position of companies E and G, firing into foxholes and searching out automatic and heavy weapons positions. They succeeded in knocking out all of them: six Browning automatic rifles (BARs), two .30-caliber (7.62-mm) machine guns, two 57-mm antitank guns, and six bazookas. Without support from these heavy weapons, the two companies were nearly helpless. But again artillery was called in to save the day.

A particularly vicious struggle took place at the western end of the line of the 2d Battalion of the 26th Infantry, where the 3d Platoon of the regiment's antitank company had been located the previous day. One of the 57-mm guns, commanded by S.Sgt. Noah Collier, destroyed three Panther tanks in succession, only to be knocked out by a panzerfaust round fired by one of the German grenadiers supporting the tank attack. Collier picked up a Browning automatic rifle and sprayed the advancing German infantrymen. He was quickly joined at the gun position parapet by two members of his crew, Cpl. Irwin Schwartz and Pfc. Donald Rose, who had grabbed their carbines. The German infantrymen fell back and took cover. A bitter firefight ensued, lasting more than an hour. Collier was slightly wounded in the leg but ignored the injury. When he heard a call for help from another GI, to the left front, he jumped up from the gun position and ran into the fog in the direction of the call. He was never seen again by his comrades.

The American artillery kept up near-continuous fire on the Germans in front of the 2d Battalion's main line of resistance (MLR). Despite this rain of shells, the Germans persisted in their attack against the Dom Butgenbach positions.

At about 0900 five German tanks hit the right of E Company and drove into the positions of G Company. Three of the tanks advanced toward the E Company command post (CP) in a house in Dom Butgenbach. Bazooka teams were unable to get into position to fire on the tanks. However, an American tank north of Dom Butgenbach was able to destroy one of the roving German tanks. A second German tank was knocked out at 1600, and the one remaining was driven away by the fire of a 90-mm SP gun. Fortunately for the Americans, the German infantry had been unable to support the attack; heavy American shelling had pinned them to the ground at the outset. The surviving German tanks were finally forced to withdraw shortly after 1600.

The 2d Battalion had been hit hard by the German attack. In Company E three men were killed, fifteen wounded, and twelve missing. Company G had started the attack with seventy-seven men; thirteen were killed, ten wounded, and twelve missing. Two American tanks and three tank destroyers had also been lost. To balance these losses, American patrols later reported enemy dead were "as common as grass." After the battle a Graves Registration unit reported 782 German dead in front of the American positions at Dom Butgenbach and Waimes. The 12th SS Panzer Division and the 3d Parachute Division, already badly hit during the actions of 16–19 December, had been gutted. Forty-seven tanks, assault guns, and tank destroyers were left smoking wrecks in front of the American positions.

Although the tenacity of the soldiers of the 26th Infantry, who had stuck to their positions during the vicious German assault, was commendable, the battle had truly been won by the awesome firepower of the American artillery. Ten battalions of artillery were eventually called into action against the German attack, and more than 10,000 rounds were expended. This cascade of high-explosive fire had kept most of the German infantry pinned down in the fields east and south of Dom Butgenbach. Although the German tanks had been able to advance into the American positions, they were not supported by infantry and consequently vulnerable. Moreover, tanks cannot hold ground without foot soldiers, so the negligible German tank successes were fleeting.

At Malmédy the 150th Panzer Brigade, SS-Lt. Col. Otto Skorzeny's erstwhile "Trojan Horse" unit, was about to make its combat debut.[4] Skorzeny had intended that his unit's mixed bag of American and imitation-American vehicles should lead SS-Lt. Col. Peiper's column as a diversion in the advance to the Meuse. Unfortunately, snarled traffic in the first days of the advance had delayed his movement to a crawl. Unable to join Peiper, Skorzeny had asked that his brigade be used as a normal combat unit. When permission was granted, he decided to act on the reports from his scouts that Malmédy was very lightly held. By attacking there, Skorzeny hoped to rip a new hole in the American lines, threatening the flanks and rear areas of the V Corps and XVIII Corps.

Unfortunately for the German attackers, Skorzeny's estimate of the defenders' strength was woefully inaccurate, as additional American forces had arrived in the village after the last German combat reconnaissance. The defenders included the 1st Battalion of the 120th Infantry, the 99th Infantry Battalion, elements of the 526th Armored Infantry Battalion, and elements of the 291st Engineer Combat Battalion.[5] The remainder of the 120th Infantry extended the line to the west and east, while six battalions of artillery were in position to support the defenders.

In the early morning of 21 December, the Germans advanced toward Malmédy in two columns. The first column, consisting of a reinforced infantry company, attacked north along the main road, Highway N-23, directly toward the town. The second column, consisting of all ten tanks in the brigade plus a battalion of infantry, advanced from the southwest on a secondary road, then onto the main Malmédy-Stavelot highway toward the town.

The American defenders had been alerted to the attack when a prisoner from Skorzeny's brigade was seized the previous night. The first German column was halted by a hastily laid minefield in front of the positions of the 1st Battalion of the 120th Infantry and was then smashed by small arms, mortar fire, and artillery. The artillery was highly effective. In what seems to have been the first use of the new VT or POZIT fuse, accurate airbursts demoralized the Germans. The remnants of the company fled after a few minutes.[6]

Skorzeny's main column caused more problems for the defenders. Although one Panther tank was damaged and withdrew after taking a hit from a towed 3" tank destroyer, and a second struck a minefield and began to burn, the rest forged on with their supporting infantry. The rain of fragments from deadly VT-fused shells began again, and many of the German infantrymen panicked and fled.

The remaining eight German tanks then forced back a platoon of the 120th Infantry's K Company and appeared ready to cross the bridge over the Warche River into the rear of the American position. However, two more Panthers were then knocked out by bazooka fire and the remaining six were driven to cover by the fire of three towed 3" guns positioned on the bluff along the road to Spa. Two M18 self-propelled tank destroyers then drove forward, knocked down with shell fire a stone wall that was protecting the Germans, and destroyed two more Panthers with armor-piercing shells. The remaining German tanks then withdrew, leaving the surviving infantry behind to be battered by intense small-arms, mortar, and artillery fire.

With the collapse of the attack, Skorzeny realized that his bid to seize Malmédy had failed miserably. He ordered the brigade to withdraw to the south. A few days later it would be withdrawn from the front and finally disbanded. The first action by the "Trojan Horse" Brigade had also been its last.

KAMPFGRUPPE PEIPER STRUGGLES FOR SURVIVAL

Elements of the 2d SS Panzergrenadier Regiment made an early-morning attempt to cross the river at Stavelot. The panzergrenadiers again bravely waded the icy water in the face of intense fire. Most never got across the river; the few who did were quickly hunted down and killed or captured.

At Stoumont another attack on Peiper's men in the Saint Edouard Sanatorium failed because the supporting tanks were unable to move forward. The enterprising commander of the 740th Tank Battalion, Col. George K. Rubel, decided to break the impasse. He commandeered a 155-mm SP gun and put it in position to open direct fire on the sanatorium.[7] Under the covering fire of the big gun, a ramp was hurriedly constructed that allowed tanks to drive over the embankment that had stymied them on the previous day. A renewed infantry assault with armor support was then mounted. This was too much for the German defenders, who abandoned St. Edouard for the last time. The civilans sheltering in the sanatorium's basement gratefully emerged to greet their American liberators. They were astounded at the devastation inflicted on the building over the preceding three days: It had been almost completely destroyed. Although shaken and tired, none of those who had taken refuge in the basement had been seriously injured during the battle.[8]

With the sanatorium finally lost, the German position at Stoumont became untenable. Peiper began to withdraw into a defensive semicircle close around the town of La Gleize. By the morning of 22 December, American artillerymen, observing from the ruins of the sanatorium, were bringing heavy fires to bear on Peiper's position. At Cheneux Colonel Tucker had decided to flank the German position with the 3d Battalion of his 504th PIR. By late afternoon his men were ready on the high ground overlooking the bridge and village. G Company, attached to the battalion, was then sent in to attack in the gathering darkness. Some of the Germans escaped, but fourteen self-propelled FLAK guns, six half-tracks, a number of assault guns, and several trucks were left behind, along with the bodies of dead SS panzergrenadiers. The capture of Cheneux had cost the paratroopers 23 killed and 202 wounded. Nearly all of these casualties were in companies B and C, leaving B Company with 18 men and C Company with 3 officers and 38 men.

Other elements of the 82d Airborne Division had less success farther south. At Trois Ponts a bridgehead on the east bank of the Salm had been established the previous night by E Company of the 505th Parachute Infantry. An attack by elements of the 1st SS Panzergrenadier Regiment, supported by assault guns, hit the company at midday. Although the company fought skillfully and was well supported by the 456th Parachute Field Artillery Battalion, the paratroopers were too lightly equipped to hold off the heavily armed panzergrenadiers. Company F was sent across the river to support them, but to no avail. The paratroopers were forced to withdraw across the river in broad daylight and were cut to ribbons, losing more than seventy men. However, German attempts to follow up with an assault crossing of the river also failed, leaving Peiper still isolated.

During the evening the situation at St. Vith, to the east of the 82d Airborne Division, had deteriorated. The 7th Armored Division and its attached units began their contraction of the "fortified goose-egg" on the east bank of the Salm (see chapter 10). However, the situation in front of the 505th Parachute Infantry remained quiet.

22 DECEMBER

The last effort of the 12th SS Panzer Division to smash the northern shoulder of the Bulge was made early on 22 December. Six tanks and elements of the 26th SS Panzergrenadier Regiment attacked the 1st Battalion of the 26th Infantry south of Butgenbach, on the right of the 2d Battalion. The tanks and an undetermined number of infantry soldiers infiltrated through the positions of A and K companies and managed to get into the town itself. Eventually an 800-yard gap was opened between the two companies.

To restore the situation, the 1st Battalion of the 18th Infantry, which had been recently relieved from its antiparatroop duties, was ordered to attack south to restore the position. B Company of the 26th Infantry was also pulled out of the line to reinforce A Company.

Under this pressure and renewed artillery fire, the German attack collapsed. By 1615 hours most of the surviving attackers had fallen back. A 200-yard gap in the line remained, however, and was not closed until the next day.

Between Butgenbach and Stavelot the American front remained quiet on 22 December. However, at La Gleize the battle against Peiper continued to rage on. With the high ground north of Stoumont in American hands, the artillery was now wreaking havoc among Peiper's men. Colonel Rubel's 155-mm SP gun was moved up during the day and again began shattering targets with direct fire. In addition, the 155-mm howitzers of the 30th Division's 113th Field Artillery Battalion began dropping in volleys of VT-fused shells, adding to the destruction. At least four other battalions, as well as numerous tanks and tank destroyers, fired into the town. La Gleize was slowly reduced to rubble and German casualties mounted. By the end of the day Peiper had decided to withdraw. Unless fuel could be gotten to him, he would have to go on foot and abandon his heavy equipment and vehicles.

Far to the south the 508th Parachute Infantry extended its lines west from the Salm near Vielsalm. The withdrawal of the 7th Armored Division from St. Vith had exposed the right flank of the 82d Airborne Division and the XVIII Airborne Corps. In addition, west of St. Vith the onrushing panzers of the LVIII Panzer Corps and the XLVII Panzer Corps also posed a major threat to the stability of the American position. South of Vielsalm there was a yawning gap in the American lines. General Ridgway had little time in which to realign his corps to meet the threat (see chapter 10).

23 December

On the front of the 1st Division on the 23d of December the principal activity was desultory artillery shoots at German columns reported moving eastward away from the battle. These columns were in fact the battered remnants of the 12th SS Panzer Division, which had been ordered to withdraw for an urgently needed rest and refitting. The 1st Battalion of the 18th Infantry relieved the 1st Battalion of the 26th Infantry, while the 2d Battalion of the 18th Infantry moved into the line southwest of Butgenbach. Between 24 and 28 December the front of the 1st Division, like that of the 2d and 99th divisions to the northeast, remained quiet as the Germans subsided into purely defensive action.

At La Gleize, SS-Lt. Col. Peiper continued to radio for permission to withdraw his battered command. Permission was finally granted late in the evening, as long as his vehicles and wounded were brought out as well. An understandably exasperated Peiper had had enough. He ordered the withdrawal to begin and directed that the radios be destroyed. On foot 800 officers and men of Peiper's command slipped east out of town, taking with them American Maj. Hal McCown, captured a few days before.[9] The column carefully slipped past American outposts and crossed the Amblève via a small wooden footbridge, led by two Belgian civilians Peiper had dragooned into serving as guides. At dawn they hid in the forests beyond the river and then continued their trek at nightfall on Christmas Eve. By dawn of Christmas Day the column, having successfully evaded the Americans, waded the Salm near Wanne and passed back into German lines. McCown, guarded by two SS troopers, was able to slip away before the column reached the Salm, during a brief firefight with an American patrol. McCown headed directly away from the column, and was shortly stopped by U.S. pickets.[10]

Peiper's original kampfgruppe had numbered about 4,800 officers and men, and approximately another 1,000 had joined him between 17 and 22 December; this meant that Kampfgruppe Peiper had suffered personnel casualties at the catastrophic rate of 86.2 percent over seven days! Peiper's matériel losses were even higher. In addition to numerous tanks, other vehicles, and weapons lost during the advance to Stoumont–La Gleize, Peiper's kampfgruppe now abandoned seven heavy Tiger-B tanks, fifty-odd medium tanks, three antiaircraft tanks, seventy half-tracks, a score of 20-mm FLAK vehicles, a dozen self-propelled 75-mm assault guns and tank destroyers, another dozen self-propelled 105-mm and 150-mm howitzers, and several dozens of other motor vehicles. All told, better than two-thirds of the offensive armored punch of the 1st SS Panzer Division had been destroyed in Peiper's failed mission.[11]

At Vielsalm the 508th Parachute Infantry covered the withdrawal of the 7th Armored Division and its attachments from the St. Vith "fortified goose-egg." By evening the last men and vehicles had crossed the Salm. The bridges were then blown in the face of the advancing Germans (see chapter 10).

Four days of desperate battle had served to stabilize the situation on and around the northern shoulder. The early shock and confusion generated by the assault by the Sixth Panzer Army had passed. The situation had clarified for the American defenders and several sharp checks had been administered to the Germans. Reserves were still rushing to the breakthrough area, including the 2d Armored Division and 75th Infantry Division, as well as the remainder of the 3d Armored Division. The position from Elsenborn west to Trois Ponts was now secure with much of the front protected by unbridged and nearly unfordable rivers.

However, the American position was far from rosy: From St. Vith southwest to Bastogne, a yawning gap still existed in the former lines of the VIII Corps. The 116th Panzer Division, with elements of the 2d SS Panzer Division following in its trail, was now far to the west of the XVIII Airborne Corps flank. Only the determination (or shortsightedness, depending on the point of view) of the German commanders to reach the Meuse had prevented them from exploiting many opportunities to roll up the American line from the flank.[12]

12

THE DEFENSE OF BASTOGNE

With the general collapse of the 28th Division's defenses along the Skyline Drive during 17–18 December, the German Fifth Panzer Army had achieved its anticipated breakthrough in the south of the planned penetration. At last relatively clear roads lay open, not only to the important transportation nexus of Bastogne, but also to the Meuse River crossings beyond. However, it had taken the Germans nearly three days to make their breakthrough, rather than the single day envisaged in the operational plans. Moreover, the roads were not as open as the Germans had hoped, for in the days it took them to crack the 28th Division's position, Generals Eisenhower and Bradley had called in reinforcements.

COMMITTING THE STRATEGIC RESERVE: 17–18 DECEMBER

The 101st and 82d Airborne Divisions of the XVIII Airborne Corps represented General Eisenhower's principal strategic reserve for the entire Northwest Europe theater of war. After their departure from the Nijmegen-Arnhem area in November, both divisions had been resting and training around Reims, and absorbing replacements for their losses in the Operation Market Garden battles. In off-duty hours, the principal diversion of the troops was barroom brawls (see chapter 1).

Both divisions were given orders to move early in the evening of 17 December, immediately after General Eisenhower decided to commit them. The suddenness of the orders caught the 101st without its commander, Maj. Gen. Maxwell D. Taylor, who was on temporary duty in the United States. (He was representing the XVIII Airborne Corps commander, Maj. Gen. Matthew B. Ridgway, at a conference in Washington, D.C., about organizational reforms for airborne divisions.) Moreover, Ridgway himself was in Britain observing the training of the 17th Airborne Division, recently arrived from the United States; he was also attending a First Airborne Army conference assessing the recent operations of the XVIII Corps in the Netherlands.

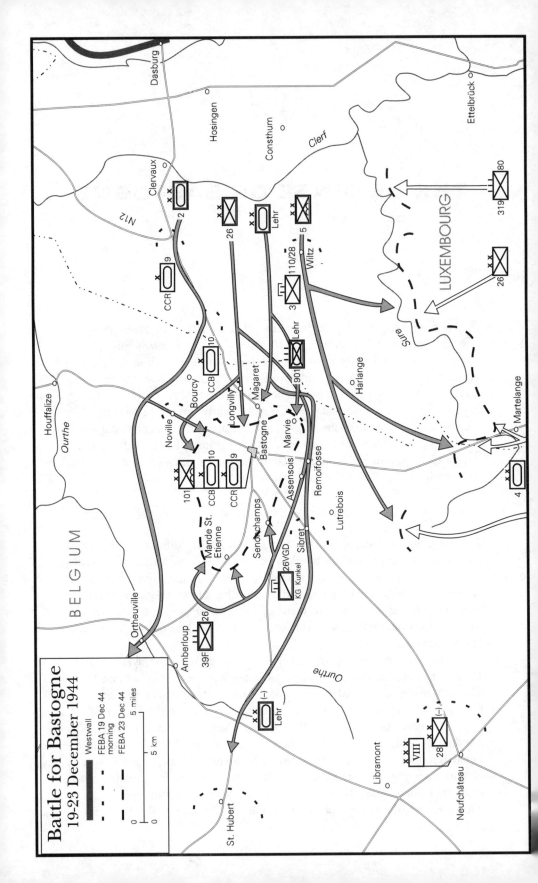

Battle for Bastogne
19-23 December 1944

Westwall

········· FEBA 19 Dec 44 morning

--- --- FEBA 23 Dec 44

0   5 km

0   5 miles

BELGIUM

LUXEMBOURG

Dasburg

Hosingen

Consthum

Clerf

Ettelbrück

Clervaux

N12

2

XX

9 CCR

26

XX

Lehr

XX

5

XX

Wiltz

110/28

3

XX

319

80

XX

26

XX

Sûre

Houffalize

Ourthe

Bourcy

10 CCB

Longvilly

Magaret

Lehr

901

XX

Harlange

Noville

Bastogne

Marvie

Assensois

Remoifosse

Martelange

101

XX

10 CCB

9 CCR

Mande St. Etienne

Sendenchamps

Lutrebois

4

XX

Ortheuville

26VGD

KG Kunkel

Sibret

Amberloup

39F

26

XX

Ourthe

Lehr (-)

XX

Libramont

VIII

28 (-)

XX

Neufchâteau

St. Hubert

Brigadier General Gerald J. Higgins, Assistant Division Commander of the 101st Division, was in Britain with Ridgway, attending the Operation Market Garden postmortem. In this hour of crisis, the "Screaming Eagles" were led by Brig. Gen. Anthony C. McAuliffe, the divisional artillery commander, while command of the corps devolved to Maj. Gen. James M. "Slim Jim" Gavin, the commander of the 82d Airborne Division.[1]

The "All-Americans" of the 82d Division were able to move first, and were on the road to the east before dawn on 18 December. The long truck columns carrying the Screaming Eagles of the 101st Airborne Division followed soon after.

The airborne troops departed from Reims so quickly that many important items of equipment, like helmets, winter clothing, sleeping bags, weapons, and ammunition, were left behind. These material shortcomings were remedied to some extent during halts by the convoys en route, but many items became available only after the units arrived in the Ardennes. Some airborne soldiers (most of whom had just returned from leave) went into action in summer uniforms with few weapons and little ammunition, and many were without jackets, sweaters, coats, and winter footgear.

The experience of Pvt. Christopher C. McEwan of the 501st Parachute Infantry, attached to the 101st Airborne, illustrates the state in which some airborne soldiers reached the combat area.[2] McEwan's weapon had been taken by the division's ordnance unit for repair and maintenance, and when the order came to move out for the Ardennes, he went armed with nothing more than "a knife in my boot." When he arrived at the division's assembly area west of Bastogne, McEwan was told to wait there until weapons were found for him and for other men in the same situation (evidently a considerable number). McEwan decided not to wait, rejoined his regiment, and ended up as a machine gunner.[3]

The actual commitment of the two airborne divisions was somewhat ad hoc, and they nearly ended up in different places. Gavin's initial plans had called for the 82d, which was in the lead, to go to Bastogne, but when he reported to Gen. Courtney Hodges at First Army Headquarters in Spa on the morning of 18 December, he was directed to divert the 82d northward toward Werbomont, which both he and McAuliffe had previously understood would be the 101st's destination. The change was effected at the village of Herbomont during the night of 18 December, where a military police post (soon assisted by Col. Thomas L. Shelburne Jr., the Provost Marshal of the 101st, and acting divisional artillery commander in place of McAuliffe) directed that division's truck columns southeast toward Bastogne.

The 101st's column was led by Lt. Col. Julian J. Ewell's 501st Parachute Infantry Regiment with the rest of the division following behind.[4] The 501st arrived at its assigned assembly area west and a little north of Bastogne proper at midnight of 18–19 December. Over the next eight or nine hours the rest of the division arrived and reached several assembly areas in and around

Bastogne, although this process was hampered by a large number of "refugee" vehicles heading west, most of these belonging to VIII Corps service units hurriedly pulling out of Bastogne. With the arrival of the 101st, Bastogne was no longer open to be taken by the advancing Germans without a fight. And, given the proven quality of the 101st, it would not be an easy fight.

The 101st Airborne Division had been activated on 15 August 1942, and was sent to England after barely a year of training and organization in September 1943. Commanded by Maj. Gen. Maxwell D. Taylor, the division first entered combat when it landed by parachute and glider behind Utah Beach in Normandy during the predawn hours of 6 June 1944. The division stayed on the ground for more than a month, fighting as infantry, before it was withdrawn to England for rest and refitting.

The 101st conducted its second airborne assault as part of the XVIII Airborne Corps in Operation Market Garden in the Netherlands on 17 September, landing around Eindhoven, thirty-two kilometers (twenty miles) behind German lines. The division was engaged in bitter combat, helping the British XXX Corps to push northward to Nijmegen and the 82d Airborne Division, and to the British 1st Airborne around Arnhem. The 101st held the main road open against repeated German efforts to sever it. The division remained in line until 27 November, when it was pulled back to Reims for refitting.

COMMITTING THE LOCAL RESERVE

On 17 December, in the converted Belgian barracks that served as the VIII Corps command post in Bastogne, Maj. Gen. Troy Middleton, the corps commander, was trying to figure out how he could hold the Germans away from Bastogne for forty-eight hours, long enough for the paratroopers to arrive. He was not concerned about the security or defense of his headquarters; he had already decided to move his command post the next day about twenty-five kilometers farther west to Neufchâteau. What was critical was to deny to the Germans, for as long as possible, the advantages they would derive from occupying Bastogne, the principal communications hub in the Ardennes region. Other than the remnants of the 110th Infantry, still delaying the German advance, Middleton had immediately available for this purpose Combat Command R of the 9th Armored Division,[5] which had not yet been in combat, plus three combat engineer battalions and an armored artillery battalion.[6] He knew these units could not stop the headlong rush of at least three German divisions for anywhere near forty-eight hours. Nevertheless, he issued orders for this handful of units to deploy east toward Clervaux and Wiltz.

Middleton got some welcome good news a short time later—the first he had received in more than thirty-six hours—when he learned from Maj. Gen. William H. H. Morris Jr., commander of the 10th Armored Division, that the 10th Armored's Combat Command B was bivouacked near Luxembourg City, only about sixty-five kilometers (forty miles) southeast of Bastogne.[7] On the evening of 16 December, General Bradley had ordered General Patton to send the 10th Armored Division to join the hard-pressed VIII Corps. Middleton had originally intended to commit the entire division north of Luxembourg City to support the 4th Infantry Division. But since then he had begun to realize that the most critical situation in his corps area was the threat to Bastogne, so he ordered Morris to send Combat Command B immediately to Bastogne. The remainder of the 10th Armored Division would remain north of Luxembourg City when it arrived.

During the night of 17–18 December, Col. Joseph H. Gilbreth's Combat Command R of the 9th Armored Division established two blocking positions on Highway N12, leading southwest from St. Vith toward Bastogne. At dawn the following morning, Col. William Roberts's Combat Command B of the 10th Armored moved out from the vicinity of Luxembourg, heading north to join in the defense of Bastogne.[8] Middleton hoped that with the equivalent of two-thirds of an armored division the German advance could be delayed long enough to permit one of the airborne divisions to occupy Bastogne. Traveling by jeep ahead of his troops, Colonel Roberts reached Middleton's headquarters in Bastogne a little before 1600 on 18 December. Middleton, whose command post was withdrawing to safer pastures at Neufchâteau, was waiting for Roberts to arrive so he could brief him on the situation.

Roberts's first combat experience had been at Château-Thierry in 1918 during World War I, and he later taught armored warfare at the Command and General Staff School. He was concerned that Middleton, who as far as Roberts knew was untutored in armored operations, would want to employ his Combat Command B in "penny packets" (a British military term for inadequately small forces). Middleton's first question only confirmed Roberts's fears: How many task forces could Roberts form?[9] Uneasily, Roberts admitted he could form three such units, each with a battalion headquarters as its command group. Middleton directed Roberts to send his three task forces to Noville (on the north side of Bastogne), Longvilly (due east of town), and Wardin (to the southeast). Roberts was unhappy with these orders, but he recognized the seriousness of the situation and figured that Middleton knew the details of the situation better than he did. As Middleton and Roberts were laying their plans, Middleton received another visitor: Brig. Gen. Anthony McAuliffe of the 101st Airborne.

McAuliffe, traveling ahead of the 101st's truck columns en route to Werbomont, had some time to spare. So he headed for Bastogne to talk to Middleton to learn more about the situation. Middleton told McAuliffe of the changes in destination of the two airborne divisions, which he knew because of a message received from First Army Headquarters. When he learned that the 101st would go to Bastogne, McAuliffe asked for Roberts's unit to be placed under the 101st. Roberts objected strenuously, and Middleton headed off a dispute by telling his two subordinate commanders that neither would have sole command and they would just have to cooperate. The meeting broke up soon after, as McAuliffe and his G-3, Lt. Col. Harry W. O. Kinnard, hurried out to lay out assembly areas for the division before darkness fell.

Anthony Clement McAuliffe was born in Washington, D.C., on 2 July 1898. He entered West Point in June 1917, a little more than two months after the United States entered World War I. Because of the desperate need for trained officers for the greatly expanded army, his class was graduated as second lieutenants on 1 November 1918, just ten days before the Germans virtually surrendered by signing the Armistice. The class was reassembled at West Point on 3 December and continued schooling for another six months as "student officers," graduating for a second time on 11 June 1919. McAuliffe, who stood twenty-sixth in a class of 300, entered the Field Artillery.

He spent seventeen years as a lieutenant before he was promoted to captain in May 1935. After graduating from the Command and General Staff School at Fort Leavenworth in July 1937, he spent two years at the Field Artillery School at Fort Sill, Oklahoma, before being sent to the Army War College in Washington, D.C. He held several important staff positions with the Supply Division of the War Department General Staff (1940–1942) before joining the 101st Airborne Division in August 1942 as a newly minted brigadier general and division artillery commander. As an airborne officer, he learned how to parachute, but commented that it was rough "for an old crock like me," thereby earning him the affectionate nickname of "Old Crock" among the 101st's soldiers. McAuliffe dropped with the 101st in Normandy on 6 June 1944, and again in Holland in mid-September.

Only 5'6" tall, but lean and energetic, McAuliffe was an effective, determined, and hard-working combat leader. Like his soldiers and subordinates, McAuliffe was not discomfited by the likelihood of being surrounded in Bastogne. He and the 101st had experienced that situation before, in Normandy as well as in Holland. Such a situation was old hat to the airborne troops.

While McAuliffe prepared for the arrival of the 101st Division, Middleton left for Neufchâteau, and Roberts stayed in Bastogne to form Combat Command B into three roughly equivalent teams as the units arrived in town. The first task force formed was Team Cherry, led by Lt. Col. Henry T. Cherry, commander of 3d Tank Battalion.[10] Roberts ordered Cherry to head eastward for Longvilly to support Colonel Gilbreth's Combat Command R (of the 9th Armored Division) but not to move east of Longvilly. Roberts sent Team O'Hara, led by Lt. Col. James O'Hara, commander of the 54th Armored Infantry Battalion, to Wardin, 5.5 kilometers (3.4 miles) east-southeast of Bastogne, astride the road to Wiltz.[11] Roberts dispatched his third task force, Team Desobry, led by twenty-six-year-old Maj. William R. Desobry, a graduate of Georgetown University and commander of the 20th Armored Infantry Battalion, to Noville, which lay 7.7 kilometers (4.7 miles) north-northeast of Bastogne on the highway to Houffalize.[12] The teams began to arrive at their positions between 1900 and 2400 on 18 December.[13]

Closing on Bastogne from north and east were elements of three German divisions, all belonging to General von Lüttwitz's XLVII Panzer Corps: Col. Heinz Kokott's 26th Volksgrenadier, Lt. Gen. Fritz Bayerlein's Panzer Lehr, and Col. Meinrad von Lauchert's 2d Panzer. These units had collectively shredded Colonel Fuller's 110th Infantry of the 28th Infantry Division over the previous three days (see chapter 7). Fortunately for the defenders of Bastogne, and especially for the two task forces of the 9th Armored's Combat Command R, these three German divisions were still partly engaged with scattered elements of General Cota's 28th Infantry Division, battering their way through the stubbornly held American positions. Some advancing columns had to make detours to find usable bridges or to avoid American positions blocking the few decent hard-surfaced roads. Many German columns were simply slowed by snow, fog, and narrow, twisting, muddy minor roads crowded with German tanks, trucks, horse-drawn vehicles and guns, and columns of soldiers.

THE ARMORED ROADBLOCKS: 18–19 DECEMBER

The troops of Combat Command R, 9th Armored, held two blocking positions on the N12 road, which led northeast from Bastogne toward St. Vith. The first of these, at the Antoniushof road junction near the villages of Lullange and Donnange, which covered the junction of the Clervaux and N12 roads, was held by Task Force Rose, led by Capt. Lawrence K. Rose.[14] The second position, at Fe'itsch near the village of Allerborn, about five kilometers southwest of Lullange and Donnange, was held by Task Force Harper, led by Lt. Col. Ralph S. Harper.[15] These two task forces together contained about thirty tanks and a little more than 1,500 men.

In addition to these armored task forces, the German advance was opposed by survivors and refugees from the 28th Infantry Division. However, these men were badly shaken. Few of them had had either a decent meal or a good night's sleep in several days, and many units had come apart in the stress of combat, so that soldiers were often separated from their comrades and leaders. Under these conditions few were capable of mustering effective resistance, but some collected around the two roadblocks while others filtered farther west.

During the morning of 18 December, the 2d Panzer Reconnaissance Battalion twice probed Task Force Rose's positions, but was driven off with the aid of B Battery's six howitzers. Tanks of the PzKw-IV battalion of the 3d Panzer Regiment joined in the attack shortly before noon, but the Germans moved slowly, waiting for tanks from the Panther battalion to arrive. By early afternoon, however, with the Panthers and PzKw-IVs in the attack, Task Force Rose was in serious difficulty with Germans on three sides. The attacking troops of the 2d Panzer Division overran the U.S. infantry positions and cleared the roadblock by 1500, but most of the U.S. tanks withdrew a short distance and maintained a determined resistance until after dark, when about a dozen surviving tanks were able to break out north toward Houffalize.

While Task Force Rose was fighting for its survival, more Germans swept southward, reaching Task Force Harper by midafternoon. The main attack, including a combination of Panthers and PzKw-IVs, began in earnest after nightfall. The U.S. tanks were caught unprepared and several were hit and burning within moments. Soon lightly armored half-tracks and armored cars were also aflame, and the firelight silhouetted the American infantrymen. The armored infantry position was swiftly overrun, and the surviving American tanks were unable to organize effective resistance and suffered heavy losses. Lieutenant Colonel Harper was killed early in the fighting, and this loss compounded the Americans' problems. The survivors of Task Force Harper fled in considerable disorder, making their way west to Longvilly and the headquarters of Gilbreth's Combat Command R. Full of stories of overwhelming German strength, some stopped there, rallying around Colonel Gilbreth's headquarters, but others were so shaken they continued on foot and by vehicle west toward Bastogne.

With the destruction of task forces Harper and Rose, Colonel Gilbreth assembled the limited forces left to him. Aside from the survivors of the two roadblocks and the headquarters and support troops of Combat Command R, these totaled perhaps thirty tanks and 1,600 men.[16] Many if not most of the stragglers that Gilbreth had collected were dazed by their experiences and not very useful as soldiers. All that most of them needed to be effective were a couple of hot meals and a few hours' sleep, but without these restoratives many men hid when the shooting began, or headed for the rear. Similar conduct was reported by other commanders during the early stages of the Ardennes campaign, and this situation was exacerbated by the scattered, confused, and uncoordinated nature of much of the fighting in the first days of the battle. (See appendix H for further discussion of American combat effectiveness.)

About 1900 on 18 December, Team Cherry's advance guard, led by Lt. Edward P. Hyduke, reached the outskirts of Longvilly to find the road and the little town packed with men and vehicles from the 9th Armored's Combat Command R. Hyduke radioed Cherry, informing him of the situation, and was told to take position just west of town. About 2000, Lieutenant Colonel Cherry arrived at Combat Command R headquarters to inform Gilbreth and his staff, much to their relief, that his team was taking up positions just west of Longvilly to block the approach to Bastogne along the Clervaux road. Cherry then returned by jeep to his headquarters, and was shot at by what he supposed were trigger-happy American stragglers in Magaret. He was mistaken: panzergrenadiers from Panzer Lehr's advance guard were in Magaret and shot at him as he sped past.

As Roberts's teams from 10th Armored's Combat Command B took their positions, the commanders of the German divisions approaching Bastogne had made decisions that granted the defenders of the American roadblocks several hours of grace before the storm broke over their heads. According to the original plan for the XLVII Panzer Corps, von Lauchert's 2d Panzer Division was to swing northwest to bypass Bastogne and continue its advance toward the Meuse. In turning north off the Clervaux road onto the Bourcy road and heading for Noville, von Lauchert unwittingly gave the American troops around Longvilly several quiet hours. Ironically, the 2d Panzer's advance toward Noville, while sparing the forces at Longvilly, would instead threaten Team Desobry of the 10th Armored's Combat Command B, which had taken position around that town.

During the night of 18–19 December, as von Lauchert's panzers and panzergrenadiers trundled toward Noville, Fritz Bayerlein's Panzer Lehr Division approached the Longvilly area from the southeast. By this stage of the battle, Bayerlein's forces should have been ahead of the slower infantrymen, but the dynamics of the fighting around Wiltz and the difficulties of march control on the narrow, winding, and muddy roads had left tanks and half-tracks intermixed willy-nilly with infantry, wagons, and horse-drawn guns. Consequently, Bayerlein's advance was slow, and Panzer Lehr's advance guard, commanded by Maj. Gerd von Fallois, did not reach Niederwampach until shortly after dark.[17] Soon after (perhaps about 1700), Bayerlein decided to take a secondary road northwest toward Magaret, eschewing the paved road west through Bras, Marvie, and Bastogne itself. He evidently hoped this lesser route would be undefended and uncrowded.[18] The road turned out to be less passable than shown on the map, and eventually degenerated to little more than a cow path before finally reaching Magaret.

As a result, Kampfgruppe von Fallois's lead vehicles and troops reached Magaret around 2000 on 18 December, just moments after Lieutenant Colonel Cherry had passed through, headed for Longvilly. The American defenders of Magaret, a small force from the 158th Engineer Combat Battalion and assorted service elements of 9th Armored's Combat Command R, held off the Germans for two hours in a confused battle fought in nearly complete darkness, but they were unable to keep the road open after Cherry passed through Magaret on his return shortly after.

By midnight advancing German troops from the 26th Volksgrenadier Division (VGD) had made contact with the American artillery positions just north of Longvilly, and had mounted several probing attacks against the gunners' positions. Under such conditions, Gilbreth ordered a withdrawal to Magaret, about four kilometers west-southwest of Longvilly and about six kilometers east of Bastogne. However, the difficulty of moving units at night, the risk of German ambushes (they heard firing from Magaret), and the potential for loss of control, which could lead to rout, persuaded Colonel Gilbreth to delay a complete withdrawal until daylight.[19] Consequently, the artillerymen had to fight off a German assault in the early-morning darkness of 19 December before they were able to pull out. Gilbreth eventually extricated the

remains of his Combat Command, including the surviving six M7 self-propelled 105-mm howitzers of the 58th and twelve M7s of the 73d Armored
Field Artillery battalions, and managed to get them into Bastogne proper,
where they joined the paratroopers of the 101st Airborne already in position
there. The long straggling column came under heavy German fire as it
wended its way laboriously westward, and suffered considerable casualties in
both men and matériel on 19 December.

Elements of Team Cherry had taken up positions near Longvilly around
2100 on 18 December, but others of Cherry's units were scattered along the
roadway from Magaret to Longvilly. The situation was complicated by the
mass of vehicles backed up along the road, unable to move past German-
occupied Magaret. Some of these vehicles belonged to Colonel Gilbreth's
Combat Command R, but others were stragglers of one sort or another, and a
fair number had been abandoned. Sometime after midnight, Cherry ordered
Capt. William F. Ryerson, in charge of the team's main body, to reopen the
road through Magaret, but ensuing developments made that order difficult to
carry out. Cherry's advance guard, commanded by Lieutenant Hyduke and
supported by four Sherman (M4) medium and seven Stuart (M5) light tanks,
had taken up positions at the western end of Longvilly, while Ryerson's main
body was tied up in the traffic jams outside of town. Meanwhile, Cherry set
up his command post in a château just south of Neffe, a small village three
kilometers east of Bastogne, and left his supply and maintenance train in Bastogne.

In Bastogne, besides his Combat Command headquarters, Roberts retained
the 420th Armored Field Artillery Battalion, B Battery of the 496th AAA (AW
or Automatic Weapons) Battalion, the headquarters elements for C Company of
the 55th Armored Engineers, D Troop of the 90th Cavalry, and C Company of
the 609th Tank Destroyer Battalion (with one platoon of four M18s), along
with assorted support units.

Before dawn on the morning of 19 December, as fighting continued
around Longvilly, Team Desobry came under attack from the bulk of
Lauchert's 2d Panzer Division, including the 3d Panzer, 2d Panzergrenadier,
and 304th Panzergrenadier regiments. Pummeled by German artillery, Desobry's troops repelled the initial German tank and infantry assaults, which
were hampered by the muddy ground (several tanks bogged in the muck were
easily picked off by American tanks and tank destroyers) and an inopportune
lifting of the fog (exposing waiting panzergrenadiers and tanks to heavy
American fire). The lifting of the fog also revealed the size of the opposing
German force: at least fifty German tanks were in view, along with several
hundred infantrymen, dozens of support weapons, and many other armored
vehicles. It was clear to Desobry that he was facing at least half a panzer division. The Germans, stung by their repulse, drew back a little, and comparative
calm settled in around Noville.

About 1430 Lt. Col. James L. LaPrade's 1st Battalion of the 506th

Parachute Infantry Regiment of the 101st Airborne Division arrived in Noville and launched a counterattack that ran headlong into a battalion-size attack by the 2d Panzergrenadier Regiment.[20] Sharp fighting produced heavy casualties on both sides, but the Americans held their positions around Noville. The paratroopers disengaged and drew back a little after nightfall. A German artillery shell hit the command post in the early evening, killing Lieutenant Colonel LaPrade and wounding Major Desobry, who was evacuated for treatment. Maj. Robert F. Harwick succeeded LaPrade as commander of the 1/506th, and Maj. Charles L. Hustead took over command of the team, which was renamed Team Hustead. Harwick also assumed LaPrade's role as commander of the combined force at Noville; Hustead's armored force fell under his command.

The fighting around Longvilly and Magaret on 19 December was bloody and confused. At dawn Lieutenant Colonel Cherry and his headquarters were isolated from the rest of his troops and came under attack by tanks and infantry from Panzer Lehr. The headquarters troops of the 3d Tank Battalion held the stone-walled château that served as Cherry's command post for several hours against repeated German tank-infantry attacks. After German grenades set fire to the buildings shortly after noon, Cherry ordered a withdrawal. Fortunately, by that time a platoon from Lt. Col. Julian Ewell's 501st Parachute Infantry Regiment of the 101st Airborne Division had arrived and was able to help cover the movement.

Meanwhile, Lieutenant Hyduke's advance guard came under heavy attack shortly after dawn from elements of Kokott's 26th VGD, supported by artillery from 2d Panzer. Heavily outnumbered and under constant artillery fire, Hyduke held on until the last of his M5 tanks were destroyed a little after 1400, and then broke his force into small groups to make their way west to Ryerson's main body.

Captain Ryerson had problems of his own. He had received Cherry's orders to reopen the road through Magaret around 1000 hours on 18 December, but turning his command around and moving along the clogged roadway, under sporadic German artillery fire, was a daunting undertaking. Despite his best efforts, he was unable to bring most of his strength to bear against the Panzer Lehr troops in Magaret until midmorning on 19 December. Ryerson's push toward and into Magaret was halted in early afternoon by German fire just outside of town. Shortly after dark a few American armored infantrymen managed to get into Magaret and seize control of the east end of town; they clung to their uncertain toehold for the rest of the night. This precarious lodgment provided access to a dirt track leading west, and Ryerson seized on this route to extricate first his wounded and then the rest of his command. They returned to American lines at Bizory, which was held by the 2d Battalion of the 501st Parachute Infantry Regiment.

Team O'Hara, occupying the southernmost of Combat Command B's armored roadblock positions, was deployed near Marvie and Wardin. For some reason, the German attackers failed to make contact with O'Hara's units, perhaps because of the pervading fog, which in some places cut visibility to less than twenty-five meters. The team's positions received some shell fire and noted the passage of stragglers from Lt. Col. Ewell's 501st Parachute Infantry during the afternoon, but was otherwise undisturbed. In midmorning, acting on order from Colonel Roberts, O'Hara sent some tanks into Wardin. The tankers found the village unoccupied and returned to their positions, although soon after noon some troops from Panzer Lehr occupied the village. Shielded from each other's view, the two forces remained until paratroopers from Ewell's 501st arrived in midafternoon.

By the evening of 19 December teams Desobry and Cherry were both heavily engaged. Although Team Cherry's combat losses had not been severe (except in Lieutenant Hyduke's advance guard), Captain Ryerson's forces were not in contact with Cherry and his headquarters, and the entire team was incapable of coordinated action. Moreover, Ryerson's forces were now involved in the same action as the 501st Parachute Infantry.[21] To the north, Desobry's defenders at Noville had been reinforced by the 1st Battalion, 506th Parachute Infantry, and both units were grimly holding on to their positions.

However badly the day might have gone for them, the armored task forces had done their job, holding the advancing Germans at bay until the paratroopers arrived. They had also confirmed General Middleton's calculation that two combat commands could do the job.

At 1900 on 19 December, Colonel Roberts was visited by an officer from the 10th Armored Infantry Battalion of the 4th Armored Division—Capt. Abe Baum, the battalion S-2 (intelligence officer), who was twenty-three years old and a native of the East Bronx. His battalion, along with the 8th Tank Battalion, had been sent north to Bastogne, and had covered 150 miles in nineteen hours since leaving their positions near the Saar River at 2300 the previous night. Captain Baum led a 400-man team into town, in part to find out where the rest of the force was supposed to go. Lieutenant Colonel Kinnard of the 101st sent him to see Colonel Roberts, who was suprised to see anyone from the 4th Armored and couldn't give Baum an answer. By this point, the two-battalion advance party from the 4th Armored had been ordered by General Patton to rejoin the division's main body south of Bastogne. Baum, along with the other officers and men of the column, turned around and drove back south to an assembly area near Arlon. They were the last organized U.S. force to move in or out of Bastogne for a week.[22]

THE SCREAMING EAGLES JOIN IN: 19–21 DECEMBER

Beginning on the morning of 19 December, after McAuliffe had consulted with Colonel Roberts, the 101st's regiments began to move out to take up their assigned perimeter positions. Colonel Ewell's 501st moved east and a little south toward Bizory, Magaret, and Marvie, while Col. Robert F. Sink's

506th headed northeast for Foy and Noville with the 1st Battalion leading the way. Lieutenant Colonel Chappuis's 502d moved northwest, probing toward Bertogne, while Colonel Harper's 327th Glider Infantry stayed around Mande–St. Etienne and covered the western approaches to Bastogne. These movements brought Ewell's regiment and Sink's lead battalion into close contact with the Germans by early afternoon on 19 December.

As we have seen, Colonel Sink's 1st Battalion, under Lt. Col. James L. LaPrade, had moved into Noville and launched an attack in early afternoon to relieve the mounting pressure on Team Desobry. Initially, McAuliffe had ordered Sink not to advance beyond the northern outskirts of Bastogne with his remaining two battalions. The 3d Battalion of Sink's 506th Parachute Infantry advanced as far as Foy by early evening and encountered German patrols nearby. It halted there for the night, receiving sporadic German artillery fire and clashing with German patrols during the hours of darkness. The 2d Battalion moved forward on the 3d Battalion's left or western flank. Colonel Sink was concerned not only with the situation at Noville, but also with his dangling right flank, where his patrols had only intermittent contact with Ewell's 501st to the south.

The German pressure on the Noville position continued through the night, and von Lauchert resumed his attacks on the morning of 20 December. By that time the eight surviving Sherman tanks had exhausted their supply of armor-piercing ammunition, and the German tanks were repelled only by the efforts of three platoons of tank destroyers, each with four M18s.[23] Shortly after noon, Major Harwick (now commander of the 1st Battalion, 506th Parachute Infantry, with Team Hustead attached) asked Colonel Roberts and General McAuliffe for permission to disengage and withdraw south toward Bastogne, since the pressure from the 2d Panzer Division was becoming too great to resist. The Americans' losses had been heavy, and the aid stations could accept no more wounded.

By the time Harwick asked for permission to withdraw, German troops from the 304th Panzergrenadier Regiment had cut the road from Bastogne to Noville by capturing the village of Foy and temporarily driving the 506th Parachute Infantry's 3d Battalion south of town. Fortunately the Americans were able to handle this situation, and McAuliffe told Harwick to hold in place for a few hours while the paratroopers of the 3d Battalion attacked up the road to clear out the Germans, and the 2d Battalion of the 502d Parachute Infantry drove northeast from Longchamps. Those American attacks made only limited headway, although the 3d/506th retook Foy. In the early afternoon, therefore, Roberts and McAuliffe ordered Harwick's paratroopers and Team Hustead to break out. The start of their march south was covered by the propitious descent of heavy fog, which obscured their withdrawal and allowed them to leave unmolested. The column took only scattered fire on the road itself, but had to drive off a blocking force from the 304th Panzergrenadier in a sharp little fight just north of Foy before reaching the relative security of American lines at Foy about 1645 hours, just as darkness fell.

Harwick's battalion had lost more than 200 killed and wounded in the fight for Noville. Team Hustead, in addition to suffering nearly as many personnel casualties, lost five M4 tanks, a dozen half-tracks, and four M18 tank destroyers, as well as other vehicles. The 2d Panzer Division suffered heavier losses: The 3d Panzer Regiment lost at least a dozen tanks, and the 2d and 304th Panzergrenadier regiments suffered more than 500 casualties between them. More seriously, Lauchert had used two precious days battering at the Noville position and had accomplished little. When he contacted Lüttwitz and Manteuffel to obtain permission to drive into Bastogne, he was told in no uncertain terms to follow the original plan and head for the Meuse. Those orders came straight from Hitler, who at this point was still obsessed with the grail of Antwerp.

South and a little east of the 506th's positions, Lt. Col. Julian Ewell's 501st Parachute Infantry encountered major enemy forces, mostly from the 26th VGD and Panzer Lehr as they moved forward during the afternoon of 19 December. Ewell's orders from McAuliffe were to move east, attack, and "clear up the situation," and to make contact with Team Cherry and find out what was going on east of Bastogne. Major Raymond V. Bottomly's 1st Battalion led the 501st's advance. The weather conditions were miserable, with sporadic rain showers contributing further to the mud amid general fog and mist. Bottomly's battalion bumped into elements of Panzer Lehr holding a roadblock at Neffe about 0930 hours. Meanwhile, Ewell had sent the 2d Battalion under Maj. Sammie N. Homan north to occupy Bizory and the dominant heights of Hill 510, and had directed Lt. Col. George M. Griswold's 3d Battalion south to take Mont and the heights south of Neffe. On that high ground, Griswold's men discovered Cherry's hard-pressed headquarters troops, and together they fell back to Mont.

During the afternoon, Homan's battalion secured Bizory, which was already in the hands of American engineers, but was unable to take Hill 510. That hill, with open slopes devoid of cover to the south and west, was held by German infantry well furnished with automatic weapons and mortars, and the paratroopers' assaults made little progress. Nine Sherman tanks that were formerly part of Combat Command R attached themselves to Homan's grateful battalion.

The advance of Capt. Claude D. Wallace Jr.'s Company I (part of Griswold's 3d Battalion) reached Wardin. This American move was interpreted by the nearby elements of the 901st and 902d Panzergrenadier regiments of Panzer Lehr as an attack against their hitherto unthreatened left flank as they continued to batter their way into Magaret. The Germans responded with a tank-infantry counterattack into Wardin shortly after noon. Company I, with only 130 officers and men, put up stiff resistance, but was forced to fall back slowly from one stone house to the next. German assault guns blew the paratroopers out of each position, and they eventually withdrew from Wardin after suffering forty casualties, including Captain Wallace, who was killed. By this time, Ewell's reports had reached McAuliffe, who ordered the 501st to dig in and hold its position.

Although most of Panzer Lehr and the 77th and 78th Grenadier regiments of the 26th VGD spent most of 19 December chopping up the American traffic jam ("column" implies too high a level of organization and common purpose) between Magaret and Longvilly, the appearance of Ewell's 501st Parachute Infantry quickly caught their attention. Bayerlein in particular had assumed from the scant contacts on the morning of 19 December that the road west to Bastogne was virtually open.[24] The new situation required a change in plans, namely the preparation for a more formal, coordinated assault toward Bastogne.

Both Kokott and Bayerlein laid plans for major attacks later in the day, but both divisions were short a good portion of their strength. Kokott's 39th Fusilier Regiment, which had been covering the capture of Wiltz, only began to move west on the muddy tracks out of the Wiltz valley on the morning of 20 December. His two grenadier regiments attacked early on the morning of 20 December with a single battalion apiece: The 77th Grenadier Regiment pushed toward Foy north of the railway embankment, and the 78th Grenadier struck at Bizory south of the embankment. Although the Germans were at first able to exploit the 1,000-yard gap between the 506th and 501st along the railway, the Americans reacted swiftly. By midmorning they isolated the company or so of German infiltrators and completely restored the line by midafternoon. Ensuring they would not be caught twice, Ewell and Sink made certain that their flanking companies were in close contact with each other. Bizory had been reinforced by the remnants of Team Ryerson (the bulk of Team Cherry's tanks and armored infantry) just before dawn, and this presence helped to repel the attack of the 78th Grenadier. The Germans at Bizory were taken aback by Ryerson's unexpected tanks, and broke off their effort before noon.

Farther south, only one battalion of the 901st Panzergrenadier Regiment had avoided the carnage and confusion around Longvilly. It made its way south and west to Marvie, and its lead company and a platoon of tanks launched an attack there about 1130. This effort made little progress, partly because Team O'Hara had been reinforced by the 2d Battalion, 327th Glider Infantry, which had taken over the positions of the tired and understrength 35th Engineer Combat Battalion in Marvie itself just minutes before. The German assault was driven back with considerable loss, and the American defenders of Marvie were unmolested for the rest of the day.

Bayerlein's 902d Panzergrenadier made a more serious attack near Neffe, but because of the disorder and confusion created by the fighting around Magaret and Marvie, the attack could not be launched until midafternoon. The German attack was pounded by fire from six American artillery battalions in Bastogne, ranging from 75-mm pack howitzers to 4.5" (114-mm) guns and 155-mm howitzers. In the face of that concentration of fire, coupled with stiff resistance from the 501st's 3d Battalion, the Germans did not press their attack.

Major changes were taking place among the German forces in front of Bastogne. Von Lauchert's 2d Panzer disengaged to positions north of Noville, but lack of fuel prohibited further movement west. Its maintenance units were busy trying to repair or salvage the dozens of vehicles damaged or disabled in the fight for Noville, and to extricate those that had gotten stuck in the muddy fields nearby. Kokott's infantrymen extended their coverage of the front line, freeing troops from both panzer divisions for other tasks. Kokott also ordered Kampfgruppe Kunkel to disengage from the front line near Bizory in the late afternoon on 20 December, and head south and then west under cover of darkness to swing around the southern side of Bastogne.[25] This move would help seal off American communications with the south and lead the way for the 39th Fusilier Regiment, which was still on the road from Wiltz. Bayerlein also disengaged his lead units and shifted the considerable weight of his division to the south around Bastogne. This effort was undertaken not only to cut the roads leading south from Bastogne but also to enable Panzer Lehr either to bypass Bastogne or to strike at it from the south.

During the night Kampfgruppe Kunkel ran into the remnants of General Cota's 28th Infantry Division (little more than assorted stragglers and a few service units) at Sibret. After a brief skirmish, the Americans withdrew south. This minor German success demonstrated that there were few if any American defenses south of Bastogne. It also indicated some promise for a push against the south side of the town.

The American defenders of Bastogne had other problems, particularly logistical ones. Since Bastogne had been the headquarters of General Middleton's VIII Corps, there were considerable stocks of supplies in dumps and warehouses, but many of the requirements of the 101st could not be met. For instance, the troops of the 101st had moved out of their billets near Reims without their full equipment loads. Shortages of small-arms ammunition in the 501st and 506th Parachute Infantry regiments had been alleviated to a degree when Colonel Roberts generously gave them access to his Combat Command's trains, but this could not be a permanent solution. Moreover, the 75-mm pack howitzers, which formed the bulk of the 101st's divisional artillery, were notably short of ammunition, although the supply of shells for the VIII Corps artillery battalions was on a better footing.[26] To add to McAuliffe's worries, during the night of 19–20 December, German raiding parties overran the 101st's service area outside Mande-St. Etienne. Although the Quartermaster and Ordnance companies suffered few losses, only eight officers and forty-four men of the medical company escaped. The loss of many of the division's medical personnel and most of its hospital supplies and equipment was serious indeed. There were some supplies in Bastogne, but nonetheless medical services were hard-pressed to provide even minimal care for the growing number of wounded.

By the morning of 21 December the tactical problems facing the 101st were less serious than its logistical situation. McAuliffe had already requested an airdrop of supplies, but the overcast skies and the degree of planning and organization necessary meant that he would probably have to hold on for two days before any succor arrived. McAuliffe therefore sharply rationed artillery ammunition, limiting most gun tubes to no more than ten rounds per day. This allowed the German columns passing north and south of Bastogne to proceed almost unhindered.

One major change in the situation on 21 December was the weather. The hitherto mild temperatures (daylight highs close to 40 degrees Fahrenheit and lows only just under freezing) had produced a good deal of fog and some rain, and left open ground so muddy that few vehicles could venture into it without getting bogged down. Temperatures fell through the day and a ground freeze set in, at last allowing motor vehicles to attempt cross-country movement.

Throughout 21 December, most of the German and American troops on the northern and eastern faces of the Bastogne pocket saw only limited action, mostly scattered skirmishing and patrols. The 2d Panzer was still waiting for fuel, although enough had arrived the previous night to enable Maj. Ernst von Cochenhausen's 2d Panzer Reconnaissance Battalion to move west toward Ortheuville. Kokott's volksgrenadiers were busy reorganizing after five days of uninterrupted combat and fanning out across the eastern and northeastern sectors of the lines to cover the gaps left by the departing panzer divisions. Bayerlein had left the 902d Panzergrenadier behind while the rest of his division moved westward, south of Bastogne. The 902d held positions in front of Marvie, facing Team O'Hara and the 327th Glider Infantry's 2d Battalion.

The main fighting of the day occurred at Senonchamps, just off the road to Ortheuville, 2,500 meters west and a little south of Bastogne, where several American artillery battalions were laagered, including Lt. Col. Barry D. Browne's 420th Armored Field Artillery. Browne, acting under orders from Colonel Roberts, had been collecting and organizing the small parties of stragglers drifting near his positions into impromptu infantry units in anticipation of a German attack. The first sign of the Germans came about 1100 hours on 21 December, when vehicles and men of Kampfgruppe Kunkel appeared south and west of Senonchamps. A hard-fought and often confused melee ensued as snow fell from heavy gray skies on hardening snow-covered ground. The 771st Field Artillery Battalion, overrun south of Villeroux, abandoned its twelve 4.5" guns and fled north. Continuing toward Villeroux, Kampfgruppe Kunkel encountered Team Pyle, a small task force assembled from stragglers from armored infantry units (perhaps 100 men in half-tracks) and fourteen M4 Shermans appropriated from the workshops of Gilbreth's

Combat Command R, and commanded by Capt. Howard Pyle. This scratch force halted Kunkel's troops for only a few minutes before it was forced to withdraw north, but this was long enough for the 755th and 969th (Colored [this was how black units were designated in the segregated U.S. Army of 1944]) Field Artillery battalions to begin withdrawal to Senonchamps. A rearguard consisting of A Battery of the 755th and the 969th's headquarters battery stopped Kunkel's advance cold with a hail of machine-gun fire. Then, while visibility dropped below 200 meters as snow fell, this rearguard made its way north. In this action the two battalions lost only one howitzer, which was disabled by a mortar shell.

At Senonchamps Team Pyle turned to make a stand to cover Browne's 420th Artillery, which was busy firing in support of paratroopers to the north and east. Fortunately, Pyle was reinforced by B Battery of the 796th AAA (AW) (SP) Battalion with M15 and M16 MGMC (Multiple Gun Motor Carriages, half-tracks with 37-mm AA guns and .50-caliber machine guns), and Team Van Kleef, another scratch armored force with five M5 light tanks and about forty infantrymen in half-tracks. Together, these forces halted the German attack; the heavy machine guns of the 769th's B Company inflicted very heavy losses on the German infantry. Kunkel decided he'd had enough for the day and broke off his attack.

C Company of the truncated 401st Glider Infantry Regiment, functioning as the third battalion of the 327th Glider Infantry Regiment, held an isolated roadblock position west of Mande-St. Etienne.[27] After dark on 21 December, German troops (probably from Panzer Lehr) cut the road to Mande-St. Etienne, leaving the company isolated from the rest of its unit with only a handful of tanks from the 10th Armored for support. Robert M. Bowen, then a staff sergeant and commander of C Company's third platoon, was told to clear the German roadblock and reopen the road to Bastogne—he was given a single Sherman tank to help. Bowen sent a squad down each side of the road, covering their advance with fire from his first squad and a machine gun to the left, and from the main gun and machine gun on the Sherman. "The Germans," wrote Bowen later, "didn't know what hit them. The fight was short and violent and when it was over 12 Germans lay dead and twenty-five more our prisoners. Sergeant Jerry Hanss, 3d squad leader, was our only casualty [with] a bullet wound in the calf."[28]

THE GERMANS ATTACK IN FORCE: 22–23 DECEMBER

The weather conditions on 22 December were unchanged: scattered snowfall, a hard freeze, and heavily overcast skies. The American logistical situation in the perimeter remained serious, as stocks of artillery ammunition continued to dwindle. For their part, the Germans were bringing up substantial reinforcements. General Brandenberger of the Seventh Army promised Lüttwitz that the 5th Parachute Division was on its way to join his troops south of Bastogne, and by dawn on 22 December elements of that division had already crossed the Arlon-Bastogne road, heading west. Lüttwitz and Manteuffel were also moving more artillery forward, although this task was made more difficult by German shortages of transport, as well as by the limited roadnet, which was already burdened by heavy traffic.

The main actions on 22 December were fought along the line of a rough arc running about four kilometers from Mande-St. Etienne to the Neufchâteau road, just north of Villeroux. In this sector, Kampfgruppe Kunkel attacked again, reinforced by one battalion of the 39th Fusilier Regiment (the other battalion probed at the 3d/327th's positions around Flamierge) and a tank-infantry kampfgruppe from Panzer Lehr. The fighting was sharp and confused, because no front lines really existed in this area, and so the day's battle had many of the characteristics of a boxing match held in pitch darkness. The German attackers made only scant progress against Pyle's and Van Kleef's tanks and the heavy firepower of the artillery, but the American defenders suffered heavy casualties. Browne, worried about his thinning infantry screen, asked McAuliffe for reinforcements. Before darkness fell, around 1630 hours, Team Watts (about 100 infantrymen commanded by Maj. Eugene A. Watts) arrived from Team SNAFU (a pool of stragglers collected by Colonel Roberts of CCA/10), and L Company of the 327th Glider Infantry Regiment arrived from the 3d/327th's positions to the northwest.[29]

C Company of the 401st Glider Infantry was in the thick of this fighting and suffered heavy losses. The lightly equipped airborne infantrymen were hard-pressed to stand up to repeated German tank-infantry attacks; there were many casualties from short-range tank gun fire. By late afternoon their positions were crumbling as ammunition ran low. Sergeant Bowen, 1st Lt. Robert Wagner, and Second Lieutenant Glynn (who had been given a battlefield commission earlier that day, and was leading two M10 TDs from the 705th TD Battalion) were wounded when a German mortar round hit just outside the aid station where they were conducting a hasty conference at 1600 to decide how to evacuate their position.

Glynn and Bowen were both out of action, but Wagner, who had been hit in the foot by a shell fragment, went back outside just after dusk (about 1715) to find out what was happening. By this time many of the surviving infantrymen in C Company were drifting to the rear, out of ammunition and unwilling to risk being overrun. Wagner tried to rally them, but at this point the Germans launched one more determined attack and smashed through the crumbling American line. Bowen, Glynn, and the other occupants of the aid station were captured by the victorious Germans. Later that night, the 327th Glider Infantry and all its attachments withdrew from the Mande-St. Etienne salient to a shorter and more defensible line a few kilometers to the east.[30]

As important as the two-day fight around Senonchamps was, 22 December has become more famous for another incident, much celebrated in American folklore. A four-man German party under a large white flag came forward to the lines of F Company, 2d Battalion, 327th Glider Infantry, on the Arlon highway shortly before noon. One of the two German officers, Oberleutnant (1st lieutenant) Hellmuth Henke of Panzer Lehr's operations section, spoke English. He informed the three-man American party that met them that they wished to speak to the American general commanding in Bastogne.[31] The Germans carried a demand for "the honorable surrender of the town."

To the U.S.A. Commander in the encircled town of Bastogne.
    The fortune of war is changing. This time, the U.S. forces in and near Bastogne have been encircled by strong German armored units. More German armored units have crossed the River Ourthe near Ortheuville, have taken Marche and reached St. Hubert, by passing through Hompré-Sillet-Tillet. Libremont is in German hands.
    There is only one possibility of saving the encircled U.S.A. troops from annihilation. That is the honorable surrender of the encircled town. In order to think it over, a term of two hours shall be granted, beginning with the presentation of this note. If this proposal is rejected, one German artillery corps and six heavy antiaircraft batteries are ready to annihilate the U.S.A. forces in and near Bastogne. The order for firing will be given immediately after the two hours' term.
    All serious civilian casualties caused by this artillery fire would not correspond with well-known American humanity.
    [signed] The German Commander[32]

    The note was presented in both German and English versions, and was ambiguously signed "The German Commander," although it originated with Lüttwitz of XLVII Panzer Corps, who knew very well that he had no massed artillery with which to make good his threat.
    The surrender note was passed along to Capt. James McAdams of F Company, then to Col. Joseph H. Harper of the 327th, and finally to McAuliffe. When McAuliffe was informed of the surrender demand by his chief of staff, Lt. Col. Ned D. Moore, he disdainfully replied "Aw, nuts!"[33] When at length he sat down to compose a formal reply, he employed that terse expression as his entire answer to the anonymous German commander.

To the German Commander:
    Nuts!
    The American Commander

    Harper gleefully volunteered to deliver McAuliffe's reply to the Germans personally. Lieutenant Henke, who spoke excellent English, was not sure what the reply meant. Henke asked Harper whether it was affirmative or negative. Harper replied that it was emphatically negative, and that "in plain English it is the same thing as 'Go to Hell!' And I will tell you something else. If you continue to attack we will kill every god damn German who tries to break into this city!" Somewhat nonplussed but certain the Americans would not surrender, Henke saluted and replied, "We will kill many Americans. This is war." The German party returned to their lines.[34]

Lüttwitz had not secured permission from his superiors for this effort, and when Manteuffel found out about it he was incensed. To try and put some teeth into what otherwise would be an empty threat, he asked the Luftwaffe to bomb Bastogne. Word of the entire incident spread quickly throughout the American troops in Bastogne, and nearly everyone was confident that the next day would bring some heavy fighting.

Fortunately for the defenders of Bastogne, 23 December dawned clear and cold: After nearly a week, a high pressure system had arrived to provide good flying weather. Not only would Troop Carrier Command be able to parachute supplies to the beleaguered Americans, but Bastogne's defenders could also expect air support from fighter-bombers, a valuable source of additional firepower. American C-47 transport planes, guided by pathfinder teams dropped in earlier, began to arrive over Bastogne about 1150 hours, and by 1500 hours 241 transports had dropped loads totaling 144 tons. A few planes were shot down or forced to turn back by German antiaircraft fire, a few more missed Bastogne, and others unfortunately dropped their parachute packs, which weighed 1,200 pounds apiece, outside the American perimeter. Still the day's airdrops considerably eased the supply situation, especially for artillery ammunition. The P-47 fighters escorting the vulnerable transports turned to strike the German positions around Bastogne as soon as the transports finished their drops. Armed with high-explosive and fragmentation bombs, napalm, and eight machine guns, eighty-two P-47s struck hard at the Germans, attacking transport and logistical concentrations, and providing direct support to American units in combat.

For their part, the Germans mounted a serious multipronged attack against the American perimeter. Colonel Kokott, whose 26th VGD and its attached 901st Panzergrenadier Regiment comprised the only available troops, was unable to commit all his forces to the attack, because his troops also had to cover most of the perimeter. Kokott planned three attacks, directed against Marvie, Senonchamps, and Flamierge, and to support these efforts he obtained tank support from the 130th Panzer Regiment of Panzer Lehr.[35] Because of its scattered deployment, all three German attacks fell on sectors held wholly or in part by units of Colonel Harper's 327th Glider Infantry.

In preparation for operations in the snow, the Germans had hurriedly painted their tanks and other vehicles white, and their infantrymen donned white snow-camouflage combat smocks. The Americans replied in kind, although their lack of experience with operations in the snow ensured that their efforts were somehat jury-rigged. They hastily whitewashed tanks and tank destroyers, half-tracks and jeeps, and many American infantrymen expropriated bed linen from civilians in and around Bastogne for hurried conversion into snow smocks.

Kokott's 39th Fusilier Regiment mounted its major effort against Flamierge with a few troops from the 78th Grenadiers assigned to the 26th Reconnaissance Battalion (under the redoubtable Major Kunkel). This was combined with an attack against Senonchamps, only five kilometers to the southeast. The Germans enjoyed some initial success, driving into Flamierge in midafternoon, but a swift counterattack by the 3d Battalion of the 327th threw them out of the village. Although ultimately unsuccessful, Kokott's attack against Flamierge did convince Harper and McAuliffe that the position of 3d Battalion's extended salient was too vulnerable, and so they pulled the battalion back to Mande-St. Etienne during the night. The attack on Team Browne at Senonchamps met with even less success, for once again the fire-power of the American tanks, artillery, and antiaircraft half-tracks stopped the Germans in their tracks. Concerned by Team Browne's situation at Senon-champs, McAuliffe sent reinforcements, but by the time elements of Team Cherry arrived at 1830 the German attack had been repelled.

The most serious of the three German attacks on 23 December was that directed against Marvie. During the daylight hours the Germans contented themselves with bombarding the village and its environs, perhaps wary of the American P-47 fighter-bombers buzzing overhead. After darkness fell, the artillery barrage increased in intensity, and the attack began in earnest about 1845. At least a battalion of the 901st Panzergrenadiers, with most of two tank companies in support, struck the positions of the 2d Battalion of the 327th Glider Infantry and Team O'Hara (which had hitherto seen only limited action). The first phase of the attack made limited headway but failed to dislodge the American defenders; it petered out around 2200. About midnight action flared up as the Germans renewed their assault and attacked with great energy and determination. The battle see-sawed for several hours, and although the Americans took out several German tanks, the panzergrenadiers of the 901st gained a foothold in the southern and western sections of Marvie by first light on Christmas Eve.

SITUATION: NIGHT OF 23–24 DECEMBER

The situation for the American defenders of Bastogne remained serious, but the supply airdrop of 23 December had eased artillery ammunition supplies considerably. McAuliffe now had all four of his airborne regiments deployed along the perimeter: Harper's 327th Glider Infantry was along the southern and western faces with Team Browne and the 326th Airborne Engineer Battalion also in line; Ewell's 501st Parachute Infantry held the southeastern face, south of the rail line; Sink's 506th Parachute Infantry covered the northeastern face; and Chappuis's 502d Parachute Infantry held the northern and northwestern faces of the American perimeter. By these deployments McAuliffe was able to employ the survivors of Team Cherry and Team Hustead as his armored reserve, using them as a sort of fire brigade to react to emergencies. Moreover, radio communication with General Middleton's VIII Corps Headquarters, and through him, with General Patton's Third Army, served to assure McAuliffe that relief from the south was simply a matter of holding on for a few more days.

On the German side, the situation at Bastogne was drawing increasing attention from Manteuffel at Fifth Panzer Army Headquarters. Although Field Marshal Model, commander of Army Group B, had obtained the 15th Panzergrenadier and 9th Panzer divisions from OKW reserves, he agreed initially to assign only Col. Wolfgang Maucke's kampfgruppe from the 15th Panzergrenadier, built around the 115th Panzergrenadier Regiment, to take part in the Bastogne battle. These were significant forces, but would they possess enough combat power to take Bastogne? Kokott and Lüttwitz knew that substantial American forces were attacking north along the Arlon highway. These were opposed by the 5th Parachute Division of the Seventh Army's LXXXV Corps, but that division was spread over a front of twenty-eight kilometers and would be hard-pressed to stop the Americans. At this point, Hitler's obsession with the Meuse River crossings began to bear its evil fruit, as he and OKW were slow to divert units and resources to the effort against Bastogne.

13

THE SOUTHERN SHOULDER BOUNCES BACK

General Patton Regroups an Army

At the Verdun conference on 19 December General Bradley had directed his Third Army commander, Lt. Gen. George S. Patton, to assume command of the VIII Corps, which was no longer able to communicate directly with First Army Headquarters. At the conference Patton had agreed to mount a counteroffensive from the south, using elements of the VIII Corps, as well as the III and XII Corps, on 22 December, or as soon as possible thereafter. He had also promised General Eisenhower that he would go directly to Luxembourg after the conference.[1]

Patton had been accompanied to the Verdun meeting on 19 December by his Deputy Chief of Staff, Col. Paul Harkins, and his senior aide, Lt. Col. Charles R. Codman. As soon as the meeting broke up, shortly after noon, Patton told Harkins to call his Chief of Staff, Maj. Gen. Hobart Gay, at Third Army Headquarters in Nancy, and, using a prearranged code, to tell him to initiate the already-planned move of the III Corps to the vicinity of Arlon. (Arlon was in Belgium, just west of the Luxembourg frontier.) When Harkins called Gay, the Chief of Staff told him to inform Patton that elements of the 4th Armored Division had actually begun to move westward on the previous night.

After studying the situation map in Bradley's office, Patton decided that he would detach from the VIII Corps the units on the critical southern shoulder of the German penetration, at the southeastern end of the VIII Corps sector, and put them under the XII Corps of Maj. Gen. Manton S. Eddy. (These were the 4th Infantry Division, Combat Command A [CCA] of the 9th Armored Division, and the newly arrived 10th Armored Division.) But Patton did not expect that Eddy could disengage from his ongoing attack in the Saar

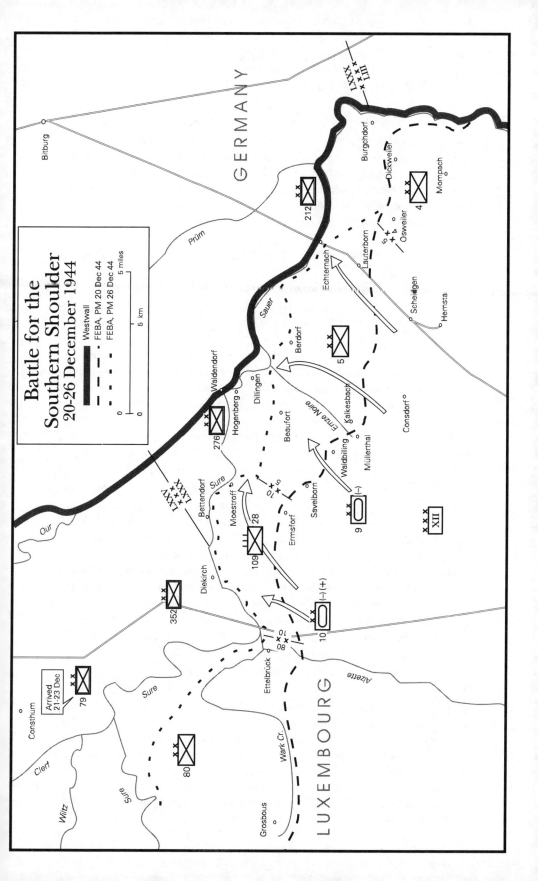

Battle for the Southern Shoulder 20-26 December 1944

Westwall
FEBA, PM 20 Dec 44
FEBA, PM 26 Dec 44

0   5 km
0   5 miles

GERMANY

Bitburg

Prüm

Sauer

Our

LUXEMBOURG

Alzette

Wark Cr.

Sure

Wiltz

Clerf

Sure

Consthum

Grosbous

Ettelbrück

Diekirch

Bettendorf

Moestroff

Ermsdorf

Savelborn

Waldbillig

Müllerthal

Consdorf

Kalkesbach

Ernze Noire

Beaufort

Dillingen

Berdorf

Echternach

Lauterborn

Osweiler

Scheidgen

Hemsta

Mompach

Dickweiler

Burgchdorf

Waldendorf

Hogenberg

LXXX

LIII

212

4

5

276

XXXI

352

79

Arrived
21-23 Dec

80

28

109

9 (-)

10

80

10 (-) (+)

XII

5

10

5

region and shift his headquarters to the vicinity of Luxembourg in less than forty-eight hours. He needed to know how well the three divisions holding the southern shoulder could stand up to the German attacks before Eddy arrived. So Patton decided to find out about the situation by calling Maj. Gen. William H. H. Morris, commander of the 10th Armored Division, which Patton had so reluctantly released to the VIII Corps on orders from Bradley on 16 December. (See chapter 9.) Since he knew Morris and trusted him, Patton believed he could get from Morris an objective assessment about the situation at the southern shoulder.

William Henry Harrison Morris Jr. was born on 22 March 1890 in Ocean Grove, New Jersey. He graduated from West Point in June 1911 as a second lieutenant of Infantry. His early assignments were troop duty in the Philippines; Tientsin, China; and Texas. After the outbreak of World War I he was assigned to the 360th Infantry Regiment of the 90th Division, and commanded a battalion in action at the Battles of St. Mihiel and the Meuse-Argonne. In the latter battle he was wounded and received the Distinguished Service Cross for exceptional gallantry in action. His service between the wars was a typical mix of attendance at or instruction in schools, troop duty, and staff assignments. In December 1940, as a colonel, he took command of the 66th Armored Regiment at Fort Benning, Georgia. In February 1942 he was assigned to command the newly activated 6th Armored Division at Fort Chaffee, Arkansas, and was promoted to major general. In early 1943 he was appointed commander of the II Armored Corps at San Jose, California. In October he became commander of the XVIII Corps. In July 1944 he learned of the death of the commander of the 10th Armored Division, which was preparing to embark for Europe. He asked Army Chief of Staff General Marshall to assign him to command that division. When asked why he was, in effect, asking for a demotion from corps to division command, he responded: "I have spent a lifetime learning how to lead troops in battle, and that's what I want to do." Marshall approved his request. Morris and his division arrived in France in September, joining the Third Army in time to take part in the battle for Metz. After the capture of that city, Morris and his division were placed in reserve to prepare for a spearhead role in the Third Army's planned offensive north of the Saar River. Late on 16 December he was ordered to take his divison north to join the hard-pressed VIII Corps in the Ardennes.

After a guarded phone conversation with Morris, Patton decided to place him in command of a "provisional corps," which would be responsible for the shoulder until the XII Corps Headquarters was ready to take over. This provisional corps would include Morris's own 10th Armored Division, the embattled 4th Infantry Division, and battered CCA of the 9th Armored Division, to which the equally battered 109th Infantry Regiment of the 28th Infantry Division was now attached.

Patton then got in his car and drove from Verdun toward Luxembourg, by way of Thionville, where the headquarters of the XX Corps was located.

Arriving at Thionville late in the afternoon, he conferred with the corps commander, Maj. Gen. Walton H. Walker, about the changes in mission, realignment of army and corps boundaries, and shifting of units between corps, which had emerged from the Verdun meeting. The XX Corps, which had been the westernmost of Patton's three corps attacking northward into the Saar region (of these, the III Corps was in reserve), was about to become the easternmost, and would have to adjust its eastern boundary somewhat to conform to a westward shift by the Seventh Army of the 6th Army Group. After about an hour of this discussion, Patton was getting ready to drive on to Luxembourg. Walker persuaded him to spend the night in Thionville because of the alarmist (and greatly exaggerated) rumors that were spreading about Operation Greif and the behind-the-lines activities of Lt. Col. Otto Skorzeny's terrorists in American uniforms.[2]

Early on the morning of 20 December Patton drove on to Luxembourg. He found the roads crowded with moving American units, mostly of the 4th Armored Division, 26th Infantry Division, and elements of the III Corps and XII Corps headquarters and corps troops. Despite the large numbers of vehicles on the roads, they were moving steadily, thanks to efficient military police traffic control.

At that time the sleepy capital of the Grand Duchy of Luxembourg was one of the most international cities in the world, and undoubtedly the most bustling. The city, including its surrounding duchy, is a north European crossroad, linking France, Germany, Belgium, and the Netherlands. Letzeburgesch is the Germanic dialect spoken by all Luxembourgers, but most of the people are also fluent in French and German, and many speak Dutch as well. In December 1944, however, the foreign language most heard on the streets of Luxembourg City was American English. Within the city limits were the headquarters of an American army group, now being joined by a field army, and an army corps plus four divisions. Also finding space someplace in the crowded city were the administrative and logistical units and headquarters of the large numbers of support units functioning under those major headquarters. American military policemen (MPs) assisted the local police in directing the heavy, predominantly military traffic.

In Luxembourg City Patton was quickly directed by MPs to the location of an advance party from the XII Corps Headquarters. General Eddy had just closed out his command post on the Saar front and was on the road to Luxembourg. Patton therefore left a message for Eddy about the establishment of the provisional corps with instructions for the XII Corps to take over when Eddy was ready to assume operational control. Patton expressed his hope that the counteroffensive would begin on 22 December. He also left word that the 5th Infantry Division, which had been attacking the day before in the XX Corps zone, was now disengaging and would be available to the XII Corps by 21 December.

Patton then visited the command post of the 80th Infantry Division, which had been hastily deployed north of Luxembourg City to protect it should the German offensive turn in that direction. He spoke to Maj. Gen. Horace L. McBride, the division commander, about his forthcoming shift to the III Corps. Before leaving Luxembourg, Patton sent messages to Major Generals Troy H. Middleton and John Millikin, commanders of the VIII and III Corps, respectively, to meet him at Arlon, where the III Corps Headquarters had just opened. He also requested that the commanders of the other two divisions of the III Corps be present at the meeting in Arlon: Maj. Gen. Hugh J. Gaffey, commander of the 4th Armored Division, and Maj. Gen. Willard S. Paul, commander of the 26th Infantry Division.

Patton then made a slight detour to visit the command posts of the 4th Infantry Division and 10th Armored Division, just north of Luxembourg. This gave him a chance to observe the attitudes of the commanders of those two embattled divisions—Maj. Gen. Raymond O. Barton of the 4th and Major General Morris of the 10th. Satisfied by his meeting with those two generals and with what he saw in their command posts, Patton drove on to Arlon.

In his conversation at Arlon with Generals Middleton, Millikin, Gaffey, and Paul, Patton expressed some concern about the risk of holding Bastogne, since the Germans would probably be able to encircle and isolate the forces in and around the town. Middleton told him that he had received a call directly from General Eisenhower about the importance of holding the town, and added that he believed the benefit of denying the road hub to the Germans was worth the risk to the 101st Airborne Division and the combat commands of the 9th and 10th Armored divisions that were holding the eastern approaches to the town. Patton was quickly convinced of the soundness of the decision and approved it. He also realized, as a result of the conversation with Middleton, that except for the units already detached to the provisional corps he could not count on any of the battered elements of the VIII Corps to take part in his planned offensive.

Patton then drove back to his headquarters at Nancy. The next day he wrote in a letter to his wife: "Yesterday I again earned my pay. I visited seven divisions and regrouped an army alone. It was quite a day, and I enjoyed it. . . ."[3]

While typically immodest, Patton hardly overstated the case—other than the implication that he had done all of this without any help from his efficient staff. He had, in fact, accomplished one of the great feats of military history: halting in its tracks an attacking army of 350,000 men and pivoting this massive force ninety degrees to be able to resume the attack in an entirely different direction in less than seventy hours. He *had* earned his pay!

THE PROVISIONAL CORPS HOLDS THE LINE

It is interesting that the opposing commanders on the southern shoulder issued very similar orders for operations beginning on 20 December, and for identical reasons. In anticipation of the early arrival of American counterattacking reinforcements, Gen. Franz Beyer of the LXXX Corps ordered the commanders of the 276th and 212th Volksgrenadier divisions (VGDs) to go on the defensive. They were to prepare for the arrival of the expected American reinforcements by consolidating, by eliminating pockets of resistance behind their main lines, and by carrying out local attacks to secure the most favorable ground for future defensive operations.

At about the same time General Morris was instructing the 4th Infantry Division, the 9th Armored Division, and CCA of his own division, to consolidate, to disengage their most exposed, leading elements, and to regroup along a shorter and stronger main line of resistance to provide a springboard for the coming offensive after the arrival of American reinforcements. The similar orders of the two corps commanders led to a number of hard-fought local engagements along the southern front on 20 December, as well as to a somewhat more orderly organization of each of the opposing lines.

Affecting General Beyer's decisions was an additional concern that did not affect General Morris: The LXXX Corps not only had the responsibility for pinning down the extreme left flank of the Seventh Army to the Westwall just west of Trier, but also had to keep contact on its right with the LXXXV Corps to assure that its divisions contributed their part to the principal mission of the Seventh Army. Like an accordion the LXXX Corps would keep contact with the LXXXV Corps, which in turn would maintain a link with leftmost of the onrushing divisions of the Fifth Panzer Army. Both Seventh Army corps would at the same time protect the left and rear of the Fifth Panzer Army and its divisions. General Beyer was worried because there was no longer any contact between the right flank of his 276th VGD and its neighbor to the right, the 352d VGD of the LXXXV Corps.[4]

The American provisional corps was deployed with the equivalent of two divisions abreast and elements of another division in reserve. On the right, east of Müllerthal and the Ernz Noire gorge, was the 4th Infantry Division with its three regiments in line: The 12th Infantry extended from the Ernz Noire to a point midway between Scheidgen and Osweiler; the 22d Infantry continued the line to the Sauer River on the east; the 8th Infantry, essentially in an observation and reserve role, covered the line of the Sauer River south to its junction with the Moselle River. The front held by the 12th and 22nd Infantry regiments was extremely rocky, rugged, and forested; although generally favoring the defenders, the terrain did provide attackers with maneuver opportunities.

On the left of the provisional corps was the 9th Armored Division (division headquarters and CCA) with two subsectors. The 109th Infantry (the depleted 1st and 3d battalions) held the line of the Wark Creek from a wide-open flank at Grosbous on the left, through Merzig, almost to Ettelbruck, where the creek joins the Sure and Alzette Rivers. The 90th Cavalry Reconnaissance Squadron was astride the Alzette River at Schieren, south of Ettelbruck, extending almost to Ermsdorf. The line from Ermsdorf to Christnach and Müllerthal was held by CCA of the 9th Armored Division, supported by the 2d Battalion of the 109th Infantry. In reserve were elements of CCR of the 10th Armored Division.

The process of consolidation, regrouping, and jockeying for position continued on both sides of the southern shoulder into 21 December. The 109th was under constant pressure throughout the day from repeated attacks all along the line by elements of the 352d VGD. (This meant that elements of the 352d Division were closer to the right flank of his 276th Division than General Beyer apparently realized at the time.)

The 276th VGD was deployed between a point north of Stegen on the right (west), through Eppeldorf, Savelborn, and Waldbillig to Müllerthal and the Ernz Noire gorge on the left (east). The principal activity in this sector on 21 December was in the vicinity of Waldbillig: Oberst Hugo Dempwolff had been ordered by General Beyer to mount a limited attack from there with his 276th VGD to seize more defensible terrain in the vicinity of Christnach.

By coincidence, Maj. Gen. John W. Leonard, commander of the 9th Armored Division, had ordered his CCA to retake Waldbillig that morning. CCA of the 9th with support from Task Force Chamberlain of the 10th Armored Division (commanded by Lt. Col. Thomas C. Chamberlain) jumped off on this offensive shortly before the German attack was scheduled to begin. The result was a protracted and hard-fought engagement over Waldbillig. By dark the Americans held the village, but withdrew about midnight.

Farther east the 212th VGD Division mounted an afternoon attack to seize good defensive terrain on high ground in the Consdorf-Scheidgen-Michelshof area. The Germans made some progress toward Scheidgen, but were unable to take the village, and were stopped in their other attempts.

That evening the 212th Division began a deliberate withdrawal back to high ground to the south and southeast of Echternach. To distract American attention from this retrograde movement, one more attack was made toward Scheidgen on 22 December. But the Americans had already begun their counteroffensive, albeit somewhat half-heartedly, and were more than ready to deal with the German attack, which incurred heavy losses, and was more spoiled than spoiling.

A "NOMINAL" COUNTEROFFENSIVE

When the German offensive had been launched on 16 December into the U.S. V and VIII Corps, the U.S. 5th Infantry Division was in reserve in the XX Corps of the Third Army, 100 kilometers to the southeast, near Saarlautern. The division had gone into the line on the night of 17–18 December, and had attacked in an easterly direction, two regiments abreast, on 18 and 19 December. On the night of 19 December the division commander, Maj. Gen. S. LeRoy Irwin, had received a call from the corps commander, General Walker, telling him to stop his attack and to prepare to move his entire division northward into Luxembourg. Irwin's reserve regiment, the 10th Infantry, was to be ready to move on an hour's notice.

Stafford LeRoy Irwin, from an old Army family, was born in Fort Monroe, Virginia, on 23 March 1893. He graduated from West Point in 1915, a member of the class "the stars fell on" a quarter of a century later. As a second lieutenant of Cavalry, he joined the 11th Cavalry and was with them during the Punitive Expedition into Mexico in 1916. Soon after that he transferred to the Field Artillery. He was bitterly disappointed that the need for trainers in the United States kept him from going overseas in World War I. Between the wars he alternated school and troop assignments across the United States and in the Philippines.

As a brigadier general, Irwin went overseas to North Africa in November 1942 in Operation Torch as the artillery commander of the 9th Infantry Division. Irwin and his Division Artillery played a major role in halting the German drive at Kasserine Pass in Tunisia in late February 1943. After serving through the remainder of the Tunisian campaign and in Sicily, the 9th Division was ordered to England in late 1943 to prepare for the invasion of Normandy. Shortly before D-Day, however, Irwin was ordered to Iceland to take command of the 5th Infantry Division. He brought the division to England in June and took it to Normandy in early July. The 5th played a major role in the breakout from Normandy in late July and early August. Irwin and his "Red Diamond" division (the nickname was derived fom the division shoulder patch) drove south through Angers, then east to cross the Seine at Fontainebleau, and on to Metz, where it was halted by the vigorous German defense of the fortified city. After several weeks of tough fighting, Irwin's division participated in the final successful assault of Metz on 19 November. The 5th continued its advance northward to reach and cross the German frontier and the Saar River. After a brief rest, it renewed the attack across the Saar on 18 December, when suddenly it was ordered to halt and to disengage.

During the night of 19 December, the 5th Division received the anticipated order for the 10th Infantry, the 818th Tank Destroyer Battalion, and the 735th Tank Battalion to move north on the next day. The infantry regiment was on the road early in the morning; the tank and tank destroyer battalions, ferried back across the Saar River during the day, were on their way to Luxembourg by 1700 hours. Meanwhile, Irwin received orders to pull the 11th Infantry out of the line after dark on 20 December. The 11th Infantry was on the road north by 1000 the next day. That night, relieved by the 95th Infantry Division, the third regiment of the 5th Infantry Division, the 2d Infantry, was pulled out of the line, and it, too, was being trucked to Luxembourg early on 22 December.

The 10th Infantry had arrived in Luxembourg City on the night of 20 December. Because of inadequate liaison between staff officers of the 5th Infantry and 10th Armored divisions, the soldiers spent the night shivering in their trucks, trying to get some sleep.

Early on 21 December General Irwin met with General Eddy and the XII Corps operations staff. Because of gains made by the 212th VGD near Echternach the previous day, and with the German attack continuing, consideration was briefly given to committing the 10th Infantry that afternoon to restore the 4th Division's lines near Scheidgen. However, when it became obvious that the 12th Infantry line was holding, General Eddy postponed until evening a decision on when and how the 10th Infantry would be committed. He did make clear to Irwin that the 10th Infantry would attack the following day. General Patton had said that there would be a counterattack beginning on 22 December and, by God, there would be a counterattack!

Manton Sprague Eddy was born in Chicago on 16 May 1892. He entered the Regular Army as a lieutenant of Infantry in 1913. He went overseas with the 39th Infantry Regiment of the 4th Division in April 1918. He served in the Aisne-Marne Offensive and was wounded in action in operations on the Vesle River in August 1918. Eddy rejoined his regiment during the Battle of the Meuse-Argonne and was soon promoted to major and given command of the 11th Machine Gun Battalion of the 4th Division. After the Armistice he marched east with his division as part of the Army of Occupation in Germany.

Between the wars Eddy's experience with troop units, schools, and staff and civilian component duties was typical of the Army's officer corps. In the 1920s and 1930s he was promoted slowly but steadily from his permanent rank of captain to colonel. In March 1942 he was promoted to brigadier general and assigned as Assistant Division Commander of the 9th Infantry Division. In June he became the division commander and was promoted to major general. In late 1942 his division was sent to North Africa and participated with distinction in the campaign in Tunisia. General Eisenhower named it as one of his two best divisions. The 9th Division took part in the Allied assault on Normandy in June 1944, and as a result of its performance Eddy was appointed commander of the XII Corps in August 1944. Eddy added to his distinction by the excellent performance of the corps during the Lorraine campaign of November 1944. In early December the XII Corps spearheaded the advance of the Third Army through the Saar region toward the Westwall. This offensive had just been renewed when the German Ardennes counter-offensive led General Patton to shift the XII Corps to the northwest to hold the right shoulder of the German penetration.

The 5th Division's 11th Infantry Regiment arrived in Luxembourg City on the afternoon of 21 December. Its commander, Col. Paul J. Black, was ordered to move into the positions of the 80th Infantry Division just north of Luxembourg City, where that division had been protecting the northern approaches to the city. The 80th Division had been ordered to attack northward on the following morning, as the right wing of the III Corps offensive. To do this it would have to pass through the positions of the 109th Infantry. At this time there was no clear boundary between the right of the III Corps and the left of the XII Corps.

General Eddy met that evening at the 4th Infantry Division command post with his four division commanders: Generals Barton (4th Infantry Division), Irwin (5th Infantry Division), Leonard (9th Armored Division), and Morris (10th Armored Division). A few hours earlier the XII Corps had formally taken over operational control from the provisional corps. Eddy attached the 10th Infantry to the 4th Division and directed that it attack around noon on 22 December to seize the initiative from the Germans and to restore the front of the 12th Infantry.

Although the counteroffensive was not very impressive, at least General Eddy could report to Third Army headquarters that the XII Corps was attacking on 22 December, as directed by General Patton. General Irwin was disappointed at this lip service to Patton's order; he did not think any significant results could be achieved by such a piecemeal effort.

Irwin was right. The 10th Infantry approached the start line on schedule, two battalions abreast, astride the road from Michelshof to Echternach with the other battalion in reserve. Virtually simultaneously a regiment of the 212th VGD mounted an attack from the north, also astride the road. This had been intended by General Sensfuss as a diversionary effort, to distract American attention from withdrawals elsewhere in the sector of the 212th Division. Under the circumstances, the German attack not only accomplished its diversionary purpose, but in effect canceled the planned attack of the 10th Infantry. Following a confused and inconclusive engagement, the Germans withdrew after dark.

Far more successful, from the American point of view, had been a peculiar incident that occurred early that morning on the front of the 109th Infantry. This followed a night of serious patrol activity and local attacks by both sides in the area south and east of Merzig. About 1,000 troops of the 3d Battalion, dug in south of the Wark Creek near Merzig, saw a column of German troops marching down the road from Ettelbruck, heading toward Grosbous. For some reason the Germans seem to have thought that the Americans had withdrawn during the night. Amazed at this scene, the Americans held their fire, but artillery forward observers alerted their gun positions. As the head of the column approached Grosbous, American artillery, tank guns, and tank destroyer guns opened fire. In a few minutes two German infantry battalions and a battalion of artillery had been smashed. The Americans counted eighteen vehicles destroyed, and they estimated that several hundred German soldiers were killed, wounded, and dispersed.[5]

The next day, back in the 4th Infantry Division sector, the 10th Infantry continued the attack begun so inauspiciously on 22 December with somewhat better results. But the troops were slowed down by bitterly cold, intermittently snowy weather. And the Germans took maximum defensive advantage of the wooded hills and steep valleys of the rugged terrain. The XII Corps could not claim any great success thus far for its counteroffensive.

THE COUNTEROFFENSIVE STARTS TO ROLL

The XII Corps operations staff had produced a new attack plan for 24 December that provided for a corps-wide attack through the current positions of the 4th Infantry Division, on a two-division—5th Infantry and 10th Armored—front. The objective was to sweep the enemy from the south side of the Sure-Sauer River in the corps zone.

In reserve behind the 5th Division and ready to exploit was a combat command of the 10th Armored Division. Covering the right flank was the newly arrived 2d Cavalry Group, responsible for observing and holding the line of the Sauer River south of the bend at Relingen. Once the 5th Division had passed through, the 4th Infantry Division was to regroup, take some replacements, rest briefly, and be ready to serve as corps reserve. Despite the complexities caused by the variety of units in the two division sectors, it was a relatively simple plan, and a good one.

The attack jumped off the next day at 1100. On the right, the 5th Division made the main effort, passing through the 4th Division positions, from Savelborn on the left to Osweiler on the right. The three regiments of the division were on line: On the right was the 10th Infantry, from Scheidgen on the west to Osweiler on the east; in the center was the 2d Infantry, from Scheidgen to the Ernz Noire gorge; the 11th Infantry on the left extended from the gorge near Christnach to Savelborn.

The 212th VGD yielded the readily defensible terrain reluctantly, and by dark still firmly controlled the high ground south of the Sauer River and east of the Ernz Noire gorge. The 2d Infantry, in the center of the sector, met the greatest resistance, as might be expected, in the rugged terrain around the gorge. Only on the left, where the 11th Infantry faced the left wing of the 276th VGD, was progress substantial, with spearheads approaching Haller by the end of the day.

Farther to the left, in the 10th Armored Division sector, progress was somewhat better. On the extreme left, the 109th Infantry (attached to CCA of the 9th Armored, which in turn was attached to the 10th Armored Division) readily overcame the right wing of the 276th Division. By 1330 the 1st Battalion of the 109th held the line of the Sure River west of Gilsdorf. By 1500 the 3d Battalion had reached Moestroff and held most of the line of the Sure River to the southwest. Between these two battalions, the 90th Cavalry Reconnaissance Squadron (attached to the 109th) had more difficulty at Gilsdorf, but with help from the 1st Battalion seized that objective shortly after dark, at 1800. The Germans blew the bridge at Moestroff as the 109th closed in. During the fighting the Americans destroyed the bridges at Gilsdorf and Bettendorf.

Farther east, however, CCA of the 9th Armored Division met with more determined resistance. On the left CCA reached Eppeldorf before being stopped, but progress elsewhere was less spectacular. By dark the 276th Division was crowded back into a bridgehead between Moestroff and Dillingen, but still held a deep salient reaching south from Eppeldorf to Haller.

Christmas Day was relatively quiet along the Sure River front, as well as along the Moestroff-Eppeldorf front of the 9th Armored. But it was no holiday in the sector where the 5th Infantry Division faced the 212th VGD. On the right of the 5th Division, the 10th Infantry fought its way slowly toward Echternach. By late afternoon the Americans had reached the heights overlooking the town and the Sauer River from which they could see German troops crossing to the north bank of the river in rubber assault boats and over a wooden footbridge near the town. With good observation, the American artillery used its new proximity fuses to place effective air bursts over the bridge and the boats, inflicting heavy casualties. The advance continued, and by dark elements of the 10th Infantry were within half a mile of the town. That night patrols entered Echternach, only to find it abandoned by the Germans. The 212th VGD was withdrawing in good order toward the Bollendorf bridge.

In the center of the 5th Division sector the 2d Infantry, after extremely tough fighting, particularly in and near the gorge, was approaching Berdorf by dark. On the left the 11th Infantry drove through Haller, and at dusk was threatening Beaufort. Sensing that the Germans to his front were close to breaking, the regimental commander, Col. Paul J. Black, continued the attack through the night. By daybreak the defenders of Beaufort began to fall back in some disorder toward Dillingen. Despite severe hammering from American artillery and fighter-bombers, both the 212th Division and the 276th Division successfully carried out classic withdrawals to their respective bridges on 26 December; the 212th to the Bollendorf bridge, the 276th to the Dillingen bridge. The 212th completed its withdrawal during the night. The 276th, under orders from Seventh Army Headquarters, held on to its bridgehead for another twenty-four hours with massive artillery support beating back all American efforts to destroy the defenders and the bridge. After dark on 27 December the Dillingen bridgehead was abandoned by the Germans, who blew the bridge before dawn.

On 26 December the 109th Infantry was released from assignment to the 9th Armored Division and the XII Corps. By 2040 all units of the 109th had been relieved in their positions along the Sure River by troops of the arriving CCA of the 6th Armored Division, now joining the XII Corps. The next morning the 109th moved by truck to rejoin the 28th Division near Neufchâteau.[6]

ASSESSMENT

The First Battle of the Sauer River had essentially been a battle between the German 212th VGD and the American 12th Infantry Regiment. Although the Americans acquitted themselves well under difficult circumstances, tactically the Germans had the best of that four-day engagement. The Second Battle of the Sauer River, which really lasted only three days, from 24 December through 26 December, had a similar outcome. Although the defenders acquitted themselves well under very difficult circumstances, the attackers (this time the Americans) generally enjoyed a tactical success. Strategically the outcome was an even greater American success and set the stage for what some believe could have been an overwhelming American victory.

By the end of the battle the XII Corps operations staff were busy on plans for a crossing of the Sure-Sauer River, a penetration of the Westwall, and an advance toward Bitburg. Apparently they favored that plan over a somewhat similar concept that would have had the corps driving almost due north, west of the Our River, toward St. Vith. In either event, the XII Corps would have been in a position to slam shut a steel door in the rear of the Fifth and Sixth Panzer armies. In retrospect, the move west of the Our, which would have avoided potential problems in storming the Westwall, appears to have been the better of the two concepts.

Remembering Patton's facetious remark at Verdun on 19 December (see chapter 9), it is hard to understand why this concept of using the relatively fresh and victorious XII Corps to cut off the German spearheads was not adopted. Bold, yes. Risky, possibly. Foolhardy, no. Had this been done, about fifteen German divisions, including most of the best armored divisions left in the German Army, might have been cut off, and it is hard to see how, even in speculation, they could have avoided destruction. Had this occurred, the Battle of the Bulge would have ended two weeks earlier than it eventually did, thousands of American and German lives would have been saved, and the war probably would have ended in February or March, instead of in May, sparing many thousands more German, British, American, and Russian lives.

Such a concept would probably have seemed too risky to Eisenhower or Bradley. But this was Patton's idea. It is very hard to understand why he did not do it on his own initiative. He gives no hint in his diaries. It is one of the many mysteries of the war.

14

THE SIEGE AND RELIEF OF BASTOGNE

Once the 101st Airborne Division was committed at and surrounded in Bastogne, it was inevitable that a major effort would be mounted for its relief. Fortunately for the 101st—and the troops of VIII Corps Artillery, Combat Command R of the 9th Armored Division, and Combat Command B of the 10th Armored Division, who also defended the vital road nexus there—plans to relieve them were already under consideration by the Allied high command by the time the Germans had completed their investment on the night of 20–21 December. By that time, major elements of Lt. Gen. George S. Patton's Third Army were already on the move to carry out that relief from their starting positions more than 150 kilometers south of the Ardennes.

Patton's Third Army had been scheduled to begin its part of the previously planned major Allied mid-December offensive on 19 December. With two corps abreast and one in reserve, it was to drive in a northeasterly direction through the Saar region to crack the Westwall, ultimately aiming for Kaiserslautern, Zweibrücken, Mannheim, and Frankfurt. For administrative reasons, early on 16 December the main effort was postponed until the twenty-first, but preliminary attacks were to begin on the twentieth. Thus it was not only remarkable but well-nigh miraculous that as early as 18–19 December one of Patton's three corps was on the move to attack toward Bastogne along a northwesterly axis—a ninety-degree change in direction—from positions 90 miles (150 kilometers) distant from its Saar region preattack positions.

Changing the course of his attack on such short notice proved that Patton was not only a fast mover, but also a skillful, sensitive, highly gifted professional commander, with a professional staff. He had anticipated the possibility of a German offensive into the thinly held VIII Corps sector of the front, and as early as 14 December had directed his staff to prepare contingency plans for a possible attack northward into the Ardennes. The command con-

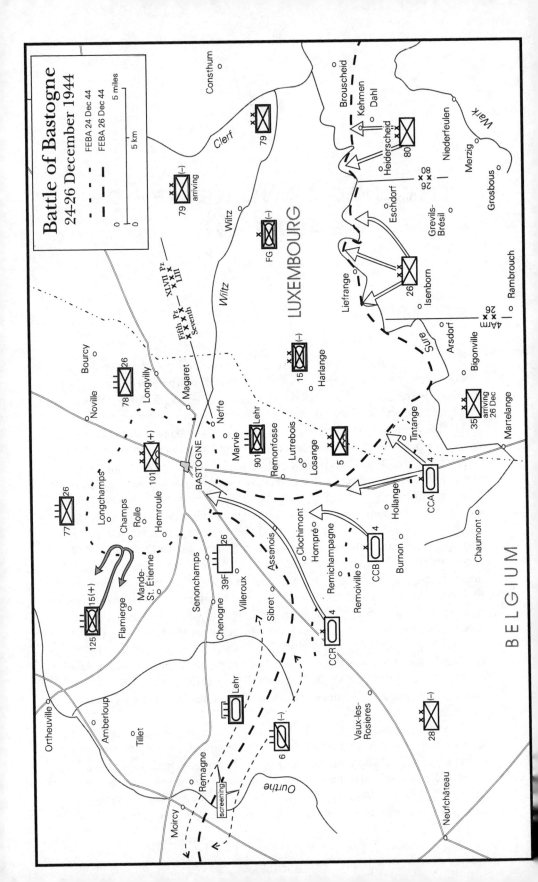

Battle of Bastogne
24-26 December 1944

FEBA 24 Dec 44
FEBA 26 Dec 44

5 km
5 miles

ference at Verdun on 19 December (see chapter 9) demonstrated the new-found professionalism of the U.S. Army. Patton's concept, as already developed by his staff, was remarkably similar to that which General Eisenhower presented at the outset of the conference. At first the Supreme Commander had been skeptical that Patton could move as swiftly as he proposed, especially over bad roads in miserable weather. Patton persisted, partly because he also saw an opportunity for driving deep into the flank of the German penetration, perhaps as far north as St. Vith, and so inflicting a massive defeat on Army Group B. In the end, he won his point, but his concept was watered down by his more cautious superiors. Forewarned, units of the Third Army were on the move as early as the evening of 18 December, before Conference at Verdun. To be fair, Patton had protested violently on 16 December when ordered by General Bradley, the 12th Army Group Commander, to send the 10th Armored Division north to assist Maj. Gen. Troy Middleton's VIII Corps to stop the offensive. The flamboyant Patton sometimes regarded an order from a higher authority that interfered with his own plans as something akin to a personal affront.

Nevertheless, Patton had begun to pay close attention to the German offensive in the Ardennes on its second day, 17 December. Following a meeting with General Bradley at 12th Army Group Headquarters in Luxembourg City on 18 December, Patton canceled the Third Army offensive, although he allowed some previously planned local attacks to be carried out.

III CORPS MOVES INTO POSITION: 20–22 DECEMBER

Patton designated Maj. Gen. John Millikin's III Corps as his primary counterattack force for a new offensive north into the Ardennes. Millikin was born in Danville, Indiana, on 7 January 1888, and was commissioned a second lieutenant of Cavalry after graduating from West Point in 1910. After service in Hawaii, on the Mexican border, and on the east coast, he went to France with the American Expeditionary Force (AEF) in February 1918, where he became Chief of the AEF's Military Police. After the war Millikin was assigned to the War Department General Staff, then served in Hawaii with the Hawaiian Division before being transferred to the Cavalry School at Fort Riley, Kansas.

Interspersed with these assignments he attended the Command and General Staff School at Fort Leavenworth, and the Army War College in Washington. In the expansion of the U.S. Army that began in the autumn of 1939, Millikin was promoted to brigadier general in October 1940 and to major general in July 1941. He served with the 1st Cavalry Division in Texas and commanded the 2d Cavalry Division in Kansas from May 1941 until April 1942. Millikin also commanded the 83d Infantry Division (May–August 1942) and the 33d Infantry Division (August 1942–October 1943). Appointed to command the III Corps, he took that headquarters overseas in August, and landed in Normandy in time to play a role in the triumphant Allied advance across northern France.

As of 19 December, the only combat division in Millikin's corps was Maj. Gen. Willard S. Paul's 26th Infantry Division. A National Guard Division with units from all six New England states, it was nicknamed the "Yankee Division." It took part in four campaigns in World War I between October 1917 and the Armistice on 11 November 1918. The 26th Division was reactivated in January 1941; under the command of Major General Paul it landed at Cherbourg and Omaha Beach in early September 1944. The 26th entered combat a month later in Lorraine as part of the Third Army's XIX Corps. It had seen considerable combat during the XIX Corps Seille-Saar campaign (8 November through 8 December), and was resting as part of the III Corps in Third Army reserve when the Germans opened their offensive in the Ardennes.

Willard S. Paul was born in Worcester, Massachusetts, on 28 February 1894, and served in World War I. He stayed in the army after the war, and by 1941 he was a colonel at Army Ground Force Headquarters in Washington. By 1942 he was commanding the 75th Infantry Division, and in 1943 he was appointed to command of the 26th Infantry Division. He took the division to France and retained that command through operations in northern France and Lorraine. The division was in Third Army reserve when it was assigned on 19 December to the III Corps for the counteroffensive against the southern face of the German Bulge in the Ardennes.

Patton also assigned two other divisions to the III Corps, both of them resting near Metz. The first of these was Maj. Gen. Horace L. McBride's 80th Infantry Division. Horace Logan McBride was born in Nebraska on 28 June 1894, and graduated from West Point in June 1916 as a second lieutenant of Artillery. He served with artillery units in combat in World War I as a captain and a major. After the war his experience included service as a student and instructor in schools, with troop units, and as a staff officer. In March 1943 he was promoted to major general as commander of the 80th Infantry Division. He took the division to England in July 1944, and after a brief period of training landed in Normandy on 3 August. McBride's division went into action near Mortain, in southwestern Normandy, on 10 August, and advanced east to take Argentan ten days later. Part of the southern jaw closing on the Falaise Pocket, the 80th turned eastward to pursue the defeated Germans into Lorraine. With the XII Corps the division took part in the Seille-Saar campaign. The performance of the division and its commander in this campaign prompted General Patton to write: "Whenever we turned to the 80th on anything we always knew the objective would be obtained." On 16 December the division was attacking northeastward, across the Saar, when the Third Army's offensive was halted due to the German Ardennes counteroffensive.

The 80th Infantry Division had been organized as a National Army division in September 1917, and went to France the following May. Its first combat experience was with the British in the Somme offensive in September 1918. It then took part in the later stages of the Meuse-Argonne campaign as part of the American First Army in October and November. The 80th Division was inactivated in May 1919 and was reactivated in July 1942 with a cadre from the 8th Infantry Division and newly drafted recruits.

The other division assigned to Millikin's corps was Maj. Gen. Hugh J. Gaffey's veteran 4th Armored Division. Hugh Gaffey was born in Hartford, Connecticut, on 18 November 1895. After graduation from the Worcester Academy in Massachusetts, he entered the University of Pennsylvania in 1916. After the United States entered World War I in April 1917, he left the university to enlist in the Army. Commissioned a second lieutenant of Field Artillery on 15 August 1917, to his regret he did not get overseas during World War I. After the United States entered World War II, he commanded the 2d Armored Division from May 1943 to April 1944, and later served as Chief of Staff of the Third Army under General Patton. At his and Patton's joint request, he was given command of the 4th Armored Division (then part of the Third Army) when the command of that division opened up in early December 1944.

The 4th Armored Division had been activated on 15 April 1941, at the same time as the 3d Armored, which also fought in the Ardennes. The division underwent extensive training and reorganization and provided cadres to help form the 8th Armored Division in January 1942. Commanded by Maj. Gen. John S. "Pop" Wood from July 1942, the 4th Armored was sent to England in January 1944 for further training. It landed at Utah Beach in Normandy on 11 July, and entered combat a little over a week later as part of the First Army's VIII Corps, taking part in the St. Lô breakout on 25 July and playing a major role in Patton's drive across Brittany. The 4th Armored continued to play a distinctive role in the Third Army's advance across France, and soon became "Patton's Favorite." The division took very heavy casualties during the Seille-Saar campaign. General Wood was sent back to the United States for a badly needed rest, and he was replaced as division commander by General Gaffey.

Patton directed III Corps Headquarters to move north from Metz to Arlon, and the three divisions were to move to forward assembly areas around Arlon and Luxembourg City. Gaffey's 4th Armored began to move on the evening of 18 December, and Combat Command B reached Longwy about midnight; the rest of the division arrived around dawn the next day.

As a result, Combat Command B of the 4th Armored was within striking distance of Bastogne by late afternoon on 20 December. Consequently, the Combat Command was temporarily assigned to Middleton's VIII Corps. The defenders of Bastogne urgently wanted the Combat Command in the city, but General Gaffey argued vigorously that his 4th Armored Division should not be scattered piecemeal across the countryside. Patton and Millikin agreed: Combat Command B was ordered to withdraw south to wait for the rest of the division. That night Combat Command B laagered near Habay La Neuve, and Combat Command A was a few kilometers away at Arlon with the remainder of the division and its trains.

The 4th Armored Division reassembled near Arlon on 21 December. The division had begun its approach march on 18 and 19 December with nearly all of its assigned tanks in the three tank battalions (8th, 35th, and 37th).[1] The road trip had taken a toll on the 8th Battalion's tanks; thirty-three broke down en route. Most of these were old vehicles in need of major overhaul or replacement after the rigors of the Seille-Saar operations. In fact, the division had received those tanks when it had arrived in England nearly a year before.[2] Thus, on 21 December the 8th Armored Battalion had only twenty combat-ready M4 Shermans.

By the time the 4th Armored Division reached Arlon, the 80th Infantry Division had moved north by road through Luxembourg City, and by the evening of 21 December had taken up positions west and northwest of Mersch with the 318th and 319th Infantry regiments forward. The 26th Division had also moved north, and by nightfall its 104th and 328th Infantry regiments were in line just south of the Niederculpach-Bissen road with the 101st Infantry and other divisional elements a few kilometers to the south. The 26th Division therefore lay between the 80th Division on the III Corps east (right) flank with the 4th Armored Division on the west (left) flank of the corps. The Third Army's 35th Infantry Division was also assigned to III Corps, and completed its withdrawal from contact with the Germans in Alsace during the daylight hours of 21 December. Finally, the 6th Cavalry Group (6th and 28th Cavalry Squadrons, Mechanized) covered the 4th Armored Division's eastern flank, and had responsibility for securing several road junctions east-south-east of Bastogne.[3]

THE GERMAN APPROACH TO BASTOGNE: 21–22 DECEMBER

Meanwhile, Gen. Hasso von Manteuffel's Fifth Panzer Army was trying to react to the changing situation around Bastogne while maintaining its drive westward toward the Meuse. The German troops in front of Bastogne were beginning to suffer from sporadic fuel and supply shortages, and although the colder temperatures hardened the muddy fields and roads and eased cross-country travel, the clearing weather after 23 December also meant that any movement during daylight was vulnerable to air attack by roving American fighter-bombers and medium bombers.

Colonel Heinz Kokott's 26th Volksgrenadier Division (VGD) retained principal operational responsibility for operations west of Bastogne. The 26th Fusilier Battalion advanced through Sibret and Chenogne to reach the Bois de Valet, and Kokott moved his divisional headquarters into the small village of Hompré, just west of the Arlon highway. At the same time, Col. Ludwig Heil-mann's 5th Parachute Division moved into position to guard the southern approaches to Bastogne.

This caused an unacceptable lengthening of the front of General der Infan-terie Baptist Kniess's LXXXV Corps line. As a result, General der Kavallerie

Count Edwin von Rothkirch und Trach's[4] LIII Corps headquarters was shifted from the extreme left of General Brandenberger's Seventh Army to its extreme right, to take over the 5th Parachute Division and other units scheduled to be committed to extend the Seventh Army's right flank westward. (The LIII Corps had previously commanded only a few fortress and replacement units.)

Rothkirch was born on 1 November 1888 at Militsch. He joined the 17th Light Dragoon Regiment as an officer cadet in early 1908, and was commissioned a second lieutenant of cavalry by June. He saw extensive frontline service in World War I, and attended the abbreviated wartime course at the Kriegsakademie in Berlin. After the Armistice, he was selected for service in the Reichswehr. As a lieutenant colonel, Rothkirch commanded the 15th Cavalry Regiment (October 1934–March 1938) and then the 2d Rifle Brigade (March–November 1938). Promoted to colonel in April 1936, he was Chief of Staff for the XXXIV Corps during the Polish campaign in September 1939. Promoted to generalmajor in March 1940, he saw no action during the 1940 campaign as commander of the 442d Local Defense Division.[5] While commander of the 330th Infantry Division (January 1942–September 1943), Rothkirch was promoted to generalleutnant. He was promoted to general der kavallerie during further staff duty, and took command of the LIII Corps on 1 November 1944.

Lead elements of the 14th Parachute Infantry moved into Sibret and Vaux-lez-Rosières, while the 15th Parachute Infantry advanced to Martelange and Bigonville nearby, effectively blocking the routes leading north from Arlon and Luxembourg City to Bastogne. The 5th Parachute Division's artillery was concentrated around the hamlets of Hompré and Hollange.[6]

Finally refueled, Colonel von Lauchert's 2d Panzer Division had begun to move on 21 December; its reconnaissance battalion reached Ortheuville. The division continued westward on 22 December, heading for the Meuse crossings near Dinant and Celles. The 2d Panzer Reconnaissance Battalion passed through Champlon and Marche before meeting stiff American resistance west of Marche about 1700. The battalion shifted its advance to the southwest and captured Hargimont early on the morning of 23 December; the division's main body was close behind.

Without its wayward regiment near Marvie (see chapter 12), Bayerlein's Panzer Lehr Division was also heading west on 22 December. Led by its reinforced reconnaissance battalion (Kampfgruppe von Fallois), the bulk of Bayerlein's division advanced through Tillet, Moicy, and Vesqueville before reaching St. Hubert. There the advance was delayed by extensive road demolitions outside town, and the division was unable to move forward until nearly midnight.

III Corps Approach to Bastogne

Units of the III Corps continued to move north and organize themselves for the attack against the southern flank of the German penetration on 22 and 23

December. During the daylight hours, elements of the corps made contact with German forces south of Bastogne. Combat Command A[7] of Gaffey's 4th Armored Division pushed up the Arlon-Bastogne highway, but was halted near Martelange by stiff resistance from elements of Colonel Heilman's 5th Parachute Division, while Combat Command B,[8] using the secondary route from Habay la Neuve, was likewise stopped near Burnon by other units of the 5th Parachute. A handful of German infantrymen (the soldiers of the 5th Parachute were dogged defensive fighters), along with an assault gun or anti-tank gun, could stop an American armored column for hours, since the rugged and often heavily wooded terrain limited off-road movement and compelled the U.S. forces to undertake costly, time-consuming, and difficult frontal attacks.

General Paul's 26th Infantry Division pushed northward just east of the 4th Armored's advance route, and was stopped when it encountered more paratroopers from 5th Parachute Division just south of Rambrouch and Grosbous. The 80th Infantry Division also had an eventful day. Its forward elements passed through the weary 109th Infantry Regiment (still attached to the 9th Armored Division) and encountered German troops at Michelbruch about 1120. Approaching Ettelbruck, the 318th Infantry became involved in a fight for the town that was still underway when darkness fell. To the west, the 319th Infantry launched a sharp attack on Merzig and was able to clear most of the town by sunset. Throughout these actions, the soldiers of Colonel Heilmann's 5th Parachute Division showed themselves to be skilled and tenacious defensive fighters, however lackluster their performance in the attack had been over the previous six days.

GERMAN DEPLOYMENTS AROUND BASTOGNE

As the III Corps laboriously pushed north, some reinforcements were assigned from OKW and Army Group B reserves to enable Brandenberger's Seventh Army to maintain contact with Manteuffel's Fifth Panzer Army. The Führer Grenadier Brigade was assigned initially to Kniess's LXXXV Corps and then to Rothkirch's LIII Corps, moving from a reserve position near Bastendorf to the vicinity of Heiderscheid.

The Führer Grenadier Brigade was formed in late summer 1944 by combining troops seconded from the Grossdeutschland Panzer Division with the outer headquarters guard at Hitler's Wolfsschanze compound in East Prussia. The brigade had barely withstood a brutal baptism of fire in East Prussia in early autumn, and although the matériel and personnel losses had been made good, there had been little time for training the replacements, and the unit's morale and confidence had not fully recovered. Nevertheless, with a total strength of just under 6,300 officers and men, and with nearly forty tanks and thirty-five assault guns and tank destroyers, the brigade was a potent miniature panzer division.[9]

Colonel Hans-Joachim Kahler, the commander of Führer Grenadier, was badly wounded by artillery fire while on a personal reconnaissance on the night of 22 December, and had relinquished command. The morale of the brigade, which was relatively poor to begin with, suffered a significant decline with the loss of Colonel Kahler. Morale was not helped by other changes in command in the brigade over the next week, as senior officers arriving with their units replaced more junior officers in a bewildering flurry.

As the panzer spearheads moved west, the volksgrenadiers were also busy. Colonel Kokott's 26th VGD of the XLVII Panzer Corps was finally able to reestablish full contact with and control over its 77th and 78th Grenadier regiments, and was also given operational control of Panzer Lehr's 901st Panzergrenadier Regiment, which was still positioned opposite the southeast face of the American pocket. During daylight on 22 December, Kokott's infantry repeatedly assaulted Senonchamps and Villeroux, but were driven back by vigorous counterattacks from Colonel Harper's 327th Glider Infantry. Only after darkness fell were the weary soldiers of 26th VGD finally able to seize both towns.

Farther to the east-southeast of Bastogne, Col. Alois Weber's 79th VGD, moving south and west out of the Clerf River valley, came under the command of Kniess's LXXXV Corps. The main body of the 79th was assembling around Landscheid by evening, but had not yet entered the front lines. Originally, this division was the 79th Infantry Division, comprising the 208th, 212th, and 226th Infantry regiments. The 79th was formed in the late summer of 1939 from reservists, in this case drawn from the Rhineland. The division saw no action during the Polish campaign, as it was still in the Saar region, and likewise saw little action during the 1940 campaign. Assigned to Army Group South, the 79th went through its baptism of fire during the invasion of Russia in the summer of 1941. Assigned to the Sixth Army, the division was essentially destroyed at Stalingrad, and re-formed in the Ukraine in the spring of 1943. By early summer, it was in action in the Kuban region before being transferred to the lower Dnieper region in early autumn. It was destroyed a second time in the Jassy (Iasi) Pocket in Bessarabia in September 1944.

The division was re-formed by renumbering the 586th VGD, which was assembling that autumn around Thorn in Lower Silesia. The 79th had only a small cadre of veterans, and even as late as mid-December it was short important items of equipment. Its strength totaled just over 10,000 officers and men; it had few motor vehicles and no antiaircraft weapons, and its self-propelled antitank company with JgPz-38(t)s was unable to join up with the division in the Ardennes.

Colonel Erich Schmidt's 352d VGD, another of Kniess's divisions, was also moving forward to contact the 79th VGD and thereby maintain a continuous front. The 914th and 916th Grenadier regiments on the 352d's left (southeast) flank advanced to Schieren, while the 915th Grenadier Regiment on the right (northwestern) flank advanced about five kilometers to Oberfeulen against virtually no opposition. Unhappily for the 352d, this advance placed it squarely in the path of the 80th Infantry Division's attack.

THE AMERICAN DRIVE FOR BASTOGNE: 23–24 DECEMBER

On 23 December, as Patton had promised Eisenhower, the battle for Bastogne began in earnest. The 4th Armored Division advanced on a nine-kilometer (5.5-mile) front. After completing a tank bridge at Martelange, Combat Command A pushed about three kilometers northward along the Arlon highway, its leading elements approaching Tintange, while most of the Combat Command was fighting about a kilometer north of its bridge.

Private Howard Peterson, of San Jose, California, was an armored infantryman with CCA/4 as it fought its way north toward Tintange. On 16 December he had been an airborne soldier with the 325th Glider Infantry Regiment of the 82d Airborne Division at Reims. The next morning he and a truckload of other airborne soldiers were in a two-and-a-half-ton truck, en route to Arlon, Belgium. These men had been grabbed from overstrength units of the 82d Division in response to an urgent appeal from the Third Army for replacements needed to bring the depleted armored infantry battalions of the 4th Armored Division up to strength. (His selection might suggest that Private Peterson had not been considered a model soldier in the 325th, but he seems to have performed well as an armored infantryman in the following days.) They arrived at Arlon on 20 December, and he joined the 4th Armored Division that day.

After the war Peterson wrote a description of his activities on the road to Bastogne on 23 December. The day was a cycle of riding on the back of an M4 tank, dismounting to fight, remounting, and moving on. The cycle was repeated several times each day. Of particular interest is his catalogue of what he wore and carried with him:

I had on my G.I. [Government Issue] "long johns," O.D. [olive-drab] pants and shirt, two pairs of socks, jump boots [relics from his recent past as an airborne soldier], four-buckle overshoes, knit sweater, banana [knit] cap, helmet, "tanker overalls," an extra pair of socks under each armpit, my "K" bar knife, my G.I. gloves, I had thrown away my gas mask, I had an ample supply of toilet paper inside my helmet, and my pockets were stuffed with "K" rations, candle stubs, cigarettes, grenades, and 2½ pound blocks of TNT complete with fuse to blow myself a hole in the frozen ground, if necessary. I had my good old M-1 [rifle] with the regulation belt load of eight clips ball [ball ammunition for standard antipersonnel use] and two clips A.P. (armor-piercing) four and one on each side, bayonet, canteen, first-aid pouch, two extra bandoliers of ammo, and three bazooka rounds.[10]

On the division's left (western) flank, Combat Command B pushed north along the west bank of the Sure River in the predawn darkness and reached Chaumont. There the unit was halted by stubborn resistance from paratroopers of the 5th Parachute Division. Combat Command B was compelled to mount a formal attack on Chaumont with artillery and air support. Elements of the 8th Tank and 10th Armored Infantry battalions fought their way into the village in midafternoon.

Soon after, the American troops were hit by a sharp German counterattack, organized by Colonel Kokott.[11] The counterattack force, comprising about a dozen assault guns from the 11th Sturmgeschütz Brigade and the 26th Antitank Battalion, with supporting infantry from the 39th Fusilier Regiment, surprised the Combat Command's forces in Chaumont and drove them from the town after a bitter fight in the gathering twilight of late afternoon. While these actions took place, Combat Command R was organized around Arlon and began to move forward toward Bigonville, east-northeast of Martelange.[12] As the 5th Parachute Division struggled to react to the 4th Armored's powerful thrusts, General Heilmann moved his headquarters west to Schloss Losange.[13]

The 26th Infantry Division advanced just over three kilometers along a front of 8.5 kilometers (5.3 miles). The 26th's 104th Infantry surprised the 352d VGD's 915th Grenadiers, who were traveling in march column with no security, and inflicted significant casualties. The light artillery battalion with the 915th, unable to resist or get off the road, was overrun and destroyed, but the infantry fell back to the area around Grosbous and Pratz, where they were isolated from the rest of the division. Colonel Schmidt and his staff were apparently unaware that the 26th Division was moving forward, and the 915th Grenadiers, expecting only patrols from the 109th Infantry, was completely surprised by the 104th Infantry. Meanwhile, the rest of the 352d fell back to Ettelbruck, in the 80th Division's sector. As the 352d recoiled from Grosbous, the 26th Division's 328th Infantry seized Wahl as it advanced on the division's left (western) flank. The 328th drove back a halfhearted counterattack by forward elements of the Führer Grenadier Brigade, which had been committed as part of the LXXXV Corps to cover the 352d's northwestern flank. By nightfall the Führer Grenadier Brigade held positions around and just south of Eschdorf and Heiderscheid, about where it had started the day.

To the east, the 80th Infantry Division continued the efforts begun the previous day. The attacks were slowed by commitment of lead elements of the 79th VGD, which together with the 352d VGD comprised the LXXXV Corps. On a front of nearly nine kilometers, the 318th and 319th Infantry regiments pushed forward about 2,400 meters, slogging through dense woods and across steep snow-covered ravines and hillsides. The 317th Infantry waited in reserve.

The 319th Infantry advanced as far north as Niederfeulen under similar difficult conditions, but was also still involved with fighting in Merzig and in the heavily wooded hills north and west of the town. The 319th's advance drove back the lead regiment of the 79th VGD, which had been readying an effort to relieve the neighboring 915th Grenadiers. To the east, the 318th

Infantry was still fighting in Ettelbruck, where additional infantry from the 352d VGD had filtered into the town. The 318th was also engaged in the hilly country on both sides of Ettelbruck, where most of the ground on the hilltops was open, but the bottom lands were covered by scraggly wooded scrub. The resolution and tenacity of the defending German troops, coupled with the scarcity of roads and the raw winter weather, slowed the 80th Division's advance.

The grueling American advance northward continued on Christmas Eve. The 4th Armored Division committed Col. Wendell Blanchard's Combat Command R to action on the secondary roads leading to Bigonville (east of Combat Command A's line of advance on the Arlon-Bastogne highway), and Blanchard's Combat Command had secured the town by sunset, driving out the defending paratroopers of the 5th Parachute Division. With three infantry regiments in line, supported by four artillery battalions, Heilmann's division was hard-pressed to hold its long front of thirty-eight kilometers (23.6 miles). Meanwhile, the 4th Armored's Combat Command A continued northward on the main highway, clearing Warnach of enemy resistance and pushing as far north as Tintange. Bloodied by the fight for Chaumont on 23 December, Combat Command B spent Christmas Eve resting and refitting around that town, on the western (left) flank of 4th Armored Division's corridor of attack.

The 4th Armored's Combat Command B reorganized and waited for replacement tanks to arrive from divisional workshops; the 8th Tank Battalion had only two platoons (eight to ten Shermans) operational. With the rest of the combat command out of action, B Troop of the 25th Cavalry Reconnaissance Squadron (reinforced by a platoon of M5 light tanks from E Company) probed as far as Grandrue. The 1st and 2d battalions of the 318th Infantry (80th Infantry Division) were temporarily attached to the division to provide additional infantry, which was particularly important for operations in the rugged, close terrain south of Bastogne. Both "borrowed" infantry battalions were understrength, each with about 450 effectives out of a full strength of around 800 officers and men.

The 26th Division pushed slowly northward, facing heavy resistance that took maximum advantage of difficult ground. The division's western boundary was moved farther west to include the sector held by the Führer Grenadier Brigade as well as lead elements of the 79th VGD. Despite strong opposition, by day's end the division had gained about 2,000 yards: The 328th Infantry was in the village of Hierheck, west-southwest of Eschdorf, moving into the steep-sided Sure River valley from the high ground around Grevils-Brésil. The 104th Infantry was just southwest of Heiderscheid.

Colonel Ben Jacobs, commanding the 328th Infantry, had the mission of taking Eschdorf. He established a task force to make the main effort, built around his 2d Battalion, to which he attached tanks, tank destroyers, engineers, and an antiaircraft platoon. The task force, commanded by Lt. Col. Paul Hamilton, moved out from Hierheck shortly after midnight on Christmas morning. F Company advanced on Eschdorf from the west while E Company approached from the east. As they entered the town, both attacking companies found themselves fiercely engaged by the alert defenders. Corporal Sam B. Peters of Little Rock, Arkansas, part of F Company's 2d Platoon, wrote the following description of the night battle:

The fighting in Eschdorf was confused and jumbled. For two days and nights there were both Americans and Germans dodging each other in the streets, buildings, barns and basements. Enemy tanks were racing up and down the town square.... My 2nd Platoon, accompanied by Capt [Reed] Seely [the company commander] crossed a small stream and moved into Eschdorf from the west. We were close enough to touch Germans during much of the night. One of the problems with night attacks with infantry troops is the inability to distinguish between friend and foe in the dark. Bumping into people with semi-automatic weapons with drawn bayonets is not a fun way to spend an evening.[14]

Nevertheless, Task Force Hamilton, joined late on Christmas Day by the 1st Battalion of the 104th Infantry Regiment, secured Eschdorf by the evening of 26 December. Peters, who was wounded during the battle, wrote that elements of the 104th "were lined up in front of the Task Force Headquarters at Hierheck as I was placed on a stretcher, strapped to a jeep and sent back to an unknown field hospital."

The Führer Grenadier Brigade was hard-pressed by the American infantry and was compelled to give ground, especially on its eastern flank, which was driven north to Heiderscheidergrund. The Seventh Army command had meanwhile reassigned the Führer Grenadier Brigade from the LXXXV Corps to the newly committed LIII Corps, where it joined Heilmann's 5th Parachute Division.

The Seventh Army also committed two more divisions assigned to the LIII Corps, the 9th and 167th VGDs. These units began to move forward from their assembly areas late on 23 December. With the roads forward clogged with traffic and subject to Allied air attack, the deployments related to this reorganization could not be accomplished swiftly.

The 9th VGD, like the 79th, came from Army Group B reserves; the 167th was sent from OKW reserves. As the 9th Infantry Division, containing the 36th, 57th, and 116th Grenadier regiments, the renamed 9th VGD had been a prewar German Regular Army division. Its home depot was at Giessen, and most of its personnel were drawn from the neighboring region of Hesse-Nassau. The 9th Infantry Division fought with distinction in the 1940 campaign. Assigned to Army Group South for the invasion of Russia in June 1941, it fought in the Ukraine throughout the opening stages of the Russian campaign. The 9th Infantry Division took part in the great southern offensive of 1942, and by early autumn had reached the foothills of the Caucasus Mountains. Following the debacle at Stalingrad, it withdrew to the Kuban peninsula that winter, and remained there through late summer 1943, when the Kuban was evacuated. It next served on the lower Dnieper in autumn 1943.

During the Soviet drive through the southern Ukraine and into the Balkans in late summer and early autumn 1944, the 9th Infantry Division suffered such severe losses while withdrawing through Rumania that it was declared combat-ineffective in early October. It was reconstituted by renumbering the 584th Division, but the new 9th VGD bore little real resemblance to the old 9th Infantry. Nevertheless, when it was committed to the Ardennes area on 28 December, the Seventh Army headquarters considered it a good division with above-average personnel, especially officers and noncommissioned officers.

The 167th VGD was raised in the early winter of 1940 as the 167th Infantry Division containing the 331st, 339th, and 387th Infantry regiments; most of its personnel were originally Bavarian reservists. The 167th fought in the French campaign and saw extensive action in Russia as part of Army Group Center. The division was transferred to Holland for rest and refit in the summer of 1942 after heavy losses during the preceding winter and spring. It returned to Russia and reentered combat in the Ukraine in early 1943. The division took part in the southern arm of the Kursk offensive in July 1943 as part of the 4th Panzer Army's XLVIII Panzer Corps, fighting alongside the 1st SS Panzer Division Leibstandarte Adolf Hitler. The 167th Infantry Division was destroyed in the Korsun Pocket in southern Ukraine in March and April of 1944.

The division was re-formed in Hungary the following September as a volksgrenadier division and benefited from obtaining a high proportion of eastern front veterans, along with a large draft co-opted from the 17th Luftwaffe Field Division then assembling in Slovakia. By mid-December, the division had nearly 12,000 officers and men, but was missing many heavy weapons and some vehicles. Its self-propelled antitank company with twelve JgPz-38(t)s did not join the division until the end of December, several days after it was committed to fighting in the Ardennes.

As these newly committed German units crept toward the front, the American attacks continued. To the east, the 80th Division ground forward slowly. The 318th Infantry, its 1st and 2d battalions detached to the 4th Armored Division, finally managed to clear and secure Ettelbruck, driving out the town's defenders, troops of the 352d VGD. During Christmas Eve day the 317th Infantry moved forward from reserve and passed through the 318th's lines, taking over the positions vacated by the transferred 1st and 2d battalions, holding the general line of the Sure River west of Ettelbruck. The 319th Infantry, on the division's left, beat off determined local German counterattacks at Heiderscheid and Kehmen.These were launched by units of the 79th VGD, which was still moving toward the advancing Americans. Two companies of the 319th were cut off on the wooded slopes leading down to the river northwest of Heiderscheid, and arrangements were made for a battalion of the 328th Infantry of the 26th Division to relieve them on Christmas Day.

Around the Bastogne perimeter, 24 December was a relatively calm day. Northwest of the beleaguered town, the lead elements of the 15th Panzergrenadier Division, Kampfgruppe Maucke assembled north and west of Longchamps in preparation for a predawn attack against the 502d Parachute Infantry's positions early on 25 December.[15] The 15th Panzergrenadier had one of the most interesting and varied unit histories in the German Army. As the 33d Infantry Division of the prewar German Regular Army, it had served in the Saar region on the French frontier during the Polish campaign, then fought particularly well in the 1940 campaign in France. As a partial reward, it was reorganized as the 15th Panzer Division in autumn 1940, and was sent to Libya as part of Rommel's Afrika Corps with the 5th Light (later 21st Panzer) Division in February through April 1941. It fought in all of Rommel's major operations in Libya and Egypt, from Abu Agheila through El Alamein. With the surrender of Panzerarmee Afrika in Tunisia in early May 1943, the division essentially ceased to exist.

Its demise was only temporary. During June and July 1943, many of its personnel who had either managed to escape from Tunisia or were returning from temporary assignments, leave, or hospital were absorbed by "Division Sizilien," a short-term ad hoc division assembled from a hodgepodge of units in Sicily. In July, Division Sizilien was redesignated the 15th Panzergrenadier Division. It took part in the defensive actions in Sicily and southern Italy from mid-July 1943 through early autumn 1944, when it was transferred north to the western front and Army Group B.

By mid-December 1944 the 15th Panzergrenadier Division was part of the reserves for Gen. Gustav von Zangen's Fifteenth Army before it was sent south into the Ardennes. It mustered nearly 11,000 officers and men, and contained fourteen tanks and nearly thirty assault guns and tank destroyers.

THE RELIEF OF BASTOGNE: 25–26 DECEMBER

The slow rate of progress by the III Corps through the unforgiving country south of Bastogne in the face of determined German resistance was frustrating to the American commanders, especially to General Patton. Some change in approach was indicated, since the three American divisions pushing north had progressed an average of barely three kilometers (two miles) per day in the past two days. Generals Millikin and Gaffey decided to shift Combat Command R of the 4th Armored Division to the west, and then send it in a northeasterly direction from Neufchâteau toward Bastogne, using a hitherto-unemployed route of advance.[16] Elements of Combat Command R began moving north from Neufchâteau about noon on Christmas Day, reentering Vaux-les-Rosières and reaching Remoiville before halting in the early evening. This move also established contact with the 28th Division's support elements and a few weary combat troops that had gathered around Neufchâteau after being driven from Vaux-lez-Rosières.[17]

On the 4th Armored Division's eastern flank, Combat Command A ground slowly north to Hollange, managing to overrun two German artillery battalions supporting the 5th Parachute Division in the Hollange-Tintange area.[18] Combat Command B pushed north to Hompré, an advance of about two kilometers.

At about the same time, the 101st Infantry Regiment of the 26th Division pushed northward to gain control of the villages of Neuenhausen and Arsdorf, bringing the regiment up to the south bank of the Sure River. This advance also maintained tenuous contact with the 6th Cavalry Group, covering the five-mile (eight-kilometer) gap between Combat Command A of the 4th Armored Division and the 101st Infantry of the 26th Division. The 26th Division's right (east) flank regiment, the 328th Infantry, advanced to Insenborn, just south of the river, driving back elements of the Führer Grenadier Brigade, which was still incomplete, although additional units arrived daily. Moreover, with the German main line of resistance now resting on the Sure River itself, the obstacles to a continued American advance were immense.

The 80th Division, advancing on a front of nearly twenty kilometers, made only very limited progress. The 319th Infantry fended off another counterattack by elements of Führer Grenadier at Heiderscheid. (American commanders noted that the Führer Grenadier's attacks were often sloppy and lethargic, but their defensive action remained determined and effective.) The 317th Infantry crept forward only 900 meters to seize Dahl and approach Kehmen, driving back troops from the 79th VGD. The 79th's defensive efforts were hampered by the cold: Hard-frozen ground prevented its troops from digging in. The 79th was also penalized by the absence of its artillery, which was still extricating itself from the traffic congestion between the Our and Wiltz rivers. In the absence of the 79th's own howitzers, Colonel Weber had to make do with a battalion of Nebelwerfer rocket launchers borrowed from the 8th Volkswerfer Brigade (VWB), weapons that were better suited to mass offensive fires because of their inherent inaccuracy.

The 3d Battalion of the 318th Infantry held its positions just north of Ettelbruck, facing the 352d VGD. That division, whose 915th Grenadiers were still surrounded by other units of the 80th Infantry Division in the woods around Grosbous, garnered some reinforcements.[19] The 352d held scattered positions thinly stretched along a 15.5-kilometer front from Ettelbruck east along the Sure River toward Echternach.

On Christmas Day Kokott also orchestrated a major attack against the Bastogne perimeter.[20] The 77th Grenadier Regiment played Santa Claus by attacking the positions of the 502d Parachute Infantry about 0330. The main infantry attack near Champs made only limited progress and was contained with comparatively little difficulty.

Two thousand yards to the southwest, in the sector of the neighboring 3d

Battalion of the 327th Glider Infantry, the attack by Kampfgruppe Maucke was quite another matter. An eighteen-tank German column with a dozen or so infantrymen clinging to each vehicle crashed through the thinly held American front lines about 0710, just before first light, and in the process driving off or destroying the thin tank destroyer screen from the 705th Tank Destroyer Battalion.

The panzers then fanned out in twos and threes, some heading for Hemroulle and the command post of the 1st Battalion of the 502d Parachute Infantry. Others were approaching Château Rolle, where the 502d's regimental command post was located. Still others aimed for points in between. One group of tanks drove toward the village of Champs itself, approaching unexpectedly from the south-southeast. They were destroyed by fire from American bazookas and guns. Most of the other German tanks were eventually hunted down and destroyed by American infantry bazookas and tank destroyers. A few of the tanks simply broke down, and one PzKw-IVH was captured intact within Hemroulle. Called in as a fire brigade, Team Cherry's tanks and armored infantry helped the paratroopers and glider infantry clean up the incursion, and the original lines were reestablished by 1400.

The fighting around Hemroulle and Champs had been very confused. The brief odyssey of Lt. Col. Ray C. Allen, commander of the 327th's 3d Battalion, serves to illustrate the situation. At about 0710, Capt. Preston E. Towns, commanding C Company of the 327th,[21] telephoned Allen to tell him that tanks were approaching his position. "Where?" the battalion commander asked. "If you look out your window now, you'll be looking down the muzzle of an 88," Towns replied.[22] Allen quickly telephoned Colonel Harper, commander of the 327th, to inform him of the proximity of German armor. "How close?" Harper asked. Allen, in an understandable hurry to get away, replied, "Right here! They are firing point-blank at me from 150 yards away. My units are still in position but I've got to run."

Allen and two of his staff officers ran outside, and although the Germans fired at them with small arms, they escaped injury. They managed to reach some woods as dawn broke. On the other side of the woods, the small party encountered paratroopers from Col. Steve Chappuis's neighboring 502d Parachute Infantry, who promptly opened fire on Allen and his companions with small arms. Pinned down, they laboriously crawled back into the woods and then circled south to reach Hemroulle. Emerging from the woods a second time, they encountered and were fired on by a hastily composed skirmish line thrown out by the 463d Parachute Field Artillery Battalion. By this point Allen had had enough. Waving a handkerchief, he persuaded the artillerymen-cum-infantry to let them come in.[23]

On the day after Christmas, the American drive northward continued. Combat Command R of the 4th Armored Division, still advancing northeast on the Neufchâteau road, cleared the German defenders from Remichampagne and the woods nearby. These Germans were a mixed bag of troops from the 26th VGD and the 5th Parachute Division, and by this stage of the battle many were rear-area service personnel, ill prepared for serious combat. Consequently, German resistance was fairly brief.

Continuing its advance, Combat Command R reached the outskirts of Assensois, about five kilometers from the center of Bastogne, in late afternoon. Shots from inside Assensois revealed that it was held by a considerable force of German defenders. Although Colonel Blanchard was in command of Combat Command R, the attack on Assensois was in fact planned and executed by Lt. Col. Creighton W. Abrams, commander of the 37th Tank Battalion,[24] in collaboration with Lt. Col. George L. Jaques, commander of the 53d Armored Infantry Battalion.[25]

Abrams was concerned about how to handle the final stages of the advance to the Bastogne perimeter because his hard-driving tank battalion was woefully understrength. Although he had thirteen M5s (out of seventeen allocated) in Company D, the other two M4 companies between them had only about ten tanks, and some of them were missing their bow gunners because available crewmen were also at a premium. His assault gun platoon had only three of its six allotted M4A3s (Shermans with a 105-mm L28 howitzer in place of the usual 75-mm or 76-mm gun). Jaques had similar problems, since the 53d Armored Infantry Battalion was short 230 officers and men, the equivalent of almost an entire infantry company, including most of his riflemen. Both lieutenant colonels wanted to achieve their objectives with a minimum of losses, because many more casualties would render their units combat-ineffective. While they had been at Combat Command R headquarters at 2000 on Christmas Day, Blanchard had ordered them to attack Sibret on 26 December. Sibret, however, was reported to be strongly held by the Germans. Expecting heavy losses if they attacked from that town, Abrams and Jaques agreed that they would avoid Sibret and take an alternate approach after they had cleared Remichampagne and their troops had assembled outside Clochimont.

Abrams, as senior officer, was in tactical control of the push for Assensois (only about 1,400 meters north of Clochimont). He radioed back about 1520 to Captain Cook, liaison officer of the 94th Armored Field Artillery Battalion at the Combat Command R command post in Remoiville, to have all available artillery prepared to fire on Assensois on call. Cook told divisional artillery to make arrangements for the 22d and 253d Armored Field Artillery battalions to reinforce this fire mission. The hastily prepared fire plan called for each battalion and a battery of the 177th Field Artillery Battalion (with four 155-mm howitzers) to fire ten volleys on call.

The assault plan quickly arranged by Abrams and Jaques had "C Team," under Capt. William Dwight, who was the battalion S-3, leading the attack. The tanks would go first, with C Company of Abrams's 37th, commanded by 1st Lt. Charles Boggess, leading the way followed by C Company of the 53d, A Company/37th Tank Battalion, and B Company/53d Armored Infantry. The other companies would remain in reserve. Boggess moved forward about 1610, and as soon as the edge of Assensois was in sight he called for the artillery to commence firing. Within a few minutes 360 rounds from thirty-six 105-mm howitzers and 60 rounds from the 155s crashed into and around Assensois. One shell landed near an American half-track on the south edge of town and inflicted three casualties, but the fire was otherwise quite accurate. The seven or eight German self-propelled antitank guns in Assensois were only able to get off a few wild rounds, and the German infantrymen were apparently completely suppressed by the American artillery.

Lieutenant Boggess radioed for the artillery to lift their fire from the southern edge of town as his column reached it. Nevertheless, some shells continued to fall in the center of town, combining with smoke from burning buildings to block out most of the fading wan winter sunlight. The infantry from C Company of the 53d dismounted while the seven operational M4s of Lieutenant Boggess's C Company of the 37th drove into town. The defenders, still stunned by the pounding they had received, put up scattered and ineffective resistance. While the main body pressed forward, Company B of the 53d Armored Infantry was left to secure the town. By 2000 resistance finally ended, and 428 German prisoners were captured.

In the meantime, Lieutenant Boggess had driven north toward Bastogne with the five tanks of C Company still under his control (two had made a wrong turn in Assensois, and were later picked up by Captain Dwight). Ahead of him, a few hundred meters beyond Assensois, Boggess saw some engineers attacking a pillbox. Uncertain of their nationality in the fading late-afternoon light, he called out to them cautiously. With considerable relief Boggess discovered that they were part of the 326th Airborne Engineer Combat Battalion, an element of the beleaguered 101st Division. It was then 1650, just after sunset. The tanks helped the engineers capture the German pillbox, and by that time Captain Dwight had arrived with C Company's two missing tanks. Dwight radioed back to Lieutenant Colonel Abrams that contact with the 101st had been made.

Alerted to Dwight's presence on the perimeter, General McAuliffe hurried to an observation post nearby. Dwight saluted him. "How are you, General?" asked Dwight. "Gee," replied McAuliffe, "I'm mighty glad to see you." In a few minutes Abrams joined Dwight's "C Team" on the Bastogne perimeter. He drove at once into Bastogne with General McAuliffe to arrange for Combat Command R's trains to enter Bastogne, along with a supply column. It was a narrow corridor, but Bastogne had been relieved.

During the night, forty supply trucks and seventy ambulances entered Bastogne, escorted by the M5s of D Company of Abrams's 37th Tank Battalion since the road was not yet fully secure. The ambulances evacuated several hundred wounded soldiers, easing the strain on the 101st's hard-pressed medical facilities, and the weary doctors, nurses, and orderlies who manned them.

The day's fighting had left Abrams's tanks very low on ammunition: B

Company's M4s had only machine-gun ammunition left, and most other Shermans had only half a dozen rounds apiece of 75-mm armor-piercing (AP) ammunition. In light of the size of the German defending force, it is clear that Abrams, Dwight, and Boggess were not exaggerating in stating that they could not have accomplished their mission without the artillery's support.

While Colonel Blanchard's Combat Command R swooped into Bastogne, Combat Command B advanced about 2,000 yards northward, moving on an axis just west of the Arlon highway. The battered paratroopers of the 5th Parachute Division gave ground grudgingly, and progress was slow and costly. Heilmann's equally battle-worn paratroopers received some badly needed succor when a kampfgruppe from the 15th Panzergrenadier Division arrived at Harlange, behind the 5th Parachute's left flank, around midday on 26 December.[26]

The 6th Cavalry Group, considerably reinforced with a battalion each of engineers and self-propelled tank destroyers, was placed under the 4th Armored Division.[27] By dark the advance elements of the 6th Cavalry were near Chaumont and in the hamlets of Remagne and Moircy on the Ourthe River. At these points, the cavalrymen made fleeting contact with patrols from Panzer Lehr's southern screening force, which was protecting the long and vulnerable flank of XLVII Panzer Corps's spearhead.[28]

While the 4th Armored Division was garnering the glory and press attention for relieving Bastogne, General Paul's 26th Infantry Division advanced about 2,000 meters all along its 10-kilometer front. On the eastern flank, the 104th Infantry captured Eschdorf from the Führer Grenadier Brigade. The 101st Infantry, which had relieved the 328th Infantry on the western flank, pushed three companies across the Sure River and took the hamlet of Liefrange from stalwart defenders, driving back the Führer Grenadier's other flank.

On 26 December, the 167th VGD was detached from the LIII Corps and assigned elsewhere, eventually coming under the command of Gen. Karl Decker's XXXIX Panzer Corps. The 9th VGD, under Col. Werner Kolb and still assigned to the LIII Corps, continued to move forward from its assembly area around Alflen, which was more than forty kilometers (twenty-five miles) east of the original German front line on 16 December.

East of the 26th Division's sector, General McBride's 80th Infantry Division also made limited progress, advancing an average of 1,200 meters on a front of just over twenty kilometers. On the division's left (western) flank, the 319th Infantry captured Ringel from troops from the 79th VGD. However, Colonel Weber was already laying plans for a counterattack against Ringel scheduled for 27 December. The 317th Infantry on the right (replacing the 3/318) entered Ettelbruck and probed northward as far as Bourscheid. Most of this effort fell on the sector of the hard-pressed 79th VGD. A few die-hard soldiers of the 352d VGD remained in Ettelbruck to contest American possession, but that division's main battle line was now outside the town. After four days of isolation, the worn and weary survivors of the 915th Grenadier finally made it back to German lines, having evaded American columns and patrols. They had been forced to abandon nearly all their transport and heavy weapons in their withdrawal, and the regiment's remnants amounted to little more than a single battalion. However, Colonel Schmidt's division was at least together again as a unit, and would be able to enjoy several days of relative quiet on the front line.

The 35th Infantry Division, commanded by Maj. Gen. Paul W. Baade, was assigned to the III Corps early on 26 December. Activated from National Guard units in Kansas, Nebraska, and Missouri in 1917, the 35th Division was sent to France in July 1918, and took part in the Meuse-Argonne campaign from September to 11 November. The division returned to the United States and was deactivated in April 1919, but remained a National Guard division. It was brought back into federal service in late December 1940. The division's shoulder patch, a Santa Fe cross (a white cross within a white wagon wheel), led to its nickname, "Santa Fe."

The 35th Division arrived in England in May 1944, and began landing at Utah Beach in Normandy on 5 July. It entered combat six days later, and played a major role in both Operation Cobra (the breakout from the Normandy Beachhead at St. Lô on 25 July) and the defeat of the German counteroffensive at Mortain on 30 July. The division was part of the Third Army's XII Corps during the drive across northern France and in the Lorraine campaign that autumn. It was withdrawn from the line on 19 December for rest and recuperation near Metz.

Paul William Baade was born in Indiana on 16 April 1889. He graduated from West Point in June 1911, and joined the 11th Infantry at Fort D. A. Russell in Wyoming. After more than a year of service with his regiment on border patrol in Texas, he went to the Philippines for three years with the 8th Infantry. Shortly after the outbreak of World War I he was assigned to the 81st Division and went overseas in July 1918. Baade, now a lieutenant colonel, distinguished himself in the Battle of the Meuse-Argonne. Between the wars his assignments were mainly school duty—both as student and instructor— plus staff assignments, and a relatively brief tour of troop duty. He returned to troop duty in June 1940, in command of the 16th Infantry Regiment of the 1st Division. In July 1941, as a brigadier general, he went to Puerto Rico to command the Mobile Force on that island. A year later he was sent to California to become the Assistant Division commander of the 35th Division. In July 1943, as a major general, he took command of the 35th.

The 35th's divisional headquarters arrived from Metz on 26 December, and the division assembled at Holtz before moving into positions along the Sure River between the 4th Armored and the 26th Infantry divisions. Anticipation of this movement had permitted the 6th Cavalry Group to shift westward and concentrate on the left (western) flank of the III Corps. At the end of 26 December, the 80th Division passed to control of Maj. Gen. Manton S. Eddy's XII Corps. At the same time, the 101st Airborne and its attached armor and artillery temporarily passed into General Millikin's III Corps.

The siege of Bastogne was over. The struggle for the Bastogne corridor had barely begun.

Official German government portrait of Adolf Hitler,
taken about 1938. Compare with his appearance
alongside Field Marshal Model in 1944.

Col. Gen. Alfred Jodl at work, date unknown but probably 1942 or earlier; captured German photo.

Sepp Dietrich at Berchtesgaden, probably summer 1942, from Eva Braun's private collection. Note "Adolf Hitler" insignia on left sleeve of his uniform, for the "Leibstandarte Adolf Hitler" SS Division.

Hasso von Manteuffel (*left*), as a lieutenant general and commander of the "Grossdeutschland Panzer Division," conferring with Col. Bronsart von Schellendorf on the eastern front, summer 1944.

Field Marshal Gerd von Rundstedt, shortly after he was captured by U.S. troops at Bad Tolz in May 1945.

Col. Otto Skorzeny, mastermind of
Operation Greif and commander of the
150th Panzer Brigade.

BELOW: Hitler (*right foreground*) congratulating
Field Marshal Walter Model (*left foreground*);
date uncertain but probably first half of 1944.

Gen. der Panzertruppen Erich
Brandenberger (*seated, center*)
signing the surrender documents
for the Nineteenth Army with
two of his staff, 5 May 1945.
Col. Joseph L. Langevin,
G-2 of VII Corps
(*standing at left*),
observes.

SS-Sturmbannführer (Major)
Joachim Peiper, mid-1943, from
Heinrich Himmler's personal photo
collection.

Formal photographic portrait of
Gen. Dwight D. Eisenhower, July 1945.

ABOVE: Field Marshal Sir Bernard L. Montgomery, in his trademark red beret, discussing operations with Maj. Gen. Matthew B. Ridgway (*right*), commander of XVIII Airborne Corps, February 1945.

Lt. Gen. Omar N. Bradley on shipboard off Goglitti, Sicily, 10 July 1943.

Lt. Gen. George S. Patton (*center*), Maj. Gen. Manton S. Eddy, commander of XII Corps (*left*), and Maj. Gen. Horace L. McBride, commander of the 80th Infantry Division (*right*), during the Lorraine Campaign, November 1944.

Brig. Gen. Anthony McAuliffe of the 101st Airborne Division, in Bastogne, 18 January 1945. This was taken when a group of U.S. commanders assembled to greet Patton.

James A. Van Fleet as a lieutenant general (February 1948–October 1949) as commander of U.S. military mission to Greece.

Maj. Gen. Troy H. Middleton (*right*) with an unidentified Army captain, on shipboard off southern Sicily, 10 July 1943.

Official portrait photo of
Lt. Gen. Courtney H. Hodges,
taken shortly after he assumed
command of the Third Army in
February 1943.

Maj. Gen. Maxwell D. Taylor, commander of the 101st Airborne Division, boarding C-47
transport (June or September 1944) for airborne assault.

U.S. Army photograph of Maj. Gen. James M. Gavin, commander of the 82d Airborne Division, January 1945.

Maj. Gen. Walter F. Lauer (*right*), commander of the 99th Infantry Division, talking with Lt. C. A. Carnavabe (with M3 "Grease Gun" submachine gun) near Rocherath, early December 1944.

Gen. Joseph Lawton Collins
as U.S. Army Chief of Staff,
11 April 1950.

German infantry advancing past column of burning U.S. vehicles (*above*) (note halftrack in right foreground) and crossing a road in front of wrecked and abandoned U.S. equipment and vehicles (*below*) during the opening stages of the Ardennes Campaign.

Patrol from the 1st Infantry Divsion searching for Col. von der Heydte's paratroopers, 17 December 1944. Note lead figure of patrol (*third from left*) is nearly hidden in foliage, although barely fifteen yards from camera.

German advance party, possibly part of the 1st SS Panzer Division "Leibstandarte Adolf Hitler," in *Kübelwagen* (German jeeplike vehicle) study road sign, probably 18 or 19 December 1944. (This is a captured photo; note effort by the censor to cross out town names on sign.)

A column of troops from the 26th Infantry
Division advancing north toward Hoscheid, as
part of the III Corps offensive to relieve
Bastogne, 23 December 1944.

Crew of M16 antiaircraft halftrack (note quadruple .50-cal. machine guns)
watch C-47s nearing Bastogne for a supply drop, 27 December 1944.

A U.S. column led by an M4 Sherman tank advances through the snow and pine woods of
the Ardennes, late December 1944. Note presence of "unofficial" mule (*right foreground*);
there were no U.S. Army pack mule units in the Ardennes.

A patrol from A Co./290th Infantry, 75th
Infantry Division, pushes forward in the
snow, 7 January 1945. (Note man with
motion picture camera in left foreground.)

ABOVE: An M5 light tank of the 771st Tank Battalion, attached to the 84th Infantry Division, advances past a wrecked German Panther tank under examination by U.S. Army Ordnance personnel, 9 January 1945.
BELOW: A disabled German Jagdpanther being examined by U.S. personnel, who have brushed the snow off its side to reveal the Germans' efforts to make it look like an American TD with a circle-in-star insignia.

Troops of the 84th Infantry Division advance across a snowy open field with tank support for a new attack on La Roche, 10 January 1945.

Pfc. William A. Mercer, an M8 armored car driver for the 90th Infantry Division's Reconnaissance Troop, uses a blowtorch to thaw his vehicle's brake pads, which had become frozen in the extreme cold, 14 January 1945.

Patrol (*above*) from G Company, 23d Infantry, 2d Infantry Division "lies low" to escape German machine gun fire near Ondenval, 15 January 1945. U.S. jeep (*left, below*) moving into the shell-torn ruins of Houffalize (see damaged sign at right), 16 January 1945.

A group of U.S. commanders assembled to greet
General Patton in Bastogne, 18 January 1945.
Note sign on building—BASTOGNE: BASTION OF
THE BATTERED BASTARDS OF THE 101ST. Lt. Gen.
Patton is shaking hands with Maj. Gen. Taylor.
Brig. Gen. McAuliffe is beside Taylor.

ABOVE: The scene of the infamous "Malmédy Massacre" (17 December 1944), during the subsequent U.S. Army investigation, 19 January 1945. Note numbered tags identifying each body.

BELOW: Snow-covered M10 tank destroyer of the 629th TD Battalion (attached to the 83d Infantry Division) in a wooded area of the Ardennes near Courtil, with its crew huddled around a fire, 20 January 1945.

U.S. infantrymen advancing into Wiltz, 22 January 1945.

Soldiers of the 23d Armored Infantry Battalion, 7th
Armored Division, advancing down road (with steep
snowbanks at roadside) near Born, 22 January 1945.

Infantry of the 82d Airborne Division and a tank of the attached 740th Tank Battalion, advancing down a forest road in the snow, 25 January 1945.

Soldiers of the 325th Glider Infantry Regiment, 82d Airborne Division, move forward with a heavily laden ammunition sled near Herresbach, Belgium, 28 January 1945.

15

CHRISTMAS HIGH-WATER MARK: THE BATTLES OF CELLES AND VERDENNE

By the evening of 23 December two German divisions—von Lauchert's 2d Panzer and Waldenburg's 116th Panzer—had pushed far to the west to spearhead the advance of the Fifth Panzer Army. The leading elements of the 2d Panzer were nearly thirty kilometers (eighteen miles) west, and a few kilometers south, of the 116th's advance unit, which was headed for Marche and the Meuse crossings near Namur.

The 2d Panzer had first been delayed by its involvement in the fight around Noville, north of Bastogne, on 19–20 December, and then had been immobilized for lack of fuel until late on 22 December (see chapter 12). Finally, able to move with fuel tanks partly replenished, von Lauchert's panzers resumed their westward advance with Kampfgruppe Cochenhausen and Kampfgruppe von Böhm[1] leading the way.

As the German columns drove westward toward the Meuse, the American First Army was reacting energetically. The VII Corps, commanded by Gen. Joseph L. "Lightning Joe" Collins, had responsibility for the sector toward which the panzers were headed. The 84th Infantry Division, part of this corps, had moved into defensive positions stretching from Hotton and the north branch of the Ourthe River south to Marche and the hamlet of Jemodenne late on 21 December.[2] The 84th was commanded by Maj. Gen. Alexander R. Bolling.

Bolling was born in Philadelphia on 28 August 1895. He enlisted in the Army shortly after the United States entered World War I in April 1917. He was sent to Officers Training School, and was commissioned a second lieutenant of Infantry in the Officers' Reserve Corps as a "ninety-day wonder" on 15 August 1917. This became a Regular Army commission on 26 October. He was assigned to the 4th Infantry Regiment, which soon became part of the

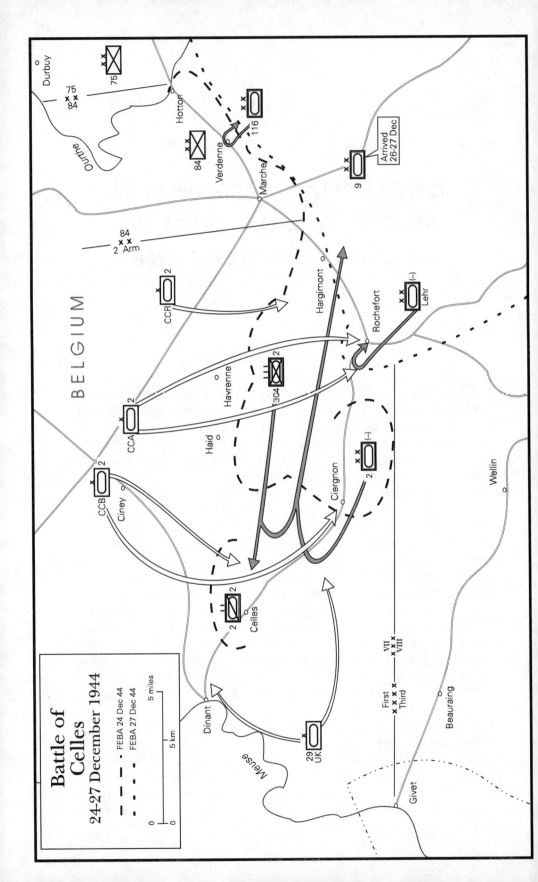

Battle of Celles
24-27 December 1944

— — — FEBA 24 Dec 44
· · · · · FEBA 27 Dec 44

0   5 km
0   5 miles

BELGIUM

Durbuy

75

75
84

Outrhe

Hotton

84

Verdenne

116

Marche

9

Arrived
26-27 Dec

84
2 Arm

CCR 2

Hargimont

Rochefort

Lehr (-)

Havrenne

CCA 2

304 2

Haid

Ciergnon

2 (-)

CCB 2

Ciney

Celles 2

2

Wellin

Dinant

Meuse

VII
VIII

First
Third

Beauraing

29
UK

Givet

3d Division. On 6 April 1918 he sailed for France with his division, and participated in the Aisne-Marne Defensive (the "Second Battle of the Marne"), and the Champagne-Marne Defensive, as well as the Champagne-Marne Offensive and the Battles of St. Mihiel and the Meuse-Argonne. After nearly a year in the Army of Occupation in Germany, he returned to the United States in October 1919.

Between the wars Bolling's service was typical of the Regular Army. When the United States entered World War II he was a lieutenant colonel and Assistant Chief of Staff, Personnel (G-1), of the Army General Headquarters, which became Army Ground Forces in March 1942. He remained in that position until, as a brigadier general, he became the Assistant Division Commander of the 8th Infantry Division in June 1943. In November he was transferred to become Assistant Division Commander of the 84th Infantry Division. In June 1944 he assumed command of the division and was soon promoted to major general.

The 84th Division of the National Army was first activated in August 1917 during World War I. It was sent to France in October 1918, but saw no action as a division, instead providing replacements for other divisions, most of which were then engaged in the great Meuse-Argonne battle. It was inactivated in January 1919 and was reactivated in October 1942, well after the outbreak of World War II. Bolling assumed command in June 1944, and it was sent overseas to England in October to complete its training. In early November the division was sent to France, then to Holland, and was first committed to battle on 18 November under the XIII Corps of the Ninth Army.

On 20 December the 84th Infantry Division was sent south to reinforce American forces opposing the northern face of the German Bulge in the Ardennes, assigned first to the XVIII Airborne Corps, then to Collins's VII Corps. General Bolling deployed the 334th Infantry in front of Hotton, the 335th around Marche, and most of the 333d in reserve behind the Marche-Hotton road, thus placing the 84th Division directly athwart the advance route of the 116th Panzer Division.

The situation in front of the 2d Panzer was less certain. The only major unit on the right (southwestern) flank of the 84th Division was the 4th Cavalry Group, which covered a line along the Lesse River.[3] However, on 23 December Maj. Gen. Ernest N. Harmon's 2d Armored Division (nicknamed "Hell on Wheels") was moving to a forward assembly area south of Liège. Harmon's division, like its sister-unit the 3d Armored, under Maj. Gen. Maurice Rose (elements of which were already engaged to the northeast),[4] was organized differently from the fourteen other armored divisions in the U.S. Army. These two divisions contained two light and four medium tank battalions in two armored regiments instead of the three mixed tank battalions in other U.S. Army armored divisions, and had a three-battalion armored infantry regiment instead of three separate battalions. Given their greater strength (252 medium tanks and 14,000 personnel as opposed to 186 medium tanks and 10,500 personnel) and long combat experience, these two divisions were formidable fighting formations, and both also enjoyed the advantage of being relatively well rested and well equipped when they entered the Ardennes fighting.

Ernest Nason Harmon was born in Lowell, Massachusetts, on 26 February 1894. After attending Norwich College in Northfield, Vermont, for one year, he entered West Point in 1913. He graduated on 20 April 1917, two weeks after the United States entered World War I, as a second lieutenant of Cavalry. He went to France in March 1918 with the 2d Cavalry, the only cavalry unit to get overseas in that war. He and his regiment fought, dismounted as infantry, in the Battles of St. Mihiel and the Meuse-Argonne. Between the wars he was a member of the U.S. Modern Pentathlon team at the Paris Olympics in 1924. In 1938, as a colonel, he became Chief of Staff to Maj. Gen. Adna R. Chaffee Jr.'s newly established Armored Force at Fort Knox, Kentucky.

In February 1942 Harmon, by now a major general, succeeded Maj. Gen. George S. Patton Jr. as commander of the 2d Armored Division. In Operation Torch, he and elements of the division landed at Safi, Morocco, south of Casablanca, on 9 November 1942. In early 1943 he went to Tunisia and acted as Deputy Commander of the II Corps at the Battle of Kasserine Pass. In April he was assigned to command the 1st Armored Division, which had been badly damaged in that battle, and revitalized the division. With elements of that division he took part in the amphibious assault at Salerno, Italy, on 9 September. After fighting through and north of Naples, Harmon and his division landed at Anzio in late January 1944. The division played a major role in the breakout from Anzio in May and June 1944, and in the subsequent northward drive to the Arno River.

Slated to be a corps commander, Harmon was instead transferred in September to the European Theater in response to General Eisenhower's urgent need for a qualified commander for Harmon's old division, the 2d Armored, which was then engaged in heavy fighting on the Belgian-German border east of Liège. In the Roer region, as part of XIX Corps in the Ninth Army, Harmon's division broke through the Westwall in October. In November it fought its way to the lower Roer River. During these months of fighting the division earned the right to its nickname, "Hell on Wheels." On 20 December the 2d Armored was ordered to join the VII Corps in the northwest Ardennes to block the German thrust toward the Meuse River.

The 2d Armored Division had been activated on 15 July 1940. During its initial training it was commanded for more than a year (January 1941–February 1942) by Maj. Gen. George S. Patton Jr., before Harmon became its second commander. After Harmon was transferred to the 1st Armored Division in April 1943, he was replaced as commander of the 2d Armored Division by Maj. Gen. Hugh J. Gaffey. The division fought successfully under Gaffey in

Sicily in July, then went to England to prepare for the invasion of France. The division landed in Normandy on 9 June 1944, and fought through the Normandy Beachhead with the V, VII, and XIX Corps. Taking part in the St. Lô breakout with the VII Corps, the 2d Armored raced through northern France, still shifting among those three corps, until it was brought to a halt in Belgium in September by stiffening German resistance. General Harmon then returned to command his old division.

Moving up behind the 2d Armored and 84th Infantry divisions was the third division of Collins's VII Corps, the 75th Infantry Division under Maj. Gen. Fay B. Prickett. Fay Brink Prickett was born in Hutchinson, Kansas, on 20 April 1893. At age fourteen he enlisted in the Kansas National Guard, serving for three years as his company's bugler and discovering an enthusiasm for military life. Prickett entered West Point in 1912 and graduated in June 1916, gaining a commission as a second lieutenant of Cavalry. He was assigned to the 10th Cavalry and took part in the Punitive Expedition into Mexico (1916–1917). He transferred to the Field Artillery in June 1917, and was sent to France late that year. By the time of the Armistice, Prickett had taken part in three campaigns and was a (temporary) lieutenant colonel commanding a battalion of the 16th Field Artillery.

Prickett graduated from the Field Artillery School at Fort Sill in 1920 and later returned to pass the Advanced Course there in June 1924. He graduated from the Command and General Staff School at Fort Leavenworth in 1930 and from the Army War College in Washington, D.C., in 1932. He then returned to West Point as commander of the Field Artillery Detachment there. With the rapid expansion of the Army after the spring of 1940, he was promoted rapidly, rising to brigadier general in mid-1942. Assigned as artillery commander of the 4th Infantry Division in August 1943, he was suddenly reassigned to command the 75th Infantry Division, which had been activated at Fort Leonard Wood, Missouri, in April. Prickett was soon promoted to major general and led the division to England in November 1944 and then to France on 13 December. The 75th was sent to Holland on 18 December, and on the next day was shifted to Belgium, where it came under the command of Collins's VII Corps.

The 75th Division had been on the European mainland and in the theater of operations for barely a week. It did not complete its assembly around the village of Durbuy, Belgium, and along the Ourthe River, until the morning of Christmas Eve. The coming battle with the lead elements of the Fifth Panzer Army would be its baptism of fire.

THE OPPONENTS MARSHAL THEIR FORCES: 23 DECEMBER

On 23 December, General Bolling's 84th Division set up a number of company-size roadblocks between Marche and the Meuse River, employing for this task the 1st Battalion of the 333d Infantry, and the 3d Battalion of the 335th Infantry. These two battalions stiffened several company and platoon-size detachments from the 29th Infantry Regiment (Separate), which had been sent forward from rear-area security duties on 21 December to cover the Meuse River crossings.[5] One platoon of the 29th was at Rochefort, and another covered the radio relay station at Jemelles.

The Communications Zone commander, Lt. Gen. John C. H. Lee, had taken several other steps to guard the important Meuse bridges. He had directed Brig. Gen. Charles O. Thrasher, commanding the Oise Sector of the COM-Z (as the Communications Zone was generally called), to send all possible reinforcements he could to stiffen the 29th Infantry Regiment. Thrasher corralled the 354th and 1313th Engineer General Service regiments, organized them as Task Force Thrasher on 20 December, and led them forward. On 22 and 23 December these troops were further reinforced by the 342d, 392d, 366th, and 1308th Engineer General Service regiments (approximately 1,300 officers and men each), the 115th Field Artillery Battalion, and the 118th regimental antitank company (both parts of the 118th Regimental Combat Team, Separate). The forces committed by Thrasher amounted to more than 8,600 officers and men.

In addition, there were six recently organized and indifferently equipped battalions of French light infantry, provided by the military governor of Metz, totaling between 3,500 and 4,000 officers and men. Late on 23 December all of these forces passed to the command of Maj. Gen. Troy Middleton's VIII Corps, responsible for the southern face of the Bulge, west of Bastogne. Bolling's 84th Division, however, remained under the VII Corps of the First Army.

Late on 23 December, leading elements of the 2d Panzer Division, with the Panzer Lehr Division close behind, skirmished with outposts of the 84th Division. These were elements of the 335th Infantry's 3d Battalion. The Germans drove the detachments back toward the battalion's main positions around Hargimont and Rochefort, five to ten kilometers southwest of Marche. Early the next morning Kampfgruppe von Böhm mounted a more serious attack and captured Hargimont from its outnumbered American defenders, opening the way for exploiting units of the 2d Panzer. The 3d Battalion of the 335th fell back to rejoin the rest of the regiment in front of Marche. At the same time, Kampfgruppe von Cochenhausen of the 2d Panzer Division drove through Harsin and Hargimont before pushing on farther west toward Buissonville. To the northeast, the 156th Panzergrenadier Regiment of the 116th Panzer Division penetrated the 334th Infantry's lines near Verdenne, advancing about a kilometer and nearly reaching the Marche-Hotton road before being halted by American reserves. Meanwhile, the elements of the 335th Infantry's 3d Battalion around Rochefort (about half the battalion) were reinforced by units of the 638th Tank Destroyer Battalion (SP) with M18 self-propelled TDs and by a platoon from the 51st Engineer Combat Battalion, which was sent to prepare the bridge in Rochefort for demolition. By this time, the American troops in Rochefort totaled about 700 officers and men under Maj. Gordon A. Bahe, commander of the 335th's 3d Battalion.

Part of Harmon's 2d Armored Division reached the VII Corps area during the day on 23 December. Combat Command A, in the lead, arrived at Ciney in the morning and established roadblocks in a semicircle south and east of town, and also set up a series of positions along the Namur-Marche road, which ran through the center of Ciney. After dark, units of 2d Panzer's Kampfgruppen von Böhm and Cochenhausen probed CCA's positions at Leignon and Haid along the Namur-Marche road. In a series of confused, small-scale firefights, the Americans were surprised and had the worst of these exchanges, which took place around 2100. Nevertheless, they held their positions and maintained control of the roadway.

During the night of 23–24 December there were further developments in the evolving encounters between Hotton and Dinant, which was on the Meuse itself, and the site of the nearest bridge. The Germans took advantage of darkness to continue their advance westward, avoiding interference from U.S. fighter aircraft, which German troops referred to with dread as "jabos," informal soldier slang for "fighter-bomber" (*jagdbomber*). Although still suffering from sporadic fuel shortages and other supply problems, the panzer columns advanced steadily. By midnight, Kampfgruppe von Böhm had reached the village of Foy-Notre Dame, a mere six kilometers from the crucial Meuse River bridge at Dinant. Before dawn on Christmas Eve, Kampfgruppe Cochenhausen had reached a shallow, roughly triangular area, bounded by the lines Leignon-Achêne-Celles-Conneux. There Major Cochenhausen's weary tankers and panzergrenadiers were able to get a few hours' rest while waiting for additional fuel for their final drive to the Meuse.

As Cochenhausen and Böhm pushed their troops forward during the day and evening of 23 December, the main body of the 2d Panzer Division, spurred on by Lauchert's personal exertions, advanced steadily northwestward. By dusk on 23 December, his units had reached Hassonville, a hamlet and crossroads about two kilometers (1.6 miles) southwest of Marche, while another column had halted in Jemelle, about two kilometers east of Rochefort.

Behind Lauchert's columns came the bulk of General Bayerlein's Panzer Lehr Division, less the 901st Panzergrenadier Regiment, which was still assigned to Colonel Kokott's 26th Volksgrenadier Division (VGD) around Bastogne. There were also detachments from the panzerjäger, FLAK, and engineer battalions on screening duty between Remagne and Wanlin (see chapter 14, note 28). During the day, Bayerlein's columns proceeded northwest and reached the outskirts of Rochefort just before dark, about 1640 hours. Faced with determined resistance from Major Bahe's force of American defenders, the Panzer Lehr troops mounted a formal assault. They spent most of the night battling for control of the town, which they had been unable to secure by dawn on 24 December.

CHRISTMAS EVE "ON THE MEUSE"

Growing German pressure on the 84th Infantry Division's blocking positions on the roadways leading to the Meuse clearly demonstrated to the higher American headquarters the seriousness of the German drive for the bridges. In response to the growing gravity of the situation, General Courtney H. Hodges, First Army commander, directed that the 3d Armored Division pass under Collins's VII Corps, giving Collins control over two infantry and most of two extra-large armored divisions.

The 116th Panzer Division's strong probe at Verdenne was reinforced during the day, and the 334th Infantry fell back to the Hotton-Marche road, searching for a more secure position. German reconnaissance troops were seen to enter the wooded area southwest of Bourdon and northeast of Verdenne itself, and the 334th spent much of the day preparing its positions in expectation of further German attacks. The Germans maintained their pressure on the 334th, keeping the important Marche-Hotton roadway under almost constant fire from small arms, machine guns, mortars, and artillery.

Late on 23 December, Col. Timothy A. Pedley Jr., commanding the 333d Infantry, ordered his 3d Battalion to counterattack southwestward toward Verdenne from its positions around Bourdon. In response to this order, K Company moved forward shortly before midnight, expecting to pass through the woods north of Verdenne and there to join forces with infantry from the 3/334 and one or two platoons of supporting tanks from the 771st Tank Battalion. These troops had been driven from Verdenne by the German attack early in the evening.

Trudging forward in the darkness, the infantrymen took a wrong turn and, a little past midnight on 24 December, approached a group of tanks whose bulk completely filled the narrow roadway. Presuming these to be the tanks of the 771st Tank Battalion, Capt. Harold P. Leinbaugh halted the company column, and ordered Sgt. Don Phelps to wake up the crewmen, and to tell them to follow the company column through the woods to attack Verdenne. Phelps pounded on the side of the nearest tank before he got a response: A dim figure rose out of a hatch and inquired, *"Was ist los?"* ("What's up?" or "What is going on?"). Phelps, startled, made no reply, and the German tanker repeated his question. Phelps recovered his wits sufficiently to take a couple of steps back and fire one shot at the German tank crewman, who yelped and dropped back into the tank. A moment later the hatch slammed shut as Phelps yelled, "They're Germans! Get down!" His words were matched by German shouts of *"Amis! Amis!"* (German soldier slang for U.S. troops).

A fierce firefight immediately broke out. The German tanks were surrounded by dug-in German infantrymen, whose security arrangements were obviously less than adequate, since they had been unaware of K Company's approach. The close-quarters firefight, eerily lit by muzzle flashes and explosions, was furious and confused, especially since much of the action took place at ranges of less than fifty yards. Captain Leinbaugh and the rest of K Company hurriedly scrambled out of the middle of the German position. Mercifully, and despite the close quarters and almost unbelievable chaos, the Americans suffered relatively few casualties, although some men, left behind in the confusion, did not make it back to U.S. lines for several hours. The 84th Division's official history, published a few years after the war, placed the German forces in this encounter at about 300 infantry and five tanks.[6] In fact, K Company had unwittingly stumbled into part of the formidable Kampfgruppe Bayer of the 116th Panzer Division: a battalion-size force of forty Panthers and PzKw-IVHs, the 156th Panzergrenadier Regiment, and supporting artillery and engineers.[7] Through a happy accident of war, K Company and the rest of the 3d Battalion, 333d Infantry, had been spared a costly battle in the wrong place. After its clash with Kampfgruppe Bayer, K Company withdrew and dug in in front of Bourdon. Colonel Pedley ordered L Company to take over K Company's task. Taking the correct route, L Company was able to rendezvous with K Company of the 3d Battalion, 334th Infantry (reduced to barely forty men), and the tanks of the 771st Tank Battalion and attack Verdenne. After several hours of difficult house-to-house fighting, they secured the town. Reinforced by more tanks from the 771st, they then repelled a German armored counterattack on Christmas morning.

To the south, the nearly isolated force of the 3d Battalion, 335th Infantry, at Rochefort fended off repeated attacks by elements of the Panzer Lehr Division. The situation was grim, because the American defenders, though resourceful and determined, were short of ammunition and other supplies. While their position was good, they were heavily outnumbered. Although authorized to withdraw in the morning, Major Bahe's troops were so closely engaged that they were unable to pull back. In late afternoon the remaining defenders finally evacuated their positions and withdrew to the west under cover of smoke grenades, leaving the remains of Rochefort to the tired troops of Panzer Lehr. Weary from a ten-hour march followed by at least twenty hours of sustained combat, the panzer crews and panzergrenadiers were too exhausted and disorganized to pursue, and the Americans escaped unhindered. Bayerlein, recognizing the state of his men, did not push them beyond sending patrols west of Rochefort. He had the rest of the division stay in place, in part to enjoy recently arrived special Christmas rations.

Farther east, near Marche, the 333d Infantry Regiment of the 84th Division had a quiet, bright, sunny day in reserve, and the men enjoyed Christmas dinner. In the afternoon the 1st Battalion was alerted to move southeast toward Verdenne. Private George Karambelas of A Company, whose home was in Alexandria, Virginia, had a premonition of disaster. His premonition hardened into near-certainty when his company was deployed in a skirmish line for a night attack without being given any information about the situation, the enemy, or the unfamiliar terrain.

The attack jumped off into a wooded area before midnight, and soon German opposition was encountered. At first it was obviously only a covering force; the Germans fell back, and the Americans continued forward through the unfamiliar woods. Karambelas and his buddies did not know it, but they were meeting the German 116th Panzer Division. Soon the enemy fire became intense, and it was obvious to some of the Americans that they were being engaged by tanks. The direction of movement now changed: The Germans advanced and the Americans fell back. Karambelas was hit in the left thigh by a fragment from a tank gun shell. As an aid man came to help him, another shell burst near them, killing the aid man instantly and wounding Karambelas again, this time in his right foot.

By this time all of the able-bodied men of A Company had disappeared, leaving only Karambelas and other wounded men in front of the advancing Germans. However, the Germans had no intention of mounting a counterattack, and they fell back to their original positions. Karambelas hobbled through the woods to the road from which the attack had started. He tried to walk to the rear, but was too weak from loss of blood, so he crawled into a ditch to rest and fell asleep. He was awakened by the sound of men walking toward him. Afraid they were Germans, he pulled out a grenade from his pocket, pulled the pin, and called out, "What company are you guys from?"

The new arrivals were from the 3d Platoon of A Company. He persuaded them to help him get to the battalion aid station, and the next morning he was put in an ambulance to begin a long evacuation process to a hospital in Paris.[8]

At Verdenne the situation was unchanged, as the 116th Panzer Division and the 84th Infantry Division faced each other, both attempting to make minor changes in their positions, but neither ready for a renewed offensive effort.

Early on Christmas Eve the 75th Division started to march south from its assembly area around Durbuy to fill the gap east of Hotton between the 84th Infantry Division and the 7th Armored Division. On the right, the 290th Infantry Regiment marched toward Hotton to move into line just to the left of the 84th Division. Farther east the 289th Infantry trudged toward Amonines and Grandmenil to link up with the 7th Armored Division. Until that day, no one in the division had heard a shot fired in anger. That situation continued for only a few more hours.

The 3d Battalion of the 289th Infantry occupied the village of Grandmenil in the early afternoon. While the troops were digging in, they received visitors from the south. These were elements of the 2d SS Panzer Division, who promptly drove the Americans out. The fighting in and around the village continued into the night. The firefight could be seen and heard by Pfc. Harold Lindstrom and his fellows of F Company of the 289th Infantry Regiment at 2200 hours about five kilometers away, as they marched down a long open slope toward Grandmenil.

The green, inexperienced soldiers of the 75th Infantry Division were about to receive a lesson in security from the veterans of the 2d SS Panzer

Division. The marching column of the 3d Battalion was suddenly swept by machine-gun fire from two or three German tanks. The column dissolved. As he lay in the snow, Lindstrom remembers being paralyzed with terror. From the sound of their voices, he knew that the Germans were no more than 100 yards away. With occasional bursts of machine-gun bullets spraying the area, he was afraid the Germans would be able to see his dark uniform standing out against the white, moonlit snow.[9]

The Germans did not exploit the situation. Obviously there were few of them—only a flanking security outpost. Slowly the officers and noncommissioned officers of the 3d Battalion regained control over their shaken troops. They pulled back, formed a defensive line, and waited through the remainder of a sleepless night for daylight to form a cohesive unit again. By midmorning on Christmas Day there was for the first time a continuous American line along the northern face of the Bulge.

While these events were taking place, General Harmon's 2d Armored Division continued its movement south and began to concentrate around Ciney. The division headquarters spent 24 December near Havelange. Harmon, who was aware of the opportunity to strike at the 2d Panzer Division's flank, had contacted the VII Corps Headquarters to get permission from General Collins to carry out this attack.[10] Collins was out visiting his forward positions, and Harmon spoke to the VII Corps artillery commander, Brig. Gen. Williston B. Palmer. By this time VII Corps had received orders from General Hodges restricting the employment of the 2d Armored. Thus Palmer had the unhappy task of persuading the aggressive Harmon to hold in place in defensive posture.

Shortly afterward, Palmer, received another telephone call—evidently over an unsecure line—this time from the First Army Chief of Staff, Maj. Gen. William B. Kean, regarding the commitment of Harmon's division.[11] Speaking in guarded terms, Kean asked Palmer if he saw "a town A and a town H on the map." Palmer, eager to authorize Harmon's attack, spied Achêne and (Le) Houisse, both *forward* of 2d Armored's positions, and thus requiring a forward movement by the division. He answered affirmatively. Kean, apparently satisfied, hung up.

Both Kean and Palmer, however, were not certain that they had fully understood each other, and had second thoughts about this conversation. Palmer sent a liaison officer to meet Collins at the 2d Armored Division's headquarters (wire communications had gone out), reporting his phone conversation with Kean. A few minutes later Kean called again, having apparently noted an unanticipated tone of enthusiasm in Palmer's voice. Kean told Palmer, "Now get this. I'm only going to say it once. Roll with the punch." Instead of an advance, this implied a withdrawal. Palmer, glancing again at the map, saw the towns of Andenne and Huy, thirty miles to the rear of Achêne and Le Houisse. Palmer recalled later that this was the only time during the war when he was "ill with disapproval."

Palmer dispatched a second messenger to Collins, reporting the change and urgently requesting the corps commander to return to his headquarters. This messenger reached Collins while he was still at Harmon's headquarters issuing attack orders for Christmas Day. Hurriedly telling Harmon to put everything on hold but to continue with preparations for the Christmas attack, Collins sped back to his own headquarters, arriving about 1830 hours.

Two hours later, Col. R. F. "Red" Akers, a staff officer from First Army, arrived to confirm the essence of Kean's second phone conversation with Palmer: On his own initiative, Collins was authorized to fall back to the line Andenne-Hotton-Manhay. Undeterred, Collins believed his understanding of the situation was more accurate than the pessimistic estimate that obviously prevailed at the First Army Headquarters. Early Christmas morning Collins issued his orders. Harmon was to proceed with his planned attack; Bolling's 84th Infantry Division would conduct holding attacks to tie down the Germans on its front.

While confusion reigned at higher headquarters, the 4th Cavalry Group came under the 2d Armored Division's tactical control. By midmorning of 24 December Combat Command A, under Brig. Gen. John Collins (no relation to "Lightning Joe" of the VII Corps), was deployed in a shallow arc from Ciney south and west to Haid. To its left around Havrenne was the 24th Cavalry Squadron, covering the right rear of General Bolling's 84th Infantry Division. A battalion of the 66th Armored Infantry Regiment had clashed with the I Battalion, 304th Panzergrenadiers (part of Kampfgruppe Cochenhausen) shortly after midnight, and before dawn on 24 December had pushed on to Buissonville. There, early that afternoon, the battalion was joined by the rest of Combat Command A. They attacked, cutting the principal road connecting Kampfgruppe Cochenhausen with the rest of the 2d Panzer Division to the east.

In reaction to this unwelcome development, General von Lüttwitz, commanding the XLVII Panzer Corps, ordered the 9th Panzer Division to relieve the main body of Colonel von Lauchert's 2d Panzer Division around Hedree and Hargimont, to permit Lauchert to mount an attack to relieve the isolated kampfgruppe. Lauchert's troops moved south a little to assemble around Jemelle during the night and prepare for their attack on Christmas Day.

The 24th Cavalry Squadron moved into Humain while the 4th Cavalry Squadron deployed as a screen between Combat Command A at Buissonville and Combat Command B around Ciney. Combat Command R spent 24 December assembling around Hogne, about five kilometers northwest of Marche, thereby also providing a backstop to both the 4th Cavalry and the 335th Infantry Regiment of the 84th Division.

CRISIS CHRISTMAS DAY: CELLES AND VERDENNE

The intensity of combat in the Celles-Hotton sector of the front rose sharply during Christmas Day, as the 2d and 84th divisions followed General

Collins's plans for the VII Corps counterattack. The 84th Division sent most of the 333d and 334th Infantry forward against the Germans in the woods northeast of Verdenne. Although the U.S. troops recaptured Verdenne itself, they made a scant impression on Kampfgruppe Bayer, whose troops displayed typical German skill in selecting good defensive terrain and typical German tenacity in holding it. However, Kampfgruppe Bayer was isolated and unable to receive supplies or reinforcements, and was confined to a relatively small area under continual American artillery fire. Faced with this strong American effort, General Siegfried von Waldenburg ordered his 116th Panzer Division to fall back a short distance to new positions south and west of the former front line. Covered by spoiling attacks, the withdrawal began after dark and was completed during the early-morning hours of 26 December.

Farther west, early on the twenty-fifth, General Harmon's armor began its counterstroke, officially understood by First Army Headquarters to be a "limited effort," but intended by both Collins and Harmon as a more serious attack. Brigadier General Isaac D. White's Combat Command B, divided into two combined-arms task forces, moved out through Achêne (Task Force A) and Conjoux (Task Force B), aiming for Celles. Task Force A's attack, shearing through German positions near Achêne, split Kampfgruppe von Böhm from Kampfgruppe Cochenhausen. For the rest of the day, Major von Böhm's reconnaissance battalion was subjected to repeated U.S. attacks from the north and west, and elements of Task Force A battled their way into Foy-Notre Dame before sunset. Task Force B, following a southerly approach to Celles, overran Conneux and Leignon before joining Task Force A in a two-pronged converging attack that took Celles in the late afternoon. These operations left both Cochenhausen's and Böhm's kampfgruppen isolated and under heavy pressure. Neither force could continue to hold its positions, much less advance, without relief.

The main body of the 2d Panzer Division moved forward through Rochefort, passing through the positions of Bayerlein's 130th Armored Reconnaissance Battalion, still weary from its exertions on 23 and 24 December. The panzers and panzergrenadiers pushed on through Ciergnon and Wanlin and probed against Custinne in late afternoon. There they were repulsed and suffered some losses, hammered by repeated U.S. air strikes and concentrated artillery fire, and facing experienced U.S. tankers from Task Force B of Combat Command A in superior positions. Bloodied and rebuffed, Lauchert's troops withdrew a little toward Wanlin. North and a little east of these actions, Combat Command A, under Brigadier General Collins, fought another battle against the combat-fresh but road-weary troops of Generalmajor Baron Harald von Elverfeldt's 9th Panzer Division.

Harald Freiherr von Elverfeldt was born in Hildesheim on 5 February 1900, and entered the German Army as an officer-cadet (fähnrich) in the prestigious and elite 1st Foot Guards Regiment in March 1918. Despite his youth, he impressed his superiors and was retained in the Reichswehr following the Versailles Treaty; in November 1919 he was promoted to lieutenant. During the years between the wars he specialized in signals, and he later passed through the Kriegsakademie in Berlin. Promoted to major in March 1937, he served as operations officer in the 3d Light Division from November 1938 through February 1940.[12] After the conquest of Poland he was promoted to lieutenant colonel (November 1939) and was assigned to the staff of the XV Panzer Corps from February 1940 through January 1941, following the 3d Light Division's conversion into the 8th Panzer Division.

During preparations for the invasion of Russia, von Elverfeldt became Chief of Staff of the new LVI Panzer Corps in March 1941, and served in that post for almost two years, during which time he was promoted to colonel. He next served as Chief of Staff for the Ninth Army under Walter Model, playing a significant role in the northern "jaw" of the abortive German offensive at Kursk in July 1943. Promoted to generalmajor in September, he next served as Chief of Staff of the Seventeenth Army. After a brief stint as senior operations officer of the Senior Troop Leaders' Course (*Lehrgang für Höhere Truppenführer*) from February to September 1944, he took command of the 9th Panzer Division on 16 September 1944.

The 9th Panzer Division was formed in the winter of 1939–1940 when the 4th Light Division, largely recruited in Austria, was converted to a full-fledged panzer division in anticipation of the campaign in the west. The 9th Panzer had its combat debut in France, where it moved further than any other German division. It also served with distinction in the Balkans in spring 1941 and in the Ukraine from June 1941 through 1942. Transferred to the central sector of the Russian front, the 9th Panzer took part in the Kursk offensive of July 1943 before being transferred back to the Ukraine. Sent to southern France in early 1944, the 9th Panzer suffered severe losses in the retreat northward in September, and was rebuilt around Venlo and Aachen during the autumn. Ordered into the Ardennes only on 22 December, the 9th Panzer had almost 14,000 officers and men (counting attached units) with twenty-seven PzKw-IVH, eleven Panther, and fourteen Tiger-I tanks and twenty-four StuG-III and JgPz-IV assault guns.[13] The division was also extensively equipped with more than sixty of the brand-new triple-mount 15-mm heavy antiaircraft machine guns.

Elements of the 9th Panzer drove the 24th Cavalry Squadron out of Humain in the morning, and went on to seize Havrenne before being halted just short of Buissonville. Combat Command A, which was trying to reach Rochefort, mounted a strong counterattack during the afternoon, driving the Germans back from Buissonville and retaking Havrenne. The 24th Cavalry launched attack after attack to retake Humain, but despite the cavalrymen's best efforts the village was still in German hands when darkness fell. Frustrated, the 24th Cavalry broke off contact with the Germans and set up roadblocks along the secondary routes leading north and east from Havrenne toward Marche and Hogne. Meanwhile, holding the prospect for more punishment for the Germans on the morrow, Combat Command R spent Christmas completing its assembly around Hogne and preparing for combat.

To the south of the day's main actions, the weary troops of Panzer Lehr spent the day recuperating after their exertions and losses of the two previous days. Bayerlein's units were repeatedly pummeled by U.S. artillery and air attacks, convincing evidence, if any was needed, that the momentum of the campaign had begun to shift in the Allies' favor.

THE BRITISH ARRIVE

Multiplying the difficulties facing Lüttwitz and his field commanders, the 3d Royal Tank Regiment and the 23d Hussars of the British 29th Armoured Brigade (normally part of the 11th Armoured Division, but operating separately from the division during the crisis) had moved forward across the Meuse to assist the 2d Armored Division. North of the Meuse, the divisions of Lt. Gen. Sir Brian G. Horrocks's veteran XXX Corps were moving into position to hold the line of the river. The 43d "Wessex" Infantry Division and the attached 34th Tank Brigade had arrived first, covering the river line from Liège south to Huy by the late afternoon of 22 December, arriving on the river line about the same time as the 29th Armoured Brigade reached the river between Dinant and Givet. The 53d "Welsh" Infantry Division began to arrive at Namur late on 22 December, and by the evening of 24 December had moved into its positions between Namur and Givet. By that time, the Guards Armored Division had also moved into position between Huy and Namur, and the presence of the latter two divisions allowed the release of the 29th Armoured Brigade for action on the east bank of the Meuse on Christmas Day.

Christmas Day saw the arrival of two more British divisions. The 51st "Highland" Infantry Division and the attached 33d Tank Brigade reached Liège, and the 6th Airborne Division (which had dropped in Normandy) began to take over the Meuse River line from Dinant south to Givet, permitting the 53d Division to concentrate between Dinant and Namur. These movements, which were spread over several days, effectively shut the once-open door for the Fifth Panzer Army. Without firing a shot, the British XXX Corps had thrown the bolt and locked it.

AFTER CHRISTMAS: 26–27 DECEMBER

The arrival of Horrocks's XXX Corps and the culmination of the 2d Armored Division's counterstroke at Celles effectively ended any chances for Lauchert's 2d Panzer Division to reach the Meuse. Almost overnight the situation for the Germans had changed dramatically. It was no longer a matter of advancing but of surviving that now most occupied the minds of the German generals and front-line commanders. The weather remained essentially clear and cold, which enabled the Allied jabos to harass German columns continuously during the hours of daylight, restricting their major movements to the hours of darkness.

The elements of Fritz Bayerlein's Panzer Lehr Division that were near the beleaguered XLVII Panzer Corps spearhead withdrew to new positions south of Rochefort, out of the battle line. Their place was taken by units from the 2d Panzer and by General von Elverfeldt's newly committed 9th Panzer.[14] By the evening of 26 December, von Elverfeldt's troops and tanks held a five-kilometer front, and the divisional headquarters had been moved from Longchamps to Harsin during the day.

Colonel von Lauchert's 2d Panzer Division was now in trouble. Kampfgruppe Cochenhausen, isolated by the thrusts of the 2d Armored Division, had been surrounded for two days, pummeled by artillery and air strikes and unable to receive ammunition or fuel. The remainder of the division, which was little larger than the surrounded kampfgruppe, had been making repeated but unsuccessful efforts to reach the isolated units. Heavy losses and the long-anticipated arrival of the 9th Panzer Division led Lauchert to disengage his weary units in midafternoon on 26 December, moving to a quieter area southeast of Rochefort to regroup. As this move took place, Lauchert shifted his headquarters from Jemelle southeast to Wavreille.

Recognizing that his battered troops could not hold on much longer without succor, Maj. Ernst von Cochenhausen (commander of the 304th Panzergrenadier Regiment, around which the kampfgruppe was built) mounted a successful but costly breakout effort. Soon after midnight on 27 December, he and his surviving men abandoned most of their remaining heavy equipment and vehicles and moved out to the southeast, heading for the main body of the 2d Panzer, which was southeast of Rochefort. After a march of nearly eighteen kilometers, the remnants of Kampfgruppe Cochenhausen reached their comrades, but it was a sad reunion. The 2d Panzer had lost nearly half its transport, a solid quarter of its personnel, nearly all of its vital reconnaissance battalion, and close to two-thirds of the seventy-five tanks and forty-five assault guns that it had possessed on 16 December.

To the northeast, General von Waldenburg's 116th Panzer Division was endeavoring, like the 2d Panzer, to reunite with an isolated task force. A major daylight assault on 26 December to relieve Kampfgruppe Bayer was repulsed with heavy losses, and Waldenburg sent a radio message to Bayer to break out on his own. To assist this effort, the 116th Panzer mounted a series of small-scale attacks against the positions of the American 84th Infantry division during the night of 26–27 December. This served in part to distract the Americans, and Bayer was able to extricate not only most of his men, but a good portion of his heavy equipment and vehicles. Offsetting this good news, however, the Führer Begleit Brigade withdrew from its positions in front of Hotton for redeployment to operations around Bastogne. This compelled the 116th Panzer to expand its front by several kilometers to link up with the 560th VGD between Odeigne and the Ourthe River's north branch. The longer front line required the division to suspend any plans for further offensive operations and to assume an essentially defensive posture. This change echoed the general reorientation of the postures and goals of the Fifth Panzer Army's spearheads: Attack was no longer a real option; the goal was to survive, while hanging on to what had been gained.

These developments left the German XLVII and LVIII Panzer Corps stalled, forcing them to revert to essentially defensive roles. General der Panzertruppen Walter Krüger's LVIII Panzer Corps held a front from the vicinity of Amonines south and east to the outskirts of Marche, while General von Lüttwitz's XLVII Panzer Corps held positions from Marche south through Rochefort. The 26th VGD and about one-third of the Panzer Lehr Division, both nominally still part of the XLVII Panzer Corps, were facing the 101st Airborne Division around Bastogne.

For the American units facing these two panzer corps, the basic mission now was to maintain the initiative and exploit success. No longer were the Americans concerned about limiting damage and avoiding wholesale defeat. General Harmon's 2d Armored Division maintained its close-fought pressure on Lauchert's 2d Panzer Division. Combat Command B continued to operate with its two task forces, A and B. These two groups were involved in hard fighting all day on 26 December as they slowly cleared Kampfgruppe Cochenhausen out of the wooded areas between Celles and Conjoux. Meanwhile, Combat Command A with Combat Command R attached held its positions around Buissonville, beating off an attack from Humain by leading elements of the 9th Panzer Division. Late in the day Combat Command R launched an attack of its own to retake Humain, but made only limited progress. Humain was continually pummeled by American artillery throughout the night of 26–27 December. Finally, the 82d Cavalry Reconnaissance Squadron (Mechanized) made contact with the 29th Armoured Brigade of the British 11th Armoured Division along the line of the Lesse River during daylight on 26 December.

To the northeast of the 2d Armored's continuing brawl with the 2d Panzer, the 84th Infantry Division continued to hold its twenty-one-kilometer front. Repeated attacks against Kampfgruppe Bayer's pocket around Verdenne were repulsed, but the pocket remained under continual heavy artillery fire. German diversionary attacks around Marenne in the early evening on 26 December created enough of a distraction for the 84th Division that Bayer was able to lead his troops back to German lines during the night of 26–27 December. It is not an indictment of American tactical intelligence but rather an indication of the general unreliability of such intelligence to note that although the Americans estimated that Kampfgruppe Bayer contained about seven tanks and 700 men, Bayer's force in fact included nearly forty tanks and around 3,000 infantry and other troops.

While Bayer's kampfgruppe was extricating itself from the American encirclement, the Führer Begleit Brigade in front of Hampteau launched an attack on the evening of 26 December. Striking the American lines between Menil and Hampteau, the advancing German columns were hammered by American artillery and tank fire, and consequently made little progress before they broke off their effort after suffering considerable losses.

Action on 27 December was essentially a continuation of the operations of the previous day. The 9th Panzer continued to hold an 11.5-kilometer front from Hedree and Hargimont southwest through Rochefort, screening the battered 2d Panzer to the southeast while awaiting the arrival of its remaining elements, which were still moving forward by rail. Like the 2d Panzer the forward elements of Bayerlein's Panzer Lehr remained out of line, resting and regrouping southeast of Rochefort. Fuel supplies permitting, the division prepared to rejoin the 902d Panzergrenadier Regiment, which was still fighting near Bastogne. Farther north, the 116th Panzer remained on the defensive, expanding and strengthening its positions in anticipation of an American attack.

For the Americans, 27 December was in large part a day of recovery and regrouping. Although Harmon's 2d Armored Division had suffered only light losses in the fighting around Celles—totaling five M5 light and twenty-two M4 medium tanks, along with some 16 killed, 26 missing, and about 200 wounded—the division's component units needed time to reorganize, restock their larders, and refuel while carrying out other necessary housekeeping tasks neglected over the previous days of hard fighting. The 84th Division, blessed with inactive enemy units on its front, took the time to give its front-line soldiers a much-needed day of rest. All of the combatant units took time to repair damaged equipment and conduct necessary maintenance, while the men not otherwise occupied wrote letters home and caught up on lost sleep.

AFTERMATH

The Fifth Panzer Army's drive for the Meuse crossings had failed. It took several more days for Adolf Hitler to become fully reconciled to this fact, and the fruits of his reaction did not become apparent until the last days of the year. However, to the German commanders in the field, especially those in the leading divisions of the XLVII and LVIII Panzer Corps at the tip of the Bulge penetration, the conclusion that their drive had fallen short was inescapable. The immediate question for both the weary Germans and their elated American opponents, who for the first time in this winter campaign had witnessed a definite shift of initiative, was: What will happen next?

The Americans now held the fields over which the previous three days' battles had been waged. The relative calm gave them an opportunity to recover disabled vehicles and equipment for repair and also to count their prisoners.

For the Germans, on the evening of 27 December, the situation was more grim. The 2d Panzer Division's tank units were sadly reduced, the reconnaissance battalion was virtually destroyed, and both panzergrenadier regiments had sustained heavy personnel and equipment losses. Most of the valuable American trucks captured in the fighting around Bastogne on 20–21 December had been destroyed or abandoned, and transport shortages had again become a major problem. The other panzer formations that had fought their way through the Ardennes nearly to the Meuse were in little better shape. Panzer Lehr had been relatively lightly engaged and so had suffered comparatively few casualties. Although the 116th Panzer had been able to extricate most of Kampfgruppe Bayer from the small Verdenne pocket, it had been compelled, like 2d Panzer and Panzer Lehr, to abandon damaged and disabled vehicles and equipment. In addition to many killed and wounded, the 116th Panzer had lost nearly 600 men, many of them also wounded, captured by the Americans.

None of the leading German panzer formations had made any significant advance from its starting position on 23 December. The 116th Panzer Division had been able to gain a kilometer or so against the 84th Infantry Division, but General Bolling's infantrymen still held the important towns of Hotton and Marche. To the southwest, the 2d Panzer Division had been compelled to break off contact with the Americans and to withdraw behind a new line, a little east of its starting positions, which was now held by the newly arrived but still incomplete 9th Panzer Division. Finally, the Panzer Lehr Division had also withdrawn, taking up new positions southeast of Rochefort, preparing to move back toward Bastogne.

The causes of this obvious German failure before the Meuse were simple and straightforward. First, the Germans had suffered from the Allies' command of the air: Good flying weather had forced them to make major troop movements only at night. This was a sharp departure from the fog- and cloud-shrouded early days of the offensive, when the Germans had roved across the country at all hours, unmolested by the dreaded and deadly Allied jabos. So complete was American air superiority during the Christmas battles that, to their dismay, few German soldiers saw any Luftwaffe aircraft during the fighting.

Second, the German divisions striking toward the Meuse were no longer fresh. Although flushed with early success, all three panzer divisions had suffered numerous casualties during the week of advance to Celles and Verdenne; the officers and men were weary and some were showing signs of exhaustion and combat fatigue. In comparison, both the 2d Armored and the 84th Infantry divisions had moved into the battle area from bivouac locations where they had enjoyed at least several days of rest and quiet. Their men and equipment were in good condition, well supplied, and well maintained.

Finally, the Germans were unable to match the massive and flexible American artillery. The American artillery battalions, at divisional, corps, and

army level, repeatedly demonstrated technical superiority and enjoyed substantial numerical advantages in guns and ammunition, switching targets
within minutes and dropping awesome concentrations of high explosive virtually at a moment's notice. Lacking the American Army's wealth of communications equipment and its large pool of well-trained (and by this date, experienced) forward observers, the German artillerymen were simply unable to
match U.S. gunners' capabilities.[15] Not least among the German Army's
problems was that among the three panzer divisions wholly or partially present near the point of the Bulge, the Germans had fewer self-propelled howitzers than the Americans had in the 2d Armored Division *alone*. As one military commentator in a later age said, quantity has a quality all its own.

The German failure to reach, let alone cross, the Meuse River effectively
ended any chance for achieving any of the goals of Hitler's grand counteroffensive in the west. Unfortunately for both the German and American troops
in the Ardennes, Hitler did not yet fully realize this fact, and another three
weeks of bloody and difficult fighting lay ahead before the campaign would
finally end.[16]

16

FACEOFF: XVIII AIRBORNE CORPS VS. II SS PANZER CORPS

THE NORTHERN FACE IN FLUX: 23 DECEMBER

After the withdrawal of American forces from the "fortified goose-egg" at St. Vith on 23 December (see chapter 10), Maj. Gen. Matthew Ridgway continued his efforts to plug the yawning gap to the west and south of his XVIII Airborne Corps. On the corps left flank from Stavelot to Trois Ponts, a substantial line had been established by the 30th Infantry Division. However, from Vielsalm west to Hotton on the Ourthe River, there was only a handful of troops at "Parker's Crossroads" (see chapter 10), and scattered elements of the 3d Armored and 82d Airborne divisions to oppose the advancing Germans of the XVIII Panzer Corps, LVIII Panzer Corps, and the II SS Panzer Corps. The final collapse of Major Parker's little force on 23 December left the road to Manhay and the vital N-15 highway north to Liège and the Meuse nearly wide open. Fortunately, Parker's valiant defense had delayed the Germans long enough to allow additional newly arrived American forces to establish blocking positions just to the north.

These forces were elements of the 82d Airborne Division and the battered remnants of the defenders of St. Vith (the 7th Armored Division, CCB of the 9th Armored Division, the 112th Infantry Regiment, and the rump of the 106th Infantry Division). The first of the new arrivals was Brig. Gen. William Hoge's CCB of the 9th Armored Division, advance elements of which were sent on the afternoon of 23 December to hold Malempré, overlooking the N-15 highway southwest of Manhay. Later that day, Col. Dwight Rosebaum's CCA of the 7th Armored Division was sent to occupy Manhay, while also relieving Hoge's task force at Malempré. (CCB/9 was then to go

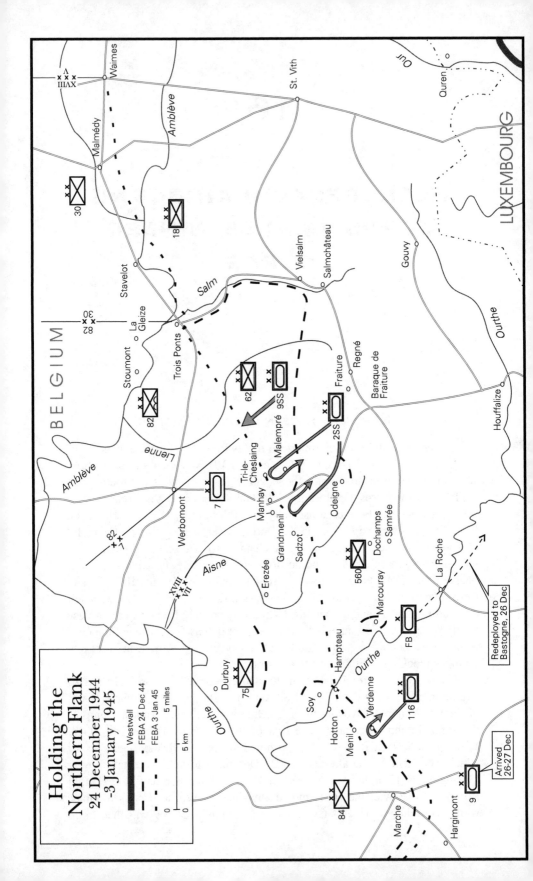

Holding the
Northern Flank
24 December 1944
–3 January 1945

Westwall
FEBA 24 Dec 44
FEBA 3 Jan 45

0   5 km
0   5 miles

BELGIUM

LUXEMBOURG

Waimes
Malmédy
Stavelot
Stoumont
La Gleize
Trois Ponts
Werbomont
Durbuy
Soy
Hotton
Menil
Marche
Hargimont
Verdenne
Hampteau
Marcouray
La Roche
Dochamps
Samrée
Baraque de
Fraiture
Regné
Fraiture
Salmchâteau
Vielsalm
St. Vith
Gouvy
Houffalize
Ouren
Manhay
Grandmenil
Erezée
Sadzot
Odeigne
Malempré
Tri-le-
Cheslaing

Amblève
Amblève
Salm
Lienne
Aisne
Ourthe
Ourthe
Ourthe
Our

XVIII
XXX
A

30
18
82 30
82 7
82
XVIII
VII

62
9SS
2SS
7
560
75
84
FB
116
9

Redeployed to
Bastogne, 26 Dec

Arrived
26-27 Dec

into XVIII Airborne Corps reserve.) At the same time, General Ridgway directed General Gavin of the 82d Airborne Division to reconnoiter a new defensive line farther north. The line that Gavin eventually chose ran generally along the line Manhay–Trois Ponts.

DISASTER AT MANHAY: 24 DECEMBER

Early on 24 December, Ridgway issued a warning order to Gavin to prepare to withdraw to the new line.[1] Although concerned for his open western flank, Gavin protested that his division had never relinquished any ground that it had gained. Furthermore, he was worried that such a withdrawal, following so closely on the withdrawal of the battered defenders of St. Vith through the paratroopers' lines, would have a devastating effect on the morale of his men.[2] However, by midmorning the question had become moot. Field Marshal Montgomery arrived at Ridgway's headquarters at Werbomont and insisted upon the withdrawal. The necessary orders were issued. Colonel Rosebaum's CCA/7 was ordered to move to high ground north of Manhay, leaving an outpost behind at the Manhay crossroads. The remainder of the 7th Armored Division was to deploy in defensive positions to the east. The 3d Armored Division, commanded by Maj. Gen. Maurice Rose, was to extend the line west to Soy and Hotton.

Maurice Rose was born on 26 November 1899 in Middletown, Connecticut. He enlisted in the 1st Cavalry Regiment, Colorado National Guard, in June 1916, and served on the Mexican border. He attended Officers' Training Camp in May 1917, and was appointed a second lieutenant, Infantry Reserve, in August. He joined the 353d Infantry Regiment at Camp Funston, Kansas, and was promoted to first lieutenant in December. He sailed to France in May 1918, and served in the St. Mihiel Offensive. After the Armistice he was assigned to the Army of Occupation in Germany, and returned to the United States in January 1920. While in Germany he was commissioned a second lieutenant in the Regular Army, and was then promoted to captain.

During the 1920s most of Rose's service was either at the Infantry School at Fort Benning or with infantry units. He transferred to the Cavalry on 1 August 1930. After graduating from the Army Industrial College in Washington in June 1941, he was assigned to command the 3d Battalion of the 13th Armored Regiment. Soon afterward he was appointed Executive Officer of the 1st Armored Brigade. In January 1942 he became Chief of Staff of the 2d Armored Division. In October 1944 he was appointed to command the 3d Armored Division in France, and soon thereafter was promoted to major general.

The 3d Armored Division had been activated in April 1941. After brief training in England, the division landed in Normandy and entered combat on 29 June 1944. As part of the VII Corps of the First Army, it participated in the breakout from Normandy in late July and early August, and continued eastward across northern France and central Belgium in August and September. After two months of inconclusive battle against the German Westwall near Aachen, the corps and the division were committed to the Roer offensive in mid-December. After initial success, their attack was halted due to the German Ardennes offensive. The 3d Armored Division was shifted south to join the XVIII Airborne Corps on 19 December.

The 2d and 3d Armored divisions were the only two heavy armored divisions in the U.S. Army. The authorized strength of the other fourteen armored divisions was 168 medium (M4) tanks, 77 light (M5) tanks, and 10,754 men. The Tables of Organization and Equipment (TO&E) of the 2d and 3d Armored divisions, however, called for 232 medium tanks, 158 light tanks, and 14,664 men.

The most serious immediate problem with the XVIII Corps, Christmas Eve plan was the role given to the 3d Armored Division, since theoretically the division was no longer an element of the XVIII Corps. The previous day the 3d Armored (minus CCB, which was engaged against Kampfgruppe Peiper near La Gleize) had been assigned to the newly arriving VII Corps, positioned just to the west of the XVIII Airborne Corps. But, in fact, only a fraction of the full division was available to General Rose, the division commander. Not only was CCB detached, but CCA was en route from First Army reserve near Eupen. Only CCR with a battalion each of light tanks, medium tanks, armored infantry, and artillery plus most of the division reconnaissance battalion and a company of engineers, was available to Rose. These had already been split into three major task forces (TF): TF Kane (commanded by Lt. Col. Matthew W. Kane) at Manhay, TF Orr (under Lt. Col. William R. Orr) at Dochamps, and TF Hogan (commanded by Lt. Col. Samuel M. Hogan), surrounded at Marcouray. In addition, Lt. Col. Walter B. Richardson's TF Richardson, the leading element of CCA, had arrived at Manhay late on the evening of 22 December. Since there was some confusion as to which of the two corps the 3d Armored Division was assigned, it was probably not important that the axis of advance of the II SS Panzer Corps was almost coincident with the seam between the XVIII Airborne and VII corps. The corps' boundary was just to the west of highway N-15, which was the locus of the proposed path of the II SS Panzer Corps.

The withdrawal of the 82d Airborne Division went very smoothly. Indeed, General Gavin later wrote, "in all the operations in which we have participated . . . I have never seen a better-executed operation than [this] withdrawal."[3] Colonel William Ekman's 505th Parachute Infantry Regiment pulled back and dug in on high ground west of Trois Ponts. Colonel Roy Lindquist's 508th Parachute Infantry Regiment fought a skillful delaying action against elements of the newly committed 9th SS Panzer Division while pulling back to new positions on the right of the 505th. Colonel Reuben Tucker's 504th Parachute Infantry Regiment continued the line farther to the right to Bras. Colonel Charles Billingslea's 325th Glider Infantry Regiment secured the division's right flank at Tri-le-Cheslaing. (All four of these regimental commanders were West Point graduates: Lindquist, the "daddy" of the group, was of the Class of 1930; Tucker was the Class of 1935; lanky, cool Billingslea was the Class of 1937; stocky, serious Eckman was the "baby" from the Class of 1938.)

General Gavin's only concern was an attack by the newly arrived Führer Begleit Brigade, which seized the small village of Regne, two miles east of Baraque de Fraiture (Parker's Crossroads).

From Regne a road led north into the valley of the Lienne Creek, the boundary between the 325th and 504th regiments. Thus the attack of the German brigade threatened the right of the 504th and the left of the 325th and the headquarters of both General Gavin and General Ridgway. Gavin directed a counterattack by the right-flank battalion of the 504th Parachute Infantry. That counterattack, supported by a company of medium tanks from CCB/9, successfully retook Regne that evening. The Americans were materially aided by the fact that Remer's Führer Begleit Brigade had been ordered to disengage so as to slip farther west to aid in the attack of the LVIII Panzer Corps at Hotton (see chapter 15).

Unfortunately the withdrawal of CCA of the 7th Armored Division at Manhay did not go smoothly. The movement that was executed that evening coincided with a renewed advance by the 2d SS Panzer Division. A column of German tanks, accompanied by dismounted panzergrenadiers, drove north on the N-15 highway, preceded (at least in American accounts) by a captured Sherman tank as a sort of Trojan Horse.

CCC/7, exhausted from its ordeal at St. Vith and caught while in the confusion of the withdrawal, easily succumbed to the surprise attack. The outpost at the Manhay crossroads was overwhelmed in minutes; seven medium tanks were lost without firing a shot. The Germans then penetrated the main position north of Manhay, again surprised and dispersed the defenders, and destroyed ten more tanks. The bewildered men of CCA fell back to the north and east, relinquishing their hold on the high ground north of Manhay.

Colonel Rosebaum, who had just been recommended for a Silver Star because of his superb defensive performance north of St. Vith a few days earlier, was the scapegoat for this disaster at Manhay. Reluctantly, in response to direct orders from General Ridgway, General Hasbrouck relieved Rosebaum of command of CCA/7. His replacement was Col. William S. Triplet, a West Point graduate of the Class of 1924, the "Thundering Herd."[4]

The German attack also cut off a minor force at Belle Haie, southeast of Manhay. This was Task Force Brewster, composed of seven tanks and an armored infantry platoon from Task Force Richardson, the leading element of Brig. Gen. Doyle A. Hickey's recently arrived CCA of the 3d Armored Division, and two companies of the 509th Separate Parachute Infantry Battalion.[5] All were under the command of Maj. Olin F. Brewster, Colonel Richardson's Executive Officer. Major Brewster attempted to withdraw to Malempré, but the Germans knocked out a tank at either end of the column, blocking the road. The survivors then fled on foot to the American lines where Brewster—to his astonishment—was admonished for abandoning government equipment by General Rose, who ordered court-martial charges prepared against the major for cowardice before the enemy. Brewster was never brought to trial, however, and the charges were eventually dropped.[6]

The American position along the north face of the German penetration had been hastily cobbled together on 21 and 22 December, thanks largely to the denial of St. Vith to the Germans. Despite the pessimism of Field Marshal Montgomery, who was apparently more respectful of German determination than the Americans, there was even talk of an early counteroffensive in the north. On 23 December, however, the Germans began to bypass St. Vith, and on Christmas Eve they had full use of the captured road hub: The American position between the penetration and the Meuse was completely unraveling.

As a result, the Germans seemed to have a clear exit from the Ardennes to the Condroz Plateau and the Meuse Plain south of Liège. General Gavin's right flank was again exposed to envelopment, threatening the entire front of the XVIII Corps. In light of Monty's expressed pessimism and his later exaggerated claims of Anglo-American cooperation in averting disaster, it is hard to undertand why he did not immediately commit the five-division British XXX Corps, which was fully available just north of the Meuse River, to restore the First Army's apparently sundered line. What were the field marshal's motives in leaving the outnumbered Americans to fight their battle unaided when substantial, well-rested British reinforcements were so close at hand? It is difficult to give him the benefit of any doubt.

On Christmas Eve Brig. Gen. Bruce Clarke's CCB/7, depleted to less than one-third its standard strength by its defensive effort at St. Vith, received an augmentation of at least one soldier: Cpl. Kenneth Neher, whom we last saw pulling himself from a manure pile in St. Vith late on 21 December. Neher had tried to rejoin the 38th Armored Infantry Battalion that night, but he soon got lost and kept running into groups of Germans infiltrating into St. Vith. At dawn he took shelter in an empty farmhouse west of St. Vith and slept fitfully through the day. That night he continued to walk to the west, keeping to forest lanes, but met no one, friend or foe. Finally, on Christmas Eve he found his battalion near Stavelot. Describing the incident after the war, he said that he was able to find "a house with a bathtub, where I took a most refreshing and enjoyable bath."[7]

Presumably Neher had finished his bath before CCB/7 was again on the move. General Ridgway had ordered General Hasbrouck to commit CCB from reserve to retrieve the defeat of CCA at Manhay. Before dark Clarke's men were again back in a defensive line, attempting to stop another German armored attack. Surprisingly, the German drive slowed, then halted. This was due less to the effectiveness of the exhausted General Clarke and his men than to the German execution of their mission. Fortunately for the Americans, the German threat was not as serious as it appeared. The attacking German force constituted less than half of the 2d SS Panzer Division. The main punch of the attackers was in the division's mixed panzer battalion (two companies of Panzer IVs and two companies of Panthers), which was finally in action after a frustrating series of fuel shortages that had delayed its entry into battle. In addition, most of the divisional reconnaissance battalion was available. However, the division's infantry elements, its panzergrenadier battalions, were still advancing on foot or bicycle, having sacrificed most of their mechanized mobility in the effort to get sufficient fuel to the panzers. Of the division's six infantry battalions, less than half were available to support the attack. Artillery support was also meager, consisting of only a single battalion of 105-mm howitzers. Once again logistical deficiencies were robbing the Germans of the fruits of their tactical competence.

Furthermore, Gen. Heinz Lammerding, commander of the 2d SS Panzer Division, had no intention of continuing the drive to the north. He was under orders to support the attack of the LVIII and XLVII Panzer corps west of the Ourthe River. As such, the attack to seize Manhay had been executed only to open maneuvering room for the division and other elements of the II SS Panzer Corps that were on the way to drive west and northwest to Hotton, Erezee, and Soy.

ANOTHER FAILURE AT MANHAY: 25 DECEMBER

On Christmas morning 1944 the situation appeared bleak for the tired, overextended elements of General Ridgway's corps. The 7th Armored Division, including its attached units, was a battered shell: CCA had been effectively routed at Manhay; CCB had been reduced to less than twenty medium tanks and the equivalent of a company of infantry; and CCR was still badly disorganized from the mauling it had received in its withdrawal over the Salm on 23 December. General Hoge's CCB/9 was in little better shape. Both the 112th and 424th Infantry regiments were numerically no more than half-strength due to battle casualties, frostbite, and battle fatigue, and at less than half-effectiveness due to exhaustion. The 82d Airborne Division was also suffering from severe casualties and fatigue. The 30th Infantry Division was in better physical shape than the other elements of the corps, but was still fully occupied with holding the 1st SS Panzer Division south of the Amblève River.[8]

In an effort to bolster the strength of the line north of Manhay General Ridgway requested that the 289th Infantry Regiment of the 75th Infantry Division be assigned to his command. (The 75th Division was already attached to the VII Corps.) General Hodges readily approved the request. For most of the remainder of the battle the 75th Division would be committed with its elements attached to other divisions: the 290th Infantry Regiment with the 3d Armored Division, the 289th Infantry Regiment with the XVIII

Airborne Corps, and later the 291st Infantry Regiment with the 2d Armored Division in the VII Corps. The divisional artillery battalions supported their assigned infantry regiments or reinforced the fires of the divisions to which the regiments were attached.[9]

During the last hours of Christmas Eve and the first hours of Christmas morning General Ridgway and General Collins of the VII Corps hurriedly put together a plan to regain the high ground around Manhay. By early morning on 25 December Col. Douglas B. Smith's 289th Infantry Regiment was in line north of Manhay with orders to support an attack by CCA of the 3d Armored Division against Grandmenil, just west of Manhay. At the same time, General Hasbrouck's 7th Armored Division, with a reorganized battalion of the attached 424th Infantry Regiment making the main effort, would retake Manhay.

The attack made slow progress on both axes of advance. General Ridgway was particularly dissatisfied with the progress of the 289th Infantry Regiment, which was disorganized by a German spoiling attack that erupted down the road from Grandmenil to Erezee. This attack was finally halted when a German tank was knocked out, blocking further advance down the road. The 289th's attack thus started late and was both hesitant and poorly executed. An exasperated Ridgway then appeared at the 3d Battalion Headquarters and, at least according to one account, bypassed the chain of command to give direct orders to the battalion commander to "take the next ridge in thirty minutes or be relieved of command."[10] In spite of Ridgway's warning, and whether or not the story is true, the green infantrymen of the 289th were unable to advance until the first elements of CCA/3, Task Force McGeorge (commanded by Maj. K. T. McGeorge), arrived on the scene. The American tankers were almost immediately bombed and strafed by American fighter-bombers who mistook them for Germans. By evening, little progress had been made in the drive on Grandmenil.

The 7th Armored Division also met fierce resistance in its efforts to retake Manhay. The division, now almost completely fought out, accomplished little. Ridgway again appeared near the front attempting to inspire the exhausted men forward. His effort was to no avail. By evening virtually no progress had been made in the effort to recapture Manhay.

THE TIDE CHANGES AT MANHAY: 26 DECEMBER

General Ridgway was keenly disappointed by the failure of the drives on Grandmenil and Manhay. He remained determined to continue the effort, however, and ordered additional reinforcements for the 7th Armored Division, bringing the 3d Battalion of the 517th Parachute Infantry Regiment forward from corps reserve. At the same time, the corps artillery was directed to mass eight battalions for a time-on-target concentration (TOT) on Manhay to support the attack. (The TOT was an American artillery innovation in which, giving due consideration to the greatly varying times of flight from widely separated battery and battalion positions, the projectiles arrive to explode simultaneously on or over the selected target with devastating effect.)

The continuous assaults by the Americans and the fighting of the past days had seriously eroded the strength of the 2d SS Panzer Division. An attempt had been made to divert attention from Manhay by an attack on the lines of the 325th Glider Infantry Regiment near Tri-le-Cheslaing, but this had been pushed back with heavy casualties. In addition, the clearing weather had released the American fighter-bombers to roam at will over the German rear areas.

It was clear to General Lammerding that his division could not hope to hold on against the growing American strength. As a result, he ordered the preparation of a fallback position south of Manhay.

By late evening of 26 December the 289th Infantry Regiment, with the support of the 3d Armored Division's tanks, was finally able to recapture Grandmenil. At the same time, the 3d Battalion of the 517th Parachute Infantry Regiment was able to push on and recapture the rubble that remained after the massive artillery preparation on Manhay. The crisis on the XVIII Airborne Corps right flank was over. In conjunction with the VII Corps Christmas battles taking place to the west, the American GIs had managed finally to seal the gaps opened in the first days of the German offensive.

THE FIGHT AT "SADSACK": 27 DECEMBER

Following the recapture of Grandmenil and Manhay, the Germans made one more serious effort to penetrate the lines of the XVIII Airborne Corps. On the morning of 27 December, elements of the 9th SS Panzer Division and the 62d Volksgrenadier Division (VGD) attacked the 3d Battalion of the 508th Parachute Infantry Regiment between the Salm River and the Lienne Creek.

The initial German attack was successful in overrunning much of the battalion's front-line positions. However, inspired by their commander, Lt. Col. Louis G. Mendez, Jr., the men of the battalion refused to collapse and fought on from their foxholes. Mendez was a West Pointer of the Class of 1940. When the German tanks drove on into the rear of the position the paratroopers rallied and pinned down the accompanying German infantry. Without infantry support the German tanks became vulnerable to tank destroyers and bazooka teams and were picked off one by one. Mendez then directed a counterattack with the assistance of a company from the reserve 2d Battalion and restored the 3d Battalion's front.

Meanwhile, southwest of Grandmenil, near Odeigne, the II SS Panzer Corps was preparing for another drive to the northwest with the 12th SS Panzer Division attacking through the positions of the 2d SS Panzer Division. The attack was scheduled for midnight, 27–28 December. Because of delays in movement caused by clogged roads and fuel shortages and an unexpected shift of elements of the 12th SS Panzer Division to the Bastogne front, the attack began with a mixed force from the 25th Panzergrenadier Regiment and Kampfgruppe Krag of the 2d SS Panzer Division, which was commanded by Maj. Ernst Krag and consisted of the reconnaissance battalion, a battalion of assault guns, and two infantry companies from the 2d SS Panzer Division.

Part of the German assault force, moving in the dark through extremely rugged terrain, got lost. But most of Kampfgruppe Krag advanced up a creek line without opposition through a gap of more than 1,000 meters between the 1st and 2d battalions of the 289th Infantry, which was attached to CCA of the 3d Armored Division. At 0200 the infiltrating Germans reached the village of Sadzot about 2,000 meters behind the front lines. The village was occupied by a 4.2" mortar unit, the 87th Chemical Battalion, and a tank destroyer platoon. The surprised Americans rallied quickly, however, and a bitter battle ensued for the village.

Word of the German penetration soon reached the CCA commander, Brig. Gen. Doyle Hickey, who committed the 509th Parachute Infantry Battalion, which was near Erezee, to take the village and plug the gap in the front lines. In the darkness the paratroopers ran into Major Krag's kampfgruppe, and a confused and hard-fought struggle ensued. The battle continued into the morning, when American artillery provided crucial support to the outnumbered paratroopers. By 1100 the Germans in Sadzot were cut off, but the battle was enlarging. German reinforcements advanced into the gap between the two battalions of the 289th, and General Hickey committed the 2d Battalion of the 112th Infantry.

The battle in and around Sadzot and farther south raged in a heavy fog throughout the day. The paratroopers pushed the Germans back, opening the way for an assault by the 2d Battalion of the 112th, which finally sealed the gap in the line of the 289th Infantry early on 29 December. Mutual exhaustion of Germans and Americans ended the battle for Sadzot, which had been dubbed "Sadsack" by the paratroopers of the now woefully depleted 509th Battalion.[11]

29 DECEMBER 1944–3 JANUARY 1945

The last days of 1944 and the first days of 1945 saw little action along the northern face of the German penetration, where the fronts of three American corps—VII, XVIII, and V, from west to east—had now established a firm, coherent line. Units were shuffled about, replacements were absorbed, and plans for a counteroffensive were made. Little combat occurred beyond clashes between opposing patrols and the usual harassing and interdiction fires of the artillery.

On the front of the XVIII Airborne Corps, preparations for the forthcoming counteroffensive involved a number of changes in organization. The 30th Division and 82d Airborne Division remained in the front lines. The 82d

Division was reinforced by the whole of the 517th Parachute Regimental Combat Team and the 551st Separate Parachute Battalion. The 7th Armored Division, CCB of the 9th Armored Division, the remnants of the 106th Division (essentially just the 424th Regimental Combat Team), the 112th Infantry Division of the 28th Division, and the 509th Separate Parachute Infantry Battalion, all passed into corps reserve. One major personnel change was the relief of General Hoge from command of CCB/9 and his appointment as Deputy Commander of the XVIII Airborne Corps under General Ridgway.

The Germans were making similar realignments. The failure of the II SS Panzer Corps to smash its way through the XVIII Airborne Corps, combined with the earlier failure of the drive by the I SS Panzer Corps on Elsenborn and the initial success of the Fifth Panzer Army attack farther south, had resulted in a major shift among the German forces in the Bulge.

On 27 December the LXVII Corps was detached from the Sixth Panzer Army and attached to the Fifteenth Army. The change meant that the Sixth Panzer Army was no longer responsible for the Elsenborn sector. Theoretically this meant that the army was now better aligned to continue the drive on the Meuse and to support the advance of the Fifth Panzer Army. Practically, of course, it was now no longer possibile to renew the drive to the north.

By 3 January much of the remaining strength of the Sixth Panzer Army had been stripped away and sent to the vicinity of Bastogne. The army now controlled three corps: the LXVI Corps with the 12th and 560th VGDs; Corps Group Felber with the 18th and 62d VGDs; and the II SS Panzer Corps with the 2d SS Panzer and the 116th Panzer divisions. Even the obvious loss of two panzer divisions from the army's roster does not adequately illustrate the loss of combat power for the Germans on the northern face of the Bulge. All six of the divisions remaining in the army had been badly hurt in the previous two weeks of fierce combat. The volksgrenadier divisions had all lost heavily in manpower and, with the possible exception of the 18th, were no longer capable of offensive action of any kind. The panzer divisions, although neither had been as roughly handled as the 2d Panzer Division had been by the 2d Armored Division in the Christmas battles, were seriously weakened in both armor and infantry strength. Whether or not they retained sufficient combat power to be able to hold back the expected American counteroffensive was a matter of conjecture for both the German and American high commands.

AT THE SHOULDER

During all of this activity along the volatile northern face of the Bulge west of Malmédy, the northern shoulder itself (Butgenbach and the Elsenborn Ridge) remained firm and was hardly tested by the Germans.

Private First Class Bert H. Morphis from Oregon had joined B Company, 1st Battalion, of the 26th Infantry Regiment of the 1st Infantry Division as a replacement rifleman on 13 June 1944 in Normandy. He was wounded at

Aachen on 20 September, and was still in the hospital when the 26th Infantry was committed to desperate battle at Butgenbach on 18 December (see chapters 5 and 11). He rejoined six days later after dark on Christmas Eve. After the war he reported that Butgenbach "was covered with a thick mantle of snow, silvery white in the moonlight. To top it off there was not a sound of war to be heard. Everything was deathly quiet in the snow."

Christmas Day was also quiet at the shoulder with no hint of the deadly struggles taking place farther west near Manhay. B Company was served a Christmas dinner that Morphis described as "turkey and the trimmings. . . . It was great." He ate his dinner standing up in a stable, underneath the farmhouse that served as the company command post, with the farmer's cattle looking on.

Morphis's description of the last week of December and the early days of January provides a vivid picture of general conditions throughout the Bulge and of the situation at the northern shoulder.

We started pushing the Bulge back slowly. We would move forward a short distance and dig in, advance again and dig in, and so on, sometimes three or four times a day. . . . And this was no ordinary "digging in." It was bitterly cold, and the ground was covered with two to three feet of snow. The ground was frozen so deeply and so hard it was almost impossible to penetrate. So we carried quarter pound blocks of TNT with detonators to loosen the frozen crust. With a pickaxe we would dig a small hole to accommodate the TNT, set it off then proceed to dig our foxhole. For this purpose we carried full size picks and shovels to expedite the frequent digging in. Moreover, since we were fighting in dense forest, we carried axes and crosscut saws. An open foxhole provided little protection from "tree bursts" from artillery shelling. Therefore it was necessary to put a cover of logs and soil over our foxholes. Our practice was to dig a hole just deep enough to work in, cut logs to provide a cover, cover the logs with dirt, then crawl inside and finish digging the hole to size. Frequently we would no sooner finish a shelter than we would move and leave it. I don't recall ever being so tired! Once I had a hole just about deep enough to cover, but instead I woke up much later lying on top of my shovel where I had fallen sound asleep while digging. Fortunately there had been no "tree bursts" in my vicinity.

I think everyone's most vivid memories are of the numbing cold. Mine certainly are! The cold was enough of an adversary without the Germans. Just staying alive took all one's ingenuity. I remember being on an outpost right in front of the German lines where the choice seemed to be between moving and being shot, or lying perfectly still and freezing to death. Somehow we survived, I with trench foot on only one great toe. . . . Food was always a problem. Our cooks were great about bringing hot food right up to the front lines when it was possible at all. However, most of the time during this period it was just not possible. I remember one two-week period when every morning and evening they brought each of us one Spam sandwich and a cup of coffee. When they started out it was all hot, but by the time they got to the front it was all cold. . . . But I was certainly glad when we got some "C" rations we could heat up and have a hot meal. We got a large supply of rations at one time, and almost immediately got orders to move out. We had to leave most of the rations behind; so we ate all we could before we left. I ate six cans of meat and beans and almost died from the overdose.[12]

17

ALLIED AND GERMAN STRATEGIC AND ORGANIZATIONAL DECISIONS

The Christmas battles, the relief of Bastogne on 26 December, and the subsequent course of the fighting on both flanks of the German penetration in the next day or two, revealed to both the German and Allied high commands that the course and nature of the battle had changed substantially. (There was one possible exception to this among the higher commanders: Hitler stubbornly insisted that one more intensive effort by his exhausted troops would bring them to and across the Meuse.)

The major change in the battle situation, clear to all senior commanders on both sides, was the fact that the Germans no longer dominated the battle-field as they had for nearly ten days. Further, while it was evident that the German offensive had not yet been definitively repulsed, unless the Germans were going to pull an unexpected rabbit out of a hat, the initiative was slipping from them, and was inexorably passing back to the Allies. Both sides thus recognized the need for new decisions, and both set about making these decisions. For the Allies, now including the French as well as the Americans and the British, the process was complicated by inevitable national differences and by clashes of personalities.

ALLIED STRATEGIC DECISION MAKING

From the beginning, General Patton saw in the German salient an opportunity to cut off and destroy a substantial element of the German Army. He had first expressed this view publicly at Verdun on 19 December. But he also recognized that the first task of a hard-pressed defender is to prevent an initially successful enemy from converting tactical success into a decisive strategic victory. In other words, the defender must do what is necessary to avoid los-

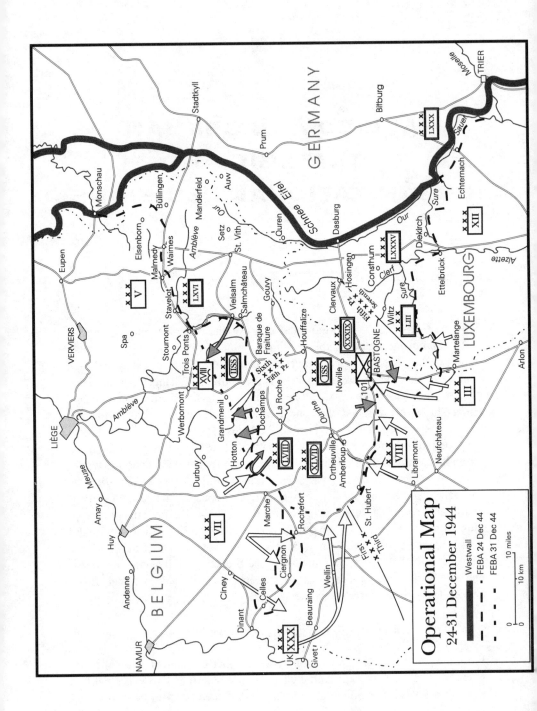

Operational Map
24-31 December 1944

Westwall
FEBA 24 Dec 44
FEBA 31 Dec 44

0   10 miles
0   10 km

GERMANY

BELGIUM

LUXEMBOURG

TRIER

Moselle

Bitburg

Stadtkyll

Prum

Echternach

Sauer

Sûre

XII

LXXX

Monschau

Eupen

Malmedy

Waimes

Büllingen

Elsenborn

Manderfeld

Auw

Our

Setz

St. Vith

Schnee Eifel

Ouren

Dasburg

Diekirch

Consthum

Hosingen

Clervaux

Ettelbrück

Martelange

Arlon

LXXXV

LIII

III

Alzette

Clerf

Wiltz

Sûre

Fifth Pz

Seventh

Ambléve

VERVIERS

LIÈGE

Spa

Stoumont

Trois Ponts

Stavelot

Vielsalm

Salmchâteau

Gouvy

Houffalize

Noville

BASTOGNE

101

Sixth Pz

Fifth Pz

La Roche

Ourthe

Dochamps

Grandmenil

Baraque de Fraiture

V

LXVI

XVIII

ISS

ISS

XXXXVII

VIII

Werbomont

Hotton

Durbuy

Ambléve

Meuse

Amay

Huy

Andenne

NAMUR

Dinant

Celles

Ciney

Ciergnon

Rochefort

Marche

Wellin

Beauraing

Givet!

St. Hubert

Ortheuville

Amberloup

Libramont

Neufchâteau

VII

CVIII

XLVII

UK XXX

First

Third

ing the war or battle before he can give serious attention to the actions required to win it. In the circumstances of this campaign, there were three essential Allied defensive tasks that took priority over all else: (1) hold the shoulders to limit the width of the German salient and thus indirectly its depth, (2) slow down the hostile advance by obstructing key movement axes, and (3) contain enemy spearheads to prevent a rear-area collapse.

The first of these tasks had been accomplished by about 20 December in the vicinity of Elsenborn in the north and Echternach in the south. The second task was accomplished between 19 and 26 December at St. Vith and Bastogne. The third task was accomplished in and around Celles on the twenty-fifth and twenty-sixth. Catastrophe having thus been averted, the Allies were now free to devise a new war-winning strategy, or to resume the one in effect when the German offensive disrupted it.

The plan that had been in effect was General Eisenhower's "broad front" strategy. Ike had adopted this as early as August 1944 and had adapted it to the somewhat changing circumstances of the Allied advances across France and the Low Countries in subsequent months. In early December, just before the German counteroffensive, this strategy had crystallized in plans for a main effort in the north, across the Rhine into the northern Ruhr region by Field Marshal Montgomery's 21st Army Group, and two secondary efforts by General Bradley's 12th Army Group: an offensive by the Ninth and First American armies across the Roer River toward and across the Rhine near Cologne, just south of the Ruhr; and another offensive, farther south, by the American Third Army through the Saar region to and across the Rhine near Frankfurt. There would be ancillary offensives still farther south by the 6th Army Group through Germany's Rhineland Palatinate and French Alsace, to and across the Rhine between Mannheim and the Swiss border.

This "broad front" strategy had been consistently and vehemently—almost bitterly—opposed by British Field Marshal Montgomery, who believed that the bulk of Allied resources should be concentrated in one area to overwhelm the enemy in conformance with the Principle of War that the British call "Concentration," and which American field manuals refer to as "Mass." Citing largely geographical and terrain reasons, Monty argued that that main effort should be in the north, directed toward the readily traversable area of the North German Plain, and under his command in the 21st Army Group.

Less vehemently, but just as firmly, American Generals Bradley and Patton had also opposed the "broad front" strategy. Their reasons were somewhat similar to Monty's. They also urged Concentration or Mass, but within the 12th Army Group in general, and Patton's Third Army in particular. This Bradley-Patton strategic concept was partly doctrinal (an American predilection for the Principle of Mass), partly chauvinistic (the Americans were providing the bulk of Allied forces, and so they felt that the offensive should be run by Americans), and very largely personal.[1] Although they tried to hide it, except from each other, Bradley and Patton both disliked Montgomery, and (somewhat unfairly) considered him to be an overly cautious—indeed, timid—commander, whose procrastination they believed would prolong the war. This was based in part on Monty's record, from 1942 on, of avoiding offensive operations unless he had an overwhelming preponderance of strength. This opinion had been reinforced in the previous six months, first by Montgomery's delays in breaking out of the Normandy Beachhead and, second, in reinforcing the airhead at Arnhem.

Before the German counteroffensive, Eisenhower rejected both of the "narrow front" recommendations for reasons that were partly military (essentially based on logistical considerations), partly political (to avoid appearing to favor either the Americans or British), and partly personal (a cautious man, Ike saw less risk in the "broad front" strategy). He had rebuffed Monty's most recent effort to raise the issue at Maastricht in early December. (See "Disagreement at Maastricht" in chapter 2.) Soon after the German offensive began, and the penetration broke direct communications between Bradley's headquarters and the headquarters of the Ninth and First armies, it will be recalled that Ike had placed both of those armies under Montgomery and his 21st Army Group headquarters. (See "Monty to Stage Center," chapter 9.) Eisenhower had made very clear his intention that this was only a temporary command adjustment, and that the Ninth and First armies would return to Bradley's command as soon as a linkup of the First and Third armies permitted a resumption of overland lines of communication between the headquarters of the 12th Army Group and the two northern armies.

"THIS MONTY BUSINESS"

Montgomery, however, saw in the situation created by the German penetration an opportunity finally to achieve the two objectives most dear to his heart: first, to become in fact, and probably in name, the overall Allied ground force commander on the western front, and second, to put into effect his "narrow front" strategy in the north, under the 21st Army Group. This was undoubtedly on his mind when he spoke on the telephone to Maj. Gen. Jock Whiteley, the British deputy G-3 in SHAEF Headquarters, on 19 December to suggest that he should be put in command of all American forces north of the German penetration. (See "Monty to Stage Center," chapter 9.) There was, of course, sound military logic behind that suggestion, and Eisenhower followed that course of action because of the logic.

It is not clear whether Monty was directly or indirectly behind criticism of Eisenhower's leadership that began to appear in the British press about 20 December, shortly after the scope and dimensions of the German offensive and breakthrough became evident. British war correspondents, particularly those assigned to Montgomery's headquarters, began attributing the German success and American failures to Eisenhower's decisions, particularly to the fact that he retained personal control over the ground forces of the Allied Expeditionary Forces. These correspondents suggested that the German breakthrough never would have happened had Montgomery been the overall ground force commander, as (these journalists suggested) he should by all rights have been. The appearance of these stories was attributed to Monty's influence by many senior American officers, including Bradley and Patton.

One reason for suspecting that Montgomery might have personally dropped a hint along these lines to the British correspondents may be found in the memoirs of Monty's Chief of Staff, Maj. Gen. Francis de Guingand.[2] Whether or not he was aware of any such effort by Monty, there is no question that de Guingand did everything within his power to offset such activity and to repair the damage done to Allied unity of effort and purpose by the British press criticisms. At one point during this period of tension in Anglo-American relations, de Guingand, who was unswervingly loyal to his commander while retaining the respect and friendship of American commanders and staff officers, spoke informally to a number of Allied correspondents at SHAEF to reassure them about what he called "this Monty business."[3]

The press-induced tension in Allied relations was at its height on 28 December when Montgomery and Eisenhower had a conference on Eisenhower's train at Hassalt, in the Netherlands, near Monty's headquarters. The purpose of the meeting was to plan for an Allied counter-counteroffensive against the German Bulge in the Ardennes.

Much of the meeting, however, was devoted to discussion of the renewed Allied offensive to the Rhine, once the Bulge had been eliminated. Eisenhower agreed with Montgomery that the main effort should be in the north by the 21st Army Group. (This, of course, had been the plan before the German offensive.) To assure adequate strength in that main effort, Ike agreed to leave the U.S. Ninth Army under the 21st Army Group. (It had already been agreed that the First Army would return to Bradley's 12th Army Group as soon as the First and Third armies linked up—presumably near Houffalize.) It is apparent from the subsequent correspondence that Monty then expressed his opinion that since he was in command of the main effort, he should also exercise operational command over the 12th Army Group, which was to make the secondary effort. This, of course, would mean that Monty would be the overall ground force commander in fact, and probably in name, for the final Allied offensive into Germany. Eisenhower apparently did not comment on this expression of opinion by Monty, assuming that the Britisher would realize that this was inconsistent with his (Eisenhower's) previously stated opinion on the subject.

Monty knew Ike well enough so that he should not have confused lack of comment with acquiescence. Nevertheless, this is what he did, in his enthusiasm for achieving his heart's desire. Interestingly, he communicated his version of the results of this meeting with Eisenhower to Gen. Sir Alan Brooke, British Army Chief of the Imperial General Staff. Even through Monty's eyes and words, Brooke seems to have assessed Ike's reaction better than Monty did! In his diary he wrote: "Monty has had another interview with Ike. I do not like the account of it. It looks to me as if Monty, with his usual lack of tact, has been rubbing into Ike the results of not having listened to Monty's advice!"[4]

The next day, 29 December, Montgomery followed up on what he thought was his triumph with a letter to Eisenhower, telling Ike how he should handle the assignment of overall ground force command to him. In giving a directive about this to Bradley, Monty didactically instructed Ike, "I therefore consider that it will be necessary for you to be very firm on the subject, and any loosely worded statement will be quite useless." He even told Ike how he should word the directive: "I suggest your directive should finish with this sentence: '12 and 21 Army Groups will develop operations in accordance with the above instructions. From now onward full operational direction, control, and coordination of these operations is vested in the C.-in-C. 21 Army Group, subject to such instructions as may be issued by the Supreme Commander from time to time.'" He then added: "I put this matter up to you again only because I am so anxious not to have another failure."[5]

It is not clear from his memoirs, or from other sources, whether Ike had given even the slightest thought to accepting Montgomery's almost insulting ploy to become the Allied ground force commander.[6] But if he had, steel was put into his backbone by a message he received that very same day (30 December) from General Marshall in Washington. Marshall had apparently heard rumors of Montgomery's effort to become overall ground force commander, and had read predictions in the British press that this would occur.

"My feeling is this," Marshall's message ran, "Under no circumstances make any concessions of any kind whatsoever. You not only have our complete confidence but there would be a terrible resentment in this country following [appointment of Montgomery as commander over an American army group]. I am not assuming you had in mind such a concession. I just wish you to be certain of our attitude on this side."[7]

Also on this day General de Guingand became concerned about the speculation in the British press, and about the possible reaction to this in Eisenhower's headquarters. He telephoned General Smith, Eisenhower's Chief of Staff, at the SHAEF Advance headquarters at Reims. Smith told him about the reaction of Ike and the staff (British officers as well as American) to Monty's arrogant letter of 29 December. As de Guingand wrote in his memoirs, "Since I was perhaps in closer touch with opinion in the outside world than my commander could be, I sensed that a difficult stage in Anglo-American relations had been reached and so I flew down and spent a night with Bedell Smith. . . . I had a chat with the Chief of Staff and . . . later in the evening we both went and had a long talk to the Supreme Commander."[8]

De Guingand discovered that, after discussing the matter with senior members of his staff, Ike had decided to inform the Combined Chiefs of Staff, through General Marshall, that they would have to choose between him and

Montgomery. There was little doubt in de Guingand's mind that Monty would lose that contest.

He told Eisenhower that his chief did not realize that his letter would precipitate such a crisis, and asked the Supreme Commander to wait for one day before sending his message to Marshall. De Guingand said that he was certain that, once Montgomery was aware of the storm he had aroused, he would not only back down, he would cooperate wholeheartedly.

At first neither Eisenhower nor his British deputy, Air Chief Marshal Sir Arthur Tedder, would agree to this. But, after General Smith urged Ike to give de Guingand a chance to talk to Monty, Eisenhower apparently agreed to delay his message for one day. Despite bad weather, early the next day de Guingand rushed back to Monty's headquarters and explained the situation to Monty. De Guingand reports (and Montgomery confirms) that Monty was genuinely surprised when he learned about the tempest his letter had stirred up.[9] It matters not whether he was really that naive. What matters is what he did. He at once drafted the following message to Eisenhower:

Dear Ike, I have seen Freddie and understand you are greatly worried by many considerations in these very difficult days. . . . I'm sure there are many factors which have a bearing quite beyond anything I realize. Whatever your decision may be you can rely on me one hundred percent to make it work. . . . Very distressed that my letter may have upset you and I would ask you to tear it up. Your very devoted subordinate Monty.[10]

The next day (1 January) Eisenhower responded:

Dear Monty, I received your very fine telegram this morning. I truly appreciate the understanding attitude it indicates. With the earnest hope that the year 1945 will be the most successful for you of your entire career, as ever, Ike.[11]

Ike did not tear up Monty's letter, but he did figuratively tear up his planned letter to the Combined Chiefs through Marshall. However, in a covering letter sending his plan to Monty that same day, Eisenhower had some pointed comments, including the following:

In the matter of command I do not agree that one Army Group commander should fight his own battle and give orders to another Army Group commander. . . . You know how greatly I've appreciated and depended upon your frank and friendly counsel, but in your latest letter you disturb me by predictions of "failure" unless your exact opinions in the matter of giving you command over Bradley are met in detail. . . .[12]

MONTY'S PRESS CONFERENCE

As de Guingand would have put it, Monty was "a good boy" thereafter, with one possible exception. This was when he held a press conference on 7 January, the purpose of which he described in his memoirs as follows:

I was perturbed at this time about the sniping at Eisenhower which was going on in the British press. So I sent a message to the Prime Minister and said that in my talk to British and American correspondents about the battle I proposed to deal with the story of the battle. I would show how the whole Allied team rallied to the call and how teamwork saved a somewhat awkward situation. I suggested I should then put in a strong plea for Allied solidarity. . . . The Prime Minister agreed. . . .[13]

While there can be little doubt as to the sincerity of Monty's intentions, the result was just the opposite of what he said he intended. He highly praised the courage and steadfastness of the American troops and their leaders. But he implied that the German early successes had been due to American laxity and ineptitude. He suggested that the situation was quickly restored primarily due to his own leadership, skill, and vigor. He also attributed to the very few British troops that he committed to the battle a far greater role and involvement than they had in fact had.

De Guingand later wrote: "I was not present, but from all accounts he was rather 'naughty,' or human enough to adopt the 'what a good boy am I' attitude." Exacerbating the inevitable negative effect of Monty's performance was a German psychological warfare coup, which is best described by a British journalist and historian, Chester Wilmot, as follows:

Writing after the war, Bradley . . . said: "When Montgomery's statement reached us, via the B.B.C. [British Broadcasting Corporation, the official British radio], my acutely sensitive staff exploded with indignation." Bradley correctly reports his staff's reaction, but he does not reveal the true source of the information. My [Wilmot's] dispatch to the B.B.C. was picked up in Germany, rewritten to give it an anti-American bias and then broadcast by Arnhem Radio, which was then in Goebbels's hands. Monitored at Bradley's H.Q., this broadcast was mistaken for a B.B.C. transmission and it was this twisted text that started the uproar.[14]

Despite his problems with "this Monty business," it is noteworthy that, a little over five years later, when Eisenhower was selected by the NATO alliance as the first Supreme Allied Commander, Europe (SACEUR), he recommended that Monty be his Deputy SACEUR. They served harmoniously together in that relationship in Paris for two years.[15]

ALLIED ASSESSMENTS, DECISIONS, AND PLANS

Eisenhower was also to some extent involved in the tactical/operational decision-making process. In fact, as indicated above, it was for the purpose of discussing tactical decisions that Eisenhower traveled to meet Montgomery on 28 December. Unlike Hitler, who was really Ike's counterpart as overall commander in chief in Western Europe, Eisenhower endeavored to avoid involvement in tactical details. However, as ground force commander, he was the counterpart of Rundstedt, and thus was responsible for overall tactical plans and concepts.

The relief of Bastogne on 26 December, following the smashing of the German spearhead at Celles on Christmas Day, made it evident that the time had come for the Allies to seize the initiative from the Germans and to return to the business of winning the war. The obvious first step in this return was to undo the damage that the Germans had done by creating the penetration or bulge. Apparently equally obvious, however, particularly in light of the events of the previous ten days, was the possibility that residual German combat power was such that the Germans could still interfere with the execution of whatever plans the Allies should design.

In fact, the possibility of renewed German interference with Allied plans was undoubtedly given more weight than it deserved. The intelligence sections of all of the major Allied general staffs, having been so thoroughly surprised by the unanticipated power of the German offensive, had now swung like a pendulum to the other extreme. The G-2s—from SHAEF, through the army groups, and the armies down to the corps—were now attributing to the Germans fancifully unrealistic capabilities. And, with one or two exceptions, the commanders were as apprehensive as their G-2s about the possibility of more German surprise attacks.

Nevertheless, again with one or two possible exceptions, these commanders were not fundamentally defeatist, and indeed had regained much of their former confidence about the inevitability of a relatively early Allied victory. And so, with generally comparable enthusiasm, but with widely varying degrees of urgency, these commanders and their staffs were now considering the various courses of action that would enable them to resume the prospective invasion of Germany.

There were four possible courses of action for dealing with the Bulge, and a few possible variants among these.

First, the Bulge (once contained) could at least theoretically be ignored.

Second, the nose of the salient could be punched in, and the Germans driven back to their starting point over the routes on which they had advanced.

Third, the Allies could take advantage of the bulge within the bulge (the Bastogne salient) to reduce the larger salient quickly, and to cut off those Germans who had advanced farther west.

Fourth, they could strike across the base of the salient, to cut off all of the Germans who had taken part in the penetration, as Patton had suggested at Verdun on 19 December.

There seem to have been no advocates of the first option. No responsible commander seems to have given any thought to the possibility that such a deep salient inside the Allied lines could be allowed to remain while resuming the offensive to the east.

There was at least one advocate of the second solution. Montgomery advocated direct but deliberate pursuit eastward of the Germans who had been defeated at Celles on Christmas Day. While the First Army held the northern flank of the corridor and the Third Army held the southern flank, the British XXX Corps, beefed up with American units, would act as a piston to push the Germans back.

The third solution appealed to most of the senior Allied generals, including Eisenhower, Bradley, and (apparently) Hodges. This was envisaged as simultaneous, converging attacks of the Third Army north from Bastogne and of the First Army south from the Hotton–Trois Ponts line, to meet near Houffalize.

The fourth solution, a drive to cut and seal off the base of the salient, from the vicinity of Diekirch in the south, and of Elsenborn in the north, was favored by Patton, and by at least one of the corps commanders, Joseph Lawton Collins, commander of the First Army's VII Corps. Patton envisaged the point of convergence to be somewhere between St. Vith and Prüm, depending on whether the southern axis was west or east of the Our-Sauer River line. Collins, who envisaged the northern arm as a drive south by his corps from the Malmédy area, seems to have been thinking of convergence in the vicinity of St. Vith.

For Patton, the argument in favor of the fourth solution was simple. "If you got a monkey in a jungle, hanging by his tail," he wrote in his diary (and repeated in a press conference on 1 January), "It is easier to get him by cutting off his tail than kicking him in the face."[16]

Collins discussed his idea with both General Hodges and Field Marshal Montgomery. On one occasion, when Monty was visiting his command post (probably 26 December) the American general and British field marshal seriously discussed the matter. Monty expressed his concern about the possibility of a new German offensive north toward Liège. When Collins pointed out that this would require the Germans to overwhelm "such top-flight divisions" as the 1st, 2d, 9th, and 30th Infantry divisions, the 2d and 3d Armored divisions, and the 82d Airborne Division, Monty shifted his position to raise a different objection. The roadnet south from Malmédy was inadequate to supply a corps offensive. Collins says he responded, "Well, Monty, maybe you British can't but we can."[17]

Collins submitted his plan to General Hodges on 27 December. In light of Montgomery's known objections, however, as an alternative he recommended a drive on Houffalize. Hodges approved the alternative.

Patton's diary, and two books based on the diary and other Patton letters and papers, not only reveal his views on this issue, but also explain—even though only by inference—why his views were not accepted.[18]

Shortly after 20 December Patton had moved his advanced command post to Luxembourg, where he was near Bradley. His diary reveals that the two generals met and consulted frequently, particularly at meals.

On 27 December Patton and Bradley agreed on the desirability of "an attack across the Sauer River at Echternach up the corridor to Bonn."[19] This would have been a drive through Bitburg and Prüm, which would have effectively slammed shut the door on the base of the German Ardennes penetration. "The possibilities of such an attack were very alluring, but in order to make it a success, at least three more divisions were necessary; that is three more in addition to the 11th Armored and 87th Infantry which Bradley had succeeded in getting released to me. Troops were not available, so the show fell through." Patton does not say, however, that Bradley's agreement was only lip service, since the army group commander had insisted that the 11th and 87th divisions be kept west of Bastogne, so that Patton could not use them for the attack north from Echternach.[20]

By 29 December Patton seems to have been reluctantly reconciled to the fact that he would not have a chance to exercise the fourth option, and that he would have to settle for a half-loaf by an attack from Bastogne north to Houffalize (the third option). However, on 3 January he thought he saw a chance to set the stage for the fourth option. He had arranged to have the 90th Infantry Division, under aggressive and competent Maj. Gen. James A. Van Fleet, shifted from the XX Corps to the Bulge front. He planned to commit the 90th in the XII corps sector, and then to try to shift one or two other divisions east, in order to have the strength that Bradley felt essential for the attack north of the Sure River. In this way he apparently hoped to persuade Bradley to let him initiate the fourth option.

However, Patton seems to have been outmaneuvered by Bradley. The army group commander rarely interfered with Patton's exercise of command of the Third Army. In this case, however, he persuaded Patton to commit the 90th Division to an offensive to eliminate the German salient southeast of Bastogne. "I let myself be overpersuaded by him in this connection and assume full responsibility for the error of subsequently engaging the 90th Division too far west."[21]

That he had not given up all hope of carrying out the fourth option is also revealed in another diary entry on 4 January: "I want to attack north from Diekirch but Bradley is all for putting new divisions in the Bastogne fight. In my opinion, this is putting good money after bad. In this weather, on the defensive, the Germans can hold us well enough so that we can never trap them there, whereas if we attack close to the base, they will have to pull out and we will regain the ground and probably catch just as many Germans as the other way." This entry was made after a discouraging day at the front, where he saw how skillfully the Germans held their positions near Bastogne. He concluded the entry with a paragraph that was uncharacteristically downbeat, but characteristically objective: "We can still lose this war. . . [T]he Germans are colder and hungrier than we are, but they fight better." He repeated this theme in a letter to his wife the next day: "Those Germans are vicious fighters."[22]

In his diary on 10 January Patton wrote about "the Germans having more nerve than we have. . . ." The immediate occasion for this remark was because he had been ordered to call off an attack and to send a division to protect Luxembourg because Allied intelligence thought they detected a threatening German force buildup near Trier. It was, however, also an expression of his frustration at not being able to carry out the fourth option.

Although Bradley and Eisenhower frustrated Patton by their caution, he knew that they were less cautious than Montgomery. Eisenhower and Bradley were also frustrated by Monty's caution. The British field marshal would not only not consider the fourth option, he was even reluctant to commit himself to the third. Having given Montgomery responsibility for the northern flank of the German penetration, Eisenhower resolutely refrained from meddling in how Monty carried out that responsibility. But Ike was concerned by Monty's apparent refusal even to consider a counterattack in the north after the Elsenborn shoulder had been solidified (about 20 December) and Peiper's task force eliminated (24 December). Indirectly, by queries and through liaison officers, Ike was able to convey to Montgomery his hope that the field marshal would order an early attack. Therefore, when he learned at a staff meeting on the morning of 27 December that Montgomery was ready to consider an attack, Ike exclaimed: "Praise God, from whom all blessings flow."[23] He immediately arranged to meet Monty the next day to discuss plans for coordination of attacks from north and south.

The flap about command was not the only controversy emerging from the conference on 28 December. Eisenhower was certain that Montgomery had committed himself to have the First Army begin the attack toward Houffalize on 1 January. Thus, when the attack did not take place, Ike had another reason to be annoyed with Monty. But the field marshal insisted that he had not agreed to attack before 2 or 3 January, and said he was now ready to make a commitment for the third.

So, finally, there was Allied agreement, and a plan of action, to carry out the third option for elimination of the Bulge.

GERMAN ASSESSMENT

By late afternoon on Christmas Day, it had become clear to the senior German commanders directly involved with the Ardennes offensive, and to those (like General Jodl of OKW) at higher headquarters, that the drive through the Ardennes had been halted. Although the situation was scarcely disastrous, and the offensive combat power of the German forces in the Ardennes was still considerable, they were no longer advancing, and in a few cases were being driven back by powerful American counterattacks.

In the north, Dietrich's Sixth Panzer Army had been completely frustrated in its effort to reach the Meuse River via the Amblève valley. The exhausted infantry divisions of the LXVII Corps facing Elsenborn Ridge were preparing for one more effort, but that was not likely to bring success. To the south, the 18th and 62d Volksgrenadier divisions (VGDs) of the LXVI Corps (originally the northern wing of Manteuffel's army, but transferred to

Dietrich late on 24 December, following the fall of St. Vith) had taken over the front held by the 1st SS Panzer Division "Leibstandarte Adolf Hitler" of the I SS Panzer Corps, now being pulled out of the front line. The southern wing of Dietrich's army, General der Waffen-SS Willi Bittrich's II SS Panzer Corps, had been committed in the renewed drive for the Meuse through St. Vith and Vielsalm.[24] Bittrich's divisions mounted initially unsuccessful attacks toward Manhay, and it soon became clear that they were not going to be able to make much forward progress.

In Manteuffel's Fifth Panzer Army sector, the leading divisions of the LVIII and XLVII Panzer Corps were also stalled: the 116th Panzer Division had failed to crack the 84th Infantry Division's positions in front of Verdenne and Hotton, and near Celles the 2d Panzer Division was fighting for its life against the American 2d Armored Division. Nor had the situation around Bastogne changed significantly, and three serious German attacks had failed to break the perimeter of the 101st Airborne Division.

Finally, the six divisions of Brandenberger's Seventh Army[25] were being roughly handled by the hard-driving fresh divisions of the III and XII Corps of Patton's Third Army. Unless they were reinforced, or the pressure against them somehow reduced, the troops of Brandenberger's army would be wholly unable to protect the southern flank of Manteuffel's army to the north and west.

THE GERMAN HIGH COMMAND REACTS

Hitler was frustrated by the situation, especially after the days of heady success early in the offensive. He believed the current ebb to be the result of a failure by German field commanders to follow his plan, and was little inclined to hear explanations of bad roads, bad weather, insufficient training and equipment, poor communications, Allied airpower, or anything else. He dismissed all of these as mere excuses.

General Alfred Jodl was a professional staff officer and an experienced as well as skillful military technician. He was also one of the few such officers in the German Army whom Hitler trusted, and in his position as Chief of Staff at OKW, he had to tread a fine line, balancing his commitment to military professionalism with his duty to Hitler as commander in chief.

At first, Jodl and his subordinates at OKW had little success in persuading Hitler that some new orders and directives were needed in order to avoid more extensive reverses or incipient disaster. However, at length the compelling facts and logic of the OKW staff began to have an impression on the dictator. In the late-day briefing on 26 December, Jodl was at last able to tell Hitler: "My Führer, we must face facts squarely. We cannot force the Meuse."[26]

Jodl's flat statement to Hitler echoed the sentiments of Field Marshal von Rundstedt (Supreme Commander in the West, or Oberbefehlshaber [OB] West), Field Marshal Model (commander of Army Group B), and General

von Manteuffel. Rundstedt, a Prussian general of the old school, was generally disgusted with Hitler and the Nazis, but was too much the apolitical professional soldier not to carry out his duties as best he could. Model, more personally loyal to Hitler, was a younger and more energetic commander. Even
so, Model had not been pleased with Hitler's plan for the Ardennes offensive,
but was generally unwilling to gainsay his Führer in public. Manteuffel also
had a reputation as an energetic and talented field commander, and had made
an impressive record on the eastern front. Manteuffel had also supported the
"Small Solution" attack plan, aiming to encircle Allied forces with a pincer
movement on Liège, as a more rational and realistic alternative to Hitler's
"Big Solution" grander design (see chapter 2).

The American relief of Bastogne the same day (26 December) had infuriated Hitler. Stymied in his desire to have the offensive reach and cross the
Meuse, Hitler had begun to search for an alternate and achievable goal for the
Ardennes offensive. The capture of Bastogne provided a convenient replacement for the lost grail of Antwerp. That redirection of Army Group B's main
effort governed German operations for most of the next two weeks, and led to
a series of bitter battles around Bastogne.

Although it was held as near-gospel by most panzer commanders that their
proper offensive role as armor was to bypass strongpoints and other centers of
resistance and leave them to be attended to by the infantry, that doctrine may
have been mistaken in respect to Bastogne. That town was such an important
road junction that it is possible to criticize General von Lüttwitz, commander
of the XLVII Panzer Corps for pulling the 2d Panzer Division away from
Noville and the north face of Bastogne on 23 December in order to renew the
drive for the Meuse crossings. Although Lüttwitz was certainly following
orders, emphasized by Manteuffel, which reflected Hitler's goals for the offensive, he was also in a position to assess the strength of American resistance at
Bastogne, the importance of the town for success of the German offensive, and
the German resources that he could bring to bear. Essentially, Lüttwitz's decision to swing the 2d Panzer west toward Dinant was reasonable, but in retrospect—and with the advantages of hindsight—it may have been an error.

There must be a question, though, whether an error-free German decision
was possible and, if so, whether it could have produced success. The choices
had become extremely difficult, and the German commanders increasingly
faced a series of Hobson's choices.

THE FIFTH PANZER ARMY ALTERS DIRECTION

Field Marshal Walter Model, commander of Army Group B and one of the
Führer's favorite (and most successful) field commanders, was too closely
subject to Hitler's immediate attention to order any actions that would result
in relinquishing hard-won ground or altering objectives. Instead, General von
Manteuffel assumed the decision-making duty, although with Model's tacit

approval at every step. Manteuffel began issuing his directives at once, and before dawn on 27 December the German military machine in the Ardennes was beginning to shift its main line of operations.

First, Manteuffel shifted the newly committed Führer Begleit (Escort) Brigade of Col. Otto Remer from the LVIII Panzer Corps front opposite Hotton to the thinly held sector west of Bastogne, to provide some "teeth" for a renewed attack against the American defenders of that town. Second, the Fifth Panzer Army commander directed that Lauchert's badly battered 2d Panzer Division be withdrawn eastward through Rochefort, falling back behind the new, defensive positions of the XLVII Panzer Corps's 9th Panzer and Panzer Lehr divisions.

Until this time General von Lüttwitz had bifurcated responsibility both for the operations against Bastogne, and for the Marche-Rochefort sector to the west as far as the tip of the Bulge. Now Manteuffel simplified Lüttwitz's problem. The XLVII Panzer Corps would retain responsibility primarily for the western sector around Rochefort. Operations around Bastogne were to be directed by experienced Lt. Gen. Karl Decker and his XXXIX Panzer Corps headquarters, just released from OKW reserve. Decker took control of the 26th VGD, part of the Panzer Lehr Division, and other units on the northern and eastern faces of the Bastogne salient. Finally, however, Decker's corps was temporarily subordinated to Lüttwitz's XLVII Panzer Corps (over von Lüttwitz's strong protests—he did not want the still-bifurcated responsibility), thus briefly creating Armeeabteilung (Army Command) Lüttwitz.[27]

Karl Decker was born on 30 November 1897 in Borntin in Pomerania. He had entered the German Army as an officer-candidate in September 1914, securing a lieutenant's commission in the 54th Infantry Regiment in July 1915. Selected to remain in the postwar Reichswehr, he volunteered for duty with the new panzer troops in the mid-1930s. He served in the Polish campaign as a lieutenant colonel commanding the 38th Antitank Battalion of the 2d Panzer Division. Decker commanded the 1st Battalion of that division's 3d Panzer Regiment during the campaign in France the following year, and became commander of the regiment in mid-May 1941, on the eve of the invasion of Russia. He was promoted to colonel in February 1942, and commanded the 21st Panzer Brigade from June to September 1943. Still a colonel, he took command of the 5th Panzer Division in September 1943, and was promoted to generalmajor that December and to generalleutnant the following June. Decker, assigned to command the XXXIX Panzer Corps on 15 October 1944, was a dedicated, courageous, and hard-driving commander, who had gained a reputation for getting the job done even under very trying conditions.

THE SIXTH PANZER ARMY REDIRECTS ITS EFFORT

At the same time that these command changes were taking place in the Fifth Panzer Army, the Sixth Panzer Army on the northern face of the Bulge was also undergoing a change of objective and some alterations of its command structure. Colonel General Dietrich and his panzers had been wholly unable to widen the breakthrough north of Vielsalm. The recent ordeal of Kampfgruppe Peiper was a clear signal that they were unlikely to be able to widen the gap in the near future. Accompanying the shift of the main effort from the Sixth Panzer Army sector south to the Fifth Panzer Army's sector was a shift of troops and resources toward Manteuffel's army at the expense of Dietrich's.

Parallel to the concentration of forces in the south around Bastogne, Army Group B and OKW had adjusted the northern front covered by Dietrich's Sixth Panzer Army. On 27 December, the LXVII Corps, exhausted from its exertions against the strong American positions in the Elsenborn Ridge area, was turned over to the Fifteenth Army.

Although this move deprived Dietrich of the services of four infantry divisions (3d Parachute Division and 12th, 246th, and 277th VGDs), all of them had suffered heavily in combat, both because of effective American resistance and because most of their infantry were poorly trained replacements. The restructuring, in fact, allowed Dietrich to concentrate his remaining resources toward making a breakthrough in the Manhay sector.

Meanwhile, Gen. Wilhelm Mohnke's 1st SS Panzer Division Leibstandarte Adolf Hitler, the unit to which Peiper's kampfgruppe belonged, disengaged from its sector around Trois Ponts and fell back on St. Vith. There, German supply and repair troops worked furiously to cobble together an operational panzer battalion from the armored detritus left over from the destruction of Peiper's kampfgruppe and Leibstandarte's other battles with the Americans.

The sector that had been held by the 1st SS Panzer Division now came under the control of the 18th and 62d VGD of the LXVI Corps, originally part of the Fifth Panzer Army, now under the Sixth. West of the LXVI Corps sector, the II SS Panzer Corps (with the 2d SS Panzer "Das Reich" and the 9th SS Panzer "Hohenstaufen" divisions) was to continue efforts to batter its way through the U.S. XVIII Airborne Corps. The 12th SS Panzer Division "Hitlerjugend" was sent forward to support the II SS Panzer Corps attacks, effectively leaving the I SS Panzer Corps with only the remnants of Mohnke's 1st SS Panzer Division. As soon as that division had completed its hasty and half-baked refit at St. Vith, it was to move to the Bastogne area where it would join with other reinforcement divisions released from OKW reserves to attempt the capture of Bastogne. It was sent south on 28 December to provide the major combat power for General Decker's XXXIX Panzer Corps.[28]

GERMAN CONCENTRATION AGAINST BASTOGNE

The withdrawal of the 1st SS Panzer Division and the shift of effort in Dietrich's sector southwest to the Manhay area, were only part of Hitler's change of plan. During the last week of December, additional changes took place. By that time, the 167th VGD and most of the 3d Panzergrenadier Division had also arrived to reinforce Decker's corps, while the Führer Begleit Brigade had arrived on the western face of the Bastogne salient, near Hubermont, to stiffen the forces of the XLVII Panzer Corps in that area, which otherwise consisted primarily of the 115th Panzergrenadier Regiment of the 15th Panzergrenadier Division. Together, these forces undertook the first German effort to reclose the ring around Bastogne, a limited attack launched on 30–31 December.

Additional forces soon followed. The 340th VGD arrived in the Bras-Benonchamps sector of the west face of Bastogne at the beginning of January, and came under the command of Gen. Hermann Priess's I SS Panzer Corps, which had taken responsibility for the northern face of the Bastogne salient, a line running from Wardin (east of Bastogne) westward to a point about two kilometers northeast of Mande–St. Etienne. This new sector for Priess's corps was at first held only by the newly arrived 340th VGD and the 77th and 78th Grenadier regiments of Kokott's battle-worn 26th VGD,[29] but Priess was reinforced by the 9th SS Panzer Division "Hohenstaufen" and the 12th SS Panzer Division "Hitlerjugend."

Thus, by 2 January, facing the Americans of the III and VIII Corps in and around Bastogne there were three German corps, in which there were three SS panzer divisions, most of two panzergrenadier divisions, one parachute division, and three volksgrenadier divisions, along with two panzer brigades and elements of another panzer division (Panzer Lehr). Moreover, Manteuffel had also worked hard to concentrate artillery and other supporting arms to work with this aggregation of combat divisions.

Facing this formidable German concentration the U.S. III and VIII corps fielded four armored, one airborne, and three infantry divisions. Against these experienced and well-equipped units of Patton's hard-driving Third Army, the German force was not quite enough.

The command changes in the final days of 1944 were not the last rearrangement the Germans were to make in the Ardennes. They did, however, set the pattern for the remainder of the campaign, and presaged the shift of the most intense action from the north to the south. For the first two weeks of January, the focus of German activity was directed by Manteuffel's Fifth Panzer Army toward the Bastogne area. The shift of the SS Panzer divisions away from Dietrich's command to Manteuffel's is clear illustration of the failure of the Sixth Panzer Army to achieve significant battlefield success.

ASSESSMENT

That the German Army could manage such a shift of effort and forces in unfavorable terrain and under conditions of enemy air superiority and uncertain supplies (especially of motor fuel), and do it all in the middle of winter, is testimony to the enduring quality of that army and its leadership. In the face of these difficulties, the shift in effort took several days to effect, and indeed the entire task was not completed until the beginning of January.

Unfortunately for the Germans, and despite their best efforts, they were not able to recover the momentum of the battle. Determined efforts to isolate and capture Bastogne would produce nothing but high casualty lists for both sides, along with further diminution of the German Army's waning combat capabilities. Had the Germans broken off their efforts in the Ardennes in late December, once the drive on the Meuse had failed, the forces available for the defense of western Germany would have been considerably greater, and it is unlikely that the forces controlled by OB West, despite the huge losses of the Ruhr encirclement, would have collapsed in late March and early April. (Indeed, one might speculate that that encirclement would not have been likely to occur.) On the other hand, by late December 1944 the complete defeat of Germany was really only a matter of time. The continuing struggle in the Ardennes served to prevent the Allies from mounting any major operations until late January, although the time purchased for Germany by continuing the battle was extremely costly in terms of troops and equipment. Hitler's decision to continue the offensive was foolish, and unjustifiably wasteful of German lives. Whether it significantly shortened or lengthened the war is debatable.

18

THE CONTINUING BATTLE
FOR BASTOGNE

THE SITUATION AROUND BASTOGNE AFTER CHRISTMAS

The reorientation of German offensive efforts against Bastogne, which had been decided upon by the high command just after Christmas (see chapter 17), ran headlong into the continuing offensive of Patton's Third Army. Patton was pushing his troops hard not only because it was in his nature to press his offensives energetically, but because he knew that it was essential to relieve the pressure on General Hodges's First Army and to stop the momentum of the German offensive. The First Army had been hard hit in the fighting for St. Vith and the "fortified goose-egg." Patton believed that this, coupled with Field Marshal Montgomery's cautious instincts, precluded any early counteroffensive from the north to slow the German drive. The situation was both a frustration for Patton, because the Third Army would have to bear the brunt of the fighting, and a balm to his egotistical nature. If the Third Army was going to do all the work, it would get all the credit and glory, too.

The corridor that the 4th Armored Division had opened into Bastogne was at first very tenuous. Major General Millikin's III Corps, especially Major General Gaffey's 4th Armored, did its utmost to widen the corridor and make land communications with Bastogne more secure. Fortunately for the Americans, the German forces immediately available to interfere with their efforts were spread thin. The principal German formations sent toward Bastogne as reinforcements before Christmas, the 9th and 167th Volksgrenadier divisions (VGDs), were thrown piecemeal into fighting east of town as they arrived. These divisions joined the 5th Parachute Division, the Führer Grenadier Brigade, and the 901st Panzergrenadier Regiment of the Panzer Lehr Division, all heavily engaged in resisting the northward drive of the III Corps 26th, 35th, and 80th Infantry divisions.

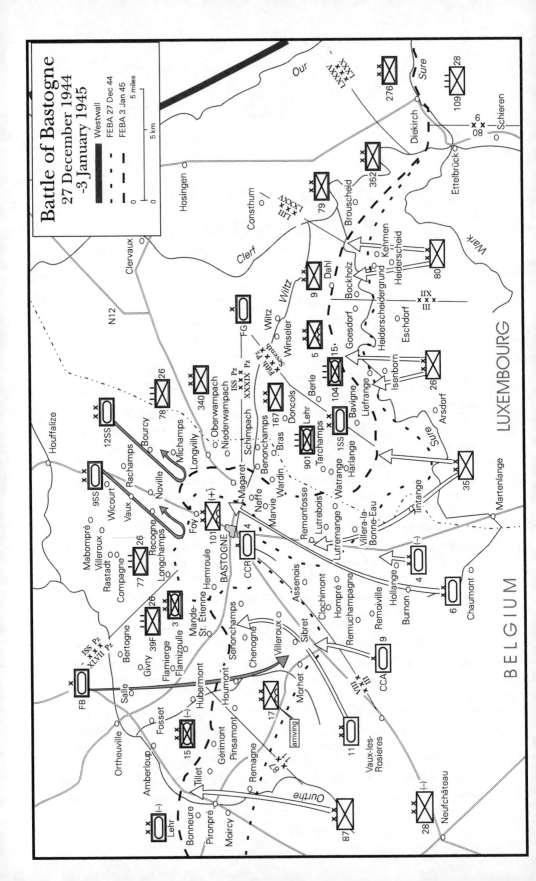

Battle of Bastogne
27 December 1944
-3 January 1945

Westwall
FEBA 27 Dec 44
FEBA 3 Jan 45

0   5 km
0   5 miles

This was the situation at the beginning of eight days of nearly continuous, confused combat south, east, north, and west of Bastogne. This battle was fought in bitterly cold weather along a front of about sixty miles, extending from St. Hubert in the west, around the Bastogne salient, to Ettelbruck in the east. Both sides had offensive missions, and in a fashion unusual in warfare, the determined opposing commanders—Manteuffel and Brandenberger on one side, Patton on the other—refused to relinquish the initiative. For the first three of these nine days the activities all along the front were sustained, but essentially local, as both sides jockeyed for position while building up their strengths by calling in additional forces to take part in their planned offensives. There followed two days of most intensive combat, as the two offensives jumped off almost simultaneously, and then each ground to an abrupt halt. While the Americans had slightly the better of these two bloody days of battle, they were unable to advance significantly. Since both sides had expected success, both sets of commanders exhorted and prodded their fighting subordinates to even greater efforts, while they and their staffs reassessed the situation, juggled units, and committed more forces to the battle. The climax was reached in roaring combat through the first two days of the new year. By 3 January American superiority in numbers, matériel, and supplies began to assert itself. Slowly the lines began to move northward as the exhausted Germans, still fighting bitterly and skillfully, began to relinquish ground all along the line.

SOUTH OF BASTOGNE: 27 DECEMBER

The relief of Bastogne on the day after Christmas left the German divisions on the southern face of the Ardennes salient in an awkward position. They were arrayed in an irregular circle facing the town from all directions. But with the road to Bastogne from the south now reopened that circle was broken, and Patton's Third Army had driven a wedge into the southern flank of Manteuffel's Fifth Panzer Army. By dawn on 27 December most of the Fifth Panzer and Seventh armies were involved in the battle for Bastogne, facing the Third Army's III and XII corps, with Major General Middleton's VIII Corps preparing to reenter combat.[1] The westernmost German units in the Bulge were the 2d, 9th, and Lehr panzer divisions, all under the command of Lüttwitz's XLVII Panzer Corps. Bayerlein's Panzer Lehr Division was the only one of these three actively engaged, with a screen composed of its anti-tank, engineer, and FLAK battalions (later most of the division) on a thirty-five-kilometer front. This thin screen faced the 6th Cavalry Group, which itself was screening the assembly areas for the 11th Armored and 87th Infantry divisions, roughly between Wanlin and Remagne. The British 29th Armoured Brigade had also moved forward to take positions west of the cavalry. However, these Allied units did little more than patrol and probe cautiously at their opponents.

Southeast of Panzer Lehr's screen lay the interlaced positions of the 115th Panzergrenadier Regiment[2] of the 15th Panzergrenadier Division (clustered around the village of Sibret, about five kilometers southwest of Bastogne) and the Führer Begleit Brigade, which was still arriving from Manhay to the north, where it had been holding a position on the left of the 116th Panzer Division (see chapter 15). On 27 December these units were just west of Bastogne, while the battle-weary and overextended 26th VGD held positions that not only partly screened the assembly areas of the Führer Begleit Brigade and the 115th Panzergrenadier Regiment, but also faced the American positions northwest, north, and northeast of the town. This was a front of twenty-seven kilometers, from Mande–St. Etienne north and east past Noville, then southeast to the vicinity of Benonchamps. The American perimeter north of Bastogne, facing these German units, consisted of Combat Command R of the 4th Armored Division near Assensois and Mande–St. Etienne, then continuing eastward to Neffe, the 327th Glider Infantry, the 502d Parachute Infantry, and the 506th Parachute Infantry regiments of the 101st Airborne Division.

The 3d Panzergrenadier Division was expected to arrive from the OKW reserve within a few days, between 28 and 30 December, and would assemble behind the screen of the 26th VGD. Before that happened, though, Colonel Kokott's meager forces were so thinly stretched that he had to employ support and technical troops to help his depleted infantry units hold this front, which stretched 5,600 meters from Sibret northwest to Pinsamont. To further complicate the situation, three other German volksgrenadier divisions were moving into position on the east side of Bastogne, marching slowly over the miserable, muddy, icy, twisting roads already clogged with supply columns and support units.

On 27 December, the 26th VGD's feldersatz (field replacement) battalion,[3] along with the 901st Panzergrenadier Regiment of General Bayerlein's Panzer Lehr Division, were transferred to the command of newly promoted General Heilmann's 5th Parachute Division. East and south of the 26th VGD's left-flank positions, essentially from the vicinity of Magaret south toward Lutrebois, the German front lines were held by detachments and patrols from the 78th Grenadier and the 901st Panzergrenadier regiments. This area was assigned to the 167th and 340th VGDs, although only the lead elements of the former were anywhere in the area on that day. The 167th VGD had been released from OKW reserves, and the 340th from Fifteenth Army reserves (see chapter 14).

The other German infantry division bound for the east side of the Bastogne perimeter was the 340th VGD. This unit, containing the 694th, 695th, and 696th Infantry regiments, had originally been formed as the 340th Infantry Division in January 1941 with East Prussian personnel. Initially serving in rear-area and garrison duties, mostly in northeastern France, the division was transferred to the Russian front in May 1942. The 340th served on the southern sector of the front and suffered heavy losses in fighting around Kiev (November 1943–January 1944). Badly mauled again in the spring of 1944, the division's remnants were withdrawn for refitting that summer and reformed as a volksgrenadier division in Germany in early autumn through the inclusion of the still-incomplete 572d Division. It was first committed to combat in the Jülich area in November, where it suffered heavy casualties. The division had not recovered from those losses when it was transferred to the Ardennes. Commanded by Oberst Theodor Tolsdorff, the division contained an unusually high proportion of veterans. However, it had only about 7,600 officers and men (barely 75 percent of authorized manpower), and its assault gun company had only nine of fourteen authorized JgPz-38(t)s when the division was transferred to the Seventh Army in the last week of December.

While the 340th and 167th VGDs were arriving as rapidly as the miserable roads would permit, about 70 percent of Col. Werner Kolb's 9th VGD had arrived in its planned assembly areas by 27 December. The 9th VGD was prepared to relieve the thinly stretched and battered Führer Grenadier Brigade along the Sure River.[4] This undertaking was complicated not only by the slow arrival of the volksgrenadiers (the remainder of the division[5] did not reach the area for another three days), but also by the continuing attacks of the 26th Infantry Division, pushing hard into the Sure valley from the south.

Werner Kolb was born in Burbach on 27 July 1895, and joined the 55th Infantry Regiment in early August 1914, just after the start of World War I. Although he won a field commission as a lieutenant of reserves in November 1915, he left the army in 1919, shortly after the end of the war, and returned to civilian life. He was recalled to duty as a senior lieutenant when the army expanded in 1938, and led a company in the 36th Infantry (part of the 9th Infantry Division) in Poland in 1939 and in France in 1940. Promoted to major in August 1940, he led the II Battalion of the 36th Infantry in the invasion of Russia in 1941. He served continuously on the eastern front, gaining promotion to lieutenant colonel in April 1943, and rising to command of the 36th Infantry in July 1943. Kolb was promoted to colonel and took command of the 9th VGD that November. Thus he was one of the few veterans of the old 9th Infantry Division to serve with its successor, the 9th VGD, when that division was committed to action in the Ardennes in December 1944.[6] An infantry commander of considerable experience, he was a dependable rather than brilliant officer, typical of the methodically efficient men on whom the German Army depended for much of its day-to-day operation.

Farther east, the 79th and 352d VGDs held the front line for the LXXXV Corps, covering the front from the hamlet of Tadler east to Gilsdorf. These German troops faced the 80th Infantry and part of the 5th Infantry divisions, both part of Major General Eddy's XII Corps. The rest of the 5th Infantry Division and the 4th Infantry Division faced the LXXX Corps, containing the 212th and 276th VGDs across the Sauer River between Gilsdorf and Echternach. The four volksgrenadier divisions of the LXXXV and LXXX Corps were all on the defensive, and were under heavy American pressure, especially from the 80th Infantry Division. Since Eddy's corps had driven north nearly to the banks of the Our and Sauer Rivers, his troops were able to relax a little. The bulk of the Third Army, and most of General Patton's attention, were concentrated on the Bastogne corridor. The battered troops of the LXXX Corps were grateful for a respite and did nothing to provoke an American response.

The relief corridor created by Combat Command R of the 4th Armored on 26 December entered the perimeter just southeast of the center of the 327th Glider Infantry Regiment's sector. This left most of the 327th Glider Infantry Regiment west and north of the corridor, while the 3d Battalion, which was on the right and south of the 501st Parachute Infantry Regiment, faced the 901st Panzergrenadier Regiment around Marvie and Neffe.

The 901st had been left behind when the Panzer Lehr Division swung south of Bastogne on 23–24 December, and by 27 December held the extreme right (northwest) flank of the Seventh Army's LIII Corps. Left of the 901st, and to the southeast, recently General Heilmann's 5th Parachute Division was heavily engaged not only with Combat Commands A and B of Gaffey's 4th Armored Division, but also with the 35th Infantry Division. Heilmann's division was supported by the remainder of the 15th Panzergrenadier Division, held in reserve east of Harlange.[7]

West of the Corridor: 27–29 December

On 26 December the 9th Armored Division, which was essentially the division headquarters and Combat Command A, was transferred by Third Army Headquarters from the XII Corps to the VIII Corps. Relieved by Combat Command A of the 6th Armored Division early that day, by evening CCA/9 was on the road westward to a new assembly area two kilometers northeast of Neufchâteau. Before noon on 27 December CCA/9 was moving northeastward, along the Neufchâteau-Bastogne highway toward Bastogne. Led by Task Force (TF) Collins (under Lt. Col. Kenneth W. Collins), CCA's mission was to attack Sibret, which was held by elements of the 26th VGD and the Führer Begleit Brigade, to help the weary troops of CCR/4 widen the corridor that they had created the previous day.

This advance by CCA/9 coincided with the first German effort to reinvest Bastogne, which was an attack by Colonel Otto Remer's Führer Begleit Brigade west of the corridor in the vicinity of Sibret late on 27 December. The brigade's attack had barely begun before it was struck on its right flank by TF Collins, supported by fighter-bombers. The Americans drove through Sibret to the edge of Chenogne, while the Germans hastily changed front from east to south.

Although delayed by American mines laid when the VIII Corps retreated through the area nine days before, TF Collins tried to secure Sibret during the afternoon. Collins's single tank company, shooting at everything in sight, drove most of Sibret's defenders (from the 115th Panzergrenadier Regiment) into the cellars, but was unable to capture the town. Collins's forces also clashed with some of Remer's Führer Begleit troops. TF Karsteter (under Lt. Col. Burton W. Karsteter), which had been following TF Collins, swung northeast to avoid getting caught up in the fight at Sibret, and pushed into Villeroux. Karsteter's column, led by his two tank companies, was unable to secure the village before darkness fell, due mostly to lack of infantry support, and withdrew in early evening. The day's fighting had consisted of a series of uncoordinated meeting-engagement contacts between advancing opponents, neither of whom had really expected to encounter any significant enemy. Sibret was now in no-man's-land.

On 28 December, the bulk of the Führer Begleit was occupying a 4.5-kilometer sector of the line, but its renewed attack through Sibret made no headway. Fortunately for the Germans, an American counterattack delivered in the same area where the fighting had taken place the previous day also made no real progress. Combat Command A of the 9th Armored became even more heavily involved in fighting in the Sibret-Chenogne area. Although TF Karsteter had been unable to clear Villeroux completely the previous day, on 28 December, after a ferocious bombardment by Allied fighter-bombers and a heavy pounding from VIII Corps artillery, the last Germans were driven out of the village's smoking ruins. TF Collins enjoyed less success; its attack was delayed until nearly noon by a persistent ground fog. Advancing from Sibret northwest toward Chenogne, it came under heavy enfilading fire from the Führer Begleit Brigade. After surpressing this fire, Collins suspended his advance and laagered for the night. Sibret, however, was now in American hands.

Meanwhile, Generalmajor Walter Denkert's 3d Panzergrenadier Division had been ordered from the LXVII Corps into the Fifth Panzer Army area on 26 December, but was still moving into position on 27 December. Walter Denkert was born on 23 February 1897 in the port city of Kiel. He entered the German Army as a wartime volunteer on 22 August 1914, and gained a reserve lieutenant's commission in the 23d Infantry Regiment. Like most reserve officers, he was not selected for the postwar Reichswehr, and he left active duty on 30 September 1919 to become a policeman. He was brought back into active duty as a major and commander of the antitank company in the 22d Infantry Division's 65th Infantry Regiment on 15 October 1935.

Denkert, promoted to lieutenant colonel in March 1939, commanded the II Battalion of the 271st Infantry Regiment (part of the 60th Infantry Division) in Poland and France, and then served in a series of staff posts from December 1940 to July 1941. He next commanded the 47th Infantry in the redesignated 22d Airlanding Division (Motorized) for two months: July–August 1941. He was promoted to colonel in February 1942 while commanding the 8th Motorized Infantry Regiment of the 3d Motorized Infantry Division. Beginning in September 1942 he next served with the 19th Panzer Division and was promoted to generalmajor in early June 1944. In October he took command of the 3d Panzergrenadier Division. Denkert was an experienced and able, but not exceptional, commander. His staff assignments, despite his lack of formal staff training, indicated considerable intelligence and ability.

The 3d Panzergrenadier Division was a prewar Regular German Army infantry division, manned largely by Prussian recruits. It fought in the 1939 and 1940 campaigns, and was motorized in the autumn of 1940, becoming the 3d Motorized Infantry Division. The division served in Army Group Center during the opening stages of the invasion of Russia, and then took part in the Stalingrad campaign as part of Army Group South. It was virtually destroyed in the Stalingrad encirclement, and was re-formed in France during the spring of 1943 as the 3d Panzergrenadier Division, essentially by renumbering the 386th Panzergrenadier Division. The newly re-formed division was sent to Italy in the autumn of 1943 and saw extensive combat there before it was brought north in the late summer of 1944. Heavily engaged in Lorraine and the Aachen area in October and November, it was hastily rebuilt in late November and early December. As of late December the 3d Panzergrenadier Division comprised about 11,500 officers and men (about 75 percent of full strength) with twenty-five StuG-IIIGs and eleven JgPz-IVs. The division had adequate transport and fairly generous allotments of half-tracks and armored cars, but was short 75-mm antitank guns, automatic antiaircraft guns, and light infantry howitzers.

On 28 December, as the 3d Panzergrenadier finally began to assemble northeast of Bastogne, it was briefly assigned to Decker's XXXIX Panzer Corps before being subordinated to the XLVII Panzer Corps. Finally, with its headquarters located in Tronlé, the 3d Panzergrenadier Division moved into the front line, occupying about 3.5 kilometers of front on the northwestern face of the Bastogne salient on the afternoon of 29 December.

On 29 December, Remer's Führer Begleit Brigade was subordinated to Denkert's 3d Panzergrenadier Division in preparation for a renewed attack to close the American corridor into Bastogne. Determined American attacks on Führer Begleit's center and left (eastern) flank made no progress. Remer was able to move his headquarters forward from Tronlé to Renaumont, not far from the brigade's artillery concentration around Rechrival, about 2.5 kilometers to the northeast.

Nearby, TF Collins turned back a German attempt to retake Sibret on the morning of 29 December. Colonel Kokott of the 26th VGD had organized a counterattack employing a company of the division's engineer battalion, but the attack column literally stumbled into a U.S. position and fifty men were killed in a few minutes before the company scattered back into the woods. After this success, TF Collins attempted to capture Chenogne, but failed.

Collins's tank company lost four Shermans to German high-velocity antitank fire. Although some of Collins's troops entered the town, they were driven out by a determined German counterattack.

TF Karsteter's mission was to seize Senonchamps farther east. After an initial advance, the task force came under German fire (presumably from the newly arrived 3d Panzergrenadier Division) from the Bois de Fragotte. In the ensuing firefight both sides took considerable losses, especially in vehicles. Although four American tanks drove into Senonchamps, they were unable to stay since the American armored infantry had been pinned down and could not follow.

The cumulative losses suffered by CCA/9 left it with only one and a half companies of armored infantry (out of three), and twenty-one M4 Sherman medium tanks (out of about fifty), although there were seventeen M5 Stuart light tanks still operable. In other words, three days' fighting had cost it half of its combat strength.[8] The Germans had also suffered: Führer Begleit Brigade had 200 battle casualties, along with the loss of about a dozen tanks and again as many assault guns; about 350 men of the 15th Panzergrenadier were killed, wounded, or missing, and a modest assortment of vehicles and heavy weapons lost. German equipment losses were lower than those suffered by U.S. forces, mostly because the Germans had less equipment, especially tanks, to begin with.[9]

EAST OF THE CORRIDOR: 27–29 DECEMBER

Fortunately for the 26th VGD's immediate future, Kokott had been informed that General Mohnke's 1st SS Panzer Division was moving south to take up positions around Bras, south of his left flank. From there, Mohnke's division was to attack southwestward and sever the American corridor into Bastogne in conjunction with attacks by the Führer Begleit and 3d Panzergrenadier on the opposite face of the corridor. However, the 1st SS Panzer had been reassigned to the Fifth Panzer Army only on the morning of 28 December, and began moving south that afternoon. By early the next evening, Mohnke had moved his division south despite fuel shortages and snarled traffic and established his headquarters at Longvilly. There, under the command of General Decker's XXXIX Panzer Corps, the 1st SS Panzer made preparations to launch its attack on 30 or 31 December.

The other divisions assigned to Decker's corps were volksgrenadier units released from OKW reserve, or reassigned from elsewhere in Army Group B. The 167th VGD, commanded by Generalleutnant Hans-Kurt Höcker, was released from OKW reserve on 27 December, but was still moving to its forward assembly area over the next two days.[10] Höcker was able to get his leading regiment into the front line on the afternoon of 29 December, occupying a small sector southeast of Bastogne around Bras, with his headquarters near Grümelscheid. Colonel Theodor Tolsdorff's 340th VGD had been taken out of Fifteenth Army reserve and sent south after the offensive began, and had come under Fifth Panzer Army command on 26 December. The 340th VGD continued its march south over the next week, but it was slowed by poor road conditions, limited supplies, and Allied air attack, to say nothing of having to share the roads with supply columns. Tolsdorff's division would not be ready for combat in the Bastogne area until 3 January 1945, and by that date he had established his headquarters at Bourcy.[11]

When Colonel Kokott relinquished control of the 901st Panzergrenadiers and the 26th VGD's feldersatz battalion to General Heilmann's 5th Parachute Division, they became part of the Seventh Army's LIII Corps, commanded by General von Rothkirch. That corps also contained the Führer Grenadier Brigade and Colonel Werner Kolb's 9th VGD. (See chapter 14 for a discussion of the arrival of these units and their actions before 27 December.)

Heilmann's 5th Parachute Division, ordered to defend in place, held a 15.5-kilometer front on 27 December, facing the American 35th Infantry Division and Combat Commands A and B of the 4th Armored Division. American attacks that day advanced about 1,500 meters, driving back the stubborn defenders of the 15th Parachute Infantry Regiment. Continued American attacks on 28 and 29 December made little progress. The 14th Parachute Infantry (on the division's right, or northwest flank) held positions around Lutrebois and Villers-la-Bonne-Eau, and the divisional engineer battalion (5th Fallschirmpioniere Battalion) held the line from Villers-la-Bonne-Eau to Harlange. The immediate vicinity of Harlange was in the hands of the 15th Parachute Infantry, and the line as far west as Bovigny was held by the 13th Parachute Infantry.

East of Heilmann's division lay the battered Führer Grenadier Brigade around Nothum, facing the left (western) wing of the 26th Infantry Division. Behind the left flank of the LIII Corps and not yet involved in the battle was Colonel Kolb's 9th VGD, facing the rest of the 26th Infantry Division. By 29 December Kolb's headquarters was located in Wiltz, and the division was assembling just north of the village of Moertrange, about two kilometers northwest of Wiltz, but was not complete until the next afternoon.

General Gaffey's 4th Armored Division was still astride the Bastogne-Arlon highway, where it had been fighting for several days in its drive to break through to Bastogne. The somewhat unexpected success of Gaffey's Combat Command R on 26 December left most of that unit inside the Bastogne perimeter, with the remaining two-thirds of the division engaged around Hompré and Sainlez, several kilometers south of Bastogne, and east of the corridor. The 4th Armored Division's widely spread positions extended over thirty-seven kilometers. On 27 December Combat Command R managed to clear out most of the German troops still holding out in Assensois (part of the 26th VGD's 39th Fusiliers).

Most of the III Corps action on 28 December was undertaken by the infantry divisions. To the east, the 26th Division suffered more than 100 casualties as it pushed northward, but made little progress over broken ground and against the determined resistance of Heilmann's paratroopers. The 35th Division, in the center, attacked toward Villers-la-Bonne-Eau, but its advance ground to a halt in the face of very heavy German fire southwest of that hamlet. The 6th Armored Division was transferred from Eddy's XII to Millikin's III Corps at 0230 on 29 December. It moved west to an assembly area around Habay la Neuve, in preparation for the Third Army offensive northward from Bastogne. The 1st and 2nd battalions of the 318th Infantry, which had been under the 4th Armored Division, were returned to the 80th Infantry Division, which had itself passed to General Eddy's XII Corps two days before.

On 28 December General Gaffey and his subordinate commanders were able to consolidate the 4th Armored's positions considerably. Combat Command A advanced about 800 meters and captured Sainlez and Livarchamps, while on the west side of the Arlon highway Combat Command B pushed past Hompré. Combat Command R cleared the woods north of Assensois and this success, coupled with the capture of Villeroux (about 2,000 meters to the west) by TF Karsteter of CCA/9 made the corridor into Bastogne considerably more secure. (See above.) Although cargo aircraft had continued their missions into Bastogne, suffering heavy losses from German FLAK, by the evening of 28 December sufficient supplies were entering the town by road to allow the costly airlift to be called off.

On 29 December the 4th Armored Division continued to strengthen its hold on the corridor into Bastogne. Combat Commands A and B cleared the southern approaches to Bastogne northeast of Assensois and northwest of Remonfosse. Combat Command R pulled away from the northwestern edge of the corridor, where Combat Command A of the 9th Armored Division was now engaged, and moved into the area east of Hompré, where Germans from the 901st Panzergrenadiers still held a section of the Arlon highway, and were perilously close to the corridor.

To the south and east of Bastogne, the 35th Division continued its northward offensive on the right flank of the 4th Armored's push. With fewer good roads and more hills and forested terrain in its sector, the 35th made slower progress. Nonetheless, able to exploit the 4th Armored's successes, the division made good headway on 27 December. The 137th Infantry Regiment advanced northward by truck, using a bridge at Tintange emplaced by the 24th Armored Engineer Battalion. The 2d Battalion of the 137th Infantry took Surré, about 2,500 meters northeast of Tintange, but the advance of the 137th's 3d Battalion was stalled by a German pillbox near Livarchamps. On the division's right flank, the 320th Infantry took Boulaide and Bascheiden (both east of Surré) without opposition, the defending paratroopers having withdrawn.

During 28 December, the 137th Infantry took Betlange, and advance elements pushed into the hamlet of Villers-la-Bonne-Eau and the village of Lutrebois just to the north. It took the 3d Battalion of the 137th Infantry all day to overwhelm the German pillbox near Livarchamps, testimony to German tenacity as well as to skill in siting fortifications and making effective use of terrain. North of the 137th Infantry's positions, the 134th Infantry prepared to attack eastward and push the Germans back from the Arlon highway. These successes were largely ephemeral because a strong and determined counterattack by the 5th Parachute Division nearly recaptured Lutrebois and Villers-la-Bonne-Eau on 29 December. Nevertheless, by evening the 134th Infantry's 3d Battalion had won tenuous control of Lutrebois. Just to the south, two companies from the 137th Infantry shared Villers-la-Bonne-Eau with a company of German parachute engineers. The 320th Infantry, still attacking northward toward Harlange, had been caught up in a fierce and bitter battle around the Fuhrman Farm, about 1,200 meters southwest of the town. These three days of fighting cost the 35th Infantry Division about 150 casualties, mostly wounded.

On the III Corps right flank, the 26th Infantry Division was confronted with a shortage of decent roads and with forbidding, rugged, heavily wooded country. The division advanced across the Sure River during 27 December with the 101st Infantry on the left and the 104th on the right. Two companies from the 104th Infantry reached Esch sur la Sure, while the 101st Infantry captured Liefrange and advanced into Kaundorf and Bavigne. Progress continued on 28 December, as the 104th Infantry pushed 3,700 meters north to capture Bourscheid, and the 101st Infantry (on the left) advanced more than 2,700 yards before evening, and was in the process of clearing the twin villages of Mecker-Denkedt. On 29 December the 101st Infantry cleared Nothum and consolidated its control over Bourscheid, although the 104th made comparatively little progress. During this fighting the 26th Division incurred about 280 casualties, nearly twice as many as suffered by the neighboring 35th Infantry Division. The 5th Parachute Division, struggling to hold off both American divisions, lost nearly 300 officers and men during the same period. This was fierce fighting.

BUILDUP WEST OF THE CORRIDOR

On 29 December Brig. Gen. Charles S. Kilburn's 11th Armored Division began to assemble between Vaux-lez-Rosières and Neufchâteau. Delayed by icy roads and snow on the 137-kilometer (85-mile) approach march from the west and by a limited capacity bridge across the Meuse, only Combat Command A had reached the assembly area by late afternoon on 29 December. This was in time to receive an attack order from the VIII Corps about 1800. The remainder of Kilburn's division had to prepare its attack plans on the march, and went directly from march column to assault formations. This hasty procedure and the accompanying lack of preparation help to account for the 11th Armored's lackluster performance over the next several days.

Charles Solomon Kilburn was born in Silver City, New Mexico, on 2

January 1895. He graduated from West Point on 20 April 1917, two weeks after the United States entered World War I, as a second lieutenant of Cavalry. Although he got to France in World War I, it was as a War Department–American Expeditionary Force Courier; to his regret, he did not get into combat. Between the wars he was an aide-de-camp to two Army Chiefs of Staff: Generals John L. Hines and Malin C. Craig. In 1941, as a colonel, he took command of the 8th Cavalry Regiment of the 1st Cavalry Division, and later commanded the 3d Cavalry Brigade of that division. In August 1942, as a newly promoted brigadier general, he was assigned to the recently activated 11th Armored Division as the commander of Combat Command A, at Camp Polk, Louisiana. In March 1944 he became the division commander, succeeding Maj. Gen. Edward H. Brook. Kilburn took the division to England in November. The 11th Armored crossed the English Channel to Normandy on 15 December 1944, just in time to be rushed to the Ardennes front.

Major General Frank L. Culin Jr.'s 87th Infantry Division assembled southwest of Libramont in preparation for its role in the VIII Corps attack against the tip of the Bulge. Frank Lewis Culin Jr. was born in Seattle, Washington, on 31 March 1892. He graduated from the University of Arizona with a bachelor of science degree in 1915, and received an M.S. degree from the same school the following year. He was commissioned a second lieutenant in the Regular Army on 30 November 1916. After graduating from the Army Service School at Fort Leavenworth in April 1917, he was posted to the 30th Infantry in Texas. After promotion to captain in August, Culin sailed with his regiment to France in December. His regiment participated in the Aisne, Aisne-Marne, and Meuse-Argonne campaigns. He returned to the United States in October 1918.

Culin spent more than six years as a professor of military science and tactics at three different institutions of higher learning: Spring Hill College in Mobile, Alabama; the University of Florida in Gainesville; and the University of Oregon at Eugene. He was promoted to major in November 1928 and to lieutenant colonel in October 1938. In May 1941 he was assigned to command the 32d Infantry Regiment of the 7th Division at Fort Ord, California. He was promoted to colonel in October.

After Pearl Harbor, Culin was promoted to brigadier general. He served as Assistant Division Commander of the 10th Light Division (Pack, Alpine: later redesignated the 10th Mountain Division) from July 1943 to April 1944. Promoted to major general, Culin was reassigned to take command of the 87th Infantry Division in April 1944 and led the division to France in early December.

The 87th Division was first activated in August 1917 during World War I. It went overseas to France in September 1918 but saw no combat, and was inactivated in January 1919. The 87th Infantry Division was reactivated on 15 December 1942 and arrived in France in December 1944. It went to Metz, where it was assigned to the XII Corps of the Third Army. The 87th performed relatively well in a few brief engagements in the Saar region near the German border, until its attacks were halted because of the German Ardennes offensive. Withdrawn from the line, the division was placed in SHAEF Reserve on Christmas Eve. On 29 December it was ordered north to join the VIII Corps of the Third Army southwest of Bastogne.

IN AND AROUND BASTOGNE: 27–29 DECEMBER

Around Bastogne, the 101st Airborne Division and its attached units (an assortment of artillery battalions, along with parts of Combat Command R of the 9th Armored Division and the surviving portions of Colonel Roberts's Combat Command B of the 10th Armored Division) concentrated on holding their positions and providing what support they could to the other divisions of Millikin's III Corps. Although the supply situation had notably improved, most of the airborne troopers were tired and cold, and the psychological strain of battle had taken some toll.[12] Consequently there was little change in the situation on 27 and 28 December. On 29 December, however, the 327th Glider Infantry Regiment, elements of the depleted 9th Armored's Combat Command R, and Combat Command B of the 10th Armored recaptured Marvie southeast of Bastogne. These forces also made contact about 500 meters west of Marvie with advancing units of the 35th Infantry Division at 1800.

On 28 December Colonel Kokott was able to reduce the front of the 26th VGD to twenty-four kilometers, but American attacks captured Villeroux and Isle le Pré. On the next day Kokott was able to shorten his front still further, to only 21.5 kilometers, a more reasonable frontage for a division that now numbered, with attachments, less than 9,600 officers and men. The previous three days' fighting had cost Kokott's division more than 300 casualties, many of them captured or missing. The 101st Airborne Division had suffered 250 casualties during the same period.

THE GERMAN AND AMERICAN ATTACKS: 30–31 DECEMBER

By the night of 29–30 December, the Germans had gathered two panzer brigades, most of two panzergrenadier divisions, an SS panzer division, a parachute division, a regiment-size panzergrenadier kampfgruppe, and four volksgrenadier divisions around Bastogne—a total of more than eight division-equivalents with nearly 100,000 soldiers.[13] These troops were organized into three corps (XXXIX Panzer, XLVII Panzer, and LIII). It was symptomatic of the pressure under which the Germans operated, and the resulting rather haphazard nature of their effort against Bastogne, that these forces were under the operational command of two different armies: the Seventh Army for the LIII Corps and the Fifth Panzer Army for the two panzer corps. Moreover, two more SS Panzer divisions and SS-General Hermann Priess's I

SS Panzer Corps headquarters—another 30,000-plus men—were en route to the battle area.

General Manteuffel had held a command conference on the afternoon of 29 December to acquaint his division commanders with their responsibilities in the coming battle and with the overall goals of this offensive. Simply put, the commander of the Fifth Panzer Army planned coordinated attacks against both faces of the corridor into Bastogne. The Führer Begleit Brigade and the 3d Panzergrenadier Division were to attack from the west, through Sibret toward the southeast, while 1st SS Panzer Division Leibstandarte, supported by the 167th VGD, attacked from the east to the southwest through Lutrebois. The objective was to close the corridor. The 15th Panzergrenadier Division and 26th VGD, both of which had suffered heavily in previous fighting, would screen the northern portions of the Bastogne salient.

Simple though the German objective may have been, the situation was not at all straightforward. By coincidence, at the same time Manteuffel had chosen for his attacks, General Patton had ordered the VIII and III Corps to attack northward to relieve the pressure on Bastogne. Thus there was the unusual situation of two embattled armies mounting simultaneous offensives in a clear-cut clash of opposing objectives. That the Germans were able to operate effectively under these circumstances testifies to their flexibility and skill.

On 30 December Panzer Lehr Division's thickening screen guarding the southeastern flank of the XLVII Panzer Corps came under increasing pressure from the advancing 87th Infantry Division. Bayerlein shifted additional forces south from the main body of the division, now in positions near Rochefort and Wellin. The 345th Infantry surrounded Remagne, and the 346th Infantry in the Bois de Lambay Fays cut the St. Hubert–Bastogne road. Local German counterattacks at Vesqueville and Hatrival were repulsed and did little to slow the Americans. On New Year's Eve, the small German garrisons in Moircy and Remagne managed to slip away to the north. Panzer Lehr had been driven back nearly six kilometers (3.7 miles) during the last days of December. This fighting cost Culin's division only about 80 casualties, while Panzer Lehr suffered about 280 killed, wounded, and missing (although close to half of those losses were inflicted in fighting farther north by units from Collins's VII Corps).

As its sister-regiments of the 87th Division pushed northward, the 347th Infantry, in divisional reserve southwest of Seviscourt, prepared to move up and relieve the 345th Infantry on New Year's Day. In response to the growing threat from the south, Bayerlein moved his headquarters from St. Hubert to Lavacherie, and shifted most of his forces to the south, so that contact to the north with Lauchert's battered 2d Panzer Division was maintained only by patrols.

To the east of Panzer Lehr, other German units of the XLVII Panzer

Corps continued their struggle with Combat Command A of the 9th Armored Division. To reflect the changing situation and unit positions on the American side, on 30 December CCA/9 and the 101st Airborne Division were transferred from Millikin's III Corps to Middleton's VIII Corps.

To the west Combat Command A of the 11th Armored, advancing on that division's left flank through Rondu, encountered little or no enemy resistance before it met up with the 345th Infantry at Remagne. Remer's Führer Begleit Brigade, however, was at last able to launch its planned counterstroke to the southeast on 30 December. Although it made good initial progress, it ran headlong into a strong American tank force outside Sibret, and its advance was halted. This tank force comprised Combat Command B of the 11th Armored Division and TF Collins (of the 9th Armored's Combat Command A). Together, after halting the Führer Begleit, they occupied Morhet before advancing as far as Lavaselle during the afternoon of 30 December.

There was considerable action for the 11th Armored Division on the last day of 1944, as Combat Command B pressed on to capture Chenogne and Houmont. By evening Führer Begleit had been driven back nearly 2,000 meters, and was fighting desperately to halt the American advance. It managed to repel several small-scale American attacks along its 8.5-kilometer front but received little help from units of the 15th Panzergrenadier Division that were still arriving in the area. These units, including divisional support and service units, were intended to back up the kampfgruppe built around the remains of the 115th Panzergrenadiers. However, they had lost matériel and become disorganized on their long march to the battle area and required several days for rest, reorganization, and reequipment before they were battle-ready.

Combat Command A of the 9th Armored Division was still operating with TF Collins and TF Karsteter. TF Collins had a busy day on 30 December, as it initially bore the brunt of the Führer Begleit Brigade's main attack, which began about 0730 hours. Resisting vigorously, Collins's tankers and armored infantrymen finally halted the German advance between Sibret and Chenogne, aided by the arrival of 11th Armored's Combat Command B, which had begun moving north from its assembly area that morning. Combat Command A of the 9th engaged in further fighting on New Year's Eve, as both task forces struggled northward toward the Bastogne–St. Hubert road.

Just east of the Führer Begleit's battles, Denkert's 3d Panzergrenadier also mounted its planned attack on 30 December, but met with even less success. Denkert's attack was halted almost as soon as it began, and by midday the 3d Panzergrenadier was fighting hard to halt an American advance. Denkert's task was all the harder because most of his tanks and a good portion of his artillery still had not arrived. To compensate for this, Remer's brigade had been placed under his command early on 30 December. This command rearrangement gave Denkert control over close to two divisional equivalents, at least on paper, but all the panzergrenadier troops were short subunits or equipment, and Remer's brigade had taken losses in the recent fighting as well as in its operations with the Sixth Panzer Army earlier in the month. As the first hours of 1945 drew near, Denkert's troops held the American attacks to minor gains, but they had been unable to reduce the corridor into Bastogne, which had been their objective.

On 30 December Combat Command A of the 11th Armored was driven out of Remagne by a counterattack from Panzer Lehr, and was unable to fight its way back into town. Frustrated, Combat Command A withdrew and was replaced by a battalion from the 345th Infantry. That battalion was slowly advancing into the town as the year ended.

Finally, the 11th Armored's Combat Command R captured Pinsamont and Acue, and cleared most of the Bois de Haies de Magery. The lack of progress by the 11th Armored Division and the rough handling received by Combat Commands A and R on 30 and 31 December attracted some attention from General Patton, who was not pleased with what he considered General Kilburn's uninspired direction of the division.

The last fighting of 1944 west of Bastogne had been costly for the units of both armies. Denkert's 3d Panzergrenadier suffered 240 casualties; the neighboring 15th Panzergrenadier had 110 killed, wounded, and missing. Panzer Lehr had lost 40 killed, 148 wounded, and 76 missing. There were 87 casualties in the Führer Begleit Brigade on 30 December, but only 14 on New Year's Eve. On the American side, the 11th Armored Division suffered more that 340 casualties, most of them wounded. The 9th Armored's Combat Command A was unscathed on 30 December, and suffered only a handful of wounded and no deaths on the last day of 1944.

North of Bastogne on 30 December, Kokott's 26th VGD lent artillery fire support to the attacks by the panzer and panzergrenadier units on its right flank. With the failure of these efforts and the consequent transition to defensive posture, elements of Kokott's division withdrew to new positions in front of Senonchamps, just east of the Bois de Fragotte. The 101st Airborne Division, which generally faced Kokott's volksgrenadiers north of Bastogne, lent support to the 11th Armored Division's drive on its left. The following day, while still providing artillery support to the 11th Armored, the 101st made no major ground attacks of its own and generally maintained its positions. Scattered local American attacks probed the 26th VGD's lines, but generally made no significant gains. The exception came on the division's extreme right flank, where elements of CCA/4 captured the small village of Neffe, barely 2,000 meters east of Bastogne. The 26th VGD lost 340 battle casualties, further eroding the strength of that hard-working division.

To the east of the 26th VGD's sector, Decker's XXXIX Panzer Corps was still awaiting the arrival of its assigned units during the final hours of the year. The 167th VGD had moved forward to occupy a five-kilometer sector east of Marvie by first light on 30 December. Its offensive failed to gain ground, hamstrung by the failure of Mohnke's 1st SS Panzer Division Leibstandarte Adolf Hitler to make much progress in its own attack on the volks-grenadiers' southern (left) flank. On New Year's Eve, the 167th VGD tried to hold its positions, but the left flank was driven back nearly 1,000 meters by renewed American attacks from Gaffey's 4th Armored Division. Contributing to the discomfiture of the 167th VGD, General Höcker was still waiting for the remaining units of his division to arrive.

Although Mohnke's 1st SS Panzer Division was in position with its head-quarters at Longvilly by first light on 30 December, its offensive met with lit-tle more success than any of the other German attacks that day. The Germans managed to drive the defending Americans out of the hamlets of Lutrebois and Villers-la-Bonne-Eau, which they had captured just the day before. Con-centrated on a 2,000-meter front around Lutrebois, the Leibstandarte was nev-ertheless weak in armor and other heavy equipment,[14] its officers and men were combat-weary and fatigued, and the defending Americans were well sup-plied and in good spirits. Moreover, some of the divisional train was still in transit from Vielsalm. Adding to the physical and tactical difficulties, the SS troopers did not cooperate at all with the neighboring paratroopers of the 5th Parachute to the south: One SS officer tried to have the commander of the 14th Parachute Infantry Regiment court-martialed for incompetence a few days later, and the bad feeling between the divisions was mutual. At the same time, the attacking Germans were mauled by elements of the 4th Armored, along with troops from the 35th Infantry Division, just west of Lutrebois. U.S. troops destroyed fifteen German tanks and assault guns in a sharp action.

On 31 December the Leibstandarte was driven back about a kilometer by the attacking 35th Infantry Division, although the Germans retained the two villages they had captured the day before for a net two-day gain of perhaps 1,500 meters. Aside from the action at Lutrebois, the 4th Armored spent the last days of 1944 continuing its efforts to expand and consolidate the corridor into the Bastogne salient. The American attack at Lutrebois was therefore part of the same stroke that had pushed back the southern wing of the 167th VGD. The units of the 4th Armored were able to take advantage of the appearance of Maj. Gen. Robert W. Grow's 6th Armored Division on their right to reduce their division's frontage from twenty-two kilometers to a little over seven, thereby preparing for further offensive action in the Lutrebois-Neffe zone.

The 6th Armored Division had been passed from the XII Corps to Mil-likin's III Corps in expectation of going over to the attack on New Year's Eve. The attack could have begun on 30 December, but CCB became tangled up in the 11th Armored Division's columns as they moved north over the same roads, and CCB was delayed by ten hours. CCA of the 6th Armored was able to attack on New Year's Eve, advancing toward Wardin and capturing Neffe. CCB spent most of the day extricating itself from Bastogne, where it was still ensnared with the 11th Armored Division's trains.

Just to the south and east of the sectors held by the 4th and 6th Armored divisions lay the 35th Infantry Division. The Leibstandarte counterattack at

Lutrebois struck the division hard, and compelled a withdrawal of about two kilometers, yielding both Villers-la-Bonne-Eau and Lutrebois itself. Three rifle companies were virtually destroyed, and only the intervention of tanks from the neighboring 4th Armored Division helped to restore the situation in the afternoon. The 35th Division's new main position solidified in a north-south line along the Remonfosse-Livarchamps road.

Nevertheless, on New Year's Eve, the 35th Infantry Division mounted an attack as part of a planned III Corps effort to push northeast and reduce the German salient around Harlange. The 134th Infantry's attempts to recapture Lutrebois were driven off with heavy losses, and the 137th Infantry's effort to relieve the remnants of two companies in Villers-la-Bonne-Eau were also unsuccessful, thwarted by the 14th Parachute Infantry in the woods around the village. The 320th Infantry, still southeast of Harlange around the Fuhrman Farm, continued to hold its positions.

Casualties mounted during the fighting east and southeast of Bastogne in the last days of December: for the 101st Airborne, 17 killed, 121 wounded, and 19 captured or missing; for the 4th Armored Division, 22 killed, 82 wounded, and 16 missing (mostly on New Year's Eve); and for the 6th Armored, 1 man killed and 14 wounded, all on 31 December. Nearly all the 35th Infantry Division losses (16 killed, 257 wounded, and 304 missing) were associated with the confused fighting around Lutrebois on 31 December. The Germans were also bloodied in these battles. The 1st SS Panzer suffered nearly 400 battle casualties; the 167th VGD lost about 350 officers and men. Colonel Tolsdorff's 340th VGD, as yet unengaged, suffered no battle losses.

General von Rothkirch's LIII Corps, the most westerly and right-hand of the Seventh Army's three corps, was not supposed to play a major role in the Fifth Panzer Army attack against the Bastogne corridor on 30–31 December. Indeed, Rothkirch's divisions had troubles of their own, most of which were provided by the relentless northward advance of the 35th and 26th Infantry divisions. Heilmann's long-suffering 5th Parachute Division fortunately saw little action on either day, as the 35th Division's attentions were directed to the Lutrebois–Villers-la-Bonne-Eau area. The kampfgruppe of the 15th Panzer-grenadier Division was still out of the line, occupying an area around the hamlet of Watrange about 1,000 meters north of Harlange. It saw little action on 30–31 December, and was still receiving new equipment.

Unlike the hard-hit 35th Division, Major General Paul's 26th Infantry Division drove northward from the Sure River toward Wiltz, despite rugged wooded terrain and an appallingly poor roadnet. Advancing on a 10-kilometer front on 30 December, the division gained 1,800 meters. On 31 December a German counterattack near Nothum temporarily stopped the division, but after the attackers lost several tanks, the 101st Infantry Regiment was able to restore the situation by 1800 hours.

Unlike the Leibstandarte, Colonel Kolb's 9th VGD was still relatively fresh. Kolb launched a counterattack on 30 December on a four-kilometer front between the hamlets of Liefrange and Esche. This effort, undertaken to help cover the disengagement of the battered Führer Grenadier Brigade, was repelled with heavy losses. On the next day, the 9th VGD completed its relief of the brigade and, despite its losses, occupied a fourteen-kilometer front just north of the Sure River. This at last allowed the Führer Grenadier Brigade, still suffering from the loss of its commander, Colonel Kahler, on 22 December, to withdraw from the line and rest as it was transferred to the Fifth Panzer Army reserve. The 406th Volksartillerie Corps's III Battalion was transferred back to its parent unit when the Führer Grenadier Brigade withdrew.

Casualties, especially for the Germans, had been heavy; for the 5th Parachute, 48 killed, 172 wounded, and 183 captured and missing; for the 9th VGD, 29 killed, 63 wounded, and 103 missing; for the Führer Grenadier Brigade, 28 killed, 57 wounded, and 100 missing. The Americans suffered fewer casualties; for the 26th Infantry Division, 21 killed, 266 wounded, and 28 missing.

In this sharp clash of opposing objectives around Bastogne, the last days of 1944 brought greater battlefield success to the troops of Patton's Third Army than to their German opponents. Despite some small-scale local successes, the first effort by the Germans to close the Bastogne corridor had failed entirely. Unfortunately for Hitler's reoriented goal, Allied airpower and the growing strength of U.S. Army forces were not likely to give the Germans another chance.

THE NEW YEAR'S FREE-FOR-ALL: 1–2 JANUARY 1945

The German command was unwilling to concede the battle to the Americans, despite their inability to advance and the heavy losses suffered over the two previous days. To the west of Bastogne, the bulk of Bayerlein's Panzer Lehr Division was engaged with General Culin's advancing 87th Infantry Division between St. Hubert and the vicinity of Pironpré. Stretched over a front of twenty-eight kilometers and missing the 901st Panzergrenadier Regiment, Bayerlein's troops were hard-pressed to hold the Americans. The 347th Infantry Regiment, on the right (eastern) flank of the 87th Infantry Division, attacked north from Moircy and Remagne toward the St. Hubert–Morhet road on New Year's Day. The 1st Battalion of the 347th Infantry pushed patrols across the road east of Pironpré, but these advance elements were driven back by a late-afternoon Panzer Lehr tank counterattack. The 347th Infantry's 3d Battalion pushed straight north from Moircy and took Jenneville around midday, but was unable to advance further.

On 2 January the 347th Infantry, still frustrated by the German strongpoint at Pironpré, adopted an unusual solution. The 1st Battalion swung east of the crossroads and captured Gérimont, while the 3d Battalion attacked to the west and captured the village of Bonnerue. This left a gap between the two battalions, and the regimental reserve, the 347th Infantry's 2d Battalion, was sent forward to take Pironpré on 3 January. By the evening of 2 January the 87th Infantry Division had advanced more than five kilometers (3.3 miles) in two days. A Panzer Lehr counterattack launched in the afternoon from St. Hubert, moreover, failed to recover the Bois de Lambay Fays. This fighting cost the 87th Division 37 killed, 85 wounded, and 46 missing. Panzer Lehr fared better in the casualty exchange with 24 killed, 69 wounded, 30 missing.

Farther east, the 11th Armored Division continued its advance, employing all three combat commands in line. The U.S. attack against the 8.5-kilometer front held by Remer's Führer Begleit Brigade began at 0900 on New Year's Day. The brigade was driven out of Pinsamont, and was compelled to withdraw the units on its left flank when elements of the 3d Panzergrenadier were forced out of Chenogne. That day Combat Command R, operating on the division's western (left) flank, pushed through Magerotte toward Brul and Pinsamont. In the center, Combat Command A attacked toward Rechrival starting about 0900, and advance elements reached Hubermont. During the afternoon, CCA was subjected to a strong German counterattack, but blunted this effort and held on to its morning gains. On the division's northeastern flank, Combat Command B captured Houmont and secured Chenogne.

The main body of Deckert's 15th Panzergrenadier Division[15] remained in reserve between the Führer Begleit Brigade, which received the brunt of the 11th Armored's attack, and the Panzer Lehr Division. As the German situation west of Bastogne grew more grave, Deckert's kampfgruppe entered the line on 2 January, holding a 3.5-kilometer sector by dusk. Meanwhile, the main body of Denkert's 3d Panzergrenadier was defending against strong American attacks around Chenogne. On New Year's Day, the defenders were driven back 1,500 meters, losing Chenogne, and established a new defensive line in front of Rechrival.

The 11th Armored's attacks continued on 2 January, supported by heavy concentrations of U.S. artillery and frequent air strikes. The 11th Armored's front expanded as Combat Command B captured Mande-St. Etienne, and Combat Command R maintained firm contact with the 87th Division to the left. Troops of Combat Command B drove the 3d Panzergrenadier back another two kilometers, to the edge of Mande-St. Etienne. On the first days of the new year, the 11th Armored had advanced a total of 5,100 meters (3.2 miles), roughly keeping pace with the division on its left. The 11th Armored's gains had not come cheap: 29 killed, 217 wounded, and 36 missing. This brought the "butcher's bill" for the division's first four days in combat to 626 officers and men, or close to 6 percent of the division, a high loss rate. The 3d Panzergrenadier lost nearly 40 killed, 120 wounded, and 115 missing during the first two days of 1945; Führer Begleit Brigade suffered about 40 killed, 80 wounded, and 30 missing. The 15th Panzergrenadier lost 7 killed, 30 wounded, and 25 missing, the majority of them on 2 January, when the bulk of the division had reentered the line.

The 17th Airborne Division ended its guard duty along the Meuse River and moved east to assemble north of Neufchâteau on 2 January. This brought the division under the command of Middleton's VIII Corps. Its entry into the battle line west of Bastogne was planned for 4 January.

To the east of Denkert's 3d Panzergrenadier, the bulk of the 26th VGD's 39th Fusilier Regiment withdrew into reserve positions around Rastade and Compogne on New Year's Day except one isolated kampfgruppe that was still holding out in Senonchamps. The doughty soldiers of the 9th Armored's Combat Command A (with the survivors of Combat Command B of the 10th Armored attached) continued their drive northward on 1 January. TF Karsteter cleared the Bois de Fragotte and entered Senonchamps late in the afternoon. After nightfall, Karsteter's tanks withdrew from Senonchamps, but the infantry remained in town, engaged in close combat with the defenders, who were part of the 39th Fusiliers. The next day, the isolated German garrison at Senonchamps was relieved by a counterattacking force from the 3d Panzergrenadier, and was able to withdraw after dark. TF Karsteter moved into town after the fusiliers departed. Elsewhere along the 26th VGD's front, the division's units were driven back more than two kilometers on New Year's Day alone, losing Magaret and Bizory east of Bastogne. That same day, Kokott's division came under the command of Priess's I SS Panzer Corps, which assumed responsibility for the front north and east of Bastogne.

During the first daylight hours of 1945 the lead elements of the I SS Panzer Corps assembled in and just south of Houffalize. The corps brought with it the 9th SS Panzer Division "Hohenstaufen" and the 12th SS Panzer Division "Hitlerjugend." Both were formidable formations, but had suffered considerable wear and tear during the early fighting in the Sixth Panzer Army sector. By the morning of 2 January, SS-Colonel Hugo Kraas's 12th SS Panzer was in position northeast of Bastogne, while SS-Colonel Sylvester Stadler's 9th SS Panzer, with CP at Houffalize, was still moving into position north-northwest of the town.

Kokott's 26th VGD had its front line reduced from 15.5 to 13 kilometers by the arrival of the SS panzers. In addition to the 26th VGD and the 9th SS and 12th SS Panzer divisions, Priess's I SS Panzer Corps also included Tolsdorff's 340th VGD assembling around Longvilly behind the 26th VGD's left (southeast) flank. During 2 January, the leading regiment of the 340th VGD entered the line near Benonchamps to cover the final stages of the division's assembly, clashing briefly with elements of the 6th Armored Division.

The rightmost division of Middleton's corps, the 101st Airborne Division, held a front line of only seventeen kilometers on 1 January, further reduced to fourteen kilometers the next day. On 2 January, troops of the 506th Parachute Infantry Regiment pushed eastward to cover the left flank of the 6th Armored Division, advancing north toward Bourcy. Otherwise, the second day of the new year was, to their undoubted relief, relatively quiet for the troops of the 101st Airborne.

Major General Grow's 6th Armored Division had entered the line on

New Year's Eve as the left-wing division of Millikin's III Corps, immediately east of the 506th Parachute Infantry Regiment. However, Combat Command B did not reach its intended start line until the early-morning hours of New Year's Day, delayed by the massive traffic jam with the 11th Armored's columns south and west of Bastogne. Despite that delay Combat Command B advanced and captured Bizory and Hill 510 against very slight opposition from the 78th Grenadier Regiment of the 26th VGD on the morning of 1 January. The combat command then wheeled west-southwest to capture Magaret. There, the 6th Armored's Combat Command A took over while CCB pushed on toward Arloncourt. Troops from Combat Command B captured Arloncourt but held it only briefly before a counterattack by Hitlerjugend (12th SS Panzer) troops drove them out.

On 2 January, Combat Command A of the 6th Armored took Wardin, losing fifteen M4 Sherman tanks, while Combat Command B pushed northeast to capture Oubourcy, Michamps, and Benonchamps. Another attempt to take Arloncourt failed, and around twilight elements of the newly arrived 12th SS Panzer Division mounted a powerful counterattack, retaking both Oubourcy and Michamps. Wardin was also recovered by the Germans, greatly reducing the 6th Armored Division's gains for the day. The 6th Armored's drive northeastward cost it 13 killed, 107 wounded, and only 5 missing; the neighboring 101st Airborne lost 13 killed, 77 wounded, and 3 missing. The elements of I SS Panzer Corps that were engaged suffered more heavily. Kraas's 12th SS Panzer lost 40 killed, 110 wounded, and about 45 missing; Tolsdorff's 340th VGD suffered 6 killed, 24 wounded, and 11 missing, all on 2 January. On the same day Stadler's 9th SS Panzer lost nearly 40 killed, 115 wounded, and 35 missing.

To the south (left) of the new positions of the I SS Panzer Corps lay Decker's XXXIX Panzer Corps, containing the 1st SS Panzer Division, the 167th VGD, and the 901st Panzergrenadier Regiment of Panzer Lehr. Both the SS troopers and the volksgrenadiers had held their hard-won gains from the last days of 1944 against repeated U.S. attacks. The last elements of the 167th VGD finally arrived on New Year's Day, having struggled forward over icy roads in the face of near-continuous air attacks. By dusk on 2 January, the XXXIX Panzer Corps held a front of about twelve kilometers, seven of them the responsibility of the 167th VGD.

The arrival of Grow's division relieved Gaffey's 4th Armored Division of the burden of the offensive it had carried for the preceding ten days. The 4th Armored spent most of New Year's Day holding its positions between Lutrebois and Villers-la-Bonne-Eau in relative peace and quiet. On 2 January Combat Command B was transferred to Middleton's VIII Corps as the corps reserve, while the rest of the division held a seven-kilometer front near Lutrebois and Remonfosse.

Major General Baade's 35th Infantry Division continued its attacks along the arc from Lutrebois to Fuhrman Farm, facing the junction of sectors held by the XXXIX Panzer Corps and Rothkirch's LIII Corps of the Seventh Army. An attack on New Year's Day by the 134th Infantry against Lutrebois from the west and northwest made no significant progress against the 1st SS Panzer Division, and two companies were isolated behind enemy lines. The 137th Infantry's attack to retake Villers-la-Bonne-Eau likewise made no headway against the 14th Parachute Infantry.The 320th Infantry's efforts to seize the Fuhrman Farm were also frustrated by the 104th Panzergrenadier Regiment of the 15th Panzergrenadier Division. General Baade's division faced difficulties not only from the Germans, but also from the icy roads and the overcast skies, replete with scattered snow squalls. The weather cleared briefly in the afternoon, only to close in again at dusk.

On 2 January the 35th Division continued its attacks. The 134th Infantry gained a toehold in Lutrebois and began clearing the village, now largely in ruins. The two isolated companies began to filter back to U.S. lines. The 1/134 came under fire from troops of the 6th Armored Division operating south of Wardin, who supposed the 35th Division's soldiers were Germans in U.S. uniforms (the pernicious result of the rumors engendered by Skorzeny's commandos and his short-lived 150th Panzer Brigade). Fortunately, only two men were killed and a few more wounded. The 137th Infantry continued to try to batter its way into Villers-la-Bonne-Eau, but again made little progress in the face of stubborn resistance from the 14th Parachute Infantry. On the division's southeastern flank, after another day of unsuccessful attacks, the 320th Infantry was promised tank support from the 4th Armored Division in the ongoing battle for Fuhrman Farm.

East of the 320th Infantry's fight at Fuhrman Farm, General Paul's 26th Infantry Division continued its drive toward Wiltz, pushing north against the 9th VGD, which held a fifteen-kilometer front. Behind the 9th VGD's lines, the Führer Grenadier Brigade was in reserve, enjoying a respite from frontline combat. On New Year's Day the 26th Division made no significant advance, due largely to a strong counterattack by volksgrenadiers on the 101st Infantry's front around Nothum. On 2 January the 26th Division's overall progress amounted to 1,200 meters. The 328th Infantry moved north into the battle line from divisional reserve, advancing in the Nothum area on the division's left flank. This left all three of the division's infantry regiments in line, each with two battalions forward and one in reserve. The 104th Infantry, on the division's right flank, was still trying to get a secure foothold in Roullingen.

The casualties continued to mount: The 4th Armored lost 16 killed, 49 wounded, and 3 missing in the first days of January; the neighboring 35th Infantry Division lost 20 killed, 166 wounded, and 70 missing, the result of heavy combat between Lutrebois and Fuhrman Farm. The Germans, hammered by superior U.S. artillery and, at least occasionally in daylight, by U.S. fighter-bombers, had heavier casualties. The Leibstandarte lost 60 killed, 160 wounded, and 45 missing, mostly in the ongoing struggle around Villers-la-

Bonne-Eau. The dwindling 5th Parachute Division about 20 killed, 55 wounded, and 20 missing.

THE GERMAN TIDE EBBS: 3–4 JANUARY

On 3 January, the 87th Infantry Division pushed northward toward St. Hubert. The advance by the 347th Infantry reached the outskirts of Tillet, while the 346th Infantry made similar progress, advancing about 1,700 meters (a little over a mile). To the east, Maj. Gen. William Miley's 17th Airborne Division had moved forward to take up an eleven-kilometer length of front line between the 87th Infantry and the 11th Armored divisions, with the 11th Armored side-slipping to the right. The 513th Parachute Infantry relieved Combat Command A of the 9th Armored and Combat Command B of the 11th Armored, while the 194th Glider Infantry relieved Combat Commands A and R of the 11th Armored on the division's right flank.

In the afternoon the 17th Airborne Division attacked northward, northwest of Bastogne, on a front of about eight kilometers. This attack made little progress due to poor reconnaissance and inadequate artillery support, both situations exacerbated by the haste with which the operation was undertaken. The airborne troops were thrown back with heavy losses by the defending soldiers of Remer's Führer Begleit Brigade and the nearby 3d Panzergrenadier.

Attacks by the 3d Panzergrenadier Division and its associated units struck Kilburn's 11th Armored Division, which had already been discomfited by the previous three days' combat, in which it had lost about seventy tanks, a third of the division's total. The disoriented and disorganized armored division gave ground under this pressure. Patton was so disappointed with the performance of both the 11th Armored and 17th Airborne divisions on 3 January that he considered relieving both of their commanders. He did eventually relieve Kilburn (in March), but Miley and his division soon redeemed themselves in Patton's eyes (see chapter 20).

The 101st Airborne Division also engaged in considerable combat on 3 January. A German attack mounted by the 9th SS Panzer Division's 19th Panzergrenadier Regiment hit the northwestern sector of the former Bastogne perimeter near the village of Longchamps with with close to thirty tanks and assault guns.[16] The 2d Battalion of the 502d Parachute Infantry bore the brunt of this action, suffering almost 120 casualties. The attackers were driven off by a combination of the paratroopers' zeal and determination and heavy artillery support.

A major role in this bloody engagement was played by C Battery of the 81st Antitank-Antiaircraft Battalion, attached to the 502d Parachute Infantry Regiment. The battery was normally equipped with six 57-mm antitank guns (British "six-pounders"), but one of these had been lost in earlier fighting near Longchamps. One of the remaining five guns, commanded by Sgt.

Joseph O'Toole, of Vincennes, Indiana, was emplaced just behind the crest of a knoll overlooking the Compogne-Longchamps road just north of Longchamps. The gun was well dug in, so that only the barrel was barely above the snow. The gun position was well integrated into the MLR (Main Line of Resistance) of the 502d Parachute Infantry Regiment. The other four guns were similarly emplaced nearby.

The German attack began about 1330. With substantial artillery support, the tanks and infantry of the 19th Panzergrenadiers were deployed on both sides of the road from Compogne. As the German tanks approached, O'Toole and his crew opened fire. They first hit a PzKw-VI Tiger, taking the turret off with the second hit. When the gun hit another tank, the Germans realized that they were opposed by an accurate antitank gun crew, and began to concentrate fire on O'Toole, his men, and their gun. The German counterfire soon destroyed O'Toole's gun and seriously wounded him and three of the four other members of the crew.

However, eight more German tanks were knocked out by the other four guns of C Battery in the next few minutes, before three of them were destroyed by German counterfire. But while the German tanks concentrated on the C Battery antitank guns, American artillery and the paratroopers' machine guns took a heavy toll on the advancing German infantry. Several more tanks were also knocked out by bazookas of the 502d. Unable to break through, the SS panzergrenadiers slowly pulled back, leaving more than fifty dead on the bloodstained snow north of Longchamps.[17]

To the east, the 2d and 3d battalions of the 501st Parachute Infantry slogged into the dense Bois Jacques, east of Foy, in midafternoon and cleared its southern reaches. However, they were thrown back by a powerful attack from the 26th Panzergrenadier Regiment of the 12th SS Panzer Division at about 1530, which drove south along the railway embankment into their partially exposed right flank. Coordination with the neighboring 50th Armored Infantry Battalion of the 6th Armored Division was poor, and this contributed significantly to the success of the German attack. TF O'Hara, including elements from the 101st and Combat Command A of the 10th Armored, was brought up to block German attacks and restore the situation. After nightfall, the 502d's infantry in the Bois Jacques withdrew south of the woods.

In Millikin's III Corps the 6th Armored Division repelled attacks west of Michamps delivered by elements of the 12th SS Panzer Division supported by the surviving dozen or so seventy-five-ton King Tiger tanks of the 506th Schwere Panzer Abteilung. The 6th Armored Division also directed heavy artillery fire against German troop concentrations, hammering units of the Hitlerjugend around Arloncourt, Bourcy (the 12th SS Panzer headquarters), and Michamps. Just to the south, efforts by other units of the 6th Armored to clear high ground near Wardin and secure the road junction south of the village were blocked by stubborn German resistance and local counterattacks delivered by troops of Tolsdorff's 340th VGD.

The 35th Infantry Division managed to capture about two-thirds of Lutrebois and secure the crossroads west of Villers-la-Bonne-Eau, but an attempt to push on and take Harlange was frustrated. The Leibstandarte division continued to stymie the 35th Division's efforts to capture Lutrebois. East of Harlange, the 26th Division continued its attacks north of Kaundorf and Mecker-Dunkrodt, but made only slight progress in the expansion of its bridgehead north of the Sure River.

Middleton's VIII Corps continued its northward offensive on 4 January, but the weather over most of the Ardennes had worsened markedly, with heavy clouds and scattered snowfalls. The 87th Division was stopped cold by determined resistance from Panzer Lehr units in fortified positions in and around Pironpré. The 17th Airborne Division launched its attack in the middle of a snowstorm with abysmal visibility (down to fifty meters or less in some places), and in those conditions coordination and effective control were virtually impossible. Compounding the 17th Airborne's problems, their advance provoked a strong enemy reaction in the Pinsamont-Rechrival-Hubermont area from Remer's Führer Begleit Brigade, and in the swirling melee that followed both sides suffered heavily. Some companies in the 513th Parachute Infantry were especially hard-hit, losing nearly 50 percent of their personnel.

Fighting on 3 and 4 January cost the 87th Infantry Division 14 killed, 91 wounded, and 44 missing; the 11th Armored lost 14 killed, 55 wounded, and 23 missing, all on 4 January. The 17th Airborne's baptism of fire on 4 January cost that division severely, with 38 killed, 167 wounded, and 70 missing. The VIII Corps's German opponents suffered considerably less: The Führer Begleit Brigade lost 5 killed, about a dozen wounded, and 5 missing, and Panzer Lehr's casualties were lighter. The 3d Panzergrenadier totals were higher, with about 20 killed, more than 70 wounded, and about 60 missing. The two portions of the 15th Panzergrenadier (one, less heavily engaged, on the east side of Bastogne under the XXXIX Panzer Corps) lost about a dozen killed, 60 wounded, and 50 missing.

Attacks by the I SS Panzer Corps and the 15th Panzergrenadier Division of the XLVII Panzer Corps made virtually no impression on the 101st Airborne Division north and west of Bastogne, but produced some severe close-in fighting along the American trench and foxhole lines. Repeated strong counterattacks compelled Combat Command B of the 6th Armored to withdraw from its exposed forward positions near Wardin, abandoning both that village and nearby Magaret to the 12th SS Panzer Division. The 50th Armored Infantry and 88th Tank battalions, and TF Kennedy (built around the 69th Tank Battalion) bore the brunt of Hitlerjugend's attack, and were forced to withdraw about 1,100 meters. These battles cost the 101st Airborne 53 killed, 393 wounded, and 91 missing, a 4.1 percent personnel loss in just two days. The 6th Armored also suffered heavily with 52 killed, 215 wounded, and 41 missing, a 2.97 percent personnel loss. The 12th SS Panzer had lost fewer personnel, about 40 killed, 110 wounded, and 40 missing. The neighboring 340th VGD lost 80 killed, 300 wounded, and 150 missing, much of this from U.S. artillery. The nearby 167th VGD got away much more lightly, losing only about 12 killed, 35 wounded, and 40 missing.

The 35th Division, holding a fifteen-kilometer front, continued its offensive against the right flank of von Rothkirch's LIII Corps. The 134th Infantry finally finished clearing Lutrebois. By this time, few structures in the village were still standing. The drive toward Harlange by the 137th and 320th Infantry regiments was still stalled by the 5th Parachute Division. The fighting on 3–4 January resulted in 18 killed, 202 wounded, and 148 missing from the 35th Division, while the paratroopers of the 5th Parachute, benefiting from their defensive posture, did not lose as many men, with about 13 killed, 50 wounded, and about 20 missing.

To the east, operating on a front of just under ten kilometers, the 26th Division made some progress against the 9th VGD. The 101st and 328th Infantry regiments pushed north about 500 meters, but the 104th Infantry had little to show for the day's efforts. The rugged terrain with its dense covering of pine forest, coupled with the thin network of poor roads and narrow trails, considerably aided the German defensive efforts. The 26th Infantry Division losses for 3–4 January were relatively heavy, amounting to 37 killed, 282 wounded, and 48 missing; the 9th VGD lost about 15 killed, 40 wounded, and 25 missing.

By the evening of 4 January, the German efforts to capture Bastogne, or at least to cut the land corridor south of town, had failed completely. The attacks by the 9th SS and 12th SS Panzer divisions had led to hard fighting and considerable casualties on both sides, but had not seriously threatened even local breakthroughs, to say nothing of posing a real threat to Bastogne. Some of the U.S. Army units operating around the perimeter of the Bastogne salient had difficult experiences and suffered heavily at the hands of their more experienced German opponents. Nevertheless, by this time the Germans had essentially lost the initiative, and were able to mount only local counterattacks. The German forces in the Ardennes continued to behampered by logistical difficulties. Their supply routes into the salient were fewer and narrower than those available to the Americans and were under frequent air attack, while at least two-thirds of their matériel and supplies moved not by trucks but by slower horse-drawn transport. All of these conditions contributed to an increasingly daunting German situation in the Ardennes.

Because of this state of affairs, the panzer divisions that had arrived from the Sixth Panzer Army had been able to undertake limited only attacks. Their diminished strength and piecemeal arrival had precluded full-scale coordinated offensives, and many of their attacks were merely reactions to American success. Most of the German infantry divisions in the Bastogne area, along with the mobile formations that had been in the area since before Christmas, were also inexorably slipping onto the defensive as the weight of the Third Army offensive wore them down. However, while the Germans' capacity for large-scale offensive action was withering, their ability to sustain prolonged and determined defensive operations remained high, and their practice of delivering sharp, forceful small-scale counterattacks as part of their defense had not faltered.

As the U.S. offensives developed from north and south, the Germans soon recognized the American goal of effecting a juncture at Houffalize. That small town became the focus of the next two weeks of fighting.

19

COUNTEROFFENSIVE IN THE NORTH

O n the evening of 26 December, after General Bradley received reports of the outcome of the overwhelming victory of the U.S. 2d Armored Division over the German 2d Panzer Division east of Dinant (see chapter 15), the 12th Army Group commander tried to call Eisenhower at Versailles. Ike was away from the headquarters, so Bradley spoke to "Beetle" Smith, the SHAEF Chief of Staff. "As near as we can tell," said Bradley, "the other fellow's reached the high-water mark today. He'll soon be starting to pull back—if not tonight, certainly by tomorrow." In that same conversation he said: "Can't you people get Monty going in the north?"[1]

CONTINUING STRATEGIC DEBATE

Monty, however, was not convinced that the German offensive had run its course. For reasons not supported by any intelligence assessment, he had convinced himself that there would be at least one more German surge, directed northward, across the northern face of the salient, toward Liège. The failure of the intelligence community to forecast the initial German offensive of 16 December was reason enough not to rely on intelligence reports; however, Monty's fear of a revitalized German offensive seems to have been based on little more than the British field marshal's innate caution.

In presenting this concern to Eisenhower at their meeting at Hassalt a day and a half later, Monty insisted that it would be militarily unsound to mount a counteroffensive in the north until this renewed German drive had been halted. Ike expressed doubts about the possibility of a renewed German thrust, and did not accept the military validity of Monty's argument that the possibility of such a thrust should preclude an Allied offensive from the north. He had visions of Montgomery indefinitely postponing any action in the north; this would allow the Germans to reinforce their defenses again the

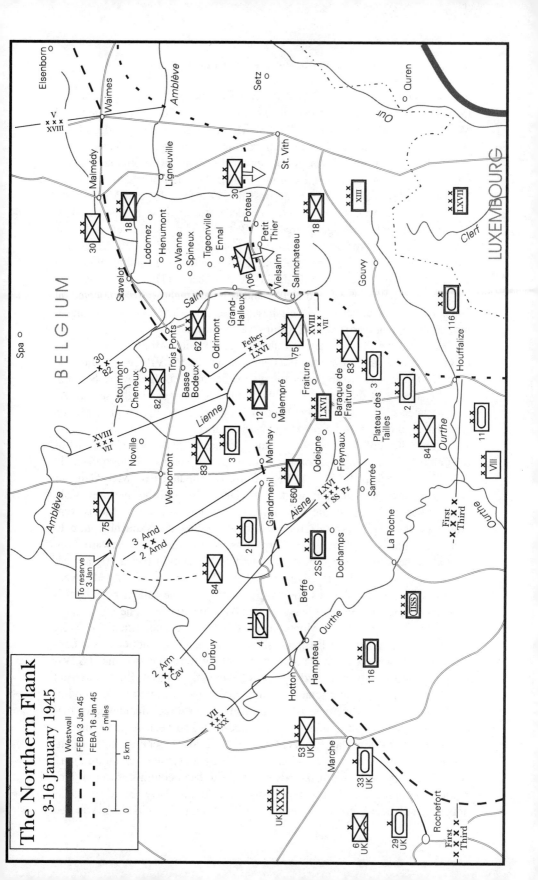

The Northern Flank
3-16 January 1945

Westwall

FEBA 3 Jan 45
FEBA 16 Jan 45

0 ___ 5 km
0 ___ 5 miles

northward push of Patton's Third Army near Bastogne, while withdrawing their battered and exposed forces in the nose of the salient. Ike insisted, and Monty finally agreed, that regardless of what the Germans might do, Monty should initiate a counteroffensive in the north by 3 January, at the latest.[2]

At least three times in the following week, Monty, who obviously had a high regard for Major General Collins, visited the VII Corps commander at his command post at the Château de Bassines, near the village of Mean, north of Marche. Ridgway seems to have attended most of these meetings.[3] Both American generals forthrightly urged the British field marshal to unleash their two corps in counteroffensive. According to Collins, Monty argued that "the northern front had not yet been stabilized, a requisite under traditional tactical concepts before a counterattack should be launched." (This, of course, was the argument he had presented to Ike, and which Eisenhower had rejected, at Hassalt.) The Americans did their best to convince him that this technical military argument was specious. Monty was unmoved.[4]

Nor—as we have seen in chapter 17—would Montgomery accept Collins's strong suggestion that the counterattack by his VII Corps should be mounted farther east, from the northern shoulder of the Bulge toward St. Vith, in order to cut off the largest possible number of Germans in the salient. As Collins later wrote: "As always happens in such cases, the umpire, Monty, won that argument. But there were no hard feelings."[5]

Monty did, however, permit Collins to concentrate the VII Corps east of the Ourthe River, in preparation for an offensive drive toward Houffalize. He belatedly moved up the British XXX Corps, commanded by Maj. Gen. Sir Brian Horrocks, into the area west of the Ourthe to hold the line previously held by the 2d Armored and 84th Infantry divisions. However, Monty kept Horrocks under 21st Army Group command, rather than attaching him to Hodges's First Army. The XXX Corps was to hold the line westward from Hotton to the nose of the salient southwest of Marche; in fact its right wing elements, the 6th Airborne Division and the 29th Armoured Brigade, were deployed in the 12th Army Group zone, in front of the salient nose, which was receding as the Germans began to pull back toward Bastogne.

It can be argued that Montgomery should have committed the XXX Corps in this area before Christmas, since the British corps not only was concentrated, but was closer to that critical part of the front than was the U.S. VII Corps and most of the scattered divisions being assigned to it. But to have put the XXX Corps into the line at that time would have meant the likelihood of substantial British casualties. Although there is no direct documentary evidence, there can be little doubt that Montgomery had been secretly directed by Field Marshal Sir Alan Brooke, Chief of the Imprial General Staff in London, and possibly even by Churchill, to hold British casualties to a minimum.[6] It has been suggested that if the XXX Corps had been committed in that area before Christmas the German offensive would not have been halted as abruptly and decisively as occurred when General Harmon's 2d Armored

Division smashed the German 2d Panzer Division on 25 and 26 December near Celles. That argument is probably specious, however, in light of the proven fighting qualities of the XXX Corps, from corps commander through all ranks. Nevertheless, it would have meant that the VII Corps could have been ready for the counteroffensive even earlier than it was. Given Montgomery's mind-set, however, this probably would not have altered the course of events.

The shift east of the Ourthe meant that the axis of the VII Corps, which was to make the main effort in the coming counteroffensive, was the Liège-Manhay-Baraque de Fraiture-Houffalize-Bastogne highway.

It is interesting that in discussing the preparations for the counteroffensive and the decision to drive toward Houffalize rather than St. Vith, John Eisenhower, in his account of the Battle of the Bulge, backhandedly supports Monty's operational concept (if not its timing), and the acceptance of that concept by his father, Ike. Young Eisenhower wrote: "This scheme [directing the VII Corps counterattack toward Houffalize] meant squeezing the Bulge at the waist—rather than from the shoulders along the Skyline Drive, which any commander would prefer if it were feasible; but the fighting had to be done where the troops were, and the troops were in Bastogne. So Houffalize was actually the only feasible meeting place."[7]

That argument ignores the fact that both Patton and Collins had earlier argued in favor of converging drives of the VII and XII Corps from the shoulders toward St. Vith.[8] It also suggests that it would have been difficult to move the forces less than 50 miles in a different location; yet such moves were being made frequently by Allied forces. And conveniently forgets that, had they been willing to take the negligible risk involved, both Eisenhower and Bradley could have allowed Patton to assemble adequate forces in the XII Corps for such an operation, and that Eisenhower could have overruled Montgomery so far as the deployment and commitment of the VII Corps was concerned. In other words, Ike eschewed a strategically decisive counterstroke in favor of a half-measure. As Patton rather justly remarks in his diaries, Eisenhower and Bradley were both cautious—too cautious, he thought. But, Patton added, they were not as cautious as Monty.[9]

The only pressure placed by Eisenhower on Montgomery was on 28 December when he insisted that Monty should initiate the Houffalize half-measure option by 3 January, a delay of at least seventy-two hours beyond what both Collins and Ridgway—the two corps commanders directly concerned—considered feasible and desirable.

PLAN AND DEPLOYMENTS FOR THE ALLIED COUNTEROFFENSIVE

Based on guidance received from 21st Army Group Headquarters, the First Army counteroffensive plan called for the main effort to be made by the VII Corps, deployed between the Ourthe and Lienne Rivers, a two-division southward thrust east and west of the Manhay-Houffalize axis. The XVIII Airborne Corps was to protect the left flank of the VII Corps, and to make a secondary attack effort east of the Lienne River with its axis of advance generally along the Salm River from Trois Ponts to Vielsalm. The First Army's other corps— the V Corps, holding the northern shoulder, on the army's left—was to remain on the defensive.

Collins's VII Corps now consisted of five divisions, plus a cavalry group and twelve corps artillery battalions. Although it was to play no part at the outset of the offensive, at dawn on 3 January the 75th Division held a seventeen-kilometer front from Hampteau (just southeast of Hotton) on the Ourthe River, eastward to Grandmenil, just west of Manhay. Once the counteroffensive began, however, the 4th Cavalry Group would take over the extreme right of the corps, on a front extending about seven kilometers from Hampteau eastward to the Aisne River. The 2d Armored Division, reinforced by a regiment of the 84th Infantry Division, was to pass through the center and left of the 75th Division, and attack southward on a front of about ten kilometers, from the Aisne River almost to the Liège-Bastogne highway at Manhay.

To the left of the 2d Armored Division, the 3d Armored Division, reinforced by a regiment of the 83d Infantry Division, was to attack on a front of about nine kilometers from Manhay to the Lienne River. This division sector included the main highway. The two armored divisions were to advance abreast, on either side of the highway axis, toward Houffalize. Behind the 2d Armored Division was the remainder of Maj. Gen. Alexander R. Bolling's 84th Infantry Division, with the mission of mopping up behind General Harmon's tanks. The remainder of the 83d Division, commanded by Maj. Gen. Robert C. Macon, had a similar role, mopping up behind General Rose's 3d Armored Division. The 75th Division, which was to pull back to the rear once the 2d Armored Division passed through, would go into corps reserve. In fact, however, it was to come under First Army's control as the army's reserve.

General Ridgway's XVIII Airborne Corps now consisted of three divisions—82d Airborne, 30th Infantry, 7th Armored—and the rough equivalent of a fourth: the 106th Infantry Division, which essentially consisted of the 424th Infantry, plus two major attachments—the 112th Infantry Regimental Combat Team (RCT) of the 28th Infantry Division and Combat Command B of the 9th Armored Division. While the rump 106th Infantry and the 7th Armored divisions were resting and absorbing replacements after their bitter struggle at St. Vith (see chapter 10), the corps front was held by the other two divisions. Major General James Gavin's 82d Airborne Division was on the right, between the Lienne and Amblève-Salm rivers, a front of about ten kilometers. Farther east, the 30th Infantry Division, commanded by Maj. Gen. Leland S. Hobbs, was stretched out over about fifteen kilometers south of Malmédy, from the Lienne River on the right (west) to Waimes on the left (east).

GERMAN DEPLOYMENTS

Opposing these two American corps was a much-depleted Sixth Panzer Army, recently reorganized and now consisting of only three corps, each of two divisions. On the left, opposite the British XXX Corps and the right wing of the U.S. VII Corps, was the II SS Panzer Corps, commanded by General der Waffen-SS Willi Bittrich. On the right of Bittrich's corps was the 2d SS Panzer Division "Das Reich," with a front of about eight kilometers, astride—but mostly to the east of—the Ourthe River. On the left was the 116th Panzer Division, overextended on a front of nearly twenty kilometers, its right overlapping that of the U.S. VII Corps, but with most of its strength opposite the British XXX Corps.

The center corps of the Sixth Panzer Army was the LXVI Corps of General der Artillerie Walter L. Lucht. On the left of this corps was the 560th Volksgrenadier Division (VGD), its center opposite Manhay, and overlapping the right of the 3d Armored Division and the left of the 2d Armored Division. The right of Lucht's corps was held by the 12th VGD, with its left opposite the 3d Armored Division and its right opposite the right wing of the XVIII Airborne Corps.

East of the LXVI Corps was the right wing of the Sixth Panzer Army, a corps-size task force called Group, or Corps, Felber, commanded by General der Infanterie Hans Felber.

Felber's hastily constructed corps had been committed just two days earlier, when the I SS Panzer Corps had been shifted south to spearhead a new drive against Bastogne (see chapter 18). Facing the XVIII Airborne Corps, Felber's corps consisted of two divisions: the 62d VGD on the left and the 18th VGD on the right.

THE VII CORPS DRIVES SOUTH: 3–11 JANUARY

At 0830 on 3 January the two armored divisions of the VII Corps launched their attacks. For a change it was not snowing, but the weather was bitterly cold. The ground was frozen under a snow cover of nearly a foot with frequent deeper drifts. However, the freeze was not deep enough to permit even the lightest armored vehicles to traverse the marshes that covered much of the Plateau des Tailles, which lay between the advancing Americans and Houffalize. This meant that the armor was road bound, and the narrow, high-crowned roads were treacherously icy.

A low overcast precluded any of the air support that had been planned to help the counteroffensive get off to a good start. The weather would be much the same for the following two weeks with one significant exception: It snowed on many of those subsequent days. On only three days of the fortnight was tactical air support possible, and on only one of those days were the American planes able to participate for more than a few hours. Thus, one of the major Allied advantages—overwhelming airpower—was not available during most of the period of the offensive toward Houffalize.

In addition to an environment decidedly unfavorable to attackers, the Americans were opposed by resourceful, courageous defenders who, while outnumbered, were sufficiently numerous to enable them to fight on more-or-less equal terms with the attackers. The overall American numerical superiority was probably about two to one, and rarely could the attackers take advantage of the initiative and their substantial artillery superiority to bring combat power odds of more than three to one to bear against critical objectives. Clausewitz, recognizing the advantages conferred upon a defender by defensive posture and the effects of terrain, was fond of writing that "defense is the stronger form of combat."[10] By this he meant that the strength of the defender is multiplied by some indefinite factor, the value of which depends on the nature of the terrain and the strength of the defender's position. On the front of the Sixth Panzer Army in early January of 1945 that multiplying factor could not have been less than two: virtually canceling out the two-to-one numerical odds in favor of the Americans.[11]

By evening of 3 January, nevertheless, the American attackers had advanced about three kilometers, with some spearheads five kilometers from the start line. The largest villages to be wrested from the German defenders were Malempré, east of the highway, and Freyneux, to the west. It was much the same on the following days, except the advance was much slower.

On 4 January the 290th Infantry Regiment of the 75th Division, which had been in reserve, moved into the line. It was on the night of the corps, southeast of Hotton, with its right on the Ourthe River. The 1st Battalion took the village of Magoster, and the next day advanced through Beffe with little opposition. Private First Class Charles R. Miller, of Tallahassee, Florida, was a scout in the first platoon of A Company. On the night of 5 January, in a foxhole in front of his platoon, Miller heard movement behind a nearby hedge. Twice he quietly whispered a challenge and got no response. He took a grenade from his musette bag and was about to pull the pin and throw it over the hedge, when the hedge parted—revealing the dark shape of a cow.

The 1st Battalion of the 290th stayed all the next day in its position southeast of Beffe, overlooking the Ourthe River. On 7 January the battalion attacked to the south with A company on the left and B Company on the right. The Germans to their immediate front had withdrawn during the night. Miller and another scout were in the lead, advancing through a wooded area, when the other scout, a recent replacement, fired his rifle. Miller, seeing nothing to his front, called to the other scout to ask what he was shooting at. "Nothing," replied the recruit. "I caught the trigger on a button on my overcoat." Miller, a veteran now, with more than a week of combat under his belt, told the other man to lock his weapon until he saw something to shoot at. The advance continued.

Less than 500 yards further into the woods, Miller saw another soldier, possibly 30 yards to his front. He and the stranger looked at each other: With camouflage nets on them the German and American helmets looked similar. Miller decided that the other man was a German; he dropped to a prone position and fired, wounding the other man. After crying out, the wounded man took shelter in a foxhole and began shooting back at Miller. Realizing that the German (he was now certain of this) was closer to the other scout than to him, Miller called and told him to shoot. The other scout responded, "I can't, my rifle won't work." In the excitement he had forgotten to unlock it.

At this point Miller's platoon leader ran up, and flopped down a few yards behind him. "Quit firing!" he called out. "You are shooting at B Company."

"B Company, Hell!" Miller replied. "The woods are full of Germans." At that moment Miller's words were confirmed by a long burst from a German machine gun, which went over their heads, and sprayed the nearby trees. The lieutenant then ordered a BAR man (a soldier equipped with a Browning automatic rifle, really a light machine gun) to join him and Miller, and to open fire in the direction of the German machine gun. After a desultory exchange of fire it became obvious to the A Company men that the Germans, using classic delaying tactics, had pulled back. Again the advance continued.[12]

This is the way it was all along the VII Corps front for the next few days. By 5 January the 2d Armored Division had fought its way into Odeigne, just east of Freyneux. On the next day the 2d Armored had all of Odeigne, and the 3d Armored had reached Fraiture and was approaching the nearby Baraque de Fraiture road intersection, known to the Americans as "Parker's Crossroads" (see chapter 10). The total advance of the 3d Armored Division had been about eight kilometers in four days; the 2d Armored had advanced about seven kilometers in the same time.

The German resistance had been consistently bitter and effective. The 2d Armored suffered 44 killed, 321 wounded, and 26 missing between 3 and 6 January, while the 3d Armored lost 45 killed, 329 wounded, and 23 missing over the same period. Every American gain had been followed by a German counterattack, which often drove the attackers back to their starting point. At best, progress was "two steps forward, one step back." The Germans were exhausted, and their morale was low. Few among them did not realize that the war was lost. Yet the determination, skill, courage, and imagination of their resistance aroused the reluctant admiration of the Americans. German losses were also heavy: The 12th VGD had lost about 80 killed, 240 wounded, and more than 300 captured and missing during 3–7 January, while losses in the neighboring 560th VGD were generally similar.

The following day, 7 January, was snowy. But the attackers were able to match the fighting qualities of the defenders. The 3d Armored Division took Parker's Crossroads, while farther west the 2d Armored Division cut the La Roche–Salmchâteau road east of Samrée.

The necessity for the armor to be roadbound on icy, treacherous roads forced the infantry to play a greater role in the offensive than General Collins had originally intended. By 7 January the 84th Division, with two regiments abreast, had pulled into line west (to the right) of the 2d Armored Division. Similarly, on the left, the uncommitted units of the 83d Division were in line east (left) of the 3d Armored Division.

Hitler's reluctant recognition on 8 January of the failure of his offensive had some effect on the command structure of the German defenders, but had little practical effect on the battlefield struggle. He permitted a withdrawal of the salient nose back to the Ourthe River—a decision that affected only the Fifth Panzer Army—and he ordered the Waffen-SS units to be disengaged. Dietrich was to turn over his small portion of the front to the Fifth Panzer Army and to withdraw his Sixth Panzer Army Headquarters back to the vicinity of St. Vith, around which the two SS Panzer corps and the four SS Panzer divisions were to rally as soon as they could be readily withdrawn from the battle.[13] Theoretically this would establish a reserve to protect against a possible Allied counteroffensive from the shoulders. Practically, however, the move gave to Hitler a strategic reserve, which could be committed elsewhere on the eastern or western fronts.

The German withdrawal and reorganization had little effect on the bitter fighting on most of the U.S. VII Corps front. On the extreme right of the corps, however, the pace of the advance quickened slightly as German units farther west pulled back to the Ourthe. On 10 January patrols from the 4th Cavalry Group entered La Roche. West of the Ourthe River the British encountered little or no resistance, but nevertheless keyed their advance to that of the Americans east of the river. This, of course, was consistent with Montgomery's obvious desire to avoid a major British involvement.

On 9 January the 83d Infantry Division had assumed the major offensive role on the east (left) wing of the VII Corps. This was a reflection of the effect on the 3d Armored Division tanks of increasingly marshy ground, and reduced roadnet on the Plateau des Tailles. Making the division's main effort was the 1st Battalion of the 330th Infantry Regiment.

Early on 10 January the headquarters of the 1st Battalion of the 330th lost radio contact with A Company. The battalion commander decided to send a new radio—SCR 300—to A Company. Private John R. Nordblom was selected as the deliveryman. He was carried to the known vicinity of A Company on the back of a tank of Company C, 774th Tank Battalion, attached to the infantry battalion. Arriving near the presumed location of the missing company, Nordblom jumped off the tank, radio strapped to his back, and headed across an open, snow-covered field to find the company command post. The antenna of the radio made a good target, and nearby Germans opened fire. Nordblom was hit in the side and hip, and dropped in the snow.

An M4 tank of C/774 pushed through the snow toward the wounded man, firing its machine gun to suppress the Germans. The tank reached Nordblom, the tank commander jumped out, laid him on the back of the tank, and jumped back inside. Still firing its machine gun at the Germans, the tank hightailed it to the rear and to the battalion aid station, where Nordblom received preliminary treatment, before being evacuated to a field hospital. The radio was finally delivered to A Company later that day.[14]

Also on 10 January the 2d Armored Division captured Samrée, and by the next day the infantry units on both wings of the VII Corps had crossed the La Roche–Salmchâteau highway. After repulsing German counterattacks, the offensive paused briefly, while the armored divisions performed long-overdue maintenance.

THE XVIII AIRBORNE CORPS OFFENSIVE

The mission assigned to General Ridgway's corps by the First Army was to advance southward toward the Houffalize–St. Vith highway, its movements conforming generally to those of the VII Corps on its right. The advance was related to phase lines, which were changed almost daily, in accordance with the pace of the VII Corps offensive. Gavin's 82d Airborne Division was on the right of the XVIII Corps; Hobbs's 30th Infantry Division was on the left. The 7th Armored Division and the one-regiment 106th Infantry Division were in reserve.

General Hobbs's 30th Infantry Division, to which the 112th Infantry RCT was attached, held a front nearly twenty kilometers in length from just east of the Salm River eastward to Waimes. Initially the 30th Division was to hold its positions, except for a feint or diversion south of Malmédy on the first day of the offensive, 3 January.

Having incurred substantial casualties in fighting in late December, and having had no replacements, Gavin's 82d Airborne was severely under-strength. However, the attachment of the independent 517th Parachute Infantry Regiment (plus its RCT companion, the 460th Parachute Field Artillery Battalion, but minus its 2d Battalion, which was still attached to the 7th Armored Division) and the independent 551st Parachute Battalion, brought Gavin's division to approximately full strength. From left to right (east to west) his attacking units were deployed as follows: 517th Parachute Infantry, commanded by Col. Rupert Graves, with the 551st Parachute Battalion attached; 325th Glider Infantry Regiment, commanded by Col. Charles Billingslea, in the center; and Col. William E. Ekman's 505th Parachute Infantry Regiment. In reserve were the 504th Parachute Infantry Regiment, commanded by Col. Reuben H. Tucker, and Col. Roy E. Lindquist's 508th Parachute Infantry Regiment.

On the first day of the offensive, 3 January, the 517th quickly took Trois Ponts. Although German resistance was determined, the other two regiments had little trouble keeping pace with the advance of the VII Corps on the right. On this and subsequent days their commanders—and, particularly the division commander, Gavin—complained that they were unduly constrained by the phase lines, which forced them to conform with the VII Corps advance. Nevertheless, while the terrain was probably slightly less rugged than that in which the VII Corps was operating, and the opposition possibly slightly thinner on the ground, the paratroopers' advance was not easy. They had the same miserable weather to contend with, and their German opponents fought just as tenaciously. Casualties in the division were very high, totaling 138 killed, 647 wounded, and 44 missing over the first four days of the attack.[15] While Gavin claimed that his right wing regiment—the 505th—could have reached the Salm River on 4 January if it had not been constrained by phase lines, this is doubtful.

The 30th Division joined the offensive on 6 January, attacking southward from Stavelot toward Spineux and Wanne, with the main effort being made on the division's right by the attached 112th Infantry Regiment. These towns, plus Wanneranval, were occupied the next day.

In the following days, despite miserable weather, both divisions advanced slowly but steadily toward their objectives. On 9 January the 106th Division was committed on the right of the 30th Division, taking over the sector that had been held by the 112th Infantry.[16] By 10 January the 82d Airborne had completely cleared the triangle formed by the Salm River and the Vielsalm-Odrimont road, and had secured a bridgehead across the Salm River near Grand-Halleux. On the next day Maj. Gen. Fay B. Prickett's 75th Infantry Division moved in to relieve the 82d Airborne Division, which was pulled back to reserve to lick its wounds.

VII CORPS DRIVES TO HOUFFALIZE

On 12 January, after a very brief lull, all four VII Corps front-line divisions pushed south of the La Roche–Salmchâteau road onto the Plateau des Tailles. The pace quickened on 13 January, as spearheads of the 3d Armored Division reached the Houffalize–St. Vith road, north of the east fork of the Ourthe River. On the right, the 2d Armored Division was within seven kilometers of Houffalize.

The inexorable advance of the Americans south and north of Houffalize, and the heavy casualties being incurred by the German defenders (divisions in the front line were, on average, each losing about 150 men per day)[17] might have been enough to convince Hitler that his troops could no longer hold a significant salient in the Ardennes, and that a withdrawal to the Westwall was inevitable. However, events on the east front facilitated his formal recognition of this fact. On 12 January the Soviets launched their powerful 1945 Winter Offensive in southern Poland. Massive buildups of Soviet forces to the north and south were detected by German intelligence, making it evident that the offensive would spread north into East Prussia and south into Hungary.

Thus, when Field Marshal von Rundstedt appealed to Hitler on 14 January to authorize a further withdrawal in the Ardennes to positions east of the

Salm River, Hitler readily approved, and demanded that the withdrawal of the Sixth Panzer Army, the two SS Panzer corps and four SS Panzer divisions, be expedited.[18] He refused, however, to approve Rundstedt's and Model's recommendation for a phased withdrawal back to the Rhine River. He insisted that further withdrawals be halted at the Westwall.

The result was that on 15 January the 2d Armored Division and the 84th Infantry Division found that the 116th Panzer Division and other elements of the LXVI Corps were withdrawing across the Ourthe River west of Houffalize. Patrols from the 2d Armored Division entered Houffalize late in the day, to find it abandoned by the Germans. Early on 16 January a patrol from the VII Corps 2d Armored Division met a patrol from the VIII Corps 11th Armored Division southwest of the town. The First and Third armies were again in contact with each other, exactly one month after their link had been ruptured at Losheim by the German offensive.

Farther east the 3d Armored Division advanced across the Houffalize–St. Vith Road, while the 83d Infantry Division pushed to the southeastern slopes of the Plateau des Tailles, and into the Salm River valley, southwest of Salm-château and the right wing of the XVIII Airborne Corps.

The linkup of the First and Third U.S. armies at Houffalize was immediately reported to SHAEF Headquarters. Orders were issued at once ending the temporary attachment of the First Army to the 21st Army Group. The order was effective at midnight, 17–18 January. The 12th Army Group was no longer a one-army group. However, as he had promised Monty, Ike left the Ninth Army under British command.

THE XVIII CORPS (A/B) ADVANCES TOWARD ST. VITH

When the XVIII Airborne Corps resumed its offensive on 13 January, the resistance of Corps Felber, which that day was redesignated the XIII Corps, was as determined and vigorous as it had been during the previous ten days. Opposite the XVIII Corps was the 18th VGD, holding a line running generally northeasterly from just north of Vielsalm to where the Malmédy–St. Vith highway crosses the Amblève River. General Ridgway's plan was to have his left and center divisions—the 30th and the 106th—attack southward against the main positions of the 18th VGD, while his right-flank division, the 75th, held in position west of the Salm River, north and south of Vielsalm, placing enfilading fire on the defending Germans. The main effort would be on the left, by the 30th Infantry Division. It was planned that when the Germans had begun to fall back in the face of the attacks from the north, the 75th would cross the Salm, envelop the left flank of the 18th VGD, and drive eastward to link with the 30th Division somewhere northwest of St. Vith. As a result the 18th VGD would either be encircled, or destroyed, or driven in disorderly withdrawal to the south and east. Once the 30th and 75th Infantry divisions linked up, of course, the 106th Division, in the center, would be pinched out.

Much to Ridgway's annoyance the 30th Division, which had developed a reputation as a "fighting division," advanced less than three kilometers on 13 January. Particularly disappointing was the performance of the 119th Infantry Regiment, attacking down the Malmédy–St. Vith road on the division's left. That evening Ridgway summoned General Hobbs, his Assistant Division Commander, Brig. Gen. William K. Harrison, and the division Chief of Staff, Col. Richard W. Stephens, to his headquarters. There Ridgway gave Hobbs a severe dressing-down, as he expressed his keen disappointment with the 30th Division and with its leadership. When he spoke of the poor performance of the 119th Infantry, Hobbs told Ridgway that he had already relieved the regimental commander, Col. Roy G. Fitzgerald. Somewhat mollified, Ridgway told Hobbs that the division would be expected to take its initial objectives the next day; implicit was the threat that failure to take the objectives would result in relief of the division commander. The division took those objectives before noon the next day, at a cost of 33 killed, 114 wounded, and 106 missing.

Meanwhile, the 106th Division had attacked into the German positions south of Stavelot. The 517th Parachute Infantry Regiment had been attached, giving General Perrin two infantry regiments: the 517th plus his own 424th Infantry. The 424th Infantry, on the right, was to make a holding attack against the German line, which extended northeastward from the Salm River near Tigeonville to the vicinity of Henumont, south of Stavelot. The 517th Parachute Infantry, on the left, was to cross the Amblève River, attack on a narrow front to penetrate the German line near Lodomez, and envelop the right of the German line facing the 424th.

After overcoming fierce resistance on 13 January, the 106th Division fully accomplished its initial mission on the next day. The penetration by the 517th was successful, and the two regiments drove the Germans back to an east-west line running generally from Ennal in the west to Poteau in the east. The relatively inexperienced and badly battered 106th Division, with only two regiments, actually made better progress those two days than did the full-strength, veteran 30th Division on its left.

As the 30th and 106th divisions continued their offensives on 15 January, there was little diminution in the effectiveness of German resistance. Unlike the LXVI Corps to its left, the XIII Corps had not received any orders to withdraw. Thus, when the 75th Infantry Division started its attack toward Vielsalm on 15 January, it made little progress. Some of the frustrations experienced by the division on that and earlier days were described after the war by Lt. Robert H. Justice, of E Company, 2d Battalion, 291st Infantry Regiment.

On the 9th of January, following a three-day rest with baths, clean clothes, and hot meals, the regiment left Creppe-Spa in the early hours of the evening. Marching for eleven hours, over 22 miles of icy roads and knee-deep snow, the regiment arrived at Basse Bodeux, Belgium, at 0500 hours. The hike lasted all through the night, and it shall never be forgotten by the men who made it. It was bitter cold, and marching had to be done on roads that were icy, on country roads that were filled with snow, across fields and through snow drifts, sometimes two feet deep.

Completing relief of the 82nd Airborne Division, the next few days were spent in sending out patrols and preparing for a prospective attack on the enemy near Grand Halleaux.

On the morning of January 15th, the 291st went into its first attack as a regiment. [Previous commitments had been made by battalions, usually attached to more experienced units.] The objective was high ground, outside Grand Halleaux, where the enemy was strongly entrenched.

The 2nd Battalion with an exposed left flank attacked from Grand Halleaux toward Petit Thier. "E" and "G" Companies led the attack with "F" Company in reserve. Both companies were pinned down during the day by heavy enemy fire.

This town will be remembered for a lifetime by the survivors of this engagement. ... The men of the 2nd Battalion, 291st Infantry ... had many factors that were against them. But we held what ground we took that day and suffered heavy casualties.

Our main obstacles that day were not only the enemy—but again snow—OD [olive drab] clothing. We were like ducks on a pond, and it was our first offensive action. . . .[19]

The next day Ridgway visited the 75th Division and spoke to its commander, General Prickett. Ridgway and the First Army commander, General Hodges, had had reason to discuss the division's earlier, less than satisfactory, performance during its brief baptism of fire in late December. Hodges had suggested that Prickett's leadership had been deficient, and that he should be relieved. Ridgway had apparently responded that he thought Prickett should be given a "full test in battle," and Hodges had concurred. Ridgway was still willing to give Prickett another chance, as a result of his visit to the division on 16 January, until the very end of his conversation with the division commander. They were in a regimental command post. Before leaving, Ridgway asked Prickett what corps headquarters could do to help him. Prickett responded, "Just pray for me."[20]

As Ridgway wrote in his memoirs, "Now I believe in the power of prayer as deeply as any man, but the tenor of this reply, made in the presence of his officers, shocked me. It indicated an attitude of mind totally lacking in self-confidence, in the aggressive spirit that dangerous moment called for." Ridgway continued: "I called him outside, explained to him the implications of his statement, and the disastrous effect it could not help but have on the spirit of his subordinates. Then, with deepest regret, for he was a good friend whom I deeply admired, I ordered his relief."[21]

Ridgway's message was understood in the 75th Division. The next day, 16 January, the 75th began to move across the front of the 106th Division, under a new commander, Brig. Gen. Ray E. Porter. Two days later its patrols had made contact with those of the 30th Division south of Poteau.

The stage was set for the final battle of the Bulge campaign.

20

"OLD BLOOD AND GUTS" SUPPRESSES DOUBTS

"The Americans' 'Small Solution'"

After the unsuccessful conclusion of the last serious German attacks directed toward the capture of Bastogne on 3–4 January, the initiative on the southern face of the Ardennes salient clearly lay with General Patton's Third Army. The major question facing the Americans was how best to utilize their hard-won advantage and reduce the "Bulge"—as the salient was now known to every American serviceman from private to general—in the shortest time and with the least cost. As we have seen, Patton especially favored a combined drive from both shoulders of the salient: While his XII Corps was advancing toward Bitburg there would be a corresponding thrust from the First Army through Prüm into the German Eifel. This bold plan would have compelled the Germans to retreat hastily, or else let most of their forces in the Ardennes be encircled and lost. Such an offensive, however, required speed, reasonably good weather, and an adequate roadnet to handle the mechanized forces needed. There was an excellent highway from Luxembourg City through Echternach to Bitburg (dubbed—for unknown reasons—the "Honeymoon Trail" by the Third Army staff).[1]

However, the roadnet southeast of the Elsenborn Ridge, which would have to be employed by the mechanized formations of Hodges's First Army in such an offensive, was less suitable for such a major effort. Considering the heavy traffic they would have to bear, the roads were narrow, winding, often unsurfaced, and worn by heavy traffic over the previous three weeks of battle. With this consideration in mind, reinforced by an understandable reluctance to take risks in the aftermath of the Germans' surprise the previous month, neither Bradley (Patton's immediate superior) nor Eisenhower supported Patton's plan. As we have seen, Montgomery, in debating the matter with General Collins, commander of the VII Corps, had already ruled out such an offensive action from the north (see chapter 17). With the three most senior Allied commanders opposed to the idea, Patton's proposal was dropped, much to his disappointment.

Frustrated by this determination, which effectively scotched any possibility of a First Army thrust from the north to match that of the Third Army from the south, the Allied commanders proposed a less effective offensive plan. Driving from north and south against the "waist" of the Bulge (instead of against the "shoulders"), the First and Third armies would meet at or near Houffalize, a small town on the Ourthe River about fourteen kilometers north-northeast of Bastogne. Hopefully, this effort would cut off the armored spearhead of the Fifth Panzer Army, and then drive on to St. Vith and Clervaux to eliminate the Bulge. By mid-January, Field Marshal von Rundstedt would refer to this decision and its resulting offensive as "the Americans' 'small solution,'" in contrast to the much more dangerous (for the Germans) "big solution" directed against the shoulders of the Bulge.

THE SITUATION ON 5 JANUARY

The Germans having failed in their attacks against Bastogne and the land corridor into town by 5 January 1945, Patton's Third Army was prepared to begin the drive on Houffalize. Third Army troops had a secure hold along the entire southern flank of the Ardennes salient, from the vicinity of St. Hubert in the west to Echternach, about seventy-seven kilometers (forty-eight miles) to the east-southeast. General Middleton's VIII Corps held the left flank, essentially the front west of Bastogne. General Millikin's III Corps was concentrated in the Bastogne salient proper, and as far east as Ettelbruck. Finally, General Eddy's XII Corps covered the remainder of the front, facing the battered volksgrenadier divisions of the Seventh Army's LXXXV and LXXX corps.

The left-flank, or most western, division of Middleton's corps was Major General Culin's 87th Infantry Division that—stiffened by the 761st Tank Battalion and the French 4th Parachute Battalion assigned to the division to cover its left flank—faced Bayerlein's Panzer Lehr Division from the vicinity of St. Hubert to Gérimont. To the east of Culin's division lay Maj. Gen. William L. Miley's 17th Airborne Division,[2] which only two days before (3 January) had moved forward from the Meuse River to take over the positions of the 4th and 11th Armored divisions, and Combat Command A of the 9th Armored Division.

William Maynadier Miley was born in Fort Mason, California, on 26 December 1897, the son and descendant of Army officers. He was appointed to West Point from Illinois in 1915, and graduated in June 1918 as part of the abbreviated wartime program. Commissioned a second lieutenant of Infantry, he attended the Infantry Service School at Fort Sill for three months before going to the 48th Infantry at Fort Servier, South Carolina. Miley did not get overseas before the Armistice, but served briefly with the 1st Division on occupation duty in Germany (June–September 1919).

Miley spent the years between the wars in a variety of troop command, school, and staff assignments. He was promoted to major in April 1940, and in October took command of the 501st Parachute Infantry Battalion. Promoted to lieutenant colonel in June 1941 and to temporary colonel in February 1942, he became commander of the 503d Parachute Infantry Regiment in March 1942. He was promoted to temporary brigadier general on 25 June 1942, and served first as Assistant Division Commander of the 96th Infantry Division and then briefly commanded the 1st Parachute Brigade. Miley next served as Assistant Division Commander of the 82d Airborne Division from September 1942 to February 1943. After promotion to temporary major general, he took command of the 17th Airborne Division when it was activated on 19 April 1943 at Camp Mackall, North Carolina. The division, comprising the 193d and 194th Glider Infantry regiments and the 507th (attached) and 517th Glider Infantry regiments, underwent training in North Carolina and Tennessee before moving to Britain in August 1944.[3] After further training in Britain, the 17th Airborne was flown to Reims, France (23–25 December 1944), and then marched by road to Neufchâteau, where on 3 January it joined General Middleton's VIII Corps, and officially relieved the 28th Infantry Division.

The arrival of the 17th Airborne allowed General Kilburn's 11th Armored Division to go into corps reserve to recover and reorganize from the battering it had received over the preceding several days. Gaffey's hard-fighting, veteran 4th Armored Division continued to hold a seven-kilometer front northwest of Assensois.

East of the VIII Corps zone lay the front held by Millikin's III Corps. On the corps left flank was Maj. Gen. Maxwell D. Taylor's 101st Airborne Division, holding just over 15 kilometers on the northern and eastern faces of the Bastogne perimeter. Beginning in the salient just southeast of the 101st Airborne's sector was a 14-kilometer front between Marvie and Magaret held by Maj. Gen. Robert Grow's 6th Armored Division. To the right (south and east) of the 6th Armored's front lay Maj. Gen. Paul Baade's 35th Infantry Division, holding a 15-kilometer front. Finally, the right flank of the III Corps was held by Maj. Gen. Willard Paul's 26th Infantry Division along a 9.5-kilometer front.

Next in line in the Third Army's front was General Eddy's XII Corps. The western portion of the XII Corps sector was held by Maj. Gen. Horace L. McBride's 80th Infantry Division, stretched over twenty-two kilometers from Heiderschied east to Ettelbruck along the Sure River. East of McBride's division lay the positions of Maj. Gen. S. Leroy Irwin's 5th "Red Diamond" Infantry Division, which stretched for about twenty-nine kilometers along the Sure-Sauer River, from the vicinity of Diekirch east to where the Ernz Noire

(Schwarz Ernz) creek flows north from its ravine into the Sauer River between Beaufort and Berdorf. The 5th Division's forward positions rested on the south bank of the river, where its occupants could clearly see their German opposites on the north bank. The easternmost unit of Eddy's corps, holding the southern shoulder of the Bulge salient, was Brig. Gen. Harold W. Blakeley's 4th "Ivy" Infantry Division.[4] The 4th Division's sector ran for more than thirty-five kilometers from the Ernz Noire east to Echternach and then bent south to follow the Sauer River to its junction with the Moselle.

On the German side of the southern face of the Bulge, opposite the VIII, III, and XII corps of the Third Army, lay four German corps of the Fifth Panzer and Seventh armies. On the extreme right, or west, facing the 17th Airborne Division, was the left, or southern, flank of the XLVII Panzer Corps. This was a hodgepodge of units around Tronlé controlled by the 3d Panzergrenadier Division, now reduced by heavy combat to shadows of their former selves.[5]

Next, facing the tough but weary airborne troops of the "Screaming Eagles" were elements of the 26th Volksgrenadier Division (VGD), the west or right flank unit of General Priess's I SS Panzer Corps.[6] Northeast of Bastogne, the 9th SS Panzer Division "Hohenstaufen," had just received orders to move north into reserve and revert to the control of the Sixth Panzer Army. Most of its positions were taken over by troops from the neighboring 12th SS Panzer Division "Hitlerjugend," which occupied positions immediately to the south and east. Due east of Bastogne lay the 340th VGD.

Southeast of Bastogne was Corps Decker,[7] including the 167th VGD, the 1st SS Panzer Division, and Panzer Lehr's long-separated 901st Panzergrenadier Regiment. The boundary between the Fifth Panzer and Seventh armies began at the tip of the German salient southeast of Bastogne. There the 1st SS Panzer and 5th Parachute divisions, belonging to two corps, each under a different army, occupied a triangular salient around Harlange, which had been the focus of the 35th Division's attentions since Christmas Eve.

To the east of the salient were the 5th Parachute Division and 9th VGD divisions of General von Rothkirch's LIII Corps, part of General Brandenberger's Seventh Army. Farther east were the 79th and the 352d VGDs, which together comprised General Kniess's LXXXV Corps. The left flank of the southern face of the Bulge was held by General Beyer's LXXX Corps, consisting of the 276th and 212th VGDs. Farther east and southeast were a few static second-rate fortress and garrison battalions.

These German forces on the southern front of the Ardennes salient appeared formidable on paper. Indeed, they were numerous and still possessed considerable defensive fighting power. However, their capacity for offensive action or for rapid movement had dwindled, and in some cases had vanished. The troops were tired, cold, often hungry, increasingly discouraged, and continually harassed by repeated Allied air attacks and nearly omnipresent American artillery fire. The units had generally taken heavy personnel casualties and had also suffered extensive matériel losses, especially in transport. In comparison, the Americans opposing them benefited from Allied command of the air, as well as from the usually efficient U.S. Army logistics and service systems. Most of the American troops in the Ardennes had by this time been exposed to combat, often under very trying conditions, and had consequently "seen the elephant" and gained valuable experience and considerable confidence in their own abilities. None of these conditions boded well for the battle-weary Germans.

PATTON'S DRIVE NORTH: 5–7 JANUARY

Although the cessation of large-scale German offensive efforts against Bastogne did not mark an immediate change in the character of the battle, the initiative had finally and thoroughly passed to the Third Army. As the month of January wore on, the Germans were compelled to react, as best their increasingly battered forces and strained supply system would permit, to American attacks and movements. There were only a few exceptions, such as in some of the fighting west of Bastogne during this period. Nor had the Germans been so badly hammered that they had given up responding to American attacks with sharp counterattacks.

In Middleton's VIII Corps sector on 5 January, the 87th Infantry Division continued its efforts to advance past Pironpré and Bonnerue, but made little progress against determined resistance from Panzer Lehr's screening forces, now reinforced by elements of the division's main body. Although the 17th Airborne Division's 194th Glider Infantry Regiment had to withdraw about 1,500 meters to the vicinity of Pinsamont and Houmontin in the face of determined attacks by the Führer Begleit Brigade, the 513th Parachute Infantry captured Mande–St. Etienne on 5 January, and held the village against a local German counterattack in the afternoon. The next day both U.S. divisions pushed forward, with the 87th mounting a limited attack against Tillet, where it encountered stubborn resistance from the Führer Begleit Brigade. General Culin committed the 761st Tank Battalion from division reserve. This was an African-American outfit (other than artillery battalions, the only black ground combat unit in the European Theater), which had fought with distinction in the Lorraine campaign of November and early December, and had gained the praise of General Patton for its performance.[8] After a slight advance, the tankers were also stopped by the determined German defense. On the next day efforts by both infantry and armor to take Tillet were repulsed by the Germans, with heavy losses on both sides.

General Gaffey's 4th Armored Division, with Combat Command B in VIII Corps reserve, remained quiet on both days. The division had yet to recover fully from its intense efforts in November and early December in Lorraine, and was able to take advantage of this lull to carry out maintenance and administrative tasks that had been deferred during active operations.

On 7 January, the 87th Infantry Division continued its efforts to capture Tillet, tangling with elements of both the Panzer Lehr Division and the Führer Begleit Brigade. The 345th Infantry relieved the 347th Infantry in early morning, allowing the 347th to assemble, relatively undisturbed, for another attack later in the day. Advance elements of the 347th Infantry occupied parts of Tillet by nightfall, an advance of 2,000 meters.

In the 17th Airborne Division's sector, the 193d Glider Infantry Regiment held its positions, while the 194th Glider Infantry pushed northward to capture Rechrival, Millomont, Renaumont, and Hubermont. However, two sharp counterattacks on the night of 7–8 January by units from the Führer Begleit Brigade recaptured Millomont and Renaumont. Meanwhile, the 513th Parachute Infantry had advanced nearly 2,300 meters to reach the southern outskirts of Flamierge by midday of 7 January, but withdrew about 400 meters after nightfall, thus forestalling a planned counterattack by elements of the 3d Panzergrenadier Division. The 4th Armored Division remained quiet, undertaking no significant operations before 10 January.

This period began slowly for Millikin's III Corps, as the 6th Armored Division recuperated a little on 5 January from the exertions of the first days of 1945. The 35th Infantry Division spent the day probing around the battered ruins of Lutrebois, but accomplished little, as resistance from the 1st SS Panzer Division was both skillful and fanatically determined. The next day the 6th Armored was busy repelling heavy attacks from the 12th SS Panzer Division to its north. The fighting was bitter, but the weariness of the "Hitlerjugend" troopers and their shortages of equipment (especially armored vehicles) hampered their progress. The 35th Division attacked into the wooded ground northeast of Lutrebois, while holding its hard-won positions around Villers-la-Bonne-Eau. Repeated 1st SS Panzer Division "Leibstandarte" attacks against those positions led to the commitment of the 6th Cavalry Squadron to help stiffen the American lines there. On 7 January the 6th Armored was once more involved in heavy combat against German tank and infantry attacks, mostly in the Neffe-Wardin sector. A limited attack by the 35th Division nearly reached the Lutrebois-Lutremange road, tangling once more with the "Leibstandarte." The 35th Division, in close combat with the SS troops did not notice the departure of the 901st Panzergrenadier Regiment of the Panzer Lehr Division, which began to withdraw to rejoin its parent unit on the western side of the Bastogne salient.

The front of General Eddy's XII Corps remained generally quiet for more than a week. The battle-weary volksgrenadiers facing the XII Corps were grateful to have escaped with their lives and were unwilling to provoke another American reaction. On 6 January the 80th Division (on the corps' left or west flank) sent its 319th Infantry across the Sure River near Heiderscheidergrund, and captured the nearby hamlets of Goesdorf and Dahl. After this brief flurry of activity, calm settled in once more, and there was little activity on the XII Corps front until 11 January.

PATTON'S DRIVE CONTINUES: 8–9 JANUARY

In the west, the Germans reacted to the 87th Division's successes by initiating a set of large-scale counterattacks on 8 January. Although none of these efforts by the Panzer Lehr Division and Führer Begleit Brigade broke through the 87th Division's front line, they compelled the 345th and 347th Infantry regiments to withdraw an average of 2,000 meters, abandoning the recently captured settlements of Bonnerue and Tillet. This unexpected German resurgence led General Culin to commit all three of his infantry regiments to counterattack; the comparatively fresh and rested 346th Infantry assumed the brunt of offensive action. The 346th encountered heavy resistance from elements of Bayerlein's Panzer Lehr Division and gained little ground, although it continued to attack Tillet after nightfall. The 345th Infantry made better progress, capturing the high ground about 2,700 meters west-northwest of Gérimont, an advance of nearly three kilometers. In reaction to the division's slow advance and the strong opposition, Patton lent Culin the 691st Tank Destroyer Battalion (towed) and the 12th Infantry (part of the XII Corps 4th Infantry Division). Already supporting the 87th Division were the 761st Tank Battalion and the French 4th Parachute Battalion.

The fighting on the outskirts of Tillet was particularly intense on 9 January for A and C companies of the 761st Tank Battalion. One of A Company's platoon leaders, S.Sgt. Henry H. Conway of Chicago, became separated from the rest of his platoon. He put his tank into hull defilade (all of the tank except the top of its turret and its gun were protected from enemy observation and fire by an undulation of the ground), and for an hour he engaged sixteen German tanks. His tank was hit, and the rear hatch was blown off, but Conway held on until he was rescued by the arrival of other tanks from the 761st.

The platoons of C Company, under Capt. Charles A. Gates, were all commanded by enlisted men: Staff Sergeants Frank C. Cochrane of Beacon, New York, and Moses E. Dade, of Washington, D.C., and Sgt. Theodore Windsor of Cleveland, Ohio. Cochrane led his platoon throughout the day, even though his tank was hit three times. The turret top of Dade's tank was shot off by a German 88, but the tank was not otherwise damaged, and Dade continued to operate it. Windsor's tank was also hit; it was knocked out of action, with its driver killed. Windsor got into another tank from which he continued to lead his platoon. But that tank hit a mine and lost a track; then it was also knocked out by German antitank fire. Windsor and two unwounded companions—Sgt. William H. McBurney and Pvt. Leonard J. Smith, both from New York City—dismounted. Alternately crawling and running through freezing snow and ice, they reached safety, and were able to return to the 761st after dark.[9]

As the 87th Division continued its seesaw struggle for Tillet and Bonnerue with dogged German opponents from the Panzer Lehr Division and Führer Begleit Brigade, the paratroopers from Miley's 17th Airborne Division, eager to redeem their disappointing performance on 4 January, were themselves involved in a close-fought struggle for the approaches to Flamierge. Strong German tank-infantry counterattacks during 8 January forced the division to fall back over 1,800 meters along a 3.6-kilometer front south of Flamierge. In the confusion, most of one battalion of the 513th Parachute Infantry was cut off on the outskirts of Flamierge. On 9 January the isolated force from the 513th Parachute Infantry exfiltrated to American lines, little the worse for wear. German attacks around Flamierge continued unabated, taking advantage of poor flying weather to hammer their opponents while they had a respite from the jabos.

On 8 January the III Corps prepared for a major attack the next day. Patton had disengaged Maj. Gen. James A. Van Fleet's 90th Infantry Division from its front-line positions in the XX Corps zone facing the Saar several days earlier.[10] The Third Army commander had then moved Van Fleet's division north by truck to assemble behind the right (southeast) flank of the 35th Division and adjoining left (west) flank of the 26th Division. At the same time, the 6th Armored Division, having weathered the German attacks of the two preceding days, recovered some of the ground it had lost east of Wardin and Neffe, pushing back troops from the 12th SS Panzer Division.

Before dawn on 9 January Van Fleet's 90th Division moved forward to the attack, the spearhead of Patton's renewed offensive against the southern flank of the Ardennes salient. The presence of the 90th Division was completely unsuspected by either Rothkirch's LIII Corps or the 5th Parachute Division. Benefiting from almost complete tactical surprise, Van Fleet's infantry advanced between the 35th and 26th divisions and plowed into the junction between the right (west) flank of the 5th Parachute and the positions of the 104th Panzergrenadier Regiment of the 15th Panzergrenadier Division. The attackers took Berle and advanced nearly 2,000 meters through difficult terrain in numbing cold (the low for the day was −6 degrees Fahrenheit, or −21 degrees Centigrade).

As part of Patton's general offensive, the 26th Division pushed forward to capture Bavigne and the heights northwest of the village. The 6th Armored's Combat Command A and the 35th Division's 134th Infantry advanced along the low ridge southeast of Marvie and feinted toward Wardin. To the south, the 137th Infantry attacked Villers-la-Bonne-Eau, with mortars and artillery pummeling the charred ruins of the hamlet yet again.

Unknown to the Americans, 9 January was the date on which Hitler, at last recognizing the failure of the German efforts to capture Bastogne, finally bowed to reality and authorized the withdrawal of General von Lüttwitz's XLVII Panzer Corps from the exposed western tip of the Ardennes salient. Characteristically, the Nazi dictator did not permit a withdrawal all the way to Houffalize, but only to an intermediate position stretching from Dochamps to Longchamps. Hitler also ordered the withdrawal of two volksartillerie corps from the Ardennes for assignment elsewhere, a sure sign that his enthusiasm for operations there had waned, and that his attention was shifting elsewhere. That day also marked the departure of Corps Decker from the scene, with General Decker finally following the XXXIX Panzer Corps headquarters units, which had left the Bastogne area on 4–5 January. Hitler also began the process of disengaging his beloved SS panzer divisions for hasty refit and offensive operations against the Soviets in Hungary.

On 9 January, as the III Corps offensive developed, Middleton's VIII Corps continued its push north. Culin's 87th Infantry Division, now operating with thirteen infantry battalions (instead of its normal nine), pushed on toward Tillet. The 346th Infantry finally secured the village, its elusive and costly goal, as the neighboring 345th Infantry regained the positions it had reached on the evening of 7 January. Miley's 17th Airborne Division, however, temporarily suspended further offensive operations, instead consolidating its positions and preparing to take over part of the neighboring 101st Airborne Division's long front-line sector. The 101st, on the right flank of the VIII Corps, renewed its attack north toward Noville, and cleared out a portion of the Bois Jacques east-southeast of Foy. The brunt of the confused fighting was borne by the 501st Parachute Infantry. The inability of the 6th Armored and 35th Infantry divisions to push forward on 501st's right (eastern) flank limited the paratroopers' advance. Progress was also limited by the confused nature of the fighting, much of it occurring at very close range among the snow-covered trees, where it was difficult for commanders to maintain control over, and keep in touch with, their units. For the two days' fighting on 8 and 9 January, the 101st suffered 15 killed, 124 wounded, and only 2 missing, most of those losses sustained on 9 January. The 87th Division lost 16 killed, 116 wounded, and 38 missing; the neighboring 17th Airborne sustained 68 killed, 297 wounded, and 125 missing, the bulk of these on 9 January.

Elsewhere in the VIII Corps zone, early on 10 January, Combat Command A of the 4th Armored passed through the forward positions of the 6th Armored and attacked northeastward toward Bourcy, together with the 506th Parachute Infantry of the 101st Airborne. However, later in the day, in response to a directive from the 12th Army Group, Patton reluctantly ordered the 4th Armored Division to disengage and move south to Luxembourg, suspending this operation.

The divisions of Millikin's III Corps were also busy on 10 January. The 6th Armored Division, still recovering from the stress and strain of fighting on 7 and 8 January, limited its activities to lending artillery support to nearby VIII Corps attacks. Troops of the 35th Division finally fought their way into Villers-la-Bonne-Eau and the high ground immediately northwest of the hamlet. Just to the south, the 6th Cavalry Group's 6th Cavalry Squadron captured Betlange, and the 28th Cavalry Squadron fought its way into Harlange. The cavalrymen dismounted from their jeeps and half-tracks to attack as infantry, employing their plentiful allotment of heavy weapons to considerable effect.[11] Continuing its attack, the corps main effort, one regiment of the 90th Division seized the heights overlooking Doncols, while another attacked German strongpoints around Trentelhof with little success. On the corps right flank, advance elements of the 26th Division reached the heights southwest of Winseler.

Two days of American attacks had severely shaken the positions of Seventh Army and Fifth Panzer Army units around Bastogne, especially southeast of town. The surprise appearance of the 90th Infantry Division had struck a severe blow against the exhausted 5th Parachute Division, weakened by three and a half weeks of steady combat, often against heavy odds. Facing most of two U.S. divisions with ample artillery and tank support, the 5th Parachute was outnumbered by nearly four to one, and outgunned by an even greater margin. Adding to General Heilmann's problems, the advances of the 35th Division in the Villers-la-Bonne-Eau area (combined with the withdrawal of the 104th Panzergrenadier Regiment to join the rest of the 15th Panzergrenadier Division), had compelled the 14th Parachute Infantry Regiment to disengage and shift east to join the rest of the 5th Parachute Division. Unfortunately, the 14th Parachute Infantry's march route took it across the path of the 90th Infantry Division, and it suffered heavy losses before it was able to escape to the northeast. The two days of combat between the 90th Infantry and the 5th Parachute divisions cost the Americans 72 killed, 182 wounded, and 12 missing, while the vastly outnumbered Germans lost an estimated 100 killed, 320 wounded, and 130 captured or missing in action.

THE HALT: 10–11 JANUARY

Just as the Germans began their disengagement from the tip of the Bulge salient, and as the offensives launched by Hodges in the north, and especially by Patton in the south, began to gather momentum, the Allied high command called a halt. Sensitive about the possibility of further German surprises in the aftermath of the Ardennes offensive, British and American (particularly American) military intelligence officers and units were seeing ghosts in every closet.

The German Nordwind offensive in Alsace, launched by General von Obstfelder's First Army on 1 January, doubtless contributed to the unease and suspicions of Allied intelligence personnel. Operation Nordwind fell upon Gen. Alexander M. Patch's Seventh Army. Patch's divisions, which were rather thinly stretched in order to cover the extended front left when Patton's divisions had moved north to the Ardennes, were hard-pressed to halt the German drive. Nonetheless, by the end of the first week of January the crisis in Alsace had passed, although the preoffensive front lines were not restored until mid-February. Perhaps catching some hints of the Fall Luxembourg operation,[12] which had been proposed to Hitler by OKW in midautumn but discarded by him, American intelligence staffs at SHAEF and 12th Army Group warned of the potential for a damaging German attack from Trier directed against Luxembourg City.

Bradley, understandably leery of being surprised for a second time in less than a month, and with Eisenhower's approval, ordered Patton to send a division south to screen Luxembourg from a possible German advance from Trier. Patton's objection was typically furious, voiced with considerable heat in a telephone conversation with Bradley in Luxembourg City. Bradley was adamant, however, and to Patton's intense frustration, he was obliged to comply. He pulled the 4th Armored Division out of line late on 10 January and sent it south.

This was less a sacrifice on Patton's part than it might seem, for Gaffey's division was overdue for a rest, and much of its equipment (it was down to fewer than fifty M4 tanks, less than one-third of its authorized tank strength) was badly in need of overhaul, major maintenance, or replacement. Moreover, Patton was aware of the division's situation, and the 4th Armored had seen little serious action for more than a week. (In fact, this is why he selected the division to make the move to Luxembourg.) In that context, Patton's loudly voiced protest to Bradley was to some extent pro forma. As frustrating and distracting as the "Trier threat" was for Patton and his corps commanders, the shift of a single division had little noticeable impact in the field, and passed almost unnoticed by the Germans, who had enough worries of their own.

Meanwhile, the bitter struggle for Tillet had come to an end, following a house-to-house assault by the 346th Infantry Regiment of the 87th Division through 10 January and into the next day. Among the many men of that regiment who distinguished themselves in the engagement, prominent was Lt. Glenn J. Doman, commander of the 1st Platoon of K Company.

Making use of bazookas, machine guns, and particularly grenades, Doman and his men took several houses before they were cut off by a German counterattack. With the assistance of artillery support called in by radio Doman broke up that attack and another that followed an hour later. After seven hours, and under renewed attack by German armor and infantry, Doman's platoon used up all of its ammunition and had to withdraw, the men carrying with them the one soldier of the platoon who had been wounded.[13]

By evening of 11 January Tillet was completely in the hands of the 87th Division. The Germans, having again brilliantly performed the classic delaying action in which they were so proficient, had withdrawn to establish new defensive positions a few kilometers to the north and east.[14]

ON TO HOUFFALIZE: 11–12 JANUARY

In the VIII Corps sector, Culin's 87th Infantry Division continued its seemingly endless slog northward. Taking advantage of the withdrawal of elements of Panzer Lehr, on 11 January the 347th Infantry finished clearing the Haies-de-Tillet wood and took control of Bonnerue, Pironpré, and Vesqueville without opposition. The French 4th Parachute Battalion entered St. Hubert in the afternoon, and the 346th Infantry reached the outskirts of Lavacherie several hours after dark, about 2030. On the next day the 87th Division pushed ahead to seize the small settlements of Tonny, Amberloup, Lavacherie, Orreux, Fosset, and the important crossroads near Sprimont. Patrols reported that there were no Germans in Menil, between Orreux and Fosset.

In the 17th Airborne Division's sector to the east, the Germans also fell back on 11 January, allowing the Americans to consolidate the approaches to Heropont, Flamierge, Flamizoulle, and Mande-St. Etienne. The next day, with the 602d Tank Destroyer Battalion (self-propelled M18s) attached from the neighboring 11th Armored Division, the division resumed its advance. The airborne troopers recaptured Flamierge against slight resistance, but patrols discovered that Flamizoulle was heavily mined. Having to send for engineers and wait for them to clear a path through town imposed a delay of several hours. Elsewhere in the division sector advancing airborne infantrymen encountered light screening and delaying forces left behind by the Führer Begleit Brigade and the 3d Panzergrenadier Division, especially around Hubermont, Renaumont, and the hamlets just to the southwest. The 11th Armored Division, still in VIII Corps reserve on 11 January, moved forward to take over a four-kilometer sector of the 101st Airborne Division's front during the following day.

While the VIII Corps advanced on 11 and 12 January, the divisions of Millikin's III Corps also pressed forward. The weary divisions of Rothkirch's LIII Corps and Priess's I SS Panzer Corps were finally forced to abandon the salient southeast of Bastogne. In fact, the dimensions of the "Harlange salient" had been considerably reduced over the previous three days by III Corps attacks, all of which were converging on Bras, a village about 7.5 kilometers east-southeast of Bastogne. The 6th Armored Division, having taken over the positions formerly held by Gaffey's 4th Armored, pushed eastward and cleared the now thinly held, scattered woods just south of Wardin.

The 35th Division, still facing the dedicated and resolute soldiers of 1st SS Panzer Division, made only limited gains in its continued attacks in the Lutremange-Lutrebois area. Some elements of the division cleared Watrange but were unable to fight their way into Tarchamps before making contact with units of the 26th and 90th divisions near Sonlez. The day's actions decreased the 35th Division's front from nearly thirteen kilometers to under ten, as it was being "squeezed out" by the other two divisions, pushing up from the south. The bulk of the 90th Division cleaned up the Trentelhof strongpoints and crossed the Bastogne-Wiltz road. Farther east, the right-flank elements of the 26th Division strengthened their positions near the Sure River, facing the 9th VGD.

In the midst of this American offensive, subject to the unwelcome attentions of most of three U.S. infantry divisions, lay the unraveling remnants of the 5th Parachute Division, struggling to escape east toward Wiltz. The rapid and unexpected advance of the 90th Infantry Division during 9–11 January had left the 5th Parachute with its lines of supply and communication nearly severed. The 14th Parachute Infantry Regiment had essentially been overrun by Van Fleet's advancing infantry during the same period. By nightfall on 11 January, the division had essentially ceased to exist as an organized force, having suffered close to 50 percent casualties in two of its infantry regiments, along with loss of nearly all of those units' heavy weapons and transport. Indeed, those soldiers of the 13th and 15th Parachute Infantry regiments who had managed to escape did so only by filtering through the tenuous American positions around them during the long, cold nights of 10–11 and 11–12 January. By the morning of the eleventh, Priess and Rothkirch were struggling to form a new defensive position along a line from Wiltz northwest along the Wiltz River to the vicinity of Longvilly and Benonchamps.

American offensive action on 12 January was more modest. Combat Command A of the 6th Armored finally fought its way into Wardin, capturing the village before pushing on to within a few hundred meters of Bras. Nearby the 90th Division's 357th Infantry finished securing Sonlez and then pushed on to take the high ground southeast of Bras. The 359th Infantry repelled a strong counterattack by the 1st SS Panzer Division, directed against the crossroads just east of Doncols. The 1st SS Panzer had been pulled into reserve on 11 January, and this counterattack was undertaken as a desperate emergency measure to open an escape route for the remnants of the 5th Parachute Division. However, the 90th Infantry Division, backed by its own attached tanks, held firm against these efforts, which petered out around dusk.[15]

Farther east, in the XII Corps zone, the 80th Infantry Division moved forward again on 11 January. Division units advanced to capture Buchholz-sur-Sure and took possession of the commanding heights south of Borden, driving back troops from the relatively fresh 79th VGD and the battered 352d VGD of the LXXXV Corps. After this flurry of action, the XII Corps sector was quiet on 12 January.

DECLINING GERMAN RESISTANCE: 13–14 JANUARY

Middleton's divisions continued their drive to the northeast on 13 and 14 January. The 345th Infantry of the 87th Division captured Spirimont by late morning of 13 January in the face of very light opposition. At the same time, the 347th Infantry pushed toward Ortheuville from Lavacherie, encountering no enemy resistance, and captured its objective about noon. The following day began with similar progress, but a junction on the left with British Major General Bols's 6th Airborne Division of the XXX Corps left Culin's division out of contact with the Germans. With the 6th Airborne advancing on its northern (left) flank and Miley's 17th Airborne on the eastern (right) flank, the 87th Division had been "pinched out" by early afternoon on 14 January. In anticipation of this, Third Army Headquarters that afternoon ordered the 87th Division to shift eastward to Eddy's XII Corps. There it was slated to relieve the 5th Infantry Division around Echternach. By evening of 14 January the 87th Division had withdrawn to the line of the Ourthe River, and the 346th and 347th Infantry regiments were on their way by truck to join the 4th Infantry Division.[16]

Like its neighbor to the west, the 17th Airborne Division also encountered only light resistance as it pressed northward. On 13 January, advance elements of the 507th Parachute Infantry Regiment reached the outskirts of Givry, while the 194th Glider Infantry occupied Salle and the 517th Parachute Infantry remained in Flamierge. Encountering only scattered German patrols and rear-guard parties on 14 January, the 507th Parachute Infantry captured Bertogne while the 194th Glider Infantry seized Givroulle and Wigny. After dark, the 193d Glider Infantry was detached to the neighboring 11th Armored Division, lying just east of the 17th Airborne. All of this shifting and reorientation was made necessary by the changing geography of the battle. With a shortening front line, as the Bulge contracted, the American forces in the Ardennes spent a good deal of time in mid-January adjusting boundaries and moving locations in order to keep in contact with the Germans, who were withdrawing steadily eastward toward the Our River.

The 11th Armored Division occupied a front of nearly six kilometers on the night of 12–13 January. On the morning of the 13 January, it attacked north toward Bertogne and Houffalize with the 41st Cavalry Reconnaissance Squadron screening its right flank. Combat Command A attacked on the right, and by evening had enveloped a rear-guard force from the 15th Panzergrenadier Division in Bertogne against very light resistance.[17] Combat Command R advanced on the division's left, and had covered about three kilometers by dusk, keeping pace with Combat Command A. The 41st Cavalry had a more interesting day, fending off an attack by two dozen German tanks and assault guns and destroying four of them.[18]

By the morning of 14 January the 11th Armored's front had expanded to 7.4 kilometers, and the division continued its attacks northward. While Combat Command A cleared Bertogne, Combat Command B passed through the front lines of the 101st Airborne Division to the east and drove north through the 101st's 506th Parachute Infantry, which was approaching Foy. Considerably in advance of the remainder of the division, elements of CCB/11 dashed into Noville in midafternoon, but withdrew before nightfall in the face of several strong German probes and an uncertain situation. Meanwhile, Combat Command R advanced and secured Recogne, and the 41st Cavalry also advanced north.

On 13 January the 506th Parachute Infantry of the 101st Airborne Division continued its northward advance to seize Foy on the road through Noville to Houffalize. At the same time the 327th Glider Infantry attacked northeast toward Bourcy, advancing through the lines of the 501st Parachute Infantry in the Bois Jacques. On the next day the 101st Airborne continued its attack north toward the rough line Noville-Rachamps-Bourcy. During the day the 506th Parachute Infantry troops in Foy were driven out of town by a sharp

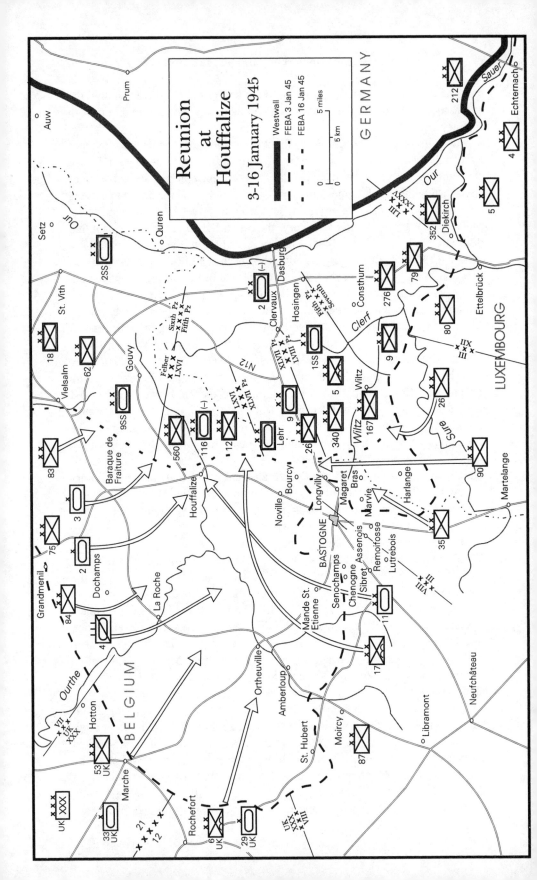

**Reunion
at
Houffalize**

3-16 January 1945

Westwall
FEBA 3 Jan 45
FEBA 16 Jan 45

5 miles
0
5 km
0

German counterattack, but a prompt counter-counterattack by the paratroopers regained the village before dusk.

In the III Corps zone on 13 January, the 6th Armored Division continued its northward drive. Combat Command B cleared part of Magaret. Farther east, the 90th Division captured Bras and nearby Hill 530, thereby "pinching out" the 35th Division. The 26th Division, making firm contact with the 90th, advanced into positions east and northeast of Doncols.

The following day, Combat Command A of the 6th Armored cleared the woods east of Wardin and captured Benonchamps, while Combat Command B secured Magaret. The 90th Infantry Division drove north-northeast toward Niederwampach, and the 26th Division on its right pushed patrols up to the Wiltz River. Farther east, the XII Corps sector remained generally quiet, although the Germans were expecting an American offensive in this area.

As the American lines drew closer to Houffalize, the intensity of opposition decreased. The Germans had pulled most of their forces to the east to avoid encirclement, and left only relatively small delaying and rear-guard forces to hamper the American advance. Although these rear-guard forces were not numerous, they were dedicated and resolute, demonstrating repeatedly the German Army's well-honed skills at small-unit tactics, making optimum use of the jumbled, wooded terrain of the Ardennes, so well suited to defense. The Germans reasoned that every day they were able to prolong the battle in the Ardennes was one more day before the Allies would launch their expected drive into the Rhineland.

HOUFFALIZE AT LAST: 15–17 JANUARY

As its front contracted, Middleton's VIII Corps pressed its advance to the north and east. On 15 January the 87th Division lent its 345th Regimental Combat Team to the neighboring 17th Airborne Division, temporarily leaving General Culin in command only of his divisional services and a handful of reconnaissance units in what amounted to a rear-area assembly zone south of the Ourthe River. That day patrols and the lead elements of the 17th Airborne Division pushed up to the southern banks of the Ourthe River, while the 193d Glider Infantry advanced into the town of Vaux.

The 11th Armored's Combat Command A drove through Compogne and Rastadt to reach the outskirts of Vellereux. There, however, unexpectedly strong German resistance in the Rau de Vaux defile compelled CCA/11 to withdraw to the west. Combat Command B swung around Noville to the east, bypassing the village and leaving it to be occupied by the 506th Parachute Infantry.

On 16 January the 87th Infantry and 17th Airborne divisions made contact along the Ourthe River with the British 51st "Highland" Infantry Division, part of Lt. Gen. Sir Brian Horrocks's XXX Corps. The 87th and 17th had little other activity, since the previous day's advances by the 11th Armored Division had left them out of contact with the enemy.

On 16 January Combat Command A of the 11th Armored captured Vellereux and pursued retreating German troops through Mabompré. Combat Command B advanced northeast through Wicourt and gained high ground south of Houffalize on either side of the highway. Pushing on ahead of the bulk of Combat Command B that morning, Task Force Greene (under Maj. Michael J. L. Greene, a 1941 graduate of West Point) clashed in a sharp firefight with a German rear-guard force on the outskirts of Houffalize.[19] As the firefight ended, Greene saw dim figures and vehicles up ahead and sent a patrol to investigate. The patrol soon came back, jubilant: They had encountered troops from the 41st Armored Infantry Regiment of the 2d "Hell on Wheels" Armored Division. At 0905 hours the First and Third armies had reestablished contact!

To the south, the attack of the 101st Airborne Division's 502d Parachute Infantry Regiment was halted outside Bourcy. However, the neighboring 506th Parachute Infantry had more success, capturing Vaux and Rachamps.

In the III Corps zone, Task Force Lagrew of the 6th Armored's Combat Command A advanced into Longvilly, while the 35th Division's 320th Infantry attacked and took Michamps. Just to the southeast, the 90th Division continued its drive to (and through) Niederwampach, capturing the nearby hamlets of Oberwampach and Shimpach.

After a discouraging day at the front, on 4 January Patton had written in his diary: "We can still lose this war. . . The Germans are colder and hungrier than we are, but they fight better." Twelve days later, after recording in his diary the meeting at Houffalize of elements of the First and Third armies, "Old Blood and Guts" showed that he no longer had doubts about the outcome of the war. "This restores Bradley to the command of the First Army . . . and terminates the German offensive." The next day he wrote, "We are going to attack until the war is over."[20]

21

RETURN TO ST. VITH

While the fall of Houffalize had marked the return to normal command relations between Hodges's First Army and Bradley's 12th Army Group, it by no means signaled the end of fighting in the Ardennes. That end was, however, clearly growing closer.

The Germans, for their part, continued to resist with skill and determination, employing small forces of infantry and armored vehicles to delay advancing American columns. At the same time, their tired and overworked transport units were strained to the utmost trying to move troops and supplies into the relative safety of Germany. Hammered by relentless Allied air attacks and the seemingly omnipresent American artillery, and hampered by fuel shortages, snowstorms, and icy roads, the German retreat from the Ardennes was a true odyssey for the units involved.

THE FINAL PHASE BEGINS

The first phase of the Allied counteroffensive was concluded by the juncture of the First and Third U.S. armies at Houffalize on 16 January 1945. The second and final phase of the counteroffensive was formally initiated by the official return of the First Army to the 12th Army Group at midnight on 17–18 January. The second-phase offensive was to be a double-envelopment operation by six corps, three each from the First and Third armies.

The concept was that of a classical double-envelopment. In the center of the two-army front three corps were to carry out a simple holding attack. Two more corps would undertake a relatively shallow envelopment from the north; a third corps would carry out a comparably shallow envelopment from the south. The three corps in the center were, from north to south, the First Army's VII Corps (Maj. Gen. J. L. Collins) and the Third Army's VIII and III Corps (Major Generals Troy H. Middleton and John Millikin), facing generally east from Houffalize and Bastogne. The VIII and III corps were initially to limit their activities to demonstrations; the VII Corps, on the other hand,

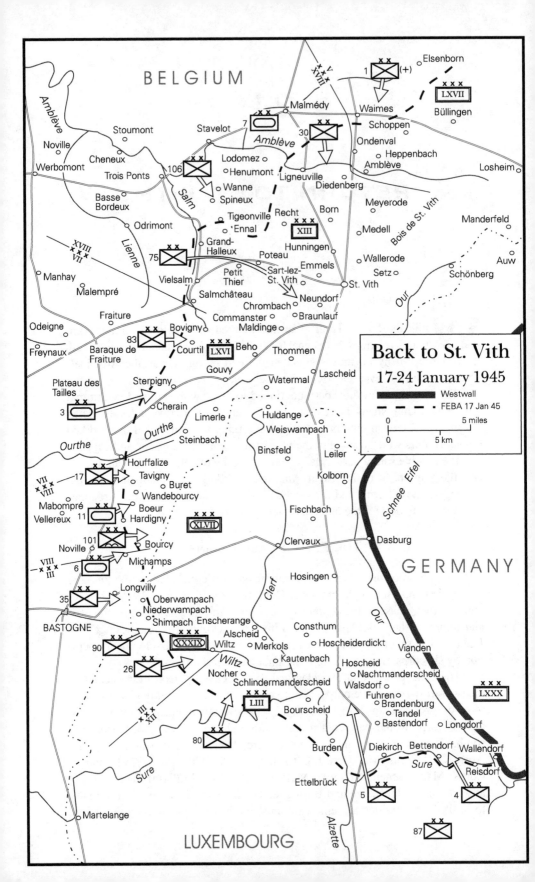

Back to St. Vith

17-24 January 1945

▬▬▬ Westwall

▬ ▬ ▬ FEBA 17 Jan 45

0 ——————— 5 miles

0 ——————— 5 km

BELGIUM

GERMANY

LUXEMBOURG

Ambléve

Elsenborn

Malmédy

Waimes

Büllingen

LXVII

Stavelot

Schoppen

Ondenval

Heppenbach

Ambléve

Losheim

Stoumont

Noville

Cheneux

Werbomont

Trois Ponts

106

Lodomez

Henumont

Ligneuville

Diedenberg

Meyerode

Bois de St. Vith

Manderfeld

Wanne

Spineux

Recht

Born

Medell

Auw

Schönberg

Basse Bordeux

Odrimont

Tigeonville

Ennal

Hunningen

Wallerode

Setz

Grand-Halleux

Poteau

Emmels

Petit Thier

Sart-lez-St. Vith

St. Vith

Our

Manhay

Malempré

Vielsalm

Salmchâteau

Neundorf

Fraiture

Bovigny

Chrombach

Braunlauf

Commanster

Maldinge

Odeigne

Freynaux

Baraque de Fraiture

83

Courtil

LXVI

Beho

Thommen

Gouvy

Lascheid

Plateau des Tailles

Sterpigny

Watermal

3

Cherain

Limerle

Huldange

Steinbach

Weiswampach

Ourthe

Binsfeld

Leiler

Houffalize

Tavigny

Kolborn

17

Buret

Wandebourcy

Fischbach

Mabompré

Vellereux

11

Boeur

Hardigny

XLVII

Clervaux

Dasburg

101

Bourcy

Noville

Michamps

Hosingen

6

Longvilly

35

Oberwampach

Niederwampach

Shimpach

Enscherange

Consthum

Hoscheiderdickt

Vianden

BASTOGNE

90

XXXIX

Wiltz

Merkols

Hoscheid

Nachtmanderscheid

LXXX

26

Kautenbach

Walsdorf

Fuhren

Nocher

Schlindermanderscheid

Brandenburg

Tandel

LIII

Bourscheid

Bastendorf

Longdorf

80

Burden

Diekirch

Bettendorf

Wallendorf

Reisdorf

Ettelbrück

5

4

Martelange

Sure

Alzette

87

Ambléve

Salm

Lienne

Ourthe

Clerf

Our

Schnee Eifel

Sure

XVIII

V

1

30

7

75

VII

VIII

VIII

III

III

XII

LUXEMBOURG

was to continue to attack east from Houffalize until pinched out by the advance of the right wing of General Ridgway's XVIII Airborne Corps, one of the two corps carrying out the envelopment from the north. The other enveloping corps in the north was the V Corps under Maj. Gen. Clarence Huebner. The envelopment in the south was to be done by the Third Army's XII Corps under Maj. Gen. Manton S. Eddy, which had been waiting impatiently to be unleashed for more than three weeks. The opening moves in this phase of the Allied counteroffensive had actually begun in the north on 15 January.

There were seven German corps in the now-shallow Bulge. The northern shoulder was held by the Fifteenth Army's LXVII Corps, generally facing the U.S. V Corps. Next came the two corps of General Dietrich's much-reduced Sixth Panzer Army, with the XIII Corps on the right and the LXVI Corps on the left. Next came the Fifth Panzer Army, also reduced to two corps in line: the XLVII Panzer Corps, generally opposing Middleton's VIII Corps, and the LVIII Panzer Corps, facing the U.S. III Corps. Next came the two corps of General Brandenberger's Seventh Army: the LIII Corps on the right and the LXXX Corps, which was still holding the left shoulder of the Bulge.

SOUTH TOWARD ST. VITH

The V Corps began its offensive from the northern shoulder of the Bulge early on 15 January. Actually only one division of the V Corps—the 1st Infantry Division, commanded by Brig. Gen. Clift Andrus—was involved in this offensive. (Until his very recent assignment as V Corps commander when Maj. Gen. Leonard T. Gerow departed to take command of the Fifteenth Army, General Huebner had commanded the 1st Division since the invasion of Sicily in the summer of 1943.) The other two divisions of the corps—the 2d and 99th Infantry divisions (under Major Generals Walter M. Robertson and Walter E. Lauer, respectively)—were still facing east, just north of the shoulder that their resistance had created on 17–18 December. However, the 2d Division's 23d Infantry Regiment was attached to the 1st Division for the offensive.

Driving south toward St. Vith, the 1st Division's main effort was made on its right by the attached 23d Infantry, along the axis of the Waimes–Ondenval–St. Vith road. Coordinated with the attack of the 23d Infantry was a simultaneous drive by the 117th Infantry Regiment of Maj. Gen. Leland Hobbs's 30th Infantry Division, on the left of the XVIII Airborne Corps, west of the highway. The objective of the 117th Infantry was to seize the high ground overlooking Ondenval from the west. Once the Ondenval defile was cleared by the 23d and 117th Infantry regiments, recently promoted Maj. Gen. Robert W. Hasbrouck's 7th Armored Division, in XVIII Corps reserve, was to pass through to seize St. Vith. The weather was atrocious, and remained so for several days. The temperature was frequently only a little above 0 degrees

Fahrenheit; any warming into the 20-degree range was invariably accompanied by heavy snow. The attacks by the two regiments were severely hampered by these conditions.

Opposing the attacks was the German 3d Parachute Division, now commanded by Generalmajor Richard Schimpf, who had replaced Gen. Walther Wadehn on 11 January. This was the left-wing division of General Otto Hitzfeld's LXVII Corps, and thus was the extreme southern unit of the German Fifteenth Army. As the attacking Americans slowly but surely pressed into and beyond Ondenval, it became obvious to Field Marshal Model that the attack threatened the rear and the lines of communication of the two corps of the Sixth Panzer Army to the west and southwest. So, on 17 January, he shifted the LXVII Corps to the control of General Dietrich's Sixth Panzer Army Headquarters.

Dietrich, in compliance with Hitler's orders of 8 January, was assembling the I SS Panzer Corps and II SS Panzer Corps in the St. Vith area. By this time he had collected there most of the battered remnants of those corps' four panzer divisions: 1st SS Panzer, 2d SS Panzer, 9th SS Panzer, and 12th SS Panzer. He had not yet, however, relinquished to the Fifth Panzer Army control of, and responsibility for, the front from Houffalize northeast to the shoulder. As the Americans pressed on slowly past Ondenval, Dietrich committed elements of the I SS Panzer Corps artillery to reinforce the fires of the artillery of the 3d Parachute Division and of the XIII and LXVII corps in the region south and southwest of Ondenval. He then reinforced the 3d Parachute Division with contingents of tanks from all four of his SS Panzer divisions, to strengthen their counterattacks. As a result the American drive was slowed still further.[1]

The fight for the Ondenval defile raged for five days. A major German counterattack, supported by tanks, was repulsed by the 23d Infantry on 18 January. The following day, in a swirling snowstorm, the Americans drove southward a few hundred more yards, finally approaching the Amblève River. On 20 January the 7th Armored Division passed through the 23d Infantry on the left (on the Waimes-Ondenval road) and the 117th Infantry on the right (on the Malmédy-Ligneauville road), and pushed southward toward German-held St. Vith. These, of course, were the same two roads that the 7th had followed just thirty-two days before, en route to St. Vith, when the town was still held by Americans.

EAST FROM HOUFFALIZE

The linkup of the First Army's VII Corps with the Third Army's VIII Corps at Houffalize effectively pinched out the right wing of the VII Corps: the 2d Armored and 84th Infantry divisions. The 3d Armored and 83d Infantry divisions, however, swung generally eastward on 17 and 18 January, heading toward St. Vith, astride the Houffalize–St. Vith highway, and the eastern (or northern) fork of the Ourthe River. The advance was bitterly opposed by the German LXVI Corps. Despite this tough resistance, by evening of 18 January the 3d Armored Division had advanced to the east of Cherain and Sterpigny, while to the north and east the 83d Infantry Division was fighting the tenacious German defenders of Courtil, and approaching Bovigny.

Still farther north and east, on 17 January, the 75th Infantry Division of General Ridgway's XVIII Airborne Corps occupied Vielsalm, which had been evacuated by the Germans. On the left of the 75th Division was the 290th Infantry Regiment, which reached the southern side of the crossroad at Poteau before dark, just as the 119th Infantry of the 30th Infantry Division reached Poteau from the north. Late on 18 January the 75th Division began a new offensive. On the extreme left of the division was the 1st Battalion of the 290th Infantry Regiment.

Private First Class Charles R. Miller, whom we last saw near Beffe and Odeigne (see chapter 19), was still one of the scouts of A Company of the 290th. To his disgust, he had been required to give up his M1 rifle for an M3 submachine gun (so-called "grease gun"). The weather had turned bitterly cold, and Miller discovered that his new weapon would not fire. Remembering early experiences when he had been a BAR man, he took the clip out of his gun, stuffed toilet paper into the receiver, and set fire to it. The gun was now operable, and through the slow advances of 19 and 20 January Miller kept it warm and working by firing an occasional round into the ground.[2]

To the northeast of the 75th Division, the 119th Infantry of the 30th Division was approaching both Recht and Born from the north. Resistance of the German XIII Corps, opposite the XVIII Airborne Corps, was as determined as was that of the LXVI Corps opposite the VII Corps. Counterattacks were frequent.

Despite the fierce German opposition, by evening of 20 January the 30th Division held the ridgeline marked by the Bois de Born (just west of the village of Born), through the Bois d'Emmels (south of Recht and east of Poteau) and Grand Bois, southwest of Poteau. There the right of the 30th Division joined the left of the 75th Division, whose line continued southwest toward Bovigny, and the left flank of the VII Corps.

THE THIRD ARMY SHIFTS EMPHASIS

Southeast of Houffalize the VIII Corps was facing east, on a narrowed three-division front. In the north, just south of the east fork of the Ourthe River, was Maj. Gen. William M. Miley's 17th Airborne Division. In the center was Brig. Gen. Charles S. Kilburn's 11th Armored Division. On the right flank of the corps, was Maj. Gen. Maxwell D. Taylor's 101st Airborne Division. The opposition, still fighting vigorously despite its terrible losses the previous week north of Bastogne, was General Heinrich von Lüttwitz's XLVII Panzer Corps.

Nevertheless, the tempo of battle had been reduced along the fronts of these two corps, which had been battling each other so wildly for more than two weeks. On 17 January the 101st Airborne Division captured Bourcy and Hardigny, thereby completing the clearing of the territory between Bastogne and the Ourthe. On 18 and 19 January, the divisions of the VIII Corps reverted to a defensive stance, with the 11th Armored Division taking over the line from Houffalize south to Hardigny while the 17th Airborne Division took responsibility from Hardigny south to Bourcy. The 101st Airborne Division fell back into reserve. On 20 January, discovering that the enemy units facing it had fallen back, CCR/11 pushed forward about 3,000 meters to seize the hamlets of Boeur, Tavigny, and Wandesbourcy, as well as the Bois aux Chênes wood.

South and southeast of the VIII Corps, the U.S. III Corps was facing the XXXIX Panzer Corps of the Fifth Panzer Army and the right wing of the LIII Corps of the Seventh Army. The four divisions of the III Corps continued the line of the VIII Corps to the south, with the 6th Armored on the left, and the 35th Infantry, 90th Infantry, and 26th Infantry divisions in line to the right almost as far as Wiltz. The 6th Armored Division continued its drive eastward. On 17 January the division encountered heavy resistance on the Bourcy-Longvilly road, while to the south the 90th Division had to fend off German counterattacks threatening to recover Oberwampach. On the next day the German effort to retake Oberwampach continued, the situation now worsened by heavy German shelling of the little town.

Nevertheless, the tempo of battle was clearly reduced. This was due in part to the fact that along these fronts the opponents had fought each other to a state of semiexhaustion in the bitter struggle for Bastogne. It was also due to the fact that the dynamic Third Army commander, Gen. George S. Patton, had shifted his attention farther east to the XII Corps front along the Sure River.

In the XII Corps sector the 87th Division relieved the 5th Infantry Division on 16 and 17 January. This permitted the 5th Infantry Division to assemble in preparation for making the main effort in an attack northward, west of the Our River, against the southern shoulder of the Ardennes salient. In less than twenty-four hours the 5th Division was ready to attack through the 87th Division, in the center of the corps line, heading for the Skyline Drive. The 4th Division was on the right, just west of the Our River; the 80th Division was on the left; the 87th Division would drop back into corps reserve.

The XII Corps attack, masked by an opportune snowstorm, opened at 0300 hours on 18 January. It came as a considerable surprise to the Germans of the 212th and 352d Volksgrenadier Divisions of the LIII Corps. The lead companies from the 4th and 5th Infantry divisions crossed the Sure River between Reisdorf and Ettelbruck in assault boats. Concealed by darkness and falling snow, the assault troops swiftly established themselves on the river's left bank, then pushed northward quickly. Meanwhile, the 87th Infantry Division demonstrated against German positions to the west, while still farther west the 80th Division seized the village of Nocher.

Patton described the attack and the weather in his diary as follows: "Eddy jumped off in a London fog which turned to rain and sleet. We are going forward but are mostly delayed by the ice."[3]

Opposite the 4th and 5th Infantry divisions was the weak German 352d VGD, led by Generalmajor Erich Schmidt, of Gen. Franz Beyer's LXXX Corps. (Schmidt had been promoted on 1 January 1945.) Thanks to surprise, by evening the Americans had advanced nearly four kilometers north of the Sure River. Meanwhile, farther west, General McBride's 80th Infantry Division had driven the left wing of General von Rothkirch's German LIII Corps back to the Wiltz River east of Wiltz.

Nevertheless, despite surprise, and despite their desperate shortage of men and weapons, the German reaction was quick and remarkably effective. General Brandenberger shifted most of the army and corps artillery from behind the LIII Corps to support the LXXX Corps. He also shifted some units from the LIII Corps to form blocking positions on the Skyline Drive and to cover the approaches to two bridges north of Vianden. At the same time Field Marshal Model shifted the battered Panzer Lehr Division and then the 2d Panzer Division from the Fifth Panzer Army to the Seventh Army, and sent General von Lüttwitz's XLVII Panzer Corps Headquarters to command these two armored divisions. Largely because of fuel shortages, these moves had less immediate effect than the shifts by General Brandenberger.

By this time Model had received permission from Hitler through Rundstedt to pull all of his troops out of the Bulge and back to the Westwall (see chapter 17). He therefore ordered a general withdrawal of the Fifth Panzer Army to the Westwall. To make sure that the left wing of the Fifth Army would not be trapped by the advance of the XII Corps, he ordered the construction of another bridge over the Our River north of Vianden.

The 4th and 5th Infantry divisions continued their advance on 19 January, pressing the battered volksgrenadiers very hard. The two divisions cleared Bettendorf, Diekirch, and Bastendorf, although German positions along the Sure just north of Reisdorf continued to hold out against the Americans. The XII Corps advanced further on 20 January, although German resistance was becoming more organized. The 4th Division cleared the triangle formed by the junction of the Our and Sure Rivers, and bypassed Longdorf to occupy Tandel. The 5th Division took the high ground near the village of Brandenburg. To the northwest, the 80th Division's 318th Infantry occupied Burden without serious opposition.

These successes posed a threat of encirclement to Rothkirch's LIII Corps. This danger prodded the corps units into a nearly panicked headlong retreat. Actually, because of the weather, the American advance did not move swiftly enough to seriously threaten the LIII Corps with encirclement. To the German commanders in the field, however, the possibility was sufficiently real to force a precipitous withdrawal on 19 and 20 January, as they knew all too well how slowly their own overburdened columns would crawl eastward.

They were also aware that the bridges across the Our, emplaced six weeks before, were neither numerous nor secure from Allied air attack. The resulting emergency efforts to get heavy equipment and transport to the relative safety of the east bank created considerable confusion and numerous traffic jams.

The snowfall that had begun in the predawn hours of 18 January escalated into a full-scale blizzard during the next two days. Despite heroic efforts by the Germans and Americans to keep the roads open, many lesser routes were closed by drifts (some more than two meters deep), and movement in many areas became virtually impossible until 21 or 22 January. The Germans, suffering from fuel shortages, were especially hard-pressed, as their snowplows lacked fuel. On the other hand, the appalling weather imposed a sharp brake on Allied operations. It not only severely limited ground movement, but also grounded Allied aircraft, preventing aerial artillery observation and canceling reconnaissance flights and planned close air support missions.

By 21 January the U.S. 5th Infantry Division, making the XII Corps main effort, had fought its way north on the Skyline Drive to a position almost due west of Vianden. However, the 4th Division, on the corps right, along the Our River, had not been able to keep pace with the 5th. This was largely because of the determined defense of the German units covering the approach to the German bridge south of Vianden.

Farther west, as the 5th Division spearheads pressed north, General von Rothkirch still feared that the left flank units of his LIII Corps were in danger of encirclement. These units continued their precipitous withdrawal during the afternoon of 21 January, offering rewarding targets to the American artillery.

The next day was unexpectedly bright and clear. Four groups of fighter-bombers of the XIX Tactical Air Command had been assigned to support the XII Corps, and they took to the air shortly after dawn. As the day wore on, and rich German targets continued to be available, more American aircraft joined in attacks against withdrawing units of the LIII Corps and the armored elements of the XLVII Panzer Corps, which were moving east to join the Seventh Army. After the war General Brandenberger commented that these American air attacks were the first time in the Ardennes that "the situation in the air was similar to that which had prevailed in Normandy."[4]

RETURN TO WILTZ

General Patton had rightly anticipated that the offensive of his XII Corps (combined with the First Army drive to St. Vith) would force a general German withdrawal, and on 19 January alerted the VIII and III Corps that they should be ready to resume the offensive on the 21st. Heavy patrolling by the divisions of these corps soon revealed that the Germans were, indeed, withdrawing.

On 21 January, as the snowfall ebbed and the skies cleared, the Third Army's northern boundary was shifted northward a few kilometers, so that the VIII Corps sector now included the Bois de Rouvroy northeast of Buret. At the same time, Millikin's III Corps took over the sector around Bastogne from Middleton's VIII Corps.

In the III Corps sector the 11th Armored and 17th Airborne divisions pushed forward against slight opposition, with CCA/11 occupying Buret and troops from the 17th Airborne advancing northeast of Tavigny. The following day the 17th Airborne's advance passed through Steinbach and Limerle, while CCA/11 entered the Bois de Rouvroy and crossed the border from Belgium into Luxembourg. By 23 January it was obvious that continuing advances on both flanks by the VII and III corps would soon "pinch out" the VIII Corps sector. The 11th Armored and 17th Airborne divisions spent most of the day solidifying their contacts on both flanks and conducting extensive patrols. As so often happens, though, the situation did not develop as expected. Third Army Headquarters changed the corps boundaries. On 24 January the 17th Airborne Division was assigned an additional front-line sector formerly given to the 6th Armored Division. The VIII Corps sector was expanded to the south, at least temporarily eliminating any possibility that the corps would be pinched out. The 17th Airborne pressed on eastward toward Thrommen and Landscheid.

On 21 January Millikin's III Corps opened a major effort to advance to the northeast toward St. Vith, a difficult undertaking in view of the terrain, weather, and stubborn German resistance. Nevertheless, the 6th Armored and 90th Infantry divisions advanced several kilometers. Elements of the 26th Division and the 6th Cavalry Group entered the battered town of Wiltz and began to clear scattered German resistance from the town and its environs. In the town, the advancing American troops discovered survivors of the 28th Division's 110th Infantry Regiment, hidden by kind Luxembourg citizens at considerable risk to themselves, since the Germans had overrun Wiltz in mid-December.[5] Thus the liberation of Wiltz, like that of Clervaux a few days later, was an occasion of great joy and considerable festivities.

On 22 January the advance continued. On the next day, the III Corps axis of advance was shifted from northeast to east, allowing the expansion of the VIII Corps sector that we have already noted. The 357th Infantry of the 90th Division attacked across the Clerf River, capturing Binsfeld, while the 28th Cavalry Squadron advanced to the vicinity of Clervaux.

By 23 January the 26th Infantry Division, the right wing of the III Corps, had moved beyond Wiltz, and was well east of the Wiltz River north and west of the town. The corps front line ran generally to the northeast, roughly along the Belgium-Luxembourg border.

CLEARING THE SKYLINE DRIVE

General Eddy's XII Corps continued its offensive, although by 21 January the axis of advance had shifted slightly to the northeast (this shift, in turn, led to the reorientation of the III Corps advance on 23 January). The advance was slow. The 80th Division's 317th Infantry was unable to cross the Our River just north of Bourscheid. On 22 January the 4th Division gained ground on the west bank of the Our, and seized Walsdorf, but was unable to clear the village of Führen. The 5th Division, still advancing to the north and west, took the commanding ridgeline east of Nachtmanderscheid. Nearby, the 80th Division advanced into the Wiltz area, using routes opened earlier by the 6th Cavalry Group. The German bridges across the Our were by this time within easy range of American artillery, and it was a continual struggle for the Germans to keep the bridges open, even at night. The situation had worsened markedly for the Germans on 22 January when the weather cleared, and much equipment was lost when Allied fighter-bombers struck the crowded roads west of the Our.

On 23 January the 4th Division finally took Führen, after three days of fighting, but the 5th Division was unable to capture either Nachtmanderscheid or Hoscheid. The 319th Infantry of the 80th Division pressed across the Wiltz River and captured Merkols. By nightfall the bulk of the XII Corps was either on the lower Our River, or within easy striking distance of the west bank. The next morning the XII Corps consolidated its control of the riverbank. The 4th Division occupied the bank from Vianden to the confluence of the Our and Sauer Rivers at Wallendorf.

Farther west the 5th Infantry Division, in the center of the XII Corps zone, continued to drive north along the Skyline Drive, although the pace was slowed significantly by the arrival in the Vianden area of the XLVII Panzer Corps and its two panzer divisions. However, American concern about German armored counterattacks was not fulfilled. Even if the Germans had had sufficient strength to make effective counterattacks—which they did not—they were acutely short of fuel and also short of ammunition.

The 80th Division completed its capture of Kautenbach and also seized Alscheid and Enscherange. By this time only scattered rear-guard packets of Germans were west of the Our in the XII Corps zone. The bridges had been taken up or destroyed, and all that was left for the Americans was mopping up.

It was now evident to General Patton that there was no possibility that the offensive of the XII Corps could cut off significant German forces in the diminished salient. He decided, therefore, to have his two leftmost corps—the VIII and the III—attack straight to the east, across the front of the XII Corps, to the Our River just north of Vianden. The XII Corps would then face east, putting the three lefthand corps of the Third Army in line along the Our River, just west of the Westwall, and ready for a renewed advance to the east.

On to the Our River

The final Bulge offensive of the VIII and III Corps began on 23 January. German resistance was generally that of rear-guard delaying tactics. The snow-covered terrain impeded the advance more than did German defenders. The 35th Infantry Division, nevertheless, found that the Germans defending Weiswampach were still formidable opponents. Private First Class Jim Graff of C Company of the 134th Infantry Regiment was bitter when supporting tanks turned back late on 24 January, leaving him and his comrades at the mercy of German tanks and dug-in machine guns. As he wrote later, there were "too many casualties from rifle companies [like his C Company] attacking across snow-swept fields into woods and fortified towns."[6] Nevertheless, the dogged advance continued, and on 26 January the 35th Division held Weiswampach. At that point the 35th was relieved by the 90th Infantry Division.

By the evening of 26 January the 90th Division of the III Corps had occupied Leiler, on the Our River at the junction of Luxembourg, Belgium, and Germany. To the north the VIII Corps extended to meet the XVIII Airborne Corps, just south and east of St. Vith. Once again there was a St. Vith salient; this time it was held by the Germans, and faced west.

South of the 90th Division the remainder of the VIII Corps approached the Our River as the Germans completed a successful and skillful withdrawal. From Kolborn south to Vianden, however, General Brandenberger's Seventh Army dug in just east of the Skyline Drive and held a shallow bridgehead little more than a kilometer in depth.

After having spent a quiet and uneventful day on 25 January, the VIII Corps moved forward again on the next day, heading northeast into the region north of Weiswampach. The corps gained additional frontage, acquiring the 90th Infantry Division in its positions to the south. The 17th Airborne Division, whose forward positions lay beyond Watermal, was relieved by the 87th Infantry Division. On 27 January the 87th captured several villages south of St. Vith, while the 90th Division continued to clear the west bank of the Our River.

Immediately to the south, the III Corps also continued to press toward the German frontier and the Our River. By the morning of 25 January the bulk of the corps was east of the Clerf River, with the Skyline Drive as its next immediate goal. CCB of the 6th Armored Division gained positions on either side of the Weiswampach-Huldange road. To the south, the 101st Infantry Regiment of the 26th Division and elements of the 6th Cavalry Group occupied Clervaux. There they discovered, for the second time in a week, American soldiers who had been hidden in the ruined town by Luxembourgers since the 2d Panzer Division had captured the town six weeks before. On 26 January, after a major reshuffle of unit positions within the III Corps, the 90th Infantry, having taken over the 6th Armored Division's positions, was shifted to the VIII Corps. Meanwhile the 6th Armored and elements of the 17th Airborne Division took over the former 90th Division positions. The 26th Division secured the Skyline Drive from Fischbach south nearly to Hosingen. The III Corps sector was mostly quiet on 27 January.

The XII Corps continued to push to north and east. On 26 January the 4th

Division began to withdraw from the front line. As this transpired, the 5th Division's 11th Regimental Combat Team pushed into Hoscheiderdickt, and, to southwest, the the 5th Cavalry Reconnaissance Troop captured the tiny but impressively named hamlet of Schlindermanderscheid. The 80th Division worked at expanding its bridgehead on the east side of the Clerf River. The 76th Infantry Division began to relieve the 87th Infantry Division in position.

On 27 January, the leading elements of the 5th Division continued their advance. To the north, the 80th Division's 317th Infantry seized the high ground overlooking the village of Hosingen from the west. The advance brought the division up to the west bank of the Our River, largely ending its offensive drive.

Back to St. Vith

Meanwhile, much further north and west, on the First Army front, there had been a lull in the narrowed VII Corps sector. On 21 January, just to the northeast, in the XVIII Airborne Corps sector, the 75th Infantry Division approached Sart-lez-St. Vith, while the 7th Armored Division battled determined German resistance in Born. To the east the 1st Division encountered similar desperate resistance in and around Schoppen.

On 22 January Hitler ordered the Sixth Panzer Army to move from the western front to the east, where the Soviet offensive was picking up momentum. This order included the army's two SS Panzer corps and four SS Panzer divisions, plus the Führer Begleit and Führer Grenadier brigades. This meant, of course, the withdrawal of the SS units that had been stiffening the XIII Corps south of Ondenval and north of St. Vith.

As a consequence of the resultant thinning of the German lines, on 23 January there was a general advance all along the First Army front west of the shoulder. In the VII Corps sector the 84th Division, which had passed through the 83d Division, advanced with support from the 3d Armored Division to seize Gouvy and Beho. In the XVIII Corps sector the 75th Infantry Division occupied Commanster and Sart-lez-St.-Vith. Since the 17th Airborne Division of the VIII Corps had seized Steinbach and Limerle, to the south, the VII Corps was now pinched out. The 30th Infantry Division moved into Ober Emmels and Nieder Emmels to the northeast. The 7th Armored Division, to which the 509th Parachute Infantry Battalion was attached, continued its drive through Born, cleared Hunningen, approached Wallerode, and reached the outskirts of St. Vith. Only in the V Corps sector did German resistance seem undiminished, and the 1st Division made negligible gains.

With German resistance waning, the American troops on the narrowing northern front continued to press forward. The 7th Armored retook all of St. Vith on 24 January, then drove back a German counterattack from the vicinity of Wallerode. To its right the 30th Infantry Division reached Crombach and Neundorf, but was pinched out as the 75th Division occupied Braunlauf and

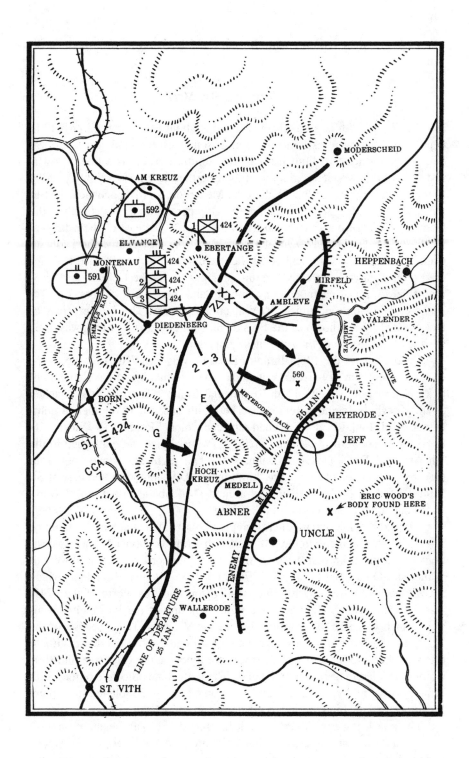

MODERSCHEID

AM KREUZ

592

ELVANCE

1 424

EBERTANGE

MONTENAU

424

591

2 424

HEPPENBACH

MIRFELD

3 424

XX 1

7 X

DIEDENBERG

AMBLEVE

VALENDER

EMMELS RAU

I

2 - 3 L

560
X

BORN

E

MEYERODER BACH

25 JAN.

517 424

G

MEYERODE

JEFF

CCA
7

HOCH-
KREUZ

ABNER

MEDELL

MLR

ERIC WOOD'S
BODY FOUND HERE
X

UNCLE

ENEMY

WALLERODE

LINE OF DEPARTURE
25 JAN. 45

ST. VITH

Maldinge and made contact with 7th Armored Division patrols south of St. Vith.

THE BOIS DE ST. VITH

Just east of St. Vith is a broad forested ridge about five to ten kilometers in depth and about twenty kilometers from its southwest terminus just east of St. Vith to its northeastern limit just east of Büllingen. There is a line of towns just west of this wooded region, with their northeasterly axis roughly parallel to that of the ridge: St. Vith, Wallerode, Meyerode, and Heppenbach. Just to the east of the ridge, and also running roughly parallel to it, is a stretch of the German-Belgian frontier terminating in the north—just east of the ridge—at the little German border town of Losheim, on the east end of the Losheim Gap. The ridge, the Gap, and all of the place names just mentioned had figured prominently in the early fighting precipitated by the German Ardennes offensive in mid-December—one month and one week before the 7th Armored Division reoccupied St. Vith on 24 January. The southern part of that wooded ridge, known as the Bois de St. Vith or St. Vith Forest, was to be the site of the last act of the Ardennes campaign.

On 20 January the 106th Infantry Division was in XVIII Airborne Corps reserve, in the Stavelot–Trois Ponts area. The two major combat elements of that division were still its 424th Regimental Combat Team and the attached 517th Parachute Infantry Regiment. The 424th had a new regimental commander, Col. John R. Jeter, who had replaced Colonel Reid on 18 January. On the twentieth both the 424th and the 517th were alerted to be attached to the 7th Armored Division. On 23 January the two regiments moved out from their bivouac area and joined the 7th Armored Division north and east of St. Vith. The 424th bivouacked in and around Diedenberg, just north of Born, and about eight kilometers north of St. Vith.

All next day the two regiments prepared for a dawn attack on 25 January. The 424th was on the extreme left of the 7th Armored Division line, its positions extending from just west of Amblève in the north to just northwest of Wallerode. On its right was the 517th Parachute Infantry Regiment, which was in the center of the 7th Armored Division line. Just north of the 424th was the 16th Infantry Regiment, the right-flank unit of the 1st Infantry Division, which was also the extreme right of the V Corps. The objective of the 7th Armored Division was to seize the high ground of the Bois de St. Vith, to establish the base for a line of departure for a new major offensive into Germany scheduled to begin on 28 January. The immediate objective of the 424th Infantry was to bypass the German strongpoint in Amblève, to capture Meyerode and the high ground to the north and east of that village.

The attack toward Meyerode and the Bois de St. Vith began at dawn— 0715—on 25 January. In a day of bitter fighting, the 424th seized its assigned intermediate objectives, occupied the village of Medell, reached the outskirts

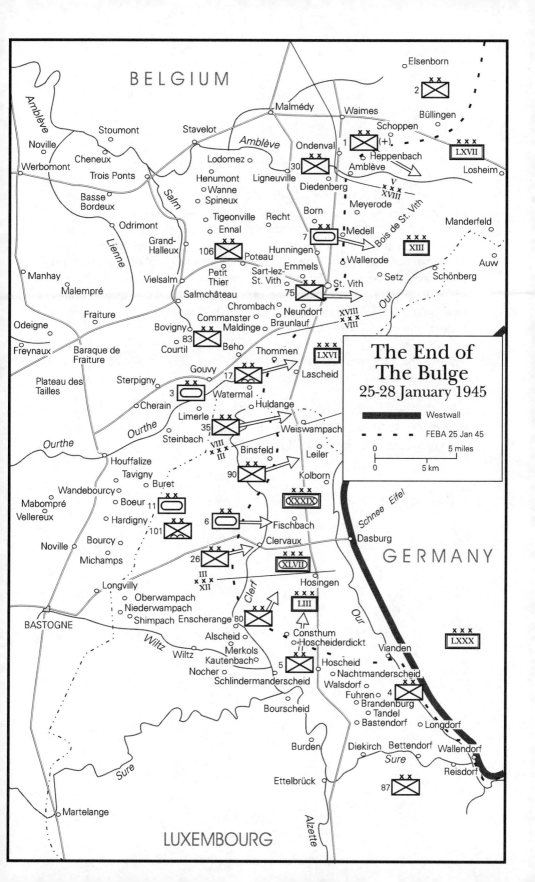

The End of
The Bulge
25-28 January 1945

Westwall

FEBA 25 Jan 45

0   5 miles

0   5 km

BELGIUM

GERMANY

LUXEMBOURG

Amblève

Stoumont

Stavelot

Malmédy

Waimes

Elsenborn

2

Noville

Cheneux

Werbomont

Trois Ponts

Lodomez

Amblève

Ondenval

Schoppen

Büllingen

1 (+)

Heppenbach

LXVII

Henumont

Ligneuville

Diedenberg

Amblève

Losheim

Wanne

Spineux

30

V

Basse
Bordeux

Salm

Tigeonville

Recht

Born

Meyerode

XVIII

Odrimont

Grand-
Halleux

Ennal

Hunningen

7

Medell

Bois de St. Vith

Manderfeld

Manhay

Lienne

Petit
Thier

Poteau

106

Sart-lez-
St. Vith

Emmels

Wallerode

XIII

Auw

Vielsalm

Setz

Schönberg

Malempré

Salmchâteau

75

St. Vith

Our

Fraiture

Chrombach

Neundorf

Bovigny

Commanster

Braunlauf

XVIII

Odeigne

Baraque de
Fraiture

Maldinge

VIII

83

Beho

Freynaux

Courtil

Thommen

LXVI

Plateau des
Tailles

Sterpigny

Gouvy

17

Lascheid

Cherain

3

Watermal

Huldange

Ourthe

Limerle

Steinbach

35

Weiswampach

Ourthe

VIII
III

Binsfeld

Leiler

Houffalize

Tavigny

Buret

90

Kolborn

Wandebourcy

Boeur

11

XXXIX

Mabompré
Vellereux

Hardigny

6

Fischbach

Noville

Bourcy

101

Clervaux

Dasburg

Michamps

26

XLVII

Longvilly

III
XII

Hosingen

Oberwampach

Schnee Eifel

Niederwampach

Shimpach

Enscherange

80

LIII

Our

LXXX

BASTOGNE

Alscheid

Consthum

Wiltz

Merkols

Hoscheiderdickt

Vianden

Wiltz

Kautenbach

5

Hoscheid

Nocher

Schlindermanderscheid

Walsdorf

Nachtmanderscheid

Fuhren

4

Brandenburg

Tandel

Bourscheid

Bastendorf

Longdorf

Burden

Diekirch

Bettendorf

Wallendorf

Sure

Sure

Reisdorf

Ettelbrück

87

Sure

Martelange

Alzette

of Meyerode, and pushed into the western slopes of the Bois de St. Vith. On 26 January Meyerode was occupied, and the assigned objective area consolidated.

THE END OF THE BATTLE

There is nothing in the war diary or S-3 reports of the 424th Infantry Regiment to show that any of its men realized the relationship of their battle line on 26–27 January to the tragedy that had shattered their division nearly six weeks earlier. On the far side of the ridge they had just captured—not more than four kilometers away—was the village of Schönberg, and the sites where the 422d and 423d Infantry regiments had surrendered on 19 December. It is likely, however, that some men of the 424th did realize that they were within ten kilometers of the area that their regiment had defended so staunchly in mid-December.

Thus the 424th Infantry, which had played a major role in the opening battle of the Ardennes campaign of 1944–45, was also a major player in the last engagement of that campaign. A new battle and new campaign were about to commence.

At dawn on 28 February the 82d Airborne Division attacked eastward through the 424th and 517th regiments to begin the first Allied offensive of 1945 into Germany. The Battle of the Bulge had ended!

EPILOGUE

The Battle of the Bulge or, more properly, the Ardennes campaign, was one of the most dramatic episodes of World War II. It was conceived by Hitler as an operation that could change the outcome of a war that even he could see Germany was obviously losing. The concept, the onset, the denouement, and the results all raise major questions about the concluding months of World War II. Here are what we consider to be the sixteen most important questions:

1. Could the German counteroffensive have succeeded?

2. What were the relative merits of Hitler's "big solution" and his generals' proposed "small solution"?

3. Did the German counteroffensive change the outcome of the war?

4. Should the Americans have anticipated the German counteroffensive?

5. How important were the redeployment orders issued by General Bradley late on 16 December?

6. Who should receive credit for those redeployments: Eisenhower or Bradley?

7. Should Eisenhower have placed the northern front under Field Marshal Montgomery?

8. Did Montgomery make a positive or negative contribution to the final Allied victory?

9. Should the Allied counteroffensive have attacked at the shoulders instead of the waist of the German salient?

10. What is the truth about the Malmédy massacre?

11. Why did the Germans miss early opportunities on the north flank of the Bulge?

12. Was Lt. Col. Peiper a war criminal or a bold leader?

13. What was the role of airpower?
14. What was the role of artillery?
15. How did American generalship compare with German generalship?
16. How did the German soldier compare with the American soldier?

Here are our answers to those questions:

1. COULD THE GERMAN COUNTEROFFENSIVE HAVE SUCCEEDED?

During World War I, under somewhat similar circumstances although German defeat was not yet obviously inevitable, the German high command (for all practical purposes, Gen. Erich Ludendorff) launched a similar offensive in early 1918.[1] That offensive came even closer to success than did Hitler's Ardennes offensive of December 1944. It can be argued that if the Allied Supreme War Council had not met at Doullens and Beauvais in March 1918 and appointed Gen. Ferdinand Foch to supreme command, the German offensive might have been successful and resulted in a negotiated, stalemated peace rather than the clear-cut German defeat that occurred later that year. It can also be argued that what happened was inevitable under the circumstances and that the Germans were bound to be defeated.

No such debate is possible for the campaign in late 1944. The Allies had a supreme commander. Despite an amazingly determined and skillful performance, the Germans did not have the resources necessary to carry Hitler's concept to its planned conclusion unless the Allies collapsed—and the Allies were too battlewise and too strong for that. On the other hand, the only alternative was to await inevitable defeat: Hitler's plan was doomed from the beginning. This does not mean, furthermore, that the German offensive might not have had a significant effect on the course of the war, or that an Allied victory was assured within a month of the initiation of the offensive.

2. "BIG SOLUTION" VS. "SMALL SOLUTION"

Hitler's "Big Solution" was for the German armies to cross the Meuse River and drive to Antwerp, destroying Allied forces north of the line Bastogne-Brussels-Antwerp. The "Small solution" favored by Field Marshals von Rundstedt and Model was for a double envelopment, with the northern arm based in the Geilenkirchen area, and the southern envelopment that planned by Hitler, through the Ardennes, with the two armies meeting near Liège. Neither solution would have changed the ultimate outcome of the war. One possible difference is that the "Small Solution" might have resulted in fewer German casualties, a less catastrophic German defeat, and Allied victory delayed by a few weeks or months.

3. DID THE GERMAN OFFENSIVE CHANGE THE
WAR OUTCOME?

The Germans had already lost the war. Without the catastrophic casualties and matériel losses of the Ardennes campaign, and by using cautiously and penuriously the human and matériel resources that were in fact so recklessly squandered in the Ardennes, the Germans probably could have substantially slowed the Allied offensives of early 1945. in both the east and the west. Thus the war might possibly have been prolonged until summer or early fall of 1945. In this case, of course, there must be a question as to where the first atomic bomb would have been employed.

4. SHOULD THE AMERICANS HAVE ANTICIPATED THE
GERMAN COUNTEROFFENSIVE?

Frederick the Great reputedly said: "It is no disgrace to be defeated; it is a disgrace to be surprised." Even granting the clarity of vision that accompanies hindsight, it is difficult to understand how the Allies, particularly the Americans, allowed themselves to be so completely surprised by the German counteroffensive. As discussed in chapter 4, even though the Germans exercised strict security, there was enough evidence available to Allied intellegence authorities about the coming offensive that it should have been detected.

Nevertheless, under the circumstances, the events of the previous six months had provided Allied intelligence analysts with a seemingly logical basis for assuming that the Germans were incapable of such a major offensive effort. So it is difficult to attribute to the Allied intelligence community the classic mistake of attempting to fathom the enemy's intentions while ignoring its capabilities. The Allied G-2s apparently *thought* they were assessing hostile capabilities. But that meant that they did ignore much evidence.

The problem, basically, was *interpretation* of the experience of the previous six months. Secure in the belief that the Allies could not lose the war, the Allied intelligence officers had become arrogant. Furthermore, at the higher levels of command—where the underestimate of German capabilities was most serious—the intelligence officers had come to rely too much on information from ULTRA (see chapter 4). And German security measures denied ULTRA an opportunity to obtain information about the German plans.

5. HOW IMPORTANT WERE THE REDEPLOYMENT ORDERS
ISSUED BY GENERAL BRADLEY LATE ON 16 DECEMBER?

There can be little doubt that the principal reason why the Germans never reached the Meuse River was the four-to-six-day delay in their timetable caused by the protracted American defense of St. Vith. There can be even less doubt that the timely arrival of the 7th Armored Division late on 17 December was the reason why St. Vith held as long as it did. It was General Bradley, then visiting at SHAEF Headquarters at Versailles, who called his headquarters late on 16 December to order the movement of the 7th Armored Division to the VIII Corps sector.

If the Germans had been more successful at St. Vith, they almost certainly would have reached, and possibly crossed, the Meuse River. Allied casualties would have been substantially higher, and Allied recovery would have been considerably delayed.

Thus Bradley's decision to shift the 7th Armored Division from the left wing of the Ninth Army to the right wing of the First was one example of Allied tactical competence that led to the German defeat.

That same evening Bradley also ordered General Patton to send the 10th Armored Division from the Third Army's XX Corps to support the right wing of the VIII Corps, the southern shoulder of the Bulge. Patton, who had another important mission for the 10th Armored Division and who thought that the Germans were only making local attacks in the Ardennes, protested but Bradley insisted.

The arrival of part of the 10th Armored Division to support the 4th Infantry Division did not have consequences as momentous as the redeployment of the 7th Armored Division. Nonetheless, if it had not been for the timely arrival of the 10th Armored, the American right shoulder of the salient might have become unhinged, seriously delaying the American recovery. However, the subsequent decision of Maj. Gen. Troy Middleton of the VIII Corps to deploy a major portion of that division to slow the German advance on Bastogne may have been equally momentous. It can be argued that otherwise the Germans would have taken Bastogne and thus would have reached, and possibly crossed, the Meuse.

6. WHO SHOULD RECEIVE CREDIT FOR THOSE REDEPLOYMENTS: BRADLEY OR EISENHOWER?

In his memoirs, *A Soldier's Story*, Bradley implies that the decision to move the 7th and 10th Armored divisions and the timing of his action to implement the decision were his alone.[2] In his later book with Clay Blair, *A General's Life*, Bradley admits that like General Patton he at first thought the initial reports of the German offensive merely indicated local German counterattacks. However, he credits Eisenhower for sensing that the situation was more serious and for urging him to take early action to meet the threat. It was in response to Eisenhower's urging that he decided to move the two divisions and to issue the necessary orders to his headquarters and to Patton.[3]

In his book *Crusade in Europe*, Eisenhower paints a picture ever-so-slightly different. Bradley's second account requires us to take at face value Ike's assertion that "I was immediately convinced that this was no local attack." Using the collegial "we" he shares with Bradley (and key members of his staff) an agreement that the 7th and 10th Armored divisions should be moved immediately to the support of Middleton's VIII Corps.[4]

There thus appears little doubt that Ike deserves the credit for *coup d'oeil* in recognizing the seriousness of the situation, and in then promptly determining what needed to be done. (This may reveal why, in the late 1920s, he was first in his class at the Command and General Staff School.) In any event, it is quite evident that Eisenhower's discussion with Bradley was critical in this process. Eisenhower has not been given sufficient credit for this truly momentous decision.

7. SHOULD EISENHOWER HAVE PLACED THE NORTHERN FRONT UNDER FIELD MARSHAL MONTGOMERY?

There are at least five reasons why this question must be answered with a reluctant yes. There are at least three reasons for suggesting that the answer could well have been no.

First, there can be no question that by 19 December the progress of the German offensive had cut all direct lines of communications between Bradley's headquarters at Luxembourg and the headquarters of the First and Ninth armies. Bradley had made a mistake in putting his headquarters so far forward and so far toward the right flank of his army group. Eisenhower is correct when he writes: "[I]t was completely impossible for Bradley to give to the attack on the southern shoulder the attention that I desired and at the same time keep properly in touch with the troops in the north who were called upon to meet the heaviest German blows."[5]

Whatever one may think of Monty and his extreme caution, he was a strong commander. In the early days of the German offensive, General Hodges, the First Army commander, was not able to exercise strong command in the north, because he had to devote too much of his attention to the physical danger of his command post, which was in the path of the main German offensive, directly and severely threatened by Kampfgruppe Peiper. In the face of the threat, of course, Hodges finally moved his command post. But, during the period of the threat, and for a day or two thereafter, First Army Headquarters was not operating at optimum efficiency. Thus, placing Monty over Hodges assured strength of command in the north, when such strength would otherwise have been far from certain.

Furthermore, the German penetration had clearly divided the Allied front into two great segments, demanding the personal attention of the overall ground force commander, who was Eisenhower, particularly with respect to the allocation and commitment of reserves. It would have been impossible, or at least inappropriate, for him to try to exercise personal control had a single subordinate been in command of both of the separated fronts.

Having already committed the XVIII Airborne Corps, it was obvious to Eisenhower that there was only one other major, battle-ready Allied force available as a reserve should the Germans make a clear breakthrough. This was the British XXX Corps. Theoretically, as Supreme Commander and simultaneously the Allied ground force commander, Eisenhower could have ordered the transfer of the British XXX Corps to Bradley's command, but this could have aroused British resentment and strained Allied relationships. The surest way of having that corps available if needed would be to keep it under Montgomery's command and to make it Montgomery's responsibility to make the commitment.

Of these four reasons, the fourth was probably the most important. And, in fact, even though the XXX Corps played a very minor role in the fighting, its commitment to the line permitted the redeployment of the U.S. VII Corps to make the main effort of the Allied counteroffensive thrust in the north in early January.

There was a fifth reason. On 20–21 December Monty seems to have been the only senior Allied commander—with the exception of General Hasbrouck, commanding the 7th Armored Division and the so-called "fortified goose-egg" around St. Vith—who recognized how close that goose-egg was to being completely encircled by the Germans. He insisted that the goose-egg be evacuated. Since Monty was so overcautious in so many other respects, it is easy to ignore this one instance when he was absolutely right. His decision undoubtedly saved the 7th Armored Division from being either destroyed or horribly damaged.

The first argument in favor of Bradley retaining control of both sides of the salient is that by radio, airplane, and multilink telephone, he could have retained sufficiently close contact with the First and Ninth army commanders to exercise command properly. And he could readily have moved his command post from Luxembourg to a more centralized location in the rear of all three of his armies, from which direct telephone connections to the two northernmost armies could have been arranged in a few hours.

Second, had Bradley been responsible for both the northern and southern shoulders of the salient, he would have been forced to leave more personal initiative to Patton in the south. While Bradley was nowhere near as cautious as Montgomery, he was far too cautious for Patton's liking; his physical presence literally "next door," and his close attention to the way Patton was running the Third Army greatly inhibited Patton's freedom of action. (Nonetheless, he was completely loyal to Bradley.) It seems quite likely that without Bradley's presence in Luxembourg, Patton would have unleashed the XII Corps up the Skyline Drive early in January, with consequences that could have been momentous.

Third, had Bradley been in overall command of the north and south flanks of the Bulge, the counteroffensive in the north would undoubtedly have been launched at least three days before it actually was, which might have resulted in some German units being cut off west of Houffalize.

On balance, however, we believe that the reasons for supporting Eisenhower's decision slightly outweigh those against the decision.

8. DID MONTGOMERY MAKE A POSITIVE OR NEGATIVE CONTRIBUTION TO THE FINAL ALLIED VICTORY?

With the exception of his decision that saved the U.S. 7th Armored Division and its attached units, Montgomery's participation in the chain of command for the Battle of Bulge probably affected the Allied cause more negatively than positively, delaying the Allied recovery. His only other decision that contributed positively to the outcome of the battle was the delayed and half-hearted commitment of the XXX Corps opposite the northwest corner of the German salient, but Eisenhower could have demanded that without putting Monty into the chain of command.

Nevertheless, as noted above, this sole significant British contribution to the battle was achieved painlessly with Montgomery in command in the north. And also, as noted above, there were other positive reasons for putting a British commander—and Monty was the only one possible—in command in the north.

We have seen, however, that Montgomery's unfortunate personality, combined with his extremely cautious nature, came close to disrupting Allied harmony. Thus it is possible to say that while it was the right decision to place the northern flank of the Bulge under Montgomery, he did not significantly contribute to the Allied success.

9. ALLIED COUNTEROFFENSIVE: ATTACK AT WAIST OR AT SHOULDERS?

The Allied high command provides good examples of three types of competent military commanders. First there is the slow, cautious, careful type who wishes to leave nothing to chance. Montgomery was the exemplar. Then there are other generals who recognize the truth of the proverb attributed to Napoleon, "You can't make an omelet without breaking eggs," but who wish to break no more eggs than necessary. Eisenhower and Bradley fit this category. Then there are bold, aggressive commanders who, without being foolhardy, recognize that great results in battle demand at least some risks. American exemplars of this type in the Battle of the Bulge were Patton and Collins.

As early as 19 December, at the Verdun conference, Patton had urged that the Allied response to the German offensive should be a counteroffensive to cut off the enemy spearheads. As soon as he was involved in the battle and had a chance to voice his recommendations, Collins had expressed the same point of view.

But Patton was overruled by Bradley, and Collins by Montgomery. Eisenhower, frustrated by Montgomery's passivity, was willing to settle for a half-measure: an offensive to cut off the waist of the German penetration at Houffalize, a relatively cautious option also favored by Bradley. Patton, unable to gain approval for the bolder step of a counteroffensive at the shoulders to cut off all Germans inside the salient, carried out his orders from Bradley with only private grumbling about the "tentmaker."[6]

It could be argued that the XII Corps offensive toward the Skyline Drive made no spectacular advance when finally unleashed on 18 January. Nor did the V Corps offensive east of St. Vith, about the same time, move very rapidly. But two things must be remembered.

First, the Germans had already withdrawn most of their troops from the salient without having had any significant elements cut off. Thus they had far larger forces near the shoulders than they would have had if these offensives had been staged in early January. This is why the American final offensives in the Bulge moved so slowly. (And, of course, the weather was more favorable to the defender than to the attacker.)

Second, when finally launched, the American offensives from the northern and southern shoulders stimulated a precipitate German withdrawal. Since they had already extracted most of their troops from the depth of the salient, however, the completion of the withdrawal was relatively easy for the Germans.

It is no wonder that when Field Marshal von Rundstedt recognized the limited nature of the American counteroffensive, he somewhat contemptuously referred to it as "the American small solution." Thus it was clear what Rundstedt would have done if he had been an American with the resources available to the Americans.

10. WHAT IS THE TRUTH ABOUT THE MALMÉDY MASSACRE?

In appendix G is presented what we believe to be an objective and balanced assessment of the Malmédy Incident of 17 December 1944. Some of its points bear repetition:

• There was without question a war crime committed by members of Kampfgruppe Peiper, who shot down and murdered in cold blood a large if indeterminate number of disarmed American prisoners of war.

• The true dimensions of the crime were seriously obscured by the almost equally criminal misconduct of a substantial number of Americans who were responsible for the interrogation and the prosecution of German prisoners— Waffen-SS soldiers—accused of the original war crime and who either encouraged or participated in illegal treatment of prisoners.

• During the war, and particularly later in the Ardennes campaign, Americans were also guilty of the war crime of killing disarmed prisoners of war. One need only quote from the diary of General Patton, who wrote on 4 January: "There were . . . some unfortunate incidents in the shooting of prisoners. (I hope we can conceal this.)"[7] But this in no way excuses the original German crime.

One reason (although no excuse) for such incidents, of course, was the effect of propaganda that had both publicized and distorted the Malmédy incident.

• There is some basis for the widespread assumption that Waffen-SS soldiers were more prone to commit such war crimes than were other German or American soldiers.

11. WHY DID THE GERMANS MISS EARLY OPPORTUNITIES ON THE NORTH FLANK OF THE BULGE?

During the early days of the German offensive there were several missed opportunities for Kampfgruppe Peiper and for other elements of the Sixth Panzer Army to advance northward to seize supplies (particularly fuel) and to disrupt seriously the rear areas of the First Army and the V Corps. It has been suggested by some historians that the failure to exploit these opportunities is an indictment of German leadership and/or evidence of German rigidity and inflexibility.

We do not agree. In most of these cases the only way that the Germans could have discovered the opportunities would have been to conduct extensive and time-consuming patrolling to the north. It is not an indictment that they did not conduct such patrolling, because this could have impaired their performance of their assigned mission, which was, in essence, to drive northwestward to the Meuse west of Huy as rapidly as possible before turning northward toward Antwerp. To have taken the time to find these opportunities, and even to have exploited the opportunities, would have seriously jeopardized the timely accomplishment of their primary mission. (It is irrelevant that, for other reasons, they did not accomplish their mission.)

12. WAS LT. COL. PEIPER A WAR CRIMINAL OR A BOLD AND HONORABLE LEADER?

On the basis of the evidence available regarding his performance as the commander of Kampfgruppe Peiper, including the Malmédy incident, it is clear that Peiper was a competent leader. We have direct evidence from Major McCown that, during the several days that McCown was his prisoner, Peiper behaved honorably. And, while there is reason to believe that orders were issued in the 1st SS Panzer Division that prisoners would not be taken, we have no direct evidence that Peiper issued such orders. Furthermore, he did take 170 American prisoners of war before he led his men back to the German lines. It is almost certain that he had no direct personal responsibility for the murder of the American prisoners of war near Malmédy.

On balance, we are prepared to give Peiper the benefit of the doubt and accept the unquestioned evidence of his soldierly performance as commander of Kampfgruppe Peiper.

13. WHAT WAS THE ROLE OF AIRPOWER?

Airpower played both a negative and a positive role in the campaign.

In a negative sense, the absence of Allied airpower in the early days of the campaign was a very great contribution to the initial German successes. Airpower had become a major element in the overall Allied military superiority in the west, beginning with preinvasion operations before the landings on the beaches of Normandy. It may be questioned whether the Allies could have landed successfully in Normandy without air superiority—almost to the point of air supremacy. Superior airpower had been an important ingredient in the Allied successes in breaking out of the Normandy Beachhead and in driving the Germans back to their frontiers in August and September.

Thus the ability to operate in an environment free of Allied airpower greatly facilitated the initial German offensive. And there can be no question that the American defensive efforts and the subsequent American counteroffensive were aided greatly by the occasional presence of large numbers of aircraft providing close support and interdicting the German lines of communications.

Yet the German drive was halted by American ground troops, often without the benefit of air support. And the American counteroffensive rolled forward, day after day, even though on most days no air support was available. Thus, on balance, Allied airpower played a major role in the German defeat. But it was not decisive.

14. WHAT WAS THE ROLE OF ARTILLERY?

There can be no doubt that American artillery played a decisive role not only in the outcome of the Ardennes campaign, but in the outcome of the war. For reasons that need not be elaborated here, during World War II American field artillery was the best in the world in terms of the tactics and technique of fire support. There was little to choose between the artillery weapons of the opponents. But American weapons were considerably more numerous, were much more plentifully supplied with ammunition, and were employed with far more sophisticated fire-direction techniques. This was as true in the engagement of targets of opportunity as it was in carefully preplanned prepared fires. Particularly important was the American ability at short notice to mass the fires of a number of widely separated artillery battalions on targets of opportunity, with devastating effects.

As a result, even the most successful German attacks were hampered by superior American artillery firepower more effectively employed. And many German attacks that might have been successful were stopped by that highly effective firepower. When the Americans were attacking, they had much less interference from German artillery because of the extremely efficient counterbattery performance of American medium and heavy artillery. Attacking infantrymen were aided by accurate and often massive fire support of light and medium artillery.

15. HOW DID AMERICAN GENERALSHIP COMPARE WITH GERMAN GENERALSHIP?

In appendix H there is a discussion of general German combat performance in the Battle of the Bulge. Leadership, of course, is a major element of combat performance, and it is obvious that the Germans compared very favorably with the Americans in terms of overall leadership. But generalship is an exceptional form of leadership, not readily susceptible to statistical analysis. It cannot be compared by means of a computer program like overall combat performance of the opposing armies, which involves many units in many engagements.

At the higher levels of generalship, it would appear that there was little to choose between the two armies. Theoretically von Rundstedt was the opposite number of Eisenhower, but in fact, because of the tight control over operations exercised by Hitler, a direct comparison is impossible. With the exception of his willingness to accept a half-measure by making the final counteroffensive toward Houffalize rather than along the Skyline Drive, Eisenhower's professional performance was almost flawless, even if it cannot be characterized as brilliant or inspired. His initial reaction to the German offensive was particularly praiseworthy.

At the army group level were Bradley and Montgomery on the Allied side and Model on the German. As was the case with Rundstedt, the rigid control exercised by Hitler prevented Model from exercising any significant qualities of generalship, although he earlier and later gave evidence that he unquestionably was a general of far more than average ability.

As to the two Allied army group commanders: Montgomery was a careful, cautious general, unwilling to take the risks demanded of great generalship, but certainly a competent professional, whose strong—if peculiar—character lifted him above the pedestrian. Bradley, an equally competent professional, whose strong but more orthodox characteristics also lifted him well above the pedestrian, was probably on balance a better general than Montgomery.

Three German army commanders participated in the Ardennes campaign: Dietrich, Manteuffel, and Brandenberger. Sepp Dietrich was miscast as an army commander. He was a relatively simple, rough-hewn soldier who would have been above his level of competence as a division commander, although he probably would have been an outstanding colonel of military police. He owed his position to his loyalty as a Waffen-SS soldier to Hitler. The performance of his headquarters, which was competent but not exceptional, was due essentially to the typical efficiency of German Army and Waffen-SS staff officers.

Both Manteuffel and Brandenberger were typical of high-ranking German Army officers: skilled professionals who always performed well under the best and worst of circumstances. Manteuffel seems also to have had at least a touch of genius which, as an army commander, he was able to display in this campaign more readily than von Rundstedt and Model (although both of these generals were probably of comparable abilities).

On the Allied side there were two American Army commanders: Hodges and Patton. Like their German opposite numbers both were skilled professionals, although it is doubtful if Hodges was as competent as either Manteuffel or Brandenberger. Patton, on the other hand, was something else. He was probably the most gifted general of any of those being discussed here. He was one of the three or four best American generals of World War II, and perhaps one of the ten best generals of American military history.

The German corps commanders as a group were typical products of the German military system: skilled, competent professionals, most of whom performed magnificently under the most difficult and trying circumstances. But at least four of the Americans were of comparable capability: Collins, Ridgway, Middleton, and Eddy.

The relatively limited evidence suggests that the quality of the German division commanders was on average slightly higher than that of their American counterparts. However, there were at least four American division commanders as competent as the best of the Germans: Robertson of the 2d Infantry Division, Harmon of the 2d Armored Division, Gavin of the 82d Airborne Division, and Hasbrouck of the 7th Armored Division.

16. HOW DID THE GERMAN SOLDIER COMPARE WITH THE AMERICAN SOLDIER?

It is unfair to speak of the performance of generals without at least some consideration of the magnificent performance of the rank and file on both sides. Rarely in history have the soldiers of opposing armies fought so fiercely while being so evenly matched, and with such little difference in their soldierly qualities. As shown in appendix H, the Germans had the advantage of a military system that was the most professional in the world for its time, and possibly for all time. (That system was not operating at its best in late 1944 and early 1945.) Yet the average American performance was almost on a par with, and in three or four divisions (such as the 1st and 2d Infantry and 82d and 101st Airborne) probably as good as, the best of the Germans'.

In devotion to duty, courage, steadfastness in hardship, and loyalty to country and national traditions, the Germans and Americans were equally matched.

APPENDIX A

BACKGROUND ON THE BATTLE OF THE BULGE

Winter came early to the soldiers facing each other in eastern Belgium and Luxembourg along the western front in mid-December 1944. On the night of 15–16 December, as those on one side shivered in foxholes, trenches, and dugouts, those on the other side blew on cold fingers and stamped frigid feet as they moved into assembly areas covered with light snow. It is doubtful if any on either side were thinking or dreaming about how and why they were where they were. It would have been a suitable time for such reassessment.

ORIGINS

Their situations were, in fact, a logical culmination of decisions that had been made across the Atlantic Ocean in Washington almost exactly three years before. There, in mid-December 1941, shortly after the United States had been catapulted into World War II by the Japanese attack on Pearl Harbor, the political and military leaders of the United States and Great Britain had met to plan a strategy for the newly formed Anglo-American Alliance.[1] The meeting, code-named the "Arcadia" Conference, produced several major strategic Allied decisions for the prosecution of the war, but one among these was paramount: Despite American fury at Japan for the costly defeat suffered in the surprise attack on Pearl Harbor, the two allies agreed to concentrate the preponderance of their combined strength on the main objective of defeating Germany, the most formidable of the three Axis enemies—Germany, Italy, and Japan.

As the war progressed, the American partners in this decision were often tempted to stray a bit from it, particularly when they received appeals for scarce resources from Army and Navy leaders fighting the Japanese. However, when reminded by their British colleagues, the American leaders and planners remained generally faithful to the concept of "Germany first!"

Another important decision at the Arcadia Conference was to establish the Combined Chiefs of Staff (CCS), a six-man (later seven-man) committee made up of the British Chiefs of Staff Committee and the American Joint Chiefs of Staff, to plan the details of Allied war strategy under the general supervision of Prime Minister Winston S. Churchill of the United Kingdom and President Franklin D. Roosevelt of the United States. The members of the British Chiefs of Staff Committee were the Chief of the Imperial General Staff, Army Field Marshal Sir John Dill; The First Sea Lord, Admiral of the Fleet Sir Dudley Pound; and Chief of the Air Staff, Air Chief Marshal Sir Charles Portal. (Later Sir John Dill became the senior British military representative in Washington and was replaced as Chief of the Imperial General Staff by General soon-to-be Field Marshal Sir Alan Brooke.)

The newly formed American Joint Chiefs of Staff (JCS) consisted of Gen. George C. Marshall, Chief of Staff of the U.S. Army; Adm. Ernest J. King, Chief of Naval Operations; and Lt. Gen. Henry H. Arnold, Chief of the Army Air Corps. Later, Adm. William H. Leahy, former Chief of Naval Operations, and now Chief of Staff to the President, became the Chairman of the JCS.

The Germany-first decision had been reconfirmed in the subsequent meetings of these leaders, at the "Symbol" Conference at Casablanca in Morocco, January 1943; at the "Trident" Conference in Washington in May; at the "Quadrant" Conference in Quebec in August; at the "Sextant" and "Eureka" conferences in Cairo and Teheran in November–December 1943; and at the "Octagon" Conference in Quebec in September 1944.[2]

"ULTRA," THE MOST-SECRET "WEAPON"

One reason for the Allies' early decision to concentrate on the defeat of Germany was their respect for, and fear of, German scientific and technical prowess. Their ongoing effort to produce an atomic bomb led the Allies to assume that German scientists were working on a similar project, and this concern was heightened by Hitler's frequent public threats to use new "secret weapons." In fact, the Germans had seriously considered the possibility of developing an atomic weapon, but had come to the conclusion that it was not feasible at that time.[3] Therefore they had, with considerable success, focused their "secret weapon" research on flying bombs, jet aircraft, and ballistic missiles.

The Anglo-American Allies, however, had had even more remarkable success on two highly secret intelligence projects, both devices designed to read the secret codes of their enemies. (By this time cryptography had become dependent upon extremely complex and mathematically sophisticated electric coding machines, in many ways the forerunners of modern computers.) Before the war American cryptographic analysts had built a machine that could read the principal Japanese diplomatic and military codes. Early in the war the British had developed even more complex machines that could read German military codes.

Interestingly the Germans, even though they were able to break some of the Allied codes, were confident from the beginning to the end of the war that their far more sophisticated encoding machine, called "Enigma," could never be duplicated.[4] They were wrong! Furthermore, the machine was first duplicated before the war by the scientists of Poland, a country scorned by the Germans. Even more interestingly, the British and French, who had been generally aware of the existence of Germany's Enigma machine, had not even come close to duplicating it.

In an act of Allied loyalty and generosity perhaps unparalleled in history—while Poland was being overwhelmed by Germany in 1939, and Polish horse-cavalrymen were being slaughtered by German tanks and machine guns—Polish scientists delivered copies of their version of the Enigma machine to French and British colleagues.[5] The Polish machine was not an exact duplicate of the German machine and could not quickly be adapted to constant German improvements and modifications of their machines. Nonetheless, it was workable and could read many German messages. There was nothing else like it outside of Germany.

France was defeated and overrun by Germany in 1940 before French cryptographers were able to gain significant benefit from the machines received from Poland. However, like the Poles before them, the French were able to conceal from the Germans their versions of the Enigma machine.

The British had made somewhat more progress than the French at a secret installation in a former country home about fifty miles north of London: Bletchley Park.[6] They were reading a substantial proportion of intercepted German radio messages, and had established a system—by then given the code name "ULTRA"—for rapidly getting important intelligence information from these messages into the hands of senior military commanders who could use it.

By early 1944 the ULTRA system was operating smoothly. There was a Special Liaison Unit (SLU) at each British and American army and higher-level headquarters responsible for delivering the decoded information directly to the commander. ULTRA information had already contributed to Allied victories in North Africa, the Mediterranean, and Italy.[7]

CROSS-CHANNEL INVASION

At "Trident" President Roosevelt and Prime Minister Churchill approved the recommendation of the CCS for a major cross-channel invasion of German-occupied western Europe in 1944. From that time on the preparations for that invasion, code-named Operation Overlord, became the major focus of the attention of the Allies.[8] On 24 December 1943 Roosevelt and Churchill appointed American Gen. Dwight D. Eisenhower, then commanding Allied forces in the Mediterranean, to be the Supreme Allied Commander (SAC) for the invasion of Europe. Eisenhower, takng over an existing planning staff called COSSAC (Chief of Staff to the Supreme Allied Commands), which had been set up by the CCS at the Casablanca Conference in January 1943, established Supreme Headquarters Allied Expeditionary Forces (SHAEF) in London early in February 1944. In May he informed the CCS that his Allied force was ready to begin the invasion.

On 6 June 1944 British and American forces under General Eisenhower's command began their assault on Fortress Europe, landing on the Normandy coast between the Cotentin Peninsula and the Seine Estuary.[9] Overall commander of the landing forces—designated the 21st Army Group—was British Gen. Sir Bernard L. Montgomery. Under him were the British Second Army, commanded by Lt. Gen. Sir Miles C. Dempsey, and the U.S. First Army, under Lt. Gen. Omar N. Bradley.

Aided greatly by support from Allied air forces, despite vigorous and skillful German resistance, the Allied ground forces established a beachhead, which was slowly expanded across northern Normandy, west of the Seine River, over the next eight weeks.

BREAKOUT, PURSUIT

On 25 July the U.S. First Army, again with massive air support, initiated Operation Cobra, the breakout of Allied forces from the Normandy Beachhead.[10] As the U.S. Third Army, commanded by Lt. Gen. George S. Patton, poured out through a gap in the German lines created by the First Army near Avranches, Bradley relinquished command of the First Army to Lt. Gen. Courtney H. Hodges. Bradley then assumed command of the newly established 12th Army Group, whose principal elements were the American First and Third armies. At the same time a new Canadian First Army, commanded by Lt. Gen. H. D. Crerar, came into line beside the British Second Army, as part of Montgomery's 21st Army Group. With two army groups in the field, Eisenhower now took over command of Allied ground forces in Europe: the U.S. 12th Army Group and the British 21st Army Group.

German resistance remained tenacious and skillful. On 7 August all available panzer divisions were flung toward Avranches in a desperate effort to plug the gap and to cut off those elements of the Third Army that had already passed through. However, fighting with equal desperation, by 12 August the 30th Infantry Division of the First Army (and other units) repulsed the German tanks at Mortain, then threw them back.[11] The Germans were now overwhelmed by the power of the Allied air and ground offensive. As their shattered forces withdrew across northern France toward the Low Countries and Germany, they were vigorously pursued by the two American armies of Generals Patton and Hodges, on the right of a long Allied line.

To their left the British 21st Army Group was also driving northeastward across the Seine River toward the Low Countries. The advance of the four Anglo-American armies was so rapid in August that Allied logisticians, without the benefit of the unloading facilities of a major seaport, were unable to keep them adequately supplied with fuel and other supplies. In early September the Allied advance slowed to a crawl, then came to a standstill, as tanks and trucks literally ran out of gas.

The Germans had suffered severely during the bloody fighting in Normandy, and heavy losses continued as they were driven in considerable disorder across northern France. By late August the German armies in the west were on the verge of collapse. But the Allied slowdown, then halt, in early September provided a respite for the Germans, and they promptly took advantage of it. When the Allies, supplies partially replenished, again began to move in mid-September, they unexpectedly found themselves faced by a reinvigorated German Army.

By this time the Allies had a solid line of forces from the North Sea to the Swiss border. On 12 September the U.S. Seventh Army, which had landed on the coast of southern France on 15 August, pulled into line beside and east of the Third Army near Dijon.[12] To its right was the newly established First French Army, made up from troops that had landed with the Americans in southern France. American Gen. Alexander Patch commanded the Seventh Army; French Gen. Jean De Lattre de Tassigny commanded the First French Army. The two armies were combined under the 6th Army Group, commanded by American Lt. Gen. Jacob L. Devers. This army group was also literally at the end of its logistical tether, since it was still being supplied over the beaches of the French Riviera, thence up the Rhône River valley, and eastward into Burgundy, Alsace, and Lorraine.

ANTWERP AND THE WESTWALL

When the Allied advance was slowly renewed in mid-September, the first major objective was to capture and open the seaport of Antwerp, in order to ease the still-difficult supply situation. On 13 September British spearheads reached Antwerp, but the Germans still held the sea approaches to the port up the Scheldt estuary, as well as the principal land approaches across northern Belgium and the southern Netherlands.[13] On 17 September newly promoted Field Marshal Montgomery's 21st Army Group, supported by the First Allied Airborne Army (consisting of the British 1st Airborne Division and the American 82d and 101st Airborne divisions) initiated Operation Market Garden.[14] This was a bold plan to turn the German right flank in the Low Countries, and to establish an Allied bridgehead north of the Lek, or Niederrhein (lower Rhine) River. (Incidentally, it would also give the Allies control of the land approaches to Antwerp.) The operation was partially successful, with the attackers seizing the crossings over the Maas (Lower Meuse) and Waal rivers near Nijmegen. However, they were unable to secure the lower Rhine crossing at Arnhem because of a combination of bad luck and skillful, determined German resistance. In another month of hard fighting, however, the British seized both banks of the Scheldt, to open the 120-kilometer-long water channel from Antwerp to the North Sea. But it took another month for engineers to repair the port facilities, which the Germans had destroyed before leaving the city. The first Allied supply convoy reached Antwerp on 28 November.[15] The great seaport now became the Allies' principal logistical base.

Meanwhile, farther south, the Americans slowly drove the Germans back to the German border and the Westwall (commonly—and incorrectly—known to the Allies as the Siegfried Line). There were now three American armies in the 12th Army Group; on 4 October the Ninth Army, commanded by Lt. Gen. William H. Simpson, came into the line near Maastricht, to the left (north) of the First Army, and to the right of the Canadian First Army.[16]

That same day the U.S. Third Army closed in on the German defenses of Metz. On 21 October, after bitter street fighting, the First Army's VII Corps, spearheaded by the 1st Infantry Division, captured Aachen, and made the first significant breach in the Westwall.[17]

General Eisenhower now ordered a general advance to clear the area west of the Rhine River. To reach the open Rhine valley it was necessary first to cross a major tributary, the Roer, which flowed northward through hilly, forested terrain, just east of the German border. A key element of the offensive plan was to seize the Roer River dams, near Schmidt in the Hürtgen Forest, so that the Germans could not block the approach to the Rhine by flooding the lower Roer valley. However, the planned offensive received a severe setback on 2–7 November when the Germans decisively repulsed the 28th Division of the First Army's V Corps, which had the mission of capturing Schmidt and clearing the Hürtgen Forest. In the following month other elements of the Ninth and First armies enlarged the Aachen breakthrough gap in the Westwall, and reached the Roer River. However, the advance halted until the dams could be captured.

On 13 December Patton's Third Army captured Metz and battled its way across the Seille River.[18] That same day the V and VII corps of the First Army mounted a new offensive into the Hürtgen Forest, toward Schmidt and the Roer River dams. The main effort was by the V Corps, on the right.

SITUATION: 15 DECEMBER 1944

With three significant exceptions, the battle line across western Europe on 15 December 1944 was similar to that which existed when the Germans launched Operation Yellow on 10 May 1940 to begin the Battle of Flanders, the offensive that was to culminate forty-two days later in the surrender of France. Allied troops were, for the most part, deployed just west of Germany's western borders, held there by Wehrmacht defenders in the fortifications of the Westwall.

The first exception to a similarity in the 1940 and 1944 battle lines along the frontiers was in the north. There, in 1944, the Allies had liberated Belgium and the southern Netherlands, holding roughly the line of the lower Rhine and Maas Rivers, leaving the Germans occupying most of the Netherlands. The second exception was the breach in the Westwall near Aachen, with troops of the Ninth and First Armies deployed into Germany as far as the lower (northern) Roer River. The third exception was farther south, in southern Alsace, where the Germans, opposed by the Franco-American 6th Army Group, held a large bridgehead west of the Rhine, the so-called "Colmar Pocket."

Save for the terrain, however, most of the similarities between the 1940 and 1944 situations were superficial. The differences were great. Nevertheless, the Germans were, in fact, hoping that they could magnify the similarities, and reduce the differences, because they were planning on an offensive for which Hitler, at least, had hopes and dreams of matching the brilliant 1940 victory.[19]

The starting point for that hope was, indeed, largely related to the fact that the terrain situation along the frontiers had hardly changed in four and a half years. In 1940 the formidable difficulties of operating in the heavily forested, hilly Ardennes region had led the Allies—the French in particular—to assume that they would have little to fear from German offensive operations in the Ardennes. The Germans, observing the French deployments and anticipating their assessment, therefore decided to make their main effort in the Ardennes, and it was their massing of combat power in that region which had assured their remarkable victory.

The observable similarity of Allied reactions to the terrain in 1944 and 1940 gave the Germans some reason for hope that if they could overcome or offset their major disadvantages they could again achieve overwhelming superiority in the Ardennes and accomplish a breakthrough comparable to that of 1940. In light of the terrible defeats that Germany had suffered on the western, eastern, and Italian fronts in the summer of 1944, the Allies believed that Germany was close to collapse and did not have the capability to undertake major offensive operations. They did not expect anything more than local counterattacks that fall or winter. The Germans were well aware of this Allied frame of mind.

Furthermore, Allied deployments in the west showed that they put the possibility of local counterattacks lowest in the Ardennes. Since they were generally on the offensive, all along the front, the Allies preferred to concentrate forces in regions where the terrain was most suitable for offensive operations, and less good for German defense. Their offensive plans were obviously focused on the Aachen-Roer area north of the Ardennes, and in the Third Army sector to the south. Deployed in the Ardennes was the thinned-out U.S. VIII Corps, which included in the lines one green, totally inexperienced division—the 106th—and one exhausted and depleted division, recovering from its recent defeat near Schmidt—the 28th.

One of the three principal differences between 1944 and 1940, however, was that in 1944 the Allies, mostly battle-hardened, were under a single, coordinated command. In 1940 the Allies, including the Dutch and Belgian armies, had nominally had a slight numerical ground force superiority, but there was little coordination among the Allies. It can be argued, furthermore, that the Germans had a combat effectiveness superiority, which was a "multiplier" effectively increasing their combat power in 1940 to a value at least equal to that of the Allies. In 1944 the overall numerical superiority of the Allied armies was close to two to one. While the Germans probably retained a slight combat effectiveness superiority, it was negligible in comparison to the near-overwhelming Allied numerical superiority.

In 1940 their near-equality of ground combat forces gave the Germans an opportunity to maneuver their troops, tanks, and aircraft in such a way as to mass an overwhelming combat power superiority in the region where they expected the Allies to be weakest: the hilly Ardennes Forest of northeastern France and southeastern Belgium. In 1944 German resources were so limited that even the most effective economy of force could provide only a relatively slight numerical ground superiority for offensive operations in a small geographical area. Their only hope for augmenting this limited superiority sufficiently to mount a successful offensive would be another "multiplier": the effect of surprise, if it could be achieved. And this hope was not great unless they could find a way to overcome another great Allied advantage, which constituted the second principal difference between 1940 and 1944.

This difference was the disparity of air forces and airpower. In 1940 somewhat contradictory records suggest that the Germans had a slight numerical and qualitative superiority in the air. But they did have a much more effective command organization that allowed them to concentrate their airpower rapidly at decisive points of their own choosing. Thus, they were able to outmaneuver the Allies in the air—as on the ground—to assure effective airpower superiority.[20] On the western front, this was a major factor in the overwhelming German victory. The situation was very different in 1944. The Luftwaffe had not quite been driven out of the skies, but it was definitely dominated by Allied air superiority. The Allies had a tremendous numerical superiority in the air, approximately 7,900 first-line planes to less than 1,800 German aircraft—more than four to one. The qualitative difference, if there was any, was negligible or may even have favored the Allies.

However, the Germans could hope that the third principal difference between the situations in May 1940 and December 1944 might offset this inferiority in the air. This was the predictability of bad weather in the Low Countries in December. Rain, snow, and particularly fog would severely limit air operations, including reconnaissance, during that time of year.

Hitler had high hopes for the offensive planned for 16 December. His generals were far less sanguine. However, they were loyal soldiers and were prepared to do their best in carrying out the orders of their chief of state.[21] And their best would turn out to be very good indeed.

APPENDIX B

THE ALLIED FORCES IN THE ARDENNES

I. U.S. FORCES IN DECEMBER 1944

BACKGROUND

On 30 June 1939 the United States Regular Army totaled 187,893 men, including 22,387 men in the Army Air Corps. On the same date the National Guard totaled 199,491 men. Major formations included nine infantry divisions, two cavalry divisions, and a single mechanized cavalry brigade in the Regular Army and eighteen infantry divisions in the Guard. All of these were at minimal peacetime strengths, equipment was lacking, and most of what was available was either obsolescent or obsolete. While the Regular Army was well trained, the state of training of the National Guard units varied from fair to poor.

The outbreak of war in Europe two months later led to the gradual expansion of the Army. On 27 August 1940, Congress authorized the induction of the National Guard into federal service for a period of twelve months and then increased the authorized strength of the Regular Army. On 16 September 1940 the first peacetime draft in U.S. history was passed by Congress. However, like the Guard, the Regular Army inducted draftees for only one year of service. Fortunately, following testimony by Army Chief of Staff Gen. George C. Marshall on 7 August 1941, Congress approved, by the narrow margin of one vote in the House of Representatives, an indefinite extension of service for the Guard, draftees, and Reserve officers.

Despite these measures, expansion was slow. On 31 December 1941, twenty-four days after the attack on Pearl Harbor, the Army consisted of 1,685,403 men (including 275,889 in the Air Corps) in twenty-nine infantry, five armored, and two cavalry divisions. While this increase of 435 percent in two and a half years was a magnificent achievement, shortages of equipment and trained personnel were still serious. And the total strength was negligible in relation to the requirements of a two-front war. Over the following three and a half years the Army expanded an additional 492 percent, to a total of 8,291,336 men in eighty-nine divisions: sixty-six infantry, five airborne, sixteen armored, one cavalry (two more were formed but later disbanded), and one mountain division.[1]

On 16 December 1944 forty-three of those divisions were deployed in the European Theater of Operations (ETO), including two airborne divisions, ten armored divisions, and thirty-one infantry divisions. At the same time, sixteen more divisions were preparing to join them. One armored division had already deployed from England to the Continent and was on its way to the front, and one airborne division was in England awaiting shipment to France. One additional armored division and two infantry divisions had completed training in England and were committed to battle before 16 January 1945. One airborne division, three armored divisions, and seven infantry divisions were completing training in England or the United States in anticipation of deployment to the European theater, but were not deployed as complete units prior to the end of the Battle of the Bulge.[2]

ORGANIZATION[3]

Chief of the Army Ground Forces Lt. Gen. J. Lesley McNair was the final arbiter on Army organization.[4] He campaigned tirelessly to reduce overhead in U.S. divisions, insisting on as much streamlining as possible. There were two reasons for this. First, shipping space was at a premium for not only combat but also support units, and all supply items (including food to feed the population of Britain) had to be shipped from the United States to England. Second, McNair and other planners realized that the U.S. manpower pool was not inexhaustible. Industry and farming in the United States, and the massive expansion of the Navy, Marine Corps, and Army Air Corps all absorbed vast numbers of men. The 213-division army envisaged in the Victory Program of 25 September 1941 was never even close to being achieved; it proved to be difficult enough to man the 89 divisions eventually fielded.[5]

An adjunct to McNair's efforts to streamline the divisions was his effort to pool all nondivisional combat assets in the Army into homogeneous battalion-size units. Pooled units were to be held by corps or armies and were to be attached to divisions as required. Artillery, engineers, tanks, tank destroyers, antiaircraft artillery, and infantry units were all components of the pool. Group and brigade headquarters units were created to control manageable aggregations of the large number of pool units.

ARMOR

The first U.S. armored formations larger than brigades were formed on 15 July 1940 when the 1st and 2d Armored divisions were activated. The Armored Force was expanded by three additional divisions in 1941, nine in 1942, and two in 1943. The initial divisional organization was tank-heavy, with one three-regiment armored brigade (a total of six light and three medium battalions, with 368 tanks) and a single two-battalion infantry regiment. This organization was similar to contemporary European practice.[6] Field tests and reports on early operations soon showed that this organization was too cumbersome and efforts were made to streamline and balance the armored division. It was reorganized on 1 March 1942: The armored brigade headquarters was replaced by two "combat command" headquarters, armored strength was reduced to two three-battalion regiments, and the armored infantry regiment was expanded to three battalions. This organization later became known as the "heavy" armored division. Further combat experience resulted in another major organizational change on 15 September 1943. The existing heavy armored divisions were converted to a new "light" division organization.[7] By August 1944, all armored divisions had been reorganized as light divisions except the 2d and 3d Armored divisions, which retained the heavy division organization. All tank battalions in the light divisions and in separate tank battalions were organized similarly; in theory they were interchangeable.

The standard U.S. medium tank was the M4 "Sherman." The M4 was designed in April 1941, with the first prototype being completed in September 1941. Following testing, it was standardized for production in October 1941; production began in early 1942. The M4 was highly advanced at that time; probably only the Soviet T-34 was superior. However, under the stimulus of combat experience, tank design was changing rapidly, particularly in the German Army; thus the armor protection and firepower of the M4, adequate for conditions in 1942 and 1943, were insufficient in 1944.[8] The tank was originally designed with a short-barreled, medium-velocity 75-mm tank gun. The armor-piercing capability of this piece, however, was inadequate to penetrate the armor of new German tanks, and by late 1944 it was being replaced by a long-barreled, high-velocity 75-mm gun (commonly known as the 76 mm) with good penetration capability and increased accuracy. However, the less-capable gun remained in service in large numbers, as supplies of newly built and rebuilt tanks with the 76-mm gun remained scarce. The combination of weak armor protection and a poor gun was only partially made up for by the tank's mechanical reliability, its rapid electric-hydraulic turret traverse mechanism, its stabilized gun, and particularly its numbers.[9]

A number of M4s were designed or specially equipped for specialized roles. These included standard M4s equipped with dozer blades, mine-clearing tanks, recovery vehicles, and an assault gun variant with a 105-mm howitzer. Six M4 assault guns were in the assault gun platoon of the standard tank battalion headquarters company. A very important variant was the M4A3E2 or "Jumbo." This was a standard M4 that had been fitted with additional armor—substantially increasing its protection. The M4A3E2 was, in fact, better protected than the vaunted German "Panther," albeit the German tank had a better gun. The M4A3E2 was produced in small numbers (254 were built); however, Ordnance workshops in the ETO, working with armorplate produced by French steel mills or with salvaged armorplate, converted a large number of M4s in Europe to the M4A3E2 standard. It is uncertain exactly how many were available in Europe (Third Army workshops alone had converted about 200 by December 1944), but, despite their small numbers, they had helped even the odds in tank-versus-tank duels against the panzers. The M4A3E2s were scattered throughout the theater: Most of the armored divisions had 20 or 30; separate battalions occasionally would have a platoon of 4 or 5.

The standard light tank was the M5 "Stuart." It mounted a 37-mm gun and was lightly armored. Like the M4, the M5 had a number of variants, most important of which was an assault gun variant equipped with a 75-mm howitzer that was designated the M8 assault gun. This was found in cavalry squadrons and in the armored infantry battalion. The usefulness of the M5 had long been in question and it was slowly being replaced by the M24 "Chaffee," which had heavier armor and a 75-mm gun.

The light armored division was organized with a Division Headquarters and Headquarters Company, two Combat Command Headquarters (known as Combat Command A [CCA] and Combat Command B [CCB]), a Reserve Combat Command Headquarters (CCR),[10] three tank battalions (each with three medium and one light tank companies), three armored infantry battalions, three eighteen-gun artillery battalions, a cavalry reconnaissance squadron (battalion), an engineer battalion, and division services. The division was commanded by a major general, the combat com-

US Armored Division

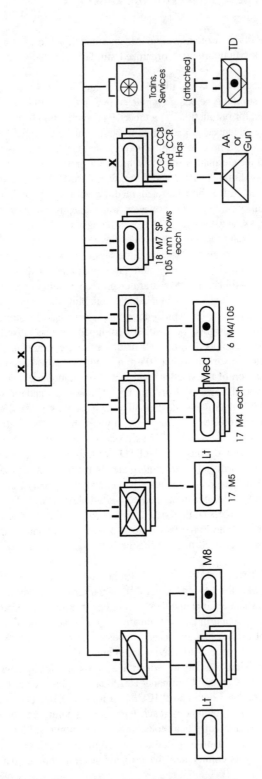

10,500 men, 168 medium and 77 light tanks, 450 halftracks, 54 SP M7 105 mm howitzers, 17 M8 and 18 M4 105 mm assault guns, 54 armored cars, 1,031 motor vehicles, 8 light aircraft.

mands by a brigadier general (the assistant division commander) and two colonels. The division included 77 light tanks, 168 medium tanks, 18 M4 assault guns, 17 M8 assault guns, 54 M7 105-mm SP (self-propelled) artillery pieces, and 54 armored cars. Total personnel strength was 10,754.

The heavy division organization was almost the same, except that the three tank battalions were replaced by two three-battalion tank regiments (each regiment's first battalion consisted of three light tank companies; the second and third battalions each had three medium tank companies) and the three armored infantry battalions were organized as a regiment under a single regimental headquarters. Thus, while the light division had three light and nine medium tank companies, the heavy division had six and twelve, respectively. The heavy division's armament included 158 light tanks, 232 medium tanks, 25 M4 assault guns, 17 M8 assault guns, 54 M7 105-mm SP artillery pieces, and 54 armored cars. Total personnel strength was 14,664.

Separate tank battalions were standardized as medium battalions, which were identical to those in the light armored division, or as light battalions, which were identical to the light battalions in the heavy armored division. The medium battalions' armament consisted of seventeen light tanks, fifty-four medium tanks, and six M4 assault guns. Personnel strength was 724. The light battalion of three companies included fifty-six light tanks and three M8 assault guns. Personnel strength was 532.

Normally at least one armored division was assigned to a corps. In addition, a corps could have an armored brigade or group headquarters assigned to it to control the separate tank battalions assigned to the corps. However, in practice the massing of separate tank battalions under a controlling headquarters was rarely done in the ETO, and the armored brigades and groups became administrative formations only. Theoretically armored divisions were to act as the maneuver reserve for the corps and were to be employed to break through enemy fronts ruptured by infantry assault. The armored division was to conduct deep pursuit of the enemy once the front was broken through. In practice, the width of the front in Europe meant that armored divisions were often used in defensive roles, for which they were not designed. A critical weakness was the fact that the infantry component of the division was too small to withstand the attrition of long-term defensive or offensive missions.

Nevertheless, the flexible organization of the armored division permitted it to be adapted to many situations. Typically, the two combat commands acted as headquarters to which battalion task forces were assigned. Armored tactics emphasized combined arms action. Cross-attachment of tank and infantry companies into battalion combat teams was practiced extensively—a practice that was facilitated by the flexible design of the division. The Reserve Combat Command was not designed as an operational combat headquarters, but it was frequently pressed into such service. In many cases one of the numerous armored or tank destroyer headquarters formations (brigades and groups) that had proved to be redundant was assigned to armored divisions to augment the capabilities of the Reserve Combat Command.

Forty separate armored battalions eventually served in Europe. They were normally assigned on the basis of one per infantry division. However, not all infantry divisions had a battalion attached. Although in theory tank battalions could be assigned to an armored brigade or group headquarters, this was never done. Usually when a separate battalion was assigned to an infantry division it retained that affiliation throughout the war. As a result, many infantry divisions developed a high degree of coordination with their associated tank battalions.

US "Heavy" Armored Division

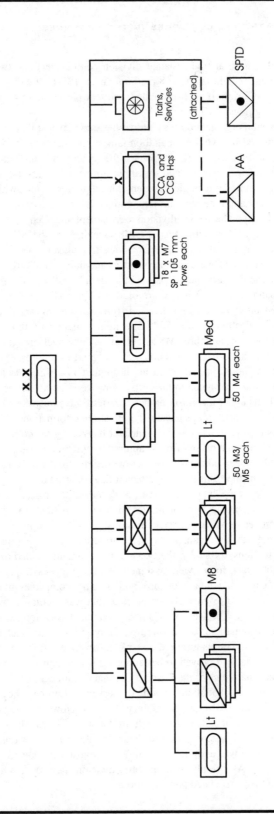

14,500 men, 232 medium and 158 light tanks, 640 halftracks, 54 SP 105 mm howitzers, 18 M4 105 mm and 14 M8 75 mm how. assault guns, 54 armored cars, 1,242 motor vehicles.

TANK DESTROYERS

An important adjunct to the armored formations was the Tank Destroyer Force. The example of the awesome power of the German blitzkrieg in 1940 resulted in the creation of separate antitank battalions within the U.S. infantry division in 1940. In 1941 General McNair decided that the ideal method of countering massed armored formations would be to deploy a highly mobile reserve of antitank guns, grouped at corps or army. As a result, the antitank battalions were removed from the divisions and, in an effort to foster an aggressive image of their role, were renamed tank destroyer (TD) battalions. The first TD battalions were all self-propelled units—an extemporaneous collection of truck-borne 37-mm antitank guns and old French 75-mm field guns mounted on half-tracked chassis. Following the experience of the Tunisian campaign a number of the battalions were converted from SP to towed guns. This was a deliberate imitation of German practice. Unfortunately, it was not realized that the Germans made extensive use of towed antitank weapons only because of necessity: They desired SP carriages for all of their antitank guns but had insufficient means to produce them.

By 1944 the error had been seen. Towed guns had proved to be too heavy and immobile for efficient use in a mobile combat environment.[11] In late 1944 many of the towed TD battalions in the ETO were being reconverted to SP guns as the weapons became available.

Tank destroyer battalions were all organized with three companies, each company equipped with twelve guns, for a total of thirty-six in the battalion. The guns employed by the TD battalions in late 1944 included the M5 3" towed gun; the M10 and M18 3" SP; and the M36 90-mm SP.[12] The M10 was the first standardized self-propelled TD gun. It was lightly armored: Its chassis was a variant of the standard M4 tank and had poor cross-country mobility and speed. By late 1944 the much-improved M18 was slowly replacing the M10. While still lightly armored, and with an open turret, its improved chassis gave it very good cross-country mobility and impressive speed. (It was the fastest tracked armored fighting vehicle in the world until the introduction of the U.S.-built M1 "Abrams" tank in the 1980s.) Furthermore, the gun of the M18 was the improved long-barrel 76-mm that had greater hitting power than the older 3" gun. The M36, which was deployed in July 1944, was the most powerful antitank weapon in the U.S. arsenal. Experience with heavy German armor had showed that the 75-mm, 3", and 76-mm series of weapons had insufficient penetrating capability. The M36 was a stopgap measure. It was a marriage of the M10 chassis with the powerful 90-mm gun (like the 3" gun, it was also originally an antiaircraft weapon). With the newly developed high-velocity armor-piercing (HVAP) round, the 90-mm was easily capable of defeating all German armor, if it could get the first hit. Unfortunately, there were few of these weapons available in late 1944.

Like the mass employment of separate armor battalions, the deployment of the tank destroyers in mass to defeat enemy armored attacks was never actually practiced. Fifty-six TD battalions eventually served in the ETO. However, a number were inactivated so as to provide personnel for infantry replacements, and others served in other roles. (In the Ardennes campaign the Third Army deployed one TD battalion as an augmentation to the army's Military Police force.) One TD battalion was normally assigned to each division: SP battalions were always assigned to armored divisions, while infantry divisions might have either SP or towed battalions attached.

CAVALRY

Reconnaissance duties in the U.S. Army were performed by mechanized cavalry units. Normally a corps would have assigned to it a mechanized cavalry group, commanded by a colonel, which consisted of a headquarters and headquarters company and two mechanized cavalry squadrons. Squadrons were organized with three cavalry troops, each equipped with thirteen M8 armored cars and quarter-ton 4×4 utility vehicles (jeeps); an assault gun troop with eight M8 assault guns; and a light tank company with seventeen M5 tanks. The armored divisions' reconnaissance squadron (technically the unit was known as an "armored reconnaissance battalion" in a heavy division and as a "cavalry reconnaissance squadron, mechanized" in a light division) was identical, except that it had a fourth cavalry troop. Infantry divisions each had a single cavalry reconnaissance troop. In addition, armored regiments had a reconnaissance platoon at regimental headquarters; tank battalions had a platoon at battalion headquarters; and SP TD battalions had a reconnaissance company, while towed TD battalions had a reconnaissance platoon in each TD company.

Interestingly, the cavalry groups were almost never called to perform their primary duty: Later analysis showed that pure reconnaissance missions accounted for only 3 percent of their activities. The remaining 97 percent of missions assigned to cavalry groups were as follows: Defensive operations made up 33 percent; special operations "including acting as mobile reserve, providing for security and control of rear areas, and operating as an army information service," 29 percent; security missions "blocking, screening, protecting flanks, maintaining contact between units, and filling gaps," 25 percent; and offensive operations, 10 percent. [13] The cavalry groups were often attached either in whole or by squadron to divisions, but also could operate independently under direct control of a corps. For most missions the group would be augmented by corps or divisional tank, tank destroyer, engineer, and/or artillery assets.

INFANTRY

Forty-two U.S. infantry divisions, not quite two-thirds of the sixty-six raised in World War II, eventually served in the ETO. The first permanent divisional organization in the Regular Army had appeared in World War I. Nine of the divisions organized continued to exist (albeit at very reduced strengths) through the 1920s and 1930s. These divisions were "square," that is, their basic infantry component was four three-battalion infantry regiments in two brigades. This was felt to be un- necessarily cumbersome and so, soon after the Army expansion began (16 September 1939), the divisions were converted to a "triangular" three-regiment organization.[14] Other minor changes mainly designed to reduce personnel overhead were made between 1939 and the spring of 1944 when the northwest European campaign began.

The infantry division in the fall of 1944 had, in addition to its three infantry regiments, four artillery battalions (three 12-tube 105-mm light battalions and one 12-tube 155-mm howitzer medium battalion), an engineer battalion, a cavalry reconnaissance troop (described above), and division service troops. The division was commanded by a major general, with a brigadier general as assistant commander and a second brigadier general as division artillery commander. Total personnel strength in the division was 14,043.

US Infantry Division

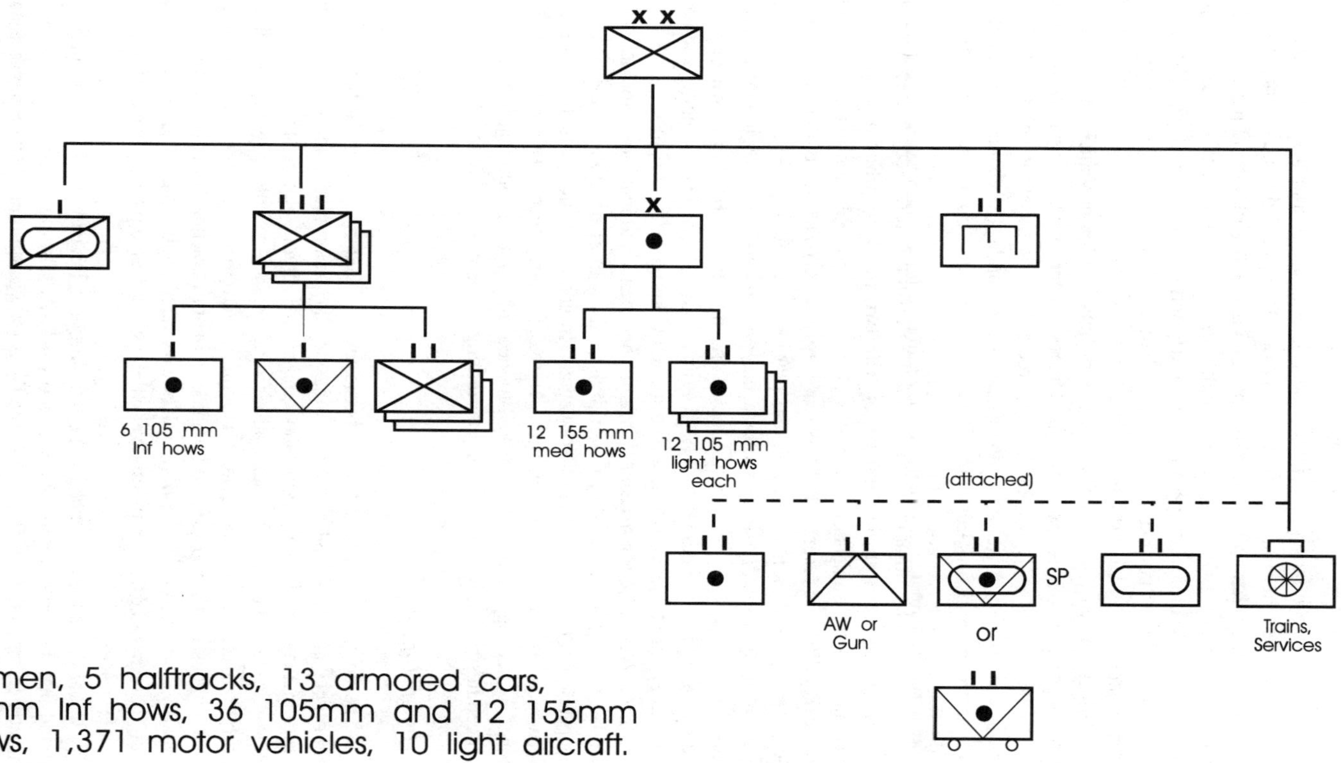

12 155 mm med hows

12 105 mm light hows each

6 105 mm Inf hows

SP

or

AW or Gun

(attached)

Trains, Services

14,253 men, 5 halftracks, 13 armored cars,
18 105mm Inf hows, 36 105mm and 12 155mm
field hows, 1,371 motor vehicles, 10 light aircraft.

Each of the infantry regiments had a headquarters and headquarters company (which included an ammunition and pioneer [A&P] platoon and an intelligence and reconnaissance [I&R] platoon), three battalions (each with a headquarters and headquarters company [which included an antitank gun platoon], three rifle companies, and a heavy weapons company), an infantry gun company (with six 105-mm howitzers), an antitank company (with nine 57-mm AT guns, in three-gun platoons, and a mine platoon), and a service company.

The infantry division did not in theory have sufficient vehicles to execute long-distance motor marches. Normally, six Quartermaster Truck Companies were attached to a division to allow it to conduct rapid road movements. However, in a pinch, vehicles in the artillery battalions, plus those in the standard division attachments (tank, tank destroyer, and antiaircraft artillery battalions) sufficed to allow most divisions to make fairly lengthy motorized movements.

The triangular organization allowed the division commander to deploy tactically with three regiments in line abreast, or with two forward in line and one in reserve. (Official doctrine suggested that on the offensive, a possible deployment was one unit forward and two in reserve, but this was rarely done.) The triangular organizations of the regiment, battalion, company, and platoon facilitated the use of similar deployments at each of the division's various echelons. In combat the regiments of a division were sometimes augmented with one of the division's 105-mm howitzer battalions and by an engineer, medical, and (if available) tank and/or TD company. Such an augmented regiment was known as a Regimental Combat Team (RCT).

There were also nondivisional infantry regiments and battalions (including Ranger battalions), organized exactly as their divisional counterparts. One of the better known independent units was the 99th "Norwegian" Infantry Battalion, which was made up of Norwegian exiles and first generation Norwegian-Americans. The 99th Battalion had gained a sterling reputation as a well-trained, hard-hitting outfit and had been badly reduced in strength by casualties in the fighting at the Westwall in the fall of 1944.

Airborne Infantry

The organization of the U.S. airborne division underwent many official (as well as semiofficial and unofficial) changes during the war. As originally conceived, the division was triangular,[15] with two two-battalion gliderborne infantry regiments, a single three-battalion parachute infantry regiment, an airborne engineer battalion (with two gliderborne and one parachute company), an antiaircraft/antitank battalion (three AAA batteries and three antitank gun companies), three gliderborne or parachute artillery battalions (usually with towed versions of the 75-mm Pack howitzer, although some battalions were equipped with lightweight M3 105-mm howitzers; there were twelve pieces per battalion), and divisional services.

Initial combat experience by the 82d Airborne Division in Sicily and Italy demonstrated that the glider regiments were too weak. As a stopgap remedy, the 401st Glider Infantry Regiment of the 101st Airborne Division was split; one battalion was assigned to the 325th Glider Infantry Regiment of the 82d Airborne Division and one to the 327th Glider Infantry Regiment of the 101st Division as the 3d Battalion of those regiments. In addition, the infantry component of the two divisions was increased for the Normandy invasion by the attachment of two nondivisional parachute regiments (the 501st and 506th) to the 101st Division and a single regiment (the 508th) to the 82d Division.

US Airborne Division

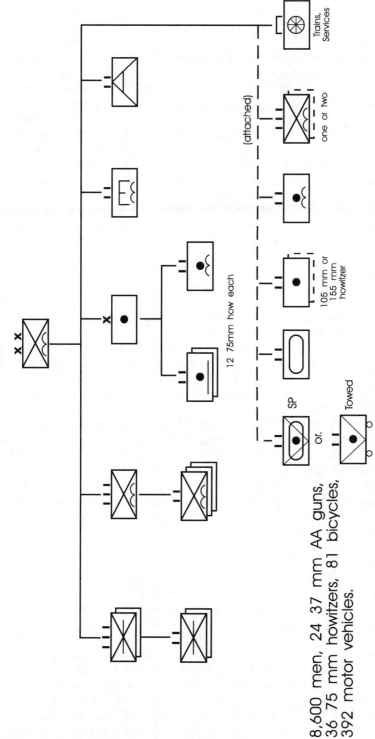

12 75mm how each

105 mm or 155 mm howitzer

SP

or.

Towed

one or two

(attached)

Trains, Services

8,600 men, 24 37 mm AA guns, 36 75 mm howitzers, 81 bicycles, 392 motor vehicles.

Note that the 82d and 101st Airborne had attached two parachute infantry regiments, each, along with a parachute field artillery battalion. Each of these divisions also contained a single three-battalion glider infantry regiment.

The 17th Airborne had two glider and two parachute regiments, and three artillery battalions. The 17th Airborne thus contained 11,000 men, and the other two divisions about 13,500 apiece.

These attachments became semipermanent and greatly reinforced the infantry strength of the two divisions. The 17th Airborne Division (which had been formed with two three-battalion glider regiments and a single parachute regiment) also had a nondivisional regiment attached, the 507th Parachute Infantry. Thus, all the airborne divisions in effect had four infantry regiments, although strengths differed slightly between divisions. The authorized strength of the various divisions (with their attachments) on 16 December was: 17th Airborne, 12,967; 82d Airborne, 12,921; 101st Airborne, 12,335.

As with the regular infantry, there were a number of separate airborne infantry regiments and battalions. One of the better known was the 509th Parachute Infantry Battalion, which had been the first U.S. airborne unit to make a combat assault in World War II in Tunisia. The battalion had won a Presidential Unit Citation at Anzio and was to win another in the Ardennes. The 509th suffered heavy casualties in the Ardennes: only seven officers and forty-eight men were left in the battalion at the end of the battle. Unfortunately, what was left of the 509th was disbanded at the end of the battle, as were many of the other separate parachute outfits, to provide badly needed replacements for the depleted airborne divisions.

Armored Infantry

The armored infantry battalion in the armored divisions (there were also a few nondivisional battalions) was organized with a headquarters and headquarters company, three rifle companies, and a service company. The battalion was very strong, with 1,031 men and many heavy weapons. Unfortunately, much of the battalion's manpower was absorbed in drivers and maintenance personnel for its extensive collection of vehicles. The battalion had seventy-two half-tracked personnel carriers, fifty-six other vehicles, and three SP 81-mm mortars. The weapons inventory, in addition to the self-propelled mortars, included nine 60-mm mortars, three M8 assault guns, nine 57-mm antitank guns, forty-nine .50-caliber heavy machine guns, and seventy-four M9 2.36" antitank rocket launchers (bazookas), as well as numerous individual automatic weapons. In comparison, a regular infantry battalion (with only 894 men) had only forty-one vehicles (all "soft-skinned," i.e., without armor); three more 81-mm mortars (albeit they were all "manpacked," i.e., broken down into component loads, each carried by a soldier); the same number of 60-mm mortars; three 57-mm antitank guns; only six .50-caliber machine guns; and twenty-nine M9 rocket launchers (bazookas).[16]

ARTILLERY

In World War I the artillery arm of the U.S. Army had fought in Europe equipped entirely with French (mostly) or British (a few) weapons. There were many reasons for this: the need for standardization in Allied arms, lack of shipping space, and lack of industrial capacity (in the short time available before the war ended) in the United States. However, another factor was that many ordnance specialists in France and Britain felt (with some minor justification) that the indigenous U.S. gun designs were not up to war-tested European standards. As a result, several years after the war the U.S. Army Chief of Staff, Gen. Charles P. Summerall (one of the most brilliant artillerymen in U.S. history) established a board of review to examine the army's ordnance requirements for the future. This (the Westervelt Board) report was impartial and farsighted, and it had dramatic consequences for the U.S. Army artillery in World War II. The board recommended that the standard divisional artillery piece be increased in caliber from 75 mm to 105 mm, while the general support weapon for the division was to be standardized as a 155-mm howitzer. Furthermore, the 120-mm corps general support gun was to be discarded in favor of a new 155-mm gun. In addition, the board recommended that designs should be begun for heavier supporting pieces of the most modern type, suitable for rapid motorized road movement. Finally, improvements in artillery communications and fire control methodology were recommended. (The fire control concepts had been pioneered by Summerall as an artillery brigade commander in France in World War I.)

The financial climate of the 1920s and 1930s delayed the development and deployment of such an improved artillery system. However, innovative Artillery and Ordnance officers continued to experiment with new gun designs and doctrine. As a result, when the Army began to expand in the late 1930s, much of the background work to modernize the artillery was already complete. Designs had been completed and prototypes developed for most of the guns and howitzers that were to see service during the war.

Divisional pieces included the M1 105-mm howitzer and the M1 155-mm howitzer. Both were excellent weapons, with good range and, particularly in the case of the 155 mm, excellent accuracy. Other new weapons were the M1 75-mm pack howitzer and the M3 105-mm howitzer. Both were lightweight and relatively short-ranged, but were ideal for use by airborne forces. The M3 105-mm piece also saw service (along with standard M1s) in the infantry regimental cannon company. The armored divisions' artillery was equipped with an SP version of the M1 105 mm, the M7 "Priest."

Nondivisional artillery included battalions equipped with these same weapons, as well as other, heavier pieces. A companion to the 155-mm howitzer was the 4.5" gun. The tube of this gun was of British design and manufacture, the carriage was that of the 155-mm howitzer. The 4.5" gun was not well liked by U.S. artillerymen, however. The shell (also British manufactured) was of low-grade steel, thick-walled and with a small bursting charge. Its range was insufficient to compensate for the relative ineffectiveness of its round. At the end of the war it was immediately withdrawn from service.

A much better weapon (and the common U.S. heavy piece) was the M1 155-mm gun, known as a "Long Tom" (an appellation that has had a long tradition in the U.S. artillery). The 155-mm gun combined long range, accuracy, and hitting power with a very well designed, highly mobile carriage. It was one of the best weapons in its class in World War II. The M12 self-propelled 155-mm gun was an interesting amalgam of the old and the new. This did not utilize the modern M1 155 mm, but rather the older, somewhat shorter-range, French-designed GPF (*Grande Puissance, Failloux*) developed in World War I. The Ordnance Department had experimentally mounted some GPFs on obsolescent M3 "Grant" tank chassis in 1942 and, after tests, 100 M12s were built—only to have AGF declare in October 1943 that there was no requirement for it. The M12 languished in storage until early 1944, when urgent requests from England for a heavy SP gun resulted in 74 being rebuilt. Seven field artillery battalions preparing for the invasion were equipped with the M12. Its mobility fully compensated for its shorter range. Heavier supporting pieces were the M1 8" howitzer, the M1 8" gun, and (very heavy indeed) the M1 240-mm howitzer. The 8" howitzer was mounted in a carriage adapted from that of the 155-mm gun and was renowned for its accuracy and hitting power.

The 8" gun and its companion piece, the 240-mm howitzer (like the 155-mm gun and the 8" howitzer, the two shared a common carriage), came into service in late 1943. When organized, the first 8" gun battalion was hastily rushed to Italy as a counter to the deadly, long-ranged German 170-mm gun. After a few teething troubles, the 8" gun proved to outrange the German piece, was as accurate, and fired a more lethal shell. The 240-mm howitzer was the heaviest artillery piece fielded by the United States in World War II. Designed to batter fortifications, it had already been invaluable in the fighting along the Westwall during the fall of 1944, but its numbers were limited.

All U.S. field artillery battalions were organized with three firing batteries, each battery usually having four tubes. Batteries in the Armored Field Artillery battalions had six M7 SP howitzers. The 240-mm howitzer battalions also had three batteries, but with only two tubes per battery. Divisional artillery was controlled by the division's artillery headquarters, usually commanded by a brigadier general. Nondivisional battalions were initially organized as two-battalion regiments. However, in 1943 the regiments were eliminated, the regimental headquarters battery became an artillery group headquarters, and the battalions became independent. Artillery groups were normally assigned to corps, which in turn often attached them to divisions. Usually two to four battalions were assigned to a group, which was under the command of a colonel. Artillery brigades were also created as headquarters formations in 1943. It was initially planned that an artillery brigade would control two or more groups, although this was rarely done in practice. Often the brigade was used to control the heavy artillery of a field army (the 32d Field Artillery Brigade in the First Army was assigned all the 8" gun and 240-mm howitzer battalions in the army). An artillery brigade was commanded by a colonel or a brigadier general.

The U.S. artillery, unlike the German, was highly mobile. The towed 105-mm howitzer battalions utilized two-and-a-half-ton trucks as prime movers. Five-ton trucks were used to pull the 155-mm howitzers. The other towed battalions were either truck drawn or, more frequently, were equipped with fully tracked M4 thirteen- or M5 eighteen-ton high-speed tractors as prime movers. Even the howitzers of the airborne division were motorized, towed by the ubiquitous (and air-portable) jeep.

All in all, the U.S. artillery arsenal was as at least as well designed as, if not better than, most of its German counterparts. Adding immeasurably to the effectiveness of the U.S. artillery was a communications and fire-control system that had no equal in the world. Forward observers of the individual artillery battalions—supported by personnel from divisional headquarters batteries, artillery brigade and group headquarters batteries, and by the highly skilled, specialist field artillery observation battalions, which were allocated on the basis of one per corps—had access, via powerful radios or extensive telephone landlines, to a formidable array of weaponry. The highly redundant observation and signal system meant that, even when all other contact between front-line units and their headquarters was lost, the artillery communications net usually remained open.

Perhaps most important, and making the U.S. artillery the best in the world in World War II, was a fire-direction system that had been developed at the U.S. Field Artillery School at Fort Sill, Oklahoma, between the wars. This was a highly refined development of the crude system Summerall had pioneered in World War I as commander of the 1st Artillery Brigade. This sophisticated system permitted rapid engagements of targets, and allowed the coordination of fires of many units from many widely separated firing positions. One of the most deadly tactics employed by the U.S. artillery was the Time-on-Target (TOT) concentration, the massing of fire from a large number of firing batteries from several battalions onto a selected target in which the times of flight from each battery were so calculated that the shells all arrived on target at nearly the same instant. The effect of a TOT was devastating both psychologically and physically to an unprepared enemy.

Further enhancing the deadliness of the U.S. artillery was the deployment and combat use in December 1944 of the new proximity fuse in artillery shells. Also known by its code designation of VT (for variable-time) or POZIT, the proximity fuse contained a tiny radar that triggered reliable detonation of the round in the air, prior to impact with the target. This significantly simplified and enhanced the lethality of "time fire" or "air bursts" by significantly augmenting the lethality of the individual round on targets on the ground. By December 1944 the German Army had developed a quite reasonable fear of the deadly U.S. artillery, a fear only matched by their fear of the omnipresent Allied air forces. Germans who had faced the more numerous Soviet artillery were unanimous in declaring that U.S. artillery, even though less numerous, was far more deadly.

Antiaircraft Artillery

The antiaircraft artillery was descended from the Coast Artillery Corps, and did not gain a separate identity until 1943. Antiaircraft units, like the tank destroyer arm, had been massively expanded in the wake of fears engendered by the German blitzkriegs of 1939 and 1940. Hundreds of battalions were formed in 1940–1943, but many had been made redundant by the almost complete Allied air superiority in 1944. Thus many battalions were disbanded to provide replacements for the infantry. However, every division had a light antiaircraft automatic weapons battalion attached. A self-propelled version of these battalions was usually attached to an armored division; a towed version was normally attached to infantry and airborne divisions. The self-propelled battalion was equipped with sixty-four mounts. Half of these were M15 combination mounts, each of which carried a single 37-mm gun and twin .50-caliber machine guns. The other 32 mounts were M16s, each carrying four .50-caliber machine guns. These were distributed equally among four batteries. The towed battalions were also equipped with sixty-four weapons, in four batteries. These were divided equally between M1 40-mm guns and M55 quad .50-caliber machine guns. Heavy antiaircraft artillery was provided by gun battalions, which deployed sixteen 90-mm guns in four batteries. The 90 mm was an accurate, high-velocity gun, also fully capable of engaging ground targets. It was similar in performance to the famous German FLAK 88, and in some ways it was superior (its data transmission system, automatic fuse-setter, and high-speed automatic rammer were second to none in design and performance). Enhancing the lethality of the 90 mm was the proximity fuse, which had originally been designed for antiaircraft use, and portable air early-warning and fire-control radar sets.

Towed battalions assigned to divisions were all designated as mobile, which indicated that there was a full complement of prime movers for the guns. Some antiaircraft battalions were designated as semimobile (SM), which indicated that there was only one prime mover per two or three guns. Semimobile battalions were only deployed for static defense of installations, for obvious reasons.

Automatic weapons battalions were normally assigned directly to a division or were part of an antiaircraft artillery group, which consisted of a headquarters and head-quarters battery and two or more attached battalions. Groups attached to a corps usually consisted entirely of automatic weapons battalions, but occasionally had one or more gun battalions as well. Most gun battalions were attached to groups held directly under an army headquarters, the groups in turn usually under the overall control of an antiair-craft brigade headquarters. Separate from army or army group control were the antiair-craft units of the IX Air Defense Command. It was originally a part of the Ninth Tactical Air Force, but in August 1944 was placed directly under SHAEF control. The IX Air Defense Command was tasked with security of the various air bases and other rear-area installations scattered throughout Belgium, France, and Luxembourg. Most of the semi-mobile battalions in the ETO were assigned to the IX Air Defense Command.

The threat of the German V-1 "buzz-bombs" to the port of Antwerp in the fall of 1944 gave the antiaircraft battalions a new mission. The Allies deployed large num-bers of antiaircraft artillery units in a corridor (known as "buzz-bomb alley") that extended from north of the town of Elsenborn almost to the sea. The southern ele-ments of this massive concentration of guns was to prove a fortuitous and welcome addition to the Allied defenses in the early days of the battle.

SUPPORT SERVICES

Engineers

It was perhaps fitting that the U.S. Army, with an officer corps heavily influ-enced by the teaching at the United States Military Academy (which was the first engineering school in the United States), should be lavishly equipped with engineer troops and equipment. Every division was supported by a three-company combat engineer battalion, which was capable of performing most engineering tasks (including demolitions, obstacle emplacement, fortification, and light bridge build-ing) for the division. When necessary, a division's engineers were augmented by additional combat engineer battalions from corps or army. Corps battalions were assigned to the command of an engineer group headquarters, which consisted of a headquarters and headquarters company and an engineer light equipment company. An engineer group normally consisted of three to six battalions; there was usually one or two groups per corps and army. Combat engineer battalions tended to have high esprit de corps; they rightly considered themselves to be elite specialists. In a pinch, the combat engineer battalions could act as infantry and did so frequently. In the Battle of the Bulge they were to prove in this role to be a vital asset to the belea-guered American Army.

In addition to the combat engineer battalions there were in the army various bridging units, heavy ponton[17] battalions (usually one to three per army), light ponton companies (usually one or more per group), and treadway bridge companies (usually one per armored division, but held at corps). The remainder of the engineer corps was made up of various specialist companies (such as heavy equipment companies, topo-graphical companies, and maintenance companies) and engineer general service regi-ments. These engineer general service regiments were indeed specialists, capable of building roads, airfields, bridges, and other permanent structures, and were lavishly outfitted with heavy construction equipment, but, unlike the combat engineer battal-ions, were neither well equipped nor trained for infantry action.

Signal Communications

Communications within the U.S. Army were provided primarily by radio, secondarily by telephone, and lastly by motorcycle dispatch riders and "runners." U.S. radios were well designed and were found at all echelons from platoon up. The small tactical sets (the famous handi-talkies or walkie-talkies) were short ranged and of temperamental reliability, but had no counterpart in any other army. The larger sets used by battalion and above were very well built FM units, that suffered from a common limitation: All were subject to line-of-sight performance, a problem that was to be a general nuisance in the hilly Ardennes and which was a factor contributing to the disaster suffered by the 106th Infantry Division. The standard field telephones (including sound-powered phones) worked well in a static situation; furthermore, many experienced divisions had supplemented their table of equipment allowance of phones with captured German equipment. However, the German bombardment that opened the offensive cut many of the wire lines, again with disastrous effects for the 106th Division.

It is notable that the decision made by General Eisenhower on 20 December to place the U.S. First Army under the command of British Field Marshal Montgomery's 21st Army Group was at least partly a result of the effect of the German offensive on Allied communications. Spearheads of the Fifth Panzer Army had forced the evacuation of radio repeater stations and had either cut or threatened to compromise the security of telephone and telegraph lines that had traversed the front behind the VIII Corps.

Transport and Logistics

The U.S. transportation and logistic network was already strained by limitations resulting from the lack of available ports and damage to the road and rail system in Europe. Rear-area communications and transportation were the responsibility of the Communications Zone (COM-Z), which was under the command of irascible, autocratic, and efficient Lt. Gen. John C. H. Lee (commonly known as "Jesus Christ Himself" Lee). The COM-Z organization moved supplies from the ports to forward supply depots within the geographic limits of the COM-Z. The supplies were then picked up by Quartermaster truck companies of the field armies and dispersed to the main army supply dumps and to corps forward supply depots. Corps and army truck units and organic divisional transportation then were utilized to move supplies forward to the divisional Quartermaster company, which in turn supplied the divisional units. Ammunition supply was performed in a similar manner, but transportation and distribution of ammunition was the responsibility of the Ordnance Corps. On occasion (frequently during the Battle of the Bulge) divisions or lower echelon units would draw directly from a main supply dump, bypassing the intervening chain.

Of the major supply items, fuel, which had been in such short supply in September and October, was no longer a problem in December. The near-static front, combined with the opening of a cross-Channel pipeline and its extension across most of France, had allowed for the stockpiling of huge quantities of gasoline (petrol), oil, and lubricants (called POL, a term inherited from the British). Many of these POL dumps were scattered throughout the Ardennes: The main First Army POL depot (more than 5 million gallons) was stockpiled in large rubber storage containers along the road leading from Stavelot to Spa.

Although POL supplies were no longer a problem in the ETO, ammunition was a nagging worry to Allied planners. In the early stages of the Army's expansion there were plans calling for a high priority in the production of 105-mm artillery shells of all types, inasmuch as these were for the standard divisional field piece. Ammunition for the heavier guns had been accorded a lower priority, under the assumption that mobile warfare would reduce the utility of the more unwieldy big pieces. Unfortunately, congressional criticism of the large overstockages of all types of artillery ammunition that had accumulated in Tunisia in 1943 forced the Army to scale back production. As a result, in late 1943 priorities had been shifted: Many plants were retooled for other ordnance production, while some 105-mm production lines were closed completely. Events in France and Germany, beginning in June 1944, changed all of these presumptions: Allied staffs in Europe discovered that the fierce German resistance encountered in the Normandy *bocage* and the Westwall had placed a premium on *all* types of ammunition—just as stockages of the 105-mm rounds, already critically short following the Normandy campaign, had begun almost to disappear. Rationing was instituted, and captured German weapons and ammunition were utilized (two ad hoc battalions were formed and equipped with German field pieces). From 11 October to 7 November 1944, the Third Army restricted expenditure of all types of artillery ammunition to a total of 76,325 rounds—about what was expended *on a daily basis* by the Third Army in late December. By 16 December the situation had become critical. In the month of December a total of 2,579,400 rounds was fired, most of it in the last fifteen days of the month. By 1 January 1945 the entire ETO stock of 105-mm ammunition was reduced to 2,524,000 rounds, a twenty-one-day supply according to War Department planning factors. This near-disastrous situation was exacerbated by the poor flying weather encountered in the fall and winter: Allied airpower was not always available to take up the slack. Although emergency measures taken in the theater and in the United States improved matters, shortages of artillery ammunition were to remain a chronic problem until the end of the war in Europe.

MANPOWER

In late 1944 a severe problem in the U.S. Army in general, and in the forces in Europe in particular, was the manpower shortage. Prewar plans to expand the Army to a total of 213 divisions were never met; a total of 89 divisions were eventually formed. Furthermore, prewar planning for replacements was found to be totally inadequate. The causes were manifold: U.S. industrial and agricultural manpower requirements could only be partially met by bringing women into the workforce; the Army was segregated, with black manpower restricted to noncombat units and a few separate combat organizations;[18] the army was forced to fight a two-front war; fear of the blitzkrieg had resulted in a huge expansion of the antiaircraft artillery and tank destroyer arms; and the requirements generated by the massive expansion of the U.S. Navy and Army Air Force had further reduced the available manpower pool. The results, by the end of 1944, were nearly catastrophic to the Army.

The lack of Infantry replacements was the most serious problem. For example, on 8 December 1944 the Third Army was short 11,000 infantrymen. This was only about 4 percent of the Third Army's total quarter-million-man strength. However, 11,000 infantrymen was equivalent to the strength of more than fifty-five rifle companies—the rifleman strength of two infantry divisions—or close to 15 percent of the infantry combat power of the army.

To meet the problem the army resorted to a number of expedients: Many antiaircraft and TD battalions were disbanded and their personnel reassigned to the Infantry; rear areas were combed of nonessential personnel; air cadets were transferred to the Infantry; the ASTP (Army Specialized Training Program), which allowed selected enlisted men to gain a college education, was discontinued; and divisions not yet deployed in the theater were ruthlessly stripped of men. Nevertheless, the problem persisted and was only solved by the collapse of Germany.

The Infantry further suffered from the Army's personnel policy, which allocated the most highly qualified and intelligent people to the specialist arms (such as Airborne, Ranger, Artillery, Armor, and Engineers). The Infantry was filled with men who had scored lowest on the AGCT (the Army General Classification Test—a type of intelligence test) and those who had not been skilled workers in civilian life. The elimination of the various special programs (ASTP, air cadets, and the like) and the reduction in specialist units had remedied matters to a degree by the end of 1944. Nevertheless, mediocre motivation and low intelligence continued to plague the Infantry.

The Army officer corps mirrored this problem to an extent. Many of the best-qualified junior officers served in specialist units or technical branches, and the Infantry was again slighted. However, the situation was better in field grade ranks and above. Combat experience had weeded out many of the less qualified (and occasionally incompetent) officers at battalion and higher levels. The promotion of the better junior grade officers gave the Army a solid core of dependable leaders. The situation was even better at division level and above. Most of the general officers were experienced professionals, who were competent if not always brilliant. Many were outstanding leaders. Brigadier Generals Robert Hasbrouck and Bruce Clarke of the 7th Armored Division, Maj. Gen. Walter Robertson of the 2d Infantry Division, Maj. Gen. Joseph Lawton "Lightning Joe" Collins of the VII Corps, and Lt. Gen. George S. Patton Jr. of the Third Army were but a few of the best who distinguished themselves in the battle.

Doctrine and Training

U.S. Army doctrine, as developed during the prewar and early-war Army expansion, emphasized mobility and combined-arms in both attack and defense. Mobility was achieved by developing reliable, robust armored and soft-skin vehicles. Unfortunately, in the case of tanks and tank destroyers, thickness of armor (and thus weight) was sacrificed in the interest of mobility to the detriment of the combat effectiveness of U.S. armored vehicles in tank-versus-tank combat. This flaw was exacerbated by General McNair's belief (later proved to be fundamentally unsound) that the armored division would not be required to engage and destroy enemy armored formations since that would be the task of the tank destroyers. Rather he visualized the armored divisions as a cavalry force to exploit gaps opened in the enemy lines by the tank-supported infantry division. The major flaw in this concept was that the lightly armored TD battalions were unable to engage and destroy enemy armor when attacking in mass, even when the TDs were deployed in concealed defensive positions. While the tank destroyers on defense were often capable of delaying and occasionally blunting armored attacks, it was found that they could rarely defeat them. Thus, instead of operating in an independent antiarmor role, TD units were semipermanently attached to infantry and armored divisions, while armored divisions were required to assume defensive as well as offensive missions. Furthermore, necessity forced the armored division into all types of offensive missions. Thus the concept of the armored division as an exploitation rather than an assault force disappeared.

Standardization in the organization of the combat arms facilitated (at least in theory) the cross-attachment of units into combined-arms combat teams. However, the close cooperation required of combined-arms teams required extensive training and combat experience to be effective. Unfortunately, early-wartime training for combat was more an exercise in the movement of troops to contact than an actual rehearsal for combat. Habits acquired from unrealistic training were too frequently found in combat: Often actions on the battlefield were dictated by rote rather than by common sense. Thus, U.S. tactics were often mechanical and, worse, predictable. This, and the lack of a coherent doctrine for cross-attachment, often resulted in mishmashes of units, confusion, and blurred (or even, occasionally destroyed) chains of command. As a result, the introduction of a "green" U.S. division into combat often resulted in disaster rather than success. Eventually, combat experience and unnecessary casualties forced commanders to change emphasis in the training regimen: By December 1944 costly experience allowed most new divisions to make an easier transition to the realities of combat, but problems still persisted.[19]

The U.S. Army had both strengths and weaknesses. However, the majority of its weaknesses were attributable to its twenty-fold expansion between 1939 and 1945. Its strengths were the results of years of hard work by a relatively few dedicated professionals in the 1920s and 1930s—work that was done by men who were almost completely unrecognized outside of their professional community. Sir Winston Churchill may have summed it up best:

I saw the creation of this mighty force—victorious in every theater against the enemy in so short a time and from such a very small parent stock. This is an achievement which the soldiers of every other country will always study with admiration and envy.

But that is not the whole story, nor even the greatest part of the story. To create large armies is one thing; to lead them and to handle them is another. It remains to me a mystery as yet unexplained how the very small staffs which the United States kept during the years of peace were able not only to build up the Armies and the Air Force units, but also to find the leaders and vast staffs capable of handling enormous masses and of moving them faster and further than masses have ever been moved in war before. [20]

II. THE BRITISH ARMY IN DECEMBER 1944

INTRODUCTION

Manpower

During the interwar years, the so-called "twenty-year armistice," Great Britain had a succession of governments, each of which attempted to cope with economic hard times (beginning in 1923, when the post–World War I boom ended) and the worsening world political situation. In this period the government was largely in the hands of the Conservative Party, led by either Mr. Stanley Baldwin or Mr. Neville Chamberlain. Chamberlain was Prime Minister from 28 May 1937, when Baldwin resigned the premiership, until 10 May 1940. Thus, the Conservatives were responsible for Britain's military posture during the crucial years preceding the outbreak of the war.

During this period, the British armed forces, and the Army in particular, were considered by military leaders to be "wholly inadequate" to their anticipated roles and missions. Since the advent of the Great Depression, British governments had been reluctant to spend large sums on defense, and a lingering strong attachment by many Britishers to the principle of disarmament, plus the prevailing spirit of pacifism, had encouraged the government in the continuance of this neglect. The Regular Army's actual strength was 95 percent of authorized strength in April 1935; two years later, its actual strength was 88 percent of authorized strength. Recruiting lagged because enlistment was voluntary, and pay and living conditions for soldiers were poor. The Territorial Army—the volunteer, militia home-defense force—was in even worse shape: In April 1936 its actual strength was 71 percent of authorized strength.

Rearmament was delayed until 1937, when the world situation had deteriorated to such an extent that it was no longer possible to ignore the unreadiness of the British armed forces. Various measures, chiefly in the nature of public relations and advertising, were taken to increase enlistments, and the speed of rearmament was accelerated after the Munich Crisis of 1938 (known in Germany as the Sudeten Crisis).

In January 1939 the War Office was reorganized to facilitate mobilization, and a short time later, in March, the government decided to double the size of the Territorial Army. This force, which was 204,000 strong in January 1939, rose to a strength of 428,000 by August 1939.

On 26 May 1939 the Military Training Act, Britain's first compulsory peacetime draft, became law. This act was soon superseded by various National Services acts, but it produced 35,000 draftees and provided valuable experience for British manpower planners and administrators in the operation of a selective service system.

The first National Service (Armed Forces) Act was passed on 1 September 1939—the day war broke out. This act provided the authority for the conscription of manpower by the services throughout the war. At the same time the Conditions of Service Act defined enlistments as running for "the duration of the present emergency."

The Army had very little trouble building up its strength. In the period June–December 1939 its strength more than quadrupled, an expansion made possible in good part by the draft and the influx of volunteers, but to an even greater extent by calling up reserves and men of the auxiliary services for active duty. By the end of the year most of the reserves and auxiliaries available had been activated, and the approximate strength of the Army stood at 1,130,000.

The expansion of the Army continued at a rapid pace during 1940, and late in the year a strength in excess of 2,000,000 men was reached, conforming to the first planned manpower ceiling or Army-wide troop basis. After 1940 wartime manpower intakes declined yearly, except 1944, when a small increase over the intake for 1943 was recorded. In 1945 just 200,700 men were enlisted. The downward trend in intakes affected the overall authorized strength of the Army, which averaged almost 2.6 million during the period June 1941–June 1945. This trend was a reflection of the diminishing, and eventually exhausted, manpower pool, which in turn limited the expansion of the Army and its ability to fulfill its worldwide mission.

The personnel replacement system, too, was affected; it began to break down during the Italian campaign (winter 1943–1944). In northwest Europe, the personnel replacement crisis in the 21st Army Group had become critical in August 1944, seriously affecting the ability of the army group to perform its mission in the Allies' overall offensive scheme.[21]

Matériel

Although serious manpower problems did not surface until late 1943, the adequacy of British matériel—both in terms of quantity and quality—was a major concern initially. The small, highly professional British Expeditionary Force (BEF), initially just four divisions sent to France immediately after the outbreak of the war, was well equipped, but the regular divisions that remained in Britain and the activating territorial divisions were equipped to a very poor standard. Even the BEF had very little tank support; Britain, as Churchill pointed out, had pioneered the development of the tank, then neglected it so much that when war broke out the country did not have a single armored division.

Eight months later, when the Germans unleashed their blitzkrieg in the west, the BEF's armored support was limited to the 1st Army Tank Brigade (two battalions) and seven poorly equipped cavalry and Yeomanry regiments, which were being organized into two brigades.

In practically every category of war equipment the British initially were deficient, especially when compared to the Germans, who, disarmed by the terms of the Versailles Treaty, were not saddled with the obsolescent "tail" of the previous world conflict. When Germany rearmed, she rearmed with modern equipment, produced by efficient war industries.

The disaster of Dunkirk made a bad situation even worse. Britain faced her enemies practically denuded of weapons. Though there was no shortage of small arms, heavy weapons in all categories were lacking. There were only 500 field artillery weapons in Britain, and just 469 tanks, of which 252 were light.

However, shielded by the Royal Air Force (and its excellent, modern fighter aircraft) and the Royal Navy, aided by the resources of the Empire-Commonwealth, and assisted by the U.S. Lend-Lease program, Britain was able to weather the crisis and rearm. Full details of British equipment at the time of the German Ardennes counteroffensive are provided below.

Doctrine

Land warfare doctrine, as it was understood by nearly all the belligerents in World War II—a corpus of fundamental principles and concepts intended to guide the actions of fighting forces in operations—was practically nonexistent in the British ground forces in World War II. One reason for this, in the words of a prescient British soldier-historian, was that doctrine was viewed with suspicion as something foreign, the British historically preferring "pragmatism and compromise between divergent views."[22] (Some may see in this the perpetuation of the British tendency to "muddle through.")

Thus, initially, British troops in combat situations were at a great disadvantage vis-à-vis their German adversaries, who had a well-developed land warfare doctrine,[23] and other advantages, such as superb, modern communications means. Moreover, the British had no prewar experience in realistic, combined-arms combat exercises, and so, lacking doctrine or even peacetime practice to draw upon, the British had to improvise. The result was that, even though the British soldier was (as he had always been) brave and disciplined, the Army as a whole was less than the sum of its parts, and even great victories, like Alamein, did not produce truly decisive results.

Alamein (October–November 1942), however, did represent a change. Guided by its commander, Gen. Bernard L. Montgomery, the British Eighth Army did achieve a remarkable success, overcoming the poor performance that had characterized many of its earlier efforts in the Western Desert (December 1940–February 1942). In general, though, it may be said that the Army had gained more from experience and trial and error than from adoption of tried-and-tested doctrine.

British Units in the Ardennes Fighting

The principal British formation involved in the Ardennes fighting was Lt. Gen. Sir Brian G. Horrocks's XXX Corps. The XXX Corps belonged to Gen. Miles Dempsey's Second British Army which, together with Gen. Henry Crerar's First Canadian Army, composed Field Marshal Sir Bernard L. Montgomery's 21st Army Group.

The XXX Corps was in Army group reserve at the outset of the Bulge campaign, preparing to move to the zone of the First Canadian Army to take part in the anticipated Rhineland battle (Operation Veritable, beginning 8 February 1945). The corps was committed on the northern flank of the Bulge, beginning on 20 December. Corps units and formations committed initially included three infantry divisions (the 51st [Highland], the 43d, and the 53d [Welsh]), one armored division (the Guards Armoured), four tank or armored brigades, one Army Royal Artillery formation (AGRA, see below), one antiaircraft artillery (AAA) brigade, one reconnaissance regiment, plus corps troops and elements of the 79th Armoured Division (Special, see below).

During the course of the Bulge fighting various units and formations were added or subtracted from the corps. Major additions included two AGRAs and the 6th Airborne Division. The principal units that saw some combat action were the 51st and 53d Infantry divisions, the 6th Airborne Division, and the 29th Armored and 34th Tank brigades. (The 29th Armoured Brigade actually belonged to the 11th Armored Division.)

Armor

Organization and Equipment

British armored divisions (excepting the specially organized 79th) were nominally 14,964 men strong, with 262 medium and 44 light tanks. There were in addition an assortment of armored cars, scout cars, carriers, half-tracks, and armored OP (observation post) tanks. The division had one armored reconnaissance regiment; one armored brigade, consisting of three armored regiments and one infantry motor battalion; one lorried (truck-transported) infantry brigade of three infantry battalions and one machine-gun company; the divisional artillery, consisting of one field regiment (twenty-four towed 25-pdr. guns), one motorized regiment (twenty-four self-propelled 25-pdrs.), one antitank regiment (forty-eight 17-pdr. antitank guns, of which twenty-four were self-propelled), one antiaircraft regiment (fifty-four 40-mm Bofors antiaircraft guns); and divisional signals, engineers, medical, support, and transport troops.

The 79th Armoured Division, formed in September 1942, was reorganized in early 1943 as a special umbrellalike organization that was responsible for all matters having to do with the specialized armored vehicles required for the cross-Channel

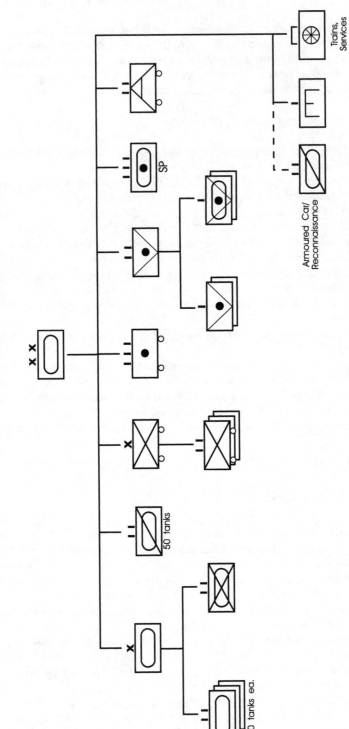

UK Armoured Division

14,500 men, 200 tanks, 24 TDs, 24 SP and 24 towed Arty, 250 halftracks and Bren carriers, 1,600 motor vehicles.

invasion and subsequent campaigns in northwest Europe. (This included concept, design, development, and operational deployment.) These special-purpose vehicles, nicknamed "funnies," included Churchill AVREs (Armored Vehicle Royal Engineers), Sherman Crabs, Sherman CDLs (Canal Defence Light—for night operations), Sherman DDs (Duplex Drive), Churchill Crocodiles, and a bewildering variety of less familiar types with similar strange designations. The principal mission of the division was to assist assault troops in the attack of deep and complex fortified belts, like the Atlantic Wall in Normandy, or the Westwall, which the Allies encountered in September 1944.

To fulfill its mission the 79th Division deployed armored amphibious assault tanks and armored vehicles specially designed to breach obstacles, like minefield-clearing tanks, carpet-layers, bridge-layers, and flamethrowers. The division was held at army group level, and its units and subunits apportioned to operational formations as needed for special tasks.

Independent armoured and tank brigades had an assigned strength of 3,400 men, 190 medium (or infantry) tanks, and 33 light tanks each. The practical difference in the two similar organizations was that the armoured brigades were equipped with U.S. M4 Shermans—many regunned with the powerful British 17-pounder—while the tank brigades were armed with the Churchill infantry tank. All light tanks were U.S. M5 Stuarts, nicknamed "Honeys" by the British. Such units had originally been intended to provide mobile, heavy, close fire support for infantry divisions, but in northwest Europe they were used frequently to reinforce and cooperate with the armoured divisions.

The principal main battle tanks of the British in this period were Shermans and Cromwells—called cruiser tanks by the British—and Churchill "infantry" tanks.

At this late period in the war a new cruiser tank, the Comet, was introduced and was being incorporated in some of the British armored formations.[24] The Comet was probably the best British tank of the war. It was considered equal to the German PzKw IV but inferior to the Panther.

TACTICS

British armor tactics envisaged the use of tanks in masses as the principal battle-field arm of decision. The infantry was to support the armor rather than vice versa as had been the case in much of the interwar planning. However, it was not often possible to employ armor in masses in northwest Europe. Great "armor battles," like Operation Goodwood (18–20 July 1944) in Normandy, near Caen, where three armoured divisions attacked on a narrow front over open terrain, were the exception. In practice, therefore, the British employed "battle groups" or "brigade groups" analogous to the American combat team and the German kampfgruppe. These were not the ad hoc groups that had been characteristic of British organization for combat in the Western Desert before the advent of Montgomery, but were very deliberately organized, semipermanent groupments of all arms that were accustomed to working together as a team.

INFANTRY

Organization

The British infantry division was nominally 18,347 strong and consisted of three infantry brigades, each of three battalions; a divisional artillery of seventy-two guns in

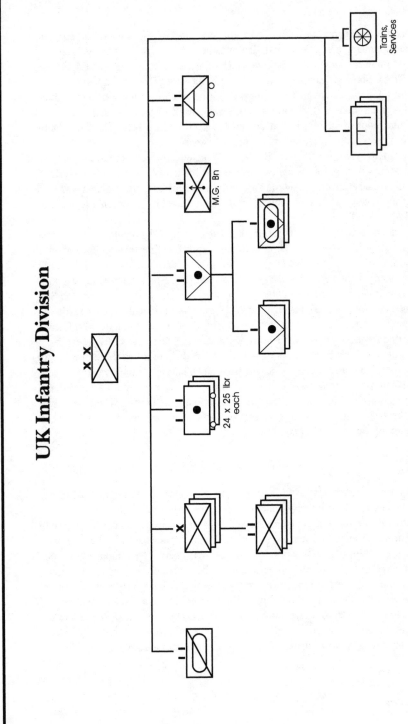

UK Infantry Division

18,000 men, 32 TDs, 70 armoured cars, 72 towed Arty,
550-600 Bren carriers, 1,800 motor vehicles.

three field regiments, one LAA regiment, and one AT regiment; one reconnaissance regiment; one MG (machine gun) battalion; and assorted combat support and combat service support troops (engineers, signals, medical, etc.).

The principal "fighting troops" in the infantry division were in the infantry brigades, each of which numbered 2,944 officers and men, in the reconnaissance regiment (793 men), in the MG battalion (697 men), in the artillery units, and Royal Engineers and Royal Corps of Signals.

AIRBORNE DIVISIONS

Of the two British airborne divisions, one—the 6th, commanded by Maj. Gen. Eric L. Bols—was deployed against the Germans in the Bulge fighting. With a nominal strength of 12,148 men, the division consisted of two parachute brigades and one air-landing (gliderborne) brigade. The division was in Britain when the Bulge fighting began and was transported to the Continent for operational deployment in Belgium, arriving on 26–27 December on the approaches to the Meuse between Dinant and Namur.

ARTILLERY

Organization

Field (light, or divisional artillery) regiments consisted of three eight-gun batteries—twenty-four guns altogether, served by 36 officers and 636 men. The standard divisional weapon was the 25-pounder in towed or self-propelled versions.

An AGRA (Army Group Royal Artillery) was a powerful artillery formation consisting of one heavy and one medium regiment. AGRAs nominally consisted of about 4,400 men and were normally allotted one to each corps, with one held at army level as a reserve. Each AGRA boasted an armament of fifty-four guns, with eight 7.2" howitzers and eight 155-mm guns (U.S.) held in the heavy regiment and forty-eight 5.5" guns. (A relatively small number of 4.5" guns were still in action with some medium regiments.) Three AGRAs, the 3d, 4th, and 5th, were available for commitment to the Bulge fighting. (The 5th AGRA was that ordinarily associated with the XXX Corps.)

Also organized under the general rubric of artillery were the Light Antiaircraft (LAA) regiments, Heavy Antiaircraft (HAA) regiments, and Antitank regiments, Survey regiments, and Air Observation Post (AOP) squadrons. LAA regiments were armed with fifty-four 40-mm AA guns. HAA regiments had twenty-four 3.7" AA guns. Antitank regiments of infantry divisions were equipped with sixteen 6-pounder and thirty-two 17-pounder AT guns; those of armored divisions were equipped largely with U.S.-built M10 SP guns, refitted with the 17-pounder, or with a new, British-built 17-pounder SP, called the Archer. This was a rearward-firing weapon that utilized the chassis of the Valentine tank with the gun crew protected by a bulletproof armored box.

Equipment

The principal British light field piece was the 25-pounder Mark II (87.6-mm) gun-howitzer, which had been introduced in late 1941 as the standard British field

UK Airborne Division

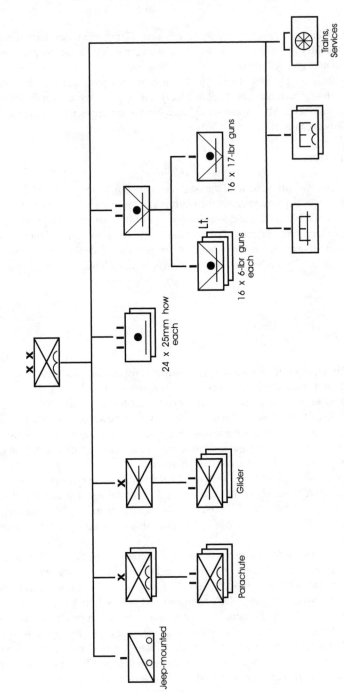

12,500 men, 48 towed Arty, 48 lt and 16 hvy AT guns.

(divisional) artillery weapon, replacing the obsolete World War I–vintage 18-pounder gun and 4.5" howitzer in the divisional artilleries.

The 25-pounder had a number of exceptional features, including an easily emplaced, wheel-like firing platform, which allowed rapid all-round traverse, and replaceable tube liners that could be quickly changed in the field. The piece could be emplaced on its firing platform in one minute and it outranged its German counterpart.

The self-propelled version of the 25-pounder was the Sexton, a Canadian-built variant of the U.S. M7 SP 105-mm howitzer motor carriage. Like the M7, the Sexton utilized the M3 Grant/M4 Sherman chassis (called the Ram by the Canadians). The gun, crew, and ready ammunition were protected by a bulletproof armored superstructure. The superstructure was not fully enclosed, but it did offer a measure of protection for the crew against blast and splinters. This, combined with the mobility of the piece, made it a weapon much superior to the towed 25-pounder.

Medium artillery weapons in the British inventory included the 4.5" gun and the 5.5" gun-howitzer. These were modern weapons introduced early in the war to replace, respectively, the obsolete 60-pounder gun and 6" howitzer as the standard corps artillery weapons of the British Army. The 4.5" gun was valued for its range (18,745 meters maximum), while the 5.5" gun-howitzer, with a maximum range of 14,630 meters, was appreciated for its "shell-power." (The 4.5" projectile weighed 55 pounds; the 5.5" round weighed 100 pounds.)

Heavy artillery weapons utilized by the British forces included 7.2" howitzers and U.S. 155-mm guns. The 7.2" howitzer was an expedient developed in late 1940 to fill a gap in the existing inventory; it was simply the old 8" howitzer of World War I retubed and mounted on a modern carriage. It threw its heavy, 200-pound projectile to a maximum range of approximately 14,200 meters, which was considered adequate at the time of its introduction. The 155-mm gun was the American "Long Tom." Crewed by fourteen men, it was capable of firing one round per minute to a maximum range of 26,860 meters (16.6 miles).

Late in the war two new super-heavy pieces were introduced in small numbers: the 240-mm and 8" howitzers. These were held in two regiments at army group and were allocated to AGRAs, that is, at corps level, for employment in long-range destructive fires, usually as part of the complex preliminary bombardments that preceded major offensive operations. Both were U.S.-made pieces and both were very accurate. The 8" howitzer weighed 15.9 tons and fired a 200-pound projectile to approximately 16,900 meters. The 240-mm howitzer fired a mammoth 360-pound projectile to approximately 23,000 meters. Its weight was 29.3 tons. Both pieces were drawn by heavy tractors, and could march at the rate of 23 mph over good, primary roads.

Doctrine

British artillery doctrine evolved rapidly in World War II after a somewhat uncertain and tentative beginning, characterized by the embarrassing dispersal of the organizational and command structure. It was not until the Battle of Alam Halfa in North Africa (31 August–4 September 1942) that the tremendous potential of the 25-pounder was realized when the gun was used in masses under centralized control for the first time.

From that point onward, British artillery doctrine developed along lines similar to those in the United States, emphasizing massed fires directed and coordinated centrally. Some have seen in this a re-creation of the tactics and techniques of 1918, but the massed fires of World War II were much more flexible because of improved observation and communications means, and were more economical.

CRITICAL OVERVIEW

Perhaps the most significant problem facing the British Army in late 1944 was the manpower crisis that had hampered its operational efficiency since late July. By then that it was apparent that the War Office had critically miscalculated the percentage of all casualties that would be sustained by the Infantry. On 28 July the number of British and Canadian infantry replacements available in-theater was just 2,837. This number was barely sufficient to replace the casualties that might be expected to result from a couple of days of intense combat.

The situation was so critical and immediate that long-range plans could not be made to deal with it, and the only workable alternative was to cannibalize some units to provide replacements for others. This expedient was put into effect in mid-August following an urgent appeal from Montgomery to the Chief of the Imperial General Staff, Gen. Sir Alan Brooke, in which Monty bluntly stated that his Infantry divisions were "so low in effective rifle strength that they can no—repeat NO—longer fight effectively in major operations" and requesting permission to "break up at once 59th Division."

The cannibalization of the 59th Division and several smaller tactical units, plus other expedient measures, helped resolve the immediate crisis, and by September 1944 a small surplus of infantry replacements had been built up behind the 21st Army Group. In January 1945 the army group had 172/3 divisions "all up to strength," backed by a replacement pool of 8,000 infantry in France. By bending all resources to the task the War Office and the army group were able to sustain this force during the final advance into Germany. However, this steady, but somewhat precarious, buildup of replacements was facilitated greatly when the British were spared the heavy casualties inflicted on their American allies in the German counteroffensive of December 1944.

APPENDIX C

THE GERMAN ARMY IN
DECEMBER 1944

The German Army had come close to destruction in both western and eastern Europe in late summer 1944, but had undergone a startling recovery in the subsequent months. Many of the divisions mauled in Normandy and then nearly destroyed in the Falaise Pocket or in the pell-mell retreat across France had been rebuilt, and new divisions had been raised or brought in from refitting in Germany or the eastern front. Still, despite the great efforts made and the near-wonders achieved, the balance of forces along Germany's western frontiers gave the Armed Forces High Command (Oberkommando der Wehrmacht, or OKW) little cause for optimism. Many German units were short of transport and lacked appropriate numbers of officers and noncomissioned officers. In the panzer divisions tanks and other armored combat vehicles were in short supply, and many units had barely half their proper allotment of some major items of heavy equipment.

THE PANZERS

Considering the impact of German blitzkrieg operations during 1939–1941, it is not surprising that the panzer divisions came to represent the power of the entire German Army. This occurred despite the fact that, even accounting for the twelve SS panzer and panzergrenadier divisions, these mechanized units amounted to barely 15 percent of the divisions in the German Army by November 1944.[1] A substantial number of these divisions[2] were assigned to the Ardennes offensive, including the 1st Leibstandarte SS Adolf Hitler, 2d Das Reich, 9th Hohenstaufen, and 12th Hitlerjugend SS Panzer divisions, and the 2d, 9th, 116th, and Panzer Lehr (130th) Panzer divisions, plus the 3d and elements of the 15th Panzergrenadier divisions.

The evaluation of German unit strengths presents some problems, largely due to German counting practices. Each major type of division (panzer, volksgrenadier, mountain, jäger, etc.) had a general basic establishment and organization pattern, which gave a strength figure known as the grundstärke, or ground strength.[3] Divisions within the major categories had individual authorizations, sometimes varying considerably from the basic pattern. The strength figure associated with these authorized levels was the soll-stärke, literally the "should-be strength," but better translated as the authorized strength. Finally, each division kept track of its actual strength, which

Panzer Division

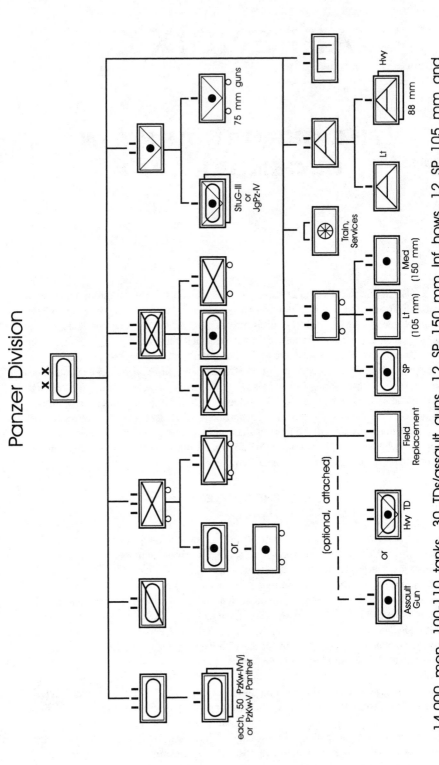

75 mm guns

StuG-III or JgPz-IV

each, 50 PzKw-Mv/J or PzKw-V Panther

or

Hw

88 mm

Lt

Train, Services

Med (150 mm)

Lt (105 mm)

SP

Field Replacement

(optional, attached)

Hw TD

or

Assault Gun

14,000 men, 100–110 tanks, 30 TDs/assault guns, 12 SP 150 mm Inf hows, 12 SP 105 mm and 6 SP 150 mm hows, 12 towed 105 mm and 12 towed 150 mm hows, 12 75 mm AT guns, 12 88 mm AA guns, 16 armored cars, 150 halftracks, 2,500 motor vehicles.

might be higher or lower than either the grundstärke or the soll-stärke. This current strength was known as the Ist-stärke, or current strength. These terms applied to both personnel and equipment levels.

A great deal of confusion arises from the Germans' precise terminology for personnel strength figures. Units recorded verpflegungsstärke (ration strength), kampfstärke (battle or combat strength), and grabenstärke (trench strength). The latter two recorded precise levels of combat and infantry personnel in the unit, while ration strength included anyone who happened to draw rations from the unit's supplies on the day in question, and so included nonunit personnel temporarily attached, or even anyone just traveling through the unit's area.

Each of the Regular Army panzer divisions nominally had a ground strength of 13,843 personnel, organized into a two-battalion panzer regiment with 105 tanks (half Panthers, the rest older Panzer-IVs); two two-battalion panzergrenadier regiments, with one of the four battalions in half-tracked carriers; a reconnaissance battalion with an armored car company and (usually) three mixed companies of infantry and heavy weapons in half-tracks, or more rarely trucks; an antitank (panzerjäger) battalion that usually contained two batteries with twenty-one self-propelled guns and one battery with twelve towed 75-mm L46 guns; an antiaircraft battalion with both heavy 88-mm and light 20-mm guns; a three-battalion artillery regiment with one battalion theoretically self-propelled; and assorted support troops.

Early in the war, panzer divisions had more tanks and comparatively less infantry. The requirements of warfare, especially defensive combat, and the severe difficulties the Germans faced in meeting their army's demands for tanks and other armored vehicles, ensured that the organization changed under the stress of war.

The SS divisions were larger, with a ground strength of more than 17,000.[4] The four SS divisions committed to the Ardennes offensive totaled between 16,000 and 20,000 personnel, with three-battalion panzergrenadier regiments, a slightly larger artillery regiment that generally included a battalion of nebelwerfers (rocket launchers), and generally an assault gun (sturmgeschütz) abteilung with twenty to thirty assault guns. The SS divisions also usually had a higher allotment of motor vehicles and of most weapons. Furthermore, the SS divisions were supposed to have first crack at new recruits. However, the four SS divisions in the Sixth Panzer Army were below their assigned strength in officers and noncomissioned officers, mostly because of the staggering losses they had suffered in Normandy, but generally had more than their allotted enlisted men.

The panzergrenadier (mechanized) divisions were organized similarly to the panzer divisions, but instead of a panzer regiment they had a single panzer battalion, which was more often than not at least partly equipped with turretless Sturmgeschütz IIIs or IVs rather than tanks. Their other units were substantially the same as those in a panzer division, although all six of a panzergrenadier division's infantry battalions were carried in trucks. The normal stregth of a panzergrenadier division in 1944 was 14,655 men.

Besides these divisions, there were several types of nondivisional panzer units. First, there were three panzer brigades: Führer Begleit (Escort), Führer Grenadier, and the 150th Panzer (Skorzeny's "Operation Greif" unit, partially equipped with captured American matériel). Their organization varied considerably. The first two could be considered small divisions. Führer Begleit had a single panzer battalion (the 102d) with twenty-eight Panzer IVs and twenty-five panzerjäger IVs and had attached the

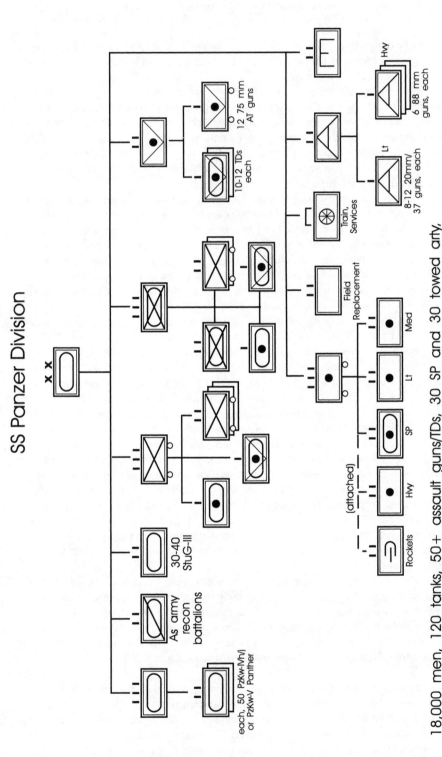

SS Panzer Division

each, 50 PzKw-IVh/J or PzKw-V Panther

30-40 StuG-III

As army recon battalions

12 75 mm AT guns

10-12 TDs each

Train, Services

Field Replacement

Hvy

6 88 mm guns, each

Lt

8-12 20mm/ 37 guns, each

Rockets   Hvy   SP   Lt   Med

(attached)

18,000 men, 120 tanks, 50+ assault guns/TDs, 30 SP and 30 towed arty, 3,000+ motor vehicles, plus 18 MRLs and 10-12 hvy arty, 25 armored cars, 180+ halftracks.

200th Sturmgeschütz Brigade with thirty-three assault guns. Führer Begleit also had a panzergrenadier regiment, a separate grenadier (infantry) battalion, a small artillery battalion, and an entire Luftwaffe FLAK regiment. Führer Grenadier had a mixed panzer battalion (the 101st) with thirty-seven Panthers and eleven Panzer IVs operational, and the attached 911th Assault Gun Brigade with thirty-one functional assault guns, plus the 99th Panzergrenadier Regiment with two infantry battalions, artillery and engineer battalions, a small reconnaissance company, and a FLAK battalion. Skorrzeny's 150th Brigade had a mixed panzer company, a large panzergrenadier battalion, an SS antipartisan unit functioning as infantry, and a reconnaissance company, and was a rather minimal brigade.

The forces committed to the Ardennes offensive also contained a number of independent self-propelled antitank and heavy tank battalions and several assault gun "brigades," which were battalion-size formations despite their designation. There were four schwere Panzerjäger (heavy tank-hunter) battalions, nominally equipped with a mix of thirty-one Jagdpanthers, Panzerjäger IVs, and Sturmgeschütz IIIs. One of these, the 519th, was attached to the Panzer Lehr Division throughout the campaign, and another (the 559th) was attached to the 12th SS Panzer Division. Other schwere panzerjäger battalions were equipped with towed antitank guns. The schwere panzer (heavy tank) battalions contained the famous and widely dreaded Tiger heavy tanks. Three of these units were committed in the Ardennes: the 501st SS (attached to Leibstandarte), the 506th, equipped with Tiger Bs (Royal or King Tigers), and the 301st, equipped with Tiger Es. Each was supposed to muster forty-five Tigers. In actual service they had fewer, typically twenty-five to thirty-five. The Tigers were formidable but mechanically unreliable, and their combat weight (62.75 tons for the Tiger E, 75 tons for the Tiger B) was too great for many bridges in the Ardennes region. Finally, there were seven assault gun brigades (nominally forty-two vehicles each, in three fourteen-vehicle companies), including the 11th Fallschirmjäger Assault Gun Brigade, which was Luftwaffe-manned and attached to the 5th Parachute Division, and the 217th Sturmpanzer Abteilung with Brummbär self-propelled 150-mm infantry guns. The 1000th and 1001st Sturmmörser companies, each with four Sturmtigers, heavily armored and mounting 380-mm rocket launchers, designed for combat in built-up areas, were also initially allotted to the Sixth Panzer Army but were withdrawn before Christmas and saw little if any action during the offensive.

The equipment in the German armored formations was generally good to excellent, although by late 1944 there was rarely enough of it. The Panther tank was particularly effective, combining well-sloped armor with the powerful 75-mm L70 (KwK-42) high-velocity gun, capable of destroying almost any British or American tank at normal battle ranges (generally about 500 meters or less). The Tigers, especially the improved Tiger B (also protected by thick, well-sloped armor), were formidable, indeed frightening, weapons, but they were few in number and so large and heavy that their tactical employment was often limited. The older Panzer IVs were mostly H models (with the 75-mm L48 gun), which comprised about half of the Wehrmacht's tank strength in the Ardennes. Although slower and less well-armed and -armored than the Panthers, they were generally a match for the older M4 Sherman tanks with their standard short 75-mm gun, although inferior to Shermans with the improved high-velocity 76-mm gun.

The Germans fielded a bewildering variety of other armored vehicles. There were at least five types of SdKfz-231,[5] -233, and -234 eight-wheeled armored cars, close to twenty models of SdKfz-250 light and -251 medium half-track armored per-

Panzergrenadier Division

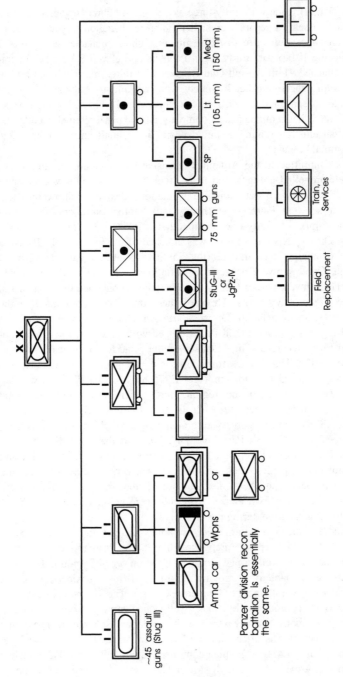

~45 assault guns (StuG III)

Armd car

Wpns

Panzer division recon battalion is essentially the same.

or

StuG-III or JgPz-IV

75 mm guns

SP

Lt (105 mm)

Med (150 mm)

Train, Services

Field Replacement

14,500 men, 45 tanks/assault guns, 30 TDs, 12 towed 150 mm Inf hows, 12 SP 105 mm and 6 Sp 150 mm hows, 12 towed 105 mm hows, 8 towed 150 mm hows, 4 towed 105 mm guns, 12 75 mm AT guns, 12 88 mm AA guns, 16 armored cars, 40 halftracks, 2,500 motor vehicles.

sonnel carriers, at least five kinds of self-propelled antitank guns, including the Jagdpanzer 38(t) or Hetzer (the [t] signified the Czechoslovak, or Tzechoslowakei in German, chassis on which the Hetzer was based), Marder, Jagdpanzer IV/K (75-mm L48 gun) and IV/L (L70 gun),[6] Jagdpanther (unofficially the JgPz V), and five models of Sturmgeschütz (StuG IIIF, IIIG, StuG 42, StuG IV, and Sturmpanzer IV/Brummbär, or "Grizzly Bear").

Many of these models remained in service because adequate numbers of the replacement models had not been produced or delivered, but the logistical burdens thus imposed caused considerable problems and made smooth operation of combat units an exacting task. That problem was magnified by a significant shortage of armored vehicle repair capacity. Consequently many damaged armored vehicles remained in repair for weeks (some, damaged before the campaign started, did not leave repair until the campaign was over), and this further limited German armor strength.

German doctrine for panzer and panzergrenadier units stressed "combined arms" principles and tactics, which the Germans referred to as einheit, or "unity." For both offensive and defensive operations, German commanders formed combined-arms teams down to the company level, combining tanks and infantry, supported by artillery, engineers, and antitank troops. Consequently, panzer and panzergrenadier divisions usually operated in two or three mutually supporting kampfgruppe (battle groups). Typically in the panzer divisions, one battle group was built around each of the two panzergrenadier regiments, and the third formed around the reconnaissance battalion.

For example, 1st SS Panzer Division "Leibstandarte Adolf Hitler" was organized into two kampfgruppen early in the battle. The lead element, known as Kampfgruppe Peiper after its commander, veteran armor officer Obersturmbannführer der Waffen-SS (Lt. Col.) Joachim Peiper, commander of the 1st SS Panzer Regiment, contained over half of that panzer regiment along with a reinforced panzergrenadier battalion, about half of the 501st SS Schwere Panzer Abteilung, and elements of the division's artillery, engineer, and FLAK units. The rest of the division, including most of the artillery, engineers, and the second panzergrenadier regiment, formed a second-echelon battle group. Kampfgruppe Peiper led the advance, but was eventually halted and surrounded in the Stavelot area, far ahead of the rest of Leibstandarte SS Adolf Hitler.[7] Peiper had to abandon his heavy equipment and lead his surviving men out on foot. While ultimately unsuccessful, Peiper's battle group was a powerful force, and for several days wreaked considerable havoc on the American units it encountered. See part IV of appendix D, "The Front on 16 December 1944," for other examples of German kampfgruppen organizations.

With adequately trained troops, which were an increasingly scarce commodity in the German armed forces by late autumn 1944, German units fought extremely well. Their tactical leadership was generally exceptional, partly because many German company-grade officers (lieutenants and captains) were recruited from promising non-commissioned officers who had been sent to officers' school, and so had considerable combat experience before becoming officers. German tactical training stressed the use of cover, surprise, and speed in the attack, and the importance of terrain and well-sited positions in the defense. However, the strain of five years of war was starting to show, and the quality of units varied greatly. Many German units, especially in the 3d and 5th Parachute and in most of the volksgrenadier divisions in the Ardennes, were badly trained and poorly led with inexperienced officers and men.

RECONNAISSANCE UNITS

One of the most important formations available to panzer and panzergrenadier division commanders was their reconnaissance battalion (Aufklärungs Abteilung). These units were usually built around an armored car company and two to four mixed companies of infantry and heavy weapons. The bulk of the battalion could be either mechanized (in half-tracks) or motorized (in trucks and motorcycles) depending on circumstances and available equipment. This force was designed not only to scout and screen for the rest of the division, but also to conduct reconnaissances-in-force, local attacks designed to find enemy strongpoints and to determine the size and disposition of enemy forces. Because of their importance to German offensive doctrine, these units were kept as close to full strength as possible. They were habitually the lead units in an advance, and often the last units to withdraw during a retreat.

In the infantry and volksgrenadier divisions, the reconnaissance battalions were replaced by a fusilier (light infantry) battalion or company, theoretically partly motorized but usually dependent on a mix of bicycles, horses, and trucks for mobility. They were not as well equipped as their mechanized counterparts, and were often employed as a division reserve infantry element. The Luftwaffe's Fallschirmjäger (Parachute) divisions did not have reconnaissance battalions, but only a small company for that purpose.

INFANTRY

Broadly speaking, there were three types of infantry divisions in the German forces committed to the Ardennes offensive. The 3d and 5th Parachute divisions already mentioned were Luftwaffe ground units. Like the Luftwaffe's antiaircraft (FLAK) units, the parachute divisions were organized, led, supplied, and supported not through the Army but through the Luftwaffe, adding another facet of complexity to the Wehrmacht's daunting logistical and support tasks. This wasteful and somewhat silly situation was the direct result of Reichsmarschall Hermann Göring's jealousy and pride.

By 1944 only a small portion of the personnel in parachute divisions were jump-qualified, and they were mostly brought up to strength with redundant ground crew and aircraft personnel, who were trained hurriedly, if at all, in infantry combat. Each division contained more than 15,000 officers and men, in three three-battalion parachute regiments, a three-battalion artillery regiment, and antitank, heavy mortar, antiaircraft, and engineer battalions. Unlike most Wehrmacht infantry-type divisions, parachute units had fully motorized transport, although neither of the divisions in the Ardennes contained their full allotment of trucks and artillery tractors. Colonel Heilmann, commander of the 5th Parachute Division (promoted to generalmajor on 1 January 1945), improvised a divisional reconnaissance battalion by motorizing one of his infantry battalions, but this innovation was not a success; contrary to Heilmann's express orders, the battalion became involved in a vicious firefight with a U.S. strongpoint early in the battle and never fully recovered.

The most common units in the Fifth and Sixth Panzer armies and the Seventh Army were the volksgrenadier divisions. Most of these had either been freshly raised since mid-1944, or were older infantry divisions that had been rebuilt on the new organizational pattern after having sustained crippling combat losses. Each such division contained three two-battalion infantry regiments, a four-battalion artillery regiment, engineer and mixed antitank-antiaircraft battalions, and a fusilier company or battalion. One of the infantry regiments was theoretically mounted on bicycles for

Fallschirmjäger Division

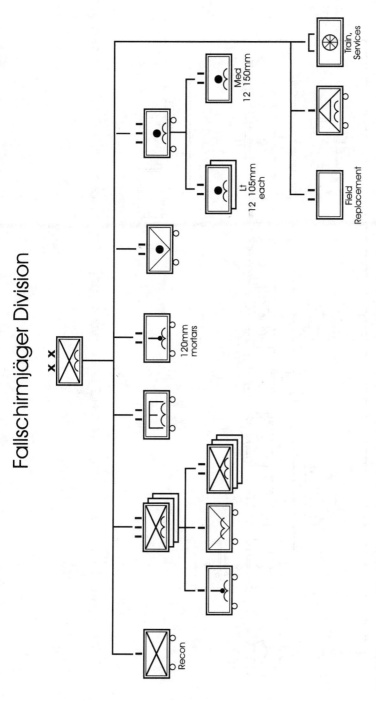

16,500 men, 24 105mm and 12 150mm motor-drawn howitzers, 18 88mm AA guns, 60+ 75mm AT guns, 2,000 motor vehicles.

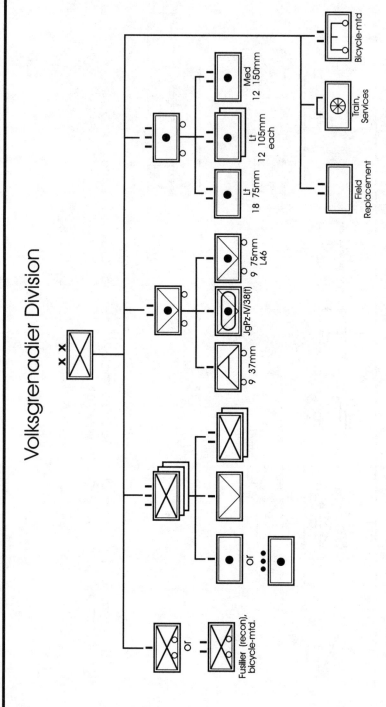

Volksgrenadier Division

11,000 men, 14 TDs, 60 lt and 18 med horse-drawn arty, 150 motor vehicles, 3,000 horses.

added mobility, although the actual level of mobility varied widely. Most of the remaining transport, including that in the artillery regiment, was horse-drawn. The infantry was to have been liberally equipped with automatic weapons (especially submachineguns and the new Sturmgewehr 44 assault rifles), mortars, and both Raketenpanzerbüchse (the German equivalent of the American bazooka) and Panzerfaust (similar in design and concept to the modern U.S. LAW) antitank weapons, but for the most part they were subject to the same equipment shortfalls as other German infantry formations.

A handful of standard infantry divisions (infanterie in German nomenclature, as opposed to the volksgrenadier) played a peripheral part in the Ardennes offensive, including the 344th, 353d, 85th, and 89th, all in the Fifteenth Army. Although similar to the volksgrenadier divisions, there were a few notable differences. An infantry division's artillery had three battalions of 105-mm howitzers instead of the two 105-mm and one 75-mm battalions in the volksgrenadiers (each type of division also had a 150-mm howitzer battalion), and officially had a fusilier battalion instead of a company. An infantry division's six infantry battalions were slightly larger than those in a volksgrenadier division, and possessed fewer automatic weapons but more mortars. These were often theoretical differences, however, as in fact there was often little difference either in organization and equipment or in personnel strength and quality between infantry and volksgrenadier units.

Most German divisions contained some towed antitank guns, although even in the infantry-type divisions one of three antitank companies had been replaced by self-propelled guns. When the war began, the standard German antitank gun was the 37-mm PAK (Panzer Abwehr Kanone, or antitank gun), but increasing tank armor had forced its replacement by the 50-mm PAK 38 in 1941–1942 and then the 75-mm PAK 40 (also known as the 75-mm L46) in late 1943 and early 1944. The PAK 40 was an effective antitank weapon, similar in capability to the 75-mm L48 gun on the PzKw-IVH, but its size and weight (16 feet long, 1.5 tons) made it unpopular with some commanders, who preferred the less effective but nimbler PAK 38 (14 feet long, 1 ton). The most effective German towed antitank gun (found only in the independent schwere panzerjäger battalions) was the 88-mm L71 PAK 41, which weighed five tons in action and was more than thirty feet long, but was sufficiently effective that no one complained about its bulk. Towed guns, because they were readily concealable, were an important component in resisting enemy tank attacks, since the Panzerfaust and Raketenpanzerbüchse, with effective ranges of under 100 meters, were essentially last-ditch weapons. By late 1944 the Germans had become very good at siting and concealing their antitank guns, as American and British tankers discovered to their sorrow on numerous occasions.

In addition to the usual mix of rifles, submachine guns, machine guns, and mortars, German infantry regiments contained a close-range antitank company equipped with Raketenpanzerbüchse. Most regiments (and some battalions) contained a gun or cannon company, equipped with the 75-mm L12 leichte infanterie geschütz (light infantry gun), effectively a small howitzer intended to give direct support to the battalion. Early in the war, German infantry regiments had a pair of 150-mm schwere infanterie geschütz (heavy infantry guns) with the lighter pieces, but by 1944 these had generally been eliminated or replaced by 120-mm mortars. Panzergrenadier regiments retained a battery of towed 150-mm infantry guns, although sometimes (especially in the panzer divisions) these were replaced by the self-propelled Gw 38 (t), with the 150-mm gun mounted on the same Czech-built tracked chassis used by the Hetzer.

German infantry doctrine, like their doctrine for panzers and panzergrenadiers, emphasized einheit and combined-arms operations. Infantry-type divisions often formed their own kampfgruppen. German training and leadership were fundamentally sound, but with most high-quality recruits drawn off into the SS, the panzers, and the Luftwaffe, the volksgrenadier and infantry divisions often fell short of the German Army's traditional élan and skill. They were also usually at the bottom of the list for new equipment and replacements, so that while most of the divisions involved in the Battle of the Bulge were at full strength to start with, they were worn down rather quickly and were unable to sustain their combat power. The lack of experienced personnel also caused problems, and a number of American units reported their enemies employing untypically (for the Germans) clumsy and costly offensive tactics.

ARTILLERY

German artillery units were generally organized in battalions of three (or occasionally two) batteries, each of four or six guns. A division's artillery element usually had four battalions (three in parachute, panzer, and panzergrenadier divisions), for a usual total of forty-two to forty-eight pieces, comparable with U.S. divisions. The most common weapons were the 105-mm leichte feldhaubitze or light field howitzer, which accounted for nearly three out of four divisional artillery pieces, and the 150-mm schwere feldhaubitze or heavy field howitzer, which comprised nearly all the remainder. There were also light 75-mm pieces (essentially the PAK 40 on a different carriage, known as the Feldkanone 40), accounting for a quarter of the tubes in most volksgrenadier divisions. Many divisions also used their heavier antiaircraft (FLAK) batteries as additional artillery, a task for which the relatively short-barreled 88-mm L56 was well suited. (That weapon was also employed as the main armament of the Tiger I heavy tank; the Tiger II or Royal Tiger employed the higher-velocity 88-mm L71, which was also used by the Jagdpanther.)

Nondivisional artillery came in a variety of calibers, and in two principal types of organization. Several larger artillery units were employed in the Ardennes fighting, notably Volksartillerie Korps (VAK) and Volkswerfer Brigaden (VWB). These last contained nebelwerfer (smoke-throwers), which were towed multibarreled rocket launchers. VWBs contained two regiments, each generally with two 15-cm battalions[8] and one 21-cm, 30-cm, or 28/32-cm battalion, and a few VWBs contained one or two batteries of self-propelled ten-barreled 150-mm Nebelwerfer mounted on Maultier half-tracks, known as the Panzerwerfer 42. The VAK were five- or six-battalion formations equipped not only with heavier weapons like 105-mm and 150-mm guns, 170-mm guns, 210-mm howitzers, and other sorts of artillery, including captured Soviet 152-mm gun-howitzers and 122-mm howitzers, but also with 75-mm L46 and 88-mm L56 flat-trajectory, high-velocity guns. (In technical artillery terms, a gun is a high-velocity, flat-trajectory weapon; a howitzer has lower muzzle velocity and a higher trajectory arc.)

Many of these units, and a great many independent artillery battalions, were short of transport. A good portion of the battalions were officially designated either bodenständige (static), teilige bewegung (partially mobile, and usually only with horses), or teilige motorisiert (partially motorized), reflecting and formalizing a total or significant shortage of transport. This general transport shortage, whether formal or not, caused two problems. First, units short of transport had trouble bringing up ammunition and distributing it to their firing batteries. Second, they had only limited mobility, and had great difficulty displacing forward. As a result, German artillery support during the first few days of the offensive was plentiful and generally adequate if not very accurate, but this advantage disappeared as the attacking units moved beyond the range of their nondivisional supporting artillery. The Germans managed to solve part of the problem by motorizing a portion of each artillery unit.

Another, and in some ways more serious, difficulty was the Germans' lack of experienced fire-control personnel, especially trained forward observers. Without a forward observation post, artillery cannot be employed effectively in indirect fire at targets close to the supported troops, and often can only be used for direct fire (that is, firing at targets visible to the guns). Not only were the Germans short of trained personnel, they were also sometimes short of radios and other specialized communication and fire control equipment. To compensate, they resorted to the First World War practice of preplanned barrages, but this was inflexible and cumbersome, and prone to mishap in rapidly changing situations. This problem was particularly acute with the VAKs, most of which lacked their nominal forward observer company. Consequently, they relied on corps and army observers, and this imposed another burden on already-strained communications nets. The VWBs, which executed only preplanned fires (the nebelwerfer could deliver a great volume of fire, but were woefully inaccurate), had no assigned forward observers, and so were largely immune to that problem, but as a consequence could not be employed in flexible fire support responsive to the needs of the supported units.

ENGINEERS, ANTIAIRCRAFT (FLAK), AND SUPPORT TROOPS

Along with each division's engineer (pioniere in German nomenclature) battalion, which served as both construction engineers for bridges and field fortifications and as combat engineers, the German forces in the Ardennes also contained a number of nondivisional engineer units. Most of these were concerned with bridge building, a necessary undertaking in the Ardennes, where the deep, fast-flowing streams were only rarely fordable. These bridge-building units came in two principal types: the Brückengerät-B (Bridging Equipment-B) and -J. The B-type was more common, and most divisions contained a B-type bridging column. Depending on subtype, a B-type column could erect a 430-foot ponton bridge with a 4.5-ton load limit, a 250-foot bridge with a 10-ton limit, or a 170-foot bridge with a 20-ton limit.

The heavier J-type bridges were more elaborate box-trestle affairs, supported by either pontons or trestles, which could bear heavier loads, up to and including tanks. Between the Seventh Army, the Fifth and Sixth Panzer armies, and Army Group B, the German forces in the Ardennes had at their disposal fourteen nondivisional Brückengerät-B and eight -J bridging columns.

In addition to bridging equipment, German engineers possessed a variety of tools and equipment for construction and demolition, including barbed wire, mines, mine-clearing equipment, digging tools, and cranes. Moreover, as specialists in the assault of fortified places, they were also equipped with flamethrowers, satchel charges, and other sorts of specialized combat equipment. In most divisions, there was a combat engineer company in each infantry-type regiment, and in panzer and panzergrenadier divisions the reconnaissance battalion also contained an engineer platoon in the weapons company. These engineer-type troops outside of the engineer battalions (Pionierbataillonen) were not members of the engineer branch, but were instead members of the branch to which their units were assigned, having been trained to perform some combat engineer functions.

The growing presence of Allied tactical aircraft over European battlefields after 1943 had compelled the Germans to increase their antiaircraft troops. Panzer and panzergrenadier divisions, and the Luftwaffe's parachute divisions, all contained antiaircraft battalions. These were known as FLAK (for *Fl*ieger *A*bwehr *K*anone, or aircraft defense cannon) units and could be under either Luftwaffe or Army control. FLAK units were either heavy, equipped with towed 88-mm or 105-mm antiaircraft guns (which could serve also as direct- and indirect-fire artillery and as antitank weapons), or light, with towed and self-propelled 20-mm and 37-mm automatic cannon. The Germans had fielded limited numbers of a newly developed 15-mm antiaircraft machine gun (evidently patterned on the Soviet 14.5-mm weapon), and were planning to introduce a new 30-mm AA gun in early 1945. Several divisions in the Ardennes had the new 15-mm machine gun, often in a triple mount, but none had received the 30-mm gun.

Both SS and Army panzer battalions had a FLAK platoon with four Wirbelwind (Whirlwind) or Möbelwagen ("Furniture Van") antiaircraft tanks, built on PzKw-IV chassis, with quadruple 20-mm automatic cannon. The Ostwind (East Wind) antiaircraft tank, with a single 37-mm gun, also sometimes appeared in these units, but was less common than the other two models. Units that had lost these tanks or never received them made do with half-tracks similarly armed. Panzergrenadier battalions also had a light FLAK platoon in their weapons company, usually equipped with six single 20-mm guns on half-tracks for the half-tracked battalion, but otherwise towed. Some divisional artillery battalions also had their own FLAK platoons.

Panzer and panzergrenadier divisions contained their own FLAK battalions, with two (sometimes three) batteries of four 88-mm heavy antiaircraft guns and four 20-mm guns each, and a light battery with six single or quadruple-mount 20-mm cannon, or single 37-mm cannon, on half-tracks or light trucks. These units always wore Army uniforms, but were sometimes Luftwaffe units (or partly manned by Luftwaffe personnel) operating under Army command. The FLAK units in the SS divisions were SS-run, although those units too often contained some Luftwaffe personnel. In infantry and volksgrenadier divisions, the FLAK element consisted of a single light battery (the third battery of the antitank battalion), with 20-mm or 37-mm guns. Parachute divisions, being Luftwaffe formations, paid great attention to their antiaircraft capabilities, and their FLAK battalions contained twelve 88-mm and eighteen or twenty-four 20-mm guns.

These antiaircraft weapons did not shoot down many Allied aircraft, but they did provide a morale benefit to German troops suffering from Allied air attacks. The FLAK battalions also provided valuable additional ground firepower. In the Korean War a few years later, U.S. troops employed the quadruple-mount .50-caliber machine guns and twin automatic 40-mm antiaircraft guns of the divisional antiaircraft automatic weapons (AAAW) battalions to halt Chinese and North Korean infantry assaults.

German support services were, like the rest of their army, soundly organized and normally well trained, but by late 1944 were suffering from both equipment shortages and poorly prepared personnel. The general lack of transport and endemic fuel shortages meant that even the panzer and panzergrenadier formations ran low on fuel as the battle wore on, and by early January some divisions began to abandon many of their vehicles because there was either no fuel to move them, or they had suffered mechanical failure and could not be repaired. The general shortage of trucks and other vehicles also hampered the flow of supplies, including ammunition and food—a situation that worsened as the vehicles were abandoned. There were numerous anecdotal American reports during the early part of the campaign of German troops stopping to gorge themselves in captured American military kitchens and to ransack supply depots.

THE LUFTWAFFE

By late 1944 the Luftwaffe was no longer the splendid instrument it had been in the opening years of the war from 1939 to 1941. The strain of resisting the Allied Combined Bomber Offensive against the German homeland (an eventuality that pre-war German planners had never considered) had severely stretched its resources, and the strain of more than five years of war was exacting a heavy toll. Although aircraft production had increased, and German aircraft were capable and effective fighting machines, they were increasingly outnumbered by the Allied air forces. Reichsmarschall Göring had been asked to provide 1,500 aircraft to support the Ardennes offensive, including 100 of the new Me-262 Schwalbe (Swallow) twin-engined jet fighter-bombers. In fact, the Reichsmarschall could promise only 1,000 aircraft, although the Luftwaffe eventually committed 1,200 aircraft overall, including about 50 jets.

Not only were the Germans numerically outmatched in the air, but the quality of their pilots had declined also. When the average life expectancy of a new fighter pilot amounted to perhaps three or four missions, fewer than 10 percent of new pilots would survive more than a few weeks. Consequently, experienced pilots were a very limited commodity, and not only for combat aircraft. Fewer than a third of Colonel von der Heydte's paratroopers (supposed to seize crossings for the advance of Kampfgruppe Peiper) actually made landfalls anywhere near the drop zone, largely because the transport pilots, inexperienced and unused to nighttime navigation, unloaded their paratroops willy-nilly all over the countryside between the Rhine and the Meuse.

Allied command of the air was such that the Luftwaffe could have only a marginal effect on operations in the best of circumstances. During the bad weather of the first days of the offensive, the Luftwaffe did manage to mount a significant level of ground support missions, but these declined in number and effect as the weather improved and as the Allied tactical air forces devoted first priority to the Ardennes battle and the German airfields supporting it. The one major Luftwaffe operation of the campaign was Operation Bodenplatte on 1 January 1945.

CONCLUSION

Taken as a whole, the situation described shows that the Germans had problems other than their relative lack of numbers and the nearly overwhelming Allied airpower. The Wehrmacht was not functioning at anything resembling peak efficiency because it lacked the support resources to do so. On the other hand, the German Army was far from beaten and remained a very capable field force. Although the Ardennes offensive probably shortened the war by exhausting Germany's last major stocks of resources—trained manpower as well as equipment—it is an open question whether saving those same resources for defense would have prolonged the war by more than a few weeks.

APPENDIX D

ORDERS OF BATTLE*
ARDENNES CAMPAIGN
16 DECEMBER 1944–
16 JANUARY 1945

I. ALLIED ORDER OF BATTLE
16–19 DECEMBER 1944

SHAEF—GEN. DWIGHT D. EISENHOWER
Allied Ground Forces—Gen. Dwight D. Eisenhower
   SHAEF Reserve
   In England:
         6th (British) AbnD—Maj. Gen. Eric L. Bols
         11th (U.S.) AD (+)—Brig. Gen. Charles S. Kilburn
            (To Continent, 17 Dec)
         17th (U.S.) AbnD (+)—Maj. Gen. William M. Miley
   On the Continent:
         XVIII (U.S.) Airborne Corps—Maj. Gen. Matthew B. Ridgway
            (First Army, 18 Dec)
         82d AbnD (+)—Maj. Gen. James M. Gavin
         101st AbnD (+)—Maj. Gen. Maxwell D. Taylor
            (TDY [CONUS])
               Acting: Brig. Gen. Anthony C. McAuliffe
            (VIII Corps, 17 Dec)
   COM-Z—Lt. Gen. John C. H. Lee
      IX (U.S.) Air Defense Command
   21st (British) Army Group—Field Marshal Sir Bernard L. Montgomery
      21st Army Group reserve:
      XXX Corps—Lt. Gen. Sir Brian G. Horrocks
         79th AD (Special) (elms)—Maj. Gen. Sir Percy C. S. Hobart
      Refitting:
         29th Arm Bde/11th AD
      First (Canadian) Army—Lt. Gen. H. D. G. Crerar

*See section V for an explanation of the format, conventions, and abbreviations used here.

I (British) Corps—Lt. Gen. J. T. Crocker
II Corps—Lt. Gen. G. G. Simmonds
 51st (British) "Highland" ID—Maj. Gen. T. G. Rennie
 6th Guards (British) Tk Bde
Second (British) Army—Lt. Gen. Sir Miles C. Dempsey
VIII Corps—Lt. Gen. E. H. Barker
XII Corps—Lt. Gen. Neil M. Ritchie
 Guards AD—Maj. Gen. Alan H. S. Adair
 43d "Wessex" ID—Maj. Gen. G. I. Thomas
 34th Tk Bde
 53d "Welsh" ID—Maj. Gen. R. K. Ross
 33d Arm Bde
 (XXX Corps, 19 Dec)
12th (U.S.) Army Group—Lt. Gen. Omar N. Bradley
Unassigned:
 94th ID—Maj. Gen. Harry J. Maloney
Ninth Army—Lt. Gen. William H. Simpson
XIII Corps—Maj. Gen. Alvan C. Gillem
 84th ID (+)—Maj. Gen. Alexander R. Bolling
 102d ID (+)—Brig. Gen. Frank A. Keating
XIII Corps reserve:
 7th AD (−) (+)—Brig. Gen. Robert W. Hasbrouck
 (VIII Corps, 16 Dec)
XIX Corps—Maj. Gen. Raymond S. McLain
 2d AD (+)—Maj. Gen. Ernest N. Harmon
Ninth Army reserve:
 30th ID (+)—Maj. Gen. Leland S. Hobbs
 (V Corps, 17 Dec)
XVI Corps (not operational)—Maj. Gen. J. B. Anderson
 75th ID—Maj. Gen. Fay B. Prickett
First Army—Lt. Gen. Courtney H. Hodges
VII Corps—Maj. Gen. Joseph Lawton Collins
 104th ID (+)—Maj. Gen. Terry de la Mesa Allen
 9th ID (+)—Maj. Gen. Louis A. Craig
 (V Corps, 18 Dec)
 83d ID (−) (+)—Maj. Gen. Robert C. Macon
 5th AD (−) (+)—Maj. Gen. Lunsford E. Oliver
VII Corps reserve:
 1st ID (+)—Maj. Gen. Clift Andrus
 (V Corps, 16 Dec)
 3d AD (−) (+)—Maj. Gen. Maurice Rose
 (XVIII Abn Corps, 19 Dec)
V Corps—Maj. Gen. Leonard T. Gerow
 8th ID (+)—Brig. Gen. W. G. Weaver
 (VII Corps, 18 Dec)
 78th ID (−) (+)—Maj. Gen. Edwin P. Parker Jr.
 2d ID (+)—Maj. Gen. Walter M. Robertson
 99th ID (−) (+)—Maj. Gen. Walter E. Lauer

V Corps reserve:
  CCB/9th AD (−)—Brig. Gen. William M. Hoge
  (VIII Corps, 16 Dec)
VIII Corps—Maj. Gen. Troy H. Middleton
  106th ID (+)—Maj. Gen. Alan W. Jones
  14th Cav. Gp—Col. Mark Devine
  28th ID (+)—Maj. Gen. Norman D. Cota
  9th AD (−) (+)—Maj. Gen. John W. Leonard
  4th ID (+)—Maj. Gen. Raymond O. Barton
VIII Corps reserve:
  CCR/9th AD (+)—Col. Joseph H. Gilbreth
Third Army—Lt. Gen. George S. Patton Jr.
  XX Corps—Maj. Gen. Walton H. Walker
  90th ID (+)—Maj. Gen. James A. Van Fleet
  5th ID (+)—Maj. Gen. S. Leroy Irwin
  95th ID (+)—Maj. Gen. H. L. Twaddle
  XX Corps reserve:
  10th AD (−) (+)—Maj. Gen. William H. H. Morris Jr.
  (VIII Corps, 17 Dec)
XII Corps—Maj. Gen. Manton S. Eddy
  6th AD (+)—Maj. Gen. Robert W. Grow
  35th ID (+)—Maj. Gen. Paul W. Baade
  87th ID (+)—Brig. Gen. Frank L. Culin Jr.
  XII Corps reserve:
  80th ID (+)—Maj. Gen. Horace L. McBride
  (III Corps, 19 Dec)
Third Army reserve:
  III Corps—Maj. Gen. John Millikin
  4th AD (+)—Maj. Gen. Hugh J. Gaffey
  26th ID (+)—Maj. Gen. Willard S. Paul
6th (U.S.) Army Group—Lt. Gen. Jacob L. Devers
  Seventh Army—Lt. Gen. Alexander M. Patch Jr.
  XV Corps—Maj. Gen. Wade H. Haislip
  VI Corps—Maj. Gen. Edward H. Brooks
  First (French) Army—Gen. J. de Lattre de Tassigny
  II Corps—Maj. Gen. G. de Montsabert
  I Corps—Lt. Gen. M. E. Bethouart

II. ALLIED ORDER OF BATTLE
20 DECEMBER 1944–16 JANUARY 1945

SHAEF—GEN. DWIGHT D. EISENHOWER
Allied Ground Forces—Gen. Dwight D. Eisenhower
SHAEF Reserve
In England:
  6th (British) AbnD—Maj. Gen. Eric L. Bols
  (To Continent, 26 Dec; XXX [British] Corps, 27 Dec)
  17th (U.S.) AbnD (+)—Maj. Gen. William M. Miley

(To Continent, 24 Dec; XVIII Corps, 25 Dec; VIII Corps, 1 Jan)
  Attached:
    507th PIR
    550th GIB
COM-Z—Maj. Gen. John C. H. Lee
  Free French troops:

2d Inf Bn	5th Inf Bn
6th Inf Bn	8th Inf Bn
9th Inf Bn	14th Inf Bn
4/2d Inf Rgt	4/20th Inf Rgt

  U.S. troops:
    29th Inf (Sep)
    118th Inf (Sep)
    115th FA Bn (105H, T)
      (Meuse Defense Line [COM-Z], 21 Dec; VIII Corps, 25 Dec)

351st Eng G/S Rgt	372d Eng G/S Rgt
398th Eng G/S Rgt	

      (XII Corps, 23 Dec)

342d Eng G/S Rgt	366th Eng G/S Rgt
392d Eng G/S Rgt	1308th Eng G/S Rgt

      (VIII Corps, 24 Dec)
  IX (U.S.) Air Defense Command (elms)—Brig. Gen. W. L. Richardson[1]

126th AAA Gun Bn (Mbl)	184th AAA Gun Bn (Mbl)
414th AAA Gun Bn (SM)	792d AAA Gun Bn (SM) (−)
204th AAA AW Bn (SM)	385th AAA AW Bn (SM)
451st AAA AW Bn (SM)	784th AAA AW Bn (SM)
787th AAA AW Bn (SM)	A/863d AAA AW Bn (SM)

      (First [U.S.] Army, 21 Dec)
21st (British) Army Group—Field Marshal Sir Bernard L. Montgomery
  21st Army Group reserve, assembling vic. Dinant-Namur-Liège:
  XXX Corps—Lt. Gen. Sir Brian G. Horrocks
    Corps Troops:

2d HC Rgt (AC)	61st Recce Rgt RAC
73d AT Rgt RA	27th LAA Rgt RA
11th Fld Co RE	209th Fld Co RE
210th Fld Co RE	211th Fld Prk Co RE

    5th AGRA

7th Med Rgt RA	64th Med Rgt RA
84th Med Rgt RA	52d Hvy Rgt RA

    106th AAA Bde

4th LAA Rgt RA	113th LAA Rgt RA
165th LAA Rgt RA	

    29th Arm Bde/11th AD
      (VIII [British] Corps, 14 Jan)
    79th AD (Special) (elms)—Maj. Gen. Sir Percy Hobart
    53d "Welsh" ID—Maj. Gen. R. K. Ross
      Attached:
        33d Tk Bde

Guards AD—Maj. Gen. Alan Adair
    (XXX Corps, 20 Dec)
43d "Wessex" ID—Maj. Gen. G. I. Thomas
    (XXX Corps, 20 Dec; VIII [British] Corps, 27 Dec)
    Attached:
      34th Tk Bde
51st "Highland" ID—Maj. Gen. T. G. Rennie
    (XXX Corps, 20 Dec; First [U.S.] Army, 22 Dec; XXX Corps,
    7 Jan)
    Attached:
      6th Guards Tk Bde
First (Canadian) Army—Lt. Gen. H. D. H. Crerar
  I (British) Corps—Lt. Gen. J. T. Crocker
  II Corps—Lt. Gen. G. G. Simmonds
Second (British) Army—Lt. Gen. Sir Miles C. Dempsey
  Army troops:
    80th AAA Bde
      86th HAA Rgt RA   99th HAA Rgt RA
    101st AAA Bde
      105th HAA Rgt RA   116th HAA Rgt RA
      (XXX Corps, 23 Dec; Second Army, 29 Dec)
  VIII Corps—Lt. Gen. E. H. Barker
  Corps troops:
    4th AGRA
      53d Med Rgt RA   79th Med Rgt RA
      121st Med Rgt RA   91st AT Rgt RA
      (XXX Corps, 21 Dec)
  XII Corps—Lt. Gen. Neil M. Ritchie
  Corps troops:
    3d AGRA
      6th Fld Rgt RA   13th Med Rgt RA
      59th Med Rgt RA   109th HAA Rgt RA
      20 & 23 Bty/59th Hvy Rgt RA
      (XXX Corps, 22 Dec; XII Corps, 11 Jan)
Ninth (U.S.) Army—Lt. Gen. William H. Simpson
    (21st Army Group, 20 Dec)
  XIII Corps—Maj. Gen. Alvan C. Gillem
    102d ID (+)—Brig. Gen. Frank A. Keating
  XVI Corps (not operational)
    75th ID—Maj. Gen. Fay B. Prickett
      (VII Corps, 22 Dec; XVIII Abn Corps, 29 Dec; VII Corps, 2 Jan
      45; XVIII Abn Corps, 7 Jan 45)
  XIX Corps—Maj. Gen. Raymond S. McLain
    2d AD (−) (+)—Maj. Gen. Ernest N. Harmon
      (VII Corps, 22 Dec)
    Attached:
      702d TD Bn (SP)
      195th AAA AW Bn (SP)

29th ID (+)—Maj. Gen. Charles H. Gerhardt
(XIII Corps, 23 Dec)
First (U.S.) Army—Lt. Gen. Courtney H. Hodges
(21st Army Group, 20 Dec)
Army Troops:
99th Inf "Norwegian" Bn
526th Arm Inf Bn
5th (Belgian) Fusilier Bn
B/125th Cav Sq
A/825th TD Bn (T)

109th AAA Gun Bn (Mbl)	125th AAA Gun Bn (Mbl)
129th AAA Gun Bn (Mbl)	136th AAA Gun Bn (Mbl)
141st AAA Gun Bn (Mbl)	142d AAA Gun Bn (Mbl)
A/782d AAA Gun Bn (SM)	
639th AAA AW Bn (Mbl)	
788th AAA AW Bn (SM)	789th AAA AW Bn (SM)
497th AAA AW Bn (SP)	467th AAA AW Bn (SP)
51st Eng C Bn	61st Eng C Bn
148th Eng C Bn	158th Eng C Bn
164th Eng C Bn	203d Eng C Bn
207th Eng C Bn	291st Eng C Bn
296th Eng C Bn	300th Eng C Bn
348th Eng C Bn	1278th Eng C Bn
364th Eng G/S Rgt	365th Eng G/S Rgt
1313th Eng G/S Rgt	

VII Corps—Maj. Gen. Joseph Lawton Collins
Corps Troops:
6th (Belgian) Fusilier Bn

738th Tk Bn (MX) (−)	759th Tk Bn (Light)
C/634th TD Bn (SP)	635th TD Bn (T)
79th FA Bn (Provisional)	87th FA Bn (105H, SP)
153d FA Bn (8″G, T)	172d FA Bn (4.5″G, T)
195th FA Bn (8″H, T)	240th FA Bn (155G, T)
266th FA Bn (240H, T)	551st FA Bn (240H, T)
552d FA Bn (240H, T)	690th FA Bn (105H, T)
980th FA Bn (155G, T)	981st FA Bn (155G, T)
991st FA Bn (155G, T)	
116th AAA Gun Bn (Mbl)	438th AAA AW Bn (Mbl)
474th AAA AW Bn (SM)	
49th Eng C Bn	237th Eng C Bn
238th Eng C Bn	297th Eng C Bn
298th Eng C Bn	
C/87th Cml Mtr Bn	

113th Cav Grp (−)
24th Cav Sq
104th ID (+)—Maj. Gen. Terry de la Mesa Allen
(XIX Corps, 22 Dec)
83d ID (−) (+)—Maj. Gen. Robert C. Macon

(XIX Corps, 22 Dec; VII Corps, 26 Dec)
Attached:
    774th Tk Bn
    629th TD Bn (SP)
    183d FA Bn (155H, T)
    193d FA Bn (105H, T)
    951st FA Bn (155H, T)
    453d AAA AW Bn (Mbl)
    A/87th Cml Mtr Bn
5th AD (−) (+)—Maj. Gen. Lunsford E. Oliver
    (V Corps, 23 Dec)
8th ID (−) (+)—Brig. Gen. W. G. Weaver
    (XIX Corps, 22 Dec)
78th ID (−) (+)—Maj. Gen. Edwin P. Parker Jr.
    (XIX Corps, 22 Dec)
VII Corps reserve, moving to vic. Huy-Marche:
84th ID (+)—Maj. Gen. Alexander R. Bolling
    (VII Corps, 20 Dec)
    Attached:
        771st Tk Bn
        638th TD Bn (SP)
        A/473d AAA AW Bn (SP)
        557th AAA AW Bn (Mbl)
V Corps—Maj. Gen. Leonard T. Gerow
        (16 Jan) Maj. Gen. C. R. Huebner
Corps Troops:

187th FA Bn (155H, T)	190th FA Bn (155G, T)
200th FA Bn (−) (155G, T)	272d FA Bn (240H, T)
751st FA Bn (155H, T)	941st FA Bn (4.5″G, T)
955th FA Bn (155H, T)	957th FA Bn (155H, T)
987th FA Bn (155G, SP)	997th FA Bn (8″H, T)
62d Arm FA Bn (105H, SP)	460th Para FA Bn (75H, T)
134th AAA Gun Bn (Mbl)	602d AAA Gun Bn (SM)
863d AAA AW Bn (SM)	
20th Eng C Bn	112th Eng C Bn
146th Eng C Bn (−)	254th Eng C Bn
296th Eng C Bn	348th Eng C Bn
300th Eng C Bn	1278th Eng C Bn
1340th Eng C Bn	
B/87th Cml Mtr Bn	

9th ID (−) (+)—Maj. Gen. Louis A. Craig
    Attached:
        746th Tk Bn
        38th Cav Sq (−)
        899th TD Bn (SP)
        186th FA Bn (155H, T)
        196th FA Bn (105H, T)
        376th AAA AW Bn (Mbl)

413th AAA Gun Bn (Mbl)

2d ID (+)—Maj. Gen. Walter M. Robertson
  Attached:
    741st Tk Bn
    99th Reconnaissance Troop/99th ID
    612th TD Bn (T)
    644th TD Bn (SP) (−)
    462d AAA AW Bn (Mbl)
    C/86th Cml Mtr Bn

99th ID (−) (+)—Maj. Gen. Walter E. Lauer
  Attached:
    801st TD Bn (T) (−)
    535th AAA AW Bn (Mbl)
    D/86th Cml Mtr Bn

1st ID (+)—Maj. Gen. Clift Andrus
  Attached:
    745th Tk Bn
    634th TD Bn (SP) (−)
    703d TD Bn (SP) (−)
    3d/C/801st TD Bn (T)
    B/200th FA Bn (155G, T)
    103d AAA AW Bn (Mbl)
    639th AAA AW Bn (Mbl)

30th ID (+)—Maj. Gen. Leland S. Hobbs
  (XVIII Abn Corps, 21 Dec)
  Attached:
  517th PIR
    551st PIB
  CCB/3d AD
    740th Tk Bn
    743d Tk Bn
    C/772d TD Bn (T)
    823d TD Bn (T)
    18th FA Bn (105H, T)
    400th Arm FA Bn (105H, SP)
    531st AAA AW Bn (Mbl)

V Corps reserve:
  CCA/3d AD—Brig. Gen. Doyle Hickey

XVIII Airborne Corps—Maj. Gen. Matthew B. Ridgway
  Corps Troops:
    509th PIB
    596th Para Eng Co

254th FA Bn (155H, T)	965th FA Bn (155H, T)
110th AA Gun Bn (Mbl)	143d AAA Gun Bn (Mbl)
563d AAA AW Bn (Mbl)	634th AAA AW Bn (−)

82d AbnD (+)—Maj. Gen. James M. Gavin
  Attached:
  508th PIR

2/401st GIR
B/703d TD Bn (SP)
3d AD (−) (+)—Maj. Gen. Maurice Rose
(VII Corps, 23 Dec)
Attached:
A/738th Tk Bn (MX)
83d Arm FA Bn (105H, SP)
486th AAA AW Bn (SP)
7th AD (+)—Brig. Gen. Robert W. Hasbrouck
Attached:
14th Cav Grp (remnants)
814th TD Bn (SP)
275th Arm FA Bn (105H, SP)
203d AAA AW Bn (SP)
106th ID (+) (remnants)—Maj. Gen. Alan W. Jones
(22 Dec) Brig. Gen. H. T. Perrin
Attached:
CCB/9th AD (−)—Brig. Gen. William M. Hoge
112th RCT/28th ID
820th TD Bn (T) (remnants)
D/634th AAA AW Bn
12th (U.S.) Army Group—Lt. Gen. Omar N. Bradley
11th AD (+)—Brig. Gen. Charles S. Kilburn
(VIII Corps, 25 Dec; XII Corps, 31 Dec; VIII Corps, 15 Jan 45)
Attached:
575th AAA AW Bn (SP)
94th ID—Maj. Gen. Harry J. Maloney
(XX Corps, 8 Jan 45)
Third Army—Lt. Gen. George S. Patton Jr.
Army Troops:
2d (French) Para Rgt
16th (French) Chasseur Bn
30th (French) Chasseur Bn
631st TD Bn (T)
A & B/119th AAA Gun Bn (Mbl)

120th AAA Gun Bn (Mbl)	128th AAA Gun Bn (Mbl)
217th AAA Gun Bn (Mbl)	411th AAA Gun Bn (Mbl)
456th AAA AW Bn (Mbl)	546th AAA AW Bn (Mbl)
550th AAA AW Bn (Mbl)	565th AAA AW Bn (Mbl)
567th AAA AW Bn (Mbl)	778th AAA AW Bn (SP)
465th AAA AW Bn (SP)	795th AAA AW Bn (SM)
776th AAA AW Bn (SM) (−)	1303d Eng G/S Rgt

1301st Eng G/S Rgt
1306th Eng G/S Rgt
293d Eng C Bn
VIII Corps—Maj. Gen. Troy H. Middleton
(Third Army, 20 Dec)

Corps Troops:

B & C/705th TD Bn (SP)
561st FA Bn (155G, T)
740th FA Bn (8″H, T)
333d FA Bn (remnants) (155H, T)
770th FA Bn (remnants) (4.5″G, T)
73d Arm FA Bn/9th AD (105H, SP)
440th AAA AW Bn (Mbl)
35th Eng C Bn
168th Eng C Bn (remnants)

559th FA Bn (155G, T)
578th FA Bn (8″H, T)
771st FA Bn (4.5″G, T)

635th AAA AW Bn (Mbl)
299th Eng C Bn

28th ID (−) (+)—Maj. Gen. Norman D. Cota
(Third Army, 8 Jan)
Attached:
707th Tk Bn (remnants)
630th TD Bn (T) (−) (remnants)
58th Arm FA Bn (105H, SP) (remnants)
687th FA Bn (105H, T)
447th AAA Aw Bn (Mbl) (−) (remnants)
44th Eng C Bn (remnants)

101st AbnD (+)—Maj. Gen. Maxwell D. Taylor (TDY [CONUS],
rejoined 27 Dec)
Acting: Brig. Gen. Anthony C. McAuliffe
Attached:
CCR/9th AD (remnants)
CCB/10th AD (remnants)
501st PIR
506th PIR
1/401st GIR
705th TD Bn (−)
463d Para FA Bn (75H, T)
333d FA Bn (155H, T) (elms)
755th FA Bn (155H, T)
775th FA Bn (4.5″G, T)
969th FA BN (155H, T)

9th AD (−) (+)—Maj. Gen. John W. Leonard
(III Corps, 20 Dec; VIII Corps, 21 Dec; First Army, 31 Dec;
Third Army, 9 Jan 45)
Attached:
109th RCT/28th ID
811th TD Bn (SP) (−)
482d AAA AW Bn (SP) (−)

III Corps—Maj. Gen. John Millikin

Corps Troops:

176th FA Bn (4.5″G, T)	177th FA Bn (155H, T)
179th FA Bn (155H, T)	255th FA Bn (105H, T)
512th FA Bn (105H, T)	731st FA Bn (155G, T)
752d FA Bn (155H, T)	776th FA Bn (155H, T)
949th FA Bn (155H, T)	
253d Arm FA Bn (105H, SP)	274th Arm FA Bn (105H, SP)
468th AAA AW Bn (SP)	
145th Eng C Bn	178th Eng C Bn
183d Eng C Bn	188th Eng C Bn
249th Eng C Bn	
3d Cml Mtr Bn	

4th AD (+)—Maj. Gen. Hugh J. Gaffey
(VIII Corps, 2 Jan 45; XII Corps, 12 Jan 45)
Attached:
735th... 704th TD Bn (SP)
489th AAA AW Bn (SP)

26th ID (+)—Maj. Gen. Willard S. Paul
Attached:
735th Tk Bn
818th TD Bn (SP)
390th AAA AW Bn (SP)

80th ID (+)—Maj. Gen. Horace L. McBride
(XII Corps, 26 Dec)
Attached:
702d Tk Bn
610th TD Bn (SP)
808th TD Bn (T) (−)
633d AAA AW Bn (Mbl)

4th ID (+)—Maj. Gen. Raymond O. Barton
(27 Dec) Brig. Gen. H. W. Blakely
(III Corps, 20 Dec; XII Corps, 21 Dec)
Attached:
70th Tk Bn
802d TD Bn (T)
803d TD Bn (SP)
81st FA Bn (155H, T)
174th FA Bn (155G, SP)
377th AAA AW Bn (Mbl)
159th Eng C Bn

III Corps reserve:
10th AD (−) (+)—Maj. Gen. William H. H. Morris Jr.
(III Corps, 20 Dec; XII Corps, 21 Dec; XX Corps, 26 Dec)
Attached:
CCA/9th AD
609th TD Bn (SP) (−)
796th AAA AW Bn (SP)
XX Corps—Maj. Gen. Walton H. Walker

90th ID (+)—Maj. Gen. James A. Van Fleet
    (III Corps, 6 Jan)
    Attached:
        712th Tk Bn
      3d Cav Grp
      6th Cav Grp (−)
        28th Cav Sq
        773d TD Bn (SP)
        807th TD Bn (T)
        241st FA Bn (105, T)
        C/558th FA Bn (155G, SP)
        537th AAA AW Bn (Mbl)
        135th Eng C Bn
        B & C/81st Cml Mtr Bn
5th ID (+)—Maj. Gen. S. Leroy Irwin
    (XII Corps, 21 Dec)
    Attached:
        737th Tk Bn
        654th TD Bn (SP)
        449th AAA AW Bn (Mbl)
95th ID—Maj. Gen. H. L. Twaddle
XII Corps—Maj. Gen. Manton S. Eddy
    Corps Troops:
        B/609th TD Bn (SP)

191st FA Bn (155H, T)	215th FA Bn (155H, T)
244th FA Bn (−) (155G, T)	273d FA Bn (155G, T)
276th FA Bn (105H, SP)	802d FA Bn (105H, T)
945th FA Bn (155H, T)	974th FA Bn (155H, T)
115th AAA Gun Bn (Mbl)	
452d AAA AW Bn (Mbl)	457th AAA AW Bn (Mbl)
91st Cml Mtr Bn	

6th AD (+)—Maj. Gen. Robert W. Grow
    (XX Corps, 21 Dec; XII Corps, 25 Dec; III Corps, 28 Dec)
    Attached:
        603d TD Bn (SP)
        777th AAA AW Bn (SP)
35th ID (+)—Maj. Gen. Paul W. Baade
    (Third Army, 23 Dec; XX Corps, 24 Dec; III Corps, 26 Dec)
    Attached:
        C/808th TD Bn (T)
        255th FA Bn (105H, T)
        448th AAA AW Bn (Mbl)
87th ID (+)—Brig. Gen. Frank L. Culin Jr.
    (XV Corps 29 Dec; XII Corps, 14 Jan 45)
    Attached:
        761st Tk Bn
        691st TD Bn
        549th AAA AW Bn (Mbl)

6th (U.S.) Army Group—Lt. Gen. Jacob L. Devers
    Seventh Army—Lt. Gen. Alexander M. Patch Jr.
        XV Corps—Maj. Gen. Wade H. Haislip
        VI Corps—Maj. Gen. Edward H. Brooks
    First (French) Army—Gen. J. de Lattre de Tassigny
        II Corps—Maj. Gen. G. de Montsabert
        I Corps—Lt. Gen. M. E. Bethouart

Allied Air Forces

United States Strategic Air Forces—Lt. Gen. Carl Spaatz
    Eighth Air Force (England)—Maj. Gen. James H. Doolittle
        1st Bomb Div (H)—Brig. Gen. Howard M. Turner
        2d Bomb Div (H)—Brig. Gen. William E. Kemper
        3d Bomb Div (H)—Maj. Gen. Earle E. Partridge
        VIII Fighter Command—Col. Benjamin J. Webster
    IX Troop Carrier Command (England)—Maj. Gen. Paul L. Williams
        (Under operational control of First Allied Airborne Army)
    Ninth Tactical Air Force (Continent)—Lt. Gen. Hoyt S. Vandenberg
        9th Bomb Div (M)—Maj. Gen. Samuel E. Anderson
            98th Bomb Wing (M)
                323d Bomb Group (M)
                    453d, 454th, 455th, 456th Bomb Sq (M)
                387th Bomb Group (M)
                    556th, 557th, 558th, 559th Bomb Sq (M)
                384th Bomb Group (M)
                    584th, 585th, 586th, 587th Bomb Sq (M)
                387th Bomb Group (M)
                    596th, 597th, 598th, 599th Bomb Sq (M)
            99th Bomb Wing (M)
                322d Bomb Group (M)
                    449th, 450th, 451st, 452d Bomb Sq (M)
                344th Bomb Group (M)
                    494th, 495th, 496th, 497th Bomb Sq (M)
                386th Bomb Group (M)
                    552d, 553d, 554th, 555th Bomb Sq (M)
                391st Bomb Group (M)
                    572d, 573d, 574th, 575th Bomb Sq (M)
            97th Bomb Wing (L)
                409th Bomb Group (L)
                    640th, 641st, 642d, 643d Bomb Sq (L)
                410th Bomb Group (L)
                    644th, 645th, 646th, 647th Bomb Sq (L)
                416th Bomb Group (L)
                    668th, 669th, 670th, 671st Bomb Sq (L)
        IX TAC (supporting First Army)—Maj. Gen. Elwood R. Quesada
            70th Fighter Wing

67th Tac Rcn Group
   12th, 15th, 30th, 107th, 109th, 153d Tac Rcn Sq
352d Fighter Group*
   328th, 486th, 487th Fighter Sq
365th Fighter Group
   386th, 387th, 388th Fighter Sq
366th Fighter Group
   389th, 390th, 391st Fighter Sq
367th Fighter Group
   392d, 393d, 394th Fighter Sq
368th Fighter Group
   395th, 396th, 397th Fighter Sq
370th Fighter Group
   401st, 402d, 485th Fighter Sq
474th Fighter Group
   428th, 429th, 430th Fighter Sq
422d Night Fighter Sq
XIX TAC (supporting Third Army)—Brig. Gen. Otto P. Weyland
   100th Fighter Wing
   354th Fighter Group
      353d, 355th, 356th Fighter Sq
   361st Fighter Group*
      374th, 375th, 376th Fighter Sq
   362d Fighter Group
      377th, 378th, 379th Fighter Sq
   405th Fighter Group
      509th, 510th, 511th Fighter Sq
   406th Fighter Group
      512th, 513th, 514th Fighter Sq
   10th Photo Rcn Group
      12th, 15th, 31st, 34th, 155th Photo Rcn Sq
   425th Night Fighter Sq
XXIX TAC (supporting Ninth Army)—Maj. Gen. Richard E. Nugent
   303d Fighter Wing
   36th Fighter Group
      22d, 23d, 53d Fighter Sq
   48th Fighter Group
      492d, 493d, 494th, 495th Fighter Sq
   373d Fighter Group
      410th, 411th, 412th Fighter Sq
   404th Fighter Group
      506th, 507th, 508th Fighter Sq
   363d Tac Rcn Group
      160th, 161st, 162d, 380th, 381st, 382d Rcn Sq

*Augmentation from Eighth U.S. Air Force

First (Prov) Tactical Air Force (Southern France)—Maj. Gen. Ralph Royce
    XII TAC (supporting Seventh Army)—Brig. Gen. Gordon P. Saville
    I (French) Air Corps (supporting First [French] Army)—Brig. Gen.
    Paul Geradot
    Fifteenth Air Force (Italy)—Maj. Gen. Nathan F. Twining
Royal Air Force—Air Chief Marshal Sir Douglas Portal
    Bomber Command (England)—Air Marshal Sir Arthur Harris
    Fighter Command (England)—Air Marshal R. M. Hill
    Second Tactical Air Force (Continent)—Air Marshal Sir Arthur Coningham
        34th Rcn Wing
            16th, 69th, 140th Rcn Sq
      No. 2 Bomber Group
        136th Wing
            418th (RCAF), 605th Sq
        137th Wing
            226th, 342d (French) Sq
        138th Wing
            107th, 305th (Polish), 613th Sq
        139th Wing
            98th, 180th, 320th (Dutch) Sq
        140th Wing
            21st, 461st (RAAF), 487th (RNZAF) Sq
      No. 83 Group (supporting Second [British] Army)
        39th (RCAF) Rcn Wing
            400th, 414th, 430th Sq
        121st Wing
            175th, 184th, 245th Sq
        122d Wing
            3d, 56th, 80th, 486th (RNZAF), 616th Sq
        124th Wing
            137th, 181st, 182d, 247th Sq
        125th Wing
            41st, 130th, 350th (Belgian) Sq
        126th (RCAF) Wing
            401st, 402d, 411th, 412th Sq
        127th (RCAF) Wing
            403d, 416th, 421st, 443d Sq
        143d (RCAF) Wing
            438th, 439th, 440th Sq
      No. 84 Group (supporting First [Canadian] Army)
        35th Rcn Wing
            2d, 4th, 168th Sq
        123d Wing
            164th, 183d, 198th, 609th Sq
        131st (Polish) Wing
            302d, 308th, 317th Sq
        132d Wing
            66th (Norwegian), 127th, 322d (Dutch) Sq

135th Wing
    33d, 222d, 274th, 349th (Belgian) Sq
145th (French) Wing
    74th, 340th (French), 341st (French), 345th (French), 485th
    (RNZAF) Sq
146th Wing
    193d, 197th, 263d, 266th Sq
No. 85 Group
    148th Wing
        264th, 409th (RCAF) Night Fighter Sq
    149th Wing
        219th, 410th (RCAF), 488th (RCAF) Night Fighter Sq

III. GERMAN ORDER OF BATTLE

OKW—ADOLF HITLER

OKW Reserve

3d PzGrenD—Genmaj. Walter Denkert
    (II SS Pz Corps, 19 Dec; LXVII Corps, 22 Dec; Fifth Pz Army,
    27 Dec; XXXIX Pz Corps, 28 Dec; XLVII Pz Corps, 29 Dec; II
    SS Pz Corps, 13 Jan; LXVI Corps, 16 Jan)

Führer Begleit Brigade—Obst. Otto Remer
    (Army Group B, 17 Dec; LXVI Corps, 18 Dec; LXXXV Corps,
    20 Dec; Sixth Pz Army, 25 Dec; LVIII Pz Corps, 26 Dec; XLVII
    Pz Corps, 27 Dec; 3d PzGrenD, 30 Dec; XLVII Pz Corps, 31
    Dec; Fifth Pz Army, 12 Jan; LVIII Pz Corps, 14 Jan)

Führer Grenadier Brigade—Obst. Hans-Joachim Kahler
    (Army Group B, 19 Dec; LIII Corps, 25 Dec; Fifth Pz Army, 31
    Dec; LIII Corps, 6 Jan; Army Group B, 12 Jan)

167th VGD (−)—Genlt. Hans-Kurt Höcker
    (LIII Corps, 24 Dec; Fifth Pz Army, 27 Dec; XXXIX Pz Corps,
    28 Dec; LIII Corps, 31 Dec; XXXIX Pz Corps, 2 Jan;
    Korpsgrüppe Decker, 5 Jan; LIII Corps, 9 Jan; LVIII Pz Corps,
    12 Jan)
    Detached:
        2d/167th Pz Jäg Bn
            (rejoined division c. 7 Jan)
        3d/167th Pz Jäg Bn

150th Pz Bde—SS-Obersturmbannführ. Otto Skorzeny (withdrawn 2
Jan 45)

Combat Group von der Heydte—Obst lt. Friedrich von der Heydte

10th SS PzD "Frundsberg" (−) (+)—SS- Brigführ. Heinz Harmel
    (Army Group G, 5 Jan)
    Attached:
        655th Hvy Pz Jäg Bn

6th SS MtnD—SS-Gruppenführ. Karl H. Brenner
    (Army Group G, c. 26 Dec)

257th VGD—Obst. Erich Seidel
(Army Group G, 16 Dec)
9th VGD
11th PzD

OB WEST—GENFELDM. GERD VON RUNDSTEDT
Army Group H—Genobst. Kurt Student
Twenty-fifth Army—Gen. d.Flieg. Friedrich
Christiansen
LXXXVIII Corps: Gen d.Inf Reinhard
First Parachute Army—Gen d.Fallsch. Schlemm
LXXXVI Corps: Gen d.Inf Püchler
II Parachute Corps—Genlt. Eugen Meindl
Army Group B—Genfeldm. Walter Model
Army Group B reserve:
79th VGD—Obst. Alois Weber
(Seventh Army, 20 Dec; LXXXV Corps, 22 Dec; LIII Corps, 12
Jan)
Enroute to Army Group B:
XXXIX Pz Corps (Korpsgruppe Decker)—Genlt. Karl Decker
(Fifth Pz Army, 23 Dec; XLVII Pz Corps, 28
Dec; Fifth Pz Army, 31 Dec)
11th PzD—Genlt. Wend von Wietersheim
(Army Group B, 22 Dec; Army Group G, 13 Jan)
9th VGD—Obst. Werner Kolb
(LIII Corps, 24 Dec)
Army group troops:
749th RR Art Bty
813th Pz Eng Co
5th OT Bde
921st, 956th, 969th, 1009th Brücko B [GE]
973th Brücko J [GE]
Fifteenth Army—Gen. d.Inf. Gustav von Zangen
Army troops:
506th Hvy Pz Bn
341st StG Bde
1513th Fst Art Bn
1st Flak Bde
2d OT Bde
885th, 922d Brücko B [GE]
914th Brücko J [GE]
XII SS Corps—Gen. d.Inf. Günther Blumentritt
Corps troops:
407th VAK [t-mot]
434th Eng Bn [t-mot]
176th ID—Obst. Landau
59th ID—Genlt. Poppe

(Korpsgruppe Felber, 26 Dec; XII SS Corps, 2 Jan)
340th VGD—Obst. Theodor Tolsdorff
    (Korpsgruppe Felber, 18 Dec; Fifth Pz Army, 26 Dec; XLVII Pz
    Corps, 31 Dec; I SS Pz Corps, 2 Jan; LVIII Pz Corps, 11 Jan)
XII SS Corps reserve:
9th PzD—Genmaj. Harald von Elverfeldt
    (Fifth Pz Army, 18 Dec; XLVII Pz Corps, 23 Dec; LVIII Pz
    Corps, 29 Dec; XLVII Pz Corps, 7 Jan)
15th PzGrenD—Obst. Hans-Joachim Deckert
    (Fifth Pz Army, 18 Dec; XLVII Pz Corps, 23 Dec; XLVII Pz
    Corps, 5 Jan; LXVI Corps, 15 Jan)
LXXXI Corps—Gen. d.Inf. Friederich Köchling
  Corps troops:
    1076th Fst Art Bty
    1301st, 1310th Fst Art Bn
    403d, 409th VAK [t-mot]
    224th Flak Bn
    16th Pz Eng Bn (replacement-training)
    7th Army Hvy Mtr Bn
  47th VGD (+)—Genlt. Max Bork
    (withdrawn 4 Jan 45)
  Attached:
    301st Hvy Pz Bn [FKL]
    319th Pz Co [FKL]
    682d Pz Jäg Bn [mot]
    Fst Pak Co 17/X
  246th VGD—Obst. Peter Körte
    (LXXIV Corps, 18 Dec; LXVII Corps, 24 Dec; LXXIV Corps,
    3 Jan)
  363d VGD (+)—Genlt. Augustin Detling
  Attached:
    627th Volga Tatar Bn
    Fst Pak Co 18/X
LXXIV Corps—Gen. d.Inf. Püchler
  Corps troops:
    628th Art Bn [bo]
    III/139th, 843d, 992d, 1193d Art
    Bn [mot]
  344th ID—Genmaj. König
    (LXXXI Corps, 21 Dec; withdrawn 27 Dec)
  353d ID (−) (+)—Obst. Koppenwallner
    (LXXXI Corps, 20 Dec)
  Attached:
    501st Fst Pak Bn
  Detached:
    1st/353d Pz Jäg Bn
  85th ID (−) (+)—Obst. Bechler
  Attached:

1st/"Hermann Göring" FJ Rgt
6th FJ Rgt
Detached:
    2d/185th Pz Jäg Bn
    3d/185th Pz Jäg Bn
89th ID (−) (+)—Genmaj. Walter Bruns
    (LXVII Corps, 27 Dec)
Attached:
    Fst Pak Co 54/X
    1308th Fst Art Bn
    170th Flak Co
Detached:
    2d/189th Pz Jäg Bn
      (rejoined division c. 22 Dec)
Sixth Panzer Army—SS Oberstgruppenführ. Josef Dietrich
    Army troops:
        8th FJ Rgt/3d FJD (en route from LXXXI Corps)
        667th StG Bde (en route)
        217th Sturm Pz Bn (en route)
        1000th, 1001st Sturm Mörser Co (en route)
        428th Art Bn [bo]
        2d, 4th Flak Sturm Rgt
        59th, 98th, 655th Eng Bn [t-mot]
        62d, 73d Eng Bn [mot]
        4th OT Bde
        1st/403d, 2d/406th, 602d Brücko B [mot]
        967th, 968th Brücko B [GE]
        844th, 851st, 895th Brücko J [mot]
        175th Brücko J [GE]
LXVII Corps—Genlt. Otto Hitzfeld
    (Fifteenth Army, 27 Dec)
    Corps troops:
        394th, 902d StG Bde (en route from Fifteenth Army)
        683d Pz Jäg Bn [mot]
        1100th Art Bn [bo]
        17th VWB [t-bew]
        403d, 405th VAK [t-mot]
272d VGD—Obst. George Kosmala
    (LXXIV Corps, 19 Dec)
326th VGD (−)—Obst. Erwin Kaschner
    (LXXIV Corps, 21 Dec; Korpsgruppe Felber, 4 Jan; XIII Corps,
    13 Jan)
Detached:
    3d/326th Pz Jäg Bn
I SS Pz Corps—SS-Gruppenführ. Hermann Priess
    (Fifth Pz Army, 31 Dec; Sixth Pz Army, 13 Jan 45)
    Corps troops:
        1098th, 1120th Art Bty [bo]

1123d Fst Art Bty
4th VWB [mot]
388th, 402d VAK [mot]
501st, 502d SS Art Bn [mot]
3d Flak Sturm Rgt (−)
277th VGD (+)—Obst. Wilhelm Viebig
(LXVII Corps; 18 Dec)
Attached:
9th SS Pz Art Rgt/9th SS PzD
12th VGD—Genmaj. Gerhard Engel
(LXVII Corps, 18 Dec; II SS Pz Corps, 19 Dec; LXVII Corps, 22
Dec; II SS Pz Corps, 30 Dec; LXVI Corps, 2 Jan; II SS Pz Corps,
15 Jan; LXVI Corps, 16 Jan)
3d FJD—Genmaj. Walther Wadehn
(LXVII Corps, 18 Dec; II SS Pz Corps, 19 Dec; LXVII Corps, 23
Dec) 519th Hvy Pz Jäg Bn (en route)
I SS Pz Corps reserve:
12th SS PzD "Hitlerjugend" (+)—SS-Standartenführ. Hugo Kraas
(II SS Pz Corps, 20 Dec; I SS Pz Corps, 23 Dec; II SS Pz Corps,
26 Dec; I SS Pz Corps, 31 Dec; Sixth Pz Army, 9 Jan; AG B, 10
Jan)
Attached:
560th Hvy Pz Jäg Bn
14th Werf Rgt/9th VWB [mot]
1st SS PzD "Leibstandarte Adolf Hitler" (+)—SS-Oberführ.
Wilhelm Mohnke
(XXXIX Pz Corps, 30 Dec; I SS Pz Corps, 3 Jan; Korpsgruppe
Decker, 5 Jan; LVIII Pz Corps, 11 Jan)
Attached:
501st SS Hvy Pz Bn
12th Werf Rgt/9th VWB [mot]
84th Lt Flak Bn
Sixth Panzer Army reserve:
II SS Pz Corps—SS-Obergruppenführ. Willi Bittrich
Corps troops:
502d SS Werf Bn [mot]
2d SS PzD "Das Reich"—SS-Brigführ. Heinz Lammerding
(Fifth Pz Army, 19 Dec; LVIII Pz Corps,
22 Dec; II SS Pz Corps, 23 Dec; LXVI
Corps, 10 Jan; II SS Pz Corps, 13 Jan)
9th SS PzD "Hohenstaufen" (−)—SS-Oberführ. Sylvester Stadler
(Fifth Pz Army, 19 Dec; I SS Pz Corps, 20 Dec; II SS Pz Corps,
23 Dec; I SS Pz Corps, 31 Dec; Sixth Pz Army, 5 Jan; II SS Pz
Corps, 6 Jan; LXVI Corps, 10 Jan; XIII Corps, 13 Jan)
Detached:
9th SS Pz Art Rgt
Fifth Pz Army—Gen. d.Pz.Tr. Hasso von Manteuffel
Army troops:

105th, 104th OT Rgt
894th, 897th, 957th Brücko J [GE]

LXVI Corps—Gen. d.Art. Walter Lucht
    (Sixth Pz Army, 22 Dec; Fifth Pz Army, 16 Jan)
  Corps troops:
    1099th Art Bn [bo]
    16th VWB [t-bew]
    10th SS Pz Art Rgt (−)/10th SS PzD
    10th SS Flak Bn/10th SS PzD
    803d Eng Bn [t-mot]
    1st/4th OT Rgt
    22d Brücko B [mot]
  18th VGD (+)—Genmaj Günther Hoffmann-Schönborn
    (Korpsgruppe Felber, 2 Jan; XIII Corps, 13 Jan)
    Attached:
      244th StG Bde
      460th Art Bn [mot]
      74th Lt Flak Bn
  62d VGD (−)—Obst. Friedrich Kittel
    (Korpsgruppe Felber, 2 Jan; XIII Corps, 13 Jan)
    Detached:
      3d/162d Pz Jäg Bn

LVIII Pz Corps—Gen. d.Pz.Tr. Walter Krüger
  Corps troops:
    116th Pz Aufkl Bn/116th PzD
    1125th Art Bty [t-bew]
    1121st Art Bn [bo]
    1350th Fst Art Bty
    401st VAK [mot]
    7th VWB [mot]
    1st Flak Sturm Rgt
    207th Eng Bn [mot]
    2d/4th OT Rgt
    4th, 850th Brücko B [mot]
  116th PzD (−)—Genmaj. Siegfried von Waldenburg
    (II SS Pz Corps, 3 Jan; LXVI Corps, 14 Jan)
  560th VGD (−)—Obst. Rudolf Bader
    (II SS Pz Corps, 28 Dec; LXVI Corps, 1 Jan; II SS Pz Corps, 11
    Jan; LXVI Corps, 13 Jan)
    Detached: (all rejoined the division c. 28 Dec)
      2d/1560th Pz Jäg Bn
      3d/1560th Pz Jäg Bn
      1st/1560th Art Rgt
      4th/1560th Art Rgt
      1129th Gren Rgt
      2d/1560th Eng Bn

XLVII Pz Corps—Gen. d.Pz.Tr. Heinrich von Lüttwitz
  Corps troops:

1119th Art Bn [bo]
766th VAK (−) [mot]
15th VWB (−) [mot]
182d Flak Sturm Rgt
22d OT Rgt
1st/409th Brücko B [mot]
846th Brücko J [mot]
2d PzD (+)—Obst. Meinrad von Lauchert
(LVIII Pz Corps, 30 Dec; XLVII Pz Corps, 5 Jan; Fifth Pz Army, 14 Jan)
Attached:
1124th Art Bty [t-bew]
5th/766th VAK
6th/766th VAK
Bty/15th VWB
600th Eng Bn [mot]
26th VGD 26 (+)—Obst. Heinz Kokott
(I SS Pz Corps, 2 Jan; LVIII Pz Corps, 11 Jan; XLVII Pz Corps, 15 Jan)
Attached:
2 Cos/130th Pz Aufkl Bn/130th "Lehr" PzD
Bty/15th VWB
1st/766th VAK
XLVII Pz Corps reserve:
130th Pz Lehr D (−) (+)—Genlt. Fritz Bayerlein
Detached:
1st/130th Pz Rgt
Attached:
559th Hvy Pz Jäg Bn
243d StG Bde
2d/766th VAK
4th/766th VAK
Bty/15th VWB
Seventh Army—Gen. d.Pz.Tr. Erich Brandenberger
Army troops:
660th Art Bty [bo]
15th Flak Rgt
47th Eng Bde [mot]
1st OT Bde
605th Brücko-Bau Bn
964th, 965th, 966th, 981st Brücko B [GE]
974th Brücko J [GE]
Seventh Army reserve:
316th Gren Rgt/212th VGD
LXXXV Corps—Gen. d.Inf. Baptist Kniess
(withdrawn 12 Jan)
Corps troops
668th Pz Jäg Bn [mot]

1092d Art Bty [t-bew]
1094th Art Bn [t-bew]
18th VWB (−) [t-bew]
406th VAK (−) [t-mot]
5th FJ Art Rgt (−)/5th FJD
LXXXV Corps reserve:
13th FJ Rgt/5th FJD
5th FJD (−) (+)—Obst. Ludwig Heilmann
(LIII Corps, 21 Dec; LVIII Pz Corps, 13 Jan)
Attached:
11th FJ StG Bde
1st, 2d, & 3d/406th VAK
Bn/18th VWB
Bn/18th VWB
Detached:
5th FJ Werf Bn
2d/5th FJ Pz Jäg Bn
352d VGD (−)—Obst. Erich Schmidt
(LXXXV Corps, 12 Jan)
Detached:
3d/352d Pz Jäg Bn
LXXX Corps—Gen. d.Inf. Franz Beyer
Corps troops:
1095th Art Bn [t-bew]
1122d Art Bn [bo]
1093d Art Bty [t-bew]
8th VWB [t-bew]
408th VAK [t-mot]
276th VGD (−)—Genmaj. Kurt Möhring
(LIII Corps, 3 Jan)
Detached:
3d/276th Pz Jäg Bn
212th VGD (−) (+)—Genlt. Franz Sensfuss
Attached:
657th Pz Jäg Bn [mot]
Detached:
3d/212th Pz Jäg Bn
LIII Corps—Gen. d.Kav. Edwin von Rothkirch
Corps troops (no divisions assigned until 21 Dec):
44th Fst MG Bn
XXIII Fst Inf Bn
212th FEB/212th VGD 212
5th FEB/5th FJD
Army Group G—Gen. d. Pz.Tr. Hermann Balck (24 Dec, Genobst.
Johannes Blaskowitz)
LXXXIX Corps—Gen d.Inf Höhne
First Army—Gen. d.Inf. Hans von Obstfelder
LXXXII Corps—Genlt. Hahn

XIII SS Corps
XC Corps—Gen d.Flieg. Petersen
Army Group Oberrhein—SS-Reichsführ. Heinrich Himmler
XIV SS Corps
XVIII SS Corps
Nineteenth Army—Gen. d.Inf. Rasp
LXIV Corps—Genlt. Thumm
LXIII Corps—Genlt. Abraham
Formed during the battle:
Corps Group Felber—Gen. d.Inf. Hans Felber
(formed 18 Dec, assigned to Fifteenth Army; Sixth Pz Army, 30 Dec; redesignated XIII Corps, 13 Jan 45)
Corps Group Decker
(formed 5 Jan, from elements of LVIII Pz Corps and XXXIX Pz Corps, assigned to Fifth Pz Army; disbanded 11 Jan)

LUFTWAFFE ORDER OF BATTLE
LUFTWAFFENKOMMANDO WEST—GENLT. JOSEF SCHMIDT
Jagdkorps II—Genmaj. Dietrich Peltz
Jagddivision 3—Genmaj. Walter Grabmann
JG 1 (3 squadrons—FW-190, Bf-109)
JG 3 (4 squadrons—FW-190, Bf-109)
JG 6 (3 squadrons—FW-190, Bf-109)
JG 26 (3 squadrons—FW-190, Bf-109)
JG 27 (4 squadrons—Bf-109)
JG IV/54 (1 squadron—FW-190, Bf-109)
JG 77 (3 squadrons—Bf-109)
Jagdabschnitt Mittelrhein—Obst. Trübenbach
JG 2 (3 squadrons—FW-190, Bf-109)
JG 4 (4 squadrons—FW-190, Bf-109)
JG 11 (3 squadrons—FW-190, Bf-109)
JG 53 (3 squadrons—Bf-109)
JG III/54 (1 squadron—FW-190, Bf-109)
SG 4 (3 squadrons—FW-190)
Fliegerdivision 3
KG 51 (elements—Me-262)
KG 66 (elements—Ju-88, Ju-188)
KG 76 (elements—Ar-234)
NJG 2 (elements—Ju-88)
NSGr 1 (elements—Ju-87)
NSGr 2 (elements—Ju-87)
NSGr 20 (elements—FW-190)

IV. THE FRONT
16 DECEMBER 1944

A. THE SIXTH PANZER ARMY ATTACK

American	*German*

1. The Monschau-Höfen Sector

First Army	*Sixth Panzer Army*

V Corps
  102d Cav Grp (−)
    38th Cav Sq
      Plt/C/893d TD Bn (SP)
    Supporting the 38th Cav Sq:
      62d Arm FA Bn (105mm, SP)
  99th ID (elms):
    3d/395th Inf
    A/612th TD Bn (T)
    Supporting the 3d/395th Inf:
    196th FA Bn (105mm, T)

LXVII Corps
  326th VGD (−) (+)
    KG (Monschau):
      1st/752d Gren Rgt
      326th Fus Co
    KG (Höfen):
      1st/751st Gren Rgt
      1st/753d Gren Rgt
      326th Pz Jäg Bn
      326th Art Rgt (−)
      326th Eng Bn
  Supporting the 326th VGD:
    683d Pz Jäg Bn (mot)
    405th VAK (t-mot)
    Rgt/17th VMB (t-bew)

2. The Wahlerscheid Sector

2d ID (+)
  99th Rcn Trp
  2d Rcn Trp
  38th RCT (38th Inf [−]):
    B/741st Tk Bn
    C/644th TD Bn (SP)
    38th FA Bn (105H, T)
  9th RCT (9th Inf [−]):
    A/741st Tk Bn
    A/644th TD Bn (SP)
    15th FA Bn (105H, T)
    C/987th FA Bn (155G, SP)
    612th TD Bn (T) (−)
  395th RCT (395th Inf (−), under 2d ID):
    Co/801st TD Bn
    924th FA Bn (105H, T)
  2d DIVARTY:
    12th FA Bn (155H, T)
    37th FA Bn (105H, T)
    Cn Co/9th Inf
    Cn Co/23d Inf
    Cn Co/39th Inf

326th VGD (elms)
  326th FEB
  1st Inf Bn
  elms/326th Art Rgt
277th VGD (elms)
  277th Fus Co
  277th FEB
  elms/277th Art Reg

Reinforcing the 2d DIVARTY:
    16th Arm FA Bn (105H, SP), 9th AD
    18th FA Bn (105H/4.5″ Rkt, T)
    B/200th FA Bn (155G, T)
2d Eng C Bn
462d AAA AW Bn (Mbl)
C/86th Chem Mtr Bn
2d ID reserve:
    23d Inf (−) (at Camp Elsenborn)
    741st Tk Bn (− A, B, C, & D)
    644th TD Bn (SP) (− A, B, & C)
Supporting the 2d ID:
    186th FA Bn (155mm, T)
    C/272d FA Bn (240mm, T)
    941st FA Bn (4.5″G, T)
    955th FA Bn (155mm, T)

3. The Krinkelt-Rocherath Sector

99th ID (−) (+)
    324th Eng C Bn
    393d RCT (393d Inf):
        Co/801st TD Bn (SP)
        370th FA Bn (105H, T)

Reserve
    CCB, 9th AD (−)
        27th Armd Inf Bn
        14th Tank Bn
        D/89th Cav Sqn (+)
        A/811th TD Bn (SP)
        B/482d AAA AW Bn (SP)
        A/811th TD Bn (SP)
        B/9th Arm Eng Bn

I SS Pz Corps
    277th VGD (−) (+)
        989th Gren Rgt
        990th Gren Rgt
        277th Pz Jäg Bn
        277th Art Rgt (−)
        Reinforcing the 277th Art Rgt:
        9th SS Pz Art Rgt/9th SS PzD
        227th Eng Bn
        277th VGD reserve:
            991st Gren Rgt

Reserve:
    I SS Pz Corps (for exploitation)
        KG 12th SS PzD:
            1st/25th SS Pz Gren Rgt (−)
        KG Müller 12th SS PzD:
            25th SS Pz Gren Rgt (−)
            12th SS Pz Jäg Bn
            2d/12th SS Pz Art Rgt
                2 Batts/12th SS Flak Bn
                1st Co/12th SS Pz Eng Bn

Supporting I SS Pz Corps:
    Werf Rgt/4th VWB

3d FJD (−) (+)
    5th FJ Rgt
    9th FJ Rgt (−)
    3d FJ Pz Jäg Bn
    3d FJ Art Rgt
    3d FEng Bn

3d FJ Hvy Mtr Bn
3d FJD reserve:
    Bn/9th FJ Rgt

Reserve:
I SS Pz Corps (for exploitation):
KG Peiper, 1st SS PzD
    3d/2d SS Pz Gren Rgt (−)
    1st SS Pz Rgt (−) (+):
        1st/1st SS Pz Rgt
        501st SS Hvy Pz Bn
    2d/1st SS Pz Art Rgt
    84th Lt Flak Bn
    3d Co/1st SS Pz Eng Bn
KG Hansen, 1st SS PzD:
    1st SS Pz Gren Rgt
    1st SS Pz Jäg Bn
    1st/1st SS Pz Art Rgt
        2 Batts/1st SS Flak Bn
        Co/1st SS Pz Eng Bn
I SS Pz Corps reserve:
1st SS Pz D (−)
    KG Sandig:
        2d SS Pz Gren Rgt (−)
        1st SS Pz Art Rgt (−)
        12th Werf Rgt/9th VWB
        1st SS Flak Bn (−)
        1st SS Pz Eng Bn (−)
    KG Knittel:
        1st SS Aufkl Bn
Supporting I SS Pz Corps
    1098th Art Bty (bo)
    1120th Afrt Bn (bo)
    1123d Fst Art Bty
    388th VAK (mot)
    402d VAK (mot)
    501st SS Art Bn
    502d SS Art Bn
    3d Flak Sturm Rgt (−)

Supporting Sixth Panzer Army:
    428th Art Bty (bo)
    749th Art Bty (from AG B)
    2d Flak Sturm Rgt
    4th Flak Sturm Rgt

Reserve:
Sixth Panzer Army reserve:
II SS Pz Corps
2d SS PzD
9th SS PzD (−)

4. The Losheimergraben Sector
(The I SS Panzer Corps Main Effort)

elms 99th Inf Div
  394th RCT (394th Inf [−]):
    Co/801st TD Bn
    371st FA Bn (105mm, T)
    801st TD Bn (T) (−)
  99th DIVARTY:
    372d FA Bn (155mm, T)
  Reinforcing the 99th DIVARTY:
    200th FA Bn (155G, T) (−)
    776th FA Bn (155H, T)
  535th AAA AW Bn (Mbl)
  D/86th Chem Mtr Bn
  99th ID Reserve:
    3d/394th Inf
    C and D/741st Tank Bn

12th VGD
  48th Gren Rgt
  27th Fus Rgt
  12th Pz Jäg Bn
  12th Art Rgt
  12th Eng Bn
    12th VGD reserve:
      89th Gren Rgt

Reserve:
  I SS Pz Corps (for exploitation):
    KG Kühlmann, 12th SS PzD:
      3d/26th SS Pz Rgt (+)
      12th SS Pz Rgt (−) (+)
      14th Werf Rgt/9th VWB (mot)
      12th SS Flak Bn (−)
      12th SS Eng Bn (−)
  KG Bremer:
    12th SS Aufkl Bn

B. THE FIFTH PANZER ARMY ATTACK

5. The Losheim Gap/Schnee Eifel Sector
(The Main Effort of the LXVI Corps)

VIII Corps
  106th ID (+)
    14th Cav Grp:
      18th Cav Sq (−)
      A/820th TD Bn (T)
        Rcn Plts/B & C/820th TD Bn (T)
    Supporting the 14th Cav Grp:
      275th Arm FA Bn (105H, SP)
    14th Cav Grp Reserve:
      32d Cav Sq

    422d RCT (422d Inf):
      589th FA Bn (105H, T)
      A/81st Eng C Bn
    106th DIVARTY:
      592d FA Bn (155H, T)
      D/634th AAA AW Bn (Mbl)

    423d RCT (423d Inf):
      B/18th Cav Sq
      C/820th TD Bn (T) (−)
      590th FA Bn (105H, T)
      B/634th AAA AW Bn (Mbl)
      B/81st Eng C Bn

LXVI Corps
  18th VGD (right wing)
    244th StG Bde
    294th Gren Rgt
    295th Gren Rgt
    18th FEB
    18th Art Rgt (−)
    Reinforcing the 18th Art Rgt:
    460th Art Bn (mot)
      18th VGD reserve:
      18th Fus Co
      18th Pz Jäg Bn (−)
      18th Eng Bn
  18th VGD (left wing)
    293d Gren Rgt
    elms/18th Pz Jäg Bn
    1st/18th Art Rgt
    74th Lt Flak Bn
  Supporting the 18th VGD:
    1099th Art Bn
    Werf Rgt/16th VWB
    10th SS Art Rgt (−)/
    10th SS PzD

Supporting the 106th ID:
  333d FA Bn (155H, T)
  771st FA Bn (4.5"G, T)
  770th FA Bn (4.5"G, T)
  965th FA Bn (155H, T)
  969th FA Bn (155H, T)
106th ID reserve:
  2d/423d Inf (at Born)
  81st Eng C Bn (−) (at St. Vith)

10th SS Flak Bn/10th
SS PzD

6. The Eigelscheid-Heckhuscheid Sector

elms 106 ID
  424th RCT (424th Inf (−):
    106th Rcn Trp
    B/820th TD Bn (T) (−)
    591st FA Bn (105H, T)
    C/81st Eng C Bn
  563d AAA AW Bn (Mbl)
  634th AAA AW Bn (Mbl) (−)
106th ID reserve (at Steinebrück):
  1st/424th Inf
Supporting the 106th ID (also
supported the 112th RCT, 28th ID):
  559th FA Bn (155G, T)
  561st FA Bn (155G, T)
  578th FA Bn (8"H, T)
  740th FA Bn (8"H, T)

62d VGD (−)
  189th Gren Rgt
  190th Gren Rgt
  162d Art Rgt
  62d VGD reserve:
    164th Gren Rgt
    162d Fus Co
    162d Pz Jäg Bn (−)
    162d Eng Bn
Supporting the 62d VGD:
  Werf Rgt/16th VWB

7. The Grosskampenberg-Sevenig Sector

28th ID (+):

  112th RCT (112th Inf):
    D/707th Tank Bn
    C/630th TD Bn (T)
    229th FA Bn (105H, T)
    C/447th AAA AW Bn (Mbl)
    C/103d Eng C Bn

VIII Corps reserve (at Trois Vierges):
CCR, 9th AD
  52d Arm Inf Bn
  2d Tk Bn
  C/89th Cav Sq (+)
  C/811th TD Bn
  C/482d AAA AW Bn (SP)
  C/9th Arm Eng Bn

LVIII Pz Corps
  116th PzD
    KG 60th Pz Gren Rgt:
      60th Pz Gren Rgt
      elms/16th Pz Rgt
      Bn/146th Pz Art Rgt
    KG 156th Pz Gren Rgt:
      156th Pz Gren Rgt
      elms/16th Pz Rgt
      Bn/146th Pz Art Rgt
  560th VGD
    KG Schumann:
      1130th Gren Rgt
      3d/1560th Art Rgt
    KG Schmidt:
      1128th Gren Rgt
      2d/1560th Art Rgt
      560th VGD reserve:
        560th Fus Co

1560th Pz Jäg Bn (−)
1560th Art Rgt
1560th Eng Bn (−)

Supporting the LVIII Panzer Corps:
401st VAK
7th VWB
1125th Art Bn (t-bew)
1121st Art Bn (bo)
1350th Fst Art Bty
1st Flak Sturm Rgt

Reserve:
LVIII Pz Corps reserve:
KG Stephan/116th PzD:
116th Pz Aufkl Bn
116th PzD (−)
KG Bayer:
16th Pz Rgt (−)
116th Pz Jäg Bn
146th Pz Eng Bn
146th Pz Art Rgt (−)

8. The Dasburg-Gemünd Sector

elms 28th ID:
110th RCT (110th Inf [−]):
28th Rcn Trp
B/630th TD Bn (T)
109th FA Bn (105H, T)
687th FA Bn (105H, T) (−)
B/447th AAA AW Bn (Mbl)
B/103d Eng C Bn

XLVII Pz Corps
2d PzD
KG Cochenhausen:
304th Pz Gren Rgt (−)
1st/3d Pz Rgt (−)
1st/74th Pz Art Rgt
Bty/273d Flak Bn
38th Pz Eng Bn (−)
KG von Böhm:
2d Pz Aufkl Bn
KG Gutmann:
2d Pz Gren Rgt (−)
1st Co/3d Pz Rgt
1st Co/38th Pz Jäg Bn
2d/74th Pz Art Rgt
Bty/15th VWB
Bty/273d Flak Bn
1st Co/38th Pz Eng Bn
2d PzD reserve:
KG Holtmeyer:
2d/2d Pz Gren Rgt
1st/304th Pz Gren Rgt
3d Pz Rgt (−)
38th Pz Jäg Bn (−)
74th Pz Art Rgt (−)

Reinforcing 74th Pz Art Rgt:
1124th Art Bty (t-bew)
5th & 6th/766th VAK
26th VGD
KG Kunkel:
26th Fus Bn
1st Co (SP)/26th Pz Jäg Bn
2d Co/130th Pz Aufkl
Bn/Pz Lehr D
Bty/1st/26th Art Rgt
Bty/15th VWB
2 Plts/26th Eng Bn
Main Body:
77th Gren Rgt
39th Fus Rgt
26th Eng Bn (−)
26th Art Rgt (−)
Reinforcing the 26th Art Rgt
1st/766th VAK
26th VGD reserve:
78th Gren Rgt
26th Pz Jäg Bn (−)
Supporting the XLVII Pz Corps:
1119th Art Bn (bo)
766th VAK (−) (mot)
15th VWB (−) (mot)
182d Flak Sturm Rgt

Reserve:
XLVII Pz Corps reserve:
Pz Lehr D (−)
KG von Fallois:
8th Co/130th Pz Rgt
3d Co/130th Pz Jäg Bn
130th Aufkl Bn (−)
4th Bty/130th Pz Art Rgt
Bty/15th VWN
Co/130th Pz Eng Bn
KG von Hauser:
901st Pz Gren Rgt
6th Co/130th Pz Rgt
243d StG Bde
2d/130th Pz Art Rgt (−)
Co/130th Pz Eng Bn
KG von Poschinger:
902d Pz Gren Rgt
130th Pz Rgt (−) (+):

                                                    5th & 7th Co/130th
                                                    Pz Rgt
                                                    559th Hvy Pz Jäg Bn (−)
                                                    130th Pz Jäg Bn (−)
                                                    130th Pz Art Rgt (−)
                                                    Reinforcing the 130th
                                                    Pz Art Rgt:
                                                      2d & 4th/766th VAK
                                                    130th Pz Eng Bn (−)
                                                    130th Flak Bn

C. THE SEVENTH ARMY ATTACK

9. The Kautenbach-Bettendorf Sector

Seventh Army

elms 28th ID

    109th RCT (109th Inf)
      C/707th Tk Bn
      A/630th TD Bn (T)
      107th FA Bn (105H, T)
      108th FA Bn (155H, T)
      A/447th AAA AW Bn (Mbl)
      A/103d Eng C Bn
28th ID reserve:
    2d/110th Inf
    707th Tk B (−)
    447th AAA AW Bn (Mbl) (−)

LXXXV Corps
  5th FJD (−) (+)
    14th FJ Rgt
      1st/406th VAK
      Bn/18th VWB
    15th FJ Rgt
      11th FJ StG Bde
      3d/406th VAK
      Bn/18th VWB
      4th/406th VAK
      5th FJ Pz Jäg Bn (−)
      5th FJ Eng Bn
  352 VGD (−)
    915th Gren Rgt
    915th 6th Gren Rgt
    352d Fus Co
    352d Pz Jäg Bn (−)
    352d Art Rgt
      352d VGD reserve:
      914th Gren Rgt
Supporting the LXXXV Corps:
  1092d Art Bty (t-bew)
  1094th Art Bn (t-bew)
  406th VAK (−)
  5th FJ Art Rgt (−), 5th FJD
  18th VWB (−) (t-bew)
  668th Pz Jäg Bn

      Reserve:
      LXXXV Corps reserve:
      13th FJ Rgt

10. The Bigelbach–Schwarz Ernz Sector

9th AD (–) (+)
  CCA:
    60th Arm Inf Bn
    3d Arm FA Bn (105mm, SP)
  CCA reserve:
    19th Tk Bn
    811th TD Bn (SP) (–)
    89th Cav Sq (–)
    482d AAA AW Bn (SP)
    9th Arm Eng Bn (–)

LXXX Korps
  276th VGD
    986th Gren Rgt
    988th Gren Rgt
    276th Pz Jäg BN (–)
    276th Art Rgt
    276th Eng Bn
  276th VGD Reserve
    987th Gren Rgt

11. The Berdorf-Echternach Sector

4th ID (elms) (+)

  12th RCT (12th Inf):
    42d AFA Bn (105H, SP)
  4th DIVARTY:
    29th FA Bn (155H, T)
  Reinforcing the 4th DIVARTY:
    81st FA Bn (155H, T)
    174th FA Bn (155G, SP)
  802d TD BN (T)
  803d TD Bn (SP)
  377th AAA AW Bn (SP)
  4th ID reserve:
    70th Tank Bn (refitting)
    4th Rcn Trp
    4th Eng C Bn

212th VGD
  423d Gren Rgt
  320th Gren Rgt
  212th Pz Jäg Bn
  657th Pz Jäg Bn (mot)
  212th Art Rgt
212th Eng Bn
  Supporting the LXXX Corps:
    1085th Art Bn (t-bew)
    1122d Art Bn (bo)
    1093d Art Bty (t-bew)
    660th Art Bty (bo)
    408th VAK
    8th VWB

Reserve:
  Seventh Army Reserves
    316th Gren Rgt/212th VGD

V. NOTES ON THE ORDERS OF BATTLE

GENERAL

The Allied Order of Battle covers two time periods, 16–19 December 1944 and 20 December 1944–16 January 1945. This was done to facilitate understanding of the profound change in the Allied command that occurred on 20 December.

The 16–19 December Order of Battle shows the assignment of divisions, corps, armies, and army groups under General Eisenhower's command at the beginning of the battle. Each entry lists the unit, followed by subordinate commands (each command level is indented to clearly show the subordination). For each unit the commander's name and rank follow its name; changes in command are shown on the next line. The final line gives changes of assignment for the unit. The change of assignment is noted by a higher formation name and a date: For example, XXX Corps, 20 Dec indicates that the unit was assigned to the XXX Corps on 20 December 1944.

All Allied army groups, armies, and corps (as well as divisions for the 12th Army Group) are shown in order from north to south along the front of the European Theater. All units that participated directly in the battle are highlighted in *italics*. (Those units that participated in the early stages of the battle are italicized for 16–19 December. However, if a unit did not participate in the latter stages of the battle, then it is not italicized for 20 December 1944–16 January 1945.) Units of the 21st and 6th Army groups are shown by army and corps only, except for those units that participated directly in the battle.

The 20 December 1944–16 January 1945 Order of Battle also lists the major non-divisional combat and combat-support formations that took an active part in the battle. Nondivisional units (except for a cavalry group and armored and tank brigades) were not shown in the 16–19 December Order of Battle for reasons of brevity. Instead, the opposing Allied and German forces in the Ardennes on 16 December are shown in section IV of this appendix, which illustrates, in diagrammatic form, the front-line dispositions and the organization for combat of the two contending sides in the various sectors of the Ardennes front, between Monschau-Höfen in the north and Wasserbillig-Echternach in the south. All nondivisional units are shown as "attached" if assigned to a division or as "army group," "army," or "corps" troops if assigned to an army or corps. Most of the U.S. group and brigade headquarters formations (Armor, Tank Destroyer, Artillery, AAA, and Engineers) are not shown; the sole exception is the cavalry groups. Although some of these formations remained relatively stable in composition, most of them frequently shifted subordinate battalions during the course of the battle. Thus, most are eliminated here for clarity and brevity. Similarly, the frequent changes of attachment (from division to division, division to corps, corps to corps, etc.) of the nondivisional formations are not shown. (A complete dissection of the various changes in attachment during the battle would double the length of this book.)

The German Order of Battle covers the period 16 December 1944–16 January 1945 with changes noted in the same manner as for the Allied Order of Battle. Some German divisions are followed by the notation "detached," which indicates that an organic element of the division was not present at the start of the battle (many had not completed organizing or equipping). A note is made if the unit joined its parent division during the battle.

KEY TO ALLIED ABBREVIATIONS

AAA   antiaircraft artillery

AAA AW   antiaircraft artillery, automatic weapons

Abn   airborne

AD   armored division

Arm   armored

AT   antitank

Bde   brigade

Bn   battalion

Bty   battery (artillery)

Brig. Gen.   Brigadier General

Capt.   Captain

Cav   cavalry

Cml Mtr   chemical mortar

Co   company

Col.   Colonel

COM-Z Communications Zone
Div division
Eng engineer
Eng C Bn engineer combat battalion
Eng G/S Rgt engineer general-service regiment
FA field artillery
Fld Co RE field company, Royal Engineers (British)
Fld Prk Co RE field park (light equipment) company, Royal Engineers (British)
Gen. General
GIB glider infantry battalion
GIR glider infantry regiment
Gld FA Bn glider field artillery battalion
Grp group
H or Hvy heavy
HAA heavy antiaircraft (British)
HC Household Cavalry (Regiment) (British)
ID infantry division
Inf infantry
L or Lt light
LAA light antiaircraft (British)
1st Lt. First Lieutenant
2d Lt. Second Lieutenant
Lt. Col. Lieutenant Colonel
Lt. Gen. Lieutenant General
M or Med medium
Maj. Major
Maj. Gen. Major General
Mbl mobile
MX mine-exploder
Para Eng Co parachute engineer company
Para FA Bn parachute field artillery
PIB parachute infantry battalion
PIR parachute infantry regiment
Prov Provisional
RA Royal Artillery (British)
RAAF Royal Australian Air Force (British Commonwealth)
RAC Royal Armored Corps (British)
RAF Royal Air Force (British)
RCAF Royal Canadian Air Force (British Commonwealth)
Rcn reconnaissance (U.S.)
RE Royal Engineers (British)
Recce reconnaissance (British)
Rgt regiment
RNZAF Royal New Zealand Air Force (British Commonwealth)
Sep Separate
SHAEF Supreme Headquarters, Allied Expeditionary Forces
SM semimobile
SP self-propelled

Sq   squadron
T   towed
TD   tank destroyer
Tk   tank

KEY TO GERMAN ABBREVIATIONS
Bde   brigade
bew   beweglich (mobile)
Bn   battalion
bo   bodenständig (immobile, stationary)
Brücko B [GE]   light bridge equipment column
Brücko B [mot]   motorized light bridging column
Brücko J [GE]   heavy bridge equipment column
Brücko J [mot]   motorized heavy bridging column
Bty   battery (artillery)
Eng   engineer
FEB   Feld Ersatz Battalion (field replacement battalion)
FJD   Fallschirmjäger Division (Luftwaffe parachute division)
FKL   Funklenk (radio-controlled demolitions)
Flak   Flieger Abwehr Kanone (antiaircraft gun)
Fliegerdivision   air division (Luftwaffe)
Fst   Festung (fortress)
Führer Begleit   Hitler's (literally leader's) escort
Fus   Fusilier (the recon/mobile reserve element in the ID and VGD; also, an
      honorific given to various infantry units)
Genfeldm.   Generalfeldmarschall
Genlt.   Generalleutnant
Genmaj.   Generalmajor
Genobst.   Generaloberst
Gren   Grenadier (an honorific given to various infantry units)
Jagdabschnitt   fighter detachment (Luftwaffe)
JG   Jagdgeschwader (Luftwaffe; fighter unit equivalent in size to U.S. group)
Kampfgruppe Combat Group   an ad hoc combat team of indefinite size
Korpsgruppe (Corps Group)   an ad hoc corps-size task force
KG   Kampfgeschwader (Luftwaffe; bomber unit equivalent in size to U.S. group)
Luftwaffe   the German Air Force; controls both air and ground formations
mot   motorisiert (motorized)
MtnD   Mountain Division
NJG   Nachtjagdgeschwader (Luftwaffe; night-fighter unit equivalent in size to U.S.
      group)
NSGr   Nachtschlachtgruppe (Luftwaffe; night ground attack unit equivalent in size
      to U.S. squadron)
Obst.   Oberst
OB West   Oberbefehlshaber West (Commander in chief West)
OT   Organisation Todt (paramilitary construction troops)
PAK   Panzer Abwehr Kanone (antitank gun)
Pz   Panzer (armored)
Pz Aufkl   Panzer Aufklärung (armored reconnaissance)

PzD   Panzer Division (armored division)
PzGrenD   Panzer Grenadier Division (motor/mechanized infantry division)
Pz Jäg   antitank (literally tank hunter)
Rgt   regiment
RR   railroad
SG   Schlachtgeschwader (Luftwaffe; ground-attack unit equivalent in size to U.S. group)
SS   Schutzstaffel (literally guard section)
StG   Sturmgeschütz (assault gun)
Sturm   assault (literally storm)
t-bew   teilebeweglich (partly mobile)
t-mot   teilemotorisiert (partly motorized)
Volks   honorific (literally people's)
VAK   Volksartillerie Korps (artillery corps; actually brigade-size)
VGD   Volksgrenadier Division
VWB   Volkswerfer Brigade (Nebelwerfer [multiple-rocket launcher] brigade)
Werf   [Nebel]werfer

UNIT HIERARCHY AND DESIGNATION

Units within armies usually follow a common convention regarding how they are designated within the overall command hierarchy. U.S., British, and German units followed similar organizational conventions (they all had platoons, companies, etc.). However, each army followed its own idiosyncratic method for identifying different units (the identity of units and their nomenclature were often steeped in tradition, particularly in the British Army). The nomenclature and method of identification used by the different armies follow, from smallest (in terms of units recorded in the order of battle) to largest:

U.S. Army	*British Army*	*German Army*
Platoon (1)	Platoon (1) or:	Zug (1)
Company (2) or:	Troop (1) (cav)	Kompanie (1) or:
Battery (art)	Company (2) or:	Batterie (art)
Troop (cav)	Battery (art)	Abteilung* (4, if part of a
Battalion (1) or:	Squadron (cav)	regiment; otherwise 1)
Squadron (cav)	Battalion (1) (3) or:	Regiment or Brigade (1)
Regiment (1)	Regiment	Division (1)
Division (1)	Brigade (1)	Korps (1) (4)
Corps (4)	Division (1)	Armee (1)
Army (5)	Corps (4)	Heeresgruppe (2) (3)
Army Group (1)	Army (5)	
	Army Group (1)	

    (1) Arabic numerals
    (2) Letters
    (3) Named
    (4) Roman numerals
    (5) Spelled-out number

*The old form "bataillon" was used only for Infantry and Engineers. All other branches named battalions "abteilung."

The Germans also used a number of ad hoc formations that were usually identified by their commanders' names. These include the kampfgruppe (battle group), which was applied either to an all-arms task force (usually a reinforced company, battalion, or regiment) or to a temporary grouping composed of the remnants of one or more depleted divisions; the korpsgruppe (corps group), a temporary grouping of two or more divisions under the command of a division headquarters (Korpsgruppe Felber was such an organization)—the headquarters was occasionally reinforced and reorganized as an actual corps headquarters; and the armeegruppe or armeeabteilung (army detachment, which was not the same as a heeresgruppe), a temporary grouping of two or more corps (or a heavily reinforced corps) under the command of a corps headquarters (the temporary subordination of the XXXIX Corps to the XLVII Corps at Bastogne on 28–31 December was such an organization).

When a unit's designation includes letters and/or numbers, separated by a diagonal line, the unit is a subunit of a larger formation. For example, 1st/B/125th Cav Sq is the 1st Platoon of B Troop of the 125th Cavalry Squadron.

The symbol (+) indicates that the unit has been reinforced; (−) indicates that a unit has detached subunits for assignment elsewhere; and " " is used to indicate a unit's honorific title.

TABLE OF EQUIVALENT RANKS

U.S. Army	German Army and Air Force	German Waffen-SS
None	Reichsmarschall	None
General of the Army	Generalfeldmarschall (Genlfeldm.)	Reichtsführer-SS
General	Generaloberst (Genobst.)	Oberstgruppenführer
Lieutenant General	General der Infanterie (Gen. d.)	Obergruppenführer
	Artillerie (Art.)	
	Gebirgstruppen (Geb.Tr.)	
	Kavallerie (Kav.)	
	Nachrichtentruppen (Na.Tr.)	
	Panzertruppen (Pz.Tr.)	
	Pioniere (Pion.)	
	Luftwaffe (Luft.)	
	Flieger (Flieg.)	
	Fallschirmtruppen (Fs.Tr.)	
	Flakartillerie (Flak.)	
	Luftnachrichtentruppen (Luft.Na.)*	
Major General	Generalleutnant (Genlt.)	Gruppenführer
Brigadier General	Generalmajor (Genmaj.)	Brigadeführer
None	None	Oberführer
Colonel	Oberst (Obst.)	Standartenführer
Lieutenant Colonel	Oberstleutnant (Obstlt.)	Obersturmbannführer
Major	Major (Maj.)	Sturmbannführer
Captain	Hauptmann (Hptm.)	Hauptsturmführer
Captain (cavalry)	Rittmeister (Rittm.)	None

	German Army	
U.S. Army	and Air Force	German Waffen-SS
First Lieutenant	Oberleutnant (Oblt.)	Obersturmführer
Second Lieutenant	Leutnant (Lt.)	Untersturmführer

In the interest of simplicity and consistency, the first reference in the text to a German officer is by his full German rank, followed by the equivalent U.S. rank in parentheses. All further reference to the officer is simply as General, Colonel, Major, etc. However, inasmuch as the SS rank of Oberführer has no equivalent U.S. rank, the decision was made to retain the original German throughout the text. In the Orders of Battle the original form of rank has been retained.

*The German service arms included:

Infanterie	Infantry
Artillerie	Artillery
Gebirgstruppen	Mountain troops
Kavallerie	Cavalry
Nachrichtentruppen	Signal troops
Panzertruppen	Armored troops
Pioniere	Engineers
Luftwaffe	Air Force
Flieger	Air crew
Fallschirmtruppen	Parachute troops
Flakartillerie	Antiaircraft artillery
Luftnachrichtentruppen	Air Force Signals troops

APPENDIX E

PERSONNEL STATISTICS

The following data on personnel statistics for the opposing forces in the Ardennes campaign are derived from the daily personnel records for units contained in the Ardennes Campaign Simulation Data Base (ACSDB). In their original format these data are too extensive to include in this work; thus, the data have been consolidated to reflect the personnel strengths and losses of the units during key periods of the campaign.

It should be noted that strengths and losses are given for *complete* divisions: Each division's totals include the strengths and/or losses for any detached units organic to that division. The totals for the strength of attachments for each division are those for nondivisional units (regiments, battalions, companies, and platoons), and do not include totals for any of the organic divisional units, which were frequently cross-attached to other divisions during the campaign. Losses are not noted for the various nondivisional units attached to corps and divisions. *Initial* strength is the unit's strength at the time it entered into combat on the date given in parentheses. *Final* strength is the unit's strength at the time it left the battle, usually on 16 January. If no dates are given, the unit participated in the campaign from 16 December to 16 January. Casualties are only those incurred during the campaign.

The strengths for armies and corps are given for the headquarters (headquarters and service support troops) and for any attached combat and combat support troops; these are designated Headquarters and Troops, respectively.

The various units are divided by echelon (army, corps, division) and by numerical order only (1st Division, 2d Division, etc.). The exigencies of combat dictated frequent shifting of the order of battle; only major changes are shown here. However, by referring to the Orders of Battle (appendix D) the reader can track the various changes in command and follow in a general sense the shifting strengths of the armies and corps.

I. AMERICAN

ARMIES

First
Headquarters Strength	Initial	48,161	Final	45,709
Troops Strength	Initial	23,410	Final	23,872

Third (19 Dec–16 Jan)
Headquarters Strength	Initial	43,021	Final	47,250
Troops Strength	Initial	18,976	Final	16,417

CORPS

III (19 Dec–16 Jan)
Headquarters Strength	Initial	5,575	Final	6,573
Troops Strength	Initial	4,462	Final	8,649

V
Headquarters Strength	Initial	6,713	Final	6,794
Troops Strength	Initial	8,012	Final	8,343

VII (22 Dec–16 Jan)
Headquarters Strength	Initial	6,713	Final	6,712
Troops Strength	Initial	17,156	Final	17,964

VIII
Headquarters Strength	Initial	6,812	Final	6,656
Troops Strength	Initial	10,616	Final	15,032

XII (21 Dec–16 Jan)
Headquarters Strength	Initial	7,120	Final	7,018
Troops Strength	Initial	7,458	Final	14,269

XVIII Abn (19 Dec–16 Jan)
Headquarters Strength	Initial	4,410	Final	6,151
Troops Strength	Initial	1,671	Final	9,663

ARMORED DIVISIONS

2d AD (24 Dec–16 Jan)
Division Strength	Initial	14,539	Final	13,355
Strength of Attachments	Initial	3,812	Final	2,703

	KIA	WIA	MIA	TOT
Casualties 16–23 Dec	3	10	0	13
Casualties 24 Dec–1 Jan	40	212	39	291
Casualties 2–16 Jan	158	943	95	1,196
Total 16 Dec–16 Jan	201	1,165	134	1,500

3d AD (19 Dec–16 Jan)
Division Strength	Initial	14,493	Final	13,968
Strength of Attachments	Initial	799	Final	2,362

	KIA	WIA	MIA	TOT
Casualties 19–23 Dec	28	170	39	237
Casualties 24 Dec–1 Jan	49	255	187	491
Casualties 2–16 Jan	177	1,055	116	1,348
Total 19 Dec–16 Jan	254	1,480	342	2,076

4th AD (20 Dec–16 Jan)

Division Strength	Initial	9,983	Final	10,207
Strength of Attachments	Initial	1,323	Final	1,274

	KIA	WIA	MIA	TOT
Casualties 20–23 Dec	3	13	2	18
Casualties 24 Dec–1 Jan	88	431	89	608
Casualties 2–16 Jan	52	188	34	274
Total 20 Dec–16 Jan	143	632	125	900

5th AD (16–22 Dec)

Division Strength	Initial	9,784	Final	9,472
Strength of Attachments	Initial	2,849	Final	881

	KIA	WIA	MIA	TOT
Total 16–22 Dec	75	306	198	579

6th AD (26 Dec–16 Jan)

Division Strength	Initial	10,876	Final	9,967
Strength of Attachments	Initial	1,256	Final	3,336

	KIA	WIA	MIA	TOT
Casualties 26 Dec–1 Jan	10	77	5	92
Casualties 2–16 Jan	124	819	197	1,140
Total 26 Dec–16 Jan	134	896	202	1,232

7th AD (17 Dec–16 Jan)

Division Strength	Initial	10,640	Final	10,492
Strength of Attachments	Initial	1,310	Final	3,005

	KIA	WIA	MIA	TOT
Casualties 17–23 Dec	42	257	126	425
Casualties 24 Dec–1 Jan	83	421	349	853
Casualties 2–16 Jan	0	8	0	8
Total 17 Dec–16 Jan	125	686	475	1,286

9th AD (16 Dec–6 Jan)

Division Strength	Initial	10,691	Final	9,184
Strength of Attachments	Initial	1,334	Final	1,163

	KIA	WIA	MIA	TOT
Casualties 16–23 Dec	72	346	665	1,083
Casualties 24 Dec–1 Jan	92	389	159	640
Casualties 2–6 Jan	10	19	4	33
Total 16 Dec–6 Jan	174	754	828	1,756

10th AD (18 Dec–16 Jan)

Division Strength	Initial	9,777	Final	9,781
Strength of Attachments	Initial	1,194	Final	1,137

	KIA	WIA	MIA	TOT
Casualties 18–23 Dec	63	326	146	535
Casualties 24 Dec–1 Jan	69	298	160	527
Casualties 2–16 Jan	2	1	0	3
Total 18 Dec–16 Jan	134	625	306	1,065

11th AD (30 Dec–16 Jan)

Division Strength	Initial	10,712	Final	9,190
Strength of Attachments	Initial	650	Final	1,093

	KIA	WIA	MIA	TOT
Casualties 30 Dec–1 Jan	31	475	30	536
Casualties 2–16 Jan	94	519	91	704
Total 30 Dec–16 Jan	125	994	121	1,240

Armored Division Summary

Total Strength (not including attachments) 101,495

	KIA	WIA	MIA	TOT
Casualties 16–23 Dec	286	1,428	1,176	2,890
Casualties 24 Dec–1 Jan	462	2,558	1,018	4,038
Casualties 2–16 Jan	617	3,552	537	4,706
Total 16 Dec–16 Jan	1,365	7,538	2,731	11,634

AIRBORNE AND INFANTRY DIVISIONS

17th AbnD (3–16 Jan)

Division Strength	Initial	12,599	Final	9,103
Strength of Attachments	Initial	1,482	Final	1,042

	KIA	WIA	MIA	TOT
Total Casualties 3–16 Jan	239	1,042	1,199	2,480

82d AbnD (19 Dec–16 Jan)

Division Strength	Initial	11,591	Final	10,683
Strength of Attachments	Initial	0	Final	0

	KIA	WIA	MIA	TOT
Casualties 19–23 Dec	34	105	53	192
Casualties 24 Dec–1 Jan	73	332	124	529
Casualties 2–16 Jan	174	853	76	1,103
Total 19 Dec–16 Jan	281	1,290	253	1,824

101st AbnD (19 Dec–16 Jan)

Division Strength	Initial	14,791	Final	11,196
Strength of Attachments	Initial	1,479	Final	1,227

	KIA	WIA	MIA	TOT
Casualties 19–23 Dec	214	1,088	198	1,500
Casualties 24 Dec–1 Jan	94	523	253	870
Casualties 2–16 Jan	275	1,614	196	2,085
Total 19 Dec–16 Jan	583	3,225	647	4,455

1st ID (17 Dec–16 Jan)

Division Strength	Initial	13,226	Final	12,991
Strength of Attachments	Initial	2,619	Final	2,817

	KIA	WIA	MIA	TOT
Casualties 17–23 Dec	38	281	123	442
Casualties 24 Dec–1 Jan	24	154	32	210
Casualties 2–16 Jan	27	227	259	513
Total 17 Dec–16 Jan	89	662	414	1,165

2d ID

Division Strength	Initial	13,300	Final	12,808
Strength of Attachments	Initial	3,876	Final	2,496

	KIA	WIA	MIA	TOT
Casualties 16–23 Dec	63	664	786	1,513
Casualties 24 Dec–1 Jan	33	166	10	209

Casualties 2–16 Jan	26	168	2	196
Total 16 Dec–16 Jan	122	998	798	1,918

4th ID

Division Strength	Initial	12,934	Final	14,225
Strength of Attachments	Initial	3,909	Final	2,461
	KIA	WIA	MIA	TOT
Casualties 16–23 Dec	113	478	717	1,308
Casualties 24 Dec–1 Jan	17	73	208	298
Casualties 2–16 Jan	14	61	37	112
Total 16 Dec–16 Jan	144	612	962	1,718

5th ID (24 Dec–16 Jan)

Division Strength	Initial	13,714	Final	14,057
Strength of Attachments	Initial	2,627	Final	2,374
	KIA	WIA	MIA	TOT
Casualties 24 Dec–1 Jan	93	745	121	959
Casualties 2–16 Jan	8	68	4	80
Total 24 Dec–16 Jan	101	813	125	1,039

8th ID (16–18 Dec)

Division Strength	Initial	12,801	Final	13,049
Strength of Attachments	Initial	3,682	Final	3,171
	KIA	WIA	MIA	TOT
Total Casualties 16–18 Dec	51	184	41	276

9th ID (18 Dec–16 Jan)

Division Strength	Initial	13,241	Final	13,711
Strength of Attachments	Initial	2,279	Final	3,798
	KIA	WIA	MIA	TOT
Casualties 18–23 Dec	12	84	3	99
Casualties 24 Dec–1 Jan	24	180	95	299
Casualties 2–16 Jan	21	158	8	187
Total 18 Dec–16 Jan	57	422	106	585

26th ID (21 Dec–16 Jan)

Division Strength	Initial	14,630	Final	11,910
Strength of Attachments	Initial	2,068	Final	2,762
	KIA	WIA	MIA	TOT
Casualties 21–23 Dec	5	73	22	100
Casualties 24 Dec–1 Jan	72	733	143	948
Casualties 2–16 Jan	137	1,218	214	1,569
Total 21 Dec–16 Jan	214	2,024	379	2,617

28th ID

Division Strength	Initial	14,254	Final	11,662
Strength of Attachments	Initial	2,742	Final	6,793
	KIA	WIA	MIA	TOT
Casualties 16–23 Dec	279	1,254	2,970	4,503
Casualties 24 Dec–1 Jan	28	119	180	327
Casualties 2–16 Jan	30	179	85	294
Total 16 Dec–16 Jan	337	1,552	3,235	5,124

30th ID (17 Dec–16 Jan)

Division Strength	Initial	14,011	Final	13,297
Strength of Attachments	Initial	3,204	Final	3,984

	KIA	WIA	MIA	TOT
Casualties 17–23 Dec	65	260	422	747
Casualties 24 Dec–1 Jan	47	270	38	355
Casualties 2–16 Jan	84	667	183	934
Total 17 Dec–16 Jan	196	1,197	643	2,036

35th ID (26 Dec–16 Jan)

Division Strength	Initial	14,179	Final	12,087
Strength of Attachments	Initial	1,913	Final	1,224

	KIA	WIA	MIA	TOT
Casualties 26 Dec–1 Jan	32	461	368	861
Casualties 2–16 Jan	92	846	547	1,485
Total 26 Dec–16 Jan	124	1,307	915	2,346

75th ID (22 Dec–16 Jan)

Division Strength	Initial	13,828	Final	12,460
Strength of Attachments	Initial	2,130	Final	3,098

	KIA	WIA	MIA	TOT
Casualties 22–23 Dec	2	4	0	6
Casualties 24 Dec–1 Jan	117	494	124	737
Casualties 2–16 Jan	93	465	108	666
Total 22 Dec–16 Jan	212	963	232	1,409

78th ID (16–18 Dec)

Division Strength	Initial	13,424	Final	12,256
Strength of Attachments	Initial	2,564	Final	2,553

	KIA	WIA	MIA	TOT
Total Casualties 16–18 Dec	149	684	472	1,305

80th ID (20 Dec–16 Jan)

Division Strength	Initial	13,934	Final	13,236
Strength of Attachments	Initial	2,684	Final	2,374

	KIA	WIA	MIA	TOT
Casualties 20–23 Dec	32	214	6	252
Casualties 24 Dec–1 Jan	180	821	628	1,629
Casualties 2–16 Jan	64	360	62	486
Total 20 Dec–16 Jan	276	1,395	696	2,367

83d ID (26 Dec–16 Jan)

Division Strength	Initial	12,361	Final	12,077
Strength of Attachments	Initial	1,998	Final	2,323

	KIA	WIA	MIA	TOT
Casualties 26 Dec–1 Jan	35	67	16	118
Casualties 2–16 Jan	473	916	232	1,621
Total 26 Dec–16 Jan	508	983	248	1,739

84th ID (20 Dec–16 Jan)

Division Strength	Initial	12,821	Final	12,837
Strength of Attachments	Initial	4,778	Final	2,699

	KIA	WIA	MIA	TOT
Casualties 20–23 Dec	9	30	12	51
Casualties 24 Dec–1 Jan	70	295	226	591
Casualties 2–16 Jan	229	1,143	184	1,556
Total 20 Dec–16 Jan	308	1,468	422	2,198

87th ID (29 Dec–16 Jan)

Division Strength	Initial	11,875	Final	11,849
Strength of Attachments	Initial	744	Final	1,412

	KIA	WIA	MIA	TOT
Casualties 29 Dec–1 Jan	19	108	15	142
Casualties 2–16 Jan	129	542	323	994
Total 29 Dec–16 Jan	148	650	338	1,136

90th ID (6–16 Jan)

Division Strength	Initial	14,180	Final	12,753
Strength of Attachments	Initial	2,005	Final	2,740

	KIA	WIA	MIA	TOT
Total Casualties 6–16 Jan	161	832	98	1,091

99th ID

Division Strength	Initial	13,642	Final	12,152
Strength of Attachments	Initial	2,838	Final	1,718

	KIA	WIA	MIA	TOT
Casualties 16–23 Dec	198	901	898	1,997
Casualties 24 Dec–1 Jan	72	307	121	500
Casualties 2–16 Jan	29	171	17	217
Total 16 Dec–16 Jan	299	1,379	1,036	2,714

106th ID

Division Strength	Initial	13,926	Final	5,344
Strength of Attachments	Initial	4,307	Final	2,255

	KIA	WIA	MIA	TOT
Casualties 16–23 Dec	254	1,013	7,237	8,504
Casualties 24 Dec–1 Jan	8	68	4	80
Casualties 2–16 Jan	102	411	164	677
Total 16 Dec–16 Jan	364	1,492	7,405	9,261

Airborne and Infantry Division Summary

Total Strength Committed (not including attachments)   295,262

	KIA	WIA	MIA	TOT
Casualties 16–23 Dec	1,518	7,317	13,960	22,795
Casualties 24 Dec–1 Jan	1,038	5,916	2,706	9,660
Casualties 2–16 Jan	2,407	11,941	4,002	18,350
Total 16 Dec–16 Jan	4,963	25,174	20,668	50,805

II. BRITISH
CORPS

XXX (19 Dec–16 Jan)

Headquarters Strength	Initial	8,643	Final	8,761
Troops Strength	Initial	7,804	Final	8,063

ARMORED DIVISIONS AND BRIGADES

Guards AD (19 Dec–16 Jan)

Division Strength	Initial	14,294	Final	14,418
Strength of Attachments	Initial	32	Final	32

	KIA	WIA	MIA	TOT
Casualties 19–23 Dec	0	1	0	1
Casualties 24 Dec–1 Jan	0	4	1	5
Casualties 2–16 Jan	4	0	0	4
Total 19 Dec–16 Jan	4	5	1	10

29th Arm Bde (19 Dec–16 Jan)

Brigade Strength	Initial	3,528	Final	3,447
Strength of Attachments	Initial	2,199	Final	2,037

	KIA	WIA	MIA	TOT
Casualties 19–23 Dec	0	0	1	1
Casualties 24 Dec–1 Jan	0	3	0	3
Casualties 2–16 Jan	12	26	8	46
Total 19 Dec–16 Jan	12	29	9	50

33d Arm Bde (19 Dec–16 Jan)

Brigade Strength	Initial	3,963	Final	3,803
Strength of Attachments	Initial	0	Final	0

	KIA	WIA	MIA	TOT
Casualties 19–23 Dec	0	0	0	0
Casualties 24 Dec–1 Jan	0	0	0	0
Casualties 2–16 Jan	7	25	1	33
Total 19 Dec–16 Jan	7	25	1	33

34th Tk Bde (19 Dec–16 Jan)

Brigade Strength	Initial	3,122	Final	3,154
Strength of Attachments	Initial	0	Final	0

	KIA	WIA	MIA	TOT
Casualties 19–23 Dec	0	1	0	1
Casualties 24 Dec–1 Jan	1	0	0	1
Casualties 2–16 Jan	0	0	0	0
Total 19 Dec–16 Jan	1	1	0	2

AIRBORNE AND INFANTRY DIVISIONS

6th AbnD (27 Dec–16 Jan)

Division Strength	Initial	13,910	Final	13,361
Strength of Attachments	Initial	704	Final	275

	KIA	WIA	MIA	TOT
Casualties 27 Dec–1 Jan	0	1	1	2
Casualties 2–16 Jan	72	194	103	369
Total 27 Dec–16 Jan	72	195	104	371

43d ID (19–27 Dec)

Division Strength	Initial	17,836	Final	17,876
Strength of Attachments	Initial	32	Final	500

	KIA	WIA	MIA	TOT
Total Casualties 19–27 Dec	1	0	0	1

51st ID (19 Dec–16 Jan)

Division Strength	Initial	17,837	Final	17,457
Strength of Attachments	Initial	0	Final	0

	KIA	WIA	MIA	TOT
Casualties 19–23 Dec	6	4	7	17
Casualties 24 Dec–1 Jan	8	14	6	28
Casualties 2–16 Jan	46	250	8	304
Total 19 Dec–16 Jan	60	268	21	349

53d ID (19 Dec–16 Jan)

Division Strength	Initial	17,968	Final	17,884
Strength of Attachments	Initial	32	Final	32

	KIA	WIA	MIA	TOT
Casualties 19–23 Dec	2	9	1	12
Casualties 24 Dec–1 Jan	0	4	3	7
Casualties 2–16 Jan	63	441	123	627
Total 19 Dec–16 Jan	65	454	127	646

British Division and Brigade Summary

Total Strength Committed (not including attachments) 92,462

	KIA	WIA	MIA	TOT
Casualties 16–23 Dec	9	15	9	33
Casualties 24 Dec–1 Jan	9	26	11	46
Casualties 2–16 Jan	204	936	243	1,383
Total 16 Dec–16 Jan	222	977	263	1,462

III. GERMAN[1]

ARMIES

Fifth Panzer

Headquarters Strength	Initial	13,153	Final	14,414
Troops Strength	Initial	0	Final	0

Sixth Panzer

Headquarters Strength	Initial	20,261	Final	19,659
Troops Strength	Initial	11,109	Final	8,537

Seventh

Headquarters Strength	Initial	14,760	Final	14,319
Troops Strength	Initial	7,391	Final	5,635

CORPS

I SS Panzer

Headquarters Strength	Initial	3,227	Final	3,153
Troops Strength	Initial	10,343	Final	3,596

II SS Panzer

Headquarters Strength	Initial	1,955	Final	1,908
Troops Strength	Initial	562	Final	916

XIII (Korps Felber) (30 Dec–16 Jan)

Headquarters Strength	Initial	1,179	Final	1,749
Troops Strength	Initial	0	Final	10,360

XXXIX Panzer (27 Dec–4 Jan)

Headquarters Strength	Initial	1,528	Final	1,524
Troops Strength	Initial	3,289	Final	0

XLVII Panzer
Headquarters Strength	Initial	4,512	Final	4,630
Troops Strength	Initial	6,162	Final	2,459

LIII
Headquarters Strength	Initial	1,773	Final	1,688
Troops Strength	Initial	1,190	Final	5,124

LVIII Panzer
Headquarters Strength	Initial	3,897	Final	3,775
Troops Strength	Initial	9,919	Final	12,840

LXVI
Headquarters Strength	Initial	4,200	Final	4,058
Troops Strength	Initial	2,933	Final	4,359

LXVII (16–27 Dec)
Headquarters Strength	Initial	1,921	Final	1,892
Troops Strength	Initial	11,311	Final	10,038

LXXX
Headquarters Strength	Initial	1,921	Final	1,836
Troops Strength	Initial	6,786	Final	6,967

LXXXV (16 Dec–12 Jan)
Headquarters Strength	Initial	1,773	Final	1,702
Troops Strength	Initial	4,705	Final	0

PANZER AND PANZERGRENADIER DIVISIONS AND BRIGADES

1st SS PzD
Division Strength	Initial	17,988	Final	14,234
Strength of Attachments	Initial	3,304	Final	1,538

	KIA	WIA	MIA	TOT
Casualties 16–23 Dec	304	920	272	1,496
Casualties 24 Dec–1 Jan	199	596	191	986
Casualties 2–16 Jan	271	763	171	1,205
Total 16 Dec–16 Jan	774	2,279	634	3,687

2d SS PzD (21 Dec–16 Jan)
Division Strength	Initial	16,970	Final	13,480
Strength of Attachments	Initial	0	Final	515

	KIA	WIA	MIA	TOT
Casualties 21–23 Dec	43	140	19	202
Casualties 24 Dec–1 Jan	292	922	167	1,381
Casualties 2–16 Jan	300	874	680	1,854
Total 21 Dec–16 Jan	635	1,936	866	3,437

9th SS PzD (20 Dec–16 Jan)
Division Strength	Initial	13,307	Final	10,305
Strength of Attachments	Initial	0	Final	0

	KIA	WIA	MIA	TOT
Casualties 20–23 Dec	96	290	106	492
Casualties 24 Dec–1 Jan	286	865	276	1,427
Casualties 2–16 Jan	324	980	310	1,614
Total 20 Dec–16 Jan	706	2,135	692	3,533

12th SS PzD

Division Strength	Initial	18,548	Final	15,475
Strength of Attachments	Initial	2,152	Final	612

	KIA	WIA	MIA	TOT
Casualties 16–23 Dec	228	802	340	1,370
Casualties 24 Dec–1 Jan	115	389	167	671
Casualties 2–16 Jan	234	611	248	1,093
Total 16 Dec–16 Jan	577	1,802	755	3,134

2d PzD

Division Strength	Initial	12,680	Final	11,560
Strength of Attachments	Initial	1,777	Final	1,532

	KIA	WIA	MIA	TOT
Casualties 16–23 Dec	45	173	37	255
Casualties 24 Dec–1 Jan	89	308	263	660
Casualties 2–16 Jan	120	360	367	847
Total 16 Dec–16 Jan	254	841	667	1,762

9th PzD (24 Dec–16 Jan)

Division Strength	Initial	13,083	Final	12,213
Strength of Attachments	Initial	793	Final	368

	KIA	WIA	MIA	TOT
Casualties 24 Dec–1 Jan	199	596	191	986
Casualties 2–16 Jan	271	763	171	1,205
Total 24 Dec–16 Jan	470	1,359	362	2,191

116th PzD

Division Strength	Initial	15,468	Final	12,328
Strength of Attachments	Initial	0	Final	0

	KIA	WIA	MIA	TOT
Casualties 16–23 Dec	190	523	355	1,068
Casualties 24 Dec–1 Jan	136	345	449	930
Casualties 2–16 Jan	76	321	503	900
Total 16 Dec–16 Jan	402	1,189	1,307	2,898

Pz Lehr D

Division Strength	Initial	12,672	Final	11,061
Strength of Attachments	Initial	2,220	Final	1,113

	KIA	WIA	MIA	TOT
Casualties 16–23 Dec	46	233	50	329
Casualties 24 Dec–1 Jan	138	504	255	897
Casualties 2–16 Jan	104	350	260	714
Total 16 Dec–16 Jan	288	1,087	565	1,940

3d PzGrenD (18 Dec–16 Jan)

Division Strength	Initial	11,424	Final	11,274
Strength of Attachments	Initial	0	Final	0

	KIA	WIA	MIA	TOT
Casualties 18–23 Dec	72	225	138	435
Casualties 24 Dec–1 Jan	101	368	207	676
Casualties 2–16 Jan	124	403	369	896
Total 18 Dec–16 Jan	297	996	714	2,007

15th PzGrenD (25 Dec–16 Jan)

Division Strength	Initial	11,181	Final	9,629
Strength of Attachments	Initial	0	Final	0

	KIA	WIA	MIA	TOT
Casualties 25 Dec–1 Jan	121	288	887	1,296
Casualties 2–16 Jan	54	230	189	473
Total 25 Dec–16 Jan	175	518	1,076	1,769

Führer Begleit Brigade (19 Dec–16 Jan)

Brigade Strength	Initial	7,003	Final	5,969
Strength of Attachments	Initial	0	Final	0

	KIA	WIA	MIA	TOT
Casualties 19–23 Dec	77	191	28	296
Casualties 24 Dec–1 Jan	124	304	52	480
Casualties 2–16 Jan	123	249	173	545
Total 19 Dec–16 Jan	324	744	253	1,321

Führer Grenadier Brigade (21 Dec–16 Jan)

Brigade Strength	Initial	6,285	Final	4,872
Strength of Attachments	Initial	640	Final	350

	KIA	WIA	MIA	TOT
Casualties 21–23 Dec	26	52	102	180
Casualties 24 Dec–1 Jan	149	300	570	1,019
Casualties 2–16 Jan	86	240	163	489
Total 21 Dec–16 Jan	261	592	835	1,688

150th PzBde (21–27 Dec)

Brigade Strength	Initial	2,955	Final	2,536
Strength of Attachments	Initial	0	Final	0

	KIA	WIA	MIA	TOT
Casualties 21–23 Dec	45	160	101	306
Casualties 24–27 Dec	20	76	48	144
Total 21–27 Dec	65	236	149	450

Armored and Mechanized Divisions and Brigades Summary

Total Strength Committed (not including attachments)				159,564

	KIA	WIA	MIA	TOT
Casualties 16–23 Dec	1,172	3,709	1,739	6,620
Casualties 24 Dec–1 Jan	2,000	5,861	3,723	11,584
Casualties 2–16 Jan	2,087	6,144	3,604	11,835
Total 16 Dec–16 Jan	5,259	15,714	9,066	30,039

FALLSCHIRMJÄGER AND VOLKSGRENADIER DIVISIONS

3d FJD[2]

Division Strength	Initial	12,474	Final	10,347
Strength of Attachments	Initial	0	Final	129

	KIA	WIA	MIA	TOT
Casualties 16–23 Dec	151	540	531	1,222
Casualties 24 Dec–1 Jan	30	156	71	257
Casualties 2–16 Jan	183	559	415	1,157
Total 16 Dec–16 Jan	364	1,255	1,017	2,636

5th FJD[3]

Division Strength	Initial	13,543	Final	5,928
Strength of Attachments	Initial	2,799	Final	1,297
	KIA	WIA	MIA	TOT
Casualties 16–23 Dec	198	802	783	1,783
Casualties 24 Dec–1 Jan	570	2,182	2,385	5,137
Casualties 2–16 Jan	232	781	401	1,414
Total 16 Dec–16 Jan	1,000	3,765	3,569	8,334

9th VGD (24 Dec–16 Jan)

Division Strength	Initial	8,730	Final	7,854
Strength of Attachments	Initial	0	Final	757
	KIA	WIA	MIA	TOT
Casualties 24 Dec–1 Jan	58	144	175	377
Casualties 2–16 Jan	156	415	345	916
Total 24 Dec–16 Jan	214	559	520	1,293

12th VGD

Division Strength	Initial	9,517	Final	6,343
Strength of Attachments	Initial	0	Final	573
	KIA	WIA	MIA	TOT
Casualties 16–23 Dec	146	445	607	1,198
Casualties 24 Dec–1 Jan	48	144	152	344
Casualties 2–16 Jan	258	786	1,065	2,109
Total 16 Dec–16 Jan	452	1,375	1,824	3,651

18th VGD

Division Strength	Initial	10,390	Final	7,552
Strength of Attachments	Initial	1,727	Final	0
	KIA	WIA	MIA	TOT
Casualties 16–23 Dec	160	488	672	1,320
Casualties 24 Dec–1 Jan	42	126	133	301
Casualties 2–16 Jan	161	425	903	1,489
Total 16 Dec–16 Jan	363	1,039	1,708	3,110

26th VGD

Division Strength	Initial	9,951	Final	6,899
Strength of Attachments	Initial	629	Final	1,705
	KIA	WIA	MIA	TOT
Casualties 16–23 Dec	210	508	294	1,012
Casualties 24 Dec–1 Jan	142	425	605	1,172
Casualties 2–16 Jan	143	388	946	1,477
Total 16 Dec–16 Jan	495	1,321	1,845	3,661

62d VGD

Division Strength	Initial	11,050	Final	7,849
Strength of Attachments	Initial	0	Final	0
	KIA	WIA	MIA	TOT
Casualties 16–23 Dec	146	445	607	1,198
Casualties 24 Dec–1 Jan	96	291	366	753
Casualties 2–16 Jan	252	719	685	1,656
Total 16 Dec–16 Jan	494	1,455	1,658	3,607

79th VGD (22 Dec–16 Jan)

Division Strength	Initial 10,116		Final	8,943
Strength of Attachments	Initial 0		Final	0

	KIA	WIA	MIA	TOT
Casualties 22–23 Dec	17	30	39	86
Casualties 24 Dec–1 Jan	134	480	221	835
Casualties 2–16 Jan	86	283	235	604
Total 22 Dec–16 Jan	237	793	495	1,525

167th VGD (24 Dec–16 Jan)

Division Strength	Initial 10,973		Final	8,948
Strength of Attachments	Initial 0		Final	920

	KIA	WIA	MIA	TOT
Casualties 24 Dec–1 Jan	66	201	271	538
Casualties 2–16 Jan	160	485	610	1,255
Total 24 Dec–16 Jan	226	686	881	1,793

212th VGD

Division Strength	Initial 10,490		Final	9,151
Strength of Attachments	Initial 661		Final	1,176

	KIA	WIA	MIA	TOT
Casualties 16–23 Dec	123	486	418	1,027
Casualties 24 Dec–1 Jan	46	95	172	313
Casualties 2–16 Jan	55	147	120	322
Total 16 Dec–16 Jan	224	728	710	1,662

272d VGD (16–19 Dec)

Division Strength	Initial 8,771		Final	8,630
Strength of Attachments	Initial 0		Final	0

	KIA	WIA	MIA	TOT
Casualties 16–19 Dec	43	95	14	152

276th VGD

Division Strength	Initial 9,320		Final	7,625
Strength of Attachments	Initial 0		Final	527

	KIA	WIA	MIA	TOT
Casualties 16–23 Dec	124	554	417	1,095
Casualties 24 Dec–1 Jan	46	95	172	313
Casualties 2–16 Jan	120	320	263	703
Total 16 Dec–16 Jan	290	969	852	2,111

277th VGD (16–27 Dec)

Division Strength	Initial 7,249		Final	6,257
Strength of Attachments	Initial 0		Final	0

	KIA	WIA	MIA	TOT
Casualties 16–23 Dec	109	356	444	909
Casualties 24–27 Dec	12	68	32	112
Total 16–27 Dec	121	424	476	1,021

326th VGD (16–21 Dec, 4–16 Jan)

Division Strength	Initial 9,083		Final	7,105
Strength of Attachments	Initial 0		Final	0

	KIA	WIA	MIA	TOT
Casualties 16–21 Dec	98	232	111	441

Casualties 4–16 Jan	110	351	513	974
Total 16 Dec–16 Jan	208	583	624	1,415

340th VGD (2–16 Jan)

Division Strength	Initial	7,147	Final	5,367
Strength of Attachments	Initial	0	Final	0
	KIA	WIA	MIA	TOT
Total 2–16 Jan	261	974	639	1,874

352d VGD

Division Strength	Initial	10,595	Final	8,512
Strength of Attachments	Initial	0	Final	834
	KIA	WIA	MIA	TOT
Casualties 16–23 Dec	176	655	615	1,446
Casualties 24 Dec–1 Jan	101	198	371	670
Casualties 2–16 Jan	55	148	121	324
Total 16 Dec–16 Jan	332	1,001	1,107	2,440

560th VGD[4]

Division Strength	Initial	11,197	Final	6,831
Strength of Attachments	Initial	0	Final	0
	KIA	WIA	MIA	TOT
Casualties 16–23 Dec	143	460	929	1,532
Casualties 24 Dec–1 Jan	124	369	496	989
Casualties 2–16 Jan	198	603	813	1,614
Total 16 Dec–16 Jan	465	1,432	2,238	4,135

Fallschirmjäger and Volksgrenadier Divisions Summary

Total Strength Committed (not including attachments) 170,596

	KIA	WIA	MIA	TOT
Casualties 16–23 Dec	1,844	6,096	6,481	14,421
Casualties 24 Dec–1 Jan	1,515	4,974	5,622	12,111
Casualties 2–16 Jan	2,430	7,384	8,074	17,888
Total 16 Dec–16 Jan	5,789	18,454	20,177	44,420

APPENDIX F

MATÉRIEL STRENGTHS IN THE ARDENNES

This appendix consists of a series of tables showing the quantities of major weapons in each division (German, U.S., and British) in the Ardennes on four important dates: 16 December and 24 December 1944, and 2 January and 16 January 1945. For both sides, units are listed from north to south, assigned to the appropriate corps and armies. The tables also show the major weapons held directly under corps and army command. The categories are, from left to right: tanks, tank destroyers and assault guns (TDs/AGs), armored cars (ACs), armored personnel carriers (APCs), towed antitank guns (Towed AT), light artillery (Lt), medium artillery (Med), heavy artillery (Hvy), and rockets. For all artillery, towed pieces are shown to the left of a slash, and self-propelled pieces to the right (34/11).

For the sake of brevity and convenience, several conventions have been adopted to simplify the tables. The tank category includes all U.S. M4 models, along with the German PzKw-IV, PzKw-V Panther, and both models of the PzKw-VI Tiger. However, U.S. light tanks (M5s, M5A1s, and a handful of new M24 Chaffees) are listed under tank destroyers since they were fast and lightly armored like the M10, M18, and M36 American TDs. German assault guns and TDs, except the half-tracks armed with 75-mm L24 howitzers or 75-mm L46 antitank guns, were more heavily armored than American TDs, and were all turretless. The APCs category includes not only the U.S. M3 and German SdKfz-250 and -251 series half-tracks, but also the British "Kangaroo" fully tracked APC (essentially an M4 Sherman with no turret) and the ubiquitous Bren carrier (accounting for the high APC totals in British infantry divisions). For the Germans, the towed AT category includes towed 88-mm (and more rarely 105-mm) antiaircraft guns often used in a ground role. The German 75-mm L46 and 88-mm L71 pieces mounted on field carriages (usually designated the FK40 and FK43, respectively) and employed as artillery, however, are counted under the light artillery category.

Light artillery consists of guns of 90-mm caliber or less and howitzers of 105-mm caliber or less. Medium artillery includes guns of 91 mm to 154 mm, and howitzers of 106 mm to 155 mm. Heavy artillery includes anything larger, up to the Germans' 355-mm (14-inch) railroad howitzers; note that U.S. M-12 self-propelled 155-mm L36 guns fall under this category. The rockets category covers German *Nebelwerfer* or multiple-rocket launchers. The SP subcategory for rockets refers to 15-cm *Nebelwerfer* mounted on half-tracks.

There are several points worth noting in these tables. First, with a few exceptions, heavy artillery is a corps-level asset. Next, very few German divisions were really well equipped, and even the best panzer divisions had relatively little self-propelled artillery compared to U.S. armored divisions. German panzer and panzergrenadier formations were also poor in armored personnel carriers compared to U.S. armored divisions. Third, the panzer divisions quickly lost tank strength when they were involved in heavy combat and, unlike the Americans, could not readily make good these losses. Finally, the wealth of U.S. industry allowed each infantry division to have a tank battalion and (generally) an SP tank destroyer battalion attached, although these were not always at full strength; typically U.S. infantry divisions have eighty or so AFVs (armored fighting vehicles), versus six to fourteen for most volksgrenadier divisions.

The status of the American 9th and 10th Armored divisions deserves some explanation. The bulk of the 9th Armored Division was employed as corps reserve for Major General Middleton's VIII Corps on 16 December. CCB/9 began the day as corps reserve for Major General Gerow's V Corps, but was transferred back to the VIII Corps during 16 December and eventually became involved in fighting in the north. CCA and 9th Armored's division troops fought in the south alongside the 4th Infantry Division, and CCR was sent to intercept the XLVII Panzer Corps east of Bastogne on 17–18 December.

The 10th Armored Division, called north from Patton's Third Army on 17 December and assigned to the VIII Corps, was also not committed as a single unit. CCB/10 moved to reinforce CCR/9 and was surrounded in Bastogne after suffering heavy losses in the roadblock battles on 20–21 December. After the relief of Bastogne, its remnants withdrew to the south and reunited with the rest of the division. The bulk of the 10th Armored Division served with the III and XII corps until it was withdrawn to refit and reorganize on 26 December and assigned to the XX Corps. The unit inventories for both divisions are shown as a division total, but the units themselves did not see action as complete entities during the campaign.

ALLIED AND GERMAN EQUIPMENT HOLDINGS

16 December 1944

Type:	Tanks	TDs/ AGs	ACs	APCs	Towed AT	Lt	Med	Hvy	Rocket
Allied Units									
First Army	2	5	39	139	12			16	
7th Armd Div[1]	149	137	85	468		/54			
V Corps		63	80			72	28		
78th Inf Div	33	21	29	41		54/18	12	/4	
99th Inf Div	15	18	20	41	18	53	24	8	
2d Inf Div	38	22	44	47	36	78	12	4/4	
VIII Corps						57	43		
106th Inf Div		41	86	120	36	63	10		
28th Inf Div	53	17	23	84	35	66	12		
9th Armd Div[2]	176	129	55	417		/54			
4th Inf Div	17	46	52	51		54	24	/12	

The *Artillery (towed/SP)* header spans the Lt, Med, Hvy, and Rocket columns.

16 December 1944

Type:	Tanks	TDs/ AGs	ACs	APCs	Towed AT	Lt	Med	Hvy	Rocket
German Units									
Sixth Pz Army	45	85			96			2	
LXVII Corps		24			36	87	44	23	108
272d VGD		8			7	71	17		
326th VGD					9	79	18		
II SS Pz Corps									24
2d SS PzD	76	68	29	217	44	36	41/3		
9th SS PzD	66	53	29	151	44	31/6	35/1		
I SS Pz Corps						76	44	41	108
1st SS PzD	97	55	16	135	42	29/2	20/13		78
12th SS PzD	70	57	20	137	42	37	29/6		84/16
277th VGD		11			7	71	17		
12th VGD		6			9	68	14		
3d FJD					30	15	10		
Fifth Pz Army					96	54	12	14	90
FB Bde	28	67	13	67	29	10	3/6		
LXVI Corps								3	108
18th VGD		28			9	79	21		
62d VGD		10			9	79	18		
LVIII Pz Corps					32	29	31	25	108/16
116th PzD	49	25	18	123	29	21/2	11/6		
560th VGD					9	79	18		
XLVII Pz Corps					32		11	3	90
2d PzD	72	49	15	149	11	13/10	37/12	8	6
26th VGD		14			10	102	12		6
Pz Lehr D	54	68	19	123	24	43	37/2		6
Seventh Army					48			2	
LXXXV Corps					36	24	36	15	84
5th FJD		18			51	36	12		24
352d VGD		6			9	79	18		
LXXX Corps						36	36	15	108/16
276th VGD					8	71	17		
212th VGD		5			45	79	18		

24 December 1944

Type:	Tanks	TDs/ AGs	ACs	APCs	Towed AT	Lt	Med	Hvy	Rocket
Allied Units									
First Army		2	15	119	9		12		
29th Armd Bde	145	23	81	193	16	/16	32	4	
V Corps							24	26/8	
9th Inf Div	47	73	48	67		66	24		
99th Inf Div			10	39	15	49	12		
2d Inf Div	34	42	32	49	27	53	12		

24 December 1944

Type:	Tanks	TDs/AGs	ACs	APCs	Towed AT	Lt	Med	Hvy	Rocket
1st Inf Div	50	73	16	53	4	54	24	4	
XVIII Abn Corps			2	19			24	12/8	
30th Inf Div	77	48	18	106	32	84/18	12		
82d Abn Div		12				56	12		
106th Inf Div (−)			8	11		16	10		
3d Armd Div	196	197	97	687	32	/70	12	/12	
7th Armd Div.	86	113	60	400		/69			
9th Armd Div[3]	107	86	41	432		/51			
VII Corps	36	76	45		33	30	36	54	
2d Armd Div	239	255	193	706		/72	12		
84th Inf Div	48	52	18	42		66	12		
75th Inf Div	57	46	18	43		54	12		
Third Army			34	73	36				
VIII Corps		24				/1	14	3	
101st AB Div		9				56	35		
28th Inf Div (−)	14	21	27	13	14	34	13		
III Corps	57	73				24	48	42	
4th Armd Div	111	124	50	497		/87	24		
26th Inf Div	56	49	42	85		54/18	24		
80th Inf Div	27	50	48	41		54	12		
XII Corps		64	80		24	12/36	60	24/12	
4th Inf Div	38	48	40	52	36	53	12		
5th Inf Div	38	47	45	30	12	66	12		
10th Armd Div	153	106	79	448		/54			
German Units									
Sixth Pz Army	33	28			96				
LXVII Corps		14			36	82	43	23	108
277th VGD		2			6	59	14		
3d PGD		39	13	55	18	32	12/4		
12th VGD		37			7	64	12		
3d FJD					24	10	8		
I SS Pz Corps						70	41	29	108
1st SS PzD	65	13	6	106	36	27/2	21/11		78
12th SS PzD	29	64	15	107	42	36	28/3		84/16
150th PzB	1	3	33	22	4				
II SS Pz Corps								10	24
9th SS PzD	56	54	32	133	42	29/6	35/10		
FBB	26	69	12	60	29	10	3/3		
LXVI Corps							3		108
18th VGD		12			9	68	16		
62d VGD		5			6	71	16		
Fifth Pz Army						54	12	12	90
9th PzD	38	22	4	138	24	15	23/11		

24 December 1944

Type:	Tanks	TDs/ AGs	ACs	APCs	Towed AT	Lt	Med	Hvy	Rocket
15th PGD	11	24	13	15	21	37	18		
LVIII Pz Corps					32	29	30	12	108/16
2d SS PzD	59	60	26	202	15	41	39/3		
116th PzD	17	23	14	87	25	23/2	11/6		
560th VGD					5	70	16		
XLVII Pz Corps					32	12	10	3	
2d PzD	29	11	13	134	10	19/9	33/11	8	18
26th VGD		10			7	72	10		
Pz Lehr D	20	54	16	117	20	25	35/4		
Seventh Army					48			2	
LIII Corps									
5th FJD		8			40	51	12		24
9th VGD		11			9	79	18		
167th VGD					5	68	14		
LXXXV Corps						24	24	3	84
79th VGD					8	63	29		
FG Bde	39	36	12	111	49	22	27		
352d VGD		2			4	58	16		
LXXX Corps						28	30	14	108/16
276th VGD		4			8	64	14		
212th VGD		3			40	83	15		

2 January 1945

Type:	Tanks	TDs/ AGs	ACs	APCs	Towed AT	Lt	Med	Hvy	Rocket
Allied Units									
First Army		30	23	73	10		12		
9th Armd Div	96	91	39	399		/54			
51st Inf Div (B)			61	594	31	72			
V Corps						12	36	40	
9th Inf Div	46	76	68	48		66	24		
99th Inf Div			14	39	34	48	12		
2d Inf Div	34	64	35	51	12	52	12		
1st Inf Div	53	51	32	18	27	54	12	4	
XVIII Abn Corps					41		24	41	
30th Inf Div	61	40	20	179	30	54/18	36	/8	
106th Inf Div (−)			5	3		16	10		
82d Abn Div	55	46				74	12		
7th Armd Div	128	65	31	416		/71			
VII Corps	36	85				12	60	42	
2d Armd Div	249	209	77	705		/72	12		
3d Armd Div	208	177	57	676		12/70	12		
75th Inf Div	55	34	44	39	23	66	12		
83d Inf Div	51	49	43	18		53	12		

2 January 1945

Type:	Tanks	TDs/ AGs	ACs	APCs	Towed AT	Artillery (towed/SP) Lt	Med	Hvy	Rocket
84th Inf Div	53	97	122	70		66	12		
XXX Corps (B)	48		144	74			114	24	
53d Inf Div			61	583	31	72			
33d Armd Bde	191	24	30						
6th Abn Div			25	25	48	51			
29th Tk Bde	152	23	81	223	16	/24			
Guards Armd Div	273	56	97	251	23	24/24			
Third Army			34	70	36				
VIII Corps		24				3/19	27	3/12	
87th Inf Div	16	6	12	17		54	12		
17th Abn Div⁴			2	30		52/18			
4th Armd Div	152	131	56	438		/54			
11th Armd Div	137	113	57	452		/54			
101st AB Div (+)		4	14			56	35	12	
28th Inf Div	12	4	4	13	14	54	12		
III Corps		57	80				24	32	
6th Armd Div	145	126	53	454		/89		/24	
35th Inf Div		28	35	2		66	24		
26th Inf Div	37	48	36	31		54	24		
XII Corps		64	80		36	24/36	60	42	
80th Inf Div	35	45	34	16		54	12		
5th Inf Div	48	50	43	18		54	12		
4th Inf Div	38	53	44	51		53	12		
German Units									
Sixth Pz Army					96				
Korps Felber									108
18th VGD		10			6	64	15		
62d VGD		3			3	69	16		
LXVI Corps						34	32	15	216/16
12th VGD		8			8	64	12		
560th VGD		4			5	66	16		
II SS Pz Corps						65	30	27	24
150th PzB	1	3	33	26	4				
2d SS PzD	28	25	12	151	35	34	31/1		24
Fifth Pz Army	19				96				
FG Bde	14	16	10	65	9	14	14		
LVIII Pz Corps							6	7	
116th PzD	12	17	14	57	17	19/1	12/5		
9th PzD	66	20	3	110	17	11	32/11		
2d PzD (−)⁵	24	17	4	104	9	14/4	10/2	6	
XLVII Pz Corps					32	9	7	3	102
Pz Lehr D	28	47	19	98	13	17	20/2		

2 January 1945

Type:	Tanks	TDs/AGs	ACs	APCs	Towed AT	Lt	Med	Hvy	Rocket
FBB	6	37	11	50	25	7	1/1		
3d PGD		29	10	52	17	31	12/4		
15th PGD		28	1	10	15	23	14		
I SS Pz Corps									
9th SS PzD	44	43	21	73	34	25/4	30/8		
12th SS PzD	21	68	13	93	41	36	28/5		30
26th VGD		4			5	64	10		
340th VGD		6			4	64	14		
XXXIX Pz Corps[6]						27	23	12	
1st SS PzD	24	10	3	47	30	19/1	15/4		24
167th VGD					5	68	24		
Seventh Army					48			2	
LIII Corps						39	40	27	16/36
5th FJD		2			50	21	8		
9th VGD		50			9	79	18		
276th VGD		2			8	59	13		
LXXXV Corps							6		84
79th VGD					8	36	28		
352d VGD		10			1	48	13		
LXXX Corps						8	24		74
212th VGD		3			38	79	15		

16 January 1945

Type:	Tanks	TDs/AGs	ACs	APCs	Towed AT	Lt	Med	Hvy	Rocket
Allied Units									
First Army		30	21	61					
V Corps						12	24	48	
9th Inf Div	46	92	87	53		66	24		
99th Inf Div	11	12	19	27	21	48	12		
2d Inf Div	28	52	22	63	11	52	12		
1st Inf Div	53	65	37	17		54	24	4	
XVIII Abn Corps					29	18	60	41	
30th Inf Div	55	35	39	172	23	54/18	12		
75th Inf Div	51	13	17	51	36	54	24		
106th Inf Div (−)	54	13	4	2		16	10		
82d Abn Div						56			
3d Armd Div	224	180	54	676	4	/72	12		
7th Armd Div	187	96	34	454		/70			
VII Corps	15	101	74		30	24	60	42/12	
2d Armd Div	250	190	74	704		/72	12		
83d Inf Div	48	33	43	18		52	12		
84th Inf Div	58	52	33	15		66	12		

16 January 1945

Type:	Tanks	TDs/ AGs	ACs	APCs	Towed AT	Artillery (towed/SP) Lt	Med	Hvy	Rocket
XXX Corps (B)	48		144	74	32		80	16	
53d Inf Div			56	597	31	72			
33d Armd Bde	191	24	30	110					
6th Abn Div			22	24	16	27			
29th Tk Bde	89	23	29	105	16	/24			
Guards Armd Div	273	56	97	251	23	24/24			
Third Army			32	58					
9th Armd Div	107	91	39	417		/54			
28th Inf Div			5	3		48	12		
VIII Corps						12/19	50	13/12	
17th Abn Div	34	6		23		40			
11th Armd Div	125	109	79	471		/54			
101st AB Div		4	14			60	12		
III Corps		87	73			12/18	36	44	
6th Armd Div	119	118	50	452		/89		/24	
35th Inf Div			4	3		66	12		
26th Inf Div	50	46	32	32		54	12		
90th Inf Div	42	43	34	16		66	12		
XII Corps		64	80		36	12/36	60	42	
80th Inf Div	35	43	36	28	12	54	12		
5th Inf Div	56	52	43	18		54	12		
4th Inf Div	38	53	52	14		52	12		
87th Inf Div			18	39	36	54	12		
4th Armd Div	141	129	53	451		/54			
German Units									
Army Group B									
12th SS PzD	23	60	10	72	37	36	25/5		30
FGB	4	5	10	62	9	14	14		
Sixth Pz Army					96				
I SS Pz Corps						15	21	20	
XIII Corps					47	34	23	12	90/18
9th SS PzD	39	33	15	40	26	19/1	26/4		
18th VGD		3				55	11		
62d VGD						50	12		
326th VGD		12			2	68	14		
LXVI Corps					32	51	40	8	102
3d PGD		18	11	43	17	27	10/4		
15th PGD		22	1	10	13	19	16		
116th PzD	9	16	14	56	21	20/1	13/4		
12th VGD		1				51	6		
560th VGD		3				51	11		

16 January 1945

Type:	Tanks	TDs/ AGs	ACs	APCs	Towed AT	Artillery (towed/SP) Lt	Med	Hvy	Rocket
II SS Pz Corps						15	21	20	
2d SS PzD	17	12	7	123	18	30	27/1		24
Fifth Pz Army					96				
2d PzD (−)	17	12	4	115	8	14/4	11/2	6	
LVIII Pz Corps					32	51	40	24	102
1st SS PzD	45	13		26	22	12/1	11/1		24
5th FJD		6			43	17	8		
167th VGD		4			2	66	13		
340th VGD		3			4	51	13		
XLVII Pz Corps					32	8	6	3	
9th PzD	33	32	1	110	16	10	28/8		
Pz Lehr D	21	44	20	95	10	17	17/2		
FBB	8	39	11	51	22	7	1		
26th VGD		1			3	58	8		
Seventh Army					96			2	
LIII Corps					48	9	20	14	/12
9th VGD		62			7	75	17		
79th VGD					8	52	26		
276th VGD		2			7	58	13		
LXXX Corps						8	24	3	84
352d VGD		8				72	24		
212th VGD		3			39	81	16		

G

MALMÉDY: MASSACRE AND TRIAL[1]

LAST ACT OF THE BATTLE

The last firefight of the Battle of the Bulge occurred before dawn on Bastille Day, 14 July 1976, in the tiny French village of Traves-sur-Saône. Later that morning the police found the body of retired Waffen-SS Colonel Joachim (Jöchen) Peiper, a bullet in his chest, beside his burnt house. Evidence that he had fiercely defended himself against the murderous firebomb and machine-gun assault of two or more assailants surrounded his body: the empty cartridges from his hunting rifle and the nearby cartridges from the guns of his assassins. Later that day the killers called the local newspaper to justify their deed: They had meted out justice to a Nazi thug, a convicted war criminal. They were never apprehended.

Peiper played a major role in the curtain-raiser of the Battle of the Bulge when he led an armored task group in a bold effort to smash through the American lines, cross the Meuse River, and lead the German Sixth Panzer Army in its planned drive to Antwerp. Troops under his command slaughtered American prisoners of war; this violation of the laws of war (the Geneva Convention) has gone down in history as "the Malmédy massacre."

After the war Peiper had been one of the principal defendants in a war-crimes trial of the German soldiers and officers accused of culpability in the Malmédy massacre. He was found guilty and sentenced to death, but the execution was not carried out. He was released from prison in 1956. Later he moved to France with his wife and children. When he received death threats in late June 1976, he sent his wife and children back to Germany but stayed in France to demonstrate that he had no personal fear of the threats.

MASSACRE AT BAUGNEZ

Almost four years after the Malmédy massacre, as the German soldiers who had been convicted of committing the crime were awaiting execution, American Judge

Leroy C. van Roden reported to the Secretary of the Army: "From the conduct of these trials, it is impossible to know whether the men being hanged are guilty or innocent."[2] It is not the purpose of the authors to second-guess Judge van Roden, but this appendix presents the known facts to allow the reader to draw his or her own conclusions.

Shortly after noon on 17 December 1944, the advance guard of Kampfgruppe Peiper approached the hamlet of Baugnez, two miles south of Malmédy, in eastern Belgium. The advance guard, a company of mechanized infantry riding in armored personnel carriers (APCs), was traveling generally west on a secondary road from Tirimont to Ligneauville. The point preceding the advance guard, six tanks and an armored half-track carrying an engineer squad, had almost reached the crossroads at Baugnez when the head of a column of about thirty American trucks traveling south on Belgian Route 32 also arrived at the hamlet. Most of these belonged to B Battery of the U.S. 285th Field Artillery Observation Battalion.

The Germans opened fire with tank guns and small arms. The American truck column halted. The Germans jumped from their personnel carriers, ordered the Americans out of their vehicles or out of nearby ditches where some of them had taken refuge, and took them prisoners. We must assume that some Americans were killed in this first encounter, but we do not know for sure.

As the Germans were rounding up their prisoners, Lt. Col. Peiper drove up in a captured jeep. That morning he had started out behind the point, but had been delayed when he stopped to interrogate a prisoner. Peiper ordered his men to search the trucks for gasoline and to clear wreckage from the road. He ordered the advance guard to continue toward Ligneauville. As he later testified at the trial, he had no interest in the prisoners; he was intent on carrying out his mission, which was to advance toward the Meuse River as rapidly as possible.

Did Peiper leave anyone behind to guard the prisoners? According to his testimony, he did not remember, nor did anyone else. Some commentators have suggested that Peiper ordered them—without guard—either to stay in place to await the arrival of infantry troops or to march eastward into captivity. It is more likely that he left a small group of guards.

The prisoners were gathered in a field beside the crossroads when the first vehicles of Peiper's main force began to pass through. In the confusion some of the Germans in the leading vehicles may have fired on the Americans, not realizing that they were prisoners. At least two German vehicles (one tank, one APC) had broken down beside the road in the vicinity and their crews were trying to repair them.

The record of the trial of the Germans accused of the massacre reveals that no examination of the background facts was made during the pretrial investigation or during the trial itself by the prosecution or by the court. Although the sequence and details of the events are not clear, the following incidents occurred:

•Some of the captured Americans tried to sneak away. There was, of course, no legal reason why they should not try to escape if opportunity presented itself. There was equally no legal reason why a German should not have shot an escaping prisoner.

•Some of the American prisoners seem to have been armed. This may be because some had retained their weapons; others may have picked up weapons lying on the ground near the crossroads. These men would have been perceived as armed enemies by the small number of Germans remaining near the crossroads.

•Shots were fired by the Germans near the prisoners; the circumstances are obscure. There might have been one or two pistol shots fired into the air as a warning to those trying to escape. These were soon followed by a volume of aimed machine-gun fire at the mass of prisoners near the crossroads. At least equally likely, the first shots could have been from the machine guns, either because of German overreaction to a perceived threat, or with murderous intent.

•Many American prisoners were killed or wounded by this German fire, although the exact number is unknown.

•About thirty prisoners escaped, most wounded, and found their way back to American units in the vicinity.

•From testimony of survivors at the trial, some of the wounded were given a murderous coup de grâce.

•There seems good reason to believe that seventy-two bodies were discovered when the crossroads was reoccupied by the Americans on 14 January. Of course, some of these may have been battle casualties from the exchange of fire before the Americans were captured, and some may have been prisoners shot while trying to escape. However, a monument erected on the site after the war lists the names of eighty-four soldiers as victims of "Nazi barbarity."[3]

AFTER THE MASSACRE

On 18 and 19 December, Peiper's task force fought its way fifteen miles farther west before its advance was halted by American resistance. Then the task force was also cut off from the rear, and on 19 December Peiper formed a perimeter around the villages of Stoumont and La Gleize. U.S. counterattacks forced Peiper to withdraw from Stoumont on 21 December. He abandoned about 80 wounded German soldiers and 20 American prisoners. He and his men held on to the mountain village of La Gleize for two more days until they ran out of fuel, food, and ammunition. From 17 through 24 December, according to one count, the task force murdered 353 U.S. prisoners (including those at the crossroads) and 111 Belgian civilians.[4]

Peiper ordered the destruction of all vehicles and heavy weapons. At 0300 on 24 December he and the remnants of Kampfgruppe Peiper began to try to break out to the east through the American ring. They abandoned 50 more wounded, under the care of a German doctor, and 150 American prisoners. They took with them only one prisoner, Maj. Hal D. McCown, commanding officer of the 2d Battalion of the 119th Infantry Regiment (of the 30th Infantry Division), who had been captured on 21 December. Early Christmas morning Peiper and about 800 surviving SS troopers of his command (originally about 3,000 men) broke through elements of the 82d Airborne Division and reached the German lines.

Major McCown escaped during one of the final skirmishes between the SS troops and the paratroopers. A few days later (6 January) he wrote a report on his experience as a POW.[5] The report includes the following information:

•Conditions were hard during the siege of La Gleize. Food and shelter were short. U.S. artillery fire was heavy, effective, and terrifying. German losses were high.

•McCown had several long conversations on a variety of general topics with Peiper, who was fluent in English.[6]

•McCown and the other American prisoners were given practically the same (inadequate) rations as the Germans, and were given the best available protection in deep cellars. None of the American prisoners reported any maltreatment while they were held in La Gleize. (At the trial the prosecution asserted that at least 175 U.S. prisoners had been murdered in the village.)[7]

THE WORD SPREADS

Some of the 30 American prisoners who had escaped the massacre at Baugnez began to reach nearby U.S. units on the evening of 17 December. The units immediately sent reports to higher headquarters. On 18 December word reached General Bradley at 12th Army Group Headquarters and General Eisenhower at SHAEF that "about 200" U.S. prisoners had been murdered near Malmédy. The news was broadcast by Radio Calais on 20 December and quickly picked up by the Allied press. It was mentioned in *Newsweek* of 25 December and *Time* of 8 January.

The Radio Calais broadcast was monitored by the headquarters of the Sixth Panzer Army, which later claimed that it had immediately initiated an investigation. By 26 December all units under command of the army had returned negative reports about such an incident.

On 30 December the U.S. State Department informed the government of Switzerland, the Protective Power, that "about 190" prisoners had been murdered. The Swiss were requested to inform the German Government. The U.S. Government expressed its expectation that the culprits would be punished and that the German Government would inform the U.S. Government through the Protective Power about the measures taken.

This triggered another German investigation. In mid-January Army Group B informed the Joint Staff (Wehrmachtführungsstab) that the investigation, which included interrogation of U.S. prisoners captured near Malmédy, had produced no evidence of a massacre. On 29 January the Joint Staff directed that the investigation should continue, reminding all subordinate headquarters that on 26 January Hitler had officially emphasized observance of the Geneva Convention. Finally, on 6 March the German Foreign Office informed the Swiss Legation that no trace of the alleged outrage had been found.[8] In light of information available to the German Government through intelligence sources about news of the Malmédy affair in the Allied press, it is hard to believe that these German investigations were very serious.

BACKGROUND OF THE TRIAL

Even though the information about the Malmédy massacre is less complete and more confused than it would have been if the matter had been properly handled by

U.S. authorities, it is evident that a serious atrocity and criminal violation of the Hague and Geneva Conventions occurred at the Baugnez crossroads shortly after noon on 17 December, and that somewhere between fifty and eighty-six American prisoners of war were murdered in cold—or at least cool—blood by their German captors. Even if, as suggested by some German commentators, this can be attributed to a panicky overreaction to the escape of some prisoners, or to weapons in the hands of others, that act was a clear and unjustifiable violation of the laws of war.

This in no way, however, justifies an apparently criminal counterreaction by victorious countrymen of the murdered soldiers, or equally criminal negligence in the application of justice, even if such reactions were stimulated by overblown war propaganda.

The propaganda had, according to one commentator, created a situation "approaching hysteria."[9] Contributing to this was the reputation of the SS; Americans made no distinction between the brutal SS guards and executioners at Himmler's concentration camps and death factories and the combat troops of the Waffen SS. Nor was the American reaction softened by the fact that these particular SS soldiers were from the Division Leibstandarte SS Adolf Hitler (Adolf Hitler SS Life Guards). At the same time that preparations were being made to try the accused perpetrators of the Malmédy massacre, evidence relating to that massacre was being presented to the War Crimes Tribunal at Nürnberg to substantiate a case that the entire SS, including the Waffen SS, was a criminal organization.[10]

Thus to all of the Americans involved in the process of criminal justice related to the trial of those accused of responsibility for the Malmédy massacre—from pretrial investigation, through preparation of the case by the prosecution, to the deliberations of members of the court-martial—there was no doubt of either the culpability or the criminality of those accused: The massacre had occurred; SS troops were responsible. Granting that many or most of those Americans involved in this process were men of goodwill, their common motivation was not to weigh evidence or to expose doubts but rather to organize the process in such a way as to assure that the guilty would be punished as quickly and efficiently as possible.

The process was facilitated by several administrative actions, some of which were questionable. After the unconditional surrender of Germany in early May 1945, it was no doubt appropriate to inform Switzerland that her role as the Protective Power had ended, since there was no longer a German government. For the same reason, but perhaps with less practical justification, the Allied military governments declared that the body of international law of the Hague Treaties was now "inapplicable."[11] On 9 May 1946, one week before the opening of the trial, the Judge Advocate's Office of the U.S. Military Government quietly changed the official status of all German "prisoners of war" to "Members of Disarmed Enemy Forces." This action was taken with the authority of the U.S. State Department, despite the disagreement and strong protests of the U.S. Army and U.S. Navy Judge Advocates General.[12] This change freed the captors of all legal obligations and deprived the prisoners of all rights under international law. Neither those accused as perpetrators of the Malmédy massacre (and related war crimes) nor their defense attorneys were informed of this change of status at the time.

The pretrial investigation began in June 1945. More than 1,000 former SS troops, now prisoners, were gathered for screening at Zuffenhausen, near Ludwigsburg. In December about 500 were transferred to a large penitentiary at Schwäbisch Hall, near Stuttgart. There the interrogation was intensified under the direction of Lt. Col. Burton F. Ellis, who was later appointed chief of the prosecution team.

There can be little doubt that a principal purpose of the interrogation process was less to obtain factual information than to induce as many of the accused as possible to make self-incriminating confessions. The most likely prospects were kept for weeks and months in solitary confinement. Because the suspects were still prisoners of war at the time, such treatment was illegal under the provisions of the Geneva Convention. When the accused were taken from their cells to be interrogated, black hoods were placed over their heads to facilitate rough (and anonymous) treatment by the guards during the march from cellblock to interrogation room.

The interrogations often took the form of mock trials. In attendance at some of these trials were individuals in the garb of priests, who took confessions and administered the last rites to those sentenced to death by the mock court. Many of the POWs later testified that after they had been found "guilty" they were promised leniency if they either prepared written confessions or incriminated fellow-prisoners.

Later accusations that the guards and interrogators used even more violent means to obtain confessions appear to be supported by firm evidence. A Schwäbisch Hall dentist testified under oath about treating patients with dislocated teeth, and one with a broken jaw. Other testimony reported black hoods covered with blood, severe bruises, and injured testicles. The citizens of Schwäbisch Hall heard howls and screams from the penitentiary at night and told their priests. Some of these reports reached Bishop Wurm of Stuttgart and Bishop Neuhaeusler, the Auxiliary Bishop of Munich, who was familiar with such treatment from the four years he had spent at Dachau during the Hitler regime.

One of the prisoners was Sgt. Arvid Freimuth. After his interrogation one night, inmates of neighboring cells heard him scream: "They have forced me to lie!" The next morning he was found dead in his cell, where he had hanged himself. A German POW who was employed as a medic in the penitentiary clinic later reported that Freimuth's body was covered with blood and bruises, and that his genitals were swollen.[13]

To what extent the treatment of the Malmédy prisoners at Schwäbisch Hall was known to higher American authorities is not clear. However, Gen. Lucius Clay related that when the Malmédy suspects did not readily confess, he ordered that they should be guarded by men who had seen the corpses at the crossroads. "And these soldiers," said Clay, "applied rather rough methods" to obtain confessions from the prisoners.[14]

By late April 1946, seventy-four prisoners were selected for trial: Peiper; 70 officers and men of his task force; Gen. Josef "Sepp" Dietrich, commanding general of the Sixth Panzer Army; Maj. Gen. Fritz Kraemer, Sixth Army Chief of Staff; and Lt. Gen. Hermann Priess, commander of the I SS Panzer Corps. The commander of the 1st SS Panzer Division, Lt. Gen. Wilhelm Mohnke, was not tried because he was a prisoner of war in Russia.

THE TRIAL

The accused were then transferred to Dachau, where the trial started on 16 May. Peiper and his men (including two battalion commanders) were charged with either committing, or ordering, or condoning the murders. The three generals were charged with having transmitted Hitler's murder orders through military channels.

Most of the accused were confronted with and acknowledged their signed confessions. A few repudiated the confessions on the grounds that they had been obtained under duress. Those who had not confessed, including Peiper and the three generals, maintained their innocence. Near the end of the trial one of the defendants who had confessed, a French national, was extradited to France. The French did not try him, and he was soon released.

Included in the evidence presented were the unsigned confessions of Sergeant Freimuth. Lieutenant William Perl, one of the prosecutors, had also been in charge of the Freimuth interrogation. He assured the court that had Freimuth not voluntarily removed himself from the process, he would have corroborated the unsigned confessions.

The following examples illustrate the pattern of the trial.

The prosecution presented the case against those accused of participating in the murders of 175 to 311 U.S. prisoners at La Gleize. According to testimony and signed confessions, the American prisoners had been lined up by their German captors on the inner side of the wall surrounding the church and the churchyard and then shot.

There are, however, some problems with this story. First, the church and churchyard were on top of a small hillock and had never been surrounded by a wall. Second, none of the surviving American prisoners held in La Gleize at the time, including Major McCown, witnessed the murders. Finally, the principal defense counsel, Lt. Col. Willis M. Everett Jr., had obtained the sworn testimony of the village priest and several villagers; they had not seen the murders, although they had seen SS medics tending both American and German wounded.[15]

There were also allegations of atrocities at Büllingen, a village of 300 inhabitants. It was charged by the prosecution that 9 Belgian civilians had been murdered there. The charge was corroborated by several confessions, but Everett was able to demonstrate that neither the mayor of Büllingen nor any of the surviving villagers were aware of these murders.[16]

On 16 July, after hearing all the testimony, the court deliberated for 140 minutes and returned a guilty verdict for all of the accused. The court then again retired to consider the sentences. Two days later the President of the Court, Brig. Gen. Josiah T. Dalbey, announced the sentences. Forty-three were sentenced to death, including Peiper; twenty-two were sentenced to life imprisonment, including Dietrich; and eight were sentenced to terms between ten and twenty years (twenty years for Priess and ten for Kraemer). The court then agreed to recommend approval of the unanimous request of all of those sentenced to death that they be shot and not hanged. (This request and recommendation were later denied by higher authority.)

THE REVIEW PROCESS

Following the trial, the record went to theater headquarters for approval, amendment, or disapproval by the Theater Commander, Gen. Lucius D. Clay. In addition to the usual review by the theater Judge Advocate General, Clay appointed a War Crimes Board of Review, also under his Judge Advocate General. As a preliminary step, he directed Lieutenant Colonel Everett, the defense counsel, to prepare a detailed petition for clemency.[17]

The reviews were not conducted in a political vacuum. The trial record reached Clay's headquarters at a time when many war-crimes trials were already under way or about to begin, not only in Europe but also in Japan and elsewhere in East Asia. Some of these trials, like General Yamashita's in the Philippines, were already controversial. If the review of the Malmédy trial raised serious questions regarding the pretrial investigation, the conduct of the trial, or the sentences, there could be implications for the other trials.

Thus it is perhaps surprising that General Clay's War Crimes Board of Review "openly accused the Army investigators of conduct at best inept, at worst unprincipled, and the Army judges of consistent bias to the advantage of the prosecution."[18] Apparently largely based on this review, General Clay announced the results of his own review of the trial record on 28 March 1948. Only twelve of the forty-three death sentences (including Peiper's) were confirmed; twenty-seven were reduced to prison sentences of varying lengths, and in four cases the charges were dismissed. Two of the twenty-two life sentences were confirmed, twelve were reduced, and in eight cases the charges were dismissed. Of the eight shorter prison sentences, five were confirmed, two reduced, and one remitted. Clay's decision did not reveal the extent to which the changes were due to faults in the process or were the result of clemency.

THE STORM

By the time the review was completed, Colonel Everett had returned to the United States and been discharged from the Army. He had loyally kept silent until General Clay's decision was announced. Although pleased with the great reductions in the severity of the sentences, he was convinced that there was no legal justification for any of the death sentences or life terms. He knew that none of the convictions had been proved beyond a reasonable doubt. Despite the fact that the Army would not give him access to the trial record, he prepared from memory a petition for a writ of habeas corpus for submission to the U.S. Supreme Court. On 18 May, however, the Court refused to accept jurisdiction.

With the executions scheduled to begin on 20 May, Everett obtained an appointment with Secretary of the Army Kenneth C. Royall on the nineteenth. As a result of Everett's presentation that day, Royall, himself a lawyer, ordered a stay of all executions (not only for the Malmédy trial, but for sixty-six other war-crimes trials that had taken place at Dachau). The stay of executions was to remain in effect until these sentences had been reviewed by a special commission that Royall appointed. The commission consisted of Judge Gordon Simpson, Judge van Roden, and Lt. Col. Charles W. Lawrence of the Army's Judge Advocate General's office.

A few days later Everett attempted to get a review of the case by the International Court of Justice at The Hague. This effort was unsuccessful, however, since the court accepted the U.S. argument that only governments could plead at The Hague, and there was no German government to protect German citizens.

The Simpson Commission submitted its unanimous report on 14 September 1948. While it criticized some aspects of the case, such as the mock trials, and some unethical practices of the prosecution, it found that those sentenced to death had committed the crimes for which they had been convicted. Nevertheless, the commission recommended that all of the Malmédy trial death sentences be commuted to life imprisonment.

Then one of the commission members broke ranks. Judge van Roden publicly accused both the Malmédy trial prosecution and the court of grave misconduct; his principal charges related to the "third degree" methods used in the interrogations.

This led to a heated political debate. Survivors of the massacre, relatives of those who had been murdered, and many patriotic veterans demanded that "justice be done" by carrying out the executions. Appeals were made to the White House in the expectation that President Harry S. Truman, a combat veteran of World War I, would support their demands for justice. Critics of the verdict were accused of anti-Semitism, since most of the prosecution team had been Jews (several of them refugees from Hitler's Germany), and the Law Member of the Court had been Col. Abraham H. Rosenfeld. Critics of the trial were also denounced as pro-Communists.

Opponents of the trial verdicts were also active. German church leaders—Cardinal Frings (Archbishop of Cologne), and Bishops Neuhaeusler and Wurm—got in touch with American Congressmen and churches. The German lawyers who had supported Colonel Everett in the defense alerted many people of influence in Europe and the United States. A significant argument was that Germany was needed as an ally against the Communist Bloc in an intensified Cold War; thus the Allies should regain the friendship of the German people by freeing victims of dubious war-crimes trials. The *Chicago Tribune* demanded that the prosecution and court of the Malmédy trial be court-martialed.[19]

The controversy reached the U.S. Senate, where a subcommittee of the Senate Armed Services Committee was established to investigate the Malmédy massacre and trial. The members were Senators Raymond E. Baldwin of Connecticut, Lester C. Hunt of Wyoming, Estes Kefauver of Tennessee, and Joseph McCarthy of Wisconsin. Not entirely by coincidence, the two Democratic members of the committee—Baldwin and Kefauver—were lawyers closely associated in their former law firms with members of the interrogation and prosecution teams (Maj. Dwight Fanton and Capt. Raphael Shumacker, respectively). At least initially, however, neither Hunt nor McCarthy seems to have held any preconceived opinions about the case, although the flamboyant McCarthy undoubtedly saw this as an opportunity for self-promotion.

McCarthy proposed that members of the prosecution team, as well as some of the convicted Germans, be given lie detector tests. Somewhat surprisingly, Lieutenant Perl, the most aggressive of the prosecutors, agreed to this. But the matter came to a vote before the subcommittee at a time when Senator Hunt was absent. Senators Baldwin and Kefauver outvoted McCarthy 2-1 on the matter. McCarthy then resigned from the subcommittee, charging in a speech on the Senate floor that its work was a shameful farce to cover up "Gestapo and OGPU tactics used by the U.S. Army."[20] The subcommittee prepared a report, then faded into oblivion.

Thus ended the last relatively impartial effort to determine what really happened near Malmédy, and in the subsequent interrogation and trial of those accused of the atrocity.

AFTERMATH AND ASSESSMENT

In April 1949 General Clay commuted six of the remaining death sentences to life imprisonment. Two years later his successor, Gen. Thomas T. Handy, commuted the last six death sentences. In 1954, when limited sovereignty was restored to West Germany by the United States, the United Kingdom, and France, a precondition was that West Germany would not reopen any of the Allied war-crimes trials. However, bilateral clemency boards were set up. Through action by these boards the prisoners were paroled one by one. The last to be released was Peiper, on 22 December 1956. He had been a prisoner for nearly eleven years, and had spent fifty-five months on death row.

What really happened at Baugnez and at the other places nearby during the week that Kampfgruppe Peiper was fighting behind the American lines? None of the many books written about the Battle of the Bulge, including the several that focus specifically on the Malmédy massacre, gives a definitive answer. However, we can speculate with reasonable confidence.

Some of the bodies later found at the crossroads were probably battle casualties. A few more may have been killed lawfully by German guards when they tried to escape from the scene of their capture. But there can be little doubt that fifty to sixty were brutally murdered when their German captors shot them in flagrant violation of the internationally recognized laws of war.

Who was responsible? Who deserved punishment for this crime? There does not appear to be hard evidence tying a policy of "take no prisoners" to Sepp Dietrich, the army commander, or to Hermann Priess, the corps commander, or to Wilhelm Mohnke, the division commander.

As the senior German commander in the vicinity, Peiper undoubtedly bears substantial guilt, even if the murders were not specifically or tacitly approved by him. He was, after all, responsible for the conduct of his men. But the fact that he later treated prisoners decently seems to mitigate his guilt. If he did order or condone a policy of "take no prisoners" at Baugnez, he did not personally adhere to that policy.

The greatest guilt, of course, was shared by the men who pulled the triggers and shot down the American prisoners in cold blood, and the officers who ordered the executions. Their actions cannot be condoned by arguing that soldiers of other armies—including the United States Army—committed similar brutal murders. But we do not know for certain who the guilty German soldiers were, because some Americans—by acts of omission and commission—prevented us from knowing. Certainly justice was not done by punishing German soldiers who had been coerced into confessions that no person in his right mind would make without coercion. Justice was not done by seeking and obtaining convictions of guilt not proved beyond a reasonable doubt, even if some of those convicted were undoubtedly guilty.

And what of the culpability of those Americans who were responsible for the coercion, and who callously used the results of coercion for the purpose of sending to their deaths men who may have been completely innocent? Their performance was nothing less than contemptible, and they were hardly less cold-blooded than the Germans who committed murder.

Germans should be ashamed of the Malmédy massacre. Americans should be ashamed of the Malmédy massacre trial.

APPENDIX H

GERMAN COMBAT PERFORMANCE

Time after time during the Battle of the Bulge German soldiers outfought their American opponents. They were not supermen. They blundered, probably about as often as the Americans. And there seems little doubt that the best of the Americans were every bit as good as the best of the Germans. Furthermore, the Americans won the battle and, eventually, the war. Yet at the height of the battle for Bastogne, on 4 January 1945, General Patton wrote in his diary: "We can still lose this war. . . . The Germans are colder and hungrier than we are, but they fight better."[1]

Why were the Germans better in combat? What was there about Germany, or Germans, or the German military system that stimulated such continuing skillful efforts among their best soldiers, and commendable efforts even from the newly inducted and poorly trained soldiers that made up a considerable portion of the Germans fighting in the Ardennes?

I first sought to find the answer to these questions more than twenty years ago. When analyzing World War II battles with the Quantified Judgment Model, I discovered that German performance or combat effectiveness was consistently superior to that of the western Allies: Americans, British, French. While the margin of superiority varied somewhat from battle to battle, it could be quantified at about 20 percent on average. In other words, my model showed that 100 German soldiers were the equivalent of about 120 American, British, or French soldiers with comparable equipment. This differential varied from unit to unit, and there were a few Allied units that could perform as well as the best of the Germans. Yet in more than 150 battles and engagements mostly at division level (although levels of aggregation ranged from regiment or brigade up to army corps), this 20 percent average German combat effectiveness performance was undeniable. This was true early in the war (my first analyses were for Salerno, Italy, in September 1943), and late in the war (one Ardennes engagement in December 1944). Against the Russians (in a smaller data base of only about fifteen battles) the average German superiority was more than 100 percent: on average, 100 German soldiers were the equivalent of 200 or more comparably equipped Soviet soldiers. This greater combat effectiveness existed whether the Germans were attacking or defending. It held when they had air superiority and when they didn't. It held when they won and when they lost.

I tried to interest the Pentagon in my quantitative finding about German combat performance. I thought that the U.S. Army might learn something useful if it were to study the German Army to find out why it possessed this persistent combat effectiveness superiority. The typical answer I got from Pentagon officials was, "Why study the German Army? We won the war didn't we?" Yes, of course we won the war. We won it because the Allies overwhelmed the Germans with numbers of men and machines. But I still asked why the Germans were better fighters than we were unit for unit. The Pentagon didn't care.

So, I wrote a book on the subject.[2] I cannot in a few pages do more than briefly summarize the results of the research and analysis that went into that book. But here are a few of my findings:

• The Germans are not and were not a "master race" as Hitler claimed. They simply organized themselves for war better than we did; they made better use of their weapons; they were more professional than we were.

• The German Army had adopted a military system that had been developed by the Prussians in 1807 after they had been overwhelmingly defeated by the French under Napoleon.

• This military system, a cultural development and not inherent to the German people, built around the superb Prussian General Staff, produced leaders and soldiers who on average fought better than their enemies, including the United States.

On the other hand, there can be no doubt that American troops fought well in the Battle of the Bulge.[3] Yet Patton was right. The Germans *were* better, at least during the first days of the battle and, on balance, in most instances for the entire campaign. It was obvious to most of them that the war was lost, yet they rarely gave up; they would keep on fighting regardless of circumstances. In close-fought battles they usually inflicted casualties on the Americans at a rate greater than the Americans inflicted casualties on them. At the same time, as an indication that their efforts were more determined than ours, they sometimes demonstrated that they would, to achieve important objectives, incur casualties at a greater rate than we did. Even when exhausted they would seize the initiative if given an opportunity. When defeated, they would counterattack; when apparently trapped, they would often find ways to escape.

In the preparation of *Hitler's Last Gamble,* I have used my latest computerized model, the Tactical Numerical Deterministic Model (TNDM), to analyze ten more Ardennes battles, simply to confirm my earlier findings, in which I had included only one Ardennes battle (the Sauer River). The results of these analyses are summarized in the table.[4] German relative combat effectiveness values (CEVs) mostly exceed 1.0 and vary from 0.77 to 1.30. (A value greater than 1.0 is performance superior to the enemy's; a value less than 1.0 is performance inferior to the opponent's.) The exception is the apparently poor German performance at Celles, discussed below. However, including the Battle of Celles, the German CEVs average around 1.05, less than the 1.2 average CEV of earlier campaigns, which warrants some analysis. The following are the principal observations emerging from such analysis:

• The average German soldier in the Ardennes campaign was not as well trained as the average American soldier. The fact that the Germans retained an average combat effectiveness superiority, even though at a lower margin than earlier in the war, was due to the continuing high standards of German professional leadership.

• The negligible German superiority at Krinkelt-Rocherath was due to the high quality of the U.S. 2d Infantry Division and the superb leadership of its commander, General Robertson.

• The relatively low German CEV at Diekirch reflects the difficulties the Germans had getting across the Our River in the sector of the 28th Division's 109th Infantry Regiment, and the exceptional performance of the 109th during the campaign.

• The even lower German CEV at Celles is due to two things. First, German records for the entire campaign are very sketchy and perhaps less reliable for this engagement. More important, however, the 2d Panzer Division was exhausted after nine days of almost constant combat and movement and was extremely short of both fuel and ammunition. Contributing further to the American superiority at Celles was the fact that the 2d Armored Division was possibly the best American armored division in Europe and was commanded by Maj. Gen. Ernest Harmon, perhaps the most skilled and most aggressive U.S. armored division commander.

• The American CEV of 1.1 (and the German CEV of 0.90) at Harlange is in fact more of a tribute to the German 5th Parachute Division than to the U.S. 90th Infantry Division. This observation is based on consideration of the exhausted condition of the German 5th FJD and its overextended line east of Bastogne, as well as the fact that, under an excellent, aggressive division commander, the U.S. 90th Division was a better-than-average U.S. infantry division. While the 5th FJD was close to collapse at the end of that battle, in fact it did not collapse.

Now, I think, we can answer the question asked at the outset of this appendix. Why were the Germans better than we were? The answer is, in brief, the superior military system noted above. Man for man, the typical German soldier was not smarter, braver, stronger, or more highly motivated than was the American soldier. But their leaders were, for the most part, more professional.

EFFECTIVENESS STATISTICS
Selected Battles: The Ardennes Campaign

Engagement	Forces	Posture	Average Strength	Casualties/ day	% Cas	Score Effectiveness	CEV*
A. Fifth Army	US: VIII C	D	50,022	1,507	3.01	2.54	
Offensive	Ge: Fifth A	A	140,144	1,269	0.91	1.08	1.09
16–19 Dec							
B. Krinkelt-	US: 2d, 99th IDs	D	26,412	696	2.64	2.48	
Rocherath	Ge: I SS Pz C	A	41,100	654	1.59	1.69	1.03
16–18 Dec							
C. Schnee Eifel	US: 106th ID	D	18,541	587	3.19	1.63	
16–18 Dec	Ge: 18th						
	VGD (+)	A	29,598	303	1.23	2.39	1.43
D. Skyline Drive	US: 110th RCT	D	6,043	406	6.72	4.10	
16–18 Dec	(28th ID)						
	Ge: XLVII Pz C	A	40,511	248	0.61	1.00	1.28
E. Diekirch	US: 109th RCT	D	4,985	259	5.20	8.75	1.30
16–19 Dec	(28th ID)						
	Ge: LXXXV C	A	32,730	436	1.33	0.79	
F. Sauer River	US: 4th ID (−)	D	9,724	345	3.55	2.79	
16–18 Dec	Ge: 212th VGD	A	15,247	271	1.78	2.63	1.13
G. St. Vith	US: 7th AD (+)	D	22,576	495	2.19	2.78	1.13
19–21 Dec	Ge: LXVI C (+)	A	48,936	628	1.28	1.01	
H. Bastogne	US: 101st	D	20,441	341	1.67	1.36	
Defense	ABD (+)						
21–26 Dec	Ge: XLVII PzC	A	30,317	277	0.91	1.13	1.11
I. Celles 25–26	US: 2d AD (−)	D–A	12,205	54	0.44	1.67	1.48
Dec	Ge: 2d PzD	A–D	7,076	204	2.88	0.76	
J. Sadzot 28–29	US: TF†	D	4,882	40	0.82	0.80	
Dec	Ge: 25th						
	PzGR (−)	A	3,199	39	1.22	1.25	1.01
K. Harlange	US: 90th ID (+)	A	16,094	176	1.09	1.32	1.10
9–11 Jan	Ge: 5th						
	FJD (−) (+)	D	7,381	212	2.53	2.39	

*CEVs are shown only for the side with superiority (greater than 1.0). CEV for the opponent is the reciprocal; for instance, the German CEV for Example A is 1.09; the US CEV is 0.92.
†TF Orr, 3d AD (+), to include Co. C, 87 Chem Bn, 509 PIBn, and 112 IR (−).

NOTES

1. BEFORE THE STORM

1. Erich Ludendorff, the operational commander of the German Army in the last two years of World War I, called 8 August 1918, "the Black Day of the German Army." It was on that day, when some German units broke and fled in the face of a determined Anglo-American offensive in northern France and Belgium, that Ludendorff realized that his war was irretrievably lost. Similarly, in August 1944, when German forces in Poland, France, and Italy were smashed by Allied offensives on three fronts, it was evident to all senior officers of Hitler's Wehrmacht that World War II had been irretrievably lost.

2. Some of Sibert's many critics believe that these words reflected his effort to seize an opportunity to use information gleaned from ULTRA without disclosing the source. There had not been a hint of any serious threat in recent ULTRA traffic. Sibert was convinced that this meant that no attack was imminent, because in the past ULTRA had invariably permitted accurate "forecasting" of German activities. But ULTRA could not be mentioned or cited except within the very limited "ULTRA community."

3. There is no evidence that Bradley had issued any such instructions.

4. Stephen E. Ambrose, *The Supreme Commander: The War Years of General Dwight D. Eisenhower* (New York, 1970), p. 552.

2. GERMAN DISPOSITIONS AND PLANS

1. There was no corresponding command for the eastern front, which was run directly from OKH (Oberkommando des Heeres, or Army High Command), but OB West and OB Southwest (under Luftwaffe Field Marshal Albert Kesselring) fell under the purview of OKW (Oberkommando der Wehrmacht). This rather peculiar command structure, which left two general staffs connected only by Hitler's personal authority, arose because Hitler, working directly through OKH, had assumed personal

operational command of the eastern front in December 1941, following German reverses early that month.

2. See appendixes C and D for a more complete discussion of German command hierarchy and organization and German military ranks.

3. The biographical sketch of Model is derived from material in T. N. Dupuy, Curt Johnson, and David L. Bongard, *The Harper Encyclopedia of Military Biography* (New York, 1992), and from Carlo D'Este's essay "Model" in *Hitler's Generals*, edited by Correlli Barnett (New York, 1989), pp. 319–33.

4. Although often referred to as the Sixth SS Panzer Army during the Ardennes offensive, the Sixth Panzer Army did not receive this designation until shortly before it took part in the Lake Balaton counteroffensive in Hungary, in mid-January 1945.

5. This oft-quoted remark, cited in Charles B. MacDonald, *A Time for Trumpets* (New York, 1985), p. 35, is derived from Charles V. P. von Luttichau, "Report on the Interview (14–19 May 1952) with Thuisko von Metzsch [one of Model's staff officers]," Operations of Army Group B and Its Role in the German Ardennes Offensive 1944, U.S. Army Center of Military History.

6. Dietrich said, "All Hitler wants me to do is cross a river, capture Brussels, and then go on and take Antwerp! And all this in the worst time of the year through the Ardennes where the snow is waist deep and there isn't room to deploy four tanks abreast let alone armored divisions! Where it doesn't get light until eight and it's dark again at four and with re-formed divisions made up chiefly of kids and sick old men—and at Christmas!" Quoted in MacDonald, *A Time for Trumpets*, p. 37, from Peter Elstob, *Hitler's Last Offensive* (London, 1971), p. 56.

7. This fact, little appreciated by historians until the 1980s, was one of the most serious failures of German industrial mobilization during the war. The Nazi doctrine of a state-sponsored family-centered social life for the nation, and women's role with Kinder, Kirche, Küche, and Kamin (children, church, kitchen, and hearth/fireplace), made the widespread employment of women workers poltically costly for the government until it was too late.

8. Biographical material for Skorzeny is drawn from the entry in T. N. Dupuy, Johnson, and Bongard, *The Harper Encyclopedia of Military Biography*. Readers are also referred to Skorzeny's memoirs—*Geheimkommando Skorzeny* (Hamburg, 1950), and *Meine Kommandounternehmen* (Wiesbaden-Munich, 1976)—and to two English-language biographies: Robert Hale, *Skorzeny's Special Missions* (London, 1957), and Charles Whiting, *Skorzeny* (New York, 1972).

9. The material for the biographical sketch of Dietrich is drawn principally from Franz Kurowski, "Dietrich and Manteuffel," in *Hitler's Generals,* edited by Correlli Barnett, pp. 411–37.

10. Rollbahn is commonly translated as "runway" but is more precisely "travel route" or "advance route." Each one was a preselected roadway designated for mechanized movement, especially for exploitation. Units not assigned to a particular rollbahn were generally not permitted to use it unless the assigned units had already passed by.

11. In Rundstedt's report to Jodl of 18 November,   on planning for the offensive, he stated that his objective was to reach the Meuse and to build bridgeheads on the first day (BA-MA RHIV 1247). Hitler agreed with this. (OKW War Diary, vol. IV, 1, p. 442.)

12. See appendices E (personnel strength) and F (matériel strength) for a more

complete analysis of German manpower and matériel allocations. See also OBWest War Diary (BA-MA RH 19 IV 76).

13. Although there were thirteen of eighteen planned infantry-type divisions (72.2 percent), the shortfall with panzer and panzergrenadier units was more serious, with only 7½ of 12 divisions (62.5 percent) present. Eventually the Germans deployed four additional volksgrenadier divisions and one panzer and two panzergrenadier divisions, with a second panzer brigade, making a total of seventeen infantry-type and eleven-plus armored or mechanized divisions and division-equivalents. That force level was not reached until the end of December, far too late to do any good for the German offensive.

3. ALLIED PLANS AND DEPLOYMENTS

1. Dwight D. Eisenhower, *Crusade in Europe* (New York, 1948), p. 210.

2. One of the coauthors of this book served twice with General Bradley. The first time was as a cadet at West Point, when then Major Bradley was the Assistant Commandant. There were two memorable contacts. One was when Bradley sternly ordered the cadet to report himself for an inadvertent infraction of Cadet Regulations. The other was when Lt. Col. Bradley arranged for the cadet to be flown by special plane as the sole passenger (it was a small plane, and the cadet's first air journey) to Mitchell Field, Long Island, to join his classmates on an "Air Corps trip," from which a brief illness had kept him. Later, as a major during World War II, the coauthor served as a battalion commander under then Maj. Gen. Bradley in the 28th Division, and observed Bradley's leadership invigorate that dispirited division.

3. See Bernard L. Montgomery, *The Memoirs of Field Marshal Montgomery* (Cleveland, 1958), pp. 268–70, and Omar N. Bradley and Clay Blair, *A General's Life* (New York, 1983), pp. 346–47.

4. Bradley and Blair, *A General's Life,* p. 347.

5. In *A General's Life* Bradley called this decision "a classic Eisenhower compromise that left me distinctly unhappy."

6. Montgomery, *The Memoirs of Field Marshal Montgomery,* p. 274.

7. The units were the 3d Parachute Division committed against the U.S. 9th and 83d divisions, along with the 341st Assault Gun Brigade, the 902d Assault Gun Brigade, the 519th Heavy Antitank Battalion, and the 403d Volksartillerie Corps. The American attack also delayed the transfer of the 246th Volksgrenadier Division from the LXXXI to the LXXIV Corps. All these units were scheduled to take part in (or, in the case of the LXXIV Corps, to support) the offensive of the Sixth Panzer Army on 16 December.

8. The 519th Heavy Antitank Battalion (which included a company of the deadly self-propelled 88-mm Jagdpanthers as well as two companies of SP 75-mm guns) was also intended to reinforce the Sixth Panzer Army's initial attack. However, it too was still at Düren, awaiting rail space for its movement to the front. It did not arrive until the offensive was nearly three days old.

The two assault gun brigades and the artillery corps were supposed to support the LXVII Corps in the crucial attack on Monschau and Höfen. Their absence left the German infantry in that sector without armored support and lacking a major part of their artillery support in their effort to block the lateral communications between the U.S. V and VII corps. Perhaps even more important was the indirect effect of the delay in transferring the 246th Division to the LXXIV Corps. That corps—already hard-pressed by the attacks of the 8th and 78th divisions—was forced to retain in line three battalions of the 272d Volksgrenadier Division holding the left of the corps sector. But the 272d was one of the three assault divisions in the Sixth Panzer Army offensive plan, and those three battalions constituted one-half of its infantry strength. There was a similar diversion of strength from the 326th Volksgrenadier Division, which was attempting to hold the crossroads at Wahlerscheid against an inexorable advance by the 2d Infantry Division.

9. It is only fair to note that the reputation of the 3d Armored Division was only slightly less prestigious than those of the 1st and 9th Infantry divisions.

10. The Allies feared that the Germans would allow forces to execute a crossing of the river and then blow the dams to create a wall of water that would destroy bridges and inundate low-lying plains of the Roer valley. The isolated attackers could then be annihilated by German reserves.

11. The 2d Division's Main Supply Route (MSR) was designated as the main road leading from Krinkelt-Rocherath to Wahlerscheid, formerly the MSR for the 99th Division. To accommodate the 2d Division, the 99th Division's route was moved some 1,500 yards to the east, where it followed a secondary road and a series of trails that ran generally east-to-west from the front lines back to Krinkelt-Rocherath.

12. Other battalions assigned to support the 78th and 99th Divisions could also be called upon if necessary. To give maximum support and flexibility (and probably to keep the congested area around Krinkelt-Rocherath clear of the impedimenta of the additional artillery battalions), the bulk of these battalions were deployed in two major groupments. One group was on the corps's far left flank to support the 8th Division and the left of the 78th Division. The second group was north of Monschau, cleverly placed so as to be able to support both the right of the 78th Division and the drive north by the 2d Division.

13. These were the 741st Tank Battalion (–), the 644th Tank Destroyer Battalion (SP) (–), the 612th Tank Destroyer Battalion (T) (–), the 462d Antiaircraft Automatic Weapons Battalion, and C Company of the 86th Chemical Mortar Battalion.

14. The casualties, including those from disease and nonbattle injuries (DNBI), for the three battalions of the 9th Infantry during the Wahlerscheid battle were as follows:

1ST BN

	13 Dec	14 Dec	15 Dec	Total
KIA	1	2	1	4
WIA	18	80	15	113
MIA	0	2	2	4
DNBI	26	89	29	144
Total	45	173	47	265

2D BN

	13 Dec	14 Dec	15 Dec	Total
KIA	1	9	9	19
WIA	64	23	39	126
MIA	4	0	9	13
DNBI	75	68	19	162
Total	144	100	76	320

3D BN

KIA	0	1	0	1
WIA	12	46	6	64
MIA	0	2	2	4
DNBI	33	65	19	117
Total	45	114	27	186

Total combat casualties 338

National Archives and Records Administration Record Group 407, Combat Interviews, 2d U.S. Infantry Division in the Breakthrough, 9th Infantry.

15. These were the 333d, 559th, 561st, 578th, 740th, 770th, 771st, 965th, and 969th Field Artillery battalions.

16. In the 28th Division as in most U.S. infantry divisions, the light artillery component consisted of three battalions, each of four 105-mm towed howitzers; the medium battalion had three batteries each with four towed 155-mm howitzers.

17. Curiously, the 42d Field Artillery was organized as a standard field artillery battalion—that is, with three firing batteries, each with four howitzers—but was equipped as an armored field artillery battalion, with M-7 self-propelled 105-mm howitzers. See the combat interviews of the 4th Infantry Division (Battle of Luxembourg), "Miscellaneous Notes from the 42d FA as Related by Lt. Col. Thomas I. Edgar, CO, and Capt. Harry L. Hooper, S-3" (NARA RG 407). The standard armored artillery battalions had three firing batteries each with six M-7 self-propelled howitzers.

4. "THE ARDENNES OFFENSIVE . . . "

1. These words appear in a memorandum to Col. Telford W. Taylor from Lt. Col. Adolph G. Rosengarten Jr., First Army ULTRA SLU, 21 May 1945, in "Reports by U.S. Army ULTRA Representatives with Army Field Commands in the European Theatre of Operations," NARA RG 457, SRH-023. Signal Liaison Units (SLUs) received decoded material from the decryption center at Bletchley Park, England, and passed the information to ULTRA-cleared personnel. The SLUs also were responsible for the security of ULTRA material. The commander of the SLU was also known simply as the SLU. For further information on the role of the SLUs in World War II, see Ronald Lewin, *ULTRA Goes to War* (London, 1978).

2. These divisions comprised 7 panzer and 13 infantry-type (2 Parachute and 11 Volksgrenadier). For additional details, see Chapter 2.

3. There were three great surprises in World War II, all accomplished by Axis forces. The first of these was the surprise achieved by the Germans in Operation Barbarossa, the invasion of Russia in June 1941. The second was the Japanese attack on Pearl Harbor in December 1941. The third, of course, was the German Ardennes offensive. Each has generated a substantial literature—many essays, a few books—devoted essentially to the intelligence considerations involved in the surprise. The purpose of most of these writings has been to determine the secret of how surprise was accomplished in order to provide guidance to future intelligence officers and commanders so that similar surprise will not be repeated. A simple—perhaps simplistic—answer to the implicit question is that a carefully designed, successful surprise plan can always be created by imaginative, thoughtful leaders. (The subsequent surprise of the Israelis by the Egyptians and Syrians in 1973 is an example.) No human intelligence can ever

anticipate all possibilities that can be dreamed up by another human intelligence. The best that a commander can do is to encourage alertness in his command so that a surprise by the enemy is unlikely to achieve decisive, disastrous results.

4. In regiments and battalions the intelligence staff was, and still is, known as the S-2 section; at division level and above it is the G-2 section, *S* standing for "staff," and *G* for "General Staff."

5. This was also known as signal intelligence, or SIGINT in the U.S. Army's lexicon of acronyms.

6. The personal experience of one of the coauthors of this book suggests that intelligence officers pay much more attention to their own ivory-tower ruminations than they do to reports from the front. I recall reporting in December 1943 that the Japanese forces in north Burma had committed 150-mm howitzers in the Hukawng valley. The area G-2 noted this report in his next intelligence summary, then disdainfully remarked, "This, of course, is impossible, since the lack of roads will not permit such deployment." When Gen. Joseph W. Stilwell visited that area of the front a few days later, I got out a pocket tape measure and laid it against the base of a Japanese dud shell. Stilwell agreed that it was 6", or 150 mm. (The name of the G-2 was Joseph W. Stilwell, Jr.)

7. See NARA RG SRH-049, "Technical Signal Intelligence Transmitted Directly to G-2, 12th Army Group, ETO from 14 August 1944 to May 1945."

8. Standard intelligence doctrine with respect to the issue of "capabilities vs. intentions" can be summarized as follows: Seize eagerly but treat with caution (lest it be disinformation) all information providing insights regarding enemy intentions. Rely primarily on hard evidence of hostile capabilities.

9. David Niven, *The Moon's a Balloon* (New York, 1973), p. 270. Lest the reader misconstrue citation of the memoirs of a Hollywood actor in this work, it should be mentioned that Niven was a prewar graduate of the Royal Military College at Sandhurst, the British equivalent of West Point. In 1942 he had assisted in the formation of "A" Squadron of Montgomery's famous "Phantom" GHQ Liaison Regiment—Montgomery's "eyes and ears" at the front. Niven commanded "A" Squadron until early 1944, when he was appointed as a liaison officer, first with the American contingent of British Lt. Gen. Frederick E. Morgan's COSSAC (Chief of Staff to the Supreme Allied Commander [designate]) staff, which was then engaged in planning for Operation Overlord, and then with its successor, SHAEF.

5. ORDEAL IN THE KRINKELTER WALD

1. Trevor N. Dupuy, Grace P. Hayes, and Curt Johnson, *Dictionary of Military Terms* (New York, 1986), p. 42.

2. Ibid., p. 27.

3. On 18 November Hitler himself gave special orders as guidelines for the method of attack (*"Richtlinien für das Angriffsverfahren der Operation 'Wacht am Rhein'"* in BA-MA 19 IV/247). The main principle for the attacking forces was—depending on the terrain—to achieve the breakthrough primarily by the infantry divisions, massively assisted by assault guns as the first echelon. The mass of the tank formations were designed for the raid to and across the Meuse. If possible they were not to be involved in the breakthrough fighting. The principal differences were in the artillery preparations. The Sixth Panzer Army began its attack with a barrage of half

an hour, while the Fifth Panzer Army rejected this approach so as not to alert the enemy. In the sector of the Seventh Army the decision about the artillery preparation was delegated to the corps commanders. There were differences of opinion between the three army commanders concerning the timing of the attack and the artillery preparation: Manteuffel preferred a night attack by infiltrating infantry forces without artillery preparation, while Dietrich and Brandenberger pointed out the inadequate training of their soldiers for such a method of attack. (See Ronke Werner, "Die Vorbereitung der Ardennen-Offensive 1944 zwischen Gmünd und Ormont," in *Militärgeschichtliches Beiheft zur Europäischen Wehrkunde*, no. 6 (December 1988).

4. Gen. der Infanterie Hitzfeld, commander of LXVII Corps, describes in his memoirs (*Ein Infanterist in zwei Weltkriegen 1898–1980*, pp. 130ff.) that for the attack on Monschau he avoided fire support of heavy artillery, because in the mountainous terrain and in view of the well-dug-in enemy forces, such fire would be nearly without effect. Field Marshal Model had agreed with Hitzfeld's estimate.

5. Route A was assigned to the reinforced I Battalion of the 25th SS Panzergrenadier Regiment and ran roughly Hollerath-Krinkelt-Elsenborn-Liège.

Route B was assigned to a much stronger force known as Kampfgruppe Müller, from the name of the commander of the 25th SS Panzergrenadier Regiment, which, minus its I Battalion, made up the largest part of the kampfgruppe. Kampfgruppe Müller was reinforced by the 12th SS Panzerjäger Battalion (with twenty-one 75-mm self-propelled tank destroyers), the II Battalion of the 12th SS Panzer Artillery Regiment (with eighteen 105-mm towed howitzers), two flak batteries, and an engineer company. Route B ran Udenbreth-Dom Butgenbach-Malmédy-Spa-Theux.

Route C was assigned to the major armored striking force of the 12th SS Panzer Division, Kampfgruppe Kuhlman, named after the commander of the 12th SS Panzer Regiment. The panzer regiment had not been fully reconstituted from its losses in the Normandy campaign and consisted of a single mixed-battalion of two PzKw-IV tank companies (thirty-three tanks) and two PzKw-V "Panther" tank companies (thirty-seven tanks). To make up the shortfall, an army tank destroyer battalion, the 560th Heavy Panzerjäger Battalion, had been assigned as the regiment's second battalion. The 560th was equipped with fourteen heavily armored, 88-mm-armed Jagdpanthers and twenty-six lighter 75-mm-armed tank destroyers. Rounding out the kampfgruppe were the III Battalion of the 26th SS Panzergrenadier Regiment in armored halftracks, and the I Battalion of the 12th SS Panzer Artillery Regiment with eighteen 105-mm towed howitzers. Route C ran Losheim-Losheimergraben-Büllingen-Waimes-Stavelot-La Gleize-Aywaille.

The remainder of the 12th SS Panzer Division was formed in two elements, both of which were prepared to move via Route C. The first was Kampfgruppe Krause, with the 26th SS Panzergrenadier Regiment (minus the III Battalion), the 12th SS Panzer Artillery Regiment (minus the I and II battalions) with eighteen 150-mm howitzers and four 105-mm guns, the 12th SS Werfer Battalion with thirty nebelwerfer multiple-rocket launchers, the 12th SS Flak Battalion, and the 12th SS Engineer Battalion (the latter two were minus elements attached to the other kampfgruppen). The second was Kampfgruppe Bremer, composed of the 12th SS Panzer Aufklärungs (reconnaissance) Battalion, which had not been fully reconstituted and was considered to be too weak to fulfill its normal role as part of the leading element of the division. In addition, the 14th Werfer Regiment (an army unit) with eighty Nebelwerfer was attached to the division.

On Route D was the soon-to-be-infamous Kampfgruppe Peiper, under the command of SS-Obersturmbannführer Joachim (Jocheu) Peiper, commander of the 1st SS Panzer Regiment, the major element of the kampfgruppe. Like the 12th SS Panzer Regiment, the 1st had been forced to reorganize as a single battalion. Two companies were equipped with the Panzer IV (thirty-four tanks) and two companies were equipped with Panthers (thirty-four tanks). The 501st SS Heavy Panzer Battalion, equipped with twenty-two massive Panzer VIb "Königstiger (King Tiger)," had been attached as the regiment's second battalion. Infantry support was provided by the III Battalion of the 2d SS Panzergrenadier Regiment in armored half-tracks. The II Battalion of the 1st SS Panzer Artillery Regiment with eighteen 105-mm howitzers was also attached, along with a company of engineers and an army light flak battalion with self-propelled 20-mm and 37-mm antiaircraft guns. Route D ran Losheim-Honsfeld-Amblève-Ligneauville-Wanne-Trois Ponts-Werbomont-Meuse.

On Route E was Kampfgruppe Hansen, named for the commander of the 1st SS Panzergrenadier Regiment. Supporting Hansen's panzergrenadiers was the 1st SS Panzerjäger Battalion with twenty-two self-propelled 75-mm tank destroyers, the I Battalion of the 1st SS Panzer Artillery Regiment with eleven towed and two self-propelled 105-mm howitzers and four towed and two self-propelled 150-mm howitzers, two flak batteries, and an engineer company. Route E ran Manderfeld-Andler-Born-Recht-Vielsalm-Grandmenil-Huy.

The remainder of the 1st SS Panzer Division was organized in the same manner as the 12th SS Division. Kampfgruppe Sandig consisted of the 1st SS Panzergrenadier Regiment (minus the III Battalion), the 1st SS Panzer Artillery Regiment (minus the I and II battalions) with twelve 150-mm howitzers and four 105-mm guns, the 1st SS Werfer Battalion with thirty Nebelwerfer multiple-rocket launchers, the 1st SS Flak Battalion, and the 1st SS Engineer Battalion (the latter two were minus elements attached to the other kampfgruppen). Kampfgruppe Knittel was composed of the 1st SS Panzer Aufklärungs Battalion. This kampfgruppe, like the 12th, was poorly prepared for a reconnaissance mission and thus relegated to security duties. Attached was the 12th Werfer Regiment with eighty multiple-rocket launchers.

6. See appendix H for a discussion of German competence in this campaign.

7. The two 280-mm pieces initially available included the fabulous K-5 (gl.), a 280-mm gun enlarged to 310-mm by removing the rifling (thus gl. for *glatt* or smoothbore), which fired a rocket-assisted 120-mm submunition round to a maximum range of 146 kilometers! Fortunately for those on the receiving end, accuracy was low: The 50 percent zone was on the order of one kilometer.

8. 99th Infantry Division Combat Interviews, 3d Battalion, 395th Infantry.

9. The 2d Infantry Division was activated in France on 26 October 1917 as the 2d Division of the U.S. Army. Like the 1st Division, it was originally organized and fought in World War I as a "square division," the infantry component consisting of two brigades of two regiments each. Unlike the other American divisions, however, one of the 2d Division's two brigades was made up of Marines. Both brigades distinguished themselves in the second major American engagement of that war: the defensive battle of Belleau Wood–Château-Thierry in June 1918. Because of the emblem on its oversize shoulder patch, the 2d Division is called the "Indian-head division."

Reorganized just before World War II as a "triangular" division, with three infantry regiments instead of four, the Marine brigade was replaced by one of the most distinguished infantry regiments of World War I—the 38th "Rock of the Marne" Regiment, which left the 3d Division when it was triangularized. The 2d Infantry Division went overseas to Northern Ireland in October 1943. It went ashore directly into combat at Normandy on 7 June 1944, the day after the initial assault landings. The division and its commander, Maj. Gen. Walter M. Robertson, distinguished themselves in bitter fighting through June and July in the slow expansion of the Normandy Beachhead. After the breakout from Normandy in early August 1944 there was more tough fighting as the division moved west into Britanny to join the battle for the heavily fortified German-held city of Brest. After the surrender of Brest, the division moved east to take over positions from the 4th Infantry Division in the German Westwall in the Schnee Eifel just east of St. Vith. In early December the 2d Division was relieved by the 106th Infantry Division and moved a few miles north to the vicinity of Elsenborn. On the basis of its outstanding performance in Normandy and Brittany, the 2d Division was selected to spearhead the drive of the V Corps toward the Roer River in mid-December.

10. A major problem for U.S. forces in the Ardennes was a characteristic of tactical voice radios. All were FM sets, which were severely hampered by the hilly, forested terrain.

11. Company A of the 47th Armored Infantry was occupied with this task for most of the next week.

12. It was not until much later that the Americans came to realize exactly how insubstantial the paratrooper threat was. Von der Heydte's battalion numbered about 1,200 men, most of whom were combat veterans, though not all were jump-experienced. The pilots of the transport group were anything but experienced: Most of the paratroopers were scattered to the four winds by the nervous pilots. Some landed near Cologne on the Rhine; very few actually arrived close to their planned drop zone. Von der Heydte was one of the few who arrived over the drop zone. Not many more than 100 men were ever assembled, some of whom had lost most of their equipment. The German paratroopers played a cat-and-mouse game with the onrushing tide of American reinforcements arriving from the north, but were never able to slow traffic seriously on the vital lateral communications roads. Von der Heydte eventually became separated from his men and surrendered at Monschau on 22 December. One regiment of the 1st Division spent most of a week chasing down reports of von der Heydte's men through the Hautes Fagnes.

13. One of these survivors was noted as being the "Commanding Officer of 'I' Company . . . without men. . . ." This was none other than Charles B. "Mac" Mac-Donald, the well-known author of *Company Commander* and *A Time for Trumpets*. How he got to the forests outside Rocherath is described in *Company Commander*.

14. From the personal recollections of Joseph Jan Kiss Jr., published in *The Bulge Bugle* (newsletter of the Veterans of the Battle of the Bulge Association), vol. XII, no. 1 (February 1993), p. 18. It is evident that Kiss's narrative places him at Krinkelt a day too soon (he would likely have arrived there late on 17 December), but otherwise his account seems entirely reliable.

15. It should be noted that throughout this narrative the term *tank* is used with some trepidation by the authors. The vehicles encountered by the 3/23d Infantry and the 1/9th Infantry on 17 December were almost certainly not tanks but the turretless tank destroyers of the 12th SS Panzerjäger Battalion. However, as the late "Mac"

MacDonald, commander of I Company of the 23d, once remarked upon being told that the tanks his men fought were neither Tigers nor Panthers, "It is irrelevant to an infantryman; if it is armored and has a big gun, then to him it is a tank."

16. 99th Infantry Division in the Ardennes, Commendation to the 196th Field Artillery Battalion by Lt. Col. McClernand Butler, commanding 3/395th Infantry.

17. 102d Cavalry Group, Action near Monschau, Statement by S-3, 62d Armored Field Artillery Battalion. According to the records, the 186th Field Artillery Battalion, also in support, fired an amazingly minuscule ninety-two rounds on 18 December; there was either something wrong with the recording or with the 186th Field Artillery Battalion.

18. 102d Cavalry Group, Action near Monschau, 23 January 1945 interview with Lieutenant Colonel O'Brien, Major Rousek, and Captain Myer (assistant S-3).

19. Robertson was meticulous in exercising his command over the 99th Division through General Lauer. This incident did not effect Lauer, and he continued to command the division through the end of the war.

20. Kiss, *The Bulge Bugle,* vol. XII, no. 1 (February 1993), p. 19.

21. It should be noted that many of the losses reported in McKinley's battalion (and others) were missing men who later rejoined their units.

22. *The Bulge Bugle,* vol. XII, no. 2 (May 1993), p. 23.

23. MacDonald, *A Time for Trumpets,* p. 244.

24. *The Bulge Bugle,* vol. XII, no. 2 (May 1993), p. 23.

25. Savard's experience is adapted from material he provided to *The Bulge Bugle,* vol. XI, no. 1 (February 1992), pp. 15–16.

6. DISASTER IN THE SCHNEE EIFEL

1. The boundary actually ran through the 14th Cavalry Group sector between C and A troops.

2. R. Ernest Dupuy, *St. Vith; Lion in the Way* (Washington, D.C., 1949), pp. 43, 44, 62 n. 4.

3. R. E. Dupuy, *St. Vith,* p. 56. Dupuy's comment on this incident is that Shakespeare was "that day running for Army in a big way. . . ."

4. See chapter 4. Allied Intelligence had had some inkling of the existence of the Skorzeny Brigade and of the nature of its possible mission. This had been noted in the G-2 Daily Periodic Report of First Army, 2 December 1944, and in First Army G-2 Estimate No. 37, 10 December 1944. See R. E. Dupuy, *St. Vith,* p. 62 n. 8.

5. R. E. Dupuy, *St. Vith,* p. 56.

6. R. E. Dupuy, *St. Vith,* p. 101 n. 2.

7. R. E. Dupuy, *St. Vith,* p. 66, refers to this weapon as a TD (tank destroyer), specifically identified as an M8. However, the 820th Tank Destroyer Battalion, which was attached to the 106th Division, had towed 3" guns, not self-propelled TDs. The records do not show that a self-propelled TD unit was in this area. Furthermore, the model designation of a self-propelled TD would have been either M18 or M36, not M8. In research for his book, Dupuy spoke and/or corresponded with Lieutenant Colonels Slayden and Williams, as well as with Lt. Col. John F. DeV. Patrick, commander of the 820th TD Battalion. However, both squadrons of the 14th Cavalry Group had M8 assault guns (which were 75-mm howitzers, the same tube as the 75-mm pack howitzer), mounted on an M5 tank chassis.

The presence of one of these at the Heuem road junction would have been quite reasonable. The ammunition for these weapons included the AP, shaped charge rounds, perfectly capable of destroying or damaging any German armored vehicle that might have been present west of Schönberg that day. It was probably one of these weapons that Lt. Col. Williams commandeered.

8. As usual, the armored vehicles in this action were reported by American participants to be tanks. It is likely that these were actually German assault guns of the 18th Volksgrenadier Division's mobile assault group, as in the earlier operations near Auw and Schönberg.

9. 106th Division, G-3 Journal.

10. R. E. Dupuy, St. Vith, p. 130 n. 15.

11. There is no record of this message in the Division G-3 file. However, it is reported in the Regimental Journal.

12. There is no record of this message in the Division G-3 file. However, it is reported in the Regimental S-3 Journal and in several interviews. There can be no doubt as to the message and its text.

13. The airdrop fiasco is reported in considerable detail in R. E. Dupuy, St. Vith, pp. 134, 135.

14. The sympathies of the farmers in this area were divided. The area had been part of Germany until the Eupen-Malmédy region was awarded to Belgium by the Treaty of Versailles in 1919. Many of the inahbitants were still pro-German. It appears, however, that a majority had become loyal Belgians, and it was from these that Wood had received food and assistance.

7. FIGHTING FOR TIME ON THE "SKYLINE DRIVE"

1. One of the coauthors served with the 28th Division during its period of Stateside training from June 1942 to July 1943. The initially poor state of training in the division was remarkably improved during the six-month tenure of Maj. Gen. Omar N. Bradley, who was division commander from June 1942 to January 1943. Bradley left to meet an urgent request for competent commanders in Tunisia. Under his successor (who took the division to England and Normandy) there was a noticeable decline in the division's effectiveness. This caused some of its men to wonder (wrongly as it turned out) whether the 28th would ever get into combat.

2. Cota's obituary in Assembly, the quarterly publication of the Association of Graduates (AOG) of the U.S. Military Academy, is an incredibly bungled job—a disgrace to the AOG and to any of Cota's classmates who survived after his death on 4 October 1971.

3. In addition to its organic units, the 112th Infantry had additional forces attached: D/707th Tank Battalion (fifteen-odd M5 light tanks), C/630th Tank Destroyer Battalion (twelve towed 3" guns), 229th FA Battalion (twelve towed 105-mm howitzers), C/447th Antiaircraft Artillery Automatic Weapons Battalion (Mobile), and C/103d Engineer Combat Battalion. In addition, VIII Corps artillery had dedicated the 770th FA (twelve towed 4.5" guns) and the 965th and 969th FA (12 towed 155-mm howitzers each) to directly support the regiment. The 229th FA was an integral part of the division.

4. Although missing its 2d Battalion, the 110th had the 28th Reconnaissance Troop, B/630th Tank Destroyer Battalion (twelve towed 3" guns), 109th FA Battalion

(twelve towed 105-mm howitzers), 687th FA Battalion (twelve towed 105-mm howitzers), B/447th AAA AW Battalion (Mobile), and B/103d Engineer Combat Battalion
attached. Of these, only the Reconnaissance Troop and the 109th FA were integral
parts of the division; the other units were attached.

5. The villages were garrisoned as follows: Heinerscheid held A Company/
110th; Marnach had B Company; Munshausen had a larger force with C Company
and Cannon Company/110th, along with B/630th Tank Destroyer (TD) Battalion
(Towed) with twelve 3" AT guns; Hosingen had K Company/110th and B Com-
pany/103d Engineer Combat Battalion. Weiler was held by I Company, Holzthum by
L Company, Consthum by M (weapons) Company, and Hoscheid by the 110th
Infantry's Antitank Company. Companies E, F, G, and H belonged to the 2d Battalion
and so were in General Cota's divisional reserve.

6. Clervaux was the Francophone name for this town. German-speaking people
(and some maps) called it Clerf. Likewise, the small river flowing through town was
the Clerf to Germans, and the Clerve to French-speakers. To avoid confusion, this
book refers to the town as "Clervaux" and to the river as "the Clerf."

7. Attached to the 109th Infantry were C/707th Tank Battalion (fifteen-odd M4
Sherman medium tanks), A/630th Tank Destroyer Battalion (Towed) with twelve 3"
guns, 107th FA (twelve towed 105-mm howitzers) and 108th FA Battalion (twelve
towed 155-mm howitzers), A/447th AAA AW Battalion (Mobile), and A/103d Engineer Combat Battalion. The 107th FA was the normal direct support artillery for the
109th Infantry; the 108th was the divisional general support battalion.

8. The biographical material on Krüger is drawn from Wolf Keilig, *Das
Deutsche Heer 1939–1945*, vol. III, *Die Generalität des Heeres im 2. Weltkrieg* (Bad
Nauheim, n.d.), p. 183. Excerpts from this work and several others concerning Ger-
man generals of World War II were kindly supplied to the coauthors by Lt. Col.-Dr.
Waldis Greiselis of the German Military Archives in Freiburg-im-Breisgau. The trans-
lations, however, are the coauthors'.

9. Biographical material on von Lüttwitz is drawn from Erwin Leufeld and
Franz Thomas, *Die Eichenlaubträger 1940–1945* (Wiener Neustadt, 1983), p. 598,
and Keilig, *Das Deutsche Heer 1939–1945*, vol. III, p. 206.

10. The biographical sketch of Kneiss is based on information from Keilig, *Das
Deutsche Heer 1939–1945*, vol. III, p. 169.

11. Blakeslee's experiences were related in a letter to *The Bulge Bugle*, vol. IX,
no. 4 (November 1990), p. 18.

12. The background material for the 560th Volksgrenadier is drawn from the files
for the Ardennes Campaign Simulation Data Base.

13. The American observations were accurate: The 560th VGD had been rebuilt
with a large draft of former Luftwaffe ground personnel.

14. Both bridges were not actually in Ouren (a situation causing some confusion). One bridge was in the village itself, while the second lay 200 or 300 meters to
the south. The latter bridge was where the attacking Germans "seemed awfully
green."

15. Information on the background of the 26th Volksgrenadier Division is drawn
from Ardennes Campaign Simulation Data Base files, and from *German Order of
Battle 1944* (New York, 1975).

16. Biographical material on Kokott comes from Keilig, *Das Deutsche Heer
1939–1945*, vol. III, p. 174.

17. Background on the 2d Panzer is drawn from the Ardennes Campaign Simulation Data Base files and from *German Order of Battle 1944*.

18. Lauchert's biography is drawn from Leufeld and Thomas, *Die Eichenlaubträger 1940–1945*, p. 419, and from Keilig, *Das Deutsche Heer 1939–1945*, vol. III, p. 192.

19. Kampfgruppe Cochenhausen contained the 304th Panzergrenadier Regiment (less the bicycle-borne I Battalion), the 1st (Panther) Battalion of the 3d Panzer Regiment (less a company), the 1st Battalion (self-propelled) of the 74th Panzer Artillerie Regiment, and the 38th Panzer Pioniere (engineer) Abteilung (less 1st Company). This force contained about 3,000 men, thirty-two PzKw-V Panther tanks, and ten SP 105-mm (Wespe) and six SP 150-mm (Hummel) howitzers.

20. Background data for Panzer Lehr are drawn primarily from the Ardennes Campaign Simulation Data Base files. The division included the Lehr Panzer Regiment and Infanterie Lehr Regiments 901 and 902.

21. Background material on Fritz Bayerlein is drawn from T. N. Dupuy, Johnson, and Bongard, *The Harper Encyclopedia of Military Biography,* p. 72, and Helmut Ritgen, *Der Geschichte der Panzer-Lehr-Division im Westen 1944–1945* (Stuttgart, 1979), passim.

22. The principal source of the discussion of the experience of Company K/3d Battalion/110th Infantry is drawn from a combat interview conducted by Capt. William J. Dunkerley with 1st Lt. Thomas J. Flynn, Company K's executive officer, outside the Moosberg POW Camp just after its liberation by U.S. Army troops on 1–2 May 1945. Thus, unlike most combat interviews, it took place several months after the events covered. Nonetheless, Flynn's account coincides with other related combat interview material. Captain Feiker, the company commander, had been killed in a POW camp in Germany during an Allied air raid, probably in March 1945. Flynn himself was evidently uncertain of the date, and it is not recorded in the combat interview.

23. Background material for the 5th Parachute Division, as well as for the biographical sketch of Generalmajor Heilmann that follows, is drawn from Roger Edwards, *German Airborne Troops* (Garden City, N.Y., 1974).

24. Background material for the 352d Volksgrenadier Division is drawn from the Ardennes Campaign Simulation Data Base and from *German Order of Battle 1944*.

25. Biographical material on von Waldenburg is drawn from Keilig, *Das Deutsche Heer 1939–1945*, vol. III, p. 355.

26. This account is continued from Lieutenant Purcell's narrative of the 112th Infantry's Cannon Company, related in a combat interview session at Hachinette, France (near Colmar), on 23 January 1945. The interview was conducted by Tec 3d grade William Henderson of the 2d Information and Historical Service, VII Corps Team, First U.S. Army.

27. "Screaming meemies" was the American nickname for Nebelwerfer rocket rounds, derived from the characteristic shrieking sound they made shortly before impact. The British called them "Moaning Minnies."

28. The rockets were actually the German Raketenpanzerbüchse 54, colloquially known as the Panzerschreck (tank terror) or Ofenrohr (stovepipe). These were similar but not identical to the U.S. 2.36" (60-mm) rocket launchers. The RkPzB 54 fired a larger 88-mm (3.46") shaped-charge projectile.

29. The 44th Engineers comprised 600 officers and men well equipped with infantry weapons; the 707th Tank Battalion contributed six damaged M4s and five

M4/105s from its assault gun platoon; the 630th Tank Destroyer Battalion deployed a half-dozen 3" antitank guns; and the battered 687th Field Artillery Battalion had available only seven of its twelve assigned howitzers. There were also some weapons from the 447th Antiaircraft Battalion, and a handful of armored cars with a few machine-gun-armed jeeps from the 28th Reconnaissance Troop.

30. This narrative is drawn from an anonymously authored section of the 28th Infantry Division's combat interview material for 16–30 December 1944, titled "The German Breakthrough/Operation of the 28th Division/16 December to 31 December 1944," which comprises thirty-one numbered typescript pages. The defense of Wiltz is covered on pp. 11–18 and the town's fall on pp. 20–22.

8. THE BATTLE OF THE SAUER RIVER

1. In Luxembourg this river is known as the Sure; the German name is Sauer. In this book we refer to that portion in Luxembourg as Sure; we refer to the portion along the German-Luxembourg border as Sauer.

2. The division's newly formed panzerjäger company was still in transit to the front when the offensive began. When it joined the division on 19 December it had only three operational vehicles.

3. The two fortress battalions were assigned to the LIII Corps, commanded by General der Kavallerie Edwin von Rothkirch, but were under the operational control of the 212th Volksgrenadier Division for the initial assault. The LIII Corps was part of the Seventh Army, but did not have any divisions assigned to it. It was given an operational role on 22 December when it was inserted between the LXXXV Corps and the LXXX Corps to take command of the 79th Volksgrenadier Division and the Führer Grenadier Brigade south of Wiltz (see chapter 12).

4. The 280/320 schweres Nebelwerfer 42 could fire either 280-mm high-explosive or 320-mm incendiary rockets from its six-barrel launcher.

5. The five battalions of the 408th Volksartillerie Corps consisted of eighteen 75-mm guns, twelve 105-mm howitzers, eighteen 105-mm guns, twelve 122-mm howitzers, and twelve 152-mm gun-howitzers. The 122-mm and 152-mm pieces were captured Russian equipment with little ammunition available. Only the 105-mm howitzers and guns had motorized prime movers; the other pieces were all horse-drawn. The two three-battalion regiments of the 8th Volkswerfer Brigade consisted of fifty-four towed and sixteen self-propelled 150-mm, eighteen 210-mm, and thirty-six 280/320-mm Nebelwerfer. Most of the brigade transport was horse-drawn except the self-propelled pieces. However, the light-weight launchers were easily towed by civilian vehicles, enough of which were obtained to allow the motorization of two 150-mm battalions. Other conventional tube-artillery support was provided by two six-piece units (one confusingly designated a battalion and the other a battery) equipped with 128-mm guns, a two-piece battery equipped with 210-mm guns, and a battalion equipped with two World War I vintage pieces—French 220-mm howitzers and Austrian 280-mm howitzers. None of these units was mobile, and only the 128-mm gun units had prime movers—only one for every three guns.

6. Maj. Gen. John W. Leonard's 9th Armored Division was the most scattered of all the units in the VIII Corps. The division never fought as a whole in the battle: At one time its three combat commands were fighting under three different corps assigned to two different armies.

7. The units were the 19th Tank Battalion, the 89th Cavalry Squadron (minus C and D troops and elements of E Troop and F Company), the 811th Tank Destroyer Battalion (SP, minus A and C companies), the 9th Armored Engineer Battalion (minus B and C companies), and the 482d Antiaircraft Automatic Weapons Battalion (SP, minus B and C batteries).

8. The 4th Division was activated in November 1917, during World War I, and moved to France in June 1918. It took part in the three major operations of the AEF in that war: the Aisne-Marne offensive, the Battle of St. Mihiel, and the Battle of the Meuse-Argonne. It returned to the United States in July 1919 and was inactivated on 1 August. Reactivated on 3 June 1940, shortly before World War II, the division was triangularized and was redesignated the 4th Infantry Division. It gets its nickname, the "Ivy Division," from its shoulder patch of four green ivy leaves.

9. "Outline," 4th Infantry Division, German Offensive, prepared by Lt. Col. William T. Gayle from information at Division Headquarters. NARA RG 407, Box 24022, Files 35 and 36.

10. A Company had seventeen mediums, all of them in repair; B Company had eight mediums, of which three were running; C Company had all eight mediums operational; D Company had fifteen lights running, most of which needed repairs.

11. Outline, 4th Infantry Division, German Offensive, p. 3.

12. The task force consisted of the 4th Engineer Battalion, the 4th Reconnaissance Troop, the 2d Battalion of the 8th Infantry Regiment, and A (–) and C companies of the 70th Tank Battalion.

13. Letter from Sam Silverman, *The Bulge Bugle,* vol. IX, no. 3 (August 1990), p. 8.

9. COMMAND DECISIONS

1. Omar N. Bradley, *A Soldier's Story* (New York, 1951), p. 465.

2. Ibid.

3. Ibid., pp. 449–50.

4. Eisenhower, *Crusade in Europe,* p. 350.

5. Arthur Bryant, *Triumph in the West* (Garden City, N.Y., 1958), p. 271.

6. For a different version of these events, see Forrest C. Pogue, *The Supreme Command; The U.S. Army in World War II* (Washington, D.C., 1954), p. 378, and Hugh M. Cole, *The Ardennes: Battle of the Bulge. United States Army in World War II. The European Theater of Operation* (Washington, D.C., 1965), p. 423. Both Pogue and Cole assert that the idea for the shifting of the command of the Ninth and First armies was Strong's, and that he discussed this with Whiteley before they both went to see Smith. Cole even asserts: "Although both officers were British, neither had broached this idea to the field marshal." The Pogue-Cole version is apparently accepted by Ambrose in *The Supreme Commander,* pp. 562–63. Obviously Cole, Pogue, and Ambrose were unfamiliar with Monty's telegram of early 20 December to Field Marshal Alan Brooke, Chief of the Imperial General Staff (CIGS) in London. In that message Montgomery flatly states that he had "told Whiteley that Ike ought to place me in operational command of all troops on the northern half of the front." (See Bryant, *Triumph in the West,* p. 271.) Charles B. MacDonald, who clearly was familiar with the Monty message, asserts that Whiteley raised the issue with Strong after a telephone conversation with Montgomery earlier in the day, when Monty made the

suggestion (*A Time for Trumpets,* p. 421). It is interesting that in *The Memoirs of Field-Marshal Montgomery* Montgomery himself sheds no light on the incident.

7. Bradley, *A Soldier's Story,* pp. 476–78.

8. See chapter 10.

9. Chester Wilmot, *The Struggle for Europe* (New York, 1952), p. 592. The same quote appears in Bryant, *Triumph in the West,* pp. 272–73. The visit is much more cordial in Sir Francis W. de Guingand, *Operation Victory* (New York, 1947), p. 429. De Guingand was Montgomery's loyal but very objective chief of staff, who accompanied the field marshal on this visit.

10. THE BATTLE OF ST. VITH

1. U.S. Army Armor School, *The Battle at St. Vith, Belgium; 17–23 December, 1944* (Fort Knox, Ky., 1966), p. 4.

2. Ibid., pp. 5–6.

3. There had been trouble from the beginning of the march: The column had been attacked several times by German aircraft, which were more active than usual. See U.S. Army Armor School, *The Battle at St. Vith,* p. 5.

4. U.S. Army Armor School, *The Battle of St. Vith,* pp. 5, 10.

5. See "Travails of the 14th Cavalry Group" in chapter 6.

6. From north to south the units in this line were: Troops C and A, 87th Cavalry Recon Squadron; Companies A and B, 38th Armored Infantry Battalion; Troop B, 87th Cavalry Squadron; elements of the 81st and 168th Engineer battalions; and Company B, 23d Armored Infantry Battalion. Elements of the 814th Tank Destroyer Battalion were located at several points in the line.

7. Cole, *The Ardennes: Battle of the Bulge,* p. 393.

8. R. E. Dupuy, *St. Vith,* p. 162. See also Cole, *The Ardennes: Battle of the Bulge,* p. 395.

9. Annex 2, 7th Armored Division After Action Report.

10. *The Bulge Bugle,* vol. XII, no. 2 (May 1993), p. 19.

11. This incident was discussed by General Clarke with one of the coauthors in the early 1980s. The vehemence of Clarke's expression of contempt for Ridgway leads me to believe that there was some interaction between the two generals shortly after the incident. I received the impression, but have no confirmation, that they never spoke to each other again during the eleven years that both continued on active duty.

12. Presumably this plan was prepared by the 7th Armored Division staff, and had been approved by General Ridgway, Commanding General XVIII Airborne Corps.

13. R. E. Dupuy, *St. Vith,* p. 173.

14. Ibid., p. 173.

15. Ibid., p. 177.

11. HOLDING THE NORTHERN SHOULDER

1. The 120th Infantry had several units attached: elements of the 291st Engineer Combat Battalion and the 526th Armored Infantry Battalion (Separate), and the 99th Infantry Battalion (Separate). The latter was nicknamed the "Norwegians," and was made up of Norwegian-Americans and native Norwegians—many of whom had fled

the German occupation of Norway and had volunteered to serve in the American Army.

2. The St. Edouard Sanatorium was run by a Catholic order to care for convalescent children and tuberculosis patients. It was a large, stout, four-story brick building.

3. These pieces were more or less equally divided between the Elsenborn front to the east and the Butgenbach front to the south, although many could reach both areas.

4. In contrast to the other two brigades, (Führer Begleit Brigade and Führer Grenadier Brigade), which were nearly divisionlike formations, the 150th Panzer Brigade was only a mixed reinforced regiment with supporting units.

5. The elements of the 291st Engineer Combat Battalion were the only troops present as far as Skorzeny knew. The other units, totaling two full-strength infantry battalions and elements of a third, arrived only in the nick of time.

6. The War Department had only recently approved General Eisenhower's request to use these newly developed fuses.

7. The exact origin of many small units like Col. Rubel's 155-mm SP was never known. It is possible that it belonged to C Battery of the 987th Field Artillery, which had been supporting the 2d Division on 16 December and had been forced to withdraw hurriedly from Krinkelt-Rocherath in the midst of the German attack.

8. For further details of the ordeal of the civilians in the sanatorium basement, see John Toland, *Battle: The Story of the Bulge* (New York, 1959), pp. 166–67, 176–77, 193–96.

9. This total contained the bulk of the hale officers and men under Peiper's command. He left behind about 380 wounded and 50 healthy SS panzergrenadiers who did not get the order to withdraw and held their positions to the last man.

10. McCown's story has been repeated often enough to be fairly familiar, and a fuller account of his experiences is given in MacDonald, *A Time for Trumpets,* pp. 455–63 and Toland, *Battle: The Story of the Bulge*, pp. 177, 193–94, 230, 261. McCown's experience as a prisoner of Peiper and his SS troops, in which the major reported that the Germans were correct and humane in their treatment of prisoners and civilians, contrasted sharply with the reputation they had acquired as a result of the Malmédy Incident (see appendix G).

11. Totals are drawn from MacDonald, *A Time for Trumpets,* p. 463.

12. The German commanders acted according to the most important objective of the offensive—to reach and to cross the Meuse. The objective was an operational, even strategic level, and not to achieve tactical success against American units on the battlefield.

12. THE DEFENSE OF BASTOGNE

1. At age thirty-seven, Gavin was the youngest division commander in the U.S. Army. It is worth noting that after the war Ridgway, Gavin, and Taylor all rose to senior posts in the U.S. Army.

2. The organization of the 101st and 82d Airborne divisions did not follow the official pattern, which called for two two-battalion glider infantry regiments and one three-battalion parachute infantry regiment. The 101st had condensed the 327th and 401st Glider Infantry regiments by giving one battalion of the 401st to the 327th and the other to the 82d Airborne. The 101st was also assigned the 501st and 506th

Parachute Infantry regiments, in addition to the 502d Parachute Infantry. The 82d Airborne contained the 325th Glider Infantry (with the 2d Battalion of the 401st as a third battalion) and the 504th and 505th Parachute Infantry regiments, with the 507th and 508th Parachute Infantry regiments attached. This peculiar situation was clarified when the divisions reorganized in March 1945.

3. Drawn from McEwan's letter to *The Bulge Bugle,* vol. X, no. 2 (May 1991), p. 10. In his letter, McEwan asked if anyone knew what had happened to the men left waiting for weapons, as he had heard they had been overrun by the Germans when they finally encircled Bastogne.

4. After the 501st Parachute Infantry came the 81st Antiaircraft Battalion, Col. Robert F. Sink's 506th Parachute Infantry, the 326th Parachute Engineer Battalion, Lt. Col. Steve A. Chappuis's 502d Parachute Infantry, and finally Col. Joseph H. Harper's 327th Glider Infantry Regiment.

5. Combat Command R, commanded by Col. Joseph H. Gilbreth, comprised the 2d Tank Battalion with fifty-odd M4 medium and fifteen M5 light tanks; the 52d Armored Infantry Battalion with close to 1,000 men; the 73d Armored Field Artillery Battalion with eighteen M7 self-propelled 105-mm howitzers; a battery of the 811th Tank Destroyer Battalion with twelve M18 tank destroyers (nicknamed "Hellcats"); and a battery of the 482d Antiaircraft Automatic Weapons (AAAW) Battalion with sixteen half-tracks: eight M15s with 37-mm L54 AA guns and twin .50-caliber machine guns, and eight M16s with quadruple-mount .50-caliber machine guns. Four M18s had been sent to help the 112th Infantry near Ouren, and four more had been sent to aid the 110th Infantry at Clervaux, although they returned. Fifteen M4 tanks had also been sent to Clervaux, and of these only three returned to Combat Command R.

6. These were the 35th, 44th, and 158th Engineer Combat battalions (Middleton sent the 44th to help defend Wiltz), and the 58th Armored Field Artillery Battalion.

7. Middleton had originally ordered Combat Command B of the 10th Armored to move the next day to support the 4th Infantry Division, hard-pressed south of the Sauer River by the attack of the Seventh Army's LXXX Corps (see chapter 8).

8. Roberts's Combat Command B comprised A, B, and D companies of the 2d Tank Battalion (thirty-five M4 medium and fifteen M5 light tanks, with six M4s armed with 105-mm howitzers); B Company of the 21st Tank Battalion (fifteen M4s); the headquarters and B Company of the 54th Armored Infantry Battalion; the headquarters, A, and C companies of the 20th Armored Infantry Battalion; the 420th Armored Field Artillery Battalion (eighteen M7 tracked 105-mm howitzers); D Troop of the 90th Reconnaissance Squadron (eight M8 armored cars, twenty jeeps, and about 150 men); and C Company of the 55th Armored Engineer Battalion. As CCB's share of the units attached to the 10th Armored, Roberts also had C Company of the 609th Tank Destroyer Battalion, with twelve M18 tank destroyers, and B Battery of the 796th Antiaircraft Automatic Weapons Battalion (SP), with eight M15 Multiple Gun Motor Carriages (MGMC) each with a 37-mm gun and two .50-caliber machine guns, and eight M16 MGMCs with four .50-caliber machine guns. The unusual allotment of three battalion headquarters permitted Roberts to deploy three independent task forces.

9. Details of the Middleton-Roberts conference are drawn from Toland, *Battle: The Story of the Bulge,* pp. 115 and 118, and MacDonald, *A Time for Trumpets,* p. 290.

10. Team Cherry contained the headquarters, A Company, and the headquarters

and one platoon of D Company, 3d Tank Battalion (seventeen M4 medium and seven M5 light tanks, and six more Shermans with 105-mm howitzers in the 3d Battalion's assault gun platoon); C Company of the 20th Armored Infantry Battalion; and a platoon each from C Company of the 55th Armored Engineers, D Troop of the 90th Reconnaissance Squadron (four M8 armored cars and about six machine-gun-armed jeeps), and C Company of the 609th Tank Destroyer Battalion (SP) with four M18 TDs—all told about 650 officers and men.

11. Team O'Hara comprised the headquarters and B Company of the 54th Armored Infantry Battalion, C Company of the 21st Tank Battalion and a platoon from D Company of the 3d (about fifteen M4 medium and four M5 light tanks), and platoons from C Company of the 55th Armored Engineers and D Troop of the 90th Cavalry Reconnaissance Squadron (four M8 armored cars and a half-dozen machine-gun-armed jeeps), totaling just under 600 officers and men.

12. Team Desobry comprised the headquarters and B Company of the 20th Armored Infantry Battalion, B Company and a platoon of D Company from the 3d Tank Battalion (fifteen medium and four light tanks), and a platoon each from C Company of the 55th Armored Engineers Battalions, C Company of the 609th TD Battalion (four M18s), and D Troop of the 90th Reconnaissance Squadron (four M8 armored cars and six machine-gun-armed jeeps), altogether a little over 600 officers and men.

13. The organization of Combat Command B's three teams is drawn from combat interview material for the 101st Airborne Division, which contains information provided by its commander, Colonel Roberts (RG 407, Box 24074, file 228, and Box 24075, files 229 and 230).

14. Task Force Rose comprised A Company, 2d Tank Battalion (fifteen M4 tanks); C Company of the 52d Armored Infantry Battalion; Battery B of the 73d Armored Field Artillery Battalion (six M7 self-propelled 105-mm howitzers); and a platoon of C Company, 9th Armored Engineers. Lullange was held by G Company, 110th Infantry, part of the 110th's 2d Battalion that had not been committed to the counterattack on the morning of 17 December, having been retained by General Cota as a last-ditch reserve (see chapter 7).

15. Task Force Harper comprised C Company, 2d Tank Battalion (about fifteen M4 Sherman tanks); A Company of the 52d Armored Infantry Battalion; and the 73d Armored Field Artillery Battalion, less Battery B (twelve M7 self-propelled 105-mm howitzers). Harper was also supported by about 100 stragglers from the 110th Infantry in Clervaux, led by Col. Theodore A. Seely, a former commander of that regiment.

16. These troops included the 58th Armored Field Artillery Battalion (assigned from VIII Corps), along with most of C Company, 9th Armored Engineer Battalion, and C Battery, 482d AAA (Automatic Weapons) Battalion SP, together with D Company of 2d Tank Battalion (about fifteen M5 Stuart light tanks) and around a dozen M4 Sherman mediums that had escaped from Wiltz or one of the task forces, and B Company, 52d Armored Infantry Battalion, in and around Longvilly.

17. Kampfgruppe von Fallois contained the 130th Panzer Aufklärungs Abteilung, a company of fifteen PzKw-IV tanks, a company of ten or twelve JgPz-IV self-propelled antitank guns (panzerjäger), a battery of artillery, and a company of engineers. General Bayerlein accompanied this force, which was named for the commander of 130th Panzer Reconnaissance Battalion.

18. This decision infuriated General von Manteuffel, who is supposed to have snapped that if Bayerlein couldn't read a map he should have one of his staff officers do it for him. This is probably unfair, since Bayerlein apparently decided to take the secondary road to Magaret after consulting a Belgian civilian about the condition of the roads. Whether Manteuffel's supposed comment was fair or not, Bayerlein's performance on 16–21 December was not up to the standards expected of a veteran panzer commander. In his memoirs, Manteuffel does not repeat the severe criticism of Bayerlein that is contained in a study he wrote for U.S. military historians while he was a prisoner of war.

19. In this context, the 101st Division's combat interview records, which include material for Combat Command B, 10th Armored Division, placed under the 101st's command, indicate that Combat Command R began to withdraw about 2300 hours on 18 December. This conflicts with the timing for the disengagement noted in other sources, but the confusing general situation could have easily   produced the discrepancy, or it might be due to the commencement of unauthorized withdrawals.

20. Like the other units of the 101st, the 506th had left its cantonment at Mormelon (near Reims) in such haste that many paratroopers lacked weapons and ammunition. Lieutenant George Rice, Team Desobry's S-4 (supply officer), hurried to Foy to snatch up what weapons and ammunition he could, and in two improvised "supply runs" managed to fill the 1/506th's most urgent needs.

21. The able and resourceful Lieutenant Hyduke and Captain Ryerson both died in a German bombing raid on Bastogne a few days later on Christmas Eve. They were killed instantly when a bomb crashed into Team Cherry's headquarters.

22. Baum's account of his last-minute run into and out of Bastogne comes from Gerald Astor, *The Blood-Dimmed Tide* (New York, 1992), pp. 227–30.

23. Major Desobry originally had only four M18 TDs. The other vehicles came from Colonel Roberts's reserve (the platoon of C Company, 609th) and the 705th Tank Destroyer Battalion, a unit assigned directly to VIII Corps that had remained in Bastogne.

24. Bayerlein's somewhat lackluster performance may have a relatively simple explanation. According to several accounts, he spent much of 19 December romancing an attractive blond American nurse captured near Magaret. The story is unusual, but Charles MacDonald put sufficient credence in it to include it in *A Time for Trumpets* (p. 295). MacDonald told one of the coauthors that following publication of the book he met a woman at a party who knew the nurse in question, but he was not able to talk to her at any length and did not get her name. So the mystery remains.

25. Kampfgruppe Kunkel consisted of the 26th Fusilier Abteilung and most of the division's antitank (panzerjäger) battalion.

26. The 101st had four artillery battalions: The 321st Glider Field Artillery Battalion (FABn) and the 377th and 463d Parachute FABn had 75-mm pack howitzers; the 907th had 105-mm howitzers identical to those in an infantry regiment's cannon company. There were also two armored FABns (Roberts's 420th and the dozen surviving M7s of Gilbreth's 73d), along with the 755th and 969th FABns with twelve 155-mm howitzers apiece, and the 771st and 775th, each with a dozen 4.5" (114-mm) guns. There were also other guns and howitzers, collected singly and in twos and threes, from "refugee" units like the 109th and 687th FABns of the 28th Division. The artillery forces in Bastogne totaled about 130 pieces.

27. See note 2.

28. Drawn from Bowen's long letter about his experiences around Bastogne during the period 19–23 December to *The Bulge Bugle,* vol. IX, no. 3 (August 1990), pp. 14–15. Bowen also recalled that C Company was 40 percent understrength, and replacements for losses suffered in Holland had not yet been made good.

29. Team SNAFU was the "holding unit" for stragglers in Bastogne, and was used as a pool for task forces and replacements. Its designation derived from a common American soldiers' expression that conveyed the fighting man's attitude toward the fortunes of war. The polite version is *S*ituation *N*ormal, *A*ll *F*ouled *U*p. The Anglo-Saxon expletive in the original expression has been replaced by "fouled."

30. See Bowen's letter to *The Bulge Bugle,* vol. IX, no. 3 (August 1990), pp. 14–15.

31. The three Americans included two sergeants, Oswald Y. Butler and Carl E. Dickinson, along with Pfc. Ernest D. Permetz, a medical aid man who spoke German.

32. Translated version drawn from John S. D. Eisenhower, *The Bitter Woods* (New York, 1969), p. 322.

33. Although this is the word he used according to several eyewitness accounts, others suggest that his reply was more profane and has been bowdlerized. Either account is possible.

34. See also Charles B. MacDonald, *A Time for Trumpets* (New York, 1985), pp. 511–13, and Rapport and Northwood, *Rendezvous with Destiny* (Washington, D.C., 1948), pp. 510–11.

35. Unlike most panzer regiments, which contained a battalion each (about fifty tanks) of PzKw-IVs and PzKw-V Panthers, the 130th Panzer Regiment contained only a single mixed battalion with twenty-seven PzKw-IVs (in the 6th and 8th companies) and thirty Panthers (in the 5th and 7th companies) on 15 December.

13. THE SOUTHERN SHOULDER BOUNCES BACK

1. See Martin Blumenson, *The Patton Papers* (Boston, 1974), pp. 598–600, and Charles R. Codman, *Drive* (Boston, 1957), pp. 231–35.

2. See "Deception, Surprise, and Operation Greif" in chapter 2. A German reviewer has questioned whether it is appropriate to call Skorzeny's soldiers "terrorists," even though they were in American uniforms. It is debatable, but we believe the description is apt.

3. Blumenson, *The Patton Papers,* p. 603.

4. To remedy this situation, General Brandenberger committed the LIII Corps near Bastogne on 20 December.

5. Interview with Lt. Col. James E. Rudder, CO, 109th Infantry; Harry G. Jackson, 1st Lt., Inf., 2d Information & Historical Service.

6. Ibid.

14. THE SIEGE AND RELIEF OF BASTOGNE

1. The 8th Tank Battalion was short one M5 light tank, the 35th was missing 4 of 53 M4 Shermans, and the 37th was short 16 M4s and an M5. This left the division with more that 160 M4s (out of a T/O&E strength of 186), and 66 of 68 M5s.

2. These data come from Combat Interviews for the 4th Armored Division (RG 407, Box 24093, file 274; Interview with Assistant Divisional G-4; 2 pages).

3.   The 6th Cavalry Squadron was detached from the 6th Cavalry Group and given the task of policing the front line between the 26th Division's left flank and the 4th Armored's right flank, while the 6th Cavalry Group Headquarters and the 28th Squadron remained to cover III Corps's extreme left flank.

4.   To avoid confusion, General von Rothkirch und Trach will be referred to as "Rothkirch."

5.   This unit, renamed the 442d Security Division, had extensive rear-area service on the eastern front.

6.   The 5th Parachute Division's artillery regiment (5th Fallschirm [Parachute] Artillerie Regiment) was understrength and extremely short of transport. To give Heilmann some mobile guns, Kneiss had assigned to his division the three mobile battalions (thirty-six pieces) of the 406th Volksartillerie Corps (VAK), and a battalion (eighteen rocket launchers) from the 18th Volkswerfer Brigade. The rest of the 406th VAK was assigned to provide general support to LXXXV Corps, and was able to move west only very slowly because of the scarcity of transport.

7.   CCA contained the 35th Tank Battalion, the 51st and 53d Armored Infantry battalions, B Battery of the 489th AAA (AW) SP Battalion, A Company of the 24th Armored Engineer Battalion, B Troop of the 25th Cavalry Reconnaissance Squadron (Mechanized), and the Divisional Artillery Headquarters with the 66th and 94th Armored Field Artillery battalions, altogether about 4,100 officers and men, sixty-odd tanks, and thirty-six M7 self-propelled 105-mm howitzers. (All organizational data for 4th Armored's combat commands are drawn from the Combat Interviews; RG 407, Box 24093, file 274.)

8.   CCB contained the 8th Tank and 10th Armored Infantry battalions, A Battery of the 489th, B Company of the 24th Armored Engineer Battalion, B Troop of the 25th Cavalry Reconnaissance Squadron, the 22d Armored Field Artillery Battalion, and support troops, totaling 2,500 officers and men, about sixty tanks, and eighteen M7 self-propelled 105-mm howitzers.

9.   The brigade's main subunits comprised a panzer battalion, a two-battalion panzergrenadier regiment, a small artillery battalion, and battalions of antitank troops, engineers, and flak. The 911th Sturmgeschütz Brigade was also attached before the brigade entered combat. The lack of experience among both officers and men, coupled with its haphazard and piecemeal commitment in the Ardennes, largely frittered away the effect of what ought to have been a powerful mechanized force.

10.   *The Bulge Bugle,* vol. XII, no. 1 (February 1993), p. 20. Although the combat veteran among the coauthors fought in the tropics rather than in a northern European winter, he finds this list neither remarkable nor surprising, with perhaps one exception. He does wonder about the three bazooka rounds and where they were carried.

11.   Kokott may have been forewarned by the capture of Combat Command B's attack orders when a liaison officer accidentally drove into German lines on the night of 23 December. The cavalry probe at Chaumont late on 23 December may also have provided warning.

12.   Through the night of 23–24 December, Combat Command R contained the 37th Tank Battalion; the 704th Tank Destroyer Battalion, Headquarters, and C Company of the 24th Armored Engineers along with most of the attached 995th Engineers (a platoon each was assigned to CCA and CCB); Headquarters and D Battery of the 489th AAA (AW) SP Battalion; and C and D troops and E Company (M5 tanks) of the 25th Cavalry Reconnaissance Squadron—in all 2,850 men with seventy-five tanks

and thirty-five TDs. Prior to this time the 4th Armored (unlike virtually every other armored division in the U.S. Army) had followed doctrine by using Combat Command R as a holding and housekeeping headquarters rather than as a third operational command.

13.   On 23 December, Colonel Heilmann was promoted to generalmajor, a rank more in keeping with his responsibilities as commander of the 5th Parachute Division.

14.   *The Bulge Bugle,* vol. XI, no. 1 (February 1992), pp. 14–15.

15.   Kampfgruppe Maucke was built around the 115th Panzergrenadier Regiment, and had one company each of tanks and assault guns, an artillery battalion, and supporting units, totaling about 4,000 officers and men.

16.   For the drive up the Neufchâteau highway, Combat Command R's organization was changed to include Lt. Col. Creighton W. Abrams's 37th Tank Battalion, Lt. Col. George Jaques's 53d Armored Infantry Battalion, the 94th Armored Field Artillery Battalion (FABn) and a battery of 155-mm howitzers from the 177th FABn, plus supporting engineers and cavalry assigned for the dash into Bastogne. These forces totaled about 2,500 officers and men with around fifty tanks and eighteen M7 105-mm howitzers.

17.   The troops of Major General Cota's 28th Division around Neufchâteau had little combat capacity by this time, because they had lost most of their unit cohesion and abandoned a good deal of equipment. However, Neufchâteau did serve as a rallying point for refugees from the 28th's overrun units, and was also the destination of the replacements now beginning to flow in.

18.   Combat Command A overran one battalion each from the 406th Volksartillerie Corps and the 18th Volkswerfer Brigade, both serving as divisional artillery for the 5th FJD. The 5th Parachute Artillery was absorbed by the 79th VGD, whose *own* artillery regiment was hopelessly bogged down in traffic crossing the Our on the overburdened German bridges.

19.   The 352d VGD was assigned a battalion from the 8th Volkswerfer Brigade, and the 5th Parachute Artillery (5th Parachute Division's artillery regiment) was placed under the 352d's control. However, without prime movers, those guns remained at Hottingen on the east bank of the Our River.

20.   This account is drawn from the 101st's combat interview material (RG 407, Boxes 21074 and 21075, files 228 to 230), and from Leonard Rapport and Arthur Northwood Jr., *Rendezvous with Destiny: A History of the 101st Airborne Division* (Washington, D.C., 1948), pp. 548–61.

21.   According to normal U.S. Army practice, this "C" Company of the 327th should be I Company, but the 3d Battalion of the 327th Glider Infantry was originally the 1st Battalion of the 401st Glider Infantry, and so the battalion retained its old company designations; therefore, 327th had *two* companies A, B, and C. To further muddy the issue, the 3d Battalion was sometimes referred to as the 1st Battalion of the 401st.

22.   It's not likely Allen would have been looking down the barrel of an eighty-eight since all the German tanks involved were PzKw-IVHs, with the 75-mm L46 gun. This is another instance, however understandable given the circumstances, of "Tiger fright."

23.   The experiences of Lieutenant Colonel Allen are drawn from Rapport and Northwood, *Rendezvous with Destiny,* pp. 552–53, and *MacDonald, A Time for Trumpets,* pp. 527–28.

24.   Abrams went on to become a general and commander of U.S. forces in Viet-

nam; he was the Chief of Staff of the U.S. Army when he died. By the winter of 1944 Abrams had an enviable reputation as a combat commander. Patton said of him, "I have only one peer as an armored commander in the U.S. Army, and that is Abe Abrams." Abrams was later awarded the Distinguished Service Cross (DSC) for his part in the capture of Assensois and the relief of Bastogne.

25.   The Assensois assault was entirely an Abrams-Jaques operation. Shortly after dark on 26 December, after Abrams had shaken hands with General McAuliffe in Bastogne, Colonel Blanchard reached Abrams by radio to ask whether it would be possible to make contact with the 101st Airborne that day. The following account of the last stage of CCR's advance and the fight for Assensois is drawn from the sixteen-page combat interview with Abrams and other officers of the 37th Tank Battalion, which is in the 4th Armored Division's combat interview file, NARA RG407, Box 24093, File 274.

26.   This battle group, slightly larger than Kampfgruppe Maucke, comprised the 15th Panzergrenadier's other infantry regiment, two artillery battalions, and the balance of other divisional assets, totaling about 6,500 officers and men.

27.   This raised its strength from less than 2,000 officers and men to about 3,500, considerably expanding the combat power of the 6th Cavalry Group.

28.   This screening force contained elements of the 130th Panzerjäger Battalion, 130th Pioniere (Engineer) Battalion, and 311th Flak Battalion, strung along a line from Remagne north and east to Wanlin.

15. CHRISTMAS HIGH-WATER MARK

1.   By this time, Kampfgruppe Cochenhausen contained the entire 304th Panzergrenadier Regiment, since the 1/304, once mounted on bicycles, was now riding in trucks captured from the Americans at Noville and elsewhere on the Bastogne approaches; three of four companies of the 1st Battalion, 3d Panzer Regiment with PzKw-V Panther tanks (the fourth company was assigned to stiffen Kampfgruppe von Böhm); the 1st (self-propelled) and 3d battalions of the 74th Panzer Artillerie Regiment; a battery of the 22d Flak Battalion; and the 38th Panzer Pioniere Battalion, less the 1st Company. Kampfgruppe von Böhm consisted of the 2d Panzer Reconnaissance Battalion, equipped with a dozen or so armored cars, four companies of infantry in half-tracked carriers, and a heavy weapons company with antitank guns and mortars.

2.   The 84th had been involved in heavy fighting around Geilenkirchen, near the Roer Dams, in late November, and had only about 13,000 of its standard complement of 14,300 men when it was committed to the Ardennes fighting.

3.   The 4th Cavalry Group comprised the 4th and 24th Cavalry Reconnaissance squadrons (Mechanized), around 1,600 officers and men with 80-odd armored cars, a few half-tracks, and numerous motor vehicles.

4.   Unlike the 2d Armored, Maj. Gen. Maurice Rose's 3d Armored Division was committed to the Ardennes fighting piecemeal. Assigned to V Corps, Combat Command B was engaged around Stavelot against Kampfgruppe Peiper, while the 3d Armored's other two combat commands (CCA and CCR) operated between the 84th Division's left flank at Hotton and the 82d Airborne Division's right flank near the Baraque de Fraiture crossroads. The 3d Armored officially came under VII Corps command on 24 December.

5.   These duties consisted, in large part, of combating near-endemic banditry in the Communications Zone. The theft was committed by Allied soldiers who were AWOL (absent without leave) and a large number of French maquis or guerrillas (whose pro-Communist faction was engaged in a war of its own with the anti-Communist Maquisards). Both groups supplied themselves by waylaying truck convoys, and the scale of their activities had made them a severe nuisance by late autumn 1944.

6.   Lt. Theodore M. Draper, *The 84th Infantry Division in the Battle for Germany* (New York, 1947).

7.   These data are from Harold P. Leinbaugh and John D. Campbell, *The Men of Company K* (New York, 1985), p. 141.

8.   *The Bulge Bugle,* vol. IX, no. 4 (November 1990), pp. 19–21.

9.   *The Bulge Bugle,* vol. XII, no. 4 (November 1993), pp. 24–25.

10.   The account that follows is drawn almost entirely from Cole, *The Ardennes: The Battle of the Bulge,* pp. 565–66. The story indicates the friction that exists in any battle, particularly when communications are less than ideal.

11.   A normal telephone line was not equipped with a scrambling device to prevent the line from being effectively tapped.

12.   His official post was I-a, senior operations staff officer, analogous to the American G-3.

13.   The Tiger tanks belonged to the 301st Heavy Tank Battalion (radio-controlled). It would normally have been composed of thirty-odd Tiger tanks and about forty radio-controlled B-IV demolition vehicles. The B-IVs were not sent into the Ardennes.

14.   Actually, the 9th Panzer Division was missing most of its artillery regiment and portions of other subunits, amounting to about two-thirds of the division's total personnel. The artillery regiment and its accompanying units were still moving forward by rail to Blankenheim until 29 December. From there, the column road-marched to Sprimont, west of Bastogne. Fuel shortages, crowded roads, blown bridges, and Allied air attacks delayed its arrival until 7 January.

15.   Major von Cochenhausen noted that U.S. artillery fire directed against his troop on Christmas Day was observed by five artillery spotter aircraft, a tactical asset rarely available to German troops by the closing days of 1944. Bayerlein also commented, after the battle, that "the Allied fighter-bombers were annoying, but the artillery was, as usual, most unpleasant."

16.   This lack of professional objectivity had been a characteristic of Hitler's military leadership since he had assumed a personal command role in December 1941.

16. FACEOFF

1.   Clay Blair, *Ridgway's Paratroopers: The American Airborne in World War II* (Garden City, N.Y., 1985), pp. 394–95.

2.   James Gavin, *On to Berlin* (New York, 1978), pp. 264–65.

3.   Ibid., p. 265.

4.   Interestingly, Triplet's experience serving in the 7th Armored Division under General Ridgway's XVIII Airborne Corps gave the colonel a very different picture of Ridgway than the St. Vith experience had given to Generals Hasbrouck and Clarke (see chapter 10). Triplet later wrote that he rated Ridgway "Number One [as a soldier]. He was a fighter, the best I've known." See Blair, *Ridgway's Paratroopers,* p. 396.

5.   The 509th was one of a number of separate airborne battalions created during the war. It was administratively attached to the XVIII Airborne Corps. General Ridgway had attached it in turn to CCA/3d Armored Division to give the tankers some added infantry support. Casualties in the battalion were so severe during the Battle of the Bulge (only seven officers and forty-eight men remained at the end of January) that the 509th was disbanded on 1 March 1945 and the survivors were incorporated as replacements within the 82d Airborne Division. See Gerard M. Devlin, *Paratrooper* (New York, 1979), p. 550.

6.   Summary relief for failure to perform to a superior's expectations was a common occurrence for American officers of all grades in World War II. The charges against Brewster were never approved by his direct superiors Colonel Richardson and Brig. Gen. Doyle A. Hickey, commander of CCA. General Rose was killed in action during fighting east of the Ruhr Pocket in March, so the matter was eventually dropped.

7.   *The Bulge Bugle,* vol. XII, no. 2 (May 1993), p. 19.

8.   By 2400 hours on 24 December the divisions comprising the XVIII Airborne Corps had suffered the following battle and nonbattle casualties:

3d Armored Division	682
30th Infantry Division	1,288
106th Infantry Division	8,981
82d Airborne Division	451
7th Armored Division	1,000*

* The losses of the 7th Armored Division are an approximation because many of the casualties were reported late due to the disorganization of the division.

9.   The splitting up of the 75th Division and its piecemeal commitment appears to reflect lack of confidence by the First Army headquarters in the reliability of the division's leadership. The division apparently had many problems in morale, training, command, and leadership. The division commander, Maj. Gen. Fay B. Prickett, was eventually relieved of his command (see chapter 19).

10.   The story may be aprocryphal, but the behavior described was typical of Ridgway, is discussed at some length in Blair, *Ridgway's Paratroopers,* pp. 398, 562, note 30.

11.   A good description of this engagement can be found in Cole, *The Ardennes: Battle of the Bulge,* pp. 601–3. The severe casualties suffered in this fight by the 509th contributed to the postcampaign decision to disband the battalion. (See note 5 above.)

12.   *The Bulge Bugle,* vol. IX, no. 3 (August 1990), pp. 20–21.

17. ALLIED AND GERMAN DECISIONS

1.   At that time forty-two American divisions were on the Continent, as opposed to nineteen British and Commonwealth divisions, with more American divisions on the way.

2.   See De Guingand, *Operation Victory,* pp. 434–35.

3.   Based on personal conversations with, and notes of, Col. R. E. Dupuy, then the chief of public relations at SHAEF Headquarters.

4.   Bryant, *Triumph in the West,* p. 279.

5.   Montgomery, *The Memoirs of Field-Marshal Montgomery,* p. 285.

6.   There are at least hints that some of Eisenhower's closest advisers feared he would accept Monty's ploy. And, as is evident from Marshall's message (see below), the American chief of staff seems to have feared that he might be under some pressure to accept. However, in *The Supreme Commander,* p. 574, Ambrose rejects this possibility, saying that the advisers "had all misjudged Eisenhower. He was not Montgomery's man. . . ." Perhaps.

7.   Pogue, *The Supreme Command,* p. 386.

8.   De Guingand, *Operation Victory,* p. 434.

9.   Montgomery, *The Memoirs of Field-Marshal Montgomery,* p. 286.

10.   Ibid.

11.   Ibid.

12.   Ibid., p. 287. There is general agreement in the narratives about this incident in Monty's memoirs, as well as those of de Guingand and Eisenhower, and in the secondary source reports of Pogue, Cole, MacDonald, and Ambrose.

13.   Ibid, p. 278.

14. Wilmot, *The Struggle for Europe,* p. 611n.

15.   The coauthor can testify personally to that relationship as a member of the original staff of that first Supreme Headquarters Allied Powers, Europe (SHAPE), 1950–1952.

16.   Blumenson, *The Patton Papers,* p. 6.

17.   J. Lawton Collins, *Lightning Joe: An Autobiography* (Baton Rouge, La., 1979), p. 292.

18.   See George S. Patton, *War As I Knew It* (Boston, 1947), and Blumenson, *The Patton Papers.*

19.   Patton, *War As I Knew It,* p. 206.

20.   Cole, *The Ardennes: Battle of the Bulge,* pp. 6–13.

21.   Patton, *War As I Knew It,* p. 213. Patton does not seem to have realized that he had been "slickered" by Bradley.

22.   Blumenson, *The Patton Papers,* p. 615.

23.   Cole, *The Ardennes: Battle of the Bulge,* p. 6.

24.   Bittrich's corps contained the 2d SS Panzer Division "Das Reich" and the 9th SS Panzer Division "Hohenstaufen," with the 12 th SS Panzer Division "Hitlerjugend" moving into position from the I SS Panzer Corps area.

25.   These included the 212th and 276th VGDs in the LXXXV Corps; the 79th and 352d VGDs in the LXXX Corps; and the LIII Corps, comprising the 5th Fallschirmjäger Division, the Führer Begleit Brigade, a kampfgruppe from the 15th Panzergrenadier Division, and the 901st Panzergrenadier Regiment of the Panzer Lehr Division. Counting all of this as "six divisions" is a bit of a simplification.

26.   Quoted in Toland, *Battle: The Story of the Bulge,*   p. 287.

27.   In fluid and dynamic situations, the Germans often created temporary higher headquarters, usually designated by the commander's name. A divisiongruppe would be a division-size formation, composed of independent battalions or parts of regiments. A korpsgruppe was a division-size or larger unit made up of regiments and pieces of divisions. An armeegruppe or armeeabteilung was a corps-size (or larger) grouping of divisions and corps. In a few cases, these temporary groupings were made permanent, and given regular numerical designations.

28.   The Leibstandarte was by this time but a shadow of what it had been on 16 December. By 28–29 December, SS-Oberfuhrer Wilhelm Mohnke's 1st SS Panzer

Division had barely thirty tanks (fourteen of them Tigers) and perhaps half a dozen assault guns and tank destroyers operational. The division had also suffered extensive personnel and transport losses, and in terms of overall combat power was hardly equivalent to a regular panzergrenadier division.

29.   Many of the infantry companies in Kokott's division had been reduced to less than forty or fifty officers and men, and his battalions were consequently little more than companies. Like most other German divisions in the Ardennes, the 26th VGD did not receive significant replacements during the battle.

18. THE CONTINUING BATTLE FOR BASTOGNE

1.   On 27 December the only combat-capable unit under the command of the VIII Corps (headquartered at Neufchâteau) was the battered and depleted—but surprisingly resilient—109th Regimental Combat Team of the 28th Infantry Division (see chapters 7 and 13), which had returned from Eddy's XII Corps on 26 December.

2.   The kampfgruppe was built around the 115th Panzergrenadier Regiment, with three motorized infantry battalions. Because of battle casualties suffered on 25 December (see chapter 14) the regiment had been reduced to little more than the equivalent of one battalion, along with a battalion of twelve towed 105-mm howitzers and a company each of PzKw-IV tanks and JgPz-IV tank destroyers (twelve or fourteen AFVs apiece) from the division's 105th Panzer Battalion. All the tanks had been lost, but about eight JgPz-IV tank destroyers remained.

3.   The German Army's feldersatz battalions were forward-area training and indoctrination units used to familiarize new recruits or replacements with a division's weapons and methods of operation. Ordinarily, the feldersatz units were too valuable to commit to combat, but in an emergency they could be used as infantry.

4.   The Führer Grenadier Brigade, which did not conform to any organizational patterns generally known to U.S. Army intelligence officers, posed some puzzles for the intelligence staff of the 26th Infantry Division. Because of its association with the Grossdeutschland Panzer Division (and because many of its personnel wore unit patches from that division), it was initially identified as that division, and it was New Year's Day before its proper identification was established.

5.   The remaining infantry regiment and artillery battalion, along with most of the division's service troops, were still en route. The units in position on 27 December were two infantry regiments, three artillery battalions, and some support troops.

6.   At the time of its commitment, the 9th VGD had about 9,130 officers and men (about 87 percent of full strength) and nearly all of its allotted weapons and equipment; it was missing all its antiaircraft guns and three of fourteen JgPz-38 (t) Hetzers.

7.   The elements of the 15th Panzergrenadier Division around Harlange included the 104th Panzergrenadier Regiment, two artillery battalions, half of the tank battalion, and most of the reconnaissance, engineer, Flak, and antitank battalions, altogether about 9,000 men and thirty-odd tanks and assault guns.

8.   These figures are taken from Cole, *The Ardennes: Battle of the Bulge,* p. 616.

9.   While U.S. casualty figures rely on complete and well-preserved unit reports from the National Archives, the German casualty figures are less accurate, and often exist only as total figures sustained by a division over several days. Therefore, the German losses presented in the text are necessarily approximations.

10.   Although relatively strong in manpower, with close to its full allotment of heavy weapons and nearly all its transport (about 300 mostly Italian trucks of doubtful reliability and close to 1,100 horse-drawn vehicles), the 167th VGD was missing its self-propelled antitank gun company and all nine of its organic 37-mm antiaircraft guns.

11.   By 3 January Tolsdorff's 340th VGD was below its theoretical strength. The division was short about 10 to 15 percent of its heavy infantry weapons (mortars, medium machine guns, infantry guns), eight of its twelve 75-mm AT guns, four 105-mm and two 150-mm howitzers, and had only six PzJg-38 (t) Hetzer SP AT guns in the antitank battalion. Also, while the division had almost 300 trucks and 47 Maultier half-track carriers, it had been reduced to just over 950 horse-drawn vehicles (about 86 percent of authorized animal transport strength).

12.   One indication of the strain of combat was the declining strength of the 101st Airborne Division. By 26 December the division's organic units had been reduced to 711 officers and 9,516 enlisted men (10,227 overall), as noted in the division's official history; see Rapport and Northwood, *Rendezvous with Destiny,* p. 593. This figure does not include the nearly 2,000-strong 501st Parachute Infantry and the 500-strong 463d Parachute Field Artillery, neither of which technically "belonged" to the 101st until 1 March 1945.

13.   The panzergrenadier kampfgruppe was the 901st Panzergrenadier Regiment of the Panzer Lehr Division. The rest of Panzer Lehr lay north and west of Bastogne, facing the 6th Cavalry Group and other units advancing against the southern face of the Bulge's tip.

14.   By the last days of December, the strength of Leibstandarte and its attached units had dwindled to 17,305 from 21,292 two weeks earlier. The division contained thirty-five tanks, twelve tank destroyers, four armored cars, forty-seven half-tracks, five self-propelled and thirty-four towed artillery pieces, and twenty-four Nebelwerfer rocket launchers. The division was missing half of its panzer regiment, half of one panzergrenadier regiment, its reconnaissance battalion, and several smaller units. The missing units and equipment had been part of Kampfgruppe Peiper (see chapters 5 and 11).

15.   The 115th Panzergrenadier Regiment, most of the divisional artillery and support units, and about half the panzer battalion.

16.   This represented the majority of the tanks and assault guns still functioning in the 9th SS Panzer Division "Hohenstaufen." Most of its panzergrenadier battalions were in similar shape, averaging less than 160 infantrymen each (about one-third of authorized rifle strength). The battalions had around 500 total personnel each, a little over half of what they were supposed to have.

17.   The story—fully consistent with the more prosaic accounts in the official reports—is told dramatically in *The Bulge Bugle,* vol. XII, no. 4 (December 1992), pp. 18–19, by then-Pfc. Eduardo Alberto Peniche of Lynchburg, Virginia. Peniche, a member of O'Toole's gun crew, was also wounded in the battle.

19. COUNTEROFFENSIVE IN THE NORTH

1.   Bradley and Blair, *A General's Life,* p. 371.
2.   Eisenhower, *Crusade in Europe,* pp. 360-61.

3.   Collins, *Lightning Joe,* p. 291.

4.   Ibid., p. 292.

5.   Ibid.

6.   There is little doubt that the United Kingdom was scraping the bottom of the manpower barrel in late 1944, and that senior government authorities had come to the conclusion that they should shift as much as possible of the manpower drain of battle-field attrition to the Americans. Bearing in mind how the United Kingdom had borne the burden of war for more than two years before U.S. entry into the conflict, this was not an unreasonable British position. It was not a matter that could be discussed with the Allies, however, particularly since the Americans were taking the bulk of the casu-alties in the war against Japan. British official sensitivity about revealing casualty fig-ures is evidenced by the fact that in the second half of 1944 official reports no longer included casualty statistics.

7.   John S. D. Eisenhower, *The Bitter Woods,* p. 4.

8.   Patton, moreover, had not wanted to get involved in Bastogne in the first place, recognizing that it would divert resources and attention from his cherished drive up the Skyline Drive.

9.   Blumenson, *The Patton Papers,* p. 608

10.   Carl von Clausewitz, *On War,* trans. Michael Howard and Peter Paret (Princeton, 1976), p. 358, and passim.

11.   For a discussion of how values for such factors can be derived, see T. N. Dupuy, *Numbers, Predictions and War* (New York 1979), chapter 3.

12.   *The Bulge Bugle,* vol. X, no. 1 (February 1991), pp. 19–23.

13.   Apparently there was considerable confusion, due to contradictory orders, in this redeployment of the SS Panzer corps and divisions.

14.   *The Bulge Bugle,* vol. VII, no. 3 (July 1988), p. 15

15.   The losses were especially heavy on 3 January, with 76 killed, 336 wounded, and 17 missing, amounting to a very high daily rate of 3.84 percent of the division's total strength of 11,184.

16.   R. E. Dupuy, *St. Vith,* chapter 14, provides the best coverage of the activities of the 106th Division and attached units for this period of the offensive.

17.   These figures are necessarily estimates, since many German casualty reports did not survive the war. Moreover, the front-line German volksgrenadier divisions in this sector had only 7,500 to 8,700 officers and men, barely half as strong as a normal U.S. infantry division with attachments. The German casualty rate—nearly 2 percent per day—was exceedingly high as a sustained rate over the many days.

18.   By this date, Dietrich's Sixth Panzer Army had operational control only of the II SS Panzer Corps, containing the 2d SS Panzer Division "Das Reich." The I SS Panzer Corps and the 1st "Leibstandarte Adolf Hitler," 9th "Hohenstaufen," and 12th "Hitlerjugend" divisions were by this time part of Manteuffel's Fifth Panzer Army and were all deployed around Bastogne. These units were soon pulled out of the line and assembled near St. Vith.

19.   *The Bulge Bugle,* vol. XI, no. 4 (December 1992), p. 25.

20.   Matthew B. Ridgway and Harold H. Martin, *Soldier: The Memoirs of Matthew B. Ridgway* (New York, 1956), p. 120. See also Blair, *Ridgway's Paratroopers,* p. 422, 564 n.

21.   Ridgway and Martin, *Soldier,* pp. 120–21.

20. "OLD BLOOD AND GUTS" SUPPRESSES DOUBTS

1. Cole, *The Ardennes: Battle of the Bulge,* p. 611.

2. Despite the U.S. Army's general dedication to organization uniformity, its five airborne divisions were anything but organizationally identical. Miley's division contained two three-battalion parachute infantry regiments (507th and 513th), two two-battalion glider infantry regiments (193d and 194th) with a separate glider infantry battalion (550th) attached to the 193d, one parachute and two glider artillery battalions, each with twelve 75-mm pack howitzers (466th Parachute, 680th and 681st Glider Battalion), and the usual support elements.

3. The 17th Airborne had started its existence with the 417th Parachute Infantry Regiment, which was replaced by the 513th in March 1944. The 507th Parachute Infantry Regiment was attached to the division after it arrived in Britain, and remained attached until it was permanently assigned to the division on 1 March 1945. At that point the 193d Glider Infantry Regiment was disbanded as part of the U.S. Army's reorganization of its airborne divisions in early 1945.

4. Blakeley had replaced Maj. Gen. Raymond O. Barton, who had been evacuated due to illness on 26 December 1944.

5. This organization is detailed in chapter 18. However, by 5 January the 104th Panzergrenadier Regiment was en route from the vicinity of Berle to rejoin the 15th Panzergrenadier Division west of Bastogne.

6. This was the bulk of the division except the 77th Grenadier Regiment, which lay near Longvilly.

7. This was the designation of the reduced headquarters establishment around Lt. Gen. Decker himself, left behind after the corps troops of the XXXIX Panzer Corps departed on 4 January.

8. The combat record of African-American (or "colored," as they were referred to at the time in official Army documents) combat units was mixed. The 761st Tank Battalion, along with the 33d and 969th Field Artillery battalions, fought in the Ardennes campaign with considerable distinction, and the record of African-American soldiers in the Alsace campaign was also excellent. On the other hand, the 92d Infantry Division (Colored) in Italy performed poorly, and that experience ensured that the 93d Infantry Division (Colored) in the Pacific was used solely for rear-area duties and garrison work. The problem was a combination of factors: poor white leadership, inadequate preparation for combat, poor understanding of what black soldiers needed to do well, and second-rate performance by some black soldiers who felt they were treated like second-class citizens.

9. Based on an article by Captain (later Lieutenant Colonel, Retired) Charles A. Gates in *The Bulge Bugle*, vol. XII, no. 1 (February 1993), p. 25.

10. The 90th Infantry Division had landed in Europe in late June 1944 and taken part in the later stages of the Normandy campaign. Its combat performance there and in subsequent operations across France and into Lorraine was, despite two changes of commanding general, significantly below par. Only after Major General Van Fleet was made division commander in mid-October did the division improve, so that by late December it was considered to be one of the best infantry divisions in northwest Europe.

11. A 740-strong cavalry squadron contained not only forty M8 armored cars, six M8 75-mm assault guns, and seventeen M5 light tanks, but also three 81-mm and

twenty-seven 60-mm mortars, along with nearly 80 machine guns and more than 200 submachine guns. By comparison, a normal U.S. infantry battalion had six 81-mm morters but only nine 60-mm mortars.

12.   This operation was one of a group of five competing plans for offensive action on the western front by the Wehrmacht in late autumn. The others were "Holland," aimed at Antwerp from Venlo, across the base of the Arnhem-Nijmegen salient; "Aachen-Liège," a double envelopment intended to recapture both those cities and encircle most of Hodges's First Army; "Luxembourg," another double envelopment that would thrust toward Luxembourg City through Trier and Metz and isolate Patton's Third Army; "Lothringen," which aimed at Nancy (and was, modified, employed as the basis for "Nordwind"); and "Alsace," directed at the recapture of Vesoul. A combination of the northern wing of "Luxembourg" and the southern wing of "Aachen-Liège" served, in part, as inspiration for Wacht am Rhein.

13.   *The Bulge Bugle,* vol. XII, no. 3 (August 1993), p. 19.

14.   The August 1993 edition of *The Bulge Bugle* (vol. XII, no. 3), pp. 19–20, reveals some controversy between veterans of the 761st Tank Battalion and those of the 87th Division as to which can claim the honor of the conquest of Tillet. There seems little doubt that the credit must go to the 87th Division, particularly its 346th Infantry Regiment. This in no way denigrates the splendid and valiant support given to the 87th Division by the all-black 761st Tank Battalion.

15.   Since the 90th Infantry Division was not really stressed by the counterattack, U.S. commanders did not realize the importance the Germans had attached to it until after the war, when German military records came to light and the real plight of the 5th Parachute Division became clear.

16.   This was to compensate the 4th Division for the 12th Infantry Regiment, still assigned to the 87th Division. The new arrangement left Culin with seven infantry battalions, and the 4th Division (assigned a more active role) with twelve infantry battalions.

17.   It is not certain whether the rear guard was from the 15th Panzergrenadier. It could have been part of the Panzer Lehr Division or even from the 3d Panzergrenadier. German records for combat units in the Ardennes were virtually nonexistent by this time.

18.   Most of these "tanks" and assault guns were probably from the 3d and 15th Panzergrenadier divisions, and there were probably few real tanks among them by this date.

19.   According to Toland, *Battle: The Story of the Bulge,* p. 362, Task Force Greene contained a light tank company (seventeen M5s), two cavalry platoons (about fifteen armored cars and fifteen jeeps), an assault gun platoon (six M8 howitzer motor carriages, an M5 chassis with a 75-mm pack howitzer replacing the M5's 37-mm L53 gun), and six half-tracks with a platoon of armored infantry—a total of 450 officers and men.

20.   Blumenson, *The Patton Papers,* pp. 625–26.

21. RETURN TO ST. VITH

1.   In his book *The Last Offensive: The European Theater of Operations, United States Army in World War II* (Washington, D.C., 1973), Charles B. MacDonald suggests that by recommitting these units that Hitler had ordered to be withdrawn,

Dietrich "risked Hitler's wrath." This is doubtful, since one of the purposes of the concentration of the SS Panzer units at St. Vith had been to provide a reserve against a possible American offensive to cut the base of the Bulge. Furthermore, Dietrich was careful not to commit any major units to the line.

2.   *The Bulge Bugle,* vol. X, no. 1 (February 1991), pp. 21–22.

3.   Blumenson, *The Patton Papers,* p. 626.

4.   As quoted by MacDonald, *Last Offensive,* p. 51.

5.   This event, the similar liberation of Clervaux a few days later, and the adventures of the Americans and their Luxembourger benefactors are reported in some detail in Toland, *Battle: The Story of the Bulge,* especially in the final chapter.

6.   *The Bulge Bugle,* vol. XII, no. 2 (May 1993), pp. 16–17.

EPILOGUE

1.   A German reviewer has challeged this parallel on the following grounds: "Comparison of the situation in 1918 with that of 1944 is very problematic. I don't agree that the circumstances were 'similar.' In 1918 the hostilities on the Eastern Front had ceased with the armistice of December 1917, followed by the Treaty of Brest-Litovsk in March 1918. With it the German High Command (Oberste Heeresleitung) was able to concentrate the majority of the German Army on the Western Front. In contrast to this, at the end of 1944 the majority of the German Army was deployed on the Eastern Front, and a major Soviet offensive was expected for January 1945." Nevertheless, we believe that the comparison is apt, with the qualifications shown.

2.   Bradley, *A Soldier's Story,* p. 465.

3.   Bradley and Blair, *A General's Life,* p. 356.

4.   Eisenhower, *Crusade in Europe,* pp. 342–44.

5.   Ibid., p. 355.

6.   In his diary, and in letters to his wife, Patton often referred to Bradley (whose first name was Omar) as "the tentmaker."

7.   Blumenson, *The Patton Papers,* p. 615.

APPENDIX A

1.   Ray S. Cline, *Washington Command Post: The Operations Divisions; The U.S. Army in World War II* (Washington, D.C., 1951), pp. 87–89.

2.   Ibid., pp. 215–33 and passim.

3.   Wilmot, *The Struggle for Europe,* p. 663.

4.   Lewin, *Ultra Goes to War,* p. 131.

5.   Ibid., pp. 48–50.

6.   Frederick W. Winterbotham, *The Ultra Secret* (New York, 1974), pp. 13–16.

7.   Lewin, *Ultra Goes to War,* p. 63.

8.   Cline, *Washington Command Post,* pp. 220–33.

9.   Mary H. Williams, *Chronology, 1941–1945: The U.S. Army in World War II* (Washington, D.C., 1960), p. 203.

10.   Pogue, *The Supreme Command,* p. 199 ff.

11.   Williams, *Chronology, 1941–1945,* pp. 244–47.

12.   Pogue, *The Supreme Command,* p. 228.

13.   Williams, *Chronology, 1941–1945,* p. 270.

14. Ibid., p. 276.
15. Ibid., p. 339.
16. Ibid., p. 294.
17. Ibid., p. 308.
18. Ibid., p. 351.
19. Cole, *The Ardennes: Battle of the Bulge,* pp. 5–18.
20. Observation by German historian, Dr. Franz Uhle-Wettler (Lieutenant General, Retired) in private communication.
21. Cole, *The Ardennes: Battle of the Bulge,* pp. 31–32.

APPENDIX B

1. Marvin A. Kreidberg, Lieutenant Colonel, Infantry, U.S. Army, and Merton G. Henry, Lieutenant, AGC, *U.S. Army History of Military Mobilization in the United States Army, 1775–1945* (Washington, D.C., pp. 549–50, 575–80, 597, 623, and passim.

2. T. Dodson Stamps and Vincent J. Esposito, eds. *A Military History of World War II,* vol. 1 (West Point, N.Y., 1952), pp. 641–47.

3. This discussion on the organization, equipment, and doctrine of the U.S. Army relies on many sources, including contemporary field manuals and Table of Organization and Equipment (TO&E) documents, as well as secondary sources that are too extensive to list in full here. (One of the coauthors contributes some personal experience as well.) For a listing of all sources relevant to this discussion consult the bibliography.

4. The Army Ground Forces was created in a major War Department reorganization of 9 March 1942. It was responsible for the organization and training of all army units other than the Air Corps. General McNair was accidentally killed by U.S. Army Air Force bombs while observing the breakout in Normandy on 25 July 1944.

5. Kreidberg and Henry, *U.S. Army History of Military Mobilization,* pp. 620–25.

6. Similar organizations were the British armored division which had two tank brigades (a total of six battalions with 337 tanks) and two infantry battalions; the German Panzer division, which had two tank regiments (also a total of six battalions but with 416 tanks) and four infantry battalions; and the French Division Cuirassée Reserve (DCR), which had two tank regiments (a total of four battalions with 158 tanks) and a single infantry battalion.

7. The 1st, 2d, and 3d Armored divisions, which were already deployed to the Mediterranean theater of operations, retained the "heavy" organization. The 1st Armored Division was converted to a "light" division on 20 July 1944, following the Rome campaign. The 2d and 3d Armored divisions retained the "heavy" organization until the end of the war.

8. U.S. tank designs also improved. However, the Army Ground Forces (AGF), with General McNair's approval, refused to sanction large-scale production and deployment of improved tanks, citing shipping space and weight restrictions and a lack of need for such a tank as reasons. This was in spite of repeated requests made by the armored forces for better tanks, following their first encounters with the powerful new German models in Tunisia and Italy during 1943. The Army Ordnance Department did design and build in small quantities—over AGF opposition—better

tanks. Only one of these, the M26 "Pershing," ever reached the ETO, but not until February 1945. It proved to be fully the equal of the fearsome German Panther. Angry American tankers declared the M26 to be just what they had asked for—in 1943.

9. The idea that the Allies overwhelmed the Germans by masses of tanks is only partially correct. In fact, by December 1944 the U.S. Army in the ETO was suffering from dangerous shortfalls in medium tank strengths. The necessity of supplying tanks to Britain, the Soviet Union, and the Pacific theater; restrictions on shipping space to Europe; and unexpectedly high attrition had severely reduced the number of tanks in the ETO. As a stopgap measure most of the separate tank battalions—and many of the battalions in the armored divisions—had been reduced from a strength of seventeen tanks per medium company, to a strength of thirteen mediums per company.

10. CCA and CCB were originally intended to have primary operational control of the division's combat elements. CCR's primary task was administrative control of units in division reserve (as the name implies); operations were to be a minor, secondary task for CCR. However, these clear distinctions were not usually observed in combat.

11. A major problem for the towed TD battalions was that the gun's prime mover, the M2 and M3 series half-track, was heavily overloaded. Gun, ammunition, crew, and other equipment weighed more than four tons—severely reducing the mobility of the half-track. A purpose-designed, fully tracked prime mover was seen as the solution. Such a vehicle was developed (the powerful, highly mobile T41 Armored Utility Vehicle, which was a derivation of the M18 self-propelled TD); however, production did not begin until October 1944. None saw service in the ETO.

12. The M5 39" gun was a hodgepodge of components, built around the tube of the obsolescent 39" antiaircraft gun, with the carriage of the 105-mm howitzer, and a simple gunshield—which surprisingly worked very well. Its main drawback, shared with all large-caliber towed antitank guns, was its two-and-a-quarter-ton weight.

13. Mary Lee Stubbs and Stanley Russell Connor, *Armor-Cavalry; Part I: Regular Army and Army Reserve* (Washington, D.C.: Office Chief of Military History, U.S. Army, GPO, 1969), p. 73.

14. The German Army had made a conversion from "square" to "triangular" divisions in 1916, during World War I.

15. The actual, as opposed to the theoretical, organization of the airborne divisions varied. The 101st Division was organized with two parachute and two glider regiments, the 82d Division with two parachute and one glider regiment. The 101st Division had three artillery battalions; the 82d Division had four.

16. The 57-mm antitank gun was an American-produced version of the British 6-pounder antitank gun. With standard armor-piercing ammunition it was only marginally effective against the flank and rear of most German armored vehicles. A new, British-designed, armor-piercing, discarding-sabot (APDS) round had proved to be highly effective, but was available only in very limited quantities (the 2d Infantry Division had six rounds per gun available on 16 December). The M9 rocket launcher was the brainchild of the pioneer American rocket designer, Dr. Robert Goddard, who had begun work on the weapon at the end of World War I. It was nicknamed the "bazooka" because of a fancied resemblance to a makeshift musical instrument played by a hillbilly comedian, Bob Burns. Early versions of the bazooka had used an unreliable, battery-powered, electrical firing mechanism. The M9 variant utilized a simpler

and more reliable, piezo-electric firing mechanism. Unfortunately, it was short-ranged, inaccurate, and the warhead was too small to be fully effective against all but the most lightly armored targets. However, despite its defects, the bazooka did provide a determined infantryman with a weapon that could penetrate the flank and rear armor of German tanks in the confusion of a close-range firefight.

17.   The word "pontoon" is properly pronounced "ponton," and beginning in World War II, that is the way it has been spelled by U.S. Army Engineers.

18.   There were a number of black combat units in the ETO; most were separate artillery units. Most were good outfits, usually with excellent esprit. A number of these were outstanding: The 969th Field Artillery Battalion was to be the backbone of the artillery in the defense of Bastogne and received accolades from generals Patton, Middleton, and McAuliffe, as well as the battered GIs of the 101st Airborne Division. The 969th's companion battalion, the 333d Field Artillery Battalion (they had originally been the 2d and 1st battalions, respectively, of the 333d Field Artillery Regiment), was in support of the 106th Infantry Division in the Schnee Eifel, where two batteries had been overrun while valiantly attempting to evacuate its howitzers. Seven howitzers were lost. The remnant of the 333d, with five remaining 155-mm howitzers, was eventually able to join the defenders of Bastogne, although two more pieces were overrun at Senonchamps outside the town. The survivors of the 333d manned their remaining three howitzers throughout the siege of Bastogne, adding their small but significant part to the defense.

19.   The German assessment of U.S. combat capability was that U.S. armor and infantry tactics were too stereotyped and predictable. Attacks were usually executed at or just after dawn and ceased at dark. Cooperation between armor and infantry was usually faulty: If one element was halted the other would withdraw rather than seek a solution to the problem, causing the attack to collapse. There were exceptions to this: The airborne divisions were well versed in small-unit infantry assault, especially at night; Maj. Gen. Terry de la Mesa Allen emphasized night attacks, infiltration, and combined-arms cooperation in his 104th Infantry Division (Allen, the former commander of the 1st Infantry Division, had been retired from command of the 1st Division, largely because of his exasperation with superiors who resisted accepting his tactical precepts, and his acerbic tongue); and both the 4th and 6th Armored divisions developed combined-arms tactics to a high degree. These divisions were all treated with caution and a degree of fear by the Germans.

20.   Churchill, *The Hinge of Fate,* vol. 4 of *The Second World War* (Boston, 1950), p. 387.

21.   Manpower data taken from Maj. Gen. A. J. K. Pigott, comp., "Manpower Problems," WO 277/, 1949.

22.   Shelford Bidwell, *Old Battles and New Defenses: Can We Learn from Military History?* (London, 1986), p. 139. See also the comments in Shelford Bidwell and Dominick Graham, *Fire-Power: British Army Weapons and Theories of War, 1904–1945* (London, 1982), passim.

23.   Interestingly, however, the Germans do not have a word for "doctrine."

24.   At the outset of the Bulge battle the 29th Armoured Brigade was being reequipped with Comets, and so was not available for commitment. However, the conversion was not complete and the brigade went into combat after drawing its old Shermans from depot.

APPENDIX C

1.   There were in the entire German ground forces 26 regular and 7 SS panzer divisions, with 12 regular and 5 SS Panzergrenadier divisions, a total of 50 mechanized divisions, compared to more than 270 infantry, mountain, horsed cavalry, parachute, and other nonmechanized divisions.

2.   The forces eventually committed to the Ardennes offensive contained five of twenty-six army Panzer divisions (19.2 percent), two of twelve army panzergrenadier divisions (16.7 percent), and four of seven SS Panzer divisions (57.1 percent). These divisions amounted to a total of eleven out of fifty panzer and panzergrenadier divisions, or 22 percent of the total.

3.   The varying allotments and strengths for each division were customarily portrayed on a graphic display called a *Gliederung* ("disposition" or "arrangement"). These showed the allotment of personnel, weapons, and other equipment items, and showed the extent to which a division's component units were under- or overstrength. They were usually produced on the first of each month. A *Grundgliederung* ("basic arrangement") was the Wehrmacht's equivalent of the U.S. Army's Tables of Organization and Equipment.

4.   The SS, or Schutzstaffel (guard force), was the Nazi Party's own security force. It had originated as a bodyguard force for senior Party officials, and also included the Sicherheitsdienst (Security Service) or SD, a sort of police, and several other branches. The Waffen-SS, or armed SS, had originated as a sort of palace guard, but had expanded during the war to more than twenty divisions by late 1944, including the seven panzer and five panzergrenadier divisions mentioned earlier.

5.   All German army vehicles had an SdKfz, for Sonderkraftfahrzeug (special-purpose vehicle), number. Outside of the Wehrmacht's weapons development office, nobody used them except to refer to half-tracks and armored cars.

6.   The "K" for *kurz* (short, for the L48 gun) and "L" for *lang* (long, for the L70 gun) referred to the relative barrel lengths of the 75-mm guns used on the two models of the JgPz-IV; the vehicles were otherwise virtually identical; ammo stowage in the JgPz-IV(l) was more limited because of the larger gun and its slightly longer ammunition, so their relative combat power was nearly the same.

7.   The Wehrmacht, which for all its efficiency was sometimes maddeningly inconsistent in its nomenclature, had a particularly hard time with the SS divisions. All of them had originally had names, and had been assigned numbers in early 1943. Thus, the Leibstandarte ("Lifeguard") SS Adolf Hitler was renumbered as the 1st SS Panzer Division "Leibstandarte Adolf Hitler," but almost any combination of both of these designations was used.

8.   Nebelwerfer batteries uniformly contained six weapons, regardless of caliber or unit.

APPENDIX D

1.   The IX Air Defense Command (ADC) was under the administrative command of the U.S. Ninth Tactical Air Force, but in effect operated under the direct operational command of SHAEF. It was responsible for the defense of Ninth Air Force airfields on the Continent and for other vital installations behind the Army

Group Rear Boundary, which was nearly synonymous with the COM-Z. It also formed a special task force known as Antwerp X to control the AAA units protecting Antwerp from the buzz-bomb threat. Unfortunately, the command structure and the areas of responsibility (many airfields and other installations guarded by the IX ADC were actually within the th Army Group Zone) were imprecise and were the cause of some friction between the IX ADC and the th Army Group.

APPENDIX E

1.   Casualty figures for German units that participated in the Ardennes offensive vary in reliability. Those that are most accurate are those for the SS and army panzer and panzergrenadier divisions and for divisions of the Fifth Panzer Army in general. Records for other units were found to be very sketchy. However, by a careful analysis of the existing records a methodology was developed to estimate with a high degree of confidence the probable distribution of casualties among the various units over time. For a complete explanation of the methodology see *ACSDB: Final Report.*

2.   Note that the initial strength of the division includes the 8th Fallschirmjäger Regiment, which did not rejoin the division until sometime in the late evening or early morning of 17–18 December. Thus, on the morning of 16 December, the division would have had a combat strength of about 9,000 men.

3.   Like the 3d Fallschirmjäger Division, the 5th Division's strength was also reduced by detachments. In his postwar account the division commander stated that many of the enlisted personnel of the division were virtually untrained. As a result, three large ersatz (replacement) battalions were formed with about 2,500 men and were attached to the LIII Corps to hold the far left flank of the Seventh Army. As the battle progressed, they were then fed forward as replacements for the enormous losses the division had taken, and the battalions were eventually disbanded. In addition, the divisional 120-mm mortar battalion had not yet arrived, and the poorly trained and equipped artillery regiment was detached to act as corps artillery; in return three corps artillery battalions and two Nebelwerfer battalions were attached to the division. These detachments reduced the combat strength of the division on 16 December to less than 10,000 men.

4.   The 560th Volksgrenadier Division was actually missing about one-third of its combat strength on 16 December. One infantry regiment, two artillery battalions, the SP panzerjäger company, the FLAK company, and an engineer company (close to 3,500 men) were all still en route from Norway via Denmark and did not rejoin the division until 28 December.

APPENDIX F

1.   The 7th Armored Division was in the process of moving south into the VIII Corps sector, and advance elements reached St. Vith after noon on 17 December.

2.   As noted in the introduction, the 9th Armored was spread in combat command packets in the VIII Corps sector. CCB/9, which had been called south from the V Corps late on 16 December, was committed to the fighting around St. Vith several hours before the lead elements of the 7th Armored arrived to join the battle there.

3.   Only CCB/9 was with the XVIII Airborne Corps; CCA/9 was with the XII

Corps near Echternach; the remnants of CCR/9 were in Bastogne with the 101st ABD.

4.   The data shown here reflect the 17th Airborne's situation on 4 January, the date when it entered combat for the first time.

5.   By this date the division's reconnaissance battalion had left to refit, except for a reduced armored car company.

6.   The data for the XXXIX Panzer Corps are for 29 December; equipment returns for 2 January were missing.

APPENDIX G

1.   This appendix is based substantially on "Malmédy—Massacre and Trial," an unpublished paper written by Lt. Gen. Dr. Franz Uhle-Wettler at the request of one of the authors. Somewhat condensed, and with many changes in emphasis and treatment to reflect an American rather than a German point of view, this appendix is in no way a paraphrase of the Uhle-Wettler paper. Nevertheless it follows the same general approach, and arrives at substantially the same conclusions. We are most indebted to General Uhle-Wettler for his contribution.

2.   Quoted by Senator Joseph McCarthy, *Congressional Record,* July 26, 1949, p. 10397.

3.   Apparently the Inspector General of the First Army visited the crossroads shortly after 14 January. He reported "approximately 120" corpses. (See Weingartner, *Crossroads of Death,* p. 67). However, at the trial the prosecution consistently referred to 72 murdered at the crossroads. In 1948–49 the Baldwin Commission (a U.S. Senate subcommittee) assumed that 86 soldiers had been murdered at Baugnez.

4.   These numbers are taken from the Baldwin Commission Report, which related numbers of murders to the locations where they were reported to have occurred. According to this report, 45 prisoners were murdered at La Gleize. (However, see note 7 for a very different number from another source.) At the trial the prosecution charged that between 538 and 749 U.S. prisoners were murdered, in addition to "over 90" Belgian civilians.

5.   The report by Major (later General) McCown is quoted (in translation) in R. Tiemann, *Der Malmedyprozess* (Osnabrück, 1990), pp. 37ff. McCown's testimony at the trial was consistent with his report, much to the annoyance of some members of the court, particularly Colonel Rosenfeld, the Law Member.

6.   Peiper had finished Oberrealschule (high school) shortly before the war, and had received the Abitur certificate, which qualified him to study at a university. The first foreign language requirement in such a school was English.

7.   This number varies considerably from that in the Baldwin Commission Report; see note 4, above.

8.   All of the German documents are reprinted in Tiemann, *Der Malmedyprozess,* pp. 66ff.

9.   Weingartner, *Crossroads of Death.*

10.   Tiemann, *Der Malmedyprozess,* p. 65 (Document 1634 PS, evidence RF 382).

11.   Director of the Legal Division, U.S. Military Government of Germany, quoted in Schöbener, *Die amerikanische Besatzungspolitik und das Völkerrecht,* p. 431. See also E. Schwinge, "Rückblick auf die Zeit der amerikanischen Besetzung," in Willms, *Handbuch der Deutschen Nation,* 1:307ff and 326.

12.   See Schöbener, *Die amerikanische Besatzungspolitik und das Völkerrecht,* pp. 236ff, 418ff, 473ff; Weingartner, *Crossroads of Death,* p. 98 n. 7; and Tiemann, *Der Malmedyprozess,* p. 93f.

13.   See Tiemann, *Der Malmedyprozess,* pp. 78ff.

14.   J. Backer, *Die deutschen Jahres des Generals Clay* (München, 1983), p. 291.

15.   Weingartner, *Crossroads of Death,* p. 148. Weingartner found the evidence: "So transparently worthless that its introduction suggested either contempt for the intelligence of the bench or confidence that any prosecution evidence, no matter how lacking in substance, would weigh in the scales against the defendants."

16.   Ibid., pp. 87, 102, 144.

17.   See Tiemann, *Der Malmedyprozess,* pp. 120ff.

18.   Weingartner, *Crossroads of Death,* p. 183.

19.   *Chicago Tribune,* 13 October 1948.

20.   Speech in U.S. Senate reprinted in translation in Tiemann, *Der Malmedyprozess,* annex 4.

APPENDIX H

1.   Blumenson, *Patton Papers,* p. 615. On that same day Patton, ever objective, also wrote: "There were also some unfortunate incidents in the shooting of prisoners. (I hope we can conceal this.)"

2.   T. N. Dupuy, *A Genius for War: The German Army and General Staff, 1807–1945* (Englewood Cliffs, N.J., 1977).

3.   My book *A Genius for War* was cited admiringly by Israeli historian Martin van Creveld in his book *Fighting Power: German and U.S. Army Performance 1939–45* (London, 1983). Van Creveld obviously leans heavily on my conclusions about the excellence of German combat performance in World War II. He then compares the American Army in World War II very unfavorably with the German Army. I strongly disagree with van Creveld in this respect. The specifics of most of his comparisons were simply very wrong. The Germans were very good; they were the best. But the Americans fought pretty well in World War II, also. We just weren't quite as good as the Germans.

4.   The following rules of thumb will be useful in interpretation of the casualty rates shown in the table:

	Regiment (4–6,000)	Division (10–18,000)	Corps & Army (Over 50,000)
Light combat	<0.6%	<0.3%	<0.1%
Normal combat	0.6–1.9%	0.3–0.9%	0.1–0.2%
Intense combat	2.0–6.0%	1.0–3.0%	0.3–1.0%
Very intense combat	>6.0%	>3.0%	>1.0%

BIBLIOGRAPHY

I. PRIMARY SOURCES

A. U.S. OFFICIAL DOCUMENTS

"After Action Report, Third U.S. Army: 1 August 1944–9 May 1945." 2 vols.

FM 101-10. *Staff Officers' Field Manual: Organizational, Technical, and Logistical Data.* Washington, D.C., 21 December 1944.

Office of the Theater Historian. *Order of Battle of the United States Army, World War II: European Theater of Operations.* Paris, December 1945.

HQ AAF, Office of the Asst. Chief of Air Staff, Intelligence. "Washington DC Weekly Summary of Enemy Air Activity." Bolling AFB Microfilm Roll A1242.

HQ, Ninth Air Force, Director of Intelligence. "Intelligence Summary." Bolling AFB Microfilm Roll B5735 (Office of Air Force History).

B. GERMAN INTERVIEWS AND REPORTS

Answers to Questions by Gen. der Panzertruppen von Lüttwitz, Commander, XLVII Panzer Corps in the Ardennes (A938).

Artillery report listing artillery strengths by armies, corps, and divisions, 10 Dec 1944. USNARA Microfilm T311, 18, 7021051-4.

"Commitment of Sixth Panzer Army in the Ardennes 1944–1945," (A924).

Heeresgruppe D (Army Group D). "Kriegstagebuch" (War Diary). USNARA Microfilm T311, Roll 17. Army Group D was virtually synonymous with Oberbefehlshaber West (OB West).

An Interview with Genobst. Alfred Jodl. Planning the Ardennes Offensive (ETHINT 50).

An Interview with Genobst. Alfred Jodl. Ardennes Offensive (ETHINT 51).

An Interview with Genfldm. Gerd von Rundstedt. The Ardennes Offensive (ETHINT 47).

An Interview with Gen. Panzer Horst Stumpff. Tank Maintenance in the Ardennes Offensive (ETHINT 61).

An Interview with Gen. der Kavallerie Siegfried Westphal. Planning the Ardennes (ETHINT 79).

An Interview with Gen. Hasso von Manteuffel, Fifth Panzer Army (11 Sep 1944–Jan 1945) (ETHINT 45); (Nov 1944–Jan 1945) (ETHINT 46).

An Interview with Obstgrf. Sepp Dietrich, Sixth Panzer Army in the Ardennes Offensive (ETHINT 15).

An Interview with Obstgrf. Sepp Dietrich, Sixth Panzer Army. Planning for the Ardennes Offensive (ETHINT 16).

An Interview with Genmaj. Rudolf Frhr. von Gersdorff. Seventh Army in the Ardennes Offensive (ETHINT 54).

An Interview with Obst. Joachim Peiper, I SS Panzer Regt. (11–24 Dec 1944) (ETHINT 10); (16–19 Dec 1944) (ETHINT 11).

An Interview with Gen. Heinrich von Lüttwitz XLVII Panzer Corps (16–24 Dec 1944) (ETHINT 41).

An Interview with Genmaj. (W-SS) Fritz Krämer LXVII Inf Corps (16–26 Dec 1944) (ETHINT 25); (16 Dec 1944) (ETHINT 26).

An Interview with Gen. Inf Baptist Kniess LXXXV Inf Corps (Nov–Dec 1944) (ETHINT 40).

An Interview with Genlt. Fritz Bayerlein. Panzer Lehr Division and 26th Volks-grenadier Division in the Ardennes (ETHINT 68).

An Interview with Genmaj. Walter Denkert. 3d Panzer Grenadier Division in the Ardennes (ETHINT 74).

An Interview with Obstlt. Otto Skorzeny. Ardennes Offensive (ETHINT 12).

An Interview with Genmaj. Otto Remer. Führer Begleit Brigade in the Ardennes (ETHINT 80).

An Interview with Genmaj. Heintz Kokott. Breakthrough to Bastogne (ETHINT 44).

An Interview with Maj. Herbert Büchs. The Ardennes Offensive (Sep–Dec 1944) (ETHNIT 34).

An Interview with Obstlt. Von der Heydte. German Paratroops in the Ardennes (ETHNIT 75).

Kriegstagebuch des Oberkommandos der Wehrmacht (Wehrmacht Führungsstab). Band IV: 1 January 1944–2 Mai 1945. Zweiter Halbband. (War Diary of High Command of the Armed Forces) Frankfurt am Main: Bernard & Graefe, 1961.

Report on the Strength of Heavy Weapons of the Panzer Divisions, 10 Dec 1944. USNARA Microfilm T311, 18, 7021020-25.

Schmidt, Lt. Gen. Beppo. Luftwaffe Operations in the West. Vol. 15, Strategic Concentration of AAA and Flying Units in the West (Luftwaffe Command West Command Area) Sep 1944–May 1945, Nov 1955. Bolling AFB Microfilm Roll K1026V.

C. British Official Documents

RAF Operations Record Book, Dec. 1944. Her Majesty's Public Records Office (HMPRO), AIR 24/301.

RAF Operations Record Book, vols. A–G, I, January 1945. HMPRO, AIR 24/304.

2d (British) Army War Diary, 1–31 Dec 1944. HMPRO, WO171/232.

XXX Corps War Diary, 15–31 Dec 1944 and Outline Order of Battle—9–30 Dec

1944, Operations Orders and Fragmentary Orders 20–31 Dec. 1944. HMPRO, WO171/346.

II. SECONDARY SOURCES

Aders, Gebhard. *History of the German Night Fighter Force, 1917–1945.* London, 1978.

Ambrose, Stephen E. *The Supreme Commander: The War Years of General Dwight D. Eisenhower.* New York, 1970.

Aschenauer, R. *Der Malmedy-Fall 7 Jahre nach dem Urteil.* München.

Astor, Gerald. *The Blood-Dimmed Tide.* New York, 1992.

Backer, J. *Die deutschen Jahres des Generals Clay* (German translation of *Winds of History—The German Years of Lucius D. Clay*). München, 1983.

Barker, A. J. *British and American Infantry Weapons of World War II.* New York, 1969.

Bidwell, Shelford. *Old Battles and New Defenses: Can We Learn from Military History?* London, 1986.

Bidwell, Shelford, and Dominick Graham. *Firepower: British Army Weapons and Theories of War, 1904–1945.* London, 1982.

Blair, Clay. *Ridgway's Paratroopers: The American Airborne in World War II.* Garden City, N.Y., 1985.

Blumenson, Martin. *The Patton Papers.* Boston, 1974.

Bradley, Omar N. *A Soldier's Story.* New York, 1951.

Bradley, Omar N., and Clay Blair. *A General's Life.* New York, 1983.

Brown, Captain Eric. *Wings of the Luftwaffe: Flying German Aircraft of the Second World War.* London, 1977.

Bruchiss, Louis. *Aircraft Armament.* New York, 1945.

Bryant, Arthur. *Triumph in the West.* New York, 1958.

Chamberlain, Peter, and Chris Ellis. *British and American Tanks of World War II.* London, 1969.

———. *The Churchill Tank.* London, 1971.

Churchill, Sir Winston S. *The Second World War.* 6 vols. Boston, 1948–1953.

Clausewitz, Carl von. *On War.* Translated by Michael Howard and Peter Paret. Princeton, 1976.

Cline, Ray, S. *Washington Command Post; The Operations Divisions; The U.S. Army in World War II.* Washington, D.C., 1951.

Codman, Charles R. *Drive.* Boston, 1957.

Cole, Hugh M. *The Ardennes: Battle of the Bulge. United States Army in World War II. The European Theater of Operation.* Washington, D.C., 1965.

Collins, J. Lawton. *Lightning Joe: An Autobiography.* Baton Rouge, La., 1979.

Congressional Record, Session on 26 July 1949.

Craven, Wesley F., and James L. Cate. *The Army Air Forces in World War II.* Vol 3, *Europe: Argument to V-E Day, January 1944 to May 1945.* Chicago, 1951.

Creveld, Martin van. *Fighting Power: German and U.S. Army Performance, 1939–45.* London, 1983.

Crow, Duncan, ed. *American AFVs of World War II.* Vol. 4 of *Armoured Fighting Vehicles in Profile* (AFVs of the World Series). Garden City, N.Y., 1972.

———. *British and Commonwealth AFVs, 1940–46.* Vol. 3 of *Armoured Fighting Vehicles in Profile* (AFVs of the World Series). Garden City, N.Y., 1971.

Data Memory Systems, Inc.(DMSI). *Ardennes Campaign Simulation Data Base: Final Report.* Fairfax, Va., 1990.

Davies, W. J. K. *German Army Handbook, 1939–1945.* New York, 1973.

Der Spiegel, no. 30/1976 (19 July).

Devlin, Gerald M. *Paratrooper.* New York, 1979.

Dierich, Wolfgang. *Kampfgeschwader (Edelweiss): The History of a German Bomber Unit, 1935–1945.* Shepperton, 1973.

Die Zeit, no. 30/1976 (23 July).

Dower, John. *War Without Mercy.* New York, 1986.

Draper, Theodore. *The 84th Infantry Division in the Battle of Germany, November 1944–May 1945.* New York, 1947.

Dupuy, R. Ernest. *St. Vith: Lion in the Way.* Washington, D.C., 1949.

Dupuy, T. N. *Attrition: Forecasting Battle Casualties and Equipment Losses in Modern War.* Fairfax, Va., 1990.

———. *A Genius for War: The German Army and General Staff, 1807–1945.* New York, 1979.

———. *Numbers, Predictions and War.* New York, 1977.

Dupuy, T. N., Grace P. Hayes, and Curt Johnson. *Dictionary of Military Terms.* New York, 1968.

Eisenhower, Dwight D. *Crusade in Europe.* New York, 1948.

Eisenhower, John S. D. *The Bitter Woods.* New York, 1969.

Ellis, Chris. *Tanks of World War II.* London, 1981.

Ellis, Chris, and Peter Chamberlain, eds. *Handbook on the British Army 1943.* London, 1975.

Elstob, Peter. *Hitler's Last Offensive.* London, 1971.

Ethell, Jeffery, and Alfred Price. *The German Jets in Combat.* London, 1979.

Franks, Norman L. R. *The Battle of the Airfields: 1st January 1945.* London, 1982.

Gander, Terry, and Peter Chamberlain. *British Tanks of World War II.* Cambridge, 1976.

Gavin, James M. *On to Berlin.* New York, 1978.

German Order of Battle 1944. Reprint of British World War II publications. London, 1975.

Girbig, Werner. *Six Months to Oblivion: The Eclipse of the Luftwaffe Fighter Force.* New York, 1973.

Green, William. *The Augsburg Eagle: Messerschmitt Bf 109.* London, 1980.

Green, William, and Gordon Swanborough. *The Focke-Wulf FW 190.* New York, 1976.

Greenfield, Kent Roberts, Robert B. Palmer, and Bill I. Wiley. *The Organization of Ground Combat Troops; United States Army in World War II; The Army Ground Forces.* Washington, D.C., 1947.

de Guingand, Sir Francis W. *Operation Victory.* New York, 1947.

Hemingway, Ernest. *Selected Letters 1917–1961.* New York, 1981.

Hoffschmidt, E. J. *German Aircraft Guns of World War I–World War II.* Old Greenwich, Conn., 1969.

Hogg, Ian. *Artillery in Color, 1920–1963.* New York, 1980.

———. *Barrage: The Guns in Action.* New York, 1970.

————. *British and American Artillery of World War II*. London, 1978.

————. *German Artillery of World War II*. London, 1975.

————. *The Guns: 1939–45*. New York, 1970.

Jung, Hermann. *Die Ardennen-Offensive, 1944/45: Ein Beispiel für die Kriegführung Hitlers*. Zürich, 1971.

Kliment, Charles. *Sdkfz 251 in Action, Armor Series #21*. Carrollton, Tex., 1981.

Kreidberg, Lieutenant Colonel Marvin A., USA, and Lieutenant Merton G. Henry, USA. *U.S. Army History of Military Mobilization in the United States Army, 1775–1945*. Washington, D.C., 1955.

Leinbaugh, Harold P., and John D. Campbell. *The Men of Company K*. New York, 1985.

Lewin, Ronald. *Ultra Goes to War*. New York, 1978.

MacDonald, Charles B. *A Time for Trumpets: The Untold Story of the Battle of the Bulge*. New York, 1985.

————. *The Last Offensive: The European Theater of Operations, United States Army in World War II*. Washington, D.C., 1973.

Macksey, Major Kenneth. *The Tanks: The History of the Royal Tank Regiment, 1945–75*. London, 1978.

Maschke, E., ed. *Zur Geschichte der deutschen Kriegsgefangenen des Zweiten Weltkrieges*. Vol. 15, *Zumsammenfassung*, München, 1974.

Maurer, Maurer, ed. *Air Force Combat Units of World War II*. The Watts Aerospace Library, USAF Historical Division Air University Department of the Air Force, New York, 1959.

Mead, Peter. *Gunners at War, 1939–1945*. Shepperton, 1982.

Meyer, G. *Die Kriegsverbrecherprozesse, in: Militärgeschichtliches Forschungsamt (Hrsg); Anfänge deutscher Sicherheitspolitik 1945–1956*. Vol. 1. München, 1982.

Meyer, Herbert. *Kriegsgeschichte der 12 SS-Panzerdivision "Hitlerjugend" Vol. II*. Osnabrück, 1982.

Milsom, John. *German Half-Tracked Vehicles of World War II: Unarmored Support Vehicles of the German Army*. London, 1975.

Montgomery, Bernard L. *The Memoirs of Field-Marshal Montgomery*. Cleveland, 1958.

Moyes, Philip J. R. *Bomber Squadrons of the R.A.F. and Their Aircraft*. London, 1964.

Mues, W. *Der Grosse Kessel*. Erwitte, 1984.

Munson, Kenneth. *German War Birds from World War I to NATO Ally*. Poole, England, 1986.

Murphy, R. *Diplomat unter Kriegern* (Diplomat Among Warriors). Berlin, 1965.

Niven, David. *The Moon's a Balloon*. New York, 1973.

Pallud, Jean Paul. *Battle of the Bulge: Then and Now*. London, 1984.

Patton, George S., *War As I Knew It*. Boston, 1947.

Perrett, Bryan. *The Churchill Tank*. London, 1980.

Philipott, Bryan. *The Encyclopedia of German Military Aircraft*. London, 1981.

Pogue, Forrest C. *The Supreme Command: The U.S. Army in World War II*. Washington, D.C., 1954.

Priller, Josef. *Geschichte eines Jagdgeschwaders: Das J.G. 26 (Schlageter) von 1937 bis 1945*. Heidelberg, 1956.

Rapport, Leonard, and Arthur Northwood, Jr. *Rendezvous with Destiny: A History of the 101st Airborne Division.* Washington, D.C., 1948.

Rawlings, John D. R. *Fighter Squadrons of the R.A.F. and Their Aircraft.* London, 1969.

Ridgway, Matthew B., and Harold H. Martin. *Soldier: The Memoirs of Matthew B. Ridgway.* New York, 1956.

Ritgen, Helmut. *Die Geschichte der Panzer-Lehr-Division im Westen 1944–1945.* Stuttgart, 1979.

Schliephake, Hanfried. *Flugzeugbewaffnung: Die Bordwaffen der Luftwaffe von der Angangen bis zur Gegenwart.* Stuttgart, 1977.

Schöbener, B. *Die amerikanische Besatzungspolitik und das Völkerrecht.* Frankfurt, 1991.

Schwinge, E. "Rückblick auf die Zeit der amerikanischen Besetzung." In B. Willms, ed., *Handbuch der Deutschen Nation.* Vol. 1. Tübingen, 1986.

Senger und Etterlin, F. M. *German Tanks of World War II: The Complete Illustrated History of German Armored Fighting Vehicles, 1926–1945.* London, 1969.

Shepherd, Christopher. *German Aircraft of World War II.* New York, 1972.

Smith, J. Richard, and Eddie J. Creek. *Jet Planes of the Third Reich.* Boston, 1982.

Stamps, T. Dodson, and Vincent J. Esposito, eds. *A Military History of World War II.* Vol. 1. New York, 1952.

Stanton, Shelby L. *Order of Battle U.S. Army, World War II.* Novato, Calif., 1984.

Stubbs, Mary Lee, and Stanley Russell Connor. *Armor-Cavalry. Part I: Regular Army and Army Reserve.* Office of the Chief of Military History, Washington, D.C., 1969.

Tanks and Weapons of World War II. New York, 1973.

Thompson, Royce L. *Tactical Air Phase of Ardennes Campaign, 16 December 1944–28 January 1945.* Office of the Chief of Military History, Department of the Army, Washington, D.C., 1950.

Tieke, Wilhelm. *Im Feuersturm letzter Kriegsjahre. II SS-Panzerkorps mit 9 und 10 SS-Division "Hohenstaufen" und "Frundsberg."* Osnabrück.

Tiemann, R. *Der Malmedyprozess.* Osnabrück, 1990.

Toland, John. *Battle: The Story of the Bulge.* New York, 1959.

U.S. Army Armor School. *The Battle of St. Vith, Belgium; 17–23 December, 1944.* Ft. Knox, Ky., 1966.

Weal, Elke C., John A. Weal, and Richard F. Barker. *Combat Aircraft of World War II.* New York, 1977.

Weingartner, J. *Crossroads of Death.* Berkeley, 1979.

White, B. T. *Tanks and Other Armoured Fighting Vehicles, 1942 to 1945.* New York, 1975.

Whiting, Charles. *Massacre at Malmedy.* New York, 1971.

Williams, Mary H. *Chronology 1941–1945; United States Army in World War II; Special Studies.* Washington D.C., 1960.

Williamson, J. *Halbkettenfahrzeuge: German Half-Track Vehicles, 1939–1945.* London, 1972.

Willms, B. *Handbuch der Deutschen Nation.* Vol. 1. Tübingen, 1986.

Wilmot, Chester. *The Struggle for Europe.* New York, 1952.

Windrow, Martin. *German Air Force Fighters of World War II*. Vol. 2. Garden City, N.Y., 1970.

Winterbotham, Frederick W. *The Ultra Secret*. New York, 1952.

Wood, Tony, and Bill Gunston. *Hitler's Luftwaffe: A Pictorial History and Technical Encyclopedia of Hitler's Airpower in World War II*. London, 1977.

Ziemssen, D. *Der Malmedy-Prozess*. München, 1952.

INDEX